Comparative Politics
Notes and Readings

Comparative Politics
Notes and Readings

Sixth Edition

Edited by

Roy C. Macridis
Professor of Politics
Brandeis University

and

Bernard E. Brown
Professor of Political Science
The City University of New York
(Graduate School and Lehman)

The Dorsey Press
Chicago, Illinois 60604

ISBN 0–256–03391–9

Library of Congress Catalog Card No. 85–73808

Printed in the United States of America

1 2 3 4 5 6 7 8 9 0 DO 3 2 1 0 9 8 7 6

Preface

It is with particular satisfaction that we have prepared the sixth edition of this book. When the first edition appeared in 1961 our aim was to introduce students to major approaches in the field of comparative politics, especially those reflecting new theories and concepts. Since then the outpouring of literature in comparative politics has been torrential, as evidenced in part by the creation of two specialized journals. We have tried to keep successive editions up-to-date by selecting choice articles and essays from a wide range of professional journals and books. The extraordinary longevity of this book is a tribute to the creativity, vigor, and significance of the work being done by students of comparative politics and, we should like to think, a vindication of our original conception of the discipline.

As in the past we have tried to furnish the student with selections from recent literature without losing sight of classic statements. The readings provide both tools of analysis and substantive studies that illustrate their utility. In selecting materials we have sought to avoid bias in favor of any single school, theory, or concept, by instead offering a balanced overview of approaches.

Three-fourths of the readings are new to this volume. The section on political change has been reorganized so as to distinguish more clearly among theories of modernization, dependency, instability, and revolution, and space has been accorded throughout to the latest theoretical developments. Greater recognition has also been given to Latin America, Africa, and other developing regions without neglecting the recent evolution of industrial societies. We hope that this volume will encourage a new generation of readers to explore and analyze the major issues of our time in a comparative perspective.

Our thanks go to many friends and colleagues for their advice and support. We are especially grateful to Professors Eric C. Browne (University of Wisconsin-Milwaukee), J. Bryan Collester (Principia College), Marcie Patton (Elmhurst College), and Mark Lichbach (University of Illinois at Chicago) for helpful suggestions. It remains difficult to do justice to all points of view within the confines of one volume, and responsibility for final choices is necessarily our own. We are also grateful, of course, to authors and publishers for granting their kind permission to reprint.

ROY C. MACRIDIS
BERNARD E. BROWN

List of Authors

Gabriel A. Almond. Emeritus Professor of Political Science, Stanford University. Author, *The American People and Foreign Policy* (1950); *The Appeals of Communism* (1954); *Political Development, Essays in Heuristic Theory* (1970). Coauthor, *The Politics of Developing Areas* (1960); *The Civic Culture* (1963); and *Comparative Politics: System, Process, and Policy* (rev. ed., 1978).

Aristotle (384–327 B.C.). A good one-volume collection is the Modern Library edition, *Introduction to Aristotle*, edited by Richard McKeon.

Crane Brinton (1898–1968). Late Professor of Ancient and Modern History, Harvard University. Author, *The Jacobins* (1930); *Nietzsche* (1941); *The United States and Britain* (1948); *English Political Thought in the Nineteenth Century* (1949); *Ideas and Men* (1950); and *The Americans and the French* (1968).

Bernard E. Brown. Professor of Political Science, City University of New York (Graduate School and Lehman). Author, *American Conservatives* (1951); *New Directions in Comparative Politics* (1962); *Protest in Paris* (1974); *Intellectuals and Other Traitors* (1980); *Socialism of a Different Kind, Reshaping the Left in France* (1982). Coauthor, *The De Gaulle Republic* (1960, 1963); *Cases in Comparative Politics* (3rd ed., 1976); *Eurocommunism and Eurosocialism, The Left Confronts Modernity* (1978).

Richard Bush. Deputy Director of the Asia Society's China Council, Washington, D.C. Author, *The Politics of Cotton Textiles in Kuomantang China, 1927–37.* (1982).

Robert F. Byrnes. Distinguished Professor of History, Indiana University. Author, *Antisemitism in Modern France* (1950); *Pobedonostev, His Life and Work* (1968). Editor, *The United States and Eastern Europe* (1967); *After Brezhnev* (1983).

Ralf Dahrendorf. Director, London School of Economics and Political Science. Author, *Class and Class Conflict in Industrial Society* (1965); *Society and Democracy in Germany* (1967); *Essays in the Theory of Society* (1968); *Life Chances* (1979); *The New Liberty* (1975); *On Britain* (1982); and many works in German.

Karl W. Deutsch. Emeritus Professor of Government, Harvard University. Author, *Nationalism and Social Communication* (1953); *The Nerves of Government* (1963); *Nationalism and Its Alternatives* (1969); *Politics and Government: How People Decide Their Fate* (1974); *Tides Among Nations* (1979). Coauthor, *Germany Rejoins the Powers* (1959); *Nation-Building* (1966).

David Easton. Professor of Political Science, University of Chicago. Author, *The Political System* (1953); *A Framework for Political Analysis* (1965); and *A Systems Analysis of Political Life* (1965). Coauthor, *Children in the Political System* (1969).

Harry Eckstein. Distinguished Professor of Social Sciences, University of California at Irvine. Author, *Pressure Group Politics* (1960); *Division and Cohesion in a Democracy, A Study of Norway* (1966). Coauthor, *Patterns of Authority* (1975). Editor, *Comparative Politics* (1963); *Internal War* (1964).

Samuel E. Finer. Gladstone Professor of Government and Public Administration, now Emeritus, University of Oxford. Author, *The Man on Horseback* (1962); *Anonymous Empire, A Study of the Lobby in Great Britain* (2nd ed., 1966); *The Life and Times of Sir Edwin Chadwick* (1970); *Comparative Government* (1974); *The Changing British Party System* (1980).

Jürgen Habermas. Director of the Max-Planck Institut, Starnberg (Germany). Author, *Toward a Rational Society, Student Protest, Science, and Politics* (1970); *Knowledge and Human Interests* (1971); *Theory and Practice* (1973); *Legitimation Crisis* (1975); *Communication and the Evolution of Society* (1979); *The Theory of Communicative Action* (1984).

M. Donald Hancock. Professor of Political Science and Director of the Center for European Studies, Vanderbilt University. Author, *Sweden, The Politics of Postindustrial Change* (1972); *The Bundeswehr and the National People's Army* (1972). Coauthor, *Politics in the Post-Welfare State* (1968).

Samuel P. Huntington. Eaton Professor of the Science of Government and Director of the Center for International Affairs, Harvard University. Author, *The Soldier and the State* (1957); *The Common Defense* (1961); *Political Order in Changing Societies* (1968); *American Politics, the Promise of Disharmony* (1981). Coauthor, *Political Power, USA/USSR* (1965); *Authoritarian Politics in Modern Society* (1970); *The Crisis of Democracy* (1975); *No Easy Choice, Political Participation in Developing Countries* (1976).

Robert O. Keohane. Professor of International Relations, Brandeis University. Author, *After Hegemony: Cooperation and Discord in the World Political Economy* (1984). Coauthor, *Power and Interdependence: World Politics in Transition* (1972). Coeditor, *Transnational Relations and World Politics* (1972).

Otto Kirchheimer (1905–65). Late Professor of Government, Columbia University. Author, *A Constitution for the Fourth Republic* (1947); and *Political Justice* (1961). Also, *Politics, Law, and Social Change, Selected Essays of Otto Kirchheimer,* edited by F. S. Burin and K. L. Shell (1969).

Harvey F. Kline. Professor of Political Science, University of Massachusetts (Amherst). Author, *Colombia: Portrait of Unity and Diversity* (1983).

David Landes. Robert Walton Goelet Professor of French History, Harvard University. Author, *Bankers and Pashas* (1958); *The Unbound Prome-*

theus (1969); *History as Social Science* (1971); *Revolution in Time: Clocks and the Making of the Modern World* (1983).

Seymour M. Lipset. Professor of Political Science and Sociology, and Senior Fellow of the Hoover Institute, Stanford University. Author, *Agrarian Socialism* (1950); *The First New Nation* (1963); *Revolution and Counterrevolution* (1968); *Emerging Coalitions in American Politics* (1978); *The Third Century* (1979); *Political Man* (rev. ed., 1981). Coauthor, *Union Democracy* (1956); *The Politics of Unreason* (rev. ed., 1978); *Dialogues on American Politics* (1978); *The Confidence Gap* (1983).

John Logue. Associate Professor of Political Science, Kent State University. Author, *Socialism and Abundance: Radical Socialism in the Danish Welfare State* (1982).

Richard Lowenthal. Emeritus Professor of Political Science, Free University of Berlin. Author, *World Communism: The Disintegration of a Secular Faith* (1966); *Model or Ally? The Communist Powers and the Developing Countries* (1977); and many works in German.

Roy C. Macridis. Professor of Politics, Brandeis University. Author, *The Study of Comparative Government* (1955); *French Politics in Transition* (1975); *Contemporary Political Ideologies* (rev. ed. 1982). Coauthor, *The De Gaulle Republic* (1960, 1963); *Foreign Policy in World Politics* (rev. ed. 1974); *France, Germany, and the Western Alliance* (1967); *Modern Political Systems: Europe* (1983); Editor, *De Gaulle, Implacable Ally* (1966) and *Political Parties* (1967).

John Stuart Mill (1806–73). Noted English philosopher and essayist. A convenient collection of his political writings is the Everyman edition of *Utilitarianism, Liberty, and Representative Government.*

Franz L. Neumann (1900–54). Late Professor of Government, Columbia University. Author, *Behemoth: The Structure and Practice of National Socialism* (1944); and *The Democratic and the Authoritarian State* (1957).

Norman H. Nie. Professor of Political Science, University of Chicago. Coauthor, *Participation in America* (1972); *Participation and Political Equality* (1978); and *The Changing American Voter* (enlarged ed., 1979).

Guillermo O'Donnell. Professor, Centro de Estudios de Estado y Sociedas, Buenos Aires (Argentina). Author, *Modernization and Bureaucratic-Authoritarianism: Studies in South American Politics* (1973).

Michel Oksenberg. Professor of Political Science and Research Associate of the Center for Chinese Studies, University of Michigan. Author, *China: The Convulsive Society* (1971); *China and America: Past and Future* (1977).

Philippe C. Schmitter. Professor of Political Science, University of Chicago. Author, *Interest Conflict and Political Change in Brazil* (1971); *Corporatism and Public Policy in Authoritarian Portugal* (1975). Editor, *Military Rule in Latin America* (1973); *Trends Towards Corporatist Intermediation* (1979); *Patterns of Corporatist Policy-Making* (1982).

Richard L. Sklar. Professor of Political Science, University of California at Los Angeles. Author, *Nigerian Political Parties* (1963); *Corporate Power in an African State: The Political Impact of Multinational Mining Companies in Zambia* (1975).

Tony Smith. Professor of Political Science, Tufts University. Author, *The End of the European Empire* (1975); *The French Stake in Algeria, 1945–1962* (1978); *The Pattern of Imperialism: The United States, Great Britain, and the Late Industrializing World Since 1815* (1981).

J. Samuel Valenzuela. Assistant Professor of Sociology, Harvard University. Editor, *Chile: Politics and Society* (1976).

Arturo Valenzuela. Professor of Political Science, Duke University. Author, *Political Brokers in Chile* (1977): *The Breakdown of Democracy in Chile* (1978).

Sidney Verba. Professor of Government. Harvard University. Author, *Small Groups and Political Behavior* (1961). Coauthor, *The Civic Culture* (1963): *Participation in America* (1972); *Caste, Race, and Politics* (1971); *Participation and Political Equality, A Seven Nation Comparison* (1978); *Injury to Insult* (1979).

Immanuel Wallerstein. Distinguished Professor of Sociology, and Director of the Fernand Braudel Center for the Study of Economics, Historical Systems and Civilization, State University of New York at Binghamton. Author, *Africa: The Politics of Unity* (1967); *The Capitalist World Economy* (1979); *The Modern World System,* 2 vols. (1980); *Historical Capitalism* (1983); *The Politics of the World Economy* (1984).

Myron Weiner. Ford International Professor of Political Science, Massachusetts Institute of Technology. Author, *Party Politics in India* (1957); *The Politics of Scarcity: Public Pressure and Political Response in India* (1962); *Party Building in a New Nation: The Indian National Congress* (1967); *Sons of the Soil: Migration and Ethnic Conflict in India* (1978); *India at the Polls, 1980* (1983). Coauthor, *India's Preferential Policies* (1981).

Howard J. Wiarda. Professor of Political Science, University of Massachusetts (Amherst). Author, *Dictatorship and Development: The Methods of Control in Trujillo's Dominican Republic* (1968); *The Dominican Republic: Nation in Transition* (1969); *Corporatism and National Development in Latin America* (1981); *In Search of Policy: The United States and Latin America* (1984). Editor, *Politics and Social Change in Latin America: The Distinct Tradition* (1974).

Contents

PART ONE

Comparative Analysis: Method and Concepts

The field of comparative politics remains in the state of flux described in the first edition of this volume some 25 years ago. There has been little theory building and cumulative empirical testing and data-collection since then. There has been also little agreement on concepts and definitions or on the scope and range of comparative analysis. The intellectual state of comparative analysis contrasts sharply with the broadening and revitalizing vision of the "comparatists" who launched their appeal for change more than 30 years ago. As Harry Eckstein pointed out, the circumstances for the development of comparative politics were then particularly propitious:

> First, the empirical range of the field has been greatly enlarged, primarily through the intensive study of non-Western systems; second, concerted attempts have been made to overcome the lack of rigor and system that characterized the field in the pre-war period to make it more scientific; third, there has been much greater emphasis upon the political role of social groups and upon political institutions that play an important role in molding political values and cognitions, loyalties, and identifications; finally, political systems have been analytically dissected and questions raised about them in terms of conceptual schemes largely imported from social sciences, above all in terms of structural-functional analysis.[1]

Two thoughtful students of comparative politics however, writing in 1970, list a set of caveats:

> Although it cannot be questioned that cross-cultural comparative research is indispensable to a developing science of politics, the problems that comparative politics specialists encounter are formidable. These range from the highly technical problems of indexing and sampling,

---

[1] Harry Eckstein and David Apter, eds., *Comparative Politics: A Reader* (New York: Free Press, 1963), p. 23.

1

to the more general problems of developing non-culture-bound categories, to the even more basic issues revolving around the rules of interpretation and the criteria for admissible explanation. . . . When this is
done they will have a more solid intellectual base for developing more
sophisticated conceptual schemes and more appropriate data processing
routines.[2]

The road to the development of a solid base of theoretical conceptualization continues to be long and uncertain. In this introductory
essay we shall trace the history of and trends in comparative politics,
identify some of the major achievements, and indicate some of the
continuing discontents.

GENERAL OBSERVATION OF TRENDS

After World War II, dissatisfaction with the state of comparative
politics was widespread. One of the editors of this volume expressed
the prevailing mood by pointing out some of the major shortcomings
of the traditional approach:

1. It dealt primarily with a single-culture configuration, i.e., the
   Western world.

2. Within this culture configuration, comparative study dealt
   mainly with representative democracies, until recently treating
   nondemocratic systems as aberrations from the democratic
   "norms."

3. This prevented the student from dealing systematically not only
   with nondemocratic Western political systems, but with colonial
   systems, other "backward" areas, and culturally distinct societies that exhibit superficially the characteristics of the representative process (e.g., India, Japan).

4. Research was founded on the study of isolated aspects of the
   governmental process within specific countries; hence it was
   comparative in name only.

The comparative study of politics was excessively formalistic in
its approach to political institutions.

1. It focused analysis on the formal institutions of government,
   to the detriment of a sophisticated awareness of the informal
   arrangements of society and of their role in the formation of
   decisions and the exercise of power.

2. In neglecting such informal arrangements, it proved to be relatively insensitive to the nonpolitical determinants of political

---

[2] Robert T. Holt and John E. Turner, eds., *The Methodology of Comparative Research* (New York: Free Press, 1970), p. 20.

behavior and hence to the nonpolitical bases of governmental institutions.

3. Comparison was made in terms of the formal constitutional aspects of Western systems, that is, parliaments, chief executives, civil services, administrative law, and so on, which are not necessarily the most fruitful concepts for a truly comparative study.

The comparative study of politics was preponderantly descriptive rather than problem solving, explanatory, or analytic in its method.

1. Except for some studies of proportional representation, emergency legislation, and electoral systems, the field was insensitive to hypotheses and their verification.

2. Even in the purely descriptive approach to political systems it was relatively insensitive to the methods of cultural anthropology, in which descriptions are fruitfully made in terms of general concepts or integrating hypotheses.

3. Thus, description in comparative government did not readily lend itself to the testing of hypotheses, to the compilation of significant data regarding a single political phenomenon—or class of such phenomenon—in a large number of societies.

4. Description without systematic orientation obstructed the discovery of hypotheses regarding uniformities in political behavior and prevented the formulation, on a comparative basis, of a theory of political dynamics (i.e., change, revolution, conditions of stability).

How was one to counter these trends and develop a more sophisticated approach to comparative study? The prescription appeared simple at the time:

1. Comparison involves abstraction, and concrete situations or processes can never be compared as such. Every phenomenon is unique; every manifestation is unique; every process, every nation, like every individual, is in a sense unique. To compare them means to select certain types or concepts, and in so doing we have to "distort" the unique and the concrete.

2. Prior to any comparison it is necessary not only to establish categories and concepts but also to determine criteria of relevance of the particular components of a social and political situation to the problem under analysis (i.e., relevance of social stratification to family system, or sunspots to political instability).

3. It is necessary to establish criteria for the adequate representation of the particular components that enter into a general analysis or the analysis of a problem.

4. It is necessary in attempting to develop a theory of politics to formulate hypotheses emerging either from the context of a conceptual scheme or from the formulation of a problem.

5. The formulation of hypothetical relations and their investigation against empirical data can never lead to proof. A hypothesis or a series of hypothetical relations would be considered proven, i.e., verified, only as long as it withstands falsification.

6. Hypothetical series rather than single hypotheses should be formulated. In each case the connecting link between general hypothetical series and the particular social relations should be provided by the specification of conditions under which any or all the possibilities enumerated in this series are expected to take place.

7. Comparative study, even if it falls short of providing a general theory of politics, can pave the way to the gradual and cumulative development of theory by (1) enriching our imaginative ability to formulate hypotheses, in the same sense that any "outsidedness" enhances our ability to understand a social system; (2) providing a means for the testing of hypotheses; and (3) making us aware that something we have taken for granted requires explanation.

8. Finally, one of the greatest dangers in hypothesizing in connection with comparative study is the projection of possible relationships ad infinitum. This can be avoided by the orderly collection of data prior to hypothesizing. Such collection may in itself lead us to the recognition of irrelevant relations (climate and the electoral system, language and industrial technology, etc.). Such a recognition in itself makes for a more manageable study of data. *Hence the importance attached to the development of some rough classificatory scheme prior to the formulation of hypotheses.*

In summary then, the major criticism of the traditional approach to the study of comparative politics was that it is centered upon the description of the formally established institutions of government; that the traditional approach was in general singularly insensitive to informal factors and processes such as the various interest groups, the wielders of social and economic power and at times even of political power operating outside of the formal governmental institutions, and the more complex contextual forces that can be found in the ideological patterns and the social organization of the system. It lacked a systematic approach.

The very word "system" causes a number of people to raise their eyebrows. It has connotations of group research that suggest the suppression of the imagination and sensitivity of the observer for the sake of conceptually determined and rigidly adhered to categories. This is far from being the case, however. A systematic approach simply involves the development of categories for the compilation of data and the interrelationship of the data so compiled in the form of theories, that is, the suggestion of variable relationships.

The development of common categories establishes criteria of relevance. Once such categories are suggested, their relevance for the compilation of data through the study of problems in as many political systems as possible should be made. For instance, if it is shown that the composition or recruitment of elites in certain political systems accounts for the degree to which the system is susceptible to change, which in turn may lead us to certain general suppositions about political stability, then a systematic approach would require the examination of the same phenomenon in a number of political systems in the light of the same general categories. While the traditional approach did not claim to be explanatory, a systematic approach claimed to be precisely this. For explanation simply means verification of hypothetical propositions. In the field of politics, given the lack of experimentation, it is only the testing of a hypothesis in as many systems as possible that will provide us with a moderate degree of assurance that we have an explanation.[3]

These general observations on the state of comparative politics appear in retrospect both modest and wistful: to develop a framework for comparison; to abandon the "country-by-country" approach in favor of comparisons of problems, processes, and institutions or the comparative testing of hypotheses was not too much to ask. Nor was it too demanding to ask for theory—virtually any theory—that spells out significant interrelationships in terms of which crucial political phenomena could be studied, compared, and evaluated. Nor was it extravagant to ask that the horizon of comparison in effect be broadened to include non-European countries. Finally, the hope that institutions—political institutions—would be studied in the context of the socioeconomic and ideological forces within which they operated was more than legitimate.

MAJOR ACHIEVEMENTS AND NEW DIMENSIONS

Some significant contributions to the study of comparative politics were made in the 1950s and 60s. Under the auspices of the Social

---

[3] For a fuller development, see Roy C. Macridis, *The Study of Comparative Government* (New York: Random House, 1955).

Sciences Research Council, a committee on comparative politics was set up in 1954 and a number of publications appeared under its auspices, most of them dealing with problems of political development. However, with the exception of the first volume that attempted to suggest an overall theory of political development, these volumes were collections of essays on specific topics: political parties, bureaucracy, political culture, and so on, without a common theoretical focus and without comprehensive coverage. They resulted from conferences held at different times in which authors "did their thing." The undertaking displayed a synthetic quality or rather an additive one. Having country specialists address themselves to common topics is no assurance that comparability of any kind will emerge and that the comparative method will be tested, that is, will yield some meaningful generalizations.

Individual authors alone or in combination with others have produced volumes that deal with significant problem areas such as political elites, socialization, political parties, interest groups, governmental structures, political development and its patterns of institutionalization, opposition, class cleavages and their reconciliation, electoral systems and their impact on representative government, totalitarian systems, constitutions, and constitutionalism and bureaucracies. Some of these studies are important contributions to our knowledge of individual countries while others are seminal works of conceptualization and theoretical building. Among those dealing with countries are the work of Ralf Dahrendorf and Karl Bracher on the impact of the Nazi system upon German society; Samuel Beer on British political parties; Stanley Hoffmann on the French Republic; Merle Fainsod on the Soviet political system; Joseph LaPalombara on Italian interest groups; Robert Scalapino on the rise of political parties in Japan, and Eckstein on Norway.[4] They have all enriched and deepened our understanding of individual political systems while at the same time raising significant theoretical questions. The list is also impressive when it comes to theoretical works. New dimensions for comparative analysis are furnished by David Easton on system theory; Karl Deutsch on communication

---

[4] The works referred to are: Ralf Dahrendorf, *Society and Democracy in Germany* (Garden City, N.Y.: Doubleday Publishing, 1967); Karl Dietrich Bracher, *The German Dictatorship: The Origin, Structure and Effects of National Socialism* (New York: Praeger Publishers, 1970); Samuel H. Beer, *British Politics in the Collectivist Age* (New York: Alfred A. Knopf, 1966); Stanley Hoffmann, *Decline or Renewal? France since the 1930's* (New York: Viking Press, 1974); Merle Fainsod, *How Russia Is Ruled,* rev. ed. (Cambridge, Mass.: Harvard Univ. Press, 1963); Joseph LaPalombara, *Interest Groups in Italian Politics* (Princeton: Princeton University Press, 1964); Robert A. Scalapino, *Democracy and the Party Movement in Prewar Japan* (Berkeley: University of California Press, 1953); Harry Eckstein, *Division and Cohesion in a Democracy: A Study of Norway* (Princeton: Princeton University Press, 1966).

theory; Seymour Lipset on participation; Beer, Sidney Verba and Gabriel Almond on political culture; Robert Dahl on the nature of political power and its various manifestations; William Kornhauser on mass society as it relates to democracy; Samuel Huntington on reevaluation of the role of political institutions in political change and development; Dahrendorf's reassessment of the role of class in contemporary politics; Barrington Moore, Jr., on totalitarianism and democracy; David Butler and Donald Stokes on the British voter; and Maurice Duverger on political parties.[5]

The field of comparative politics has as a result shown remarkable progress in at least two ways. We look upon politics in one or more countries with far greater sophistication than in the past, and we approach it with a set of general concepts, even if not always agreed upon. We are no longer satisfied with institutional studies—either descriptive or legalistic—or with the study of constitutional provisions and the formal distribution of power they set up. We probe deeper into the political elites, the socioeconomic and ideological contextual forces within which they operate, political parties and interest groups, communication mechanisms between leaders and led, the impact of economic and social change upon political participation and behavior. We seek for the fundamentals, so to speak, of a political system: stability, legitimacy, authority (or, conversely, with the reasons for instability), nonperformance, and revolutions. This is not a mean accomplishment.

But the authors and works cited here represent only an initial effort when compared to the hopes and expectations with which we began and the resources that have been made available. These works are the tip of the iceberg. There is no common theory, no generally accepted or acceptable proposition for further research, no cumulative effort in the form of data collection, data sorting, and hypothesizing. No common body of theory and knowledge has evolved to which the student of comparative politics can be directed.

For a theory to be useful, a number of requirements must be

---

[5] See: David Easton, *A Systems Analysis of Political Life* (New York: John Wiley & Sons, 1965); Karl Deutsch, *The Nerves of Government* (New York: Free Press, 1963); Seymour M. Lipset, *Political Man: The Social Bases of Politics*, rev. ed.; (Baltimore: The Johns Hopkins Press, 1981); Samuel H. Beer, ed., *Patterns of Government*, 3d ed. (New York: Random House, 1973); Gabriel Almond and Sidney Verba, *The Civic Culture* (Princeton: Princeton University Press, 1963); Robert Dahl, *Polyarchy: Participation and Opposition* (New Haven: Yale University Press, 1971); William Kornhauser, *The Politics of Mass Society* (New York: Free Press, 1959); Samuel P. Huntington, *Political Order in Changing Societies* (New Haven: Yale University Press, 1968); Ralf Dahrendorf, *Class and Class Conflict in Industrial Society* (Stanford: Stanford University Press, 1959); Barrington Moore, Jr., *Social Origins of Dictatorship and Democracy* (Boston: Beacon Press, 1966); David Butler and Donald Stokes, *Political Change in Britain* (New York: St. Martin's Press, 1969); Maurice Duverger, *Political Parties*, 3d ed. (London: Methuen, 1969).

fulfilled. The theory should be both comprehensive and parsimonious; it should be geared to the proper level of generality and abstraction to include the essentials for political analysis; it should be capable of generating hypotheses (a hypothesis is fundamentally an "if-then" proposition that can be investigated empirically); it should allow the investigators enough freedom to choose from among the empirical data the particular phenomena and structures that relate to the general concepts embedded in the theory; finally it should not prescribe one and only one research procedure but rather make it possible to use the procedure most likely to be feasible under the existing field situations. If, for instance, survey research is the *only procedure* prescribed, then it is obvious that only those countries where surveys are possible will be included. All others will have to be excluded.

Easton's theory of a political system meets many of these requirements despite the fact that his model is highly abstract.[6] The "system" is viewed as a decision-making mechanism operating within the framework of beliefs and attitudes held by the people about their regime, that is, the basic form of their government. On the one side we have "demands" constantly pressing for satisfaction, and "supports," that is, positive feelings of loyalty and attachment to the political system. On the other side we have "outputs," decisions aimed at alleviating predicaments or meeting demands. The interplay between demands and decisions affects the level and the intensity of supports that can range from very positive when the system is highly legitimate and stable, to very negative when there is widespread disobedience. The role of "socialization" in creating supports is adequately stressed to involve not simply the education and induction of the young into the system but the responsiveness of the elites to new political groups and openness to the participation of all groups in the decision-making process. "Exclusiveness" or "repression" will yield discontent and undermine the legitimacy of the system; prolonged ineffectiveness, that is, the inability to translate demands into policy, will have the same consequences. "Revolution" in this sense is the only way for certain groups to make their "inputs." Generally speaking the connecting links between inputs and the decision makers are the interest groups, other associations, and the political parties. They are transmission belts and as such they play a crucial role in keeping the system open and responsive. This is, in skeleton form, Easton's "system." It is not new—far from it. But it was formulated with great simplicity

---

[6] David Easton, "An Approach to the Analysis of Political Systems," *World Politics*, April 1957, pp. 383–400.

and could have generated a number of studies in comparative analysis. The major difficulty was its being pitched at a very high level of generality and abstraction.

INDICATIONS OF CONTINUING DISCONTENT

The most important reasons for our continuing discontent with the present state of comparative analysis lie, in our opinion, with the excessive and at times uncritical effort to apply the canons of the "behavioral revolution" to it.

Behavioralism provided a salutary emphasis upon political factors other than the governmental forms. Although their discovery was not entirely original, it opened up the study of what we may call the contextual factors within which political structures and forms develop and political roles flourish. Borrowing in great part from sociology and anthropology, behavioralism put a stress upon careful definitions of the empirical problems to be investigated and upon the formulation of hypotheses and their testing. It sharpened the tools of our analysis by introducing new techniques—surveys, interviewing, the compilation of aggregate data—in an effort to provide correlations between various socioeconomic and psychological factors and political behavior. Weighing, measuring, and correlating are among the most positive aspects of the behavioral revolution in politics. When applied to a political scene, American or foreign, of which the observers had adequate knowledge, the emphasis was most beneficial. Students picked dark or shadowy areas and threw light upon them. Their findings, or at least their observations, added to the picture we had and helped us refine it. The findings, in other words, made sense and produced new data about the system being studied because we already had a great deal of information about the system.

Where the behavioral revolution went wrong was at its two extremes—in the efforts to build "grand theory" at the one extreme, and in the study of what may well be called political trivia, at the other. In between the two lay a fertile field for study and exploration. But it is to the extremes that most of the work was directed, generally with disappointing results. This will become abundantly clear, I hope, when we discuss the following points that exemplify the state of the discipline today: its failure to establish criteria of relevance and its gross neglect of the study of governmental structures and forms.

The search for relevance and the criteria of relevance has bedeviled political thought and inquiry. It is an issue that cannot be easily resolved. Society as an overall system, that is, a set of interrelations, roles, and structures, consists of a number of subsystems for which no hard and fast boundaries can be drawn. In a sense, all that is social is also political, firmly rooted in history. What is social can be broken down analytically into subsystems, but again, the lower we move in identifying subsystems, the harder it becomes to set boundaries. The "web" is there.

Conceivably then every manifestation, every attitude or relationship, every motivation or idea in society has a relevance to politics. Politics may engender aspirations; it may shape interests; it may evoke demands; it may call for decisions; it may lead to conflicts about values and interests that necessitate arbitration. Child-rearing, the school curriculum, modes of entertainment, sex relations, to say nothing of economic interests and activities, are all *potentially* related to politics. Yet what is potential is not actual in empirical terms. In most cases and for most of the time, the great host of social, economic, and interpersonal relations has no actual relevance to politics and therefore to the discipline. Yet each and all *may* at a given time and place, and under a set of conditions that is impossible to foresee, assume a political relevance, only to subside again into an apolitical stance.

The dilemma is obvious. Should we study everything that is *potentially* political? Should we narrow our definition and, if so, how? Behavioralism provides the worst possible answer—study everything. It postulates that every aspect of political behavior relates to every aspect of social behavior. Hence we may finish by studying manifestations and attitudes and relationships that have no discernible political relevance.

To be sure, there are no a priori grounds on the strength of which one can discard this holistic approach. The element of potentiality is ever present, and our inability to develop any rules about the intricate phenomenon that accounts for the actualization of what is potential makes it impossible to condemn potentiality as a criterion of relevance. Only two closely related grounds for its rejection can be suggested. The first is what Joseph LaPalombara has called the rule of parsimony, and the second is what we call the concern with focus. Parsimony suggests that we choose those categories and concepts on the basis of which we are as sure as we can be that what we are studying is politically relevant. Concern with focus simply suggests the most direct way to get at politically relevant phenomena.

The Fallacy of Inputism

Two terms that have gained wide currency in the last decade are "input" and "output." The system converts demands into decisions.

Through the feedback mechanism, output factors influence the input side. Emphasis is placed upon the input factors, but the state is given a degree of autonomy and independence, and through a process that is by no means clear, it can influence supports and demands. The difficulty comes with the selection of the input factors, that is, with the same problem of relevance that we have discussed. Do we study again all societal manifestations on the assumption that they all make inputs? Do we consider attitudinal data, aggregate data, hard and soft data ranging from the number of hospital beds to child-father relations? Where and in what manner do we define the subject matter for study, and what is our cutoff point? Political scientists are often like thirsty people who go looking for water in a contextual Sahara when more often than not it is right there fresh from the spring—or at least from a well-chlorinated reservoir. Their search in the contextual wasteland brings only further difficulties upon them, for there is no theory, no conceptual scheme that links—in any form that is testable—the amassed socioeconomic and psychological data with the political. In fact, emphasis upon the input factors very often not only neglects the political but sometimes explicitly avoids it.

We are inclined to define what we call "inputism" as the study of society by political scientists without a political focus and very often without a political question. The job is enticingly easy. All that is needed is a questionnaire, interviewers, a pool of respondents, the *UN Statistical Yearbook,* and a countersorter or, even better, a computer. I wish to reemphasize the phrase "without a political focus and very often without a political question." When the empirical political situation and the empirical political phenomenon we are investigating make it necessary—as often happens—to study the socioeconomic or psychological factors on the input side, then such study is focused and relevant, for the input factors are analyzed to "explain" the situation we are investigating. We hypothesize that the attitude of the French military with regard to a series of political decisions or with regard to the process of decision making was, among other things, shaped by the education they received at the Jesuit schools. The linkage between the two, I believe, can be made. It will not fully explain the attitude of the military, but we think it may provide one of the first steps leading to explanation. We start with the concrete political problem. Inputism would reverse the priorities, advocating the study of the socialization of the elite groups in the French educational system, with the unwarranted expectation that such study would clarify "politics" in general and help us explain political behavior. What behavior? With regard to what problem? At what time?

Inputism tends to lead to three fallacies, that of: (1) determinism,

(2) scientism, and (3) superficiality. All three fallacies are related.

According to determinism, it is the input factors that shape political action. The political phenomenon is almost invariably reduced either to a number of nonpolitical determinants, in which case we have a multiple kind of reductionism, or to one factor, in which case we have a singlefactor reductionism. In either case, the state can play virtually no independent problem-solving or attitude-forming role. It is only through a process of feedback—not clearly understood and not easily demonstrated—that governmental action may influence the determinants that then in turn will act upon the governmental decision-making process. Politics constantly remains a dependent variable. It is, to use Bentley's expression, the parallelogram of interest action and interaction, that is, the parallelogram of all socioeconomic and psychological determinants that will shape the decision-making machinery and will determine its output. The famous "black box," as graduate students have come to know the government, is at its best a filter mechanism through which interests express themselves and at its worst a simple transmission mechanism. The role of the state is reduced to the narrow confines of an organization that channels, reflects, and expresses commands and instructions that come from "elsewhere." The hint to political scientists is obvious: study everything but the machinery of the state and its organizational structures; study the "elsewhere."

Scientism constitutes the effort to measure as accurately as possible the weight, scope, and persistence of the input factors, on the purely gratuitous assumption that they are or can be linked causally to political phenomena. The assumption is gratuitous because we have failed as yet to establish any such causal links and because it is doubtful that we ever will. The assumption is confounded when the political phenomena with which the input factors are to be linked are not clearly stated. Sometimes system theory suggests the broadest possible relationship among "concepts," rather than variables—consensus, stability, performance; sometimes it offers a very narrow-gauge hypothesis linking some political manifestation to one nonpolitical variable (for example, voting with income or race). The first attempt obviously bogs down into analytical exercise rather than empirical testing, while the second one will never attain the level of testability on the basis of which higher-level propositions can be made. Even when system theory establishes clear-cut concepts linked to empirical phenomena from which testable propositions can emerge, it is impossible to move back from the propositions to the concepts and to the overall theory through a series of verifiable tests that exclude all alternative propositions, concepts and theories. Scientism therefore leads us from hyperfactualism to hypertheorizing—the latter becoming progressively an exercise (often brilliant) in intellectual virtuosity. It lacks, however, the only thing that really counts—emipirical relevance.

Since no theory as yet offered has shown its worth in causally linking determinants with political phenomena, our efforts very often end with the superficial juxtaposition of a given determinant with a given political phenomenon—that is to say, with correlations. Since no adequate theory has been offered, however, and since we therefore have no explanation, correlational findings are a somewhat more sophisticated version of the "sun spot" theory. Lipset's book *Political Man* is an illustration of this.[7] At the end of this excellent study, the reader is not sure whether open democratic societies are affluent because they are open and democratic or whether it is the other way round.

Determinism, scientism, and correlational studies that have a distinct trait of superficiality typify the state of a discipline that has consistently eschewed the hard and persistent empirical phenomena that ought to concern it in the name of theory building and theory testing. Structures and processes and the manifestly political institutions through which decisions are made have been relegated to the level of epiphenomena. The examination and the evaluation of policies have been handed over to the journalists and politicians, and the formulation of a judgment *in the name of knowledge* is considered incompatible with the canons of a self-imposed scientific objectivity. It is these trends that account for the state of the discipline as a whole, and they affect particularly the study of comparative politics, or the comparative study of politics. The state of the discipline can be summed up in one phrase: the gradual disappearance of the political. To repeat, if government is viewed as the reflection of the parallelogram of socioeconomic and psychological and other determinants, the prescription for political science becomes a proscription of the study of government.

Yet the behavioral revolution has also had, as we have noted, beneficial effects. We shall never return exclusively to normative speculation, and we shall never be satisfied with judgments about political phenomena without the benefit of careful measurement. We shall continue to distinguish sharply between "facts" and "values," and we shall subject our postulates to a critical examination, demanding always clarity of definitions and terms. Where the propositions about behavior can be tested, we shall test them under all the canons of controlled inquiry that the social sciences have developed. We shall continue to seek to build theory, that is, a set of interrelated and interconnected propositions, each of which has direct empirical meaning and relevance, and we shall continue to

---

[7] Lipset, *Political Man,* rev. ed. (Baltimore: The Johns Hopkins Press, 1981).

develop narrow hypotheses that can be tested, that is, invariably falsified. We shall use the many tools of empirical inquiry available to us—survey opinion data, aggregate data—and in both the construction of our research and our search for the explanation of political phenomena, we shall feel free to borrow, when the occasion demands, from the theoretical sophistication of many disciplines—sociology, anthropology, economics, and psychology—and, of course, to use the empirical data that history provides.

But the time has come to qualify and reconsider our quest for a science of politics in the full sense of the term. In the last analysis this may be a contradiction in terms. There can be no science where the element of human will and purpose predominates. Politics is a problem-solving mechanism; our study must deal with it and not with the laws surrounding behavior. The ultimate irony is that even if laws could be discovered, then our discipline would be primarily concerned with an effort to explain why they are not obeyed—why the laws are really nonlaws. Natural sciences began by addressing themselves to empirical phenomena in order to understand them, explain them, and control them. The ultimate goal of the natural sciences has been to control nature. The higher the level of generalization that subsumes a number of measurable relationships, the higher the potentiality of control. It is the other way around with politics. The study of politics explicitly divorces knowledge from action and understanding from control. The laws that we constantly seek will tell us little about our political problems and what to do about them. Our concern becomes scholastic.

We therefore suggest that we reconcile ourselves to the fact that while we can have an understanding of some political phenomena, a history of politics and political movements, an understanding of the functioning of governmental forms and structures, a concern and indeed a focus on major concepts such as power, decision making, interest, organization, control, political norms and beliefs, obedience, equality, development, consensus, performance, and the like, we do not and cannot have a science of politics. We can have, at most, an art. Second, and this is the sign of the art, we may manage to arrive at some inductive generalizations based upon fragmentary empirical evidence. An inductive generalization is at best a statement about behavior. It can be derived from identical action and interaction under generally similar conditions over a long period of time in as many different contexts as possible. The behavior is not explained, but the weight of evidence allows us to anticipate and often predict it. A series of solidly supported inductive generalizations may in the last analysis be the most fruitful way to move gradually to a scientific approach, as it provides us with a rudimentary form of behavioral patterns. Our knowledge of politics is then at most an understanding of our accumulated experience. It is in this area that comparative politics has an important role to play. By carefully identifying a given behavior or structure or movement and by attempting to study it in as many settings as possible and over as long a period of time as possible, we can provide generalizations backed by evidence.

If we view our discipline as an art and if we limit its goals to inductive generalizations about politics, that is, a well-ordered and catalogued table or listing of accumulated experience, then three imperatives for research emerge, providing focus and satisfying the need for parsimony. First, we must study the practitioners of the art, the political leaders who hold office and, more generally, the governing elites that aspire to or possess political power. Second, we must study the structures and organizations and mechanisms through which the elites gain political power and exercise it, that is, the parties and other political associations. Third, we must be concerned with the governmental institutions through which demands are channeled or, just as often, by which they are generated. These imperatives do not exhaust our immediate task, but give us a starting point.

In studying the governmental elites and the institutions through which they gain and exercise power, we ought to consider the art of government as a problem-solving and goal-oriented activity. This kind of activity characterizes any art. The task of government is to identify problems (or to anticipate them) and provide for solutions. Our study then is to ask ourselves constantly, How well is the art performed? Who within the government listens, who foresees, who advises and suggests policy? What are the skills of the practitioners, and what are their objective capabilities? Finally, what is the impact of a decision upon the problem or the predicament it was designed to alleviate or to remove? The practitioner is not strictly bound by determinants. Communal life suggests and often sets goals of performance and achievement that become more than normative goals. They become in a way the "operative goals" that give direction to political action. The governing elite plays an independent role in seeking out the goals and in implementing them. Andrew Shonfield in his book on planning refers to the French planning as the result of an "elitist conspiracy."[8] More often than not decision making is an elitist conspiracy whose study and assessment would be far more rewarding than the survey and elaboration of all the input factors or the nonpolitical determinants involved.

But in the last analysis government is an act of will that can

---

[8] Andrew Shonfield, *Modern Capitalism* (London: Oxford University Press, 1965).

shuffle and reshuffle many of the determinants. Government involves choice, and the parameters are often wider than we are inclined to think. Any government will begin by surveying the conditions that appear to indicate the limits of freedom and choice; a government must always ask "what it has." But any government must also be in a position to assess what it wills. To say this is not to return to metaphysical speculation about the "will" of the state or the government. It is simply to reintroduce as integral parts of our discipline the state's performance and choices and the institutions through which they are implemented.

Relevance and Focus: A Set of Priorities

First and above all, it is our obligation to study all those organized manifestations, attitudes, and movements that press directly for state action or oppose state action. No matter what terms we use—decision making, authoritative allocation of values, regulation, adjudication, enforcement—we are concerned with the same old thing, the state. What is it asked to do? And what is it that people in a community do not want to see it do? To deny this pervasive empirical phenomenon, in the name of a given theory, is to deny our art or, for those who prefer, our science. The demand for state action or the demand that a given action cease is the very guts of politics. No science of politics—or for that matter, no science—can be built upon concepts and theories that disregard or avoid empirical phenomena. Why do the French farmers throw their peaches in the river and their beets on the highway? Why did the American students leave their comfortable homes to demonstrate in the streets? Why have American workers patterned their political demands in one way, but French workers in another? Obviously, to control, to influence, or to oppose state action.

Thus, our second priority also relates to what we have called the state, resurrecting what may appear to many graduate students to be an ancient term. We mean by it, of course, what we have always understood the term to mean, stripped of all its metaphysical trimmings. It means all the structures and organizations that make decisions and resolve conflicts with the expectation that their decisions will be obeyed: the civil service, the legislature, the executive, the judiciary, the host of public or semipublic corporations and organizations that are called upon to resolve differences and to make decisions. We include also the agencies whose function is to study facts, to deliberate about them, to identify areas of conflict, and to suggest policy decisions. The most relevant issue here is not the one that David Easton discusses, or rather suggests, that is, a theory of likely problems and predicaments—especially when the theory is pitched at a very high level of generalization.[9] What is instead important is to study the preparedness of the state to discern predicaments or problems. Potential problems can be theorized about. The actual political phenomenon, however, is the existing machinery through which problems are perceived—the agencies, the research, the flow of information, the manner in which individual values and constituency considerations enter into the minds of the men and women who work for the state—and finally includes that happy or fatal moment when the state copes with, ignores, or is simply unable to perceive the problem. The state can also, while perceiving the problem, either alleviate the predicament or suggest solutions utterly unrelated to it.

It is this second priority—the study of the state and all state agencies; their organization and performance; the scope of their decision making; the attitudes of the men and women who perform within their structures the roles of informing, studying, consulting, and deciding; and the major constituencies they serve—that has been so sadly neglected in the last decade or so. Few are the studies that focus on the state as an agency of deliberation, problem identification, and problem solving. Few are the studies of the institutions of the state in the modern developed systems. This is no accident at all. After the state was ostracized from the vocabulary of politics, we found it far more fashionable to study the systems in which there was no state, that is, the so-called developing, emerging, or new systems. The result was to eschew the urgent and nagging empirical situations in the modern and highly industrialized societies where our fate is to be decided, in order to study political phenomena and especially political development in the societies where there was no state. No wonder Huntington began to despair of studying the process of development in any terms other than "institutionalization," that is, the building of institutions with authority and legitimacy, such as the state and the party.[10]

The third priority is the study of political attitudes—the "civic culture," as Almond puts it, or what Beer calls "the structure of norms and beliefs,"[11] and what others have very loosely called ideology. But whatever name we give to them, the phenomena to be studied must point directly to the beliefs, norms, and orientations about the state (authority, scope of action, legitimacy, sense of participation, and involvement). If we are to remain strictly within

---

[9] Easton, *A Systems Analysis*, esp. chapters 4, 14, and 15.

[10] Samuel P. Huntington, "Political Development and Political Decay," *World Politics*, April 1965, pp. 383–430. See also his *Political Order in Changing Societies*.

[11] Almond and Verba, *The Civic Culture;* and Samuel Beer, *Patterns of Government* (part I, chapter 3).

the confines of relevance we must narrow our scope to those manifestations and attitudes that directly link the personal, economic, or
psychological phenomena with the political. The linkage between
"micro" and "macro" so well developed by Almond in his *Civic
Culture* in order to identify meaningful political orientations needs
to be carried a step forward. This can be done only when we reintroduce the state and its agencies and link them directly to political
orientations. Unless we take this step, we shall remain at the "micro" level. We shall not link attitudes to structures and forms, to
decisions and policies. The specifics about governmental decisions
and performance will elude us.

Finally, the fourth priority—which in a real sense is no priority
at all—relates to the study of what may be called the infrastructure
of the political world: attitudes and ideas; social, economic, and
cultural institutions; norms and values that are prevalent in any
given society, national or international. There is no reason why
we shouldn't study child rearing, the patterns of socialization, the
degree of concentration of economic power, the identification of personality types and traits, family life patterns, small groups and
private associations, religious attitudes, and so on. All of these, as
we indicated, *may* have a relevance to politics. In a number of
cases—and they are the ones that count—the relevance is only too
clear. It suggests itself by the very nature of the empirical phenomenon we are studying. It links a given organized political manifestation with a contextual factor that may explain it. It would be difficult
to understand the role of the French military up until the Dreyfus
case without knowing something about the education its members
received in Jesuit schools. But in this case we study education because we begin with the army as a political force operating within
the government and the state. We go deeper into contextual factors
in order to find an explanation of a manifest political phenomenon.

What we are trying to suggest by these priorities, then, is primarily a change of focus. Our concern is simply to pinpoint what is
political. We begin with the political; we catch it, so to speak, in
its most visible, open, and raw manifestation; we begin with the
top of the iceberg before we go deep to search for its submerged
base. We focus on the state and its agencies, on its types of action
or inaction, and on all those organized manifestations that call for
action or inaction on its part. We study the forms of decision making
and analyze and evaluate its substance. We explore its impact upon
groups, interests, and power elites within the system; we study in
turn their reactions to state actions and their counterdemands as
they are manifested through various media from political parties
down to voting.

The central focus of politics, therefore, and of the study of comparative politics is the governmental institutions and political elites,

their role, their levels of performance and nonperformance. Stating this in such blunt terms appears to be utterly naïve. Shall we return then to the descriptive study of governmental institutions? Far from it. What we are suggesting is a starting point and a focus of investigation. Any such investigation, we know today, will inevitably lead us, as it should, far and wide in search of the contextual factors (rather than determinants) within the framework of which a government operates and to which its action, its performance, and its policies may often be attributed. We shall have to probe the infrastructure, but without losing sight of either our focus or the relevant question we began our investigation with.

What accounts for a well-organized civil service? What is the impact of large-scale organizations—parties, bureaucracy, and so on—upon the citizen? Under what conditions does public opinion exercise its influence on the government? What accounts for political instability? Is an executive who is responsible to the people more restrained than one responsible to the legislature? How and under what conditions does representation degenerate into an expression of particular interests? Under what conditions do young people maintain political attitudes different from those of their parents, and at what point do they revolt? Under what conditions do ruling groups become responsive to popular demands?

We can multiply these questions, but they illustrate the point. None of them can lead to hard hypotheses and proof (or disproof). Some cannot be easily answered. But this is not too important unless we are to accept that only those questions that can lead to testing in the rigorous, and therefore impossible, meaning of the term have the freedom of the market. In fact, the questions we suggest lead to a comparative survey, both historical and contemporaneous, of some of the most crucial political phenomena: responsiveness, performance, change, development, and a host of others. Such a survey will inevitably produce inductive generalizations, perhaps in the manner of Machiavelli, but with far more sophisticated tools and greater access to data than was ever the case before. It will inevitably help us to qualify our questions and to reformulate them as hypotheses that will suggest other qualifications—new variables, if you wish—and lead to further investigation—testing, if you wish—and the reformulation of the questions—the gradual development of theory, if you like.

RECENT CONTRIBUTIONS—CLUSTERING

The vitality of a discipline lies, let us repeat, in its capacity to project theories and concepts that help us familiarize ourselves with the outside world. Comparative politics is emerging as the most comprehensive and theoretical branch of political science. We do not use the term *familiarize* pejoratively. To familiarize means to identify the facts and engage them in a dialogue in trying to find explanations. To do so intelligently, however, one must know what questions to ask. Any dialogue must lead to intellectual processes whereby certain facts are discarded because they provide no answers, while others are taken into account. In order to discard and to accept facts, one must have established certain "linkages" that make facts cluster together into patterns, so that sentences in the dialogue are meaningful. Like words, facts take on coherence, and give at least a tentative answer to questions.

Nobody will deny that students of politics today are far more familiar with the empirical processes of politics than they were in the past. Familiarization has taken place in both horizontal and vertical terms. Horizontally, the world has indeed become our oyster. A mere perusal of articles on individual countries listed in the International Political Science Abstracts will show that the Eurocentric approach no longer prevails. Indeed, a committee of the Social Science Research Council has appealed for the revitalization of European studies, especially in politics.[12] We do not imply that with the world as our oyster, new pearls of wisdom have been found. We are simply pointing out that our laboratory for comparative study has been expanded as never before, so much so as to lead to some confusion and a pause.

Comparative politics has also been greatly enriched vertically: It has gained in depth. No other branch of the political science discipline has made so much effort to relate the state to society and to seek determinants of political phenomena in the larger socioeconomic matrix. Again the contrast between now and the past is marked. Fifty years ago the march toward democracy was considered irresistible and authoritarianism but an aberration. Textbooks on European governments were the indispensable fare. Institutional structures and procedures were minutely dissected and discussed, and comparison was little more than a cataloging of institutions. Carl J. Friedrich's *Constitutional Government and Democracy*[13] provided a more rewarding analysis. But, as Harry Eckstein pointed out, certain political trends were rejected as aberrant if they did not square with commonsense criteria that in the last analysis were defined by the author's notion of human nature. Comparative government textbooks were limited both horizontally (confined to Europe) and vertically (dealing only with formal governmental and legal structures).

---

[12] Suzanne Berger et al., "New Perspectives for the Study of Western Europe," Social Science Research Council *Items* 29, no. 3 (September 1975).

[13] Carl J. Friedrich, *Constitutional Government and Democracy,* 4th ed. (Waltham, Mass.: Blaisdell, 1968).

We mentioned some of the factors that led to the expansion of the vertical dimension of comparative politics. They include the general behavioral revolution (the development of general system theories and borrowing from sociological and psychological theory) and a broadening of comparative political analysis (relating institutions to social factors such as class, status, personality, groups, culture, socialization). Especially important has been the interest in modernization and its socioeconomic determinants or correlates. The dialogue has been refined. Institutions and their performance or "outputs" are related to a multiplicity of inputs (perceptions, aspirations, outlooks, interests, claims). The enrichment of comparative politics literature has accounted, as noted, for an embarrassment of choices and perhaps a confusion of priorities.

At the scholarly level, the literature in comparative politics has led even the aficionados to distraction. There is a burgeoning subdivision of specializations—we call it clustering—not only by area or country, as in the past, but by subfields such as developmentalism, public policy, neocorporatism, culturalism, institutionalism, and political economy. Recent publications exhibit the following: (1) most of them compare political processes and a variety of political phenomena across a limited number of countries; (2) they do so with regard to a coherent categorical concept—culture, interests, elites, electoral processes, policy outputs, modernization, and so on; and (3) they propose to give an explanation, that is, to identify the factors that account for a given political process or manifestation.

What we call *clustering* amounts, at least temporarily, to the abandonment of the search for a general theory that characterized our efforts in the 60s. As Sidney Verba pointed out in a recent colloquium, "The absence of a single, unifying, integrating model and body of assumptions is clearly especially disappointing to graduate students and some young practitioners." He reported the general consensus of many comparatists that the field lacked clear focus, leadership, and an agreed-upon set of theoretical underpinnings.[14] Instead, clustering reflects a search for the development of middle-range theory capable of handling a limited number of variables applicable to a limited number of empirical situations. Typical topics include: the role of the military; the role of the military in modernization; the study of structures, including bureaucracy, in the formulation of social and public policy; the pervasive trend toward authoritarianism in developing nations; the impact of modernization on political stability and institution formation; the relationship between interests and the state in the making of public policy;

---

[14] Sidney Verba, from his unpublished paper, "Comparative Politics: Where We Have Been, Where Are We Going?" Center for International Affairs, Harvard University, 1982.

electoral processes; the impact of international economic factors on public policy; and comparative assessment of policy outputs or performance of individual states.

Political scientists in mainstream and neo-Marxist traditions have been reexamining the role of the state as an autonomous entity. There has also been a renewed interest in economic theory and models, and a renewed emphasis, in the tradition of both Marx and Weber, on historical comparative studies that single out social class and ideology as major variables. Clustering, as opposed to the search for grand theory, has given to the field a new vitality, and may ultimately pave the way to the development of some unifying models and priorities.

CHAPTER ONE

Comparing Political Systems

1

How We Compare

John Stuart Mill

There are two kinds of sociological inquiry. In the first kind, the question proposed is, what effect will follow from a given cause, a certain general condition of social circumstances being presupposed. As, for example, what would be the effect of . . . abolishing monarchy, or introducing universal suffrage, in the present condition of society and civilization in any European country, or under any other given supposition with regard to the circumstances of society in general: without reference to the changes which might take place, or which may already be in progress, in those circumstances. But there is also a second inquiry, namely, what are the laws which determine those general circumstances themselves. In this last the question is, not what will be the effect of a given cause in a certain state of society, but what are the causes which produce, and the phenomena which characterize, States of Society generally. In the solution of this question consists the general Science of Society; by which all the conclusions of the other and more special kind of inquiry must be limited and controlled.

In order to conceive correctly the scope of this general science, and distinguish it from the subordinate departments of sociological speculation, it is necessary to fix with precision the ideas attached

---

Source: John Stuart Mill, "Of the Inverse Deductive, or Historical Method," in *A System of Logic,* Book VI, chapter 10, (New York: Harper, 1846). Abridged by the editors.

to the phrase, "A State of Society." What is called a state of society, is the simultaneous state of all the greater social facts, or phenomena. Such are, the degree of knowledge, and of intellectual and moral culture, existing in the community, and in every class of it; the state of industry, of wealth and its distribution; the habitual occupations of the community; their division into classes, and the relations of those classes to one another; the common beliefs which they entertain on all the subjects most important to mankind, and the degree of assurance with which those beliefs are held; their tastes, and the character and degree of their aesthetic development; their form of government, and the more important of their laws and customs. The condition of all these things, and of many more which will spontaneously suggest themselves, constitute the state of society or the state of civilization at any given time.

When states of society, and the causes which produce them, are spoken of as a subject of science, it is implied that there exists a natural correlation among these different elements; that not every variety of combination of these general social facts is possible, but only certain combinations; that, in short, there exist Uniformities of Coexistence between the states of the various social phenomena. And such is the truth: as is indeed a necessary consequence of the influence exercised by every one of those phenomena over every other. It is a fact implied in the *consensus* of the various parts of the social body.

States of society are like different constitutions or different ages in the physical frame; they are conditions not of one or a few organs or functions, but of the whole organism. Accordingly, the information which we possess respecting past ages, and respecting the various states of society now existing in different regions of the earth, does, when duly analyzed, exhibit such uniformities. It *is* found that when one of the features of society is in a particular state, a state of all the other features, more or less precisely determinate, always coexists with it. . . .

It is one of the characters, not absolutely peculiar to the sciences of human nature and society, but belonging to them in a peculiar degree, to be conversant with a subject matter whose properties are changeable. I do not mean changeable from day to day, but from age to age: so that not only the qualities of individuals vary, but those of the majority are not the same in one age as in another.

The principal cause of this peculiarity is the extensive and constant reaction of the effects upon their causes. The circumstances in which mankind are placed, operating according to their own laws and to the laws of human nature, form the characters of the men; but the men, in their turn, mould and shape the circumstances, for themselves and for those who come after them. From this reciprocal action there must necessarily result either a cycle or a progress. . . .

But, while it is an imperative rule never to introduce any generalizations from history into the social science unless sufficient grounds can be pointed out for it in human nature, I do not think any one will contend that it would have been possible, setting out from the principles of human nature and from the general circumstances of man's position in the universe, to determine à priori the order in which human development must take place, and to predict, consequently, the general facts of history up to the present time. The initial stages of human progress—when man, as yet unmodified by society, and characterized only by the instincts resulting directly from his organization, was acted upon by outward objects of a comparatively simple and universal character—might indeed, as M. Comte remarks, be deduced from the laws of human nature; which moreover is the only possible mode of ascertaining them, since of that form of human existence no direct memorials are preserved. . . .

If, therefore, the series of the effects themselves did not, when examined as a whole, manifest any regularity, we should in vain attempt to construct a general science of society. We must in that case have contented ourselves with that subordinate order of sociological speculation formerly noticed, namely, with endeavoring to ascertain what would be the effect of the introduction of any new cause, in a state of society supposed to be fixed; a knowledge sufficient for most of the ordinary exigencies of daily political practice, but liable to fail in all cases in which the progressive movement of society is one of the influencing elements; and therefore more precarious in proportion as the case is more important. But since both the natural varieties of mankind, and the original diversities of local circumstances, are much less considerable than the points of agreement, there will naturally be a certain degree of uniformity in the progressive development of man and of his works. . . . History accordingly does, when judiciously examined, afford Empirical Laws of Society. And the problem of general sociology is to ascertain these, and connect them with the laws of human nature by deductions showing that such were the derivative laws naturally to be expected as the consequences of those ultimate ones.

It is indeed, in most cases, hardly possible, even after history has suggested the derivative law, to demonstrate à priori that such was the only order of succession or of coexistence in which the effects could, consistently with the laws of human nature, have been produced. We can at most make out that there were strong à priori reasons for expecting it and that no other order of succession or coexistence would have been by any means so likely to result from the nature of man and his position upon earth. This, however—which, in the Inverse Deductive Method that we are now characterizing, is a real process of verification—is as indispensable (to be more so is impossible) as verification by specific experience has been shown to be where the conclusion is originally obtained by the direct way of deduction. The empirical laws must be the result of but a few instances, since few nations have ever attained at all, and still fewer by their own independent development, a high stage of social progress. If, therefore, even one or two of these few instances be insufficiently known or imperfectly analyzed into its elements, and therefore not adequately compared with other instances, nothing is more probable than that a wrong empirical law will result instead of the right one. Accordingly, the most erroneous generalizations are continually made from the course of history. . . . The only check or corrective is, constant verification by psychological and ethological laws. We may add to this, that no one but a person competently skilled in those laws is capable of preparing the materials for historical generalization by analyzing the facts of history, or even by observing the social phenomena of his own time. No other will be aware of the comparative importance of different facts, nor consequently know what facts he is to look out for, or what to observe; still less will he be capable of estimating the evidence of those facts which, as is the case with most, cannot be observed directly, but must be inferred from marks.

The Empirical Laws of Society are of two kinds; some are uniformities of coexistence, some of succession. . . .

In order to obtain better empirical laws, we must not rest satisfied with noting the progressive changes which manifest themselves in the separate elements of society, and in which nothing is indicated but the relation of the fragments of the effect to corresponding fragments of the cause. It is necessary to combine the statical view of social phenomena with the dynamical, considering not only the progressive changes of the different elements, but the contemporaneous condition of each; and thus obtain empirically the law of correspondence not only between the simultaneous states, but between the simultaneous changes, of those elements. This law of correspondence it is, which, after being duly verified a priori, will become the real scientific derivative law of the development of humanity and human affairs.

In the difficult process of observation and comparison which is here required, it would evidently be a very great assistance if it should happen to be the fact, that some one element in the complex existence of social man is preëminent over all others as the prime agent of the social movement. For we could then take the progress of that one element as the central chain, to each successive link of which, the corresponding links of all the other progressions being appended, the succession of the facts would by this alone be presented in a kind of spontaneous order, far more nearly approaching to the real order of their filiation than could be obtained by any other merely empirical process.

Now, the evidence of history and the evidence of human nature combine, by a most striking instance of consilience, to show that there is really one social element which is thus predominant, and almost paramount, among the agents of the social progression. This is, the state of the speculative faculties of mankind; including the nature of the speculative beliefs which by any means they have arrived at, concerning themselves and the world by which they are surrounded.

It would be a great error, and one very little likely to be committed, to assert that speculation, intellectual activity, the pursuit of truth, is among the more powerful propensities of human nature, or fills a large place in the lives of any, save decidedly exceptional individuals. But notwithstanding the relative weakness of this principle among other sociological agents, its influence is the main determining cause of the social progress; all the other dispositions of our nature which contribute to that progress, being dependent upon it for the means of accomplishing their share of the work. Thus (to take the most obvious case first), the impelling force to most of the improvements effected in the arts of life, is the desire of increased material comfort; but as we can only act upon external objects in proportion to our knowledge of them, the state of knowledge at any time is the impassable limit of the industrial improvements possible at that time; and the progress of industry must follow, and depend upon, the progress of knowledge. The same thing may be shown to be true, though it is not quite so obvious, of the progress of the fine arts. Further, as the strongest propensities of human nature (being the purely selfish ones, and those of a sympathetic character which partake most of the nature of selfishness) evidently tend in themselves to disunite mankind, not to unite them—to make them rivals, not confederates; social existence is only possible by a disciplining of those more powerful propensities, which consists in subordinating them to a common system of opinions. The degree of this subordination is the measure of the completeness of the social union, and the nature of the common opinions determines its kind. But in order that mankind should conform their actions to any set of opinions, these opinions must exist, must be believed by them. And thus, the state of the speculative faculties, the character of the propositions assented to by the intellect, essentially determines the moral and political state of the community, as we have already seen that it determines the physical.

These conclusions, deduced from the laws of human nature, are in entire accordance with the general facts of history. Every considerable change historically known to us in the condition of any portion of mankind, has been preceded by a change, of proportional extent, in the state of their knowledge, or in their prevalent beliefs. As between any given state of speculation, and the correlative state of everything else, it was almost always the former which first showed itself; though the effects, no doubt, reacted potently upon the cause. Every considerable advance in material civilization has been preceded by an advance in knowledge; and when any great social change has come to pass, a great change in the opinions and modes of thinking of society had taken place shortly before. Polytheism, Judaism, Christianity, Protestantism, the negative philosophy of modern Europe, and its positive science—each of these has been a primary agent in making society what it was at each successive period, while society was but secondarily instrumental in making *them;* each of them (so far as causes can be assigned for its existence) being mainly an emanation not from the practical life of the period, but from the state of belief and thought during some time previous. The weakness of the speculative propensity has not, therefore, prevented the progress of speculation from governing that of society at large; it has only, and too often, prevented progress altogether, where the intellectual progression has come to an early stand for want of sufficiently favorable circumstances.

From this accumulated evidence, we are justified in concluding, that the order of human progression in all respects will be a corollary deducible from the order of progression in the intellectual convictions of mankind, that is, from the law of the successive transformation of religion and science. The question remains, whether this law can be determined, at first from history as an empirical law, then converted into a scientific theorem by deducing it a priori from the principles of human nature. As the progress of knowledge and the changes in the opinions of mankind are very slow, and manifest themselves in a well-defined manner only at long intervals; it cannot be expected that the general order of sequence should be discoverable from the examination of less than a very considerable part of the duration of the social progress. It is necessary to take into consideration the whole of past time, from the first recorded condition of the human race; and it is probable that all the terms of the series already past were indispensable to the operation; that the memorable phenomena of the last generation, and even those of the present, were necessary to manifest the law, and that consequently the Science of History has only become possible in our own time.

2

The Analysis of Political Systems

David Easton

I. SOME ATTRIBUTES OF POLITICAL SCIENCE

In an earlier work I have argued for the need to develop general, empirically oriented theory as the most economical way in the long run to understand political life. Here I propose to indicate a point of view that, at the least, might serve as a springboard for discussion of alternative approaches and, at most, as a small step in the direction of a general political theory. I wish to stress that what I have to say is a mere orientation to the problem of theory; outside of economics and perhaps psychology, it would be presumptuous to call very much in social science "theory," in the strict sense of the term.

Furthermore, I shall offer only a Gestalt of my point of view, so that it will be possible to evaluate, in the light of the whole, those parts that I do stress. In doing this, I know I can run the definite risk that the meaning and implications of this point of view may be only superficially communicated; but it is a risk I shall have to undertake since I do not know how to avoid it sensibly.

The study of politics is concerned with understanding how authoritative decisions are made and executed for a society. We can try to understand political life by viewing each of its aspects piecemeal. We can examine the operation of such institutions as political

Source: David Easton, "An Approach to the Analysis of Political Systems," *World Politics* 9, no. 3 (April 1957), pp. 383–400. By permission. Article abridged by the editors.

parties, interest groups, government, and voting; we can study the nature and consequences of such political practices as manipulation, propaganda, and violence; we can seek to reveal the structure within which these practices occur. By combining the results we can obtain a rough picture of what happens in any self-contained political unit.

In combining these results, however, there is already implicit the notion that each part of the larger political canvas does not stand alone but is related to each other part; or, to put it positively, that the operation of no one part can be fully understood without reference to the way in which the whole itself operates. I have suggested in my book, *The Political System*,[1] that it is valuable to adopt this implicit assumption as an articulate premise for research and to view political life as a system of interrelated activities. These activities derive their relatedness or systemic ties from the fact that they all more or less influence the way in which authoritative decisions are formulated and executed for a society.

Once we begin to speak of political life as a system of activity, certain consequences follow for the way in which we can undertake to analyze the working of a system. The very idea of a system suggests that we can separate political life from the rest of social activity, at least for analytical purposes, and examine it as though for the moment it were a self-contained entity surrounded by, but clearly distinguishable from, the environment or setting in which it operates. In much the same way, astronomers consider the solar system a complex of events isolated for certain purposes from the rest of the universe.

Furthermore, if we hold the system of political actions as a unit before our mind's eye, as it were, we can see that what keeps the system going are inputs of various kinds. These inputs are converted by the processes of the system into outputs and these, in turn, have consequences both for the system and for the environment in which the system exists. The formula here is very simple but, as I hope to show, also very illuminating: inputs—political system or processes—outputs. These relationships are shown diagrammatically in Figure 1. This diagram represents a very primitive "model"— to dignify it with a fashionable name—for approaching the study of political life.

Political systems have certain properties because they are systems. To present an over-all view of the whole approach, let me identify the major attributes, say a little about each, and then treat one of these properties at somewhat greater length, even though still inadequately.

1.   Properties of identification. To distinguish a political system

---

[1] David Easton, *The Political System* (New York: Alfred A. Knopf, 1953).

FIGURE 1

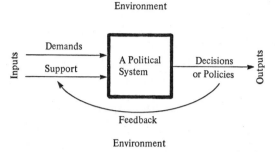

Environment

Feedback

Environment

from other social systems, we must be able to identify it by describing its fundamental units and establishing the boundaries that demarcate it from units outside the system.

a. Units of a political system. The units are the elements of which we say a system is composed. In the case of a political system, they are political actions. Normally it is useful to look at these as they structure themselves in political roles and political groups.

b. Boundaries. Some of the most significant questions with regard to the operation of political systems can be answered only if we bear in mind the obvious fact that a system does not exist in a vacuum. It is always immersed in a specific setting or environment. The way in which a system works will be in part a function of its response to the total social, biological, and physical environment.

The special problem with which we are confronted is how to distinguish systematically between a political system and its setting. Does it even make sense to say that a political system has a boundary dividing it from its setting? If so, how are we to identify the line of demarcation?

Without pausing to argue the matter, I would suggest that it is useful to conceive of a political system as having a boundary in the same sense as a physical system. The boundary of a political system is defined by all those actions more or less directly related to the making of binding decisions for a society; every social action that does not partake of this characteristic will be excluded from the system and thereby will automatically be viewed as an external variable in the environment.

2. Inputs and outputs. Presumably, if we select political systems for special study, we do so because we believe that they have characteristically important consequences for society, namely, authoritative decisions. These consequences I shall call the outputs. If we judged that political systems did not have important outputs for society, we would probably not be interested in them.

Unless a system is approaching a state of entropy—and we can assume that this is not true of most political systems—it must have continuing inputs to keep it going. Without inputs the system can do no work; without outputs we cannot identify the work done by the system. The specific research tasks in this connection would be to identify the inputs and the forces that shape and change them, to trace the processes through which they are transformed into outputs, to describe the general conditions under which such processes can be maintained, and to establish the relationship between outputs and succeeding inputs of the system.

From this point of view, much light can be shed on the working of a political system if we take into account the fact that much of what happens within a system has its birth in the efforts of the members of the system to cope with the changing environment. We can appreciate this point if we consider a familiar biological system such as the human organism. It is subject to constant stress from its surroundings to which it must adapt in one way or another if it is not to be completely destroyed. In part, of course, the way in which the body works represents responses to needs that are generated by the very organization of its anatomy and functions; but in large part, in order to understand both the structure and the working of the body, we must also be very sensitive to the inputs from the environment.

In the same way, the behavior of every political system is to some degree imposed upon it by the kind of system it is, that is, by its own structure and internal needs. But its behavior also reflects the strains occasioned by the specific setting within which the system operates. It may be argued that most of the significant changes within a political system have their origin in shifts among the external variables. Since I shall be devoting the bulk of this article to examining some of the problems related to the exchange between political systems and their environments, I shall move on to a rapid description of other properties of political systems.

3. Differentiation within a system. As we shall see in a moment, from the environment come both energy to activate a system and information with regard to which the system uses this energy. In this way a system is able to do work. It has some sort of output that is different from the input that enters from the environment. We can take it as a useful hypothesis that if a political system is to perform some work for anything but a limited interval of time, a minimal amount of differentiation in its structure must occur. In fact, empirically it is impossible to find a significant political system in which the same units all perform the same activities at the same time. The members of a system engage in at least some

minimal division of labor that provides a structure within which action takes place.

4. Integration of a system. This fact of differentiation opens up a major area of inquiry with regard to political systems. Structural differentiation sets in motion forces that are potentially disintegrative in their results for the system. If two or more units are performing different kinds of activity at the same time, how are these activities to be brought into the minimal degree of articulation necessary if the members of the system are not to end up in utter disorganization with regard to the production of the outputs of interest to us? We can hypothesize that if a structured system is to maintain itself, it must provide mechanisms whereby its members are integrated or induced to cooperate in some minimal degree so that they make authoritative decisions.

II. INPUTS: DEMANDS

Now that I have mentioned some major attributes of political systems that I suggest require special attention if we are to develop a generalized approach, I want to consider in greater detail the way in which an examination of inputs and outputs will shed some light on the working of these systems.

Among inputs of a political system there are two basic kinds: demands and support. These inputs give a political system its dynamic character. They furnish it both with the raw material or information that the system is called upon to process and with the energy to keep it going.

The reason why a political system emerges in a society at all—that is, why men engage in political activity—is that demands are being made by persons or groups in the society that cannot all be fully satisfied. In all societies one fact dominates political life: scarcity prevails with regard to most of the valued things. Some of the claims for these relatively scarce things never find their way into the political system but are satisfied through the private negotiations of or settlements by the persons involved. Demands for prestige may find satisfaction through the status relations of society; claims for wealth are met in part through the economic system; aspirations for power find expression in educational, fraternal, labor, and similar private organizations. Only where wants require some special organized effort on the part of society to settle them authoritatively may we say that they have become inputs of the political system.

Systematic research would require us to address ourselves to several key questions with regard to these demands.

1. How do demands arise and assume their particular character in a society? In answer to this question, we can point out that demands have their birth in two sectors of experience: either in the environment of a system or within the system itself. We shall call these the external and internal demands, respectively.

Let us look at the external demands first. I find it useful to see the environment not as an undifferentiated mass of events but rather as systems clearly distinguishable from one another and from the political system. In the environment we have such systems as the ecology, economy, culture, personality, social structure, and demography. Each of these constitutes a major set of variables in the setting that helps to shape the kind of demands entering a political system. For purposes of illustrating what I mean, I shall say a few words about culture.

The members of every society act within the framework of an ongoing culture that shapes their general goals, specific objectives, and the procedures that the members feel ought to be used. Every culture derives part of its unique quality from the fact that it emphasizes one or more special aspects of behavior and this strategic emphasis serves to differentiate it from other cultures with respect to the demands that it generates. As far as the mass of the people is concerned, some cultures, such as our own, are weighted heavily on the side of economic wants, success, privacy, leisure activity, and rational efficiency. Others, such as that of the Fox Indians, strive toward the maintenance of harmony, even if in the process the goals of efficiency and rationality may be sacrificed. Still others, such as the Kachins of highland Burma, stress the pursuit of power and prestige. The culture embodies the standards of value in a society and thereby marks out areas of potential conflict, if the valued things are in short supply relative to demand. The typical demands that will find their way into the political process will concern the matters in conflict that are labeled important by the culture. For this reason we cannot hope to understand the nature of the demands presenting themselves for political settlement unless we are ready to explore systematically and intensively their connection with the culture. And what I have said about culture applies, with suitable modifications, to other parts of the setting of a political system.

But not all demands originate or have their major locus in the environment. Important types stem from situations occurring within a political system itself. Typically, in every ongoing system, demands may emerge for alterations in the political relationships of the members themselves, as the result of dissatisfaction stemming from these relationships. For example, in a political system based upon representation, in which equal representation is an important political norm, demands may arise for equalizing representation between urban and rural voting districts. Similarly, demands for changes in the process of recruitment of formal political leaders, for modifications of the way in which constitutions are amended, and the like may all be internally inspired demands.

I find it useful and necessary to distinguish these from external demands because they are, strictly speaking, not inputs of the system but something that we can call "withinputs," if we can tolerate a cumbersome neologism, and because their consequences for the character of a political system are more direct than in the case of external demands. Furthermore, if we were not aware of this difference in classes of demands, we might search in vain for an explanation of the emergence of a given set of internal demands if we turned only to the environment.

2. How are demands transformed into issues? What determines whether a demand becomes a matter for serious political discussion or remains something to be resolved privately among the members of society? The occurrence of a demand, whether internal or external, does not thereby automatically convert it into a political *issue*. Many demands die at birth or linger on with the support of an insignificant fraction of the society and are never raised to the level of possible political decision. Others become issues, an issue being a demand that the members of a political system are prepared to deal with as a significant item for discussion through the recognized channels in the system.

The distinction between demands and issues raises a number of questions about which we need data if we are to understand the processes through which claims typically become transformed into issues. For example, we would need to know something about the relationship between a demand and the location of its initiators or supporters in the power structures of the society, the importance of secrecy as compared with publicity in presenting demands, the matter of timing of demands, the possession of political skills or know-how, access to channels of communication, the attitudes and states of mind of possible publics, and the images held by the initiators of demands with regard to the way in which things get done in the particular political system. Answers to matters such as these would possibly yield a conversion index reflecting the probability of a set of demands being converted into live political issues.

If we assume that political science is primarily concerned with the way in which authoritative decisions are made for a society, demands require special attention as a major type of input of political systems. I have suggested that demands influence the behavior of a system in a number of ways. They constitute a significant part of the material upon which the system operates. They are also one of the sources of change in political systems, since as the environment fluctuates it generates new types of demand-inputs for the system. Accordingly, without this attention to the origin and determinants of demands we would be at a loss to be able to treat rigorously not only the operation of a system at a moment of time but also its change over a specified interval. Both the statics and historical dynamics of a political system depend upon a detailed understanding of demands, particularly of the impact of the setting on them.

III. INPUTS: SUPPORT

Inputs of demands alone are not enough to keep a political system operating. They are only the raw material out of which finished products called decisions are manufactured. Energy in the form of actions or orientations promoting and resisting a political system, the demands arising in it, and the decisions issuing from it must also be put into the system to keep it running. This input I shall call support. Without support, demands could not be satisfied or conflicts in goals composed. If demands are to be acted upon, the members of a system undertaking to pilot the demands through to their transformation into binding decisions and those who seek to influence the relevant processes in any way must be able to count on support from others in the system. Just how much support, from how many and which members of a political system, are separate and important questions that I shall touch on shortly.

What do we mean by support? We can say that A supports B either when A acts on behalf of or when he orients himself favorably toward B's goals, interests, and actions. Supportive behavior may thus be of two kinds. It may consist of actions promoting the goals, interests, and actions of another person. We may vote for a political candidate, or defend a decision by the highest court of the land. In these cases, support manifests itself through overt action.

On the other hand, supportive behavior may involve not external observable acts, but those internal forms of behavior we call orientations or states of mind. As I use the phrase, a supportive state of mind is a deep-seated set of attitudes or predispositions, or a readiness to act on behalf of some other person. It exists when we say that a man is loyal to his party, attached to democracy, or infused with patriotism. What such phrases as these have in common is the fact that they refer to a state of feelings on the part of a person. No overt action is involved at this level of description, although the implication is that the individual will pursue a course of action consistent with his attitudes. Where the anticipated action does not flow from our perception of the state of mind, we assume that we have not penetrated deeply enough into the true feelings of the person but have merely skimmed off his surface attitudes.

Supportive states of mind are vital inputs for the operation and maintenance of a political system. For example, it is often said that the struggle in the international sphere concerns mastery over men's minds. To a certain extent this is true. If the members of a political system are deeply attached to a system or its ideals, the likelihood of their participating in either domestic or foreign politics in such a way as to undermine the system is reduced by a large factor. Presumably, even in the face of considerable provocation, ingrained supportive feelings of loyalty may be expected to prevail.

We shall need to identify the typical mechanisms through which supportive attitudes are inculcated and continuously reinforced within a political system. But our prior task is to specify and examine the political objects in relation to which support is extended.

1. The Domain of Support

Support is fed into the political system in relation to three objects: the community, the regime, and the government. There must be convergence of attitude and opinion as well as some willingness to act with regard to each of these objects. Let us examine each in turn.

1. The political community. No political system can continue to operate unless its members are willing to support the existence of a group that seeks to settle differences or promote decisions through peaceful action in common. The point is so obvious—being dealt with usually under the heading of the growth of national unity—that it may well be overlooked; and yet it is a premise upon which the continuation of any political system depends. To refer to this phenomenon we can speak of the political community. At this level of support we are not concerned with whether a government exists or whether there is loyalty to a constitutional order. For the moment we only ask whether the members of the group that we are examining are sufficiently oriented toward each other to want to contribute their collective energies toward pacific settlement of their varying demands. . . .

2. The regime. Support for a second major part of a political system helps to supply the energy to keep the system running. This aspect of the system I shall call the regime. It consists of all those arrangements that regulate the way in which the demands put into the system are settled and the way in which decisions are put into effect. They are the so-called rules of the game, in the light of which actions by members of the system are legitimated and accepted by the bulk of the members as authoritative. Unless there is a minimum convergence of attitudes in support of these fundamental rules—the constitutional principles, as we call them in Western society—there would be insufficient harmony in the

actions of the members of a system to meet the problems generated by their support of a political community. The fact of trying to settle demands in common means that there must be known principles governing the way in which resolutions of differences of claims are to take place.

3. The government. If a political system is going to be able to handle the conflicting demands put into it, not only must the members of the system be prepared to support the settlement of these conflicts in common and possess some consensus with regard to the rules governing the mode of settlement; they must also be ready to support a government as it undertakes the concrete tasks involved in negotiating such settlements. When we come to the outputs of a system, we shall see the rewards that are available to a government for mobilizing support. At this point, I just wish to draw attention to this need on the part of a government for support if it is going to be able to make decisions with regard to demands. Of course, a government may elicit support in many ways: through persuasion, consent, or manipulation. It may also impose unsupported settlements of demands through threats of force. But it is a familiar axiom of political science that a government based upon force alone is not long for this world; it must buttress its position by inducing a favorable state of mind in its subjects through fair or foul means.

The fact that support directed to a political system can be broken down conceptually into three elements—support for the community, regime, and government—does not mean, of course, that in the concrete case support for each of these three objects is independent. In fact we might and normally do find all three kinds of support very closely intertwined, so that the presence of one is a function of the presence of one or both of the other types. . . .

2. Quantity and Scope of Support

How much support needs to be put into a system and how many of its members need to contribute such support if the system is to be able to do the job of converting demands to decisions? No ready answer can be offered. The actual situation in each case would determine the amount and scope required. We can, however, visualize a number of situations that will be helpful in directing our attention to possible generalizations.

Under certain circumstances very few members need to support a system at any level. The members might be dull and apathetic, indifferent to the general operations of the system, its progress or decisions. In a loosely connected system such as India has had, this might well be the state of mind of by far the largest segment of the membership. Either in fact they have not been affected by national decisions or they have not perceived that they were so affected. They may have little sense of identification with the present regime and government and yet, with regard to the input of demands, the system may be able to act on the basis of the support offered by the known 3 percent of the Western-oriented politicians and intellectuals who are politically active. In other words, we can have a small minority putting in quantitatively sufficient supportive energy to keep the system going. However, we can venture the hypothesis that where members of a system are putting in numerous demands, there is a strong probability that they will actively offer support or hostility at one of the three levels of the system, depending upon the degree to which these demands are being met through appropriate decisions.

Alternatively, we may find that all the members of a system are putting in support, but the amount may be so low as to place one or all aspects of the system in jeopardy. Modern France is perhaps a classic illustration. The input of support at the level of the political community is probably adequate for the maintenance of France as a national political unit. But for a variety of historical and contemporary reasons, there is considerable doubt as to whether the members of the French political system are putting in anything but a low order of support to the regime or any particular government. This low amount of support, even though spread over a relatively large segment of the population, leaves the French political system on somewhat less secure foundations than is the case with India. There support is less widespread but more active—that is, quantitatively greater—on the part of a minority. As this illustration indicates, the amount of support is not necessarily proportional to its scope.

It may seem from the above discussion as though the members of a political system either put in support or withhold it—that is, demonstrate hostility or apathy. In fact, members may and normally do simultaneously engage in supportive and hostile behavior. What we must be interested in is the net balance of support.

IV. MECHANISMS OF SUPPORT

To this point I have suggested that no political system can yield the important outputs we call authoritative decisions unless, in addition to demands, support finds its way into the system. I have discussed the possible object to which support may be directed, and some problems with regard to the domain, quantity, and scope of support. We are now ready to turn to the main question raised by our attention to support as a crucial input: how do systems typically manage to maintain a steady flow of support? Without it a system will not absorb sufficient energy from its members to be able to convert demands to decisions.

In theory, there might be an infinite variety of means through which members could be induced to support a system; in practice, certain well-established classes of mechanisms are used. Research in this area needs to be directed to exploring the precise way in which a particular system utilizes these mechanisms and to refining our understanding of the way in which they contribute to the making of authoritative policy.

A society generates support for a political system in two ways: through outputs that meet the demands of the members of society; and through the processes of politicization. Let us look at outputs first.

1. Outputs as a Mechanism of Support

An output of a political system, it will be recalled, is a political decision or policy. One of the major ways of strengthening the ties of the members to their system is through providing decisions that tend to satisfy the day-to-day demands of these members. Fundamentally this is the truth that lies in the aphorism that one can fool some of the people some of the time but not all of them all of the time. Without some minimal satisfaction of demands, the ardor of all but the most fanatical patriot is sure to cool. The outputs, consisting of political decisions, constitute a body of specific inducements for the members of a system to support that system.

Inducements of this kind may be positive or negative. Where negative, they threaten the members of the system with various kinds of sanctions ranging from a small monetary fine to physical detention, ostracism, or loss of life, as in our own system with regard to the case of legally defined treason. In every system support stems in part from fear of sanctions or compulsion; in autocratic systems the proportion of coerced support is at a maximum. For want of space I shall confine myself to those cases where positive incentives loom largest.

Since the specific outputs of a system are policy decisions, it is upon the government that the final responsibility falls for matching or balancing outputs of decisions against input of demand. But it is clear that to obtain the support of the members of a system through positive incentives, a government need not meet all the demands of even its most influential and ardent supporters. Most governments, or groups such as political parties that seek to control governments, succeed in building up a reserve of support. This reserve will carry the government along even though it offends its followers, so long as over the extended short runs these followers perceive the particular government as one that is in general favorable to their interests. One form that this reserve support takes in Western society is that of party loyalty, since the party is the typical instrument in a mass industrialized society for mobilizing and maintaining support for a government. However, continuous lack of specific rewards through policy decisions ultimately leads to the danger that even the deepest party loyalty may be shaken. . . .

Thus a system need not meet *all the demands* of its members so long as it has stored up a reserve of support over the years. Nor need it satisfy even *some of the demands* of all its members. Just whose demands a system must seek to meet, how much of their demands, at what time, and under what conditions are questions for special research. We can say in advance that at least the demands of the most influential members require satisfaction. But this tells us little unless we know how to discover the influentials in a political system and how new sets of members rise to positions of influence.

The critical significance of the decisions of governments for the support of the other two aspects of a system—namely, the political community and the regime—is clear from what I have said above. Not all withdrawal of support from a government has consequences for the success or failure of a regime or community. But persistent inability of a government to produce satisfactory outputs for the members of a system may well lead to demands for changing of the regime or for dissolution of the political community. It is for this reason that the input-output balance is a vital mechanism in the life of a political system.

2. Politicization as a Mechanism of Support

It would be wrong to consider that the level of support available to a system is a function exclusively of the outputs in the form of either sanctions or rewards. If we did so conclude, we could scarcely account for the maintenance of numerous political systems in which satisfaction of demands has been manifestly low, in which public coercion is limited, and yet which have endured for epochs. Alternately, it might be difficult to explain how political systems could endure and yet manage to flout or thwart urgent demands, failing thereby to render sufficient *quid pro quo* for the input of support. The fact is that whatever reserve of support has been accumulated through past decisions is increased and reinforced by a complicated method for steadily manufacturing support through what I shall call the process of politicization. It is an awkward term, but nevertheless an appropriately descriptive one.

As each person grows up in a society, through a network of

rewards and punishments the other members of society communicate to and instill in him the various institutionalized goals and
norms of that society. This is well known in social research as the
process of socialization. Through its operation a person learns to
play his various social roles. Part of these goals and norms relate
to what the society considers desirable in political life. The ways
in which these political patterns are learned by the members of
society constitute what I call the process of politicization. Through
it a person learns to play his political roles, which include the absorption of the proper political attitudes.

Let us examine a little more closely something of what happens
during the process of politicization. As members of a society mature,
they must absorb the various orientations toward political matters
that one is expected to have in that society. If the expectations of
the members of society with regard to the way each should behave
in specific political situations diverged beyond a certain range, it
would be impossible to get common action with regard to the making
of binding decisions. It is essential for the viability of an orderly
political system that the members of the system have some common
basic expectations with regard to the standards that are to be used
in making political evaluations, to the way people will feel about
various political matters, and to the way members of the system
will perceive and interpret political phenomena.

The mechanism through which this learning takes place is of
considerable significance in understanding how a political system
generates and accumulates a strong reserve of support. Although
we cannot pursue the details, we can mention a few of the relevant
dimensions. In the first place, of course, the learning or politicization
process does not stop at any particular period for the individual;
it starts with the child and, in the light of our knowledge of learning,
may have its deepest impact through the teen age. . . .

In the second place, the actual process of politicization at its
most general level brings into operation a complex network of rewards and punishments. For adopting the correct political attitudes
and performing the right political acts, for conforming to the generally accepted interpretations of political goals, and for undertaking
the institutionalized obligations of a member of the given system,
we are variously rewarded or punished. For conforming we are
made to feel worthy, wanted, and respected and often obtain material advantages such as wealth, influence, improved opportunities. For deviating beyond the permissible range, we are made
to feel unworthy, rejected, dishonored, and often suffer material
losses. . . .

In the third place, the means used for communicating the goals
and norms to others tend to be repetitive in all societies. The various

political myths, doctrines, and philosophies transmit to each generation a particular interpretation of the goals and norms. The decisive links in this chain of transmission are parents, siblings, peers, teachers, organizations, and social leaders, as well as physical symbols such as flags or totems, ceremonies, and rituals freighted with political meaning.

These processes through which attachments to a political system become built into the maturing member of a society I have lumped together under the rubric of politicization. . . .

When the basic political attachments become deeply rooted or institutionalized, we say that the system has become accepted as legitimate. Politicization therefore effectively sums up the way in which legitimacy is created and transmitted in a political system. And it is an empirical observation that in those instances where political systems have survived the longest, support has been nourished by an ingrained belief in the legitimacy of the relevant governments and regimes.

What I am suggesting here is that support resting on a sense of the legitimacy of a government and regime provides a necessary reserve if the system is to weather those frequent storms when the more obvious outputs of the system seem to impose greater hardships than rewards. Answers to questions concerning the formation, maintenance, transmission, and change of standards of legitimacy will contribute generously to an understanding of the way in which support is sufficiently institutionalized so that a system may regularly and without excessive expenditure of effort transform inputs of demand into outputs of decision.

That there is a need for general theory in the study of political life is apparent. The only question is how best to proceed. There is no one royal road that can be said to be either the correct one or the best. It is only a matter of what appears as the given level of available knowledge to be the most useful. At this stage it appears that system theory, with its sensitivity to the input-output exchange between a system and its setting offers a fruitful approach. It is an economical way of organizing presently disconnected political data and promises interesting dividends.

3

The Crisis of the State

Karl W. Deutsch

In this present-day world, the state—and this is typically the more or less sovereign national state—is both indispensable and inadequate. It is an indispensable instrument to get many things done, to provide many needed services and to deal with many real problems. But it is inadequate to cope with an increasing number of other problems of life and death for many of its inhabitants. No state today can protect the lives of its citizens in the case of thermonuclear war against it, nor against the poisonous fall-out from thermonuclear war outside its borders. No national state can protect the world's ecology, the oceans and the atmosphere, nor can any one state solve the problems of worldwide population growth or lack of raw materials, energy or food. In all these respects, the first and basic promise of government—to protect the lives of its citizens—has become illusory.

From these and other conditions has sprung the crisis of the modern state. This is not the place to list or trace all these conditions but the general concept of crisis can be indicated. Crisis we may call a situation with three characteristics: an existing state of affairs has become untenable, or is rapidly becoming so; a new more stable and tenable pattern or arrangement is not known or does not appear practicable, due to ignorance, lack of means, lack of consensus or the pressure of countervailing interests; and the search for such

Source: Karl W. Deutsch, "The Crisis of the State," *Government and Opposition* (Summer 1981), pp. 331–43. By permission. Footnotes abridged by the editors.

a viable and practicable pattern, its establishment in practice and the decisions relating to this task all must be carried out under great pressure of time.

The growth of dangers of an order of magnitude beyond the size of the national state has accelerated since the coming of nuclear energy in 1945; other such dangers have become manifest since the 1960s and 1970s. The typical modern state is still sovereign in the sense that its actions cannot be completely steered or predicted from the outside but it is less sovereign in the sense of classic political theory in that its decisions are less highly concentrated, less consistent and less effective in controlling important classes of events. Similarly, domestic needs, demands and burdens upon the state have grown rapidly since the 1930s, often faster than the capabilities of many states to meet them. There are not many decades left to meet the expectable catastrophes which these developments portend. Experts can observe and in part calculate many aspects of the crisis before us. Many more people feel them by intuition or experience. In this situation of crisis, a more adequate development of the theory of the state becomes an urgent task.

The theoretical approach proposed here is combinatorial, somewhat similar to some of the notions of Claude Levi-Strauss and Jean Piaget.[1] It begins by distinguishing structures and functions of the state, and it divides the structures into six major structural elements and the class of functions into eight major functions or goals. This requires us to accept two lists of enumerations, which may try the patience of the reader. These lists are necessary, however, in order to generate at a later stage a number of combinations corresponding to different types of states, actual or potential.

At least some of these types will then again be listed, together with statements about some of the times and places where they may have occurred, a brief discussion about the observable sequence of their rise and decline and of some of the crises of transition from one type to another. It is hoped that this primitive combinatorial model will serve in this manner as a search device and a heuristic tool, leading to insights and hypotheses subject to subsequent confirmation, disconfirmation or specific limitations of validity.

CHANGING STRUCTURES AND FUNCTIONS OF THE STATE

By a structure we mean a process in a system that changes at a rate so slow as to be negligible for the purposes of the investigation.[2]

---

[1] J. Piaget, *Le Structuralisme*, (Paris: Presses Universitaires de France, 1972).

[2] J. G. Miller, *Living Systems* (New York: McGraw-Hill, 1976).

Another concept of structure will be introduced in a later section of this article. A process then involves a change so fast that it cannot be neglected. Thus hills and valleys are structures for the city planner but may be processes for the student of long-term geological evolution. Structures may persist for a long time because of their internal characteristics, or because of some structure-maintaining processes. Thus sand dunes are maintained by the wind, buildings by repairs, organizations by recruitment.

The structure of the state, from this point of view, consists of relatively stable configurations of interlocking occupational and social roles which we call institutions or sometimes structural groups, such as an army, a court or an office, together with such tangible appendages as buildings, installations and equipment.

Such structures of the state could be conveniently divided into six groups:

1.   Armed persons and their equipment, organized as military forces or police;

2.   Decision-makers, legislators and rulers in more or less full-time roles;

3.   Civilian personnel and their equipment, organized in services of administration and coordination; legislators and other decision-makers, military and civilians; judges and employees of courts;

4.   Employees organized to produce publicly-desired goods or installations, such as roads;

5.   Employees organized in agencies to deliver services such as education, health care, or old age pensions; and

6.   The underlying population which obeys the state to a degree that is sufficient to permit the state to function, and which may be mobilized in its demands or efforts at one time or another by the government or by social, cultural and economic processes more or less outside the government's control. It is this habitual interplay of probable popular compliance with probable state enforcement and state services that constitutes the essence of the state.

Structures can be multifunctional. Any one of these elements may take on more than one function. Rulers themselves may be armed, and so may be bureaucrats; armies may perform administrative tasks or build roads; service organizations may also produce goods; state enterprises may also perform services; and members of the general population may volunteer, or be mobilized, to supplement any or all of these specialized roles, or to substitute for them. In most cases, however, the distinction among these six structural elements of the state remains convenient, and in the long run they seem to tend to reestablish themselves in practice.

During the last 100 years, the share of the structural elements listed under 1–5, above, has increased. The share of the entire public sector in most countries has grown from about 5–10 percent of GNP in the late 19th century to about 20–45 percent in most non-Communist countries today, with the highest shares typically found in countries with higher levels of industrial development.

Each of these structural elements or subsystems, of course, may be articulated according to different levels and kinds of performance and different problems of consistency or conflict with other structures.

The functions of the state also are characterized by their plurality. By a function we mean a process which serves to maintain a larger system within which it occurs, or to maintain some element or subsystem within it, or to aid in the pursuit of the goal of a goal-seeking system, or of the goal of a goal-pursuing subsystem within it. To the extent of this effect, a process is called functional, and it is called dysfunctional to the extent of its effect in the opposite direction. Functions are subject to the principle of more or less complete functional equivalence which suggests that one and the same function often can be fulfilled more or less adequately by more than one of several different structures. Thus naval war has been waged by state-owned warships and by privateers, and education has been provided by state and non-state organizations.

Among the functions of the state, the most important ones can be grouped conveniently under nine headings which also seem to correspond fairly well to observable reality:

1. The maintenance of order and predictability in society—pattern maintenance in Talcott Parsons's language (though somewhat differing from his theory)—against external and domestic threats. Since in any unequal society some social groups or classes are more wealthy or otherwise privileged than others, the state in maintaining this order also maintains group privilege or class privilege; it is likely in turn to be supported by these privileged groups and classes and to share some of its personnel with them. This function is found in all states that endure. (A partial and temporary exception may have been China during the Cultural Revolution of the 1960s.)

2. The pursuit of expected power, wealth and higher social standing—often through force and conquest—for the state organization and its personnel, and for all or part of the population currently living under its rule. Outstanding examples were ancient Rome, Hitler's Germany and the many states striving for colonial empire in 1875–1918.

3. The pursuit of wealth through government-regulated and/or planned economic development. Examples were Colbert's France in the 17th century or the Soviet Union since 1927.

4. The pursuit of wealth by *laissez-faire* development and competition in a market based on government protection of property

and other conditions for its functioning. An example was 19th-century England, particularly after 1846.

5.   The provision of welfare through social, medical and educational services. Examples are contemporary Britain, West Germany and the states of Scandinavia.

6.   The coordination and integration of activities and attitudes within the society. To some extent, this function is universal among states.

7.   Promoting the process of adaptive learning on the level of the entire society, so as to bring about the creation of new structures of organization and patterns of behaviour in order to help the society to adapt to changes in its natural, social or political environment. An example was Japan, 1868–1915.

8.   Increasing the capabilities of the society for initiative learning through new structures and processes permitting it to initiate new relationships with its environment, enter new habitats, such as the oceans or outer space, or master new forces of nature, such as solar energy. Examples are the initiation of the development of nuclear and solar energy, space navigation and ocean-floor mining in the United States and other countries.

9.   The attainment of some specific goal, such as national independence, or change in the social order or culture. Examples can be found in the American, French, Mexican, Russian and Chinese Revolutions.

Each of these functions may also become a value in its own right in one culture or another and each function may to some extent come to overlap with one or several others, enter into a relationship of tension, conflict or else mutual reinforcement with them. Nonetheless the functions remain distinct, and we may also distinguish types of states by looking at one particular state at a particular time—but without letting the other functions disappear completely.

THE STATE AS A COMBINATORIAL STRUCTURE OF FUNCTIONS

The nine functions of the state, listed in the preceding section, seem to persist for so long and to recur so frequently across time and space that they can be treated as structural elements in a larger system of the functions of the state.

Here the notion of a combinatorial structure[3] becomes relevant. Such a combinatorial structure can be defined as a set of relatively stable elements, together with a set of rules describing the possibilities of their combination and transformation, together with the

---

[3] Piaget, *Le Structuralisme*

entire transformation group generated by these elements and rules.

To generate a manageable transformation group of this kind, we make a few simplifying assumptions:

1. In any type of state, the different functions will be of unequal importance and can be ranked in the order of that importance as measured or estimated in terms of the time, attention and resources devoted to each function, or of the percentage of the observed variance of state activity that can be accounted for by each function.

2. An approximate profile of each type of state can be indicated by the three functions most important for that type, and by their rank order, while the rest of the variance in state behaviour is assumed to be accounted for by the remaining five functions and a small error term ϵ.

Even this simple model would generate a large number of potential state types. Some of these may be impractical; others exist now or have existed in the past; and still others do not exist but may come into being in the future. For this last category, the combinatorial model may serve as a search device.

SOME TYPES OF STATES: OBSERVED
OR EXPECTABLE

Let us pick out a few combinations.

1. A traditional state, as found in medieval Europe, say in the 12th and 13th centuries, placed most stress by far on pattern maintenance, followed by power, and then on integration and coordination.

2. A state chiefly dedicated to conquest would have to put power first by far and then pattern maintenance for the conquering organization and culture, with integration and coordination in third place. Such states may have been the Norman state at the time of the conquest of England, and perhaps Spain at the time of the conquest of the New World.

3. The mercantilist states of 17th- and 18th-century Europe put first of all economic development through government regulation, closely linked to increase of state power, followed by a continuing concern for pattern maintenance.

4. The *laissez-faire* states of the mid-19th century sought above all economic development through market processes, secured by the maintenance of property rights and social privileges, and by the expansion of state power in the international arena as well as in the colonies and in semi-colonial countries.

5. The welfare states of the second half of the 20th century in Western Europe and English-speaking North America insisted in the first place on development by *laissez-faire* market forces,

combined as a second priority with greatly increased welfare policies, and joined in third place to pattern maintenance of many
parts of the social structure in accordance with a "social market
economy" as exemplified in the German Federal Republic.

6.   The mobilizing states of national or social revolutions put
goal attainment first, be it national independence or the establishment of a new social order, linked to a strong concern for power,
and then some efforts at adaptive and initiative social learning.

7.   The post-revolutionary states, such as Russia after 1917 and
China after 1949 and even more so after the mid-1970s, were most
concerned with pattern maintenance, followed by planned development in its Communist-led form, followed in turn by a concern
for integration and coordination, with welfare policies an instrument of the preceding three functions. Non-Communist post-revolutionary regimes show a similar pattern, with Communist-led central
planning replaced by efforts at development through economic regulation.

8.   What of the state in the near future, say about 2000 A.D.?
In today's highly developed countries, it may have to put heavy
stress on adaptive social learning, together with the power to implement its results, followed by a heightened concern for integration
and coordination.

9.   The learning state, say about 2100 A.D., may be able to stress
initiative learning, followed by adaptive learning and a continuing concern for integration and coordination. Most of the other
basic state functions would remain, however, at least in residual
form.

The last two state types are speculative constructions. Yet they
seem plausible to me. They contain a normative element: they imply
that one is in favour of human survival. But they also include an
important empirical element. The growing challenges such as world
population growth, limited deliveries of food, energy and metals,
weapons proliferation, and others, have been observable for one
or more decades. There is no evidence that these trends will quickly
disappear. But there are instances of adaptive and initiative learning that are observable and that suggest that these functions may
yet increase. This will require, however, corresponding changes in
regard to the other functions of the state, and even to its structures.
The seven historical types, by contrast, can be checked against the
evidence which will reveal their provisional simplicity and their
many specific inadequacies.

The crisis of transition from one state type to another would
be another topic for research, but some of them are also a part of
our experience in the world in which we live.

STATE TYPES, SYSTEM LEVELS AND THE SIZE OF STATES

In a traditional type of state, most of the socially and economically relevant decisions are either already predetermined by tradition, or made at the level of small subsystems, such as the family, the kin group, the village, the town or the city state. To a large extent, the traditional state was thus subsystem-dominant, and the remaining decision latitude of its political sector—be it a single ruler, a council of oligarchs or even a citizens' assembly—was small.

A similar basic pattern is found in many of the conquest-states of history, except that they mobilized from time to time larger numbers of men for military purposes, and that their rulers sometimes could make a larger decision as to whether to attack this or that country, and what orders to give about the treatment of some conquered population. Apart from these relatively infrequent occasions, the day-to-day routines of life for the population of such conquest states, and of the empires they founded, remained largely limited to small local units and based on the political apathy of most of the inhabitants.

The West European mercantilist state of the 16th to 18th centuries acted mainly on the level of the "national" territory. Ordinarily, however, striving to promote economic growth—and through it the growth of military or naval power—through government regulations and monopolies, both within its borders and as far as possible in the international market and arena, it did not mobilize the people in its support; only England after the 1640s could be called a nation-state in this latter sense. But this mercantilist state increasingly exercised power and collected taxes in money throughout its territories and paid its administrators in money. It was a territorial state and also a tax-collecting state in Joseph Schumpeter's sense of the term, giving rise to a paid professional bureaucracy and using increasingly elaborate written records, files and administrative routines, as noted particularly by Max Weber. These mercantilist states also conquered empires, partly resembling the empires of ancient times. They administered them superficially, with hardly any government services beyond the maintenance of order and the highly imperfect enforcement of tax laws and economic regulations—but even so, they penetrated many of the conquered lands and populations more thoroughly and with more far-reaching consequences than their predecessor had ever done.

From the 17th century mercantilist state to the *laissez-faire* state of the 19th century and the welfare state of the 20th, an increasingly large proportion of decisions was made on the nation-state level.

Though the adherents of the *laissez-faire* state were ideologically opposed to the expansion of bureaucracy and of the public sector, in fact this expansion continued during the 19th century: the introduction of compulsory primary education alone added large numbers of schoolteachers to the ranks of public employees. The welfare states of the 20th century greatly accelerated this trend, expanding by 1980 public expenditures and the public sector to more than one-third of the gross domestic product of the world's highly industrialized countries in the market-oriented world and to much higher levels in the centrally-planned industrial countries.

The modern welfare states likewise have remained on the nation-state level. Indeed, with transition from the *laissez-faire* state to the welfare state, the average size of states has tended to become smaller. For the welfare state tends to expand the scope of government—that is, the ensemble of its tasks—relatively quickly by an order of magnitude, while increasing the capabilities of government much more slowly, if at all. The result is a growing disproportion between the tasks and capabilities of government. This becomes visible as a mounting overload of government, and often as an increasing neglect of the needs and desires of marginal population groups and regions, such as ethnic or religious minorities or poor regions distant from the centre. The resulting movements of rebellion or secession are further fostered by the social mobilization of the population whose needs, demands and political capabilities also have been increasing, often faster than the capabilities of government. In the end many such secession or independence movements succeed and lead to the establishment of new and smaller nation-states, or of states endeavouring to weld their population into nations.

The discrepancy between the quickly increasing burdens upon the state and its slowly growing capabilities to provide the services demanded may continue and produce recurrent crises, both in old states and new ones. One possible response is the effort of the political regime to mobilize the activities of the population for participation in the endeavours of the government and for their active support. To the extent that this strategy succeeds, or that its equivalent is produced by the spontaneous actions of substantial parts of the population, the state becomes a mobilizing state.

Such mobilizing states sometimes have been established with an original aim of an international revolution, such as the USSR in the years 1917–19, or of a supranational revolution in the name of some pan-regional or religious ideology, such as that intended by some participants in the revolutions of Egypt in the 1950s or of Iran in 1979. In practice, however, mobilizing states usually found the effects of their appeals limited to the population of one national state, and they have ended up operating mainly at the nation-state level.

If successful, a mobilizing state eventually becomes a post-revolutionary state, putting heavy stress on maintaining and developing the main national and/or social institutions established in the revolutionary or mobilizing phase, as well as on improving political integration and coordination within its borders. These tasks again are likely to limit the main activities of the post-revolutionary state to nation-state level.

Here again, however, the inadequacy of the nation-state in coping with urgent but worldwide problems of security and survival is making itself felt. In the next three decades, 1980–2010, no state operating essentially at the nation-state level will be able to escape the crisis of the nation-state. The adaptive learning state of the next half century will have to develop new ways of internal political participation, as well as ways of participating far more thoroughly and effectively in new supranational and international organizations and endeavours, many of which will still have to be created. The same will apply to an even greater degree to the initiative learning state of the late 21st century and to its as yet unknown successors. All of these types of state will have to transcend in massive and essential ways the nation-state level.

LIMITS TO THE SIZE OF STATES

For every one of its nine basic functions, every state ordinarily must issue commands. Whatever the form of such commands—laws, decrees, court decisions or administrative regulations—most of them must appear as binding to most people at least for most of the time, if the state is to endure. That is to say, they must be obeyed to that very large extent and they must be expected to be so obeyed. The limits of the effective domain of the state are thus the limits of its probability of finding popular obedience, both in regard to the territory where its writ runs with effect, and to the set of persons who are likely to obey it. The more different populations are in their language, culture, geographic and economic conditions and in their social structure, the less likely they are to obey the commands issued by a strange and geographically, culturally and/or socially distant government. This distance in large part is social, cultural and economic, involving differences in perceptions, expectations and interests. More important than a distance between bodies, it is most often a distance between minds and between different patterns of social relationships. It can be compensated, therefore, only to a very limited extent by any technologies of transport and communication. This declining probability of obedience with increasing psychological distances of this kind has limited the size of states ever since states have existed in proportion to the activities and capabilities of their populations.

But this is not the only limit on the size of states. Popular compliance is the obverse of the government's domination, that is, of its probability of being obeyed. Such compliance can have several sources: habit, apathy, shared interests and aims, belief, or fear of enforcement by the government. This last source, fear of the government's force, is then likely to reinforce the population's habits of compliance. This role of force in government has been stressed by many political theorists from Thomas Hobbes's day to ours. Such fear depends at least in part on the credibility of the rulers' threat of highly probable punishment for disobedient subjects, and on the credibility of their promise of some substantial and highly probable reward—at least in relative terms—for obedient behaviour. If either the threat of punishment or this promise of reward or clemency ceases to be credible, the rulers' threat will lose power. This may explain why so many of the world's most cruel and fearsome rulers in the end ceased to be heeded, and why people so often have continued to resist in one way or another the superior force of rulers and nations who seemed alien to them.

Enforcement, in short, is practical only when it is directed against a relatively few and sustained by the compliance of the many, usually at least a majority, and the active support of at least a substantial group. The likelihood of such conditions for successful enforcement again tends to decline with geographic, social, cultural or economic distance, and thus contributes to limiting the size of states.

A third limiting factor rests in the finite capabilities of government. To serve any or all of the nine basic functions, governments must have channels and receptors to take in information, from within their own machinery, their own country, from its natural, technological and agricultural environment, and from the international system of foreign states and peoples. These facilities for the intake of information are inevitably limited. Other limitations apply to the memory of government, both in the heads of its personnel and in its written records, or even its electronic ones.

The limited capacities of a state organization may lead to its being overburdened, at the level of the central government or of its regional or local administration, or at several of all these levels. The more territories and populations a state incorporates within its boundaries, and the more economic and political relationships and actual or potential conflicts it enters into with other states or peoples, the more likely it is to neglect the affairs of those territories and populations which rank low on its scale of priorities, and which are thus marginal to its concerns, geographically, politically or economically. Here one might speak of a law of declining attention and responsiveness to the needs of the marginal components of expanding states. It is this declining attention and the consequent decline in governmental performance and services for these marginal regions and populations that in turn tends to bring about declining loyalties and growing resistance, and thus to limit the size of states.

These internal limits may further be reinforced from the outside by the well-known workings of the politics of the balance of power. Strong and expanding states tend to provoke fear among the governments of other states and to give rise to coalitions against them. But ancient Rome, Alexander's empire, the Ottoman empire, the Spanish empire and, in the 20th century, the British empire were not limited or defeated by any external hostile coalitions. Each of these, in the end, disintegrated mainly from within.

PART TWO

Contemporary Political Regimes

This volume is prepared on the basis of a general conception: A political system is, above all, a mechanism for the making of decisions. It is endowed with legitimacy, that is, the decisions made by the various organs of government are expected to be widely obeyed.

Decisions involve compromises among many conflicting points of view held by social groups, parties, associations, interest organizations, and regions. On the one hand, we have the governmental organs that make decisions—the legislature, the executive, the courts, and the bureaucracy. On the other hand, there are the social and economic forces and groupings, and the beliefs and values held by the members of the society about their political systems. This suggests a threefold distinction: (1) the government; (2) the "social and cultural configuration," that is, social classes, economic groups, ethnic groups, regions, interest groups and their mode of action; and (3) the pattern of values and ideologies relating specifically to political authority, permissive areas of governmental action, and the role and position of individuals and associations.

It is the interplay between social configuration, ideology, and the governmental organs that constitutes the dynamics of politics— the making of decisions. Social and economic groups, molded and patterned in accordance with the ideas people hold, press their claims upon the government. Interest groups and political parties function as conveyor belts between interest claims and governmental decisions. Political leadership sifts these claims, often provides for compromise, and articulates them in the form of pledges or decisions. It is not impossible, especially when conflicts assume a high level of intensity and when opposing sides are evenly balanced, for a political system to find itself in a situation where no decision can be made. The system is at a state of stalemate.

The efficiency of a political system can be gauged in terms of its ability to make decisions that are widely accepted. An efficient system maintains a balance between change and stability. Change is the result of constant claims that arise from the social groups because of evolving technical and economic conditions. Emerging social groups inevitably put forward demands as they gain access to positions of influence and power. Throughout the 19th century, for instance, the general theme of political change was associated with the claims of the lower middle classes and the workers (in some cases the slaves and serfs) for suffrage and political participation. As societies industrialize, these same groups organize in order to facilitate the translation of their newly acquired political influence into immediate socioeconomic benefits. Efficiency therefore depends on the nature of governmental response to the demands from groups. If existing institutions prove incapable of meeting these demands, the new groups may attempt to gain power by revolutionary means, which has disruptive effects upon the whole system.

The most persistent challenges to a political system derive from economic and technological modernization. In underdeveloped countries modernization involves literally the restructuring of society— the inculcation of new norms of behavior, the training of skilled bureaucrats, and drastic action on the basis of newly established goals. Modernization at the political level involves the identification of the masses of the people with these goals. Disciplined effort is indispensable because of the lack of available resources. These societies must rely upon their most plentiful and therefore cheapest commodity—human labor—whose effective utilization requires sacrifice and unremitting toil. Max Weber has suggested that in Western Europe the Protestant religion provided the philosophy that broke down the barriers of feudal and medieval society, secularized human motivation, and supplied incentive that made possible the Industrial Revolution. Ideologies and values in the underdeveloped societies are now undergoing similar transformations. Will these nations follow the European pattern of economic individualism, or the Communist type of collective effort with emphasis on coercion and indoctrination? Their choice will largely determine the nature of their emerging political institutions.

Problems of modernization are naturally different for the societies that have already attained a high level of industrialization. The crucial problem in economically advanced systems is to maintain a constant rate of economic growth, to develop technology rapidly and effectively in order to increase the productivity of labor, and to make the benefits of increased productivity available to all in the form of better living conditions and welfare. The government is compelled to provide a wide range of services and to enforce social justice by means of income distribution.

To summarize: We have suggested that in a political system

conflicting claims and demands are translated into accepted decisions. The claims are made by social groups. The manner in which
conflicts are expressed depends to a great degree on the nature of
ideologies and values concerning political authority. The links between the social structure and the governmental organs are political
parties, interest groups, and other associations. It is the role of
political leadership to articulate interests and conflicts, achieve a
synthesis in the form of policy, and carry it out through the governmental organs. An efficient government is able to provide for change
in a stable fashion—that is, without resort to violence on the part
of important groups. It must also be able to survive as a system
in the midst of competing nation-states.

An examination of all these propositions calls for comparative
analysis and study.

THE COMPARATIVE APPROACH

A systematic approach requires an overall view or theory of politics.
Political science has therefore borrowed extensively from sociological theory. For example, politics has been viewed by some analysts
as a system of interaction between actors (individuals and groups)
for the purpose of realizing specific goals. A political system must
perform certain indispensable (or requisite) functions in order to
survive. Certain institutions are also indispensable (or requisite)
structures for the performance of these functions. Structures differ
from one system to another and undergo profound modifications
under the impact of diverse factors—war, industrialization, economic changes, new aspirations, and new demands.

The study of politics (as for Aristotle) becomes the study of a
"system" linked organically with social structure, traditions and
ideologies, culture, and the environment within which it operates.
It may then be possible to discern significant similarities and differences that mere description of the legal forms of a state does not
suggest. Establishment of *correlations* between political, economic,
cultural, and social phenomena provides a perspective in terms of
which the dynamics of change may be understood and broad generalizations made. In essence, this is the application of scientific method
to the study of political phenomena. Hypotheses and theories about
the political process are elaborated into a rational system and then
examined critically in the light of available evidence.

The analytical approach, then, strives toward a definition of a
political system, identifies the most important structures through
which a system functions, and studies differences and similarities.
It purports to establish general propositions about political behavior. As in natural science, generalizations are stated in the form
of hypotheses involving a series of conditions. For instance, it could

be posited that if there are no serious ideological conflicts in a society and if there is a majority electoral system, then two parties will develop. It can be posited that industrialization and prosperity will, all other conditions being held in check, lead to a decrease in conflict about issues and the development of a political system concerned with the solution of concrete problems. It may be posited that economic policies endangering the status of certain social groups will provoke a strong movement of protest on the part of the threatened groups, who will seek to protect themselves even by violence—or that groups denied participation in the political system will, all other things being equal, seek to gain status and influence also by violence.

These hypotheses can be tested against reality and accordingly qualified, modified, or rejected. Field work and empirical observation are therefore indispensable for comparative study as for all forms of scientific inquiry. This kind of analysis will add to our knowledge of the conditioning factors whose presence or absence accounts for the validation or the rejection of our hypothesis. For instance, if we propose that wherever there is A (for example, a majority electoral system) then B (a two-party system) will follow and find that in one system this obtains but in another it does not, then we have to seek the reasons for this disparity. We do so by finding a series of other factors $(X, X_1, X_2, X_3, X_4, X_5,$ and so on). Our hypothesis then will be qualified to read A will follow B provided factors X_2 (religious differences, X_3 (regionalism), X_4 (ethnic groups), or others, depending upon field observation, obtain. In this manner a comprehensive explanation accounting for the differences between two systems may be given.

It is at this point that comparative analysis becomes both challenging and at the same time frustrating for the student. Rarely if ever can we provide a coherent and satisfactory generalization explaining the differences between systems. Historical and other factors give nations characteristics that are unique, that is to say, cannot be duplicated. In fact we shall find it virtually impossible to verify any hypothesis or to develop any generalization that is valid for *all* political systems. It is necessary to lengthen the chain of conditioning factors (Xs) for each political system in order to take into account individual and idiosyncratic factors. The proposal to develop general laws seems to bog down in a never-ending explanation for unique situations. Some observers contend that there are no universally valid laws. In despair they conclude that the indeterminacy and uniqueness of political behavior do not permit generalization.

It would be a serious mistake to accept this point of view. Comparative analysis can at the very least identify and perhaps explain uniqueness, which is of crucial importance. Unless we start with general concepts and hypotheses, we are not able even to draw distinctions let alone account for them. How can we tell what is unique without knowing what is general? Power, for instance, is manifested in many ways and contains many elements—religion, property, birth, administration, and so on. But these different manifestations can be distinguished, related, and understood only in terms of some general concept of power.

The Range of Comparison

The range of comparison will usually be determined by the theoretical scheme, by the formulation of a *problem* or the study of *a given area*. In all cases two crucial questions must be confronted: How do we compare? What do we compare?

Comparison may be attempted between segments of the political process in various systems, or between certain institutions, or between political systems as such, in order to clarify issues that preoccupy us. Let us take the multiparty system in France. The historian of French political institutions will describe the origin, development, ideologies, and characteristics of the French multiparty system. The student of comparative politics faced with the same problem would ask rather: What are the conditions for the existence of a multiparty system? Are they institutional?—social?—sectional?—ideological? Once the conditions have been identified, then comparison with other multiparty systems will show the relevance of some but not others, that is, comparative study may disprove the relationship between certain conditions and multipartism. We find, for instance, that analogous sectional conditions in the United States have not produced a multiparty system—or that similar electoral systems exist in both two-party and multiparty systems.

Through comparison it is possible to explain the nature of a phenomenon like a multiparty system in the light of a chain of conditioning factors, such as sectionalism, proportional representation, the cabinet's inability to dissolve parliament, and so on. The chain of conditioning factors that we find in France cannot be reproduced historically or experimentally in any other country. But this in no way lessens the need for suggesting relationships among conditioning factors for the purpose of analysis and empirical investigation. Nor does it mean that because France and Country X or Y are unique they cannot be the subject of comparison. France is indeed unique, but in an analytical sense the conditions of multipartism are general categories permitting comparison of France with other political systems. Every suicide is unique. But as Emile Durkheim demonstrated, the conditions under which people commit suicide can be analytically identified in terms of a number of broad categories.

We compare, therefore, in order to discover the conditions under which certain phenomena take place. Conditions or, more precisely, a series of conditions are hypothetically related to the phenomenon we study. The task of empirical observation is to test the validity of such hypothetical formulations. By so doing we enrich our knowledge of the factors that account for a given phenomenon until we are able to generalize about them. The presence or absence of some or others will enable us to make tentative judgments about political developments and occurrences.

Comparison may be either *static* or *dynamic*. In the first instance, we undertake an anatomy, so to speak, of political systems. Structures are described and related. In this connection classificatory tables are useful in that they suggest analogies and differences. Structures, however, must be identified in terms of the particular function they perform in a system. This is much more difficult than it may seem to be. It is essential to discern the *overt* from the *covert*, and the *manifest* from the *latent* functions. For instance, though there are striking structural analogies between the electoral system of the Soviet Union and that of the United States, their functions are wholly dissimilar. Elections in the United States are an integral part of the process of arriving at decisions over which the body politic is divided. In the Soviet Union, on the other hand, elections are used to express loyalty to the regime, and to rally the people around the policy of their leaders.

Dynamic comparison is the study of the performance of various systems. We not only identify structures through which certain functions are performed but also account for the structural variations between systems. Ultimately an effort may be made to trace out consequences of alternative courses of action, or predict in the light of a chain of conditioning factors. This last stage is indeed the most significant but at the same time the most difficult to reach.

THE SEARCH FOR NEW DEFINITIONS

Awareness of the need for a more systematic approach to the study of politics, coupled with a new appreciation of the interrelationship between social and political structures, has played havoc with the old descriptive definitions and classifications. Traditionally, a state has been described as a community of people living in a given territory with a government. Wherever there is a stable relationship between governors and governed there is a state. Thus, both Ecuador and the United States are examples of "states." But the classic definition does not tell us what to look for and where to look in order to find out how and why these two states are different. The use of categories like ideology, social configuration, and government as a decision-making mechanism aids the student in understanding similarities and differences.

A profusion of new schemes for classifying governments has been suggested in recent years. Many stem from Max Weber's distinction between three types of authority: traditional, rational, and charismatic. Gabriel Almond in his article "Comparative Political Systems" distinguishes between four major kinds of systems: consensual (primarily Anglo-American), fragmented (continental Europe), totalitarian (communist and fascist), and preindustrial. David Apter refers to political systems as dictatorial, indirectly and directly representational, and oligarchical. James Coleman refers to "terminal colonial democracy" and "colonial or racial oligarchy." In addition, he describes "stable and unstable" systems, and "underdeveloped and developing" societies. There are "transitional" societies in which Daniel Lerner tells us that we must look for a cluster of interrelated phenomena—industrialization, urbanization, literacy, participation in mass media, role differentiation, and empathy. Karl W. Deutsch develops an impressive listing of variables in order to differentiate systems on the basis of diverse combinations.

The "boundaries" of the field of politics have become blurred. In identifying the component elements of a system, Gabriel Almond lists the following "input" (primarily political) functions: political socialization and recruitment, interest articulation, interest aggregation, and political communication. The "output" (or governmental) functions are more familiar even if the terms appear to be new. They are rule making, rule application, and rule adjudication. Harold Lasswell goes a step further in describing the functions of a political system as follows: intelligence, recommendation, prescription, invocation, application, appraisal, and termination. David Easton is, as we have seen, more parsimonious. He holds that the main functions of a political system are demands, supports, and authoritative decisions—the latter determining the proper boundaries of politics. Samuel Beer discusses a political system with reference to its "political culture," the "pattern of power," the "pattern of interests," and the "pattern of policy."[1]

---

[1] The works referred to include: Max Weber, *The Theory of Social and Economic Organization* (New York: Oxford University Press, 1947), pp. 324–91; Gabriel A. Almond, "Comparative Political Systems," *Journal of Politics,* August 1956; David Apter, "A Comparative Method for the Study of Politics," *American Journal of Sociology* (November 1958), pp. 221–37; Gabriel A. Almond and James S. Coleman, *The Politics of Developing Areas* (Princeton: Princeton University Press, 1960); Daniel Lerner, *The Passing of Traditional Society* (New York: Free Press, 1958); Karl W. Deutsch, "Towards an Inventory of Basic Trends and Patterns in Comparative and International Politics," *American Political Science Review,* March 1960; Harold D. Lasswell, *The Decision Process* (Bureau of Governmental Research, University of Maryland, 1956); David Easton, "An Approach to an Analysis of Political Systems," *World Politics* (April 1957) (see Reading 2); and Samuel Beer, *Patterns of Government* (New York: Random House, 1973), pp. 3–53.

We are, therefore, as was said at the outset, in a state of flux. We are uncertain of the boundaries of political science in its relation to other social sciences and in disagreement over the significant components of political systems. But a state of flux is not necessarily a state of confusion. It may rather be an indication of healthy curiosity and intellectual ferment. The discipline is maturing as it attempts to relate political and social factors, explain behavior, and clarify problems. Description of the institutions and policies of states continues to be of crucial importance. But they are properly viewed only as parts of the "political system."

CHAPTER TWO

Democracies

4

Will More Countries Become Democratic?

Samuel P. Huntington

What are the prospects for the emergence of more democratic regimes in the world? This question has intellectual and policy relevance for the 1980s. During the 1950s and early 1960s, scholars concerned with this issue were generally optimistic that decolonization and economic development would lead to the multiplication of democratic regimes. The history of the next decade dealt roughly with these expectations, and people became more pessimistically preoccupied with the reasons for the breakdown of democratic systems. By the late 1970s and early 1980s, however, the prospects for democracy seemed to have brightened once again, and social scientists have responded accordingly. "Transitions to democracy" became the new focus of attention. The optimists of the 1950s were rather naively optimistic; those of the 1980s have been more cautiously optimistic, but the optimism and the hope are still there. . . . The purpose of this article is to use social science theory and comparative political analysis to see to what extent this new, more cautious optimism may be justified.

This issue is important for at least four reasons. First, the future of democracy is closely associated with the future of freedom in the world. Democracies can and have abused individual rights and

---

Source: Samuel P. Huntington, "Will More Countries Become Democratic?" *Political Science Quarterly* 99, no. 2 (Summer 1984), pp. 193–218. By permission. Footnotes abridged by the editors.

liberties, and a well-regulated authoritarian state may provide a high degree of security and order for its citizens. Overall, however, the correlation between the existence of democracy and the existence of individual liberty is extremely high. Indeed, some measure of the latter is an essential component of the former. Conversely, the long-term effect of the operation of democratic politics is probably to broaden and deepen individual liberty. Liberty is, in a sense, the peculiar virtue of democracy; hence, if one is concerned with liberty as an ultimate social value, one should also be concerned with the fate of democracy.

Second, the future of democracy elsewhere in the world is of importance to the United States. The United States is the world's premier democratic country, and the greater the extent to which democracy prevails elsewhere in the world, the more congenial the world environment will be to American interests generally and the future of democracy in the United States in particular. Michael Doyle has argued quite persuasively that no two liberal societies have ever fought each other.[1] His concept of liberalism differs from the concept of democracy employed in this paper, but the point may well be true of democratic regimes as well as liberal ones. Other things being equal, nondemocratic regimes are likely to pose more serious challenges to American interests than democratic regimes.

Third, "a house divided against itself," Abraham Lincoln said, "cannot stand. . . . This government cannot endure permanently half-slave and half-free." At present the world is not a single house, but it is becoming more and more closely integrated. Interdependence is the trend of the times. How long can an increasingly interdependent world survive part-democratic and part-authoritarian and totalitarian? At what point does interdependence become incompatible with coexistence? For the Soviet bloc and the Western World, that point may still be some distance in the future, but tensions arising out of the growing interaction between totally different political systems are almost inevitably bound to increase. At some point, coexistence may require a slowing down or halting of the trends toward interdependence.

Fourth, the extension or decline of democracy has implications for other social values, such as economic growth, socioeconomic equity, political stability, social justice, and national independence. In societies at one level of development, progress toward one or more of these goals may be compatible with a high level of democracy. At another level of socioeconomic development, conflicts may

---

[1] Michael W. Doyle, "Kant, Liberal Legacies, and Foreign Affairs, Part I," *Philosophy and Public Affairs* 12 (1983), pp. 213 ff.

exist. The question of the appropriateness of democracy for poor countries is, in this context, a central issue. But even highly developed societies may achieve their democracy at some sacrifice of other important values, such as national security.

In addition, if it is desirable to extend the scope of democracy in the world, obviously it is necessary to know what conditions favor that in the late 20th century. Empirical analysis is necessary to answer the question: What policies should governments, private institutions, and individuals espouse to encourage the spread of democracy? To what extent do efforts such as those of the Reagan administration have an impact, positive or negative, on the state of democracy in the world, and at what cost in terms of other social values and national goals?

The first step in evaluating the prospects for democracy is to define the dependent variable with which we are concerned. Definitions of democracy are legion. The term has been applied to areas and institutions far removed from politics. It has also been defined as an ideal impossible of human achievement. For Peter Bachrach, for instance, a democratic system of government has for its paramount objective "maximization of the self-development of every individual." Robert Dahl says a democratic political system is one which is "completely or almost completely responsible to all its citizens."[2] Such definitions may be relevant to normative political theory, but they are not very useful for comparative empirical analysis. First, they are often so vague and general that it is virtually impossible to apply them in practice. How does one judge whether a political system is attempting to maximize the self-development of individuals or is completely responsive to all its citizens? Second, democracy may also be defined in such broad terms as to make it identical with almost all civic virtues, including social justice, equality, liberty, fulfillment, progress, and a variety of other good things. Hence it becomes difficult if not impossible to analyze the relationship between democracy and other social goals.

For comparative analysis a more empirical and institutional definition is desirable, and this paper follows in the tradition of Joseph A. Schumpeter. A political system is defined as democratic to the extent that its most powerful collective decision-makers are selected

---

[2] Peter Bachrach, *The Theory of Democratic Elitism: A Critique* (Washington, D.C.: University Press of America, 1980), pp. 24, 98 ff.; Robert A. Dahl, *Polyarchy: Participation and Opposition* (New Haven: Yale University Press, 1971), p. 2. For a useful analysis of "rationalist" and "descriptive" concepts of democracy, see Jeane J. Kirkpatrick, "Democratic Elections, Democratic Government, and Democratic Theory," in *Democracy at the Polls*, ed. David Butler, Howard R. Penniman, and Austin Ranney (Washington, D.C.: American Enterprise Institute for Public Policy Research, 1981), pp. 325–48.

through periodic elections in which candidates freely compete for votes and in which virtually all the adult population is eligible to vote. So defined, a democracy thus involves the two dimensions—contestation and participation—that Dahl sees as critical to his realistic democracy or polyarchy.[3]

THE RECORD OF DEMOCRATIC DEVELOPMENT

The historical emergence of modern democratic regimes falls into four phases. What could reasonably be called a democratic political system at the national level of government first appeared in the United States in the early 19th century. During the following century democratic regimes gradually emerged in northern and Western Europe, in the British dominions, and in a few countries in Latin America. This trend, which Alexis de Tocqueville had foreseen in 1835 and which James Bryce documented in 1920, appeared to be irreversible if not necessarily universal. Virtually all significant regime changes were from less democracy to more democracy. Writing at the end of this period, Bryce could well speculate as to whether this "trend toward democracy now widely visible, is a natural trend, due to a general law of social progress."[4]

The trend was reversing, however, even as he wrote. The year 1920 was in many aspects the peak of democratic development among the independent nations of the world.[5] During the following two decades, democracy or democratic trends were snuffed out in Germany, Italy, Austria, Poland, the Baltic states, Spain, Portugal, Greece, Argentina, Brazil, and Japan. The war fought to make the world safe for democracy seemed instead to have brought its progress to an abrupt halt and to have unleashed social movements from the Right and the Left intent on destroying it.

The aftermath of World War II, on the other hand, marked another dramatic, if brief, spurt in the multiplication of democratic regimes. With the support of its allies, the United States imposed democracy on West Germany, Austria, Italy, and Japan (where it took root), and attempted to do so in South Korea (where it did

---

[3] Dahl, *Polyarchy*, pp. 4–9. See also Joseph A. Schumpeter, *Capitalism, Socialism, and Democracy*, 2d ed. (New York: Harper & Row, 1947), p. 269: "the democratic method is that institutional arrangement for arriving at political decisions in which individuals acquire the power to decide by means of a competitive struggle for the people's vote."

[4] James Bryce, *Modern Democracies*, 2 vols. (New York: Macmillan, 1921), vol. 1, p. 24.

[5] The proportion of independent states that were democratic was roughly 19 percent in 1902, 34 percent in 1920, 32 percent in 1929–30, and 24 percent in 1960. See G. Bingham Powell, Jr., *Contemporary Democracies* (Cambridge, Mass.: Harvard University Press, 1982), p. 238.

not). Coincidentally, the process of decolonization got underway with newly independent countries usually adopting at first the political forms of the imperial powers. In at least some cases, such as India, Israel, Ceylon, and the Philippines, the forms of democracy were accompanied by the substance also. Other countries, such as Turkey and some Latin American states, moved to emulate the political systems of the victorious Western powers. By the early 1950s, the proportion of democracies among the world's independent states had reached another high.

The fourth period in the evolution of democratic regimes, from the early 1950s to the 1980s, differs from the other three. In each of them, there was an overwhelmingly dominant trend, either toward the extension of democracy (1820–1920 and 1942–1953), or toward its reduction (1920–1942). In each period there were very few, if any, significant regime shifts against the dominant trend. The thirty years from the early 1950s to the early 1980s, however, were not characterized by a strong move in either direction. The trends were mixed. As we have seen, the number of democratic regimes seemed to expand in the 1950s and early 1960s, to shrink in the middle-late 1960s and early 1970s, and then to expand again in the late 1970s and early 1980s. Overall, however, the net record of change in the state of democracy in the world was not very great. It would be difficult to argue that the world was more or less democratic in 1984 than it had been in 1954. Indicative of this relative stability, albeit for a much shorter period of time, are Freedom House's estimates of the proportion of the world's population living in "free" states. In the first such estimate, in January 1973, 32.0 percent of the world's population was found to live in "free" states. In the next year, the percentage increased to 36.0 percent. During the following 10 years, except for the 2 years India was under emergency rule (when it was 19.8 percent and 19.6 percent), the proportion of the world's population living in free states never went above 37.0 percent and never dropped below 35.0 percent. In January 1984 it was 36.0 percent, exactly where it had been 10 years earlier.[6]

The overall stability in the extent of democracy does, however,

---

[6] See "The Comparative Survey of Freedom" compiled annually for Freedom House, [a private research organization in New York City], by Raymond D. Gastil, particularly *Freedom at Issue*, no. 17 (1973), pp. 2–3; no. 70 (1983), p. 4; no. 76 (1984), p. 5. Freedom House classifies a state as "free" if it rates in first or second place on a seven-place scale for both political rights and civil liberties. The countries so classified all have the minimum features of a democratic political system, at least at the time of classification. While recognizing the importance of institutionalization, the Freedom House survey does not attempt to measure the extent to which democracy has become institutionalized. Thus, its 1984 survey, published at the very beginning of 1984, rated both New Zealand and Nigeria as "free," although the latter had presumably left the category as a result of the coup on New Year's Day.

conceal some important developments in both directions. With a
few notable exceptions, almost all colonies that achieved independence after World War II shifted from democratic to nondemocratic
systems. In contrast, a few countries moved in the opposite direction.
These include Spain, Portugal, Colombia, Venezuela, Greece, and
the Dominican Republic. Several South American countries, including two with long-standing democratic systems (Chile, Uruguay)
and two with less stable populist systems (Brazil, Argentina), became bureaucratic-authoritarian states, with military governments
intent upon fairly sustained rule. By the end of 1983, however,
Brazil had made substantial progress back towards a democratic
system, and Argentina had a democratically elected government.
Many other countries (including Peru, Ecuador, Ghana, Nigeria,
and Turkey) seemed to oscillate back and forth between democratic
and undemocratic systems, in a pattern traditionally characteristic
of praetorian societies. In East Asia: Korea, Singapore, Indonesia,
and the Philippines became less democratic, Taiwan remained undemocratic; the Indochinese states succumbed to a ruthless Viet-
namese totalitarianism; and Thailand and Malaysia remained partially democratic. Finally, efforts to move Hungary, Czechoslovakia,
and Poland toward more democratic politics were halted directly
or indirectly by Soviet action.

Any estimate of the future of democracy in the world must be
rooted in an explanation of why these mixed trends prevailed between the 1950s and the 1980s, and hence whether the overall stability in the prevalence of democratic regimes in the world will continue. Ancient and modern political analysts have many theories
to explain the rise and fall of democratic regimes. To what extent
do these various and conflicting theories explain what happened
and did not happen after World War II and what could happen
in the 1980s?

Thinking about the reasons for the emergence of democratic regimes has typically had two foci. One approach has focused on the
preconditions in society that favor democratic development. A second approach has focused on the nature of the political processes
by which that development has occurred. Each will be considered
in turn.

PRECONDITIONS OF DEMOCRATIZATION

In 1970, Dankwart Rustow published a penetrating article on "transitions to democracy," in which he criticized studies that focused
on "preconditions" for democratization because they often tended
to jump from the correlation between democracy and other factors
to the conclusion that those other factors were responsible for democracy. They also tended, he argued, to look for the causes of

democracy primarily in economic, social, cultural, and psychological, but not political, factors.[7] Rustow's criticisms were well taken and helped to provide a more balanced view of the complexities of democratization. It would, however, be a mistake to swing entirely to the other extreme and ignore the environmental factors that may affect democratic development. In fact, plausible arguments can be and have been made for a wide variety of factors or preconditions that appear to be associated with the emergence of democratic regimes. To a large extent these factors can be grouped into four broad categories—economic, social, external, and cultural.

Economic Wealth and Equality

In his critique, Rustow gave special attention to an influential article published by Seymour Martin Lipset a decade earlier. In that piece, Lipset highlighted the seeming correlation between high levels of economic development and the prevalence of democratic political systems among European, English-speaking, and Latin American nations. The "more well-to-do a nation," he postulated, "the greater the chances that it will sustain democracy."[8] His study stimulated a flood of further analyses that criticized, qualified, and refined his argument. Whatever the academic hairsplittings, however, his basic point seemed to make sense. "There is," as another scholar put it in 1960, "a positive correlation between economic development and political competitiveness."[9] A quarter century later, that correlation still seemed to exist. In 1981, for instance, a comparison of the World Bank's ratings of countries in terms of economic development with Freedom House's ratings of them in terms of liberty showed these results—2 of 36 low-income countries were classified "free" or democratic, 14 out of 60 middle-income countries were so classified, and 18 out of 24 countries with industrial economies were so classified.[10] As one moves up the economic ladder, the greater are the chances that a country will be democratic.

The correlation between wealth and democracy is thus fairly

[7] Dankwart A. Rustow, "Transitions to Democracy: Toward a Dynamic Model," *Comparative Politics* 2 (1970), p. 337 ff.

[8] Seymour Martin Lipset, "Some Social Requisites of Democracy: Economic Development and Political Legitimacy," *American Political Science Review* 53 (1959), p. 75.

[9] James S. Coleman, "Conclusion," in *The Politics of the Developing Areas*, ed. Gabriel A. Almond and James S. Coleman (Princeton: Princeton University Press, 1960), p. 538.

[10] World Bank, *World Development Report 1981* (New York: Oxford University Press, 1981), pp. 134–35; and *Freedom at Issue*, no. 64 (1982), pp. 8–9. See also Seymour Martin Lipset's update of his earlier analysis, *Political Man: The Social Bases of Politics*, 2d ed. (Baltimore: The Johns Hopkins University Press, 1981), pp. 469–76.

strong. How can it be explained? There are three possibilities. First, both democracy and wealth could be caused by a third factor. Protestantism has, for instance, been assigned by some a major role in the origins of capitalism, economic development, and democracy. Second, democracy could give rise to economic wealth. In fact, however, high levels of economic wealth require high rates of economic growth and high rates of economic growth do not correlate with the prevalence of democratic political systems.[11] Hence, it seems unlikely that wealth depends on democracy, and, if a connection exists, democracy must depend on wealth.

The probability of any causal connection running from wealth to democracy is enhanced by the arguments as to why this would be a plausible relationship. A wealthy economy, it is said, makes possible higher levels of literacy, education, and mass media exposure, all of which are conducive to democracy. A wealthy economy also moderates the tensions of political conflict; alternative opportunities are likely to exist for unsuccessful political leaders and greater economic resources generally facilitate accommodation and compromise. In addition, a highly developed, industrialized economy and the complex society it implies cannot be governed efficiently by authoritarian means. Decision-making is necessarily dispersed, and hence power is shared and rule must be based on consent. Finally, in a more highly developed economy, income and possibly wealth also tend to be more equally distributed than in a poorer economy. Since democracy means, in some measure, majority rule, democracy is only possible if the majority is a relatively satisfied middle class, and not an impoverished majority confronting an inordinately wealthy oligarchy. A substantial middle class, in turn, may be the product of the relatively equal distribution of land in agrarian societies that may otherwise be relatively poor, such as the early 19th century United States or 20th century Costa Rica. It may also be the result of a relatively high level of development, which produces greater income equality in industrial as compared to industrializing societies.

If these arguments are correct, economic development in the Communist world and the Third World should facilitate the emergence of democratic regimes. Yet one must be skeptical as to whether

---

[11] This is not to argue that authoritarian regimes necessarily have higher economic growth rates than democratic ones, although they may. See Robert M. Marsh, "Does Democracy Hinder Economic Development in the Latecomer Developing Nations," *Comparative Social Research* 2 (1979), pp. 215–48; G. William Dick, "Authoritarian Versus Nonauthoritarian Approaches to Economic Development," *Journal of Political Economy* 82 (1974), pp. 817–27; and Erich Weede, "Political Democracy, State Strength and Economic Growth in LDCs: A Cross-National Analysis," (Paper presented at the Annual Meeting of the American Political Science Association, Chicago, Ill., September 1983).

such an easy conclusion is warranted. In the first place, there is the question as to what level of economic development is required to make possible the transition to democracy. As Jonathan Sunshine has conclusively shown, the countries of Western Europe generally became democratic when their per capita gross domestic products were in the range of $300–$500 (in 1960 dollars). By 1981, perhaps two-thirds of the middle-income developing countries had reached or exceeded that level of development. Most of them, however, had not become democratic. If the economic theory holds, the level of economic development necessary to facilitate the transition to democracy must be higher in the late 20th century than it was in the century prior to 1950.[12] In addition, different countries may still transit to democracy at widely varying levels of development. Spain, after all, did grow extremely rapidly during the 1950s and 1960s and did become democratic after the death of Francisco Franco in the mid-1970s. Could this have happened without the industrialization, urbanization, and development of the middle class that were central to Spanish economic growth? Quite probably not. Lopez Rodo was at least partially right when he had earlier predicted that Spain would become democratic when its per capita income reached $2,000 per head.[13] But then what about Portugal? It made a simultaneous transition to democracy, without having experienced the massive economic development of Spain and while still at a much lower level of economic well-being.

In addition, what about the experience of the southern cone states of Latin America? They too went through major processes of economic development and yet turned away from democracy, a phenomenon that led Guillermo O'Donnell to develop his theory of bureaucratic authoritarianism that posited just the opposite of the Lipset wealth-democracy theory. Instead, O'Donnell argued that economic development and particularly the strains produced by a heavy emphasis on import substitution led to the emergence of new, stronger, and more lasting forms of authoritarian rule.[14]

There is also the experience of the East Asian newly industrializing countries. In the 1960s and 1970s, these countries not only had the highest economic growth rates in the world, but they also

---

[12] Jonathan Sunshine, "Economic Causes and Consequences of Democracy: A Study in Historical Statistics" (Ph.D. diss., Columbia University, 1972), p. 115 ff.

[13] John F. Coverdale, *The Political Transformation of Spain after Franco* (New York: Praeger Publishers, 1979), p. 1.

[14] Guillermo A. O'Donnell, *Modernization and Bureaucratic-Authoritarianism: Studies in Latin American Politics* (Berkeley: University of California, Institute for International Studies, 1973), pp. 3–15, 113–14. For analysis of this theory, see David Collier, ed., *The New Authoritarianism in Latin America* (Princeton: Princeton University Press, 1979).

achieved those rates while in most cases maintaining very equitable systems of income distribution. Yet none became more democratic and two of the most notable economic achievers, Korea and Singapore, became less so.

At the same time, the economic theory may still serve a purpose in terms of focusing attention on those countries where transitions to democratic or other types of modern political systems are most likely to occur. As countries develop economically, they can be conceived of moving into a zone of transition or choice, in which traditional forms of rule become increasingly difficult to maintain and new types of political institutions are required to aggregate the demands of an increasingly complex society and to implement public policies in such a society. In the 1981 World Bank ordering of countries by level of economic development, the zone of choice might be conceived as comprising the top one third of the middle-income countries, that is, those running from Number 77 (the Republic of Korea) up to Number 96 (Spain). To these should be added Taiwan, which in terms of per capita income fits in the middle of this group. Of these 21 countries:

- Seven were democracies, including four (Spain, Venezuela, Portugal, Greece) that transited to democracy after World War II, two that became democratic on independence (Israel, Trinidad and Tobago), and one that had sustained democracy for many years (Costa Rica).

- Four were the bureaucratic-authoritarian (B-A) states of the southern cone (Brazil, Chile, Argentina, Uruguay).

- Four were the newly industrializing countries (NICs) of East Asia (the Republic of Korea, Taiwan, Singapore, Hong Kong).

- Two were Communist (Rumania and Yugoslavia).

- The remaining four (Algeria, Mexico, Iran, and South Africa) were resource rich, ideologically diverse, and politically undemocratic.

Two years later, this group of countries, now labeled by the World Bank as "upper middle income countries" had been reduced by the graduation of Spain into the category of "industrial market economies," but had been enlarged by the movement upward of Malaysia, Lebanon, and Panama, and by the Bank's transfer into it of Iraq from the category of "high income oil exporters."[15]

If the wealth theory of democracy were valid, one would predict further movement toward democracy among the twenty-odd states

---

[15] World Bank, *Development Report 1981*, pp. 134–35, and *World Development Report 1983* (New York: Oxford University Press, 1983), pp. 148–49.

in this group, perhaps particularly on the part of the East Asian NICs and the B-A states of South America. Experience suggests, however, that what is predictable for these countries in the transition zone is not the advent of democracy but rather the demise of previously existing political forms. Economic development compels the modification or abandonment of traditional political institutions; it does not determine what political system will replace them. That will be shaped by other factors, such as the underlying culture of the society, the values of the elites, and external influences.

In the late 1950s, for instance, both Cuba and Venezuela were reaching the level of economic development where the traditional sort of military despotism to which each had been subjected for years (Fulgencio y Batista Zaldivar, Marcos Pérez Jiménez) was no longer adequate for the needs of the society. These military despotisms came to their ends in 1958 and 1959. Batista collapsed in the face of an armed revolutionary movement that rapidly seized and consolidated power, nationalized private property, and installed a pervasive Marxist-Leninist dictatorship. The Pérez Jiménez regime collapsed as a result of the withdrawal of support by virtually all the major groups of Venezuelan society. That collapse was accompanied, however, by the negotiation of a series of pacts among Venezuelan leaders representing the major political and social groups that set the framework for a democratic political system. By the late 1950s, the days of traditional personalistic despotism in Cuba and Venezuela were numbered; what was not fixed was what would replace them. Fidel Castro chose to lead Cuba in one direction; Rómulo Betancourt chose to lead Venezuela in a very different one. Fifteen years later in somewhat comparable circumstances King Juan Carlos and Adolfo Suárez in Spain and António Ramalho Eanes in Portugal made similar choices on behalf of democracy. In another case, by the mid-1970s the rapid economic development of Iran had clearly undermined the basis for the shah's regime. The shah did not attempt to develop a broader, more participatory set of democratic institutions. His inaction, combined with the decision or lack of decision by the military leaders and the political skill of the mullahs, opened Iran to a religious revolution. Different and earlier decisions by Iranian leaders in the 1960s and 1970s might have moved Iran in a more democratic direction.

If the concept of a transition zone is valid, economic development produces a phase in a nation's history where political elites and the prevailing political values can shape choices that decisively determine the nation's future evolution. The range of choice may be limited. In 1981, for instance, all countries with per capita gross national products of $4,220 or more (aside from the small oil-exporting states and Singapore) were either democratic or Communist.

Conceivably, transition zone countries could make other choices. Iran is obviously in the fanatic pursuit of a different course; possibly the East Asian NICs and the Latin American B-A regimes may find other alternatives. To date, however, those countries that have come through the transition zone have almost always emerged as either democracies or as Communist dictatorships.

Social Structure

A second set of often-discussed preconditions for democracy involves the extent to which there is a widely differentiated and articulated social structure with relatively autonomous social classes, regional groups, occupational groups, and ethnic and religious groups. Such groups, it is argued, provide the basis for the limitation of state power, hence for the control of the state by society, and hence for democratic political institutions as the most effective means of exercising that control. Societies that lack autonomous intermediate groups are, on the other hand, much more likely to be dominated by a centralized power apparatus—an absolute monarchy, an oriental despotism, or an authoritarian or totalitarian dictatorship.[16] This argument can be made on behalf of groups and pluralism in general or on behalf of particular groups or types of pluralistic structure which are singled out as playing a decisive role in making democracy possible.

According to one line of argument, pluralism (even highly stratified pluralism) in traditional society enhances the probability of developing stable democracy in modern society. The caste system may be one reason why India has been able to develop and to maintain stable democratic institutions.[17] More generally, the argument is made that societies with a highly developed feudalism, including an aristocracy capable of limiting the development of state power, are more likely to evolve into democracies than those that lack such social pluralism. The record of Western Europe versus Russia and of Japan versus China suggests that there may well be something to this theory. But the theory fails to account for differences between North America and South America. Tocqueville, Louis Hartz, and others attribute democracy in the former to the absence of feudalism. The failure of democracy in South America has,

---

[16] Those who hold a more Rousseauistic conception of democracy will, of course, tend to see intermediate groups as obstacles to the realization of true democracy. For a balanced analysis of these issues, see Robert A. Dahl, *Dilemmas of Pluralist Democracy: Autonomy vs. Control* (New Haven: Yale University Press, 1982). For a general argument for intermediate groups as a bulwark against totalitarianism, see William Kornhauser, *The Politics of Mass Society* (New York: Free Press, 1959).

[17] See Lloyd I. and Susanne Hoeber Rudolph, *The Modernity of Tradition: Political Development in India* (Chicago: University of Chicago Press, 1967), pp. 15–154.

conversely, often been attributed precisely to its feudal heritage, although the feudalism that existed there was, to be sure, highly centralized.[18]

The theory that emphasizes traditional pluralism is, in a sense, the opposite of the one that emphasizes wealth as a precondition of democracy. The latter makes democracy dependent on how far the processes of economic development and modernization have gone. The traditional pluralism theory, in contrast, puts the emphasis on where the process started, on the nature of traditional society. Was it, in Gaetano Mosca's terms, primarily a "feudal" or a "bureaucratic" society? If pushed to the extreme, of course, this theory implies societal predestination: it is all determined in advance that some societies will become democratic and others will not.

The most significant manifestation of the social structure argument, however, concerns not the existence of a feudal aristocracy, but rather the existence of an autonomous bourgeoisie. Democracy, the Marxists argue, is bourgeois democracy, reflecting the interests of that particular social class. Barrington Moore has restated the proposition succinctly in a more limited formulation: "No bourgeois, no democracy."[19] This argument would seem to have much to commend it. The failure of democracy to develop in Third World countries despite their economic growth can, perhaps, be related to the nature of that growth. The leading roles have been played by the state and by multinational enterprises. As a result, economic development runs ahead of the development of a bourgeoisie. In those circumstances where a bourgeoisie has developed, however, the prospects for democracy have been greater. The move to democracy in Turkey in the 1940s coincided with the move away from the étatisme of Kemalism and the appearance of a group of independent businessmen. More significantly, the ability of a developing country to have an autonomous, indigenous bourgeoisie is likely to be related to its size. Countries with small internal markets are unlikely to be able to sustain such a class, but large ones can. This may be one factor explaining why India (with one short interlude) has sustained a democratic system, and why Brazil, which is also developing

---

[18] For elaboration of these themes, see among other: Louis Hartz, *The Liberal Tradition in America* (New York: Harcourt Brace Jovanovich, 1955), and Louis Hartz, ed., *The Founding of New Societies* (New York: Harcourt Brace Jovanovich, 1964), especially chap. V, Richard M. Morse, "The Heritage of Latin America"; James M. Malloy, ed., *Authoritarianism and Corporatism in Latin America* (Pittsburgh: University of Pittsburgh Press, 1977); Howard J. Wiarda, "Toward a Framework for the Study of Political Change in the Iberio-Latin Tradition," *World Politics* 25 (1973), pp. 206–35; Claudio Veliz, *The Centralist Tradition of Latin America* (Princeton: Princeton University Press, 1979).

[19] Barrington Moore, Jr., *Social Origins of Dictatorship and Democracy* (Boston: Beacon Press, 1966), p. 418.

a vigorous indigenous bourgeoisie, steadily moved away from bureaucratic authoritarianism in the 1970s and early 1980s. In South Africa, businessmen have been among those most active in attempting to ameliorate apartheid and broaden democracy in that country.

The seemingly important role of an autonomous bourgeoisie for the development of democracy highlights the question of the relation between economic system and political system. Clearly political democracy is compatible with both a substantial role in the economy for state-owned enterprises and a substantial state welfare and social security system. Nonetheless, as Charles Lindblom has pointed out (in a volume that otherwise highlights the conflict between the business corporation and democracy), all political democracies have market-oriented economies, although quite clearly not all market-oriented economies are paired with democratic political systems.[20] Lindblom's message would seem to be like Moore's—a market-oriented economy, like a bourgeoisie, is a necessary but not sufficient condition for the existence of a democratic political system.

Why should this be the case? At least two reasons suggest themselves. Politically, a market economy requires a dispersion of economic power and in practice almost invariably some form of private property. The dispersion of economic power creates alternatives and counters to state power and enables those elites that control economic power to limit state power and to exploit democratic means to make it serve their interests. Economically, a market economy appears more likely to sustain economic growth than a command economy (although the latter may, as the Soviet and East European cases suggest, do so for a short period of time), and hence a market economy is more likely to give rise to the economic wealth and the resulting more equitable distribution of income that provide the infrastructure of democracy.

A third source of autonomous social pressure in a democratic direction may be provided by labor unions. Historically, unions played this role in Western Europe and the United States. In the contemporary world, unions have also had a role in the struggles against the racist oligarchy in South Africa, against military rule in the southern cone, and against the Communist dictatorship in Poland. At the same time, the experience of these cases also suggests the limits on the extent to which, in the absence of affiliated political parties, labor unions can affect political change.

Under some conditions, communal (that is, ethnic, racial, or religious) pluralism may be conducive to the development of at least limited forms of democracy. In most cases of communal pluralism,

---

[20] Charles E. Lindblom, *Politics and Markets* (New York: Basic Books, 1977), pp. 161–69.

democracy can operate only on a consociational rather than a majoritarian basis.[21] And even when it is organized on a consociational basis, it will often break down as a result of social mobilization that undermines the power of elites or as a result of the intrusion of external political and military forces (as in Cyprus or Lebanon). Even in the best of circumstances, consociational democracy can often only remain stable by in effect becoming consociational oligarchy (as in Malaysia), that is, by sacrificing contestation in order to maintain representation.

External Environment

External influences may be of decisive importance in influencing whether a society moves in a democratic or nondemocratic direction. To the extent that such influences are more important than indigenous factors, democratization is the result of diffusion rather than development. Conceivably, democracy in the world could stem from a single source. Clearly it does not. Yet it would be wrong to ignore the extent to which much of the democracy in the world does have a common origin. In 1984, Freedom House classified 52 countries (many of them extremely small) as "free."[22] In 33, of those 52 countries, the presence of democratic institutions could be ascribed in large part to British and American influence, either through settlement, colonial rule, defeat in war, or fairly direct imposition (such as in the Dominican Republic). Most of the other 19 "free" countries where democracy had other sources were either in Western Europe or in South America. The extension of democracy into the non-Western world, insofar as that has occurred, has thus been largely the product of Anglo-American efforts.

Ever since the French Revolution, armies have carried political ideologies with them. As we have indicated, where American armies went in World War II, democracy followed (in four cases enduringly, in one case temporarily). Where Soviet armies went, Communism followed. Military conquest is clearly one way of extending democracy and other political systems. Historically, however, Western colonialism has been the most important means of diffusing democratic ideas and institutions. The enduring results of such colonialism have, however, been rather limited. As of 1983, no former French, U.S., Dutch, Portuguese, or Belgian colony was rated "free"

---

[21] See primarily the works of Arend Lijphart, particularly *The Politics of Accommodation: Pluralism and Democracy in the Netherlands*, 2d ed. (Berkeley: University of California Press, 1975) and *Democracy in Plural Societies: A Comparative Evaluation* (New Haven: Yale University Press, 1977).

[22] *Freedom at Issue*, no. 76 (1984), pp. 8–9.

by Freedom House. Several former British colonies were. Myron Weiner has, indeed, emphasized that *"every single country in the third world that emerged from colonial rule since the second world war with a population of at least one million (and almost all the smaller countries as well) with a continuous democratic experience is a former British colony."*[23] British rule seemingly had a significantly different impact from that of other colonial powers. Only six countries meet Weiner's condition, however, and a much larger number of former British colonies have *not* sustained democracy. The question then becomes how to distinguish among former British colonies. One possibility is that the duration of democratic institutions after independence is a function of the duration of British rule before independence. The colonies where democratic institutions appear to have taken the firmest root are those such as India, Sri Lanka, and the West Indian Anglophone states, where British rule dates from the 18th century. The record of former British colonies in Africa, on the other hand, where British rule dates only from the late 19th century, is not all that different from that of the former African colonies of other European powers.

In large measure, the rise and decline of democracy on a global scale is a function of the rise and decline of the most powerful democratic states. The spread of democracy in the 19th century went hand in hand with the Pax Britannica. The extension of democracy after World War II reflected the global power of the United States. The decline of democracy in East Asia and Latin America in the 1970s was in part a reflection of the waning of American influence.[24] That influence is felt both directly, as a result of the efforts of the American government to affect political processes in other societies, and also indirectly by providing a powerful and successful model to be followed.

Regional external influences can also have a significant effect on political development within a society. The governments and political parties of the European Community (EC) helped to encourage the emergence of democratic institutions in Spain and Portugal, and the desire of those two countries plus Greece to join the community provided an additional incentive for them to become democratic. Even beyond the confines of the EC, Western Europe has generally become defined as a community of democratic nations, and any significant departure by one nation from the democratic

---

[23] Myron Weiner, "Empirical Democratic Theory," in *Comparative Elections in Developing Countries,* ed. Myron Weiner and Ergun Ozbudun (Washington, D.C.: American Enterprise Institute, manuscript, 26 [italics in original]).

[24] Samuel P. Huntington, *American Politics: The Promise of Disharmony* (Cambridge, Mass.: Harvard University Press, 1981), pp. 246–59.

norm would clearly create a major crisis in intra-European relations. In some measure, a similar development may be taking place among the countries of the Andean Pact. The departure from the Pact of Chile and the addition of Venezuela in the mid-1970s, plus the transitions to democracy in Ecuador and Peru, then laid the basis for identifying pact membership with the adherence to democratic government.

In some regions, but most notably in Latin America, regional trends may exist. By and large, Latin American governments moved in a democratic direction in the late 1950s and early 1960s, then in an authoritarian direction in the late 1960s and early 1970s, and then once again in a democratic direction in the late 1970s and early 1980s. The reasons for these regional shifts are not entirely clear. They could be a result of four factors: simultaneous parallel socioeconomic development in Latin American societies; the triggering of a trend by the impact of one "pace-setting" Latin American society on its neighbors; the impact on Latin America of a common external influence (such as the United States); or some combination of these factors.

Cultural Context

The political culture of a society has been defined by Sidney Verba as "the system of empirical beliefs, expressive symbols, and values which defines the situation in which political action takes place."[25] Political culture is, presumably, rooted in the broader culture of a society involving those beliefs and values, often religiously based, concerning the nature of humanity and society, the relations among human beings, and the relation of individuals to a transcendent being. Significant differences in their receptivity to democracy appear to exist among societies with different cultural traditions.

Historically, as many scholars have pointed out, a high correlation existed between Protestantism and democracy. In the contemporary world, virtually all countries with a European population and a Protestant majority (except East Germany) have democratic governments.[26] The case of Catholicism, particularly in Latin countries, on the other hand, is more ambivalent. Historically, it was often argued that a natural opposition existed between Catholicism and democracy. By and large, democratic institutions developed

---

[25] Sidney Verba, "Comparative Political Culture," in *Political Culture and Political Development*, ed. Lucian W. Pye and Sidney Verba (Princeton: Princeton University Press, 1965), p. 513.

[26] For the statistical correlation between Protestantism and democracy, see Kenneth A. Bollen, "Political Democracy and the Timing of Development," *American Sociological Review* 44 (1979), pp. 572–87.

later and less surely in European Catholic countries than in Protestant ones. By and large, however, these countries also developed later economically than the Protestant countries, and hence it is difficult to distinguish between the impact of economics and that of religion. Conceivably, the influence of the latter on politics could have been mediated through its impact on economic development and the rise of an entrepreneurial class. With economic development, however, the role of the church changed, and in most Catholic countries now the church is identified with support for democracy.

Islam, on the other hand, has not been hospitable to democracy. Of 36 countries with Moslem majorities, Freedom House in 1984 rated 21 as "not free," 15 as "partially free," none as "free." The one Islamic country that sustained even intermittent democracy after World War II was Turkey, which had, under Mustapha Kemal, explicitly rejected its Islamic tradition and defined itself as a secular republic. The one Arab country that sustained democracy, albeit of the consociational variety, for any time was Lebanon, 40 to 50 percent of whose population was Christian and whose democratic institutions collapsed when the Moslem majority asserted itself in the 1970s. Somewhat similarly, both Confucianism and Buddhism have been conducive to authoritarian rule, even in those cases where, as in Korea, Taiwan, and Singapore, economic preconditions for democracy have come into being. In India and Japan, on the other hand, the traditional Hindu and Shinto cultures at the very least did not prevent the development of democratic institutions and may well have encouraged it.

How can these differences be explained? Both doctrinal and structural aspects of the religions could play a role. At the most obvious level, those cultures that are consummatory in character—that is, where intermediate and ultimate ends are closely connected—seem to be less favorable to democracy. In Islam, for instance, no distinction exists between religion and politics or between the spiritual and the secular, and political participation was historically an alien concept.[27] Somewhat similarly, Confucianism in China was generally hostile to social bodies independent of the state, and the culture was conceived as a total entity, no part of which could be changed without threatening the whole. Instrumental cultures, in contrast, are "characterized by a large sector of intermediate ends separate from and independent of ultimate ends" and hence "ultimate ends do not color every concrete act."[28] The Hindu tradition, for example,

---

[27] See Daniel Pipes, *In the Path of God: Islam and Political Power* (New York: Basic Books, 1983), pp. 48–69, 144–47.

[28] David E. Apter, *The Politics of Modernization* (Chicago: University of Chicago Press, 1965), p. 85.

is relatively tolerant of diversity. S. N. Eisenstadt has written that "the basic religious and cultural orientations, the specific cultural identity of Indian civilization were not necessarily associated with any particular political or imperial framework. . . ."[29]

As a whole, consummatory culture is thus more resistant to change, and when change comes in one significant element of the culture, the entire culture is thrown into question or is displaced and destroyed. In the instrumental culture, on the other hand, change can come gradually and incrementally. Hence, less resistance exists to the adaptation of new political forms, such as democratic institutions, and the process of adaptation can be an extended one that in itself facilitates the development of stable democracy.

With respect to the more narrowly political culture of a society, it seems reasonable to expect that the prevalence of some values and beliefs will be more conducive to the emergence of democracy than others. A political culture that values highly hierarchical relationships and extreme deference to authority presumably is less fertile ground for democracy than one that does not. Similarly, a culture in which there is a high degree of mutual trust among members of the society is likely to be more favorable to democracy than one in which interpersonal relationships are more generally characterized by suspicion, hostility, and distrust. A willingness to tolerate diversity and conflict among groups and to recognize the legitimacy of compromise also should be helpful to democratic development. Societies in which great stress is put on the need to acquire power and little on the need to accommodate others are more likely to have authoritarian or totalitarian regimes. Social scientists have attempted to compare societies along these various dimensions, but the evidence remains fragmented and difficult to systematize.[30] In addition, of course, even if some beliefs and values are found to correlate with the presence of democratic institutions, the question still remains concerning the relationship among these in a developmental sense. To what extent does the development of a pro-democratic political culture have to precede the development of democratic institutions? Or do the two tend to develop more simultaneously with the successful operation of democratic

---

[29] S. N. Eisenstadt, "Transformation of Social, Political, and Cultural Orders in Modernization," *American Sociological Review* 30 (1965), p. 668. In contrast to the Hindu tradition, Eisenstadt writes, "the identity between political and religious communities represents a very important similarity between the Chinese and Islamic societies" (p. 663).

[30] See Pye and Verba, *Political Culture;* Dahl, *Polyarchy,* pp. 124–87; Gabriel A. Almond and Sidney Verba, *The Civic Culture* (Princeton: Princeton University Press, 1963); David McClelland, *The Achieving Society* (New York: Van Nostrand Reinhold, 1961).

institutions, possibly created for other reasons, generating adherence to democratic values and beliefs?[31]

PROCESSES OF DEMOCRATIZATION

The classic model of democratization that has infused much discussion of the subject is that of Britain, with its stately progression
from civic rights to political rights to social rights, gradual development of parliamentary supremacy and cabinet government, and
incremental expansion of the suffrage over the course of a century.
It is basically a linear model. Dankwart A. Rustow's model, based
on Swedish experience—national unity, prolonged and inconclusive
political struggle, a conscious decision to adopt democratic rules,
habituation to the working of those rules—also involves a relatively
simple linear progression. These "ingredients," he has argued,
"must be assembled one at a time."[32] These linear models primarily
reflect European experience during the century ending in 1920 and
the experience of some Latin American countries (such as Argentina
until 1930 and Chile until 1973).

Two other models have generally been more relevant than the
linear model to the experience of Third World countries. One is
the cyclical model of alternating despotism and democracy. In this
case, key elites normally accept, at least superficially, the legitimacy
of democratic forms. Elections are held from time to time, but rarely
is there any sustained succession of governments coming to power
through the electoral process. Governments are as often the product
of military interventions as they are of elections. Such interventions
tend to occur either when a radical party wins or appears about
to win an election, when the government in power threatens or
appears to threaten the prerogatives of the armed forces, or when
the government appears incapable of effectively guiding the economy and maintaining public order. Once a military junta takes
over, it will normally promise to return power to civilian rule. In
due course, it does so, if only to minimize divisiveness within the
armed forces and to escape from its own inability to govern effectively. In a praetorian situation like this, neither authoritarian nor
democratic institutions are effectively institutionalized. Once countries enter into this cyclical pattern, it appears to be extremely
difficult for them to escape from it. In many respects, countries

---

[31] For arguments on the priority of democratic values, see the case Dahl makes
on Argentina, *Polyarchy*, pp. 132–40, and Jonathan Tumin's amendment of Barrington Moore in "The Theory of Democratic Development: A Critical Revision," *Theory
and Society* 11 (1982), pp. 143–64.

[32] Rustow, "Transitions to Democracy," p. 361.

that have had relatively stable authoritarian rule (such as Spain and Portugal) are more likely to evolve into relatively stable democracies than countries that have regularly oscillated between despotism and democracy (such as Peru, Ecuador, Bolivia, Argentina, Ghana, Nigeria). In the latter, neither democratic nor authoritarian norms have deep roots among the relevant political elites, while in the former a broad consensus accepting of authoritarian norms is displaced by a broad consensus on or acceptance of democratic ones. In the one case, the alternation of democracy and despotism *is* the political system; in the other, the shift from a stable despotism to a stable democracy *is a change* in political systems.

A third model is neither linear nor cyclical but rather dialectical. In this case, the development of a middle class leads to increased pressures on the existing authoritarian regimes for expanded participation and contestation. At some point, there is then a sharp break, perhaps in the form of what I have elsewhere called the "urban breakthrough," the overthrow of the existing authoritarian regime, and the installation of a democratic one.[33] This regime, however, finds it difficult or impossible to govern effectively. A sharp reaction occurs with the overthrow of the democratic system and installation of a (usually right-wing) authoritarian regime. In due course, however, this regime collapses and a transition is made to a more stable, more balanced, and longer-lasting democratic system. This model is roughly applicable to the history of a number of countries, including Germany, Italy, Austria, Greece, and Spain.

Most theories of political development in general and of democratization in particular see these processes as involving a number of different elements. The sequence in which those components appear may have important implications for the overall results of the process. Several theorists have suggested, for instance, that the preferable overall process of development for a country is first to define its national identity, next to develop effective institutions of authority, and then to expand political participation. The "probabilities of a political system's development in a nonviolent, nonauthoritarian, and eventually democratically stable manner are maximized," Eric Nordlinger has argued, when this sequence occurs.[34]

---

[33] Samuel P. Huntington, *Political Order in Changing Societies* (New Haven: Yale University Press, 1968), pp. 72–78.

[34] Eric A. Nordlinger, "Political Development: Time Sequences and Rates of Change," *World Politics* 20 (1968), pp. 494–530; Dankwart A. Rustow, *A World of Nations* (Washington, D.C.: Brookings Institution, 1967), p. 126 ff.; Leonard Binder et al., *Crises and Sequences in Political Development* (Princeton: Princeton University Press, 1971), pp. 310–313.

In somewhat parallel fashion, it has been argued that the development of broad-gauged political institutions for political participation, such as electoral and party systems, must coincide with or precede the expansion of political participation if instability and violence are to be avoided. Similarly, Robert A. Dahl emphasizes the greater probability of success in transitions to democracy (or polyarchy in his terms) if the expansion of contestation precedes the expansion of participation.[35]

All these theories thus emphasize the desirability for the eventual development of stable democracy of the expansion of political participation occurring relatively late in the sequence of change. However, given the widely accepted desirability of political participation (including in totalitarian regimes) and the major increases in social mobilization (such as urbanization, literacy, and media consumption) produced by economic development, the prevailing tendencies in the contemporary world are for participation to expand early in the process of development, and before or concurrently with contestation. This may be one reason why economic development in the Third World has not stimulated the emergence of more stable democratic regimes. At present, the one notable case where contestation has clearly developed in advance of participation is South Africa. Hence, according to the Dahl thesis, the prospects for democratic development should be greater in South Africa than elsewhere in Africa.

It is often assumed that since democracy, to a greater degree than other forms of government, involves rule by the people, the people therefore play a greater role in bringing it into existence than they do with other forms of government. In fact, however, democratic regimes that last have seldom, if ever, been instituted by mass popular action. Almost always, democracy has come as much from the top down as from the bottom up; it is as likely to be the product of oligarchy as of protest against oligarchy. The passionate dissidents from authoritarian rule and the crusaders for democratic principles, the Tom Paines of this world, do not create democratic institutions; that requires James Madisons. Those institutions come into existence through negotiations and compromises among political elites calculating their own interests and desires. They are produced when, as Rustow argued, political leaders decide "to accept the existence of diversity in unity and, to that end, to institutionalize some crucial aspect of democratic

---

[35] Dahl, *Polyarchy,* pp. 33–40; Huntington, *Political Order,* esp. pp. 32–59, 78–92. See also Richard A. Pride, *Origins of Democracy: A Cross-National Study of Mobilization, Party Systems, and Democratic Stability,* Comparative Politics Series, Vol. 1, (Beverly Hills, Calif.: Sage Publications, 1970).

procedure." The political leaders may do this because they are convinced of the ethical and political superiority of democracy and hence view democracy as a desirable goal in itself. More likely, however, they will view democracy as a means to other goals, such as prolonging their own rule, achieving international legitimacy, minimizing domestic opposition, and reducing the likelihood of civil violence, from which they will probably suffer. Hence, whatever institutions are agreed on will, in Rustow's words, "seem second-best to all major parties involved."[36] One could paraphrase Reinhold Niebuhr: the ability of elites to compromise makes democracy possible; the inclination of elites to vengeance makes democracy desirable—for the elites.

In the decades after World War II, democratic regimes have usually been introduced in independent countries through one or some combination of two processes. *Replacement* occurs when an authoritarian regime collapses or is overthrown as a result of military defeat, economic disaster, or the withdrawal of support from it by substantial groups in the population. Its leaders are killed, imprisoned, flee the country, or withdraw from politics. The leaders of the now-dominant groups, which had not been actively involved with the authoritarian regime, agree among themselves to institute a democratic system. This agreement may be reached very quickly because of previous experience with democracy and because its inauguration is seen as the "obvious" solution by the relevant political elites, as in Venezuela in 1958 and Greece in 1974. Or it may come about as a result of political struggle among elites with differing views as to the future of their country, out of which the leaders committed to democracy emerge successfully (as in Portugal in 1975–76). This process may involve, as it did in the case of Venezuela, a series of carefully negotiated pacts among the relevant groups that can cover economic policy and the role of institutions (such as the church and the army), as well as the procedures for choosing a government. One critical issue on which the constitutive elites must agree is how to treat those actively involved in the previous authoritarian regime.[37]

The alternative process for inaugurating a democratic regime might be termed *transformation*. In this case, the elites within an authoritarian system conclude that, for some reason or another, that system which they have led and presumably benefited from no longer meets their needs or those of their society. They hence take the lead in modifying the existing political system and

---

[36] Rustow, "Transitions to Democracy," pp. 355–57.

[37] John H. Herz, "On Reestablishing Democracy after the Downfall of Authoritarian or Dictatorial Regimes," *Comparative Politics* 10 (1978), pp. 559–62.

transforming it into a democratic one. In this case, while there may well be a variety of internal and external pressures favoring change, the initiative for such change comes from the rulers. Transformation involves, as Juan Linz put it, "change through *reforma* rather than *ruptura.*"[38] Notable examples include, of course, Britain in the 19th century, and after World War II, Turkey in the 1940s, Spain in the 1970s, and Brazil in the 1970s and 1980s. The leaders of the transformation process typically confront all the problems of the political reformer, having to maneuver skillfully between the stand-patters opposed to any democratization, on the one hand, and the committed dissident and opposition groups demanding the immediate dissolution of the authoritarian system, on the other. Essential to their success is that they be seen as keeping control, acting from a position of strength and not under duress, and dictating the pace of change.

The replacement process requires compromise and agreement among elites who have not been part of the authoritarian regime. The transformation process requires skilled leadership from and agreement among the elites who are part of that regime. In neither case is agreement necessarily required between elites who are within the regime and those opposing the regime. This situation makes replacement and transformation possible, since reaching an agreement between out-groups and in-groups is far more difficult than reaching an agreement among out-groups or among in-groups. Except for Costa Rica in 1948, it is hard to think of a case where a democratic system of any duration was inaugurated by explicit agreement between the leaders of a regime and the leaders of the armed opposition to that regime.

"As long as powerful vested interests oppose changes that lead toward a less oppressive world," Barrington Moore has argued, "no commitment to a free society can dispense with some conception of revolutionary coercion."[39] His thesis is that liberty and democracy can be inaugurated by bloody revolution and that such a course may well impose fewer costs than the alternative of gradual reform. When in world history, however, has violent revolution produced a stable democratic regime in an independent state? "Revolutionary coercion" may bring down an authoritarian regime, but, except again for Costa Rica in 1948, guerrilla insurgencies do not inaugurate democratic regimes. All revolutionary opponents of authoritarian regimes claim to be democrats; once they achieve power

---

[38] Juan Linz, "Crisis, Breakdown, and Reequilibration," in *The Breakdown of Democratic Regimes,* ed. Juan Linz and Alfred Stepan, (Baltimore: The Johns Hopkins Press, 1978), p. 35.

[39] Moore, *Social Origins,* p. 508.

through violence, almost all turn out to be authoritarian themselves, often imposing an even more repressive regime than the one they overthrew. Most authoritarian regimes are thus replaced by new authoritarian regimes, and a democratic succession usually requires minimum violence. "In the future as in the past," as Dahl concluded his study of this issue, "stable polyarchies and near-polyarchies are more likely to result from rather slow evolutionary processes than from revolutionary overthrow of existing hegemonies.[40]

THE PROSPECTS FOR DEMOCRACY

This brief and informal survey of the preconditions and processes conducive to the emergence of democratic regimes argues for caution in any effort to predict whether more countries will become democratic. It may, however, be useful to attempt to sum up the modest conclusions which seem to emerge from this review.

With respect to preconditions, the emergence of democracy in a society is helped by a number of factors: higher levels of economic well-being; the absence of extreme inequalities in wealth and income; greater social pluralism, including particularly a strong and autonomous bourgeoisie; a more market-oriented economy; greater influence vis-à-vis the society of existing democratic states; and a culture that is less monistic and more tolerant of diversity and compromise. No one of these preconditions is sufficient to lead to democratic development. With the possible exception of a market economy, no single precondition is necessary to produce such development. Some combination of some of these preconditions is required for a democratic regime to emerge, but the nature of that combination can vary greatly from one case to another. It is also necessary, however, to look not only at what preconditions must be present but also at the negative strength of any precondition that may be absent. The powerful absence of one favorable condition, or, conversely, the presence of a powerful negative condition, that overrides the presence of otherwise favorable conditions, may prevent democratic development. In terms of cultural tradition, economic development, and social structure, Czechoslovakia would certainly be a democracy today (and probably Hungary and Poland also) if it were not for the overriding veto of the Soviet presence. In similar fashion, extreme poverty, extreme economic inequalities, or deeply ingrained Islamic and Confucian cultural traditions could have comparable effect in Africa, Central America, or the Middle East and East Asia.

With respect to the processes necessary to bring about democratic

---

[40] Dahl, *Polyarchy,* p. 45.

development, a central requirement would appear to be that either the established elites within an authoritarian system or the successor elites after an authoritarian system collapses see their interests served by the introduction of democratic institutions. The probability of stable democracy emerging will be enhanced to the extent that the transition can be a gradual one, that the introduction of contestation precedes the expansion of political participation, and that the role of violence in the transition is minimized. The probability of democratization decreases sharply to the extent that political life in a society becomes highly polarized and involves violent conflict between social forces.

Possibility of Regime Changes

In terms of these generalizations, prospects for democratic development in the 1980s are probably greatest in the bureaucratic-authoritarian states of South America. Cultural traditions, levels of economic development, previous democratic experience, social pluralism (albeit with weak bourgeoisies outside Brazil), and elite desires to emulate European and North American models all favor movement toward democracy in these countries. On the other hand, the polarization and violence that has occurred (particularly in Argentina and Chile) could make such movement difficult. The prospects for a relatively stable democratic system should be greatest in Brazil. Beginning in the early 1970s, the leadership of the Brazilian regime began a process of *distensão*, gradually relaxing the authoritarian controls that had been imposed in the 1960s. By the early 1980s, Brazil had acquired many of the characteristics of a democratic system. The principal deficiency was the absence of popular elections for the chief executive, but those were generally viewed as certain to come sometime in the 1980s. The gradualness of the Brazilian process, the relative low level of violence that accompanied it, and the general recognition among elite groups of the importance of not disrupting it in any way, all seemed to enhance the prospects for democracy.

In Argentina, the economic and military failures of the authoritarian regime led to a much more dramatic and rapid transit to democracy in 1983. The probabilities of this replacement being sustained would seem to depend on three factors: the ability of the Alfonsín government to deal with the economic problems it confronted; the extent to which Peronista, as well as Radical, elites were willing to abide by democratic rules; and the extent to which military leadership was effectively excluded from power or came to identify its interests with the maintenance of a democratic regime. The two other southern cone countries with bureaucratic-authoritarian regimes, Chile and Uruguay, are the two South American countries that did have the strongest democratic traditions. As of 1984, however, in neither country had authoritarian rule lost its legitimacy and effectiveness to the point where it could no longer be maintained and a replacement process could occur (as in Argentina). Nor had the leaders of either regime embarked on a meaningful transformation process to democratize their system (as in Brazil). The Brazilian and Argentine changes, however, cannot fail to have impact on political development in the smaller countries.

The probability of movement in a democratic direction in the East Asian newly industrializing countries is considerably less than it is among the Latin American B-A states. The economic basis for democracy is clearly coming into existence, and if their economic development continues at anything like the rates it did in the 1960s and 1970s, these states will soon constitute an authoritarian anomaly among the wealthier countries of the world. The East Asian countries generally have also had and maintained a relatively equal distribution of income. In addition, the United States, Britain, and Japan are the principal external influences on these societies. All these factors favor democratic development. On the other side, cultural traditions, social structure, and a general weakness of democratic norms among key elites all impede movement in a democratic direction. In some measure, the East Asian states dramatically pose the issue of whether economics or culture has the greater influence on political development. One can also speculate on whether the spread of Christianity in Korea may create a cultural context more favorable to democracy.

Among other less economically developed East Asian societies, the prospects for democracy are undoubtedly highest but still not very high in the Philippines. The Marcos government is not likely to attempt to transform itself, and hence efforts to create a democratic system must await its demise. At that time, American influence, previous experience with democracy, social pluralism (including the influence of the Catholic Church), and the general agreement among opposition political leaders on the desirability of a return to democracy, should all provide support for movement in that direction. On the other hand, military leaders may not support democratic norms, and the existence of a radical insurgency committed to violence, plus a general proclivity to the use of violence in the society, might make such a transition difficult. Conceivably, Philippine development could follow the lines of the dialectical model referred to earlier, in which (as in Venezuela) an initial experience with democracy is broken by a personalistic authoritarian interlude that then collapses and a new, more stable democratic regime is brought into existence by agreement among political leaders. The

Philippine Betancourt, however, may well have been gunned down at the Manila airport.

Among Islamic countries, particularly those in the Middle East, the prospects for democratic development seem low. The Islamic revival, and particularly the rise of Shi'ite fundamentalism, would seem to reduce even further the likelihood of democratic development, particularly since democracy is often identified with the very Western influences the revival strongly opposes. In addition, many of the Islamic states are very poor. Those that are rich, on the other hand, are so because of oil, which is controlled by the state and hence enhances the power of the state in general and of the bureaucracy in particular. Saudi Arabia and some of the smaller Arab oil-rich Gulf countries have from time to time made some modest gestures toward the introduction of democratic institutions, but these have not gone far and have often been reversed.

Most African countries are, by reason of their poverty or the violence of their politics, unlikely to move into a democratic direction. Those African and Latin American countries that have adhered to the cyclical pattern of alternating democratic and authoritarian systems in the past are not likely to change this basic pattern, as the example of Nigeria underlines, unless more fundamental changes occur in their economic and social infrastructure. In South Africa, on the other hand, the relatively high level of economic development by African standards, the intense contestation that occurs within the minority permitted to participate in politics, the modest expansion of that minority to include the Coloureds and Asians, and the influence of Western democratic norms, all provide a basis for moving in a more democratic direction. However, that basis is countered on the other side by the inequalities, fears, and hatreds that separate blacks and whites.

In some small countries, democratic institutions may emerge as a result of massive foreign effort. This did happen in the Dominican Republic; in 1984 it was, presumably, happening in Grenada; it could, conceivably, happen at extremely high cost in El Salvador.

The likelihood of democratic development in Eastern Europe is virtually nil. The Soviet presence is a decisive overriding obstacle, no matter how favorable other conditions may be in countries like Czechoslovakia, Hungary, and Poland. Democratization could occur in these societies only if either the Soviet Union were drastically weakened through war, domestic upheaval, or economic collapse (none of which seems likely), or if the Soviet Union came to view Eastern European democratization as not threatening to its interests (which seems equally unlikely).

The issue of Soviet intervention apart, a more general issue concerns the domestic pattern of evolution within Communist states.

For almost four decades after World War II, no democratic country, with the dubious possible exception of Czechoslovakia in 1948, became Communist and no Communist country became democratic through internal causes. Authoritarian regimes, on the other hand, were frequently replaced by either democratic or Communist regimes, and democratic regimes were replaced by authoritarian ones. In their early phase, Communist states usually approximated the totalitarian model, with ideology and the party playing central roles and massive efforts being made to indoctrinate and mobilize the population and to extend party control throughout all institutions in the society. Over time, however, Communist regimes also tend to change and often to become less totalitarian and more authoritarian. The importance of ideology and mobilization declines, bureaucratic stagnation replaces ideological fervor, and the party become less a dedicated elite and more a mechanism for patronage. In some cases, military influence increases significantly. The question thus arises: Will Communist authoritarian regimes, absent Soviet control, be more susceptible to movement toward democracy than Communist totalitarian regimes?

The answer to that question may well depend on the extent to which Communist authoritarian regimes permit the development of a market-oriented economy. The basic thrust of communism suggests that such a development is unlikely. Communism is not, as Karl Marx argued, a product of capitalist democracy; nor is it simply a "disease of the transition" to capitalist democracy, to use Rostow's phrase.[41] It is instead an alternative to capitalist democracy and one whose guiding principle is the subjection of economic development to political control. Even if it becomes more authoritarian and less totalitarian, the Communist political system is likely to ensure that economic development neither achieves a level nor assumes a form that will be conducive to democracy.

The United States and Global Democracy

The ability of the United States to affect the development of democracy elsewhere is limited. There is little that the United States or any other foreign country can do to alter the basic cultural tradition and social structure of another society or to promote compromise among groups of that society that have been killing each other. Within the restricted limits of the possible, however, the United States could contribute to democratic development in other countries in four ways.

---

[41] Walt W. Rostow, *The Stages of Economic Growth* (Cambridge: Cambridge University Press, 1960), p. 162.

First, it can assist the economic development of poor countries and promote a more equitable distribution of income and wealth in those countries. Second, it can encourage developing countries to foster market economies and the development of vigorous bourgeois classes. Third, it can refurbish its own economic, military, and political power so as to be able to exercise greater influence than it has in world affairs. Finally, it can develop a concerted program designed to encourage and to help the elites of countries entering the "transition zone" to move their countries in a more democratic direction.

Efforts such as these could have a modest influence on the development of democracy in other countries. Overall, however, this survey of the preconditions for and processes of democratization leads to the conclusion that, with a few exceptions, the prospects for the extension of democracy to other societies are not great. These prospects would improve significantly only if there were major discontinuities in current trends—such as if, for instance, the economic development of the Third World were to proceed at a much faster rate and to have a far more positive impact on democratic development than it has had so far, or if the United States reestablished a hegemonic position in the world comparable to that which it had in the 1940s and 1950s. In the absence of developments such as these, a significant increase in the number of democratic regimes in the world is unlikely. The substantial power of anti-democratic governments (particularly the Soviet Union), the unreceptivity to democracy of several major cultural traditions, the difficulties of eliminating poverty in large parts of the world, and the prevalence of high levels of polarization and violence in many societies all suggest that, with a few exceptions, the limits of democratic development in the world may well have been reached.

5

Democracy in Africa

Richard L. Sklar

I am often asked to explain what possessed me, a white American political scientist, to undertake African studies. Usually, I reflect upon my state of mind in the mid-1950s and mention the allure of a new horizon for democracy, limned by the doctrine of self-determination for subject peoples. Even then, however, realists warned that democracy in Africa, as in Asia, would bleed and die on the altars of national consolidation and social reconstruction.[1] But democracy dies hard. Its vital force is the accountability of rulers to their subjects. Democracy stirs and wakens from the deepest slumber whenever the principle of accountability is asserted by members of a community or conceded by those who rule. Democracy cannot be destroyed by a coup d'etat; it will survive every legal assault upon political liberty. The true executioner of democracy has neither sword nor scepter, but a baneful idea. Ironically, the deadly agent is an idea about freedom.

In Africa today, freedom from want is a universal goal. Millions of lives are blighted by the effects of poverty, unemployment, malnutrition, untended illness, and inadequate education. In all countries, political leaders dedicate themselves to the cause of economic and

Source: Richard L. Sklar, "Democracy in Africa," Presidential address to the African Studies Association, 1982, *African Studies Review* 26, Nos. 3/4 (September-December 1983), pp. 11–24. Reprinted by permission of the African Studies Association and the author. Footnotes and references abridged by the editors.

[1] See the sensitive assessment by Rupert Emerson, *From Empire to Nation* (Cambridge, Mass.: Harvard University Press, 1960), pp. 272–92.

social development. Most leaders also claim to respect the principle of accountability to the people. However, the imperatives of development are far more demanding than the claims of democracy. Appalled by the human condition and waste of resources in Africa and other nonindustrial regions, many intellectuals proclaim the validity of an antidemocratic idea, to which the term "developmental dictatorship" is aptly applied.

According to A. James Gregor the principles of developmental dictatorship were first formulated by Italian Marxists during the course of intense theoretical debates before the outbreak of World War One.[2] Eventually, they came to understand that orthodox Marxism was not relevant to the social realities of their underdeveloped country. Left to itself, they reasoned, the feeble Italian bourgeoisie, fettered by its dependence upon foreign capitalists, would not create an industrial society. Fatefully, they forsook the ideal of proletarian internationalism and embraced statist nationalism in order to mobilize all talents and resources for a program of forced and rapid industrialization. With heretical abandon, they entrusted responsibility for the direction of events to an "audacious minority" or "vanguard elite."[3] Faced with a similar predicament in the 1920s, the post-capitalist regime in Moscow adopted a similar nationalist and statist strategy. Ever since, national struggles to overcome economic backwardness in many parts of the world have been intensified if not actually led by proponents of developmental dictatorship.

The hardships of developmental dictatorship are well known: liberty is suppressed; labor is regimented and exploited; freedom of movement is curtailed; personal choice is severely restricted. From his pre-revolutionary vantage point, Karl Marx advised his readers to anticipate painful transitions or "birth pangs," during the creation of new social orders. "The country that is more developed industrially only shows, to the less developed, the image of its own future."[4] Must we, now, believe that Africa, rid of external rule but bowed-down in social and economic agony, with burgeoning populations and a dearth of jobs, should or will resort en masse and in extremis to developmental dictatorship? Shall we avert our eyes from an unforeseen alternative and disregard an abundance of evidence for the thesis that Africa today is a veritable workshop of democracy?

---

[2] A. James Gregor, *Italian Fascism and Developmental Dictatorship* (Princeton, N.J.: Princeton University Press, 1979).

[3] Ibid., p. 87.

[4] Karl Marx, *Capital,* Vol. I (New York: International Publishers, 1967), pp. 8–10. Preface to the First German Edition, 1867.

Democracy in Africa is as varied as the ever-changing forms of government in more than 50 sovereign states. Democracy in Africa is an experimental process in a new generation of countries. We should study this process not only to learn about Africa, but also to refresh our knowledge about the meaning of democracy itself. As the African philosopher, Edward Wilmot Blyden, might have said, in our time, these experiments in democracy constitute "Africa's service to the world."[5]

For this assessment of democracy in Africa, I have distinguished four existing types at the level of national government and one other which has been proposed. The first type is liberal democracy, wherein the powers of government are limited by law and citizens enjoy freedom of association to compete for office in free elections at regular intervals. Numerous liberal democracies were bequeathed to Africa by the former colonial rulers; all but a few of them, however, were rudely swept away by military coups, political usurpations, and constitutional changes shortly after (or within a decade of) independence. A few hardier breeds of liberal democracy have been planted and nurtured by African statesmen themselves.

At the present time, one person in five on the continent of Africa lives in a truly liberal democracy with genuine freedom of expression and freedom of political association. (Among black Africans the percentage is higher: one in four.) The citizens of liberal democracies include an estimated 100 million Nigerians plus the citizens of five other states, namely, Botswana, The Gambia, Mauritius, Senegal, and Zimbabwe. However, the serious qualifications to which this observation is liable underscore the experimental and highly contingent nature of liberal democracy in Africa.

During the past two years, ventures in liberal democracy have been aborted by paternalistic military guardians in Upper Volta, (arguably) the Central African Republic, and Ghana. At present, liberal democracy lingers in Zimbabwe, but the political leaders of that country have expressed their strong preference for a democracy without party competition. Until the electoral victory of Mauritian socialists in June 1982, no national government in an independent African state had ever been transferred to an opposition by electoral means. Confirming the historic importance of this event, the Mauritian socialists have pledged to strengthen a constitutional guarantee of free elections at regular intervals. In The Gambia, liberal democracy nearly succumbed to an insurrection in July 1981.

---

[5] The title of an address, delivered in 1880, in which Africa's contribution to world culture is judiciously assessed. See Edward Wilmot Blyden, *Christianity, Islam and the Negro Race,* 2d Ed. (London: Whitingham, 1888).

It has since been fortified by the establishment of a confederation with a protective sister-republic, Senegal. Since the retirement of President Léopold Sédar Senghor in January 1981, Senegal has emerged as a full-fledged liberal democracy. President Abdou Diouf leads a moderate socialist party which enjoys a commanding majority in the national assembly. The party is also a haven for conservative and parasitical interest groups. To rejuvenate this party for the urgent tasks of economic reconstruction, and to defuse a potentially revolutionary opposition, President Diouf has opened the door of legality to all political parties. Inevitably, the opposition parties sparkle, like the fragments of a Roman candle, in splendid sectarian isolation. Diouf's open air treatment of illiberal dissent is a milestone for democratic socialists in Africa.

Given the large number of sovereign entities in today's Africa, and the preponderance of illiberal governments, the crucial accounting for African liberal democracy must be rendered in populous Nigeria. Scholars have pondered and variously explained the remarkable resilience of constitutional liberty in Nigerian government. Without prejudice to the importance of other explanations, notably the influence of indigenous constitutional traditions, I am particularly impressed by the impact of federalism upon Nigerian political thought. While the number of states in Nigeria's federation has varied and remains contentious, federalism per se is an article of national faith, the virtually unquestioned premise of national unity. It is instructive to recall that federalism was a shared value for rival nationalists during the colonial era;[6] it was the indispensable basis for Nigerian unity under military rule, when the threat of national disintegration loomed large. At present, nineteen states accommodate a richly textured and wondrously complex tapestry of democratic political life.

Truly federal governments are necessarily liberal governments, predicated on the division and restraint of power. In Nigeria, the rights of citizens and constituent states alike are protected by a staunchly independent judiciary. In fact, Nigeria is an exceptionally legalistic society; many political issues of great moment are finally resolved in the courts, for example, the outcome of the 1979 presidential election. Nor did the courts lose their vitality under military rule. Shorn, temporarily, of their formal constitutional independence, the judges still retained their authority in the states, where,

---

[6] Nnamdi Azikiwe, *Political Blueprint of Nigeria* (Lagos: African Book Company Limited, 1943); Obafemi Awolowo, *Path to Nigerian Freedom* (London: Faber, 1947); James S. Coleman, *Nigeria: Background to Nationalism* (Berkeley and Los Angeles: University of California Press, 1958), pp. 323–24.

in the words of a legal scholar, they performed "prodigious feats of courage" defending the rights of citizens.[7] Should constitutional government in Nigeria be suppressed once again, the potential for its early revival would be preserved by federalism, the legal profession, and the determined practice of judicial independence.

Despite its apparent vigor, liberal democracy in Nigeria is debilitated by the effects of economic anarchy and social distemper. A small minority of the population is conspicuously wealthy and privileged while the vast majority seethes with discontent. Keepers of the national conscience frequently deplore the plunder and waste of Nigeria's wealth by corrupt officials in collusion with unscrupulous businessmen. Scholars discern the portents of revolutionary mass action, particularly in the northern states, where class conflict is pronounced.[8] Disillusioned intellectuals renounce democracy and urge the merits of developmental dictatorship in one form or another. Both the Leninist and the corporatist, or Brazilian, versions have their advocates. In Nigeria, as in Senegal, liberal democracy is democracy with tears and many reservations.

A second type of democracy in Africa accepts the principle that rulers should be accountable to their subjects but dispenses with the political method of multiparty electoral competition. I shall adopt the term guided democracy for this type of government by guardians of the public weal who insist upon political uniformity. Guided democracy is, to be sure, a form of developmental dictatorship; it is classified separately because the other forms of developmental dictatorship make little or no pretense of accountability to the people on the part of exalted persons or national saviors.

The late President Jomo Kenyatta of Kenya was one of a number of African presidents who have ruled beyond the reach of accountability. When he died, in 1978, the barons of Kenyan politics and society could not imagine, nor would they have tolerated, another episode of such highly personal rule. Kenya had become a de facto one-party state in 1969, when the sole opposition party was banned. Yet the one-party political process in that country has been highly competitive; the triumphal party itself has been described as a "confederation of arenas" where the bosses of rural factions "collide" and "collude" in their "perennial struggle" for power.[9] Survey

---

[7] Okay Achike, *Groundwork of Military Law and Military Rule in Nigeria* (Enugu: Fourth Dimension Press, 1978), p. 184.

[8] Larry Diamond, "Cleavage, Conflict and Anxiety in the Second Nigerian Republic," *The Journal of Modern African Studies,* forthcoming.

[9] Robert H. Jackson and Carl G. Rosberg, *Personal Rule in Black Africa* (Berkeley: University of California Press, 1982), p. 103.

research on the electoral process tells of a well informed electorate
which imposes the norm of accountability upon its representatives;
for example, in 1979, 45 percent of the incumbent members of Parliament were defeated at the polls.[10] When, in 1982, Kenya became
a one-party state de jure, her commitment to guided rather than
liberal democracy was decisively confirmed.

During the course of a purely formal parliamentary debate on
the establishment of a one-party state, the Vice-President, Mr. Mwai
Kibaki, explained that constitutional change was needed to preclude
the election of persons who would favor experiments based upon
Marxist theories. Such theories, he argued have been disproved
by the poor economic performances of communist systems.[11] This
kind of reasoning, from a different ideological perspective, is used
by the leaders of those authoritarian regimes which have socialist
orientations to preclude the practical advocacy of capitalist ideas.
In such cases, political monopolies are justified by persons who assert the moral necessity or scientific truth of an official doctrine,
e.g., "Humanism" in Zambia, the "Third Universal Theory" in
Libya, and Marxism-Leninism in several countries.

The touchstone of guided democracy is the existence and operation of a political mechanism which can be expected to ensure the
accountability of rulers to the people. Various developmental dictatorships in Africa, both capitalist and socialist, do not pass muster
as guided democracies because their leaders rule without regard
to the principle of accountability. Those which do qualify as guided
democracies include a variety of political forms and ideological orientations. Some, such as Guinea-Bissau, Tanzania, and (arguably)
Zambia, have mass-mobilizing parties with open memberships. Others, including Congo People's Republic, Angola, and Mozambique,
have created Leninist parties with doctrinal restrictions on membership and statutes on the required accountability of leaders. In these
and other instances of one-party or, as in Libya, no-party rule, the
degree of democracy varies with the intensity of passion for political
accountability and its effective enforcement.

In socialist thought, the concept of democracy extends beyond
the precept of accountability to the idea of social justice. From that
perspective, democracy implies the effective pursuit of an egalitarian social order in addition to a government which is accountable
to the people. For the principal instance of social democracy (my
third type for this survey) in Africa I turn, necessarily, to Tanzania.

---

[10] Ibid., p. 111; Joel D. Barkan, "Legislators, Elections, and Political Linkage,"
in Joel D. Barkan with John D. Okumu, eds., *Politics and Public Policy in Kenya
and Tanzania* (New York: Praeger Publishers, 1979), pp. 83–84.

[11] *The Weekly Review* (Nairobi), June 11, 1982, p. 5.

Ever since the famous Arusha Declaration of 1967, the Tanzanian Government has endeavored to minimize social inequality and to counteract various tendencies toward class division. In the commentaries of President Julius K. Nyerere, two aspects of the quest for social equality are strongly emphasized: first, the problem of privilege, or differentials in both personal consuming power and access to public services; second, the importance of popular participation in the decision-making processes of both political and economic organizations. On the first count, impressive achievements have been recorded in reducing income differentials and providing economic, educational, health, and other essential services to the public at large. Furthermore, the conversion of public trust into personal wealth has been checked by progressive taxation, lean salary scales for the administrators of public agencies, and the enforcement of a socialist code of conduct for leaders and officials.

On the second count, that of progress toward popular and democratic participation in governmental and economic decision-making, Tanzania's record is more difficult to assess. In 1967, the sole legal party accepted an historic challenge: to build socialism in an agrarian country without resort to coercive methods of collectivization. At the same time, every effort would be made to raise the standard of living and enhance the quality of life in peasant and working class communities. However, the vast majority of rural dwellers did not respond favorably to the party's call for collectivization on a voluntary basis. Finally, at the end of its patience, the government used compulsion to move and resettle millions of peasants from their dispersed homes and farms into clustered villages between 1974 and 1976. That process, known as "villagization," has made it possible for the government to reach the entire rural population with basic services. However, the related aim of socialist farming—the collectivization of production—was, at first, deemphasized and then virtually abandoned in the face of peasant resistance, a food crisis, and the critical views of potential donors, notably the World Bank, at a time of dire need for foreign aid.

Suddenly, the socialist venture in Tanzania was awash in a sea of academic and intellectual doubt. Could rural socialism be reconciled with an acceptable level of agricultural efficiency? Had the socialist venture been sabotaged by non- or pseudo-socialist officials and their class allies in concert with antisocialist foreign powers? Those who seek honest answers to these hard questions and still believe in the viability of socialist policies in Tanzania have set great store by the party's avowed commitment to popular and democratic participation in economic and political life. They also view with concern the lack of evidence to show that workers and peasants participate effectively in the formulation and adoption of public policies. At the center of power, the ruling party itself sets a decisive example for all other institutions. In his empathetic assessment of party life, Cranford Pratt finds an "oligarchic" and "profound bias against any opposition to the leadership."[12]

If, as Nyerere maintains, democratic participation is a cornerstone of social equality, sincere socialists cannot disregard the inevitably repressive effects of legal barriers to freedom of association. Socialists of participative conviction cannot sidestep a pluralist question: Is democratic participation viable in a one-party state, where political competition is severely restricted by the virtual elimination of group rights to pursue self-determined political aims? This question, which reflects the liberal critique of guided democracy, has engaged the attention of intellectuals in several other African countries where the search for social democracy is less resolute than it has been in Tanzania. An illuminating example is the constitutional declaration of a "One-party Participatory Democracy" in Zambia. It signifies experimentation with a fourth, familiar but elusive, type of democracy, namely, participatory democracy.

The theory of participatory democracy is a product of the current era. It affirms the existence of a reciprocal relationship between democratic political institutions and participative social institutions, with particular emphasis upon the educative effects of democratic participation in the workplace.[13] In Zambia, the concept of participatory democracy was introduced as a national goal by President Kenneth D. Kaunda in 1968. Subsequently, Kaunda construed the concept to connote democratic participation in all spheres of life, so that "no single individual or group of individuals shall have a monopoly of political, economic, social or military power." To his mind, the public interest suffers when politicians monopolize political power, or soldiers monopolize military power, or intellectuals and technocrats monopolize knowledge, or publishers and writers monopolize the power of the pen, or workers monopolize power through strikes, or chiefs monopolize the power of tradition. In the near future, he forecast, participatory democracy would be practiced in all Zambian institutions, including the civil service and the army.

Objectively considered, however, the record of participatory de-

---

[12] Cranford Pratt, "Tanzania's Transition to Socialism: Reflections of a Democratic Socialist," in Bismarck U. Mwansasu and Cranford Pratt, eds., *Towards Socialism in Tanzania* (Toronto: University of Toronto Press, 1979), pp. 211, 219.

[13] As Carole Pateman observes in her pathbreaking exposition of participatory democracy, "most individuals spend a great deal of their lifetime at work and the business of the workplace provides an education in the management of collective affairs that is difficult to parallel elsewhere." *Participation and Democratic Theory* (Cambridge, England: Cambridge University Press, 1970), p. 43.

mocracy in Zambia has fallen far short of Kaunda's expectations. Careful studies attest to the very low levels of popular attachment to, or involvement in, participatory institutions in rural Zambia. The sole legal party has not become a truly popular institution. Membership in the party has dwindled to fewer than 5 percent of the population despite its availability to Zambians without restriction. A "commandist" and "paternalistic" style of administration at the local level is magnified at the national level by a domineering office of the president. As William Tordoff observes, "Ironically, no one emphasizes the virtues of participatory democracy more than the President himself, yet his own style of increasingly personalized decision-making renders its realization difficult."[14] As in Tanzania, the party-state in Zambia abhors the very idea of political pluralism. Yet the Zambian government, unlike the Tanzanian, must contend with a formidable and resourceful labor movement; indeed, the Mineworkers Union of Zambia, 60,000 strong, has never accepted the hegemony of the party in the sphere of industrial relations. Its long-term struggle for autonomy from an imperious government lies at the very heart of conflict in Zambian politics.

Truly democratic participation is self-motivated and self-determined; it is not coerced. In Africa, participatory democracy implies a commitment to the self-motivated assertion of peasant and working class interests in political affairs. But the Zambian leadership has tried to induce popular participation into channels which would be controlled by a monopolistic political party. From a democratic standpoint, however, induced participation comes close to being a contradiction in terms; indeed it is a form of coercion. And it has been rejected by the Zambian workers and peasants.

In 1981, following a spate of wildcat strikes, four leaders of the labor movement, including the chairman and secretary-general of the Zambia Congress of Trade Unions, and an eventually successful aspirant for the presidency of the Mineworkers' Union, were detained for nearly three months on charges of plotting against the government. Announcing this action, Kaunda accused the labor leadership of capitalist deviations. In 1982, Kaunda turned a corner in his personal ideology. Much to the amazement of Kaunda-watchers, most of whom were confident of his apparently unshakable commitment to nondoctrinaire "humanist" socialism, he decided that Zambia's official ideology should be Marxist (or "scientific") socialism. But this is not, after all, an arbitrary choice. Scientific socialism marks a strictly logical progression in ideology for a ruling

---

[14] William Tordoff, "Introduction," in William Tordoff, ed., *Administration in Zambia* (Manchester, England: Manchester University Press, 1980), p. 25; and Ian Scott, "Party and Administration Under the One-Party State," ibid., p. 157.

group of socialist inclination which intends to control the working class. It also signifies the maturation of basic tendencies toward an undiluted developmental dictatorship in Zambia.

As a result of Kaunda's ideological demarche, the beleaguered labor movement has acquired a powerful ally in its bid for autonomy, namely the interdenominational Christian Council of Zambia. Following his release from detention, Frederick Chiluba, chairman of the Congress of Trade Unions, is reported to have "made a point of going to church almost every day." As in Poland, the struggle for participatory democracy in Zambia has forged an alliance between two social institutions which are second to none other in popularity, namely the labor movement and the churches. Like his Polish counterpart, Lech Walesa, Chiluba stands for participatory democracy from without, rather than from within, the party.

In Zambia, as in Tanzania, the acid test for participatory democracy is the attitude of the national leadership toward self-assertion by the working class and the peasantry. Neither regime has passed that test; each has chosen to promote induced, rather than spontaneous, participation. It may be instructive to contrast these instances with the noteworthy practice of worker self-management in Algeria, inaugurated spontaneously by urban and rural workers at the end of the war for independence. For 20 years, this genuine expression of working class democracy has survived the rigors of interaction with an authoritarian government. The vitality and lasting effect of this participatory institution in Algeria is attributable to its spontaneous, as opposed to induced, genesis. By contrast, a memorable episode of induced participatory democracy under revolutionary conditions in Guinea-Bissau, called by Amilcar Cabral "revolutionary democracy," appears to have faded in the post-revolutionary, one-party state.

A fifth type of democracy has no legal guardian in Africa, but its adoption is often contemplated. Its name is consociational democracy, so christened by a Dutch political scientist, Arend Lijphart, and widely celebrated by like-minded scholars. This type of democracy is prescribed by its advocates as a long- or short-term solution to the problem of cultural, i.e., ethnic, racial, or religious, group conflict in deeply divided societies. In fact, it is a version of liberal democracy with the addition of special arrangements to protect the vital interests of cultural groups. In culturally plural societies, such as Switzerland, federalism and cantonal autonomy are exemplary consociational devices; the principle of proportionality for both political representation and the distribution of benefits is also important. In Nigeria, the constitutional requirement that political parties must reflect the federal character of the country in order to qualify for registration is one of several consociational devices which have been designed to prevent sectional domination. Consociational mechanisms and techniques are routinely used by the governments of plural societies. According to Lijphart, however, the hallmark of specifically consociational democracy, as a distinct type, is effective and voluntary political cooperation among the elites and truly representative leaders of the main cultural groups.[15]

In South Africa, the banner of consociationalism has been unfurled by legal opponents of the ruling National Party, principally the white Progressive Federal Party and *Inkatha,* a Zulu-based mass organization, acting through a multiracial commission appointed by Gatsha Buthelezi, Chief Minister of Kwazulu, in 1980. Drawing upon the ideas of Professor Lijphart, who served as a member, the commission has proposed a consociational constitution for the Province of Natal as an example for the country as a whole. The key features of this proposal include universal adult suffrage, a legislative assembly elected by means of proportional representation in electoral districts, and an executive body chosen in accordance with consociational principles. These recommendations have been rejected by the government. Meanwhile proposals for consociational democracy in South Africa have also been criticized by rigorously democratic thinkers. Heribert Adam, for one, notes that group identities and ethnic labels in South Africa have been imposed upon subject groups by the dominant group. "For example," he observes, "there are no enthusiastic Coloureds in the self-perceptions of those classified as Coloureds."[16] Furthermore, a growing number of black liberation leaders are social revolutionaries with little or no interest in consociational compromising. Increasingly, the liberation struggle involves collective demands for "redistributive" or social and, in the workplace, participatory democracy.

In divided societies, like South Africa, where revolutionary action involves a large and increasing measure of class struggle, consociational democracy cannot fulfill its promise of stabilizing social satisfaction. Yet it would be mistaken to believe that the consociational idea of self-determination for self-regarding communities is counterrevolutionary per se. Insofar as subnational group rights command

---

[15] Arend Lijphart, *Democracy in Plural Societies* (New Haven: Yale University Press, 1977). The theory of consociational democracy has a partly African pedigree, namely, the classic analysis of West African politics by the Jamaican Nobel Laureate, Sir W. Arthur Lewis, *Politics in West Africa* (London: Allen and Unwin, 1965). Lijphart, pp. 143–46, 177–81, 216–22.

[16] Heribert Adam, "Political Alternatives," in Adam and Hermann Giliomee, eds., *Ethnic Power Mobilized: Can South Africa Change?* (New Haven: Yale University Press, 1979), p. 288.

general respect, democratic movements which disregard consociational precepts do so at their peril. In Africa, the value of consociational democracy would be more clearly apparent in countries, such as the Democratic Republic of the Sudan, where the nature of cultural cleavage is less ambiguous than it is in the apartheid republic. This type of democracy should not be underappreciated because of its current association with moderate reform in South Africa.

Democracy in Africa is widely approved but everywhere in doubt. Democratic dreams are the incandescent particles of current history which gleam brightly in the sunlight of liberation only to fade beneath the lengthening shadow of grim economic realities. This survey of types may help to sort some of the problems of democracy in Africa. Liberal democracy founders in a rising tide of tears and social despair. Reflecting on two recent setbacks for liberal democracy in West Africa, an acute observer offered this judgement: "it was only the appalling economic situations in Ghana and Upper Volta, and the impotence of the respective governments faced with this situation that led to the collapse of their parliamentary systems."[17]

Social democracy introduces a standard for the just distribution of wealth and material benefits; but its success and survival cannot be ensured by redistributive policies alone. In an age of social optimism, people will not settle for the redistribution of misery and poverty. Everything depends upon the timely creation of national wealth and wealth-producing assets by means of public and collective, rather than private, enterprise. In many African countries, however, statist economic policies, espoused in the name of socialism, have discouraged or prevented the release of creative, wealth-generating energies. In Guinea, for example, the regime outlawed all private markets in 1975; private trading was made a criminal offense. State agencies were supposed to fill the void, but they were riddled with corruption and proved to be hopelessly inefficient. Economic collapse and starvation were avoided only because the law was erratically enforced and eventually allowed to lapse. In this and many other cases, statism has been mistaken for socialism.

For reasons that are, in the main, historical and contingent rather than theoretical or necessary, socialism has often been identified with statism by friends and foes alike. Increasingly that identification discredits socialism as a mode of development in the eyes of the world on the ground that statist strategies are plainly impractical and unrealistic apart from their troubling political aspects. In the past, a few countries, notably the Soviet Union and China, have constructed socialist economies with capital extracted from

---

[17] *West Africa* No. 3377 (April 26, 1982), p. 1111.

the countryside and appropriated by the state for purposes of investment and essential purchases abroad. That classic strategy is plainly unsuited to conditions in the agrarian countries of Africa for several reasons, among them rural resistance to collectivization, exponential population growth, the high cost of critical imports, and endemic problems of statist economic management. Furthermore, socialism is supposed to signify the democratization of economic life. Coercion is contrary to the spirit of socialism. Statism, the most general form of coercion, is the graveyard of socialism as well as democracy.

Participatory democracy is a logical response to the challenge of statism. Its appearance and reappearance in Africa should be a source of inspiration to democrats and, in particular, democratic socialists. However, the practice of participatory democracy cannot be regimented by the state without detriment to its integrity. Where participatory institutions have been created in factories and farms by self-motivated and self-directed workers, as in the case of Algeria, they countervail the power of the one-party state. By contrast, where participative decision-making is narrowly restricted and subject to close supervision by a party-state, as in Tanzania and Zambia, participatory democracy succumbs to the assault of guided democracy and developmental dictatorship.

Shall we conclude, with Gregor, that developmental dictatorship is the wave of the future for Africa?[18] The empirical support for that viewpoint is weak. Its sole rationale—the presumed power to produce rapid economic development—is scarcely tenable. Democracy is a far more popular alternative, but democracy must take up the challenge of development where dictatorship has failed. Africa needs a developmental democracy, a democracy without tears. Developmental democracy could represent a synthesis of all that has been learned from the many experiments with simpler types. It would probably be liberal and social, participatory and consociational all at once. From guided democracy it could inherit an appreciation for the function of leadership. The core of guided democracy could even be refined and transformed into preceptoral democracy, or leadership without political power.[19] In a complex, developmental democracy, intellectual guidance would operate by means of persuasion alone; its efficacy in Africa would be ensured by that immense respect for learning and scholarship which is a characteristic quality of modern African societies.

---

[18] A. James Gregor, *Italian Fascism and Developmental Dictatorship*, pp. 327, 333.

[19] This differs from Charles E. Lindblom's concept of a "preceptoral system," which denotes the fusion of intellectual leadership and political power by dictatorial means. *Politics and Markets* (New York: Basic Books, 1977), pp. 52–62.

Developmental democracy does not imply a specific formulation of democratic principles based upon distinctive core values, such as political liberty for liberal democracy, social equality for social democracy, popular participation for participatory democracy, or group rights for consociational democracy. The content of developmental democracy would vary with the views of democratic theorists. One such theorist, the Canadian, C. B. Macpherson, introduced the term to designate a stage in the evolution of liberal democracy, marked by the emergence, in theory and practice, of equal opportunity for "individual self-development."[20] This advance was promoted by the political doctrines of John Stuart Mill and his early 20th century successors. In our time, it is surely appropriate to broaden the meaning of developmental democracy so that it will accommodate the goals of social reconstruction in the nonindustrial countries. Developmental democracy today, should, I believe, be enlarged to encompass the core values of social, participatory, and consociational democracy as well as the specifically liberal elements of limited government and individual self-development.

Broadly conceived, developmental democracy would evoke fresh and original responses to the problems of economic underdevelopment, social stagnation, and political drift. Original thought is the heart of the matter. Gregor has shown, convincingly, that the essential ideas of developmental dictatorship were formulated during the first decade of this century by revolutionary syndicalists in Italy. By the ninth decade these ideas have surely run their course. There is no good economic reason for Africans today to propitiate the European gods of developmental dictatorship.

From the early stirrings of modern African nationalism to the onset and consolidation of political independence, Africa has resisted foreign intellectual domination. In all but a few countries, African governments conduct their foreign relations on the basis of a deep and abiding commitment to the principle of nonalignment in world politics. African statecraft reflects a determination to formulate the challenges of international relations from a self-defined standpoint. In the social thought of 20th century Africa, intellectual self-reliance is a paramount theme; it spans the ideological spectrum as indicated by its prominence in the francophonic philosophy of Negritude, the Africanist tradition of Anton Lembede and his followers in South Africa, the "African" and democratic socialism of Nyerere, and the revolutionary socialism of Amilcar Cabral. Students of social thought should recognize the quest for an intellectual synthesis and transcendence of capitalism and socialism in their

---

[20] C. B. Macpherson, *The Life and Times of Liberal Democracy* (Oxford, England: Oxford University Press, 1977), pp. 44–76.

classical and contemporary, or neoclassical, forms. In an essay entitled, "The Emancipation of Democracy," W. E. B. Du Bois assessed
the contribution of black people in America to democracy thus:

> It was the black man that raised a vision of democracy in America
> such as neither Americans nor Europeans conceived in the 18th century
> and such as they have not even accepted in the 20th century; and
> yet a conception which every clear sighted man knows is true and
> inevitable.[21]

Might this not be written of Africa's contribution to democracy
in our time?

Where shall we look for the signs of intellectual and political
synthesis which would signify the emergence of a new democracy?
Where have the forms of developmental democracy begun to take
shape? Every national workshop bears inspection, for each, in its
own way, contributes to the aggregate of democratic knowledge
and practice. Consider Zimbabwe, where revolutionary socialists
in power prepare to terminate a transitional period of liberal government in favor of a more restrictive, one-party political formula.
Their long-term objective has been described in an official document
as "a truly socialist, egalitarian and democratic society." Zimbab-
wean leaders and theorists will be challenged by the fact that there
are no models for that kind of social construction on the face of
this earth.

In pacesetting Zambia, where wage labor constitutes a comparatively large component of the total work force (more than one third),
the struggle for trade union autonomy is fundamental to the cause
of developmental democracy. But for the democratic vitality of the
labor movement, developmental dictatorship in the guise of "scientific socialism" could not be counteracted by other popular groups
in Zambia. While clergymen, businessmen, intellectuals, and professional people are, in the main, opposed to the adoption of "scientific
socialism" as an official doctrine, they could not resist it effectively
without the firm support of democratic labor. In this matter of
ideological choice, the principal restraining force on Zambia's political leadership is neither foreign capital nor the Zambian bourgeoisie; it is the Zambian labor movement.

In the Sahelian nation of Niger, a military government has proclaimed the institution of a new political order, known as "the development society." Founded upon the twin pillars of traditional youth
organizations and village-based agricultural cooperatives, the new
system of government functions through a series of elected councils,

---

[21] W. E. Burghardt Du Bois, *The Gift of Black Folk* (New York: Washington
Square Press, 1970), p. 65.

culminating in a National Development Council, which has been directed to frame an "original" and "authentically Nigerian" constitution. Here, too, the spirit of developmental democracy is abroad.

In neighboring Nigeria, the prospects for developmental democracy are enhanced by a federal system of government which provides a multiplicity of arenas for social and political experimentation. Federalism is also the essential foundation of Nigerian national unity. The relevance of that example to pan-African thought merits attention. Dictatorship may be the most formidable barrier to pan-African unity. Pan-African federalism would foster democracy at the expense of dictatorship in many countries. As a pan-African principle, federalism would also facilitate the exchange of democratic discoveries among African polities and thereby promote the growth of developmental democracy. Increasingly, African freedom would radiate African power.

Metaphorically speaking, most Africans today live under the dictatorship of material poverty. The poverty of dictatorship in Africa is equally apparent. It offends the renowned African tradition of community-wide participation in decision-making. By contrast with dictatorship, democracy is a developing idea and an increasingly sophisticated form of political organization. The development of democracy in Africa has become a major determinant of its progress in the world.

6

The Quest for Economic Democracy

M. Donald Hancock and John Logue

Throughout much of the 20th century, reform-minded politicians and trade unionists in Western Europe and North America have sought to extend worker participation in both macro- and microeconomic decisions. They have done so, as Edward S. Greenberg has observed, for a variety of potentially inconsistent reasons: to integrate employees more fully into the productive process with a view to mitigating labor conflict, to humanize the workplace, and to democratize relations between labor and private capital.[1] Modes of participation used to promote these objectives range from collective bargaining to worker representation in consultative bodies on the shop floor as well as at top levels of company management, various forms of profit-sharing, and worker ownership.

The forms and degree of worker participation in economic decisions vary considerably among the Western democracies. Workers' and union officials' access to managerial councils in Britain and the United States—"liberal" polities lacking highly centralized national trade union movements—is not securely institutionalized. But then there are corporatist systems such as Austria, West

---

Source: M. Donald Hancock and John Logue, "Sweden: The Quest for Economic Democracy," *Polity* 17, no. 2 (Winter 1984), pp. 248–69. By permission. Article and footnotes abridged by the editors.

[1] Edward S. Greenberg, "Industrial Self-Management and Political Attitudes," *American Political Science Review* 75 (1981), pp. 29–42.

Germany, Denmark, Norway, and Sweden where strong national
trade-union associations—in alliance with Social Democratic parties
continuously garnering 30 percent or more of the popular vote—
have achieved comprehensive and highly effective forms of worker
participation. Numerous American and European scholars discern
in these differences a principal explanation for contrasting patterns
of policymaking and socioeconomic performance.[2]

Beyond efforts to explain the underlying causes of different policy
outcomes in various nations or subsystems lies the necessity to assess the practical and theoretical implication of increased worker
participation for ongoing processes of political change in the advanced democracies. Academic observers and policy actors alike
concur that continuing efforts to extend employee influence in company and national economic decisions promise long-term systemic
consequences—but they differ profoundly on what these will be.
Most mainstream Social Democrats anticipate that increased
worker participation will lead to a more equitable balance between
capital and labor. This achievement would have the dual effect of
lessening employee dissatisfaction and facilitating cooperation
among labor, management, and government officials to sustain economic growth in the decades ahead. Radical left critics, in contrast,
denounce Social Democratic "reformism," alleging that it merely
co-opts workers into the established capitalist order and thereby
helps ensure its survival. On the right, many conservative politicians and spokesmen for employer interests fear just the reverse:
economic democracy bringing about the eventual expropriation of
private property and transforming capitalism into some as yet unde-
fined form of "labor socialism."

Among the advanced industrial democracies, Sweden provides
a crucial test of these alternative prospects. Since the late 1960s,
leaders of the national Federation of Trade Unions (*Landsorganisa-
tion,* or LO) and the Social Democratic Party (SAP) have sponsored
successive reform initiatives whose cumulative effect has been to
extend substantially the individual and collective rights of workers.

---

[2] Among them are David R. Cameron, "The Expansion of the Public Economy:
A Comparative Analysis," *American Political Science Review* 72 (December 1978),
pp. 1243–61; Cameron, "On the Limits of the Public Economy," *The Annals* 459
(1982), pp. 46–62; Francis B. Castles, *The Social Democratic Image of Society* (Boston:
Routledge & Kegan Paul, 1978); Arnold J. Heidenheimer, Hugo Heclo, and Carolyn
Teich Adams, *Comparative Public Policy: The Politics of Social Choice in Europe
and America,* 2d ed. (New York: St. Martin's Press, 1983); Douglas A. Hibbs, Jr.,
"Political Parties and Macroeconomic Policy," *American Political Science Review*
71 (1977), pp. 1467–87; Walter Korpi, *The Working Class in Welfare Capitalism:
Work, Unions and Politics in Sweden* (Boston: Routledge & Kegan Paul, 1978); and
Manfred G. Schmidt, "Does Corporatism Matter?" in *Patterns of Corporate Policy-
Making,* ed. Gerhard Lehmbruch and Philippe C. Schmitter (Beverly Hills, Calif.:
Sage Publications, 1982).

They have also proposed a system of compulsory wage-earner funds that will still further increase employee influence vis-à-vis private capital. The resulting public debate voicing intense nonsocialist criticism of the proposal and revealing widespread ambivalence concerning its merits even within Social Democratic ranks underscores Sweden's distinctive status as a "threshold nation" confronting an historical choice between opposing strategies of system change.

We shall attempt here to clarify the substance and likely consequences of that choice. This will entail, first, an assessment of workplace reforms enacted during the 1970s—ranging from job redesign efforts to parliamentary legislation. We will then consider whether the implementation of a national system of wage-earner funds in fact promises a fundamental transformation of Sweden's existing economic system. We focus on Sweden not for its own sake but as an instance of distinctive policy and structural innovation in response to changing economic conditions that confront all industrial democracies. Accordingly, in our conclusion we will try to look at the Swedish experience in comparative perspective.

DEMOCRATIZING WORK LIFE: "THE THIRD STAGE"

Aspirations to democratize work life in Sweden are a direct consequence of the electoral strength, ideological values, and long years of governance by the Social Democratic Party. Organized in 1889, in tandem with proliferating trade unions in the wake of rapid industrialization, the SAP soon became an important political force. In cooperation with the Liberals, Social Democratic leaders agitated successfully for suffrage reform and political democratization. The two parties formed Sweden's first democratic government in 1917 and, during three years of coalition rule, proceeded to institutionalize the present parliamentary system and introduce universal suffrage. After a desultory period of ministerial instability during the 1920s, when no party or coalition could command a stable parliamentary majority, the Social Democrats assumed long-term executive power in 1932 with the tacit backing of the Agrarian Party (now known as the Center). They governed either in coalition or alone for the next 44 years, during which time they initiated and expanded a whole array of social services, including universal retirement benefits, a national health system, and multiple financial benefits to lower-income workers and families.

Throughout their long tenure in power, the Social Democrats consistently polled nearly half of the national vote in successive national and local/regional elections—peaking at 53.8 percent in 1940 and 50.1 percent in 1968. One of their principal political assets is the LO, which represents some 90 percent of the industrial work force through its 25 member unions and contributes the bulk of the SAP's membership. In return, LO spokesmen have been allowed considerable influence in shaping party (and hence government) policy at key junctures in the nation's economic and social development. Leading examples include the formation and implementation of Sweden's highly effective active labor market policies in the early postwar period and the adoption of a controversial system of supplementary pension benefits during the late 1950s.

The Social Democrats claim historical credit for their leadership role in achieving political democracy and creating the welfare state in what they call the first two stages in Sweden's progressive democratization. Their goal for a third stage is to democratize work-place relations. Justifying it on the basis of "the traditions of the labour movement" and a "desire to humanize industrial society and make proper use of its enormous potentialities," the Social Democrats formally assert their intention

> to replace the present concentration of economic power in private hands by an order of things in which each individual is entitled as a *citizen*, *wage earner* and *consumer* to determine the direction and distribution of production, the shaping of the productive apparatus, and the conditions of working life. This will be done by engaging the *citizens* in the national planning of resource management in order to make the best use of the country's potentialities. It will be done by guaranteeing the *wage earners* influence on their work places and firms and by expanding their participation in the formation of capital and the administration of collective savings. It will be done by strengthening the position of *consumers* in relation to producers and by putting consumers themselves on a more equal footing where influence over production is concerned.

Placing the democratization of work life on par with political democracy or the welfare state may strike many outside observers as farfetched. Yet, in light of the actual developments in Sweden, the linkage is not inappropriate. After a decade of systematic reforms, even cursory visits to Swedish plants reveal that authority relations on the job are undergoing a transformation. This is not to say that Sweden has become a workers' paradise. Workers still work; managers still manage. But they do so in the context of new rules that reflect a basic shift in the balance of power at the work place.

Since the late 1960s a series of reforms has significantly strengthened the rights of individual workers and local unions vis-à-vis management. They include private and public measures to (1) redesign jobs to fit workers rather than vice versa; (2) guarantee individual rights at work; (3) increase employee influence on health and safety issues; (4) expand the scope of union-management bargaining to include the organization of production, investment policy, selection of managerial personnel, and other managerial prerogatives; and (5) institute employee representation on company boards. Together with the SAP-LO's efforts to establish a national system of wage-earner funds, these measures promise a democratization of authority on the job and in economic life as revolutionary as the centralization of power that resulted from the introduction of the factory system in the 19th century.

ERODING TAYLORISM: MANAGEMENT ADAPTS TO THE WELFARE STATE

The industrial revolution introduced not only mechanical power to replace labor but also a new pattern of work organization. The transformation of skilled crafts into repetitive, unskilled jobs demanded the imposition in industry of almost military discipline and a clear hierarchy of command. The hermetic separation of supervision and planning responsibilities from manual work was as much a cornerstone of "Scientific Management" as was the subdivision of jobs into their smallest components. Indeed, Frederick Winslow Taylor, whose name has come to grace the theory invoked to justify the maximum division of labor, cautioned that "one type of man is needed to plan ahead and an entirely different type to execute the work."[3]

In retrospect it is clear that the emphasis Taylor and his successors placed on fragmenting and disciplining labor had to do with adapting complex production processes to an unskilled labor force. In Sweden the movement away from Taylorism's modern incarnations reflects the realization that highly regimented, monotonous work processes are badly matched with the expectations and abilities of a highly educated labor force. By the late 1960s the confluence of that realization with full employment, one of the world's highest per capita income levels, high marginal tax rates, and ample welfare provisions generated employee discontent that expressed itself in alarming rates of absenteeism and turnover in routine, unpleasant production jobs. Costs soared while quality plummeted.

Management responded to these symptoms of worker malaise with a series of experiments in job redesign. Inspired by pathbreaking Norwegian precedents during the 1960s, Swedish managers proceeded to reverse the fragmentation of labor by expanding the work cycle of individual employees and organizing them into production teams which assumed many of the supervisory tasks, training

---

[3] Frederick Winslow Taylor, *The Principles of Scientific Management* (New York: Harper & Row, 1916), p. 38.

functions, and quality control responsibilities previously exercised by foremen and white-collar personnel.

The most dramatic departure has been the introduction of semi-autonomous work groups in the auto industry—the very citadel of job fragmentation and industrial discipline. The best publicized example is the assembly plant that Volvo opened in 1974 in the Baltic coastal town of Kalmar. Designed from the outset for team assembly, rather than the traditional assembly line, all aspects of the physical plant—including the division of work areas and the placement of coffee rooms and even entrances—were intended to encourage group cohesion. The plant attracted immense domestic and international attention as soon as it opened, and continues to be viewed favorably by local management and labor. Volvo officials calculate that production costs in Kalmar—despite higher transportation expenses and a lower utilization of capacity—are competitive with Volvo's more traditional and far larger Torslanda plant in Gothenburg on the west coast. According to one semiscientific study conducted at the plant, workers approve of every aspect of the job innovations but one: the steady stream of visitors, experts, students, foreign scholars, and journalists who have descended on the new facility to see it in operation.[4]

*   *   *   *   *

These examples from Volvo . . . are not unique; the movement away from Taylorism has been general throughout Swedish industry. That job redesign has been more common and more radical in Sweden than elsewhere reflects less the idealism of Swedish management than the fact that Sweden's comprehensive welfare services and full employment policies have provided workers the freedom (within limits) to pick and choose among jobs. Though job redesign does not quite recreate the kind of independence and skill that 19th-century craftsmen are supposed to have possessed, it has gone far toward restoring autonomy to production workers on the job.

EXTENDING WORKER RIGHTS

Parallel with experiments in job redesign instigated by management during the 1970s, the governing Social Democrats, prodded by union leaders, legislated a spate of reforms that have significantly enhanced the individual and collective rights of employees. Some of

---

[4] Stefan Aguren, Reine Hansson, and K. G. Karlsson, *The Volvo Kalmar Plant: The Impact of New Design on Work Organization* (Stockholm: Rationalization Council, 1976).

the bills, such as the prohibition of sex discrimination in employment (1979), are the subject of legislation in the United States. Other measures cover benefits that are governed by contract in the United States, although their terms and scope are generally much more extensive than in the latter case. Examples include provisions for seven months of paid maternity/paternity leave (1975), five weeks of paid vacation (1977) plus paid holidays, and the right to paid leaves of absence for study purposes if the study assignment is related to union work (1975). A special legislative provision accords foreign workers—who make up 7 percent of Sweden's population and a quarter or more of the labor force in many plants—the right to 240 hours of Swedish language instruction on company time at full pay (1975).

One of the most ambitious reforms enacted during the 1970s was the Employment Security Act (1974) prohibiting the dismissal of individual workers without factual basis. Under this statute, employers may not fire an employee simply because of his or her reduced ability to work; instead, an employer is obligated to reassign the worker to lighter duties. Nor are "incompatibility," "problems in cooperation," or other euphemisms for managerial caprice sufficient grounds to dismiss a worker. Where legitimate grounds for dismissal (such as the inability of a person to work at all, permanent cutbacks in production, or a plant closure) do exist, the act stipulates that individual workers receive prior notice ranging from one month for those under 25 to six months for those 45 and over. In addition, employers are required to pay full wages for layoffs exceeding two consecutive weeks or 30 days in a calendar year. The consequence of these provisions *is that the employer's interest in production stability matches that of the employee.* While the full effects of the Employment Security Act have yet to be measured, an immediate result has been to force large firms to improve their planning—at least as far as it affects unemployment levels.[5]

Alongside the extension of individual rights of workers, new legislation has accorded the unions themselves greater authority with regard to employers. Some statutory measures have simply extended contractual provisions previously restricted to local union bastions to the nation-at-large. For example, the right of shop stewards at some plants to perform union work on company time was made general by legislation in 1974. Under pressure of the threat of legislation, the LO and the SAF negotiated an agreement in 1975 that accorded local unions the right to hire outside consultants at company expense. In 1973 unions obtained the right, on

---

[5] The act apparently also deters small firms from hiring new employees as quickly as they otherwise might.

a trial basis, to appoint two representatives to the boards of Sweden's larger industrial firms; the provision became permanent in 1976. While worker representation on company boards is largely symbolic in that the employee representatives are easily voted down by management, the practice does provide local unions an important source of information concerning company intentions.

Significantly broader channels of information were established with the passage of the Employee Participation Act (*Medbestäm-mandelagen,* or MBL) in 1976. Described by some observers as the most far-reaching piece of legislation concerning employee influence in the industrial West, the MBL inspired expectations of revolutionary change when it went into effect on January 1, 1977. The revolution did not in fact occur, but the key provisions of the law are worth noting:

1.   The employers' traditional prerogative "to direct and allocate work," which had been enshrined in the statutes of the Swedish Federation of Employers (SAF) since 1906 and included in virtually every major labor contract negotiated thereafter, was struck down. The MBL eliminates the legal concept of managerial prerogatives common to other industrial democracies. Instead, all important managerial decisions—from hiring managerial personnel to investment—are subject to collective bargaining.

2.   The employer is obligated to provide the union with continual information about production, personnel policy, and the economic status of the company. In addition, unions have the right to examine corporate accounts and other records relevant to their members' interests. As a result the union can have substantial insight into the real situation of the firm and management's intentions.

3.   Management is required to negotiate with the unions all major changes prior to their implementation. If, or when, negotiations become deadlocked on the local level, and remain deadlocked after appeal to the national negotiating level, management can finally impose its decision. But it cannot do so without negotiation.

4.   The union's interpretation of contractual provisions concerning codetermination and employee rights is binding until the national Labor Court rules to the contrary.

5.   The union has veto rights over subcontracting under most circumstances.

*   *   *   *   *

Another far-reaching extension of collective influence involves health and safety. The Work Environment Act of 1974 (strengthened in 1978) brought a dramatic shift in the balance of power between employers and workers in the day-to-day operation of industrial firms. Key provisions of the law called for safety stewards on the shop floor empowered to enforce strict health and safety standards. They are accorded the same protection against dismissal as shop stewards, receive full pay from their company while in training and performing their duties, and possess the authority to shut down dangerous work processes at their own discretion. The latter provision constitutes a direct transfer of power from management to workers: the safety steward's judgment of health and safety requirements prevails over that of management until either changes are made or the steward is overruled by a government safety inspector.

The Draconian provisions of the Work Environment Act are rarely invoked. Interviews in four major plants in the metal trades in 1980, for example, revealed only one instance in which work had been shut down for safety reasons. But the threat implicit in the law has clearly induced management to improve the work environment. Most importantly, the law substantially redefines the traditional meaning of occupational health and safety. Going beyond the avoidance of industrial accidents and illness, it stresses the adaptation of work to human and social needs. Thus, it seeks to minimize monotony, stress, and isolation while according individual employees maximum influence over their work situation. Its objective, in short, is to make work congenial to those who perform it.

* * * * *

THE WAGE-EARNER FUND CONTROVERSY

The wage-earner fund proposal, which was first advanced in 1975, points toward the possibility—though not yet the certainty—of an even more sweeping change in employer-worker relations than that achieved through the reforms of the 1970s. The proposal has, therefore, become the object of an extended ideological controversy between the LO and the Social Democrats, on the one hand, and leaders of the three nonsocialist parties, the SAF, and spokesmen for individual firms, on the other. Even within Social Democratic ranks, opinions vary widely concerning the scope, timing, and even the desirability of such a system.

The controversy began—paradoxically, in light of Sweden's current economic doldrums—when the LO initiated steps to deal with the problem of "excess profits" in private industry. By the late 1960s, union spokesmen discovered that as an unintended consequence of the LO's postwar practice of "solidaristic wage policies"—defined as equal pay for equal work regardless of the profitability of particular firms—Sweden's more efficient companies had amassed considerable capital that might otherwise have been paid out in wages. Accordingly, the 1971 LO congress approved the formation of a study group to investigate the concentration of wealth and recommend steps to redistribute a portion of company profits to the advantage of employees. Rudolf Meidner, a senior LO economist, was appointed chairman of the study group. Together with two other union economists, Meidner proceeded to evaluate proposals which had been advanced earlier in Denmark and West Germany to establish branch or worker funds as a form of mandatory profit-sharing. The LO team published a Swedish blueprint for a similar venture in 1975, recommending the creation of a general and collective system of employee funds.[6] These would be generated through the transfer of a percentage of company profits in the form of shares and would be administered by union representatives. Dividend income from the shares could be used to acquire additional stock, thereby suggesting the prospect that employees could eventually acquire majority ownership of individual firms. The basic purpose of the wage-earner funds would be to enable wage-earners "to obtain not only greater influence over economic decisions but also greater power over their own work situation."[7]

The "Meidner plan," and its unanimous endorsement in a slightly modified version by the 1976 LO congress, sparked an extended public debate, both in Sweden and abroad. Rejecting the LO's concept of a compulsory system of funds based on collective ownership and control, a group of conservative economists, employed by the SAF and the Swedish Federation of Industry, proposed a voluntary program of individualized profit-sharing. In the political arena, leaders of the Center and the Moderate Unity (conservative) parties denounced the LO plan as posing a long-term threat to both the rights of private ownership and pluralist democracy. Discomforted by the fact that these attacks came on the eve of the September 1976 parliamentary election, Social Democratic chairman and Prime Minister Olof Palme sought to diffuse the controversy by referring the issue of wage-earner funds to a Royal Commission on Employees and Capital Growth which had been appointed the previous year to consider means of increasing employee influence through worker participation in capital formation. Palme's tactic failed to allay either nonsocialist criticism of the Meidner plan or widespread confusion among rank-and-file Social Democrats concerning its alleged merits. Because of public uncertainty about the fund proposal, a spirited attack by the Center Party on the Social Democrats' intention to expand Sweden's nuclear energy program, and the negative effects of various election-eve scandals, SAP

---

[6] Rudolf Meidner, in collaboration with Anna Hedborg and Gunnar Fond, *Löntagarfonder* (Stockholm: Tidens förlag, 1975).

[7] Ibid., p. 20.

strength fell to its lowest point in more than four decades (42.7 percent) in the September election. As a result, the Social Democrats had to relinquish the government to a coalition of the Center Party, the Liberals, and the Moderates.

During the subsequent six years of "bourgeois" rule, which saw considerable governmental instability, the Social Democrats and their nonsocialist opponents continued their verbal battle over the proposed wage-earner fund system. The SAP and the LO appointed a joint committee in 1977 to revise Meidner's original proposal in light of both nonsocialist and Social Democratic criticism. Responding to charges that the fund would concentrate economic power in the hands of union officials, the SAP-LO study group proposed in 1978 that the funds be established on a decentralized basis: a minimum of 24 funds, one apiece in each of Sweden's regional provinces. The committee also added an important new goal to the concept. Alongside the LO's original intention that the wage-earner funds should "complement the solidaristic wage policies," "mitigate the concentration of wealth," and "enhance worker influence in economic decisions," they were now envisaged as a means to "contribute to collective savings and capital formation for productive investments."

*   *   *   *   *

Ideological differences concerning the fund issue intensified from the fall of 1981 onward. Both the Social Democrats and the LO formally endorsed a more detailed version of their earlier proposals at national congresses held in September/October. They proposed that 24 funds should be established, each with its own governing board. Initially, a majority of the members of the boards would be designated by the unions, while the remainder would be chosen by elected regional and local government bodies. In time, the boards could conceivably be elected directly. Each of the regional funds would be financed on a dual basis: (1) through a 1 percent increase in the amount that employers pay on behalf of each worker into the ATP system, and (2) through the annual transfer of one fifth of company profits above a certain percentage of its annual income. The wage-earner funds would be invested in Swedish industries through the purchase of company shares on the open stock market. Voting power conferred by share ownership would be divided between the governing boards of the various regional funds and the local unions. As initially proposed by the SAP and the LO in 1980, dividend income would be paid into the supplementary pension system.

*   *   *   *   *

CONCLUSION

None of the workplace reforms described above is in itself revolutionary or even dramatic. Other democratic nations have enacted more sweeping measures in particular areas of the industrial process. West Germany's system of codetermination *(Mitbestimmung)*, for instance, offers workers and unions significantly more direct influence over company decisions than is the case in Sweden. Some of the American "humanization of work-life" projects are far more radical in terms of job redesign than the experiments at Volvo.[8] French and Italian judges have sentenced employers to jail for manslaughter when fatalities occurred in industrial accidents. That Sweden has become a recognized model for the democratization of work life is not due to the radicalism of any single reform; instead, it is a consequence of the scope and cumulative effect of the various measures taken together. The whole of Sweden's work-place reform, in short, is greater than the sum of its parts.

The LO has officially described this achievement as "reformism in the best sense of the word," aiming at a "fundamental transformation of society." In practice, it corresponds to Gunnar Adler-Karlsson's concept of "functional socialism": the socialization of some aspects of private ownership without touching the fact of ownership itself.[9] According to this definition, managerial privileges constitute a bundle of rights which, far from being indivisible, can be split in a variety of ways between management and labor. Among those affecting employees collectively, some—such as overseeing the day-to-day operations of the firm—remain the province of management. Other rights, such as those concerning health and safety, have become the prerogative of workers. Those affecting managerial personnel and employment have become the object of joint management-labor consultation and collective bargaining. The result is that many more functions of management have become "socialized" in Sweden than in other industrial democracies, despite the absence of a significant degree of public ownership comparable, for instance, to that in France and the United Kingdom.

In terms of the historical objectives of increased worker participation, Sweden has thus attained not only the "integration" of employees into the productive process but also far-reaching humanization

---

[8] The General Foods Gravy Train plant in Topeka, Kansas, for example, encourages workers to learn *every* job in the plant, including those normally relegated to lab technicians and production engineers. Work teams handle hiring, what firing there is, and most of the direct management of the production process, even to the point of starting production during the graveyard shift in the absence of managers or team leaders. See Daniel Zwerdling, *Democracy at Work* (Washington, D.C.: Association for Self-Management, 1978), pp. 19–29.

[9] Gunnar Adler-Karlsson, *Funktionssocialism*, 2d ed. (Stockholm: Prisma, 1970).

and democratization of workplace relations. As such, Sweden has achieved—alongside West Germany—one of the world's most fully developed systems of industrial democracy. At the same time, it should be noted that job redesign and the reforms of the 1970s—however striking in international comparison—have not yet fundamentally altered existing property relations. Just as managers still manage and workers still work, private citizens and corporations still own nearly 90 percent of Swedish industry. Whether this will remain true in the decades ahead is another matter.

The pending test of the Social Democrats' ability to move beyond industrial democracy on the level of individual plants to a more comprehensive system of economic democracy affecting the productive process of the nation as a whole is the wage-earner fund issue. Ideological conservatives speaking on behalf of individual firms, the SAF, and the nonsocialist parties who perceive wage-earner funds as a threat to private property have their ardent counterparts among those Social Democrats who support the proposal for precisely that reason. For "system-changers" within the LO and the SAP, the wage-earner funds promise the eventual transfer of ownership of Sweden's larger industrial firms from private to collective hands. Party and union moderates, on the other hand, have continually urged caution in formulating, and above all implementing, a fund system. Among them are Prime Minister Palme and other cabinet officials who have repeatedly emphasized the need for finding a compromise solution to the fund question. While the former SAF chairman, Curt Nicolin, categorically rejected the idea of an agreement with the Social Democrats in the aftermath of the 1982 election—saying, "We will not negotiate our own destruction," he subsequently relented somewhat and said: "We have our own views on the fund question but we're good Swedes and will participate in the discussion."

Despite intense nonsocialist criticism and rank-and-file ambivalence, the Social Democrats have proceeded to implement the fund proposal. As one of its first acts upon resuming office, the Palme government introduced a 20 percent tax on dividends as an initial step toward creating a wage-earner fund system. Simultaneously, the cabinet decreed that Swedish firms must deposit 20 percent of their pre-tax profits in noninterest bearing accounts with the national pension fund. (They may draw on their deposits for investment purposes but only after prior consultations with local union officials.) In April 1983, the Swedish parliament endorsed the new "profit tax" by a substantial margin (156–133).

During the summer of 1983, the Social Democrats formally proposed the creation of five regional wage-earner funds (rather than the 24 provincial funds, as envisioned in 1978). The funds are to be financed through a combination of a 20 percent tax on company profits and a marginal increase in the percentage of employer contributions to the ATP system. Moderate Social Democratic views prevailed with respect to the intermediate effects of the fund system: the government's bill restricted both the total capitalization of the regional funds to 17.5 billion Swedish crowns (the equivalent of approximately $2.19 billion) and the percentage of company shares that each of the funds may purchase (namely, 8 percent per fund for a hypothetical total of 40 percent among the five regional funds together). The Swedish parliament acted on the proposal in December 1983 along predictably partisan lines. The Social Democrats voted unanimously in favor, VPK delegates abstained, and nonsocialist deputies voted against. The plan went into effect in January 1984.

The next national election . . . will offer the Swedish electorate an opportunity to pass interim judgment on the prospective transformation of the nation's current economic system into a new mix of public and private ownership promised by the introduction of the wage-earner fund system. If the voters so endorse, the result will in fact be a threshold move toward an unprecedented version of economic democracy.

7

The World Political Economy
and the Crisis of Embedded
Liberalism

Robert O. Keohane

INTRODUCTION

The political economies of modern Western European states do not
exist in isolation, but within a context established by the international system. In pursuing policies designed to facilitate economic
growth and social cohesion, governments react not just to the interests and power of domestic groups, but to constraints and incentives
provided by the world political economy.

These international conditions affect each country differently:
each economy occupies a particular location in the international
division of labour, and changes in the environment (for example,
increasing competitiveness of exports in a particular sector from
newly industrializing countries) will affect each one in a distinctive
way. This is most obvious with respect to oil: Britain and Norway,
alone among Western European countries, are net exporters. In
other sectors there are also differences in the sensitivity of different
countries to external events: for instance, the effects of cheap Third
World textile and clothing exports on a given European country

Source: Robert O. Keohane, "The World Political Economy and the Crisis of
Embedded Liberalism," in *Order and Conflict in Contemporary Capitalism*, ed. John
H. Goldthorpe (Oxford: Clarendon Press, 1984. By permission. References abridged
by the editors), pp. 15–38.

will depend not only on the size of its textile and clothing industry, but also on whether it competes directly with such products or, as in the case of Switzerland, uses them as inputs in the production of high-quality final products.

Much of this volume seeks to explain the substantial differences among European countries in economic policy and performance during the 1970s. For this purpose it is important to understand their somewhat different locations in the world economy. This chapter, however, seeks to identify the international forces impinging on Western Europe as a whole, to establish a context for the comparison and evaluation of national policies. My argument is that these common forces are significant enough that they must be taken into account in any analysis of the European political economies, and the evolution of the welfare state, during the 1970s and 1980s.

Without an analysis of common patterns, comparative political-economic studies can be quite misleading. Analysts focusing on the domestic politics and economics of one or a few countries may ascribe patterns of behaviour and outcomes to distinctively national causes, without recognizing the degree to which common forces affecting a range of countries operate powerfully in each. Consider the example of inflation. One could have investigated inflation in the 1970s by considering it as a separate phenomenon in Britain, France, Germany, Holland, and Sweden, and by searching for its causes within each country. In each case, domestic forces could have been located that contributed to rapid increases in prices. But this would have missed a key point: that inflation was a worldwide phenomenon, which no country could singlehandedly resist. After understanding this, the analyst of domestic German policy would not seek to explain high rates of inflation simply on the basis of those policies, but would rather seek to solve the puzzle of why German inflation was so *low,* relative to the inflation rates of most other industrial countries.

An international-level analysis such as the one offered in this paper is therefore neither an alternative to studying domestic politics, nor a mere supplement to it—an afterthought in which "the international dimension" is introduced. On the contrary, it is a *precondition* for effective comparative analysis. Without a conception of the common external problems, pressures, and challenges facing European political economies in the 1970s and 1980s, we lack an analytical basis for identifying the role played by domestic interests and pressures in the various countries. Understanding the constraints imposed by the world political economy allows us to distinguish effects of common international forces from those of distinctive national ones.

My purpose in this paper is to locate the European economies in a changing world political economy, by analysing how changes in the world political economy during the last two decades have affected European societies and conditioned their policy reactions. I will emphasize constraints that the international political economy of modern capitalism places on domestic policy choices, and how these constraints may be changing.

My principal theme has to do with liberalism, or what I call, following John Ruggie, "embedded liberalism." I inquire about the preconditions for its emergence after the Second World War; the political biases that it may embody; and the sources of reactions against it that became apparent during the 1970s. My working assumption is that liberalism was acceptable in Europe for such an unprecedentedly long time largely because of the extended period of prosperity, associated with liberal policies, that lasted until the early 1970s. Conversely, in the absence of a strong ideological commitment to liberalism, economic adversity can be expected to lead to increased protectionism, as it did after the crises of 1873 and 1931. Thus my examination of the preconditions for, and reactions to, liberalism rests in part on an analysis of the international sources of economic growth. This involves a comparison between conditions in the 1950s and 1960s, which facilitated both liberalism and extensive systems of social welfare; and those of the 1970s, which sharpened conflicts between the maintenance of liberalism and the continued expansion of the welfare state.

I begin by indicating how conditions in the world political economy and American policy during the 1950s and early 1960s facilitated European economic growth and reduced the severity of dilemmas facing European governments seeking to combine capitalism, increased openness with respect to the world economy, and social welfare. Ironically, it was American hegemony that provided the basis for the development and expansion of the European welfare state.

The second section of the paper then considers the argument made by both Marxists and conservatives that international liberalism is biased in favour of conservative governments favouring capital, and against socialist or social-democratic regimes supported by labour. This claim has considerable force, although it suffers from failing to take into account different strategies that can be followed by social-democratic regimes, and different sets of institutions and policy networks that affect the feasibility of one strategy or another. Some of these strategies . . . have been much more effective than others. Thus the "bias against social democracy," allegedly inherent in international capitalism, can be reinterpreted as a bias against those forms of social democracy that do not sufficiently take account of the constraints of the market.

The third section of this paper directs our attention to some international forces that have helped to undermine liberalism (either through worsening the economic situation of Western Europe or otherwise) during the 1970s and early 1980s. I distinguish three sets of changes. First, features of the world economy that had been transmitting prosperity from one country to another began to transmit inflation and recession. The forces generating prosperity, inflation or recession can be regarded as in the first instance internal, endogenous to one society or another (although such developments in each country are surely influenced by observations of events elsewhere). Yet in an open world political economy their effects spread out beyond borders. Even if the international "transmission belts" did not change greatly, their impact was altered as they began to carry the virus of economic failure rather than the vaccine of success from one economy to another. The costs of interdependence became increasingly severe. A second change had more direct negative effects on the real incomes of Europeans: the terms of trade deteriorated after 1973, largely as a result of huge increases in oil prices. This negative shift in the terms of trade, compounded by indirect effects on aggregate demand, seems to have made liberalism more difficult to maintain, since it worsened the European economic situation. Finally, Europe was affected by the expansion of capitalism to the periphery, especially East Asia and Latin America, as reflected in the increases in exports of manufactured goods by less developed countries, especially the newly industrializing countries, to Europe over the last two decades. Although the direct economic effects of these exports may have been positive for Europe (as neo-classical economists claim), they seem to have provided a catalyst for intensified protectionism.

In the conclusion, I ask about the stability of a liberal world order. Liberalism can be regarded as a self-reinforcing system, in which declines in trade barriers both foster prosperity and weaken the inefficient sectors pressing for protection, thus creating political conditions for further liberalization. According to this perspective, disturbances and setbacks should be considered unpredictable "shocks," as the McCracken Report (OECD, 1977) suggested.[1] But

---

[1] *Towards Full Employment and Price Stability* (Paris: Organization for Economic Cooperation and Development, 1977). [Note by the editors: The above-cited McCracken Report was produced by a group of distinguished economists from OECD countries and sought to defend the view that the economic problems that had emerged in these countries could be "largely . . . understood in terms of conventional economic analysis" and that what was needed to overcome them was "better use of existing instruments of economic policy and better functioning and management of existing market mechanisms."]

liberalism can also be viewed as beset by contradictions, containing the seeds of its own destruction so that its very success undermines it. In so far as the latter is the case, the current problems of liberalism have their sources in the inherent dynamics of an open capitalist world political economy.

EMBEDDED LIBERALISM AND AMERICAN HEGEMONY

Goldthorpe has suggested that an analysis of contemporary economic failure and social conflict in the advanced industrialized countries should begin with an understanding of the political bargains that provided a basis for the successful growth of their economies, and the expansion of their welfare states, during the 1950s and 1960s. Thus he writes (Memorandum to the Study Group):

> If the current problems of western capitalist economies are to be seen as grounded in institutional and other social changes [as opposed to the McCracken Report view emphasizing exogenous shocks], then it would appear only logical to see the success of these economies in the post-war years as being likewise grounded in some form of social order or "settlement": that is, one which could provide for conditions favourable to a higher level of economic performance than now prevails. Thus, the need is indicated to understand the nature of this post-war order, as it applied both internationally and—in differing versions—within western industrial societies, as a precondition for understanding the nature of its subsequent breakdown and, in turn, the possibilities for further collapse or for reconstruction or transcendence.[2]

In my view, this settlement is well characterized by Ruggie's felicitous phrase, "embedded liberalism."[3] To understand what this concept means, it is useful to think of the political-economic choices faced by governments as falling along two dimensions:

1. *The extensiveness of the welfare state:* that is, the extent to which the state reallocates resources to individuals, firms, and groups, as compared to the allocations that would be made by markets;

2. *The degree of liberalism or protectionism* in foreign trade and international monetary policy.

---

[2] John Goldthorpe, "Introduction," in Goldthorpe, ed., *Order and Conflict in Contemporary Capitalism* (Oxford: Clarendon Press, 1984).

[3] John Gerard Ruggie, "International Regimes, Transactions and Change: Embedded Liberalism in the Postwar Economic Order," *International Organization* 36 (1982).

These two dimensions can provide the basis for a simple illustration, as shown in Table 1. In the top left of the diagram is found the classic *laissez-faire* state, characterized by market allocations and liberal foreign economic policies. This state neither reallocates income internally nor stands as a shield between world markets and the domestic economy. On the opposite end of the main diagonal is the ideal type of socialism, or closed welfare-state national capitalism, in which the state is both intimately involved in the domestic economy, and social welfare arrangements, and interposes itself between that economy and world markets.

The lower-left hand box of the diagram represents the location of a state pursuing *laissez-faire* policies at home but mercantilist ones abroad. I label this the "self-help" state. The most important example of this pattern is probably provided by the United States in the period between the Civil War and the Great Depression, culminating in the high Smoot-Hawley Tariff of 1930, enacted by a Congress and acquiesced in by an administration hostile to the development of an extensive welfare state at home. One still observes nostalgic tendencies in this direction on the part of some Americans, but the United States has not really fitted this category since the New Deal.

In combining liberalism in foreign economic relations and activist, welfare-oriented policies at home, European societies after the Second World War pursued policies that were diametrically opposed to the self-help model. These constitute what has previously been described as "embedded liberalism." Liberalism was "embedded" in the acceptance of an extensive role for the state, both in the steering of the economy and in assuring a decent life to citizens. Internationally, the form of liberalism agreed to after World War II had to be consistent with the welfare state rather than in conflict with it. Thus the constraints imposed on national economic policies by the classical gold standard were relaxed, and the pursuit of "free

TABLE 1

The Two Dimensions of Embedded Liberalism

Policies Toward World Economy	Role of the State	
	Laissez-Faire	Interventionist
Liberal	classic liberalism	embedded liberalism
Protectionist/ Mercantilist	self-help	socialism or closed national capitalism

trade" replaced by the goal of non-discrimination. Furthermore, the goal of price stability was sacrificed, when this seemed necessary to maintain an open international economy.

Embedded liberalism did not develop automatically after World War II. And it certainly was not the product of purely domestic political bargains or settlements. On the contrary, the United States devoted a great deal of thought, and huge resources, to ensuring this outcome.

Part of the American effort was ideological. The United States propagated the view that the maintenance of capitalism and the welfare state could be rendered compatible by what Maier has called the "politics of productivity."[4] Cooperation among classes would ensure rising real wages and increasing opportunities, as well as extensive social welfare benefits, to the mass of the population. Liberalism, policies of macroeconomic management, and a limited form of welfare state would reinforce one another rather than be in conflict. Liberal trade would bring economic benefits through the international division of labour.

Yet the ideological appeal of the "politics of productivity" was not sufficient to persuade Europeans to support an open capitalist system based on non-discriminatory trade. Liberalism was not deeply rooted in continental Europe, and even Britain had turned in the 1930s to protectionism, in the form of the Ottawa System of Imperial Preference. The United States self-consciously set out to create a liberal system in Germany, and sought to promote the victory of pro-capitalist coalitions in Italy and France. Furthermore, it provided both positive and negative incentives for European countries to adopt liberal external policies and to renounce what Block has called "national capitalism."[5]

The groundwork for this American policy was laid during and after World War II, in successful U.S. attempts to gain political control over the two most crucial areas of the world economy: finance and energy. Before the Bretton Woods conference of 1944, the United States apparently sought to "fine-tune" British power, keeping Britain strong enough to be able to adopt liberal trade and payments policies after the war, but too weak to be in a position to renounce American credits and follow an independent economic strategy. At the conference itself, and later in negotiations on a loan to Britain, the United States pursued its interests as the only

---

[4] Charles S. Maier, "The Politics of Productivity: Foundations of American Economic Policy after World War II," in Peter J. Katzenstein, ed., *Between Power and Plenty: Foreign Economic Policies of Advanced Industrial States* (Madison: University of Wisconsin Press, 1978).

[5] Fred Block, *The Origins of International Economic Disorder* (Berkeley: University of California Press, 1977).

large creditor country in the world economy, and the chief international banking centre. At the same time, the United States sought to establish its control over Middle Eastern oil, whether through an agreement with Britain, which proved abortive or, successfully, through the rupture of the Red Line Agreement and the re-enforcement of exclusive control over Saudi oil by American companies.

Finding its initial attempts quickly to construct a liberal world capitalist economy thwarted by the difficulties of reconstruction and the political influence of labour and the Left in Europe, the United States shifted its policies in 1947 without abandoning its basic objective: it provided massive financing through the Marshall Plan, and accepted trade and payments liberalization by stages rather than all at once. As Hirsch and Doyle comment, "such a policy was then possible because of the fundamental characteristic of the international political economy of the time: United States leadership on the basis of only qualified hegemony."[6] The United States was not strong enough to achieve its objectives exactly as it preferred; but it was sufficiently powerful to be able to find routes to achieve its goals, even if these were neither entirely direct, nor those originally preferred by the policy-makers themselves.

During the 1950s and 1960s the United States continued to pursue policies that reinforced embedded liberalism in Europe. It supported an international monetary regime of pegged exchange rates, in which it acted as the Nth country, keeping its currency tied to gold at a fixed price and allowing others to maintain exchange rates that enabled their exports to be competitive on world markets. In conjunction with the now-liberal European governments, the United States pressed for trade liberalization in a series of negotiations, culminating in the successful conclusion of the Kennedy Round, at least in so far as trade in manufactured goods was concerned, in 1967. American policy also sought, in the face of greater European reluctance, to secure most-favoured-nation treatment for Japan: between 1951 and the mid-1960s the United States pressed European governments first to admit Japan to the GATT, then to end discrimination against Japanese exports, which many of them had continued to maintain even after Japan became a Contracting Party of GATT in 1955. Yet even as it pressed for trade liberalization, the United States accepted the barriers erected by the Common Market, and its initial protests against the highly protective Common Agricultural Policy of the European Community—which itself had a major welfare component—were muted. American policy accepted

---

[6] Fred Hirsch and Michael Doyle, "Politicization in the World Economy: Necessary Conditions for an International Economic Order" in Hirsch, Doyle and Edward L. Morse, eds., *Alternatives to Monetary Disorder* (New York: McGraw-Hill, 1977).

the "embeddedness" of European liberalism in the welfare state.

By the mid-1960s it appeared that the prophets of productivity had been correct in their praise of liberalism. The development of a common market within Europe and the reduction, on the whole, of trade barriers between Europe and other industrialized areas of the world (particularly North America) had led to efficiencies resulting from economies of scale. Liberalization also increased competition within European economies, presumably resulting in positive dynamic effects. The combination of selective state interventionism and international openness seemed to have assured steady capitalist economic growth. Different countries could achieve this benign result by different combinations of demand management and export-led growth.

Europe also benefited from a peculiar sort of "invisible hand," in the form of improving terms of trade for Europe with other countries, particularly the raw materials-producing areas of the Third World. This was the counterpart to the worsening terms of trade faced by the Third World producers themselves. Such a trend was most striking in the case of oil. Prices of oil, which were around $3.00 a barrel shortly after the war, fell to $1.80 during the 1950s and remained quite stable in nominal terms until 1971. Since manufactured exports from the advanced industrialized countries were subject to inflation (albeit moderate compared to the 1970s) during this time, the real cost of oil fell between 1950 and 1971. Even after the rise in posted oil prices in 1971 from $1.80 to $3.00 per barrel, world prices of oil between 1963 and 1972 only rose at the same rate as for manufactures during that same period. The favourable trends in terms of trade that characterized the period between 1950 and 1971 provided resources that could be used by Western European governments both to enhance the benefits provided by the welfare state and to increase investment and growth. In effect, transfer payments from the primary-producing countries to the industrialized ones made it easier for the latter to satisfy the demands arising from groups within their societies.

Thus European economies in the 1950s and 1960s benefited both from liberalization of the world economy and from improving terms of trade, particularly with respect to oil. The prosperity to which these trends contributed financed the expanding European welfare states that emerged during this period and that continued to grow during the 1970s. Yet neither liberalization on a world scale (as opposed to within the six-nation European Community) nor the improving terms of trade were principally the result of European actions. On the contrary, both were highly dependent on the hegemonic leadership of the United States. American policy fostered liberal trade among the advanced industrialized countries: one could even say that the policies of the Truman administration were designed to "force Europe to be free." U.S. domination of the Middle East, and the willingness of the United States to use American oil reserves, in a crisis, to support Europe (as in 1956–57), kept oil prices low. The European welfare state was built on foundations provided by American hegemony.

THE POLITICAL BIAS OF LIBERALISM

Both Marxist and neo-classical writers have recently contended that liberal capitalism exerts pressure against social-democratic solutions to economic problems in advanced industrialized countries. For the purposes of evaluating this argument, liberal capitalism can be defined as a world system embodying arrangements for the production and exchange of goods in which three conditions are met: (1) property rights to productive resources are vested principally in private individuals and corporations; (2) production for profit takes place predominantly with wage labour, to be sold on a market; and (3) privately controlled capital and goods are able to move relatively freely across national boundaries. The hypothesis to be explored in this section is that liberal capitalism, thus defined, generates a systematic bias against social-democratic solutions to economic problems in advanced industrial countries. In so far as this hypothesis is correct, liberalism in Europe both constrained the Left from going as far as it would have liked to ensure welfare through public policy, and gave the Left (or at least its more radical elements) incentives to break out of the strait-jacket of liberalism, particularly when general economic conditions worsened.

The contention that international liberalism contains a bias against labour, and thus against social democracy and the extensive welfare state, has been employed by prominent Marxist writers. For instance, Hymer argued that openness in the world political economy favours capitalists *vis-à-vis* labour, since it leads capital to coalesce, but fragments labour.[7] Capitalists benefit politically from openness because capital is more mobile than labour and because they have superior access to information. In an open system, new investment can move abroad, and even established firms can relocate. Goods produced abroad can be exported back to home markets. Block, who also stresses the role of capital exports, argues that "the openness of an economy provides a means to combat the demands of the working class for higher wages and for economic and social reforms."[8]

---

[7] Stephen Hymer, "The Internationalization of Capital," *Journal of Econo⸗ Issues,* 6 (1972).

[8] Fred Block, *The Origins of International Economic Disorder,* p. 3.

Conservatives make a remarkably similar argument, albeit with different language and opposite normative implications. Thus the McCracken Report contends that the scope for social-democratic economic policies is limited by economic interdependence:

> Some governments may have underrated the consequence[s] of international interdependence and overrated their scope for independent action. With the improvement in international communications there are increasing signs of an international "demonstration effect" which, coupled with the greater mobility of skilled labour, may lead to a capital flight and a brain drain from countries pursuing equality strenuously with an inadequate growth rate, while in others failure to do enough about inequality creates political unrest.[9]

This argument develops, in different phrases, the essential Marxian claim that liberal capitalism benefits capital over labour and constrains governments from pursuing social-democratic policies much beyond the modal world level. In the first place, as explained further below, the transnationalization of financial flows, as capital movements become ever easier and cheaper, is likely to make it difficult for any country long to maintain a rate of profit significantly below the norm for the advanced countries, without suffering capital flight and loss of private investment. A sort of Gresham's Law may operate in which policies that reinforce the position of capital drive out policies that reduce its dominance and distribute wealth more equally. Secondly, as capital becomes more mobile, labour in the industrialized countries comes more directly into competition with labour in the less developed countries, particularly the "newly industrializing countries." Immobile labour employed in manufacturing industry becomes particularly vulnerable to competition from much cheaper labour in places such as South Korea, Mexico, or Taiwan. Thus measures that increase the real wage of labour in the advanced industrialized countries, either through pay increases or increases in welfare payments borne in whole or part by employers, will increase the incentives for firms to relocate production abroad. In a liberal world economy, the price, in terms of employment, paid by labour in return for increasing its real wage, will tend to rise, as the mobility of capital, technology, and managerial expertise increases. This development corresponds, at the international level, to the development of economic dualism, in which migrant labour plays an important role, at the level of European (or American) society.

The conservative economists draw the conclusion from these international constraints not that international interdependence is

---

[9] *Towards Full Employment and Price Stability,* pp. 136–37.

harmful (which might imply that protectionist policies would be in order), but that national social welfare objectives should be trimmed. Acceptance of international liberalism reinforces the need for what I have elsewhere called the neo-orthodox conception of a "disciplinary state."[10]

Both Marxist and neo-classical political economists argue, implicitly or explicitly, that international openness improves the bargaining position of investors *vis-à-vis* governments and other groups in society. In a closed economy, governments interested in promoting private investment need only ensure that expected rates of profits from productive investment, discounted for risk, are higher than those to be gained from holding financial instruments or engaging in speculation, and higher than the rewards anticipated from consumption. For an open economy with capital mobility, however, investment at home must also bring profits higher than those anticipated from investment abroad. If the prospective marginal rate of profit at home falls below expected returns abroad, one can expect an investment outflow and a slowing down of economic activity at home, relative to activity abroad. As a result, the minimum ordinary rate of profit that the government must allow to be generated at home in order to avoid capital outflow and a lack of investment, will be determined not simply by convention, domestic interest rates, and the willingness of investors to defer consumption, but by the marginal world rate of profit. Thus the internationalization of capital flows—the ease with which financial capital can be transferred across national boundaries—makes it more difficult for any country to institute measures that change the distribution of income against capital and in favour of labour, if this implies a marginal rate of profit significantly below that for the world as a whole. Unless the government has the ability to withstand the short-term costs (as well as potential long-term efficiency costs) of closing off its economy from the world economy, it must keep profit rates from falling too far below the world standard. At the same time, the "exit" possibilities that capitalists have available are likely to increase the efficacy of their attempts at "voice"—their ability to influence policy through the political process at home.[11]

Once an open capitalist world system has been established, it may create a bias in favour of pro-capitalist, and against socialist-leaning, governments. When Thatcher or Reagan induces a recession through tight monetary policies, as part of a strategy to control

---

[10] Robert O. Keohane, "Economics, Inflation and the Role of the State: Political Implications of the McCracken Report," *World Politics*, 31 (1978).

[11] Albert O. Hirschman, *Exit, Voice and Loyalty: Responses to Decline in Firms, Organizations and States* (Cambridge, Mass.: Harvard University Press, 1970).

inflation through reducing the rate of wage increases, the pound or dollar appreciates and funds flow into the country. This may be inconvenient for a country seeking to control its money supply or expand exports; but it does not lead to a loss of confidence in the government, and expands rather than contracts the resources at its disposal. No help needs to be sought from other governments as a result. When Mitterrand tries to stimulate demand and to nationalize selected industries, by contrast, the franc declines, France's foreign reserves are jeopardized, and assistance may be needed from the IMF or selected governments of wealthy countries. Socialist and social-democratic governments are thus induced to maintain openness. The experience of Britain's Labour party during the 1960s and 1970s illustrates the dilemma. In the face of international economic problems, reflected in payments deficits, Labour sought to resolve the contradictions it faced by abandoning socialism, and even some elements of its plans for social democracy, in the interests of maintaining business confidence. This process culminated in the decision of James Callaghan's Labour Government, in 1976, to sign a Letter of Intent to secure an IMF loan.

This argument implies that an open capitalist world financial system tends to reinforce itself. When pro-capitalist governments are in power, they have strong incentives to promote openness, not only for the sake of efficiency and gains from trade, but to reinforce the power of capital *vis-à-vis* labour. They also find that reinforcing economic openness helps their own political fortunes, since the web of interdependence thus created makes it more difficult for subsequent left-wing governments to achieve their purposes. When socialist and social-democratic governments come into power, they soon find that to avoid runs on their currencies, and financial crises, they need to gain the confidence of the business "community," and that this may require that they abandon some of their more socialist objectives.

This argument is oversimplified and potentially misleading because it ignores variations in strategies followed by social-democratic governments, and in the policy institutions and networks that those governments can use. Indeed, the contrast between the substantial success of social democracy in both Scandinavia and Austria, on the one hand, and the difficulties encountered by attempts to move to the Left in Britain and France, on the other, suggests that variations in national strategies are important determinants of success or failure. From the standpoint of the Marxist/neo-classical argument about the bias of liberal capitalism, these variations are puzzling.

The answer to this conundrum may lie in the institutions of trans-sectoral concertation involving both labour and business, that some European countries have developed: that is, in "corporatism."[12] Indeed, it may be helpful to think of the problem in terms of two ideal-typical forms of social democracy. Type A is typical of large countries such as Britain and France. It is characterized by only sporadic control of government by socialist parties; by policies of socialist governments that seek rapidly to shift the distribution of rewards from private capital to labour; and by a lack of domestic corporatist institutions permitting trans-sectoral concertation. Type B, by contrast, which is most closely exemplified by Austria and Sweden, is typical of small, open economies that need to export to survive: it is characterized by continuous left-wing rule over a long period of time, on the basis of strong union movements; by policies designed to maintain employment and improve equity in ways consistent with market incentives; and by corporatist institutions linking the state with leaders of both business and labour.

This distinction could help us to reformulate the Marxist/neo-classical argument. International capitalism does seem to exert a bias against Type A social democracy. Capital flight, or the threat thereof, typically leads to pressures on social-democratic governments in these countries to move toward the Right. That is, international capitalism *reinforces* the pressures exerted by the market against anti-capitalist policies in open, non-corporatist economies. Yet no such bias seems to exist against Type B social democracy. Capital flight does not seem to have been a serious problem for these countries during the 1970s; Sweden, for example, has maintained capital controls. Indeed, international capital markets *financed* Austrian and Swedish balance of payments deficits, permitting either an investment-led boom, as in Austria, or extensive job-training programmes, as in Sweden.

The McCracken Report suggested the existence of a "narrow path to growth" for the advanced industrialized countries after the first oil shock. This analysis by contrast, indicates that there may be a "narrow path to social democracy." Strategies for social democracy that exploit the market are more effective than those based on the assumption that market pressures can be ignored or over-ridden by the exercise of state power.

It is not clear whether small countries have an inherent advantage in designing appropriate strategies that reconcile social democracy with world capitalism. The Marxist/neo-classical argument seems to imply that small states should have more difficulty in

---

[12] Gerhard Lehmbruch, "Concertation and the Structure of Corporatist Networks," in John Goldthorpe, ed. *Order and Conflict in Contemporary Capitalism*, pp. 60–80.

coping with the pressures of world capitalism than large ones, because they are more open and because they have less power over the "rules of the game"—the international arrangements, such as those agreed to at Bretton Woods, that define the terms under which a given country can link itself to the world political economy. Furthermore, in bilateral relationships where both sides are involved with equal intensity, small states might be expected to be more constrained by the policies of larger ones than vice versa. Yet Cameron has shown that it is precisely the small European countries that have the largest state budgets, in proportion to their size: far from simply succumbing to the pressures of the world political economy, they seem to try, actively, to provide a buffer between the world political economy and their citizens.[13] Perhaps this is a result of the fact that as citizens of small countries their social democrats were acutely aware of the need to make social democracy consistent with export competitiveness. They therefore were willing to design domestic institutions and policy networks that facilitated mutual adjustment between labour and management.

In so far as a bias exists against Type A social democracy, socialist movements in such countries will have incentives to consider radical moves toward state intervention to sever key links with the world economy. Cutting oneself off from world capitalism may seem to be the only effective way of regaining autonomy, even if the economic costs are recognized as being enormous. As the international conditions fostering prosperity were undermined during the 1970s, such arguments regained some of their appeal. It is not surprising that the sympathy for measures such as these was greater on the British and French Left—especially in certain elements of the British Labour party and the French Socialists—than on the Right, or in countries which had developed effective strategies of social-democratic corporatism.

INTERNATIONAL FORCES UNDERMINING EMBEDDED LIBERALISM

Embedded liberalism is now under pressure in Europe. Protectionism and state interventionism in the economy have increased in the last decade, and tendencies toward socialism, or national capitalism, are more evident than they have been since the 1940s. The question is not whether there is a "new protectionism," but what it represents, and why the previous trend toward increasing liberalism has been reversed. From the neo-classical liberal standpoint

---

[13] David Cameron, "The Expansion of the Public Economy: A Comparative Analysis," *American Political Science Review*, 72 (1978).

protectionism is an atavistic reaction by groups that refuse to adjust to the efficiency-creating pressures of competition. For instance, Olson regards protectionism as the result of the political influence of narrowly-based, self-serving "distributional coalitions," and Baldwin, and in more extreme form Brock and Magee, following the same long line of analysis, see it as an economically perverse outcome of the competition of groups in the political market-place. Conversely, from the standpoint of Polanyi and his followers, protectionism could be regarded as an effort at self-defence by "society," against the rampages of the market-place.[14]

Polanyi's notion of action by "society" is vague and could be regarded as a mystification of more concrete political processes. The neo-classical analysis of the political economy of protectionism, on the other hand, naively incorporates the political theory of pluralism: policy outcomes are simply the result of group and sectoral pressures; the state is a virtual cipher without a political stance or ideology of its own. As a basis for description and partial explanation, pluralism is a useful notion, but it begs issues of the role and structure of the state, the sources of group interests, and the role of ideology. In this section of the present paper, I will not consider the potential sources of protectionism within European societies but rather focus on features of the *international* political economy that seem to have had negative effects on the ability of these societies to attain economic growth and to manage social conflicts. These characteristics of the world system may have intensified pressures throughout Europe for protectionism. As indicated in the introduction, I will consider three forces: (1) the transmission of prosperity, inflation and recession; (2) the deterioration of the terms of trade; and (3) the expansion of capitalism to the periphery.

From Transmission of Prosperity to Transmission of Stagflation

The construction of an increasingly open world economy in the 1950s and 1960s meant that economic growth in one country contributed to growth elsewhere. Demand for imports in prosperous economies created demand for exports in others, increasing incomes and the demand for imports in the latter. Until the late 1960s,

---

[14] Mancur Olson, *The Rise and Decline of Nations* (New Haven: Yale University Press, 1982); Robert E. Baldwin, "The Political Economy of Protectionism," in Jagdish Bhagwati, ed., *Import Competition and Response* (Chicago: University of Chicago Press, 1982); W. A. Brock and S. P. Magee, "The Economics of Special Interest Politics: The Case of the Tariff," *American Economic Review, Papers and Proceedings* 68 (1978); and Karl Polanyi, *The Great Transformation* (Boston: Beacon Press, 1944).

this beneficent pattern of exchange took place in a world economy with pegged exchange rates and great confidence in the dollar as the key currency, yet with persistent United States payments deficits that helped to maintain world liquidity. America was the chief supporter of an international financial regime that facilitated non-inflationary economic growth.

In the 1970s, international transmission mechanisms had less benign effects. From 1966 onward the United States pursued an inflationary fiscal policy associated with the war in Vietnam, and in 1971 the United States ceased to support pegged exchange rates and formally cut the linkage between the dollar and gold. The international monetary system, which continued to be highly integrated despite the changes it went through during the next few years, then carried inflation from country to country. This occurred, although by different means and perhaps to a lesser extent, under flexible as well as fixed exchange rates. Particularly during the period of greatest uncertainty about the exchange rate regime, between August 1971 and March 1973, national monetary policies in the major OECD countries were highly inflationary, perhaps partly as a result of the absence of incentives from the international regime to follow more stringent policies.

In the 1970s the rules governing both exchange rates and oil prices were much less clear, and less constraining of national policy, than they had been during the Bretton Woods era. The changes in oil prices reflected a decline in American and European control over the terms of exchange; in money, they reflected an attempt by the United States to free itself from the burdens of the Bretton Woods regime. In both cases, the result was that the structure of authority became more decentralized. Neither a well-defined set of rules, nor a hegemonic power (in conjunction with its large corporations and its allies) determined outcomes.

From this decentralized authority structure emerged a pattern of relations that is similar to what Hirschman has described in another context as a "political tug-of-war."[15] In such a situation, organizations or groups can determine the prices for their own products (that is, they have market power), but there is no central authority capable of establishing a consistent set of non-inflationary prices for all goods. Each group would prefer stable prices if it could also be assured of its desired share of the social product; but since it cannot accomplish this on its own, it demands more, in nominal terms, in the hope of gaining, or at least not losing,

---

[15] Albert O. Hirschman, "The Social and Political Matrix of Inflation: Elaborations on the Latin American Experience," in *Essays in Trespassing: Economics to Politics and Beyond* (Cambridge: Cambridge University Press, 1981).

in real terms. In this model, inflation is explained "in terms of social conflict between groups each aspiring to a greater share of the social product," and by the absence of an effective government that can authoritatively allocate shares of that social product.

Such an inflationary tug-of-war seems to have taken place between the major oil-importing countries and OPEC in the years immediately following the major price increases of 1973–74. The *nominal* price of oil had an effective floor under it, since OPEC feared the consequences of initiating a downward spiral. But the *real* price of oil could be reduced either by increases in the prices of goods sold to OPEC countries, or by declines in the value of the dollar, either of which could be facilitated by inflation in the United States. This does not mean that the United States deliberately fostered inflation to reduce the real price of oil, but it does suggest that concern about oil prices and terms of trade reduced the incentives to deal decisively with inflation. To some extent, inflation was a face-saving device by which the demands of producers for high prices could be reconciled with the desire of consumers for lower prices.

Inflationary American macroeconomic policies in 1977–78 meant that European countries paid lower prices for imported oil, since the price of oil was denominated in depreciating dollars. Yet American policy also transmitted less welcome effects to Europe. Having been unsuccessful at persuading Germany and Japan to reflate more rapidly in early 1977, the United States sought to put pressure on them by letting the dollar depreciate, therefore making German and Japanese exports less competitive against those of the United States. This led eventually to an agreement at the Bonn summit, in July 1978, by which Germany and Japan were to stimulate their economies in return for phased decontrol of U.S. oil prices and a tightening of American monetary policy. Unfortunately for these governments, the Bonn summit did not lead to a resumption of the virtuous circle of non-inflationary growth: in the fall of 1978, the dollar came under severe pressure, requiring extensive exchange market intervention, and in early 1979 the effects of the Iranian Revolution began to lead to a new escalation of oil prices.

Since the tightening of American monetary policy that took place in the fall of 1979, and particularly since the Reagan administration took office, another vicious circle of international transmission has contributed to the difficulties faced by European governments. High American interest rates have led European governments and central banks to increase their interest rates, for fear of foreign exchange crises resulting from capital flight. The consequence, of course, is that American monetarism has been imitated even by governments that do not sympathize either with its economic logic or its political biases. This is not to say, of course, that these governments had no choices: they could have sought to reflate their economies regardless of American policy. But then they would have encountered difficulties similar to those experienced by the socialist government in France since 1981: foreign exchange crises and losses of reserves, as capital fled the country for areas where real rates of return (nominal interest rates adjusted for inflation and expectations of exchange rate movements) were higher. Faced with such dilemmas, governments that are unable to sustain strategies to counteract, or even take advantage of, international constraints are under severe pressure to return to orthodoxy.

Viewed politically, the point is that the pressures transmitted by the international monetary system are not merely the results of impersonal market forces but reflect the policies of political coalitions in major countries, particularly the United States. When these policies shift, the effects are transmitted quickly throughout the system.

Thus international transmission of economic forces has had a different impact since 1971 from that of the two previous decades. Often the shift to flexible exchange rates is cited as a major source of these changes, although flexible rates are really more symptoms of disorder than cause. If national fiscal and monetary policies diverge sharply in a highly interdependent world economy but politically fragmented world system, fixed exchange rates will be impossible to sustain for long. In some respects, flexible rates may enable governments to control the effects of international disturbances more effectively—for instance, a low-inflation country can counteract the effects of inflation emanating from other countries by letting its own currency appreciate. Nevertheless, even if flexible rates are unavoidable, and have certain advantages, they do complicate the task of economic management by introducing another unpredictable variable into the managers' calculations.

The key issue, in my view, is not so much how economic effects are transmitted internationally, but what is being transmitted. Is it helpful or harmful to the recipient? The 1950s and early 1960s seem to have been characterized largely by "virtuous circles," in which non-inflationary growth in one area reinforced non-inflationary growth in another. In the last decade and a half, transmission has been characterized by "vicious circles," in which inflation and recession, perhaps generated originally within one society as a result of a combination of economic and political forces partly endogenous to it, are carried to others. International interdependence remains, but its consequences for social conflict and economic management are different.

The Deterioration of the Terms of Trade

All significant changes in the world economy have uneven effects on various countries, groups, or sectors. Furthermore, those countries, groups and sectors adversely affected by changes have differential abilities to force the costs of adjustment to change on to others. Power is, by one measure, the ability not to have to adjust to change.

Governments, of course, have to allocate the costs of adjustment among their citizens, and in particular, between capital and labour. If they are powerful in the world system, this internal adjustment may be facilitated by their ability to force foreigners to bear some of those costs. Conversely, if they are weak (or become weaker from a formerly strong situation), their internal adjustments may be rendered more difficult by adverse shifts imposed on them by others.

During the 1950s, the industrialized countries, including Europe, benefitted substantially from improving terms of trade between manufactured goods, which they exported, and primary products, of which they were net importers: these terms of trade improved by about 25 percent (from the standpoint of exporters of manufactured goods) between 1950 and 1963.[16] During the next decade (1963–72), these terms of trade were essentially stable, continuing to improve slightly in favour of manufactures: the industrialized countries' terms of trade improved by about 3 percent. Between 1973 and 1982, however, the terms of trade for these countries worsened by about 20 percent. This dramatic shift, caused largely by the huge oil price increases of that period, reflected the inability of the industrialized countries to force the costs of adjustment to higher oil prices entirely on to others: indeed, during that decade, taken as a whole, the terms of trade of the non-oil developing countries were almost stable, deteriorating only after 1977, while the terms of trade of the oil producers improved sharply.[17]

Since the deterioration in the terms of trade was essentially a result of the huge oil price rises in 1973–74 and 1979–80, we need to look somewhat more closely at the effects of those price increases on the economies of the industrialized countries. The first set of price rises led to an increased import bill for the OECD countries of $65 billion, equivalent to about 1.5 percent of their collective GNP. The second price spiral led to increased import costs of about $150 billion, equivalent to about 2 percent of OECD GNP. In addition to these terms of trade effects, the oil shocks reduced aggregate

---

[16] *Towards Full Employment and Price Stability,* Chart 9, p. 61.

[17] *World Economic Outlook* (Washington, D.C.: International Monetary Fund, 1982), Table 9, p. 150.

demand. In 1980 the OECD countries lost about 3 percent of GNP as a result of the oil price increases of the previous year; in 1981 the loss was about 4 percent.[18]

Oil price increases therefore both made the industrialized countries poorer and directly reduced their levels of economic activity. But the price rises also, of course, had an inflationary effect in the short run. In an effort to counter inflation, governments contracted their monetary and fiscal policies. This led to a further reduction in real income in these societies, which was particularly pronounced after the second oil shock. The consequent reduction in GNP was about one-fourth of 1 percent in 1980 and almost 2 percent in 1981. Thus the combined loss of output from the second oil shock amounted to about 5 percent of Gross Domestic Product (GDP) in 1980 and nearly 8 percent in 1981 for a two-year total of over $1 trillion.[19]

The immediate effects on worker-consumers in the OECD countries were cushioned by the fact that the distribution of income in 1974–75 shifted quite sharply from capital to labour, and from investment to consumption, throughout the area. Labour's share of total domestic factor income rose between 1970–73 and 1974–77 from about 69 percent to about 72 percent in Germany, from 64 to almost 70 percent in France, and from 76 to 80 percent in the United Kingdom. This had temporarily positive effects on consumption but very negative effects on private investment, with serious consequences for subsequent unemployment. After the second oil shock, in contrast, changes in labour's share of income, and in the balance between consumption and investment, were much less marked.[20] Although European societies responded to the first oil shock by trying to cushion their citizens against it, they were not able to repeat this performance. The reaction to the second oil shock, especially in Britain and the United States (in the latter, even before Reagan took office), was to follow tight monetary policies in an attempt to force the costs of adjustment on to the present population, rather than to impose it, through inflation and low investment, on the future. As we have seen, this policy was transmitted, through international markets, to other countries, even where their governments had different preferences or different theories about how the world looked.

---

[18] *Annual Report* (Basle: Bank for International Settlements, 1981), p. 40; Sylvia Ostry, John Llewellyn, and Lee Samuelson, "The Cost of OPEC II," *OECD Observer*, 115 (1982), pp. 37, 38.

[19] *Towards Full Employment and Price Stability* p. 70; Sylvia Ostry et al., "The Cost of OPEC II," p. 38; *World Energy Outlook* (Paris: OECD, 1982), pp. 63–4.

[20] *Annual Report* pp. 41, 42, 44; ibid. (1982), p. 30.

The crucial point about this is a familiar one. Governments have to allocate costs among their people, between classes and sectors. Much of political analysis is about how this is done: "who gets what, when, how?" in Lasswell's phrase. But domestic allocations depend on the allocations resulting from political struggle at the international level. Weak countries have to bear the burdens of adjustment to change: they cannot impose them on others. Unless they are being subsidized by rich allies or politically naïve bankers, their governments must allocate costly adjustments among their people—inevitably leading to discontent—or else let them be inflicted through the market (for instance, in the form of inflation). Between the 1960s and the 1980s the willingness of the United States to maintain a stable international monetary system declined. Furthermore, its ability, in conjunction with selected European governments and major oil firms, to control petroleum prices virtually disappeared. As a result, the dependence of European governments on other countries increased. The higher petroleum prices that accompanied this loss of control reduced the ability of Europeans as well as people in other oil-importing areas to purchase manufactured goods: real incomes had to fall. The corollary of this process, thrusting adjustment costs on to Europe, was that domestic allocational dilemmas were sharpened, and the task of social conflict management made more difficult.

The Rise of Exports from Less Developed Countries

During the last two decades, less developed countries (LDCs), and in particular the eight principal newly industrializing countries (NICs) of Asia and Latin America (Hong Kong, Singapore, South Korea, and Taiwan—the "gang of four"—in East Asia, India in South Asia, Argentina, Brazil, and Mexico in Latin America) have experienced rates of economic growth much above those in Europe and North America. This growth has been led by exports. Manufactured exports from LDCs rose annually by 16.2 percent between 1960 and 1976, a rate higher than the rate of export growth for industrialized countries (14.1 percent) or for all trade commodities (13.7 percent). The pace of LDC expansion was, at least at first, not seriously retarded by the oil crisis: largely as a result of the rapid growth of NIC exports, imports to both the EEC and the United States from non-OPEC developing countries increased threefold between 1973 and 1978. Although LDC exports accounted for less than 10 percent of the world market for manufactured goods in 1976, in sectors such as clothing and footwear they had increased by that time to over 30 percent of the market; and in the more technologically advanced sector of electrical machinery they increased from less than 1 percent in 1963 to 12 percent in 1977. This relative growth continued even in the recession: in 1981–82, the volume of industrial country exports remained roughly constant, but the exports of non-oil LDCs rose by about 7 percent; and preliminary figures for 1983 indicated that LDC exports continued to do relatively better than those of the industrial countries.[21]

Questions about the implications of this export growth for employment in the advanced industrialized countries have been raised with increasing urgency in recent years. Hager, for instance, has claimed that "the supply of industrial labour of the Third World will approach, for practical purposes, the infinite," and that "there is no natural equilibrium solution possible even in theory."[22] Yet OECD economists and others point out that exports from the advanced industrialized countries to the non-oil developing countries have increased almost as fast as imports in percentage terms; since exports to the LDCs of manufactured goods exceeded imports by almost a three to one ratio in 1973, the result was that the positive trade balance of the advanced countries with the LDCs, in manufactured goods, increased from $25 billion in 1973 to almost $70 billion in 1979.

These changes suggest that rapid adjustment to change has been taking place in the world trade system since 1973. Branson has documented this for the United States; whether similar patterns characterize Western European adaptation is not yet clear. Between 1973 and 1978 the United States trade surpluses in capital goods, chemicals, and agricultural products almost doubled, to approximately $26 billion, $7 billion, and $13 billion, respectively. During the same period of time, its trade deficits in consumer goods and automotive products also doubled, to about $18 billion in the former category and $10 billion in the latter. Branson infers that this reflects clear patterns of comparative advantage.[23]

The dominant view among economists is that this pattern of adjustment is good for the advanced industrialized countries as well

---

[21] *World Economic Outlook* (Washington, D.C.: International Monetary Fund, 1982), Appendix B, Tables 1 and 2, pp. 143–44; ibid. (1983), pp. 179, 185; Colin I. Bradford, Jr., "The NICs and World Economic Adjustment," in Louis Turner and Neil McMullen, eds., *The Newly Industrializing Countries* (London: Allen and Unwin, 1982), pp. 175–76; Leslie Stein, "The Growth and Implications of LDC Manufactured Exports to Advanced Countries," *Kyklos,* 34 (1981); *The Impact of the Newly Industrializing Countries on Production and Trade in Manufacturing* (Paris: OECD, 1979), Table 5, p. 24.

[22] Wolfgang Hager, "Protectionism and Autonomy: How to Preserve Free Trade in Europe," *International Affairs,* (Summer 1982), pp. 421, 420.

[23] William H. Branson, "Trends in United States International Trade and Investment Since World War II," in Martin Feldstein, ed., *The American Economy in Transition* (Chicago: University of Chicago Press, 1980), Table 3.19, p. 220.

as for the newly industrializing countries: both parties benefit, in
Ricardian fashion, from trade and the associated investment. The
conclusion of one analyst reflects the dominant neo-classical wisdom: "there seems little doubt that it is to the advantage of developed countries to absorb more LDC exports and to adjust their economies accordingly."[24] Thus the increasing economic interdependence
between advanced countries and the newly industrializing countries
is seen as a triumph of liberalism, only somewhat tarnished by
economically irrational, politically inspired protectionism.

Yet if adjustment is a reality, so is protectionism. This has been
evident both in the United States and Western Europe, but Europe
has shown stronger tendencies to act in a protectionist manner,
and considerably greater willingness to deviate from the rhetoric
of liberal trade. In textiles, the EEC has taken the lead in tightening
up the provisions of the Multi-Fiber Agreement, and in steel and
shipbuilding it has also intervened to protect old industries. Individual European countries have gone further, particularly in areas
such as automobiles and consumer electronics. The major target
of European ire was Japan, but as Turner points out, "some of
the NICs began to be sucked into such trade disputes."[25]

European resistance to Japanese and LDC imports is taking place
at levels of import penetration below those already attained by
these exporters in the U.S. market. Less than 16 percent of EEC
imports (excluding intra-EEC trade) were accounted for in 1978
by the LDCs, while the corresponding figure for the United States
was almost 22 percent. Even as a percentage of GDP, American
imports from the LDCs were almost a third higher than Europe's.
Perhaps partly as a consequence, the rate of growth of LDC imports
into the EEC between 1973 and 1978 was lower than into the U.S.
market.

It is not surprising that resistance to imports should increase
during times of economic stress. Workers facing unemployment are
strongly motivated to use political action to preserve their jobs. If
firms "satisfice," seeking to maintain customary levels of profits,
many of them will redouble their lobbying efforts in a downturn
as actual profits and earnings fall below these thresholds. Even if
firms and workers act as maximizers, they may intensify their efforts to secure protection during depressions. In such a period, their
gains are less likely to be competed away by new entrants, since
rates of return even after protection may still be too low to justify
new investment within the area enclosed by the trade barriers.

---

[24] Leslie Stein, "The Growth and Implications of LDC Manufactured Exports to
Advanced Countries," *Kyklos* 34 (1981), p. 57.

[25] Louis Turner and Neil McMullen, eds., *The Newly Industrializing Countries*,
p. 138.

Imports into advanced countries from less industrialized ones can also be expected to stir up more opposition than imports from other advanced economies. Both tentative theoretical models and experience suggest that liberalization of trade is most likely where neither country has a strong comparative advantage in the industry and the products of different firms within the industry are highly differentiated, since under these conditions firms in *both* countries can benefit from liberalization. Where advantages are all on one side, however, one finds what Bhagwati calls the "growing dominance of external products" scenario, leading to protectionist demands both from entrepreneurs (especially if cheap migrant labour is not available) and from labour.[26] In so far as protectionism results from political pressures by affected groups, therefore, one can expect it to be particularly intense against imports from LDCs, especially the well-organized NICs, with their tendency to focus suddenly on one sector or another for massive import penetration.

The findings of the literature on the political economy of protectionism are ironic, if not paradoxical. Since Europe and the United States benefit economically from LDC exports, one might expect the changing international division of labour to reinforce embedded liberalism. However, the conjunction of surplus capacity and unemployment (the results overwhelmingly of other factors) with rapid increases in NIC exports makes the NICs obvious scapegoats for advocates of protection. Wages in the NICs are low, and many of these countries have highly repressive governments; so the charge of "unfairness" is easier to make than it is with respect to the Japanese.

Thus the significance of the newly industrializing countries for European liberalism may be more indirect than direct. The NICs serve as catalysts for action to scuttle non-discriminatory patterns of trade. Mercantilists can play down the importance of exports by the advanced countries to the NICs, arguing that these will only temporarily increase in response to gains by the less developed, lower-cost trading partners. Hager, for instance, characterizes Europe as "a high cost area with decentralized real-capital formation, and hence intrinsically on the defensive. Under free trade conditions, any of the low-cost producers can decide to produce anything for the European market, constrained only by other outside competitors."[27] He thus conjures up the extraordinary spectacle of the NICs having comparative advantages over Europe in *everything*.

---

[26] Jagdish Bhagwati, "Shifting Comparative Advantage, Protectionist Demands and Policy Response," in Bhagwati, ed., *Import Competition and Response*, pp. 177–79.

[27] Wolfgang Hager, "Protectionism and Autonomy," p. 423.

From the protectionist standpoint, the existence of the welfare state makes international liberalism even more intolerable. Hager comments as follows:

> With unemployment approaching 10 percent, the full-employment-of-factors assumption of free trade welfare economics looks threadbare. The welfare state adds a twist to the classical story by insisting that the idled factor labour be paid nearly in full, as if it were still producing. The cheap shirt is thus paid for several times: once at the counter, then again in unemployment benefits for the idled workers. Secondary losses involve input industries (although in the short term their exports rise): machinery, fibres, chemicals for dyeing and finishing products.[28]

Western Europe seems more likely than the United States to follow protectionist policies during this decade. Ideological beliefs in liberalism are weaker in Europe than across the Atlantic, European industry is less dynamic technologically, and governments have more instruments available for intervention in the economy. "Industrial policy" is therefore more attractive to many European governments, especially that of France, than it is to the United States. As Woolcock notes "there are no specific trade-related adjustment policies in Western Europe. With extensive structural-policy instruments of both a selective and a non-selective nature, there is little need to introduce new policy instruments."[29]

Protectionism coupled with industrial policy is not inevitable. European protectionism would conflict with the fact that the huge debts of many less developed countries can only be serviced if those countries can continue to increase their exports. For this reason, as well as its own political-security concerns with countries such as Mexico, South Korea, and Taiwan, the United States is likely to resist pressures for extensive protection. Since not all European governments are as enthusiastic about industrial policy as the French, pressures against protectionism are likely to be strong.

Neo-classical economists have long held that a well-functioning liberal world economy provides opportunities for the poor and weak. Despite the denial of this argument by dependency theorists, the developments of the last decade in the world political economy strongly support it. The rise of the NICs was itself a consequence of liberalism. Yet the result is not the further increase in economic openness envisioned by liberals: on the contrary, the suddenness of the process, characteristic of capitalist uneven development, forces adjustment costs on to groups that are weak economically

---

[28] Ibid., p. 424.

[29] Stephen Woolcock, "Adjustment in Western Europe," in Turner and McMullen, eds., *The Newly Industrializing Countries,* p. 236.

but relatively strong politically. Polanyi's metaphor captures the effects, if not the nature of the process: "society protects itself" against the ravages of the market. Or, to use the phrases of the literature on the political economy of protectionism, groups threatened by change lobby for protection in order to create rents for themselves. The policy connotations are different but the results are the same: unless its effects are cushioned by deliberate policy, the success of liberalism, even embedded liberalism, tends to destroy the conditions for its existence.

Even within the parameters of liberal assumptions about the best long-run path of the political economy, therefore, proponents of adjustment assistance, subsidies, and other forms of support for threatened industries and workers can make a strong case. Their argument is strengthened if these measures appear, in the medium to long run, to facilitate adjustment and maintain the conditions for liberalism. From this perspective, a reduction in the rate of increase in economic interdependence could be seen as a precondition for avoiding the demise of embedded liberalism in Western Europe.

CONCLUSIONS

Behind the variety of international forces impinging on Europe from the world political economy, two closely related patterns of change seem to be crucial: the rise and erosion of American hegemony and the expansion of capitalism on a world scale. As we have seen, American dominance, and the willingness of the United States to use its resources to build a liberal international political economy, were crucial elements in the post-war triumph of embedded liberalism in Europe. Conversely, the adverse shifts in terms of trade and the transmission of economic distress that characterized the 1970s were aggravated, if not caused, by a decline in the ability and willingness of the United States to manage the world economy for its own benefit and that of its allies. Even when it would have been possible for the United States to continue managing the world political economy, to do so in a way that benefited Europe would have required more costly adjustments by the United States than it cared to make.

As American authority over the world capitalist system was eroding in the 1970s, the system itself continued to expand. The earlier expansion of the 1940s and 1950s, incorporating Europe into the Americano-centric world political economy, contributed to European economic growth and to the gradual expansion of the welfare state, even if it contained a bias against rapid increases that went beyond the modal pattern of the time. The incorporation of Japan into the system as an advanced country during the 1960s and 1970s was received with less enthusiasm in Europe, since it imposed adjustment costs on their economic and political institutions and threatened the European position at or near the top of the international division of labour. Yet throughout this period, the political bias of liberalism benefited interests, groups, and political élites that were favourable to maintaining internationally oriented capitalism.

In conjunction with the economic crises of the 1970s (which had a variety of sources), the later rise of exports of manufactured goods from the newly industrializing countries, coupled with an increasing Japanese challenge, began to generate a powerful counter-reaction. Increasing state interventionism, designed at first to cushion societies from some of the adverse effects of interdependence, threatened to overwhelm liberalism itself. The problem was not the failure of capitalism but, in Schumpeterian fashion, its success. Uneven development again took place in the 1970s, as in the 1950s—but this time the most rapid rates of growth were in East Asia rather than Europe. Not surprisingly, the reactions of Europeans to this turn of events were quite different from their response to the Marshall Plan.

Against this background it is hard to regard the problems of the world political economy in the 1970s as exogenous, unpredictable shocks, as argued in the McCracken Report. Admittedly, not all of these events seem inevitable, and misguided American policies on both oil and monetary relations had a great deal to do with the subsequent crises. Nevertheless, there is an inherent logic to the decline of hegemonic powers in a capitalist system, since their technological and organizational advantages are inherently subject to diffusion to the periphery, driven by the incentives of profit and power.[30] Equally fundamental to the hegemon's position is the relationship between power and adjustment. As we have seen, power is in part the ability not to have to adjust to change. Adjustment is a "political bad": people do not like to have to change their habits, especially if the results are psychologically and financially distressing. Voters tend to punish politicians who seek to force adjustments on to them. Yet adjustment is an "economic good": neo-classical economists never tire of singing its praises as the principal engine of growth. The economy that does not adjust does not grow.

Hegemonic powers can avoid adjustment longer than others, precisely because they are powerful. Yet this ability to evade the necessity to make unpleasant changes can itself contribute to long-term

---

[30] Robert Gilpin, *War and Change in World Politics* (Cambridge: Cambridge University Press, 1981).

decay. If weaker states adjust more readily than strong ones (not necessarily because they are more farsighted but because they have less choice), their economies will become more efficient, and they will become stronger. Japan's rapid adjustment to the 1973–74 oil shock, compared to that of the United States, is a case in point. No law prescribes that hegemonic powers will necessarily decline at any given time, but they are subject to the temptation to take the easy path. Their power gives them enough rope with which to hang themselves.

Even more than the decline of hegemony, the expansion of capitalism is the result of endogenous factors: unconstrained by state power, capitalism continuously reaches out not only for new markets and sources of raw materials, as in the past, but for new areas in which production for export can profitably take place. As new manufacturing centres enter the world system, the international division of labour becomes more extensive and interdependence grows rapidly. Yet the *political* economy of capitalism follows a more contorted path. Political reactions arise against what may seem, on efficiency grounds, to be a beneficial process. Europe, and to some extent the United States, are now going through such a reaction.

At the heart of this problem is a fundamental tension, or contradiction, in the international political economy of modern capitalism. International capitalism keeps expanding to the periphery, but depends on interventionist, self-interested states in the centre for its maintenance and support.[31] Embedded liberalism is endangered because its peculiar combination of state interventionism and international openness rested on conditions—American political dominance and the pre-eminent position of Europe in the international division of labour—that can no longer be maintained, and that indeed were undermined by the success of liberalism itself. Major adjustments must now take place: to a new form of embedded liberalism that accepts the expansion of capitalism away from Europe, uncontrolled by the United States; or toward greater self-reliance and protectionism for Western Europe, perhaps in conjunction with selected areas of the Third World. Domestic political pressures point toward protectionism, yet its economic costs, and the threat it poses to transatlantic political relations, are well appreciated in Europe as well as in the United States. One plausible compromise would incorporate elements of both cooperation and protection. "Cooperative protectionism" could limit political friction through the use of multilateral agreements, while cushioning the costs of rapid

---

[31] Robert Gilpin, *U.S. Power and the Multinational Corporation: The Political Economy of Direct Foreign Investment* (New York: Basic Books, 1975).

economic change. Such a strategy could easily degenerate to a discordant and stringent protectionism if too many concessions were made to obsolescent industries and interest groups seeking to prevent, rather than merely to delay, painful adjustments to change. Yet it offers the promise of reconciling the realities of international political and economic interdependence with demands for protection at home. Europe may have to choose, not between liberalism and protectionism in stark forms, but between defensive and discordant, or adjustment-oriented and cooperative, variants of protectionism. Its future will be affected—one is tempted to say, determined—by its reaction to this fateful choice.

CHAPTER THREE

Authoritarianism: Old and New

8

On Democracy and Tyranny

Aristotle

PREREQUISITES OF DEMOCRACY

We proceed now to inquire what form of government and what manner of life is best for communities in general, not adapting it to that superior virtue which is above the reach of the vulgar, or that education which every advantage of nature and fortune only can furnish, nor to those imaginary plans which may be formed at pleasure; but to that mode of life which the greater part of mankind can attain to, and that government which most cities may establish: for as to those aristocracies which we have now mentioned, they are either too perfect for a state to support, or one so nearly alike to that state we are now going to inquire into, that we shall treat of them both as one.

The opinions which we form upon these subjects must depend upon one common principle: for if what I have said in my treatise on Morals is true, a happy life must arise from an uninterrupted course of virtue; and if virtue consists in a certain medium, the middle life must certainly be the happiest; which medium is attainable by every one. The boundaries of virtue and vice in the state must also necessarily be the same as in a private person; for the form of government is the life of the city. In every city the people

---

Source: Aristotle, "On Democracy and Tyranny," in *A Treatise on Government,* trans. William Ellis (London: George Routledge and Sons, 1888). Abridged by the editors. Aristotle taught from 335 to 323 B.C. His writings are drawn from notes taken by his students.

are divided into three sorts; the very rich, the very poor, and those who are between them. If this is universally admitted, that the mean is best, it is evident that even in point of fortune mediocrity is to be preferred; . . .

It is also the genius of a city to be composed as much as possible of equals; which will be most so when the inhabitants are in the middle state: from whence it follows, that that city must be best framed which is composed of those whom we say are naturally its proper members. It is men of this station also who will be best assured of safety and protection; for they will neither covet what belongs to others, as the poor do; nor will others covet what is theirs, as the poor do what belongs to the rich; and thus, without plotting against any one, or having any one plot against them, they will live free from danger: for which reason Phocylides wisely wishes for the middle state, as being most productive of happiness. It is plain, then, that the most perfect political community must be amongst those who are in the middle rank, and those states are best instituted wherein these are a larger and more respectable part, if possible, than both the other; or, if that cannot be, at least than either of them separate; so that being thrown into the balance it may prevent either scale from preponderating.

. . . The middle state is therefore best, as being least liable to those seditions and insurrections which disturb the community; and for the same reason extensive governments are least liable to these inconveniences; for there those in a middle state are very numerous, whereas in small ones it is easy to pass to the two extremes, so as hardly to have any in a medium remaining, but the one half rich, the other poor: and from the same principle it is that democracies are more firmly established and of longer continuance than oligarchies; but even in those when there is a want of a proper number of men of middling fortune, the poor extend their power too far, abuses arise, and the government is soon at an end.

Other particulars we will consider separately; but it seems proper to prove, that the supreme power ought to be lodged with the many, rather than with those of the better sort, who are few; and also to explain what doubts (and probably just ones) may arise: now, though not one individual of the many may himself be fit for the supreme power, yet when these many are joined together, it does not follow but they may be better qualified for it than those; and this not separately, but as a collective body; as the public suppers exceed those which are given at one person's private expense: for, as they are many, each person brings in his share of virtue and wisdom; and thus, coming together, they are like one man made up of a multitude, with many feet, many hands, and many intelligences: thus is it with respect to the manners and understandings of the multitude taken together; for which reason the public are the best judges of music and poetry; for some understand one part, some another, and all collectively the whole. . . .

. . . For the multitude when they are collected together have all of them sufficient understanding for these purposes, and, mixing among those of higher rank, are serviceable to the city, as some things, which alone are improper for food, when mixed with others make the whole more wholesome than a few of them would be.

*   *   *   *   *

Since in every art and science the end aimed at is always good, so particularly in this, which is the most excellent of all, the founding of civil society, the good wherein aimed at is justice; for it is this which is for the benefit of all. Now, it is the common opinion, that justice is a certain equality; and in this point all the philosophers are agreed when they treat of morals: for they say what is just, and to whom; and that equals ought to receive equal: but we should know how we are to determine what things are equal and what unequal; and in this there is some difficulty, which calls for the philosophy of the politician. Some persons will probably say, that the employments of the state ought to be given according to every particular excellence of each citizen, if there is no other difference between them and the rest of the community, but they are in every respect else alike: for justice attributes different things to persons differing from each other in their character, according to their respective merits. . . .

Now the first thing which presents itself to our consideration is this, whether it is best to be governed by a good man, or by good laws? Those who prefer a kingly government think that laws can only speak a general language, but cannot adapt themselves to particular circumstances; for which reason it is absurd in any science to follow written rule; and even in Egypt the physician was allowed to alter the mode of cure which the law prescribed to him, after the fourth day; but if he did it sooner it was at his own peril: from whence it is evident, on the very same account, that a government of written laws is not the best; and yet general reasoning is necessary to all those who are to govern, and it will be much more perfect in those who are entirely free from passions than in those to whom they are natural. But now this is a quality which laws possess; while the other is natural to the human soul. But some one will say in answer to this, that man will be a better judge of particulars. It will be necessary, then, for a king to be a lawgiver, and that his laws should be published, but that those should have no authority which are absurd, as those which are not, should. But whether is it better for the community that those things which cannot possibly come under the cognisance of the law either at all or properly should be under the government of every worthy citizen, as the present method is, when the public community, in their general assemblies, act as judges and counsellors, where all their determinations are upon particular cases. For one individual, be he who he will, will be found, upon comparison, inferior to a whole people taken collectively: but this is what a city is, as a public entertainment is better than one man's portion: for this reason the multitude judge of many things better than any one single person. They are also less liable to corruption from their numbers, as water is from its quantity: besides, the judgment of an individual must necessarily be perverted if he is overcome by anger or any other passion; but it would be hard indeed if the whole community should be misled by anger. Moreover, let the people be free, and they will do nothing but in conformity to the law, except only in those cases which the law cannot speak to. But though what I am going to propose may not easily be met with, yet if the majority of the state should happen to be good men, should they prefer one uncorrupt governor or many equally good, is it not evident that they should choose the many? But there may be divisions among these which cannot happen when there is but one. In answer to this it may be replied that all their souls will be as much animated with virtue as this one man's.

. . . As for an absolute monarchy as it is called, that is to say, when the whole state is wholly subject to the will of one person, namely the king, it seems to many that it is unnatural that one man should have the entire rule over his fellow-citizens when the state consists of equals: for nature requires that the same right and the same rank should necessarily take place amongst all those who are equal by nature: for as it would be hurtful to the body for those who are of different constitutions to observe the same regimen, either of diet or clothing, so is it with respect to the honours of the state as hurtful, that those who are equal in merit should be unequal in rank; for which reason it is as much a man's duty to submit to command as to assume it, and this also by rotation; for this is law, for order is law; and it is more proper that law should govern than any one of the citizens: upon the same principle, if it is advantageous to place the supreme power in some particular persons, they should be appointed to be only guardians, and the servants of the laws, for the supreme power must be placed somewhere; but they say, that it is unjust that where all are equal one person should continually enjoy it. But it seems unlikely that man should be able to adjust that which the law cannot determine; it may be replied, that the law having laid down the best rules possible, leaves the adjustment and application of particulars to the discretion of the magistrate; besides, it allows anything to be altered which experience proves may be better established. Moreover, he who would place the supreme power in mind, would place it in God and the laws; but he who entrusts man with it, gives it to a wild beast, for such his appetites sometimes make him; for passion influences those who are in power, even the very best of men: for which reason law is reason without desire.

Tyranny

It now remains to treat of a tyranny . . . In the beginning of this work we inquired into the nature of kingly government, and entered into a particular examination of what was most properly called so, and whether it was advantageous to a state or not, and what it should be, and how established; and we divided a tyranny into two pieces when we were upon this subject, because there is something analogous between this and a kingly government, for they are both of them established by law; for among some of the barbarians they elect a monarch with absolute power, and formerly among the Greeks there were some such, whom they called aesumnetes. Now these differ from each other; for some possess only kingly power regulated by law, and rule those who voluntarily submit to their government; others rule despotically according to their own will. There is a third species of tyranny, most properly so called, which is the very opposite to kingly power; for this is the government of one who rules over his equals and superiors without being accountable for his conduct, and whose object is his own advantage, and not the advantage of those he governs; for which reason he rules by compulsion, for no freemen will ever willingly submit to such a government. These are the different species of tyrannies, their principles, and their causes.

. . . Tyrannies are preserved two ways most opposite to each other, one of which is when the power is delegated from one to the other, and in this manner many tyrants govern in their states. Report says that Periander founded many of these. There are also many of them to be met with amongst the Persians. What has been already mentioned is as conducive as anything can be to preserve a tyranny; namely, to keep down those who are of an aspiring disposition, to take off those who will not submit, to allow no public meals, no clubs, no education, nothing at all, but to guard against everything that gives rise to high spirits or mutual confidence; nor to suffer the learned meetings of those who are at leisure to hold conversation with each other; and to endeavour by every means possible to keep all the people strangers to each other; for knowledge increases mutual confidence; and to oblige all strangers to appear

in public, and to live near the city-gate, that all their actions may
be sufficiently seen; for those who are kept like slaves seldom entertain any noble thoughts: in short, to imitate everything which the
Persians and barbarians do, for they all contribute to support slavery; and to endeavour to know what every one who is under their
power does and says; and for this purpose to employ spies. . . .

     · . A tyrant also should endeavour to engage his subjects in a
war, that they may have employment and continually depend upon
their general. A king is preserved by his friends, but a tyrant is
of all persons the man who can place no confidence in friends, as
every one has it in his desire and these chiefly in their power to
destroy him. . . .

     These and such-like are the supports of a tyranny, for it compre-
hends whatsoever is wicked. But all these things may be comprehended in three divisions, for there are three objects which a tyranny has in view; one of which is, that the citizens should be of
poor abject dispositions; for such men never propose to conspire
against any one. The second is, that they should have no confidence
in each other; for while they have not this, the tyrant is safe enough
from destruction. For which reason they are always at enmity with
those of merit, as hurtful to their government; not only as they
scorn to be governed despotically, but also because they can rely
upon each other's fidelity, and others can rely upon theirs, and
because they will not inform against their associates, nor any one
else. The third is, that they shall be totally without the means of
doing anything; for no one undertakes what is impossible for him
to perform: so that without power a tyranny can never be destroyed.

9

Notes on the Theory of Dictatorship

Franz L. Neumann

DEFINITION OF DICTATORSHIP

Strange though it may seem, we do not possess any systematic study of dictatorship. The historical information is abundant, and there are many analyses of individual dictators in various countries. But there is no analysis that seeks to generalize not only from the political experience of the 20th century, but from the political systems of the more distant past. The present paper attempts to outline the theoretical problems encountered in the analysis of dictatorship and to indicate whatever answers now can be supplied.

By dictatorship we understand the rule of a person or a group of persons who arrogate to themselves and monopolize power in the state, exercising it without restraint.

The first question raised by this definition is whether the Roman dictatorship and the absolute monarchy should be included in its scope.

It seems more appropriate to classify the Roman dictatorship (prior to Sulla) not as a dictatorship properly speaking, but as a form of Crisis Government. This may seem arbitrary, for the very word "dictator" derives from Roman constitutional law. Nevertheless, the Roman dictatorship was a magistracy, clearly defined in

Source: Reprinted with permission of the publisher from Franz L. Neumann *The Democratic and Authoritarian State* (New York: Free Press, 1957). Copyright 1957 by The Free Press, a corporation. Abridged by the editors.

authorization, scope, and duration, and it ought not to be confused with a political system in which power is arrogated by an individual or a group, and which does not circumscribe either the scope or the duration of dictatorial power. The Roman dictator was appointed by one of the consuls for a period not to exceed six months, to defend the country against an external enemy or to cope with internal dissension. He was duty-bound to appoint at once a Master of the Horse for the command of the cavalry; he had no authority to change the constitution, to declare war, to intervene in civil law suits, or to impose new fiscal obligations upon Roman citizens. Within these limits, the sovereign power of the Roman people was concentrated in his hands. The consuls became his subordinates; the tribunician power of intercession did not apply against his acts; nor could a citizen condemned in a criminal trial invoke the normal right of appeal *(provocatio)* against him.

The Romans resorted to dictatorship because the collegiate nature of the magistracy, including the consulate, and the one-year restriction on its term, made the conduct of war extremely difficult. But the dictatorship itself was to prove unsuitable for wars of long duration. By the end of the fourth century it was already in decline, reappearing in irregular forms during the Punic Wars and disappearing at the end of the Second Punic War (201 B.C.). From then on, the Roman dictatorship (e.g., Sulla's and Caesar's) changes its character radically.

The second problem that our definition raises is the relation between monarchy and dictatorship. The title of the absolute ruler—whether he is designated King, Emperor, Leader, or Duce—is not decisive here. This was already recognized by Aristotle, who held the rule of kings among non-civilized (non-Hellenic) peoples to be "similar to that of tyranny" and who defined his fifth type of kingship, the case "where a single power is sovereign on every issue, with the same sort of power that a tribe or a polis exercises over its public concerns," as a *Pambasileia,* an all-kingship or super-kingship.

Actually, from the standpoint of the exercise of power the absolute monarch is a dictator, but from the standpoint of the legitimacy of power, he is not. We may speak of legitimate monarchical rule whenever accession to power is constitutionally regulated by heredity or by election and monarchical rule is generally accepted as the normal form of government. These criteria are rather vague—but so is the actual situation. In the history of political and constitutional thought, the ruler who comes to power through a *coup d'état (absque titulo)* is held to be an usurping tyrant, but he may rid himself of this stigma if he succeeds in formally establishing his rule and that of his line, which then becomes "legitimate." On the other hand it was also generally held that a monarch who acceded to the throne legitimately could degenerate into a tyrant through his acts *(quoad exercitio)*. Thus, while one may distinguish in principle between monarchy and dictatorship, one must realize that the principle suffers many exceptions and that, consequently, certain forms of the absolute monarchy must also be treated as forms of dictatorship.

Our definition, furthermore, envisages dictatorship only in the state, and in no other social organization. There may be situations in which absolute power of a party boss or of the pater familias may help us understand the mechanisms leading to a dictatorship or serving to maintain its power. But there is as yet no convincing evidence that the dictatorial structure of social organizations necessarily leads to or facilitates political dictatorship. An example is the ambiguity of the social and psychological role of the so-called "authoritarian family."[1] The authoritarian (quasi-dictatorial) family may lead, as some maintain, to a more ready acceptance of political dictatorship,[2] but dictatorship may also be promoted (and more frequently, perhaps) by the decay of traditional authority, by the very undermining of the authority of the father. The relation between political and social forms of authoritarianism must, therefore, be taken as a special problem, and not as an automatic correlation.

Moreover, we deliberately do not distinguish among a dictator, a tyrant, and a despot. Tyranny and despotism have no precise meaning. One usually associates despotism with oriental dictatorships, whereas tyranny is often used to designate any system of government that either in its origin or in its practice is tainted by unconstitutional practices or characterized by lack of restraints. Both words are emotionally charged and exhibit in varying degrees rejection and resentment of these systems of government.

Rejection of the terms *tyranny* and *despotism* does not mean, however, that within the general definition of dictatorship there are no subtypes. A number of distinctions are significant.

The first pertains to the scope of the political power monopolized by the dictator. The dictator may exercise his power through absolute control of the traditional means of coercion only, i.e., the army, police, bureaucracy, and judiciary. We may call this type a *simple dictatorship*.

In some situations, the dictator may feel compelled to build up

---

[1] Which, however, need not necessarily be a dictatorial family, because the power of the *pater familias* may well be founded in reason: "rational authority."

[2] T. W. Adorno et al., *The Authoritarian Personality* (New York: W. W. Norton, 1950).

popular support, to secure a mass base, either for his rise to power or for the exercise of it, or for both. We may call this type a *caesaristic dictatorship,* which, as the name indicates, is always personal in form.

Even this combination of monopolized coercion and popular backing may be insufficient as a guarantee of power. It may be necessary to control education, the means of communication and economic institutions and thus to gear the whole of society and the private life of the citizen to the system of political domination. The term for this type is *totalitarian dictatorship.* It may be either collective or personal, that is, it may or may not have a caesaristic element.

It need hardly be mentioned that these classifications are ideal types which will only approximate historical realities. They will help us, however, to understand the structure of the various cases of dictatorship.

CAESARISTIC DICTATORSHIP

The simple dictatorship—whether it be military or bureaucratic, the rule of a junta, a caudillo, or even an absolute monarch—is exercised primarily through the control of what one may call the classical instruments of rule: army, police, bureaucracy, judiciary. This limitation is due less to self-imposed restraints than to the absence of any need for more extensive controls. Simple dictatorship usually occurs in countries where the masses of the people lack political awareness, where politics is the affair of small cliques who compete for favors and hope to gain prestige and wealth by association with the dictator. The mass of the people pay taxes and may have to serve in the army, but otherwise have little to do with political life. The only social controls which may be needed are bribery and corruption of a few influential individuals in order to tie them closely to the system.

In the *caesaristic dictatorship* a new element enters: the need for popular support. The term *caesarism* was apparently coined by Romieu in his little book *L'Ere des Césars* (1950) and its climate most adequately described by Guizot, Louis Philippe's Prime Minister after the revolution of 1830.

"Chaos," says Guizot, "is now hiding under one word—democracy. This is now the ultimate and universal word all seek to appropriate as a talisman. The Monarchists say: Our Monarchy is a Democratic Monarchy; it differs essentially from the ancient monarchy and is adapted to modern conditions of society. The Republicans say: The Republic is Democracy governing itself. This is the only form of government in harmony with democratic society, its principles, its sentiments, and its interests.

"Socialists, Communists, Montagnards wish that the Republic should be pure and absolute democracy. This is for them the condition of its legitimacy.

"Such is the power of the word democracy that no government or party dares to exist or believes it can exist without inscribing that word upon its banner."[3]

Caesarism becomes a necessity when the masses tend to become politically articulate.

*   *   *   *   *

TOTALITARIAN DICTATORSHIP

Totalitarian dictatorship, to which our attention now will be directed, ought not to be confused with caesarism. Up to the 19th century at least, caesaristic dictatorship does not necessarily lead to a totalitarian system, nor is the totalitarian state necessarily the result of a genuine caesaristic movement. Totalitarianism is thus a separate problem. For the purpose of a brief discussion the modern totalitarian dictatorship may be reduced to five essential factors.

The first of these is the transition from a state based upon the rule of law (the German *Rechtsstaat*) to a police state. The rule of law is a presumption in favor of the right of the citizen and against the coercive power of the state. In the totalitarian state this presumption is reversed. Details need not concern us here, since the power of executive agencies in totalitarian states to interfere at discretion with life, liberty and property may be taken as the best-known feature of this kind of dictatorship.

The second factor is the transition from the diffusion of power in liberal states to the concentration of power in the totalitarian regime. This concentration may vary in degree as well as form. But there is no role in any totalitarian state for the various liberal devices of diffusing power, such as separation of powers, federalism, a functioning multiparty system, bicameralism, etc.

These first two elements, however, are to be found in the absolute monarchy as well as in the totalitarian dictatorship. What distinguishes totalitarianism politically is the third element, namely, the existence of a monopolistic state party. Such a party is required because the traditional instruments of coercion do not suffice to control an industrial society, and all the less so since bureaucracies and armies may not always be reliable. The monopolistic party is a flexible instrument which provides the force to control the state

---

[3] Guizot, *La Démocratie en France* (Leipzig, 1849), p. 2.

machine and society and to perform the gigantic task of cementing the authoritarian elements within society together.

Moreover, the monopolistic party involves a socio-psychological aspect pertaining to what is commonly called a "mass" society. Since modern totalitarian dictatorships arise, almost without exception, within and against democracies (weak though the democratic structures may have been), the totalitarian clique has to assume the shape of a democratic movement and to retain this façade even after it has come to power. In other words, it is forced to practice the ritual of democracy even though the substance is totally denied.

The role of the monopolistic party involves the fourth element of the totalitarian dictatorship: the transition from pluralist to totalitarian social controls. Society ceases to be distinguished from the state; it is totally permeated by political power. The control of society, now as important as the control of the state, is achieved by the following techniques:

1. The leadership principle—to enforce guidance from the top and responsibility to the top.

2. The "synchronization" of all social organizations—not only to control them, but to make them serviceable to the state.

3. The creation of graded elites—so as to enable the rulers to control the masses from within and to disguise manipulation from without, i.e., to supplement bureaucracies in the narrow meaning of the term with private leadership groups within the various strata of the population.

4. The atomization and isolation of the individual, which involves negatively the destruction or at least weakening of social units based on biology (family), tradition, religion, or cooperation in work or leisure; and positively the imposition of huge and undifferentiated mass organizations which leave the individual isolated and more easily manipulable.

5. The transformation of culture into propaganda—of cultural values into saleable commodities.

The final factor in totalitarianism is the reliance upon terror, i.e., the use of noncalculable violence as a permanent threat against the individual. Care must be taken, however, not to define a totalitarian dictatorship simply as rule of violence. Without it, it is true, such regimes could not survive. But they could not endure for any length of time without considerable identification by the oppressed people with its rulers.

These, in brief outline, are the features of the most repressive of political systems. What distinguishes it from absolutism is not primarily the caesaristic element, for this was also characteristic of the absolute monarchy in certain periods of its history, but rather the destruction of the line between state and society and the total politicization of society by the device of the monopolistic party. This is not merely a question of more or less political power. The difference is one of quality, not quantity. Where, as in the absolute monarchy, power is primarily exercised through the traditional bureaucratic instruments of coercion, its operation is governed by abstract, calculable rules, although their execution often may be arbitrary. Absolutism, therefore, already contains the major institutional principles of modern liberalism. Totalitarian dictatorship, on the other hand, is the absolute negation of these principles because the main repressive agencies are not courts and administrative bodies, but the secret police and the party.

A fully developed totalitarian dictatorship is the form an industrial society may adopt if it should become necessary to maximize its repressive elements and eliminate its liberal ones. But totalitarian dictatorship is not the child of modern industrialism alone. Sparta . . . may be . . . an illuminating earlier experiment.

*   *   *   *   *

DEMOCRACY AND DICTATORSHIP

If we review the various types of dictatorships outlined above, we are forced to conclude that the usual confrontation of liberal democracy vs. dictatorship as an antithesis of good and evil, cannot be maintained from a historical point of view. Moralizing about political systems makes it difficult to understand their functions. The relationship between democracy and dictatorship is not as simple as is sometimes stated.

1. Dictatorships may be an implementation of democracy. But this refers to emergency dictatorships with functions similar to the classical Roman type, which we prefer to classify as a kind of magistracy.

2. Dictatorships may be the preparation for democracy. We may then speak of an educational dictatorship.

3. Dictatorships may be the very negation of democracy and thus be a totally regressive system.

Pisistratus' rule is probably a classical example of an educational dictatorship. As Werner Jaeger puts it: "The masses were still politically inexperienced, so that democracy was far away: it could not come until the aristocracy had been brought low by the Pisistratic tyrants." We may add that the great function of the Pisistratidae was the creation of an Athenian national (or collective) spirit. This was done by facilitating the emergence of a "middle class," which

Aristotle believed to be the social prerequisite of democracy. Hence, without the work of Pisistratus the regimes of Cleisthenes and Pericles would hardly be conceivable.

It is well to remember that the Marxist-Leninist conception of a dictatorship of the proletariat was democratic precisely in this sense of a preparatory dictatorship. The concentration of power in the hands of the proletariat was to be used to abolish class rule altogether and to herald a new epoch of freedom in a classless society. That it was not this expectation but the very opposite which materialized cannot be discussed in detail here. However, we may cite the basic reasons why, under modern conditions, every dictatorship tends to be a totalitarian dictatorship and to involve the negation of democracy.

The democratic ideology has become so universal that Guizot's statement seems even truer today than it did in 1848. All modern dictatorships arose from democratic conditions. This is true of Italy, Germany, Spain, Argentina, and perhaps even of the USSR, although to a lesser degree.

The dictator is therefore compelled to seek mass support and, having obtained it, to practice the ritual of democracy even if its substance is withheld. As Engels already saw, a *coup d'état* seems hopeless against a modern army; the dictator can come to power only with the help or toleration of the army, but to sustain his power, he depends on a mass base.

There is, however, an important distinction between the Fascist-Nazi type and the Bolshevik. In the former, the dictator could rely upon substantial sectors of the traditional ruling groups (industry, finance, agrarians, army, bureaucracy, judiciary) which were committed to a minimum of formal legality since overt rebellion would have jeopardized their own status and security. Consequently, the dictatorship in its rise to power had to play the democratic game (compare Hitler's strategy before his Beer Hall Putsch of 1923 and afterwards). And once it had attained this goal, the requirements of competition with the outside world and the need to secure the active or passive co-operation of industrial labor, led the Nazi-Fascist type of dictatorship to present itself as a higher and nobler form of democracy.

For the Bolsheviks the need for mass support is of a different nature. The original theory of the dictatorship of the proletariat as the dictatorship of the majority over a minority was compatible at least with one version of democracy. But the Russian proletariat was a small minority in 1917, and with the Bolshevik rejection of Trotsky's theory of a permanent revolution, the democratic mass base had to be secured from among the peasants. When this was not voluntarily forthcoming the Bolshevik regime evolved into a full-blown totalitarian dictatorship.

But even in agrarian, colonial, and semi-colonial countries, where democracy did not exist or was inadequately practiced, modern dictatorship tends to become totalitarian. Today every nation experiences democracy vicariously. Due to the world-wide scope of communications, even the most backward peoples have become aware of democracy and want it, awakening mass consciousness usually taking the form of a demand for national emancipation. Consequently, here too a dictator must attempt to be a Caesar by acting out the democratic ritual even if he is compelled to go on towards a totalitarian regime.

THE SOCIAL FUNCTION OF DICTATORSHIP

Neither the attraction of a democratic ideology nor the scope of the dictatorship can fully explain the phenomena of caesarism and totalitarianism. An understanding of the social function of dictatorship would require a comprehensive analysis based upon the following elements:

1.   The economic system.
2.   The class relationship.
3.   The personality structure.

In each historical situation these factors—economic, social, and psychological—must be treated as a unity, not as isolated, independent causes. An index of changes in these elements will frequently—I would even say invariably—be found in the intellectual and artistic trends of a given period, i.e., in philosophy, literature, and the arts. I should like to indicate certain principles that may help in the search for the causes and functions of the various types of dictatorships.

In terms of *class relationships*, the function of dictatorship may be related to three basic and recurring situations:
1.   Disenfranchised and insurgent social classes demand recognition of their interests which the political power-holders refuse to grant. There are two alternatives, depending upon the political maturity of the ascending classes:

If they are politically mature—as the bourgeoisie in England in the 17th or in France in the 18th century—caesarism will be merely a transitory phenomenon (Cromwell and Robespierre). The new classes, in power and commanding a majority, will for various reasons demand a liberal political system.

But if they are not mature, or too weak, the caesaristic movement will become a dictatorship as in the case of Pisistratus, Cola di Rienzo, or Lenin.

2. The second case is the attempt of a social class threatened with decline and striving to preserve its status and power. Dictatorship may then arise as an attempt to preserve the status quo. The most striking examples are Sparta, to a lesser extent the half-hearted efforts of Napoleon I, and probably the regimes of Franco and Perón.

3. The third possibility is the attempt of what one might call doomed classes to change radically the socioeconomic situation, to reverse it, and to install a political system that would restore them to their old preeminence. This is the kernel of the German and Italian Fascist movements.

These class relationships must be studied in the light of changing economic systems. Totalitarianism, although not a new phenomenon, is determined in its modern form by the features of an industrial society. Modern industrialism is politically ambivalent because it contains and intensifies two diametrically opposed trends in modern society: the trend toward freedom and the trend toward repression. Sociologists usually define this as the problem of "moral lag," holding that the growing potentialities of modern technology outstrip the progress of "morality." This may or may not be true, but it is not, in my opinion, the decisive factor.

It is easy to say that technology is neutral politically and socially, so that any desired result can be attained depending upon the persons who use it and upon their aims. Technological optimists (like Georges Sorel and Thorstein Veblen) hold that only the full development of technological resources and their efficient utilization (e.g., exclusion of "conspicuous consumption"), can bring mankind to its highest perfection. We do not challenge this statement, but should like to explore some of its implications.

Large-scale technology on the one hand may imply the total dependence of the industrial population upon a complex, integrated mechanism, which can be operated only in a highly organized, stratified, and hierarchic system. This system must instill the virtues of discipline, obedience and subordination—no matter who owns the means of production. Thus, modern industrialism preaches the very virtues which every authoritarian political system seeks to cultivate. These virtues are repressive because they are opposed to man's self-determination.

On the other hand, the very opposite virtues may also be strengthened by technology: self-reliance, awareness of one's power and, most particularly, the feeling of solidarity—that is, a spirit of cooperation as opposed to authoritarianism.

THE PSYCHOLOGICAL PROCESSES
OF DICTATORSHIP

These two antagonistic trends of industrialism are, in my opinion, essential for the understanding of modern dictatorship. The authoritarian element facilitates the rise of a dictatorship. But the cooperative aspect forces the dictatorship to find some way of replacing solidarity based on a rational interest (such as class interest) with some other identification that does not undermine but rather strengthens the dictatorship. Mussolini tried corporatism; Hitler, the doctrine of folk-community; Stalin, that of the classless socialist state. But in varying degrees all these identifications were a fake. That they nonetheless "succeeded" leads us to our final problem: the psychological processes connected with dictatorship. The basic problem is anxiety and fear and their function in political life.

Freud has defined anxiety as an "increase in tensions arising from nongratification of [the individual's] need."[4] Anxiety is thus always present—at least potentially—as a situation or a state of indefiniteness. Fear, in turn, is the recognition of a specific danger.

Therefore, external dangers, arising in specific situations and from specific objects, are experienced in the light of internal anxiety, which then becomes externalized and activated.

But this externalization of anxiety through fear is by no means always dangerous to the personality. One may distinguish three functions of fear:

1. Fear as a warning.
2. Fear as protection.
3. Fear as destruction.

Thus, an external danger may well have a kind of monitoring function: it may warn the individual that something terrible may happen to him. And the reaction to the threat may then perform a protective or even cathartic function. It may not only remove the concrete danger, but allay the anxiety as well and thus make the individual more free. On the other hand, fear may activate anxiety (particularly neurotic anxiety) to the point of making it destructive. (Indeed there are psychoanalysts who derive anxiety from destructive impulses.) Hence, in some individuals, fear becoming operative or latent anxiety may either paralyze the personality and make it incapable of defense (depressive anxiety) or heighten its aggressive instincts (persecutory anxiety).

This bare (and rather thin) analysis of certain terms of individual

---

[4] Sigmund Freud, *The Problem of Anxiety,* trans. H. A. Bunker (New York: W. W. Norton, 1936), p. 76.

psychology may now be put to use in understanding the rise of totalitarian movements and the operation of the totalitarian state.

As an illustration let me again take the Spartan state. Plutarch says, ". . . [T]he Spartans dealt with them [the Helots] very hardly: for it was a common thing to force them to drink to excess, and to lead them in that condition into their public halls, that the children might see what a sight a drunken man is; they made them to dance low dances, and sing ridiculous songs. . . ." Then they assassinated them. There is little difference between the Spartan aristocracy's behavior toward the Helots and the Nazis' treatment of the Jews. The ancients were well aware of the fact that the passive element in the Spartan character was fear, that this fear was systematically cultivated and that the Spartans' famous courage in battle was nothing but fear of being stigmatized if they failed in their military duty. The actual or feigned fear of the Helots is the integrating principle of the Spartan ruling class, their anxieties being activated into aggressiveness and destruction. The totally repressive character of Sparta (as compared to Athens) rests precisely in this fact.

In totalitarian movements (as contrasted with totalitarian states), there appears a similar element. A distinction should be made between the Nazi-Fascist movement and Lenin's party prior to 1917. The Bolshevik party at that time was not a totalitarian movement, nor may Lenin (in contrast to post-1928 Stalin) be considered a totalitarian leader. The Bolshevik party then did not manipulate fear; this is a later development which began with the defeat of the revolutionary movements in Western Europe.

In contrast, the Nazi-Fascist movement activated the anxieties of the middle classes and turned them into channels of destruction which were made legitimate by means of the masses' identification with a leader, the hero. The nature of such identification has already been discussed by Freud.[5] This phenomenon appears in all caesaristic and totalitarian movements, in various degrees, of course, and with varying historical functions.

---

[5] Sigmund Freud, *Group Psychology and the Analysis of the Ego*, trans. S. J. Strachey (New York: W. W. Norton, 1949).

10

Tensions in the Bureaucratic-Authoritarian State and the Question of Democracy

Guillermo O'Donnell

CONCERNING THE STATE

The state is fundamentally a social relationship of domination or, more precisely, one aspect—as such, comprehensible only analytically—of the social relations of domination.[1] The state supports and organizes these relations of domination through institutions that usually enjoy a monopoly of the means of coercion within a defined territory and that generally are viewed as having a legitimate right to guarantee the system of social domination. As such, the state should be understood from and within civil society, though in its objective, institutional form it appears to be, and proclaims itself to stand, above society.

Source: Guillermo O'Donnell, "Tensions in the Bureaucratic-Authoritarian State and the Question of Democracy," in *New Authoritarianism in Latin America,* ed. David Collier (Princeton: Princeton University Press, 1980), pp, 286–302. By permission. Article abridged by the editors.

[1] This discussion represents a revision of the conception of the state which was implicit in my essay "Reflections on the Patterns of Change in the Bureaucratic-Authoritarian State," *Latin American Annual Review* 13, no. 1 (Winter 1978), pp. 3–38. I now view this earlier conception as excessively focused on the institutional features of the state. Unfortunately, I can only briefly introduce here the most indispensable elements of this revised conceptualization. For a more complete discussion, see my "Apuntes para una teoría del Estado" (Documento CFDES/G.E. CLACSO/No. 9, Centro de Estudios de Estado y Sociedad, Buenos Aires, 1977).

What interests us here is a type of capitalist state. As such, it maintains and structures class domination, in the sense that this domination is rooted principally in a class structure that in turn has its foundation in the operation and reproduction of capitalist relations of production. These relations of production are the "heart of civil society," within which we view the state as the strictly political aspect of the social relations of domination. From this perspective the state is, first and foremost, a relation of domination that articulates in unequal fashion the components of civil society, supporting and organizing the existing system of social domination. What makes this support effective are certain objective manifestations of the state—its institutions and the law. Yet the true meaning and consequences of these can be understood only in terms of their being the objective manifestations of certain aspects of the system of domination in society.

I wish to stress two interrelated themes regarding the state— first, its analytic reality as the political aspect of certain social relations of domination, and, second, its concrete objectification as a set of institutions and legal norms. By keeping in mind the interrelation between these two faces of the state—analytic and concrete— one can see the falsity of the claim by the state's institutions to embody a rationality that is distinct from and superior to that of civil society, as well as the corresponding falsity of denying the state's fundamental role in articulating civil society in an unequal (or more precisely, contradictory) fashion.

Further, the apparent separation of the institutions of the state from civil society fosters the emergence of diverse linkages or "mediations" between the opacity and fractionalization of that which is "private"—i.e., civil society—on the one hand, and the "public" and universalistic role (for the population within its borders) in which the state institutions usually present themselves to ordinary consciousness. I do not have space to develop here the reasoning that underlies this conclusion, but the state is usually also the organizational focus of consensus within society, from which it derives the basis for its own legitimation. In order to achieve consensus, these institutions must appear as *the* state, as agents of a general interest of a community—the nation—that transcends the reproduction of daily life in civil society. The reification of the state in its institutional objectifications obscures its underlying role as guarantor of domination within society; yet—inasmuch as it implies that state and society appear to be separate—it tends to generate various mediations between them through which consensus tends to be created. The state ultimately is based on coercion, but it usually is also based on consensus, which both encompasses and conceals coercion.

The principal mediation alluded to above is the nation. I mean by nation the collective identities that define a "we" that consists, on the one hand, of a network of solidarities superimposed upon the diversity and antagonisms of civil society and, on the other hand, of the recognition of a collectivity distinct from the "they" that constitutes other nations. The nation is expressed through a dense symbolism epitomized by the flag and national anthem, as well as by an official history that mythologizes a shared, cohesive past and extols a collective "we" which should prevail over the cleavages (not only those between social classes) of civil society.

There are two other fundamental political mediations. One is citizenship, in the double sense of: (1) Abstract equality which—basically by means of universal suffrage and the corresponding regime of political democracy—is the foundation of the claim that the power exercised through the institutions of the state by the occupants of governmental roles is based on the consent of the citizens; and (2) the right to have recourse to juridically regulated protection against arbitrary acts on the part of state institutions. The second mediation is the *pueblo* or *lo popular*.[2] This mediation is based on a "we" that derives neither from the idea of shared citizenship, which involves abstractly equal rights, nor from the idea of nation, which involves concrete rights which apply equally to all those who belong to the nation without respect to their position within society. *Pueblo* and *lo popular* involve a "we" that is a carrier of demands for substantive justice which form the basis for the obligations of the state toward the less favored segments of the population.

Normally, in a capitalist state the subject of the state is the citizen, who has the right, which is not systematically denied, to lodge claims of substantive justice before the appropriate state institutions. Of course, this right is actually limited by the systematic inequalities that arise from the underlying class structure of society and from other forms of social inequality. Nonetheless, this right is partially real, and the belief in its existence is normally an important element of consensus, which entails challenging neither the domination which is exercised in society nor the role of the state as the agent or representative of the general interest of the nation.

The efficacy of this idea of the nation, along with that of citizenship and *lo popular*, allows the state institutions to appear as agents which achieve and protect a general interest—that is, the general interest of a "we" that stands above the factionalism and

---

[2] Translator's note: These two terms are not translated because the most nearly equivalent terms in English, *people* and *popular*, have different meanings. The meaning intended by O'Donnell is indicated in the text above.

antagonisms of civil society. Moreover, the effective functioning—
as an institutional reality and in terms of subjective acceptance
on the part of a large portion of relevant social actors—of the ideas
of citizenship and *lo popular* usually provides a consensual basis
for the exercise of power, and ultimately of coercion, by the state
institutions. They do this because the basis of state power must
appear to reside outside the state itself. The state can only be legitimated by appearing to reside in external referents whose general
interest the state institutions are supposed to serve. These external
referents are normally the nation, jointly with citizenship and
pueblo, which represent the intersection of an abstractly equal "we"
(i.e., citizenship) and a "we" which is concretely unequal (involving
the tutelage of the less favored portion of society, i.e., the *pueblo*).
From these referents there usually emerge collective identities that
stand above the class cleavages that can potentially arise from civil
society. Because the state appears separated from society and objec-
tified in its institutions, these institutions cannot by themselves
legitimate the power they exercise except by means of the collective
referents whose general interests they claim to serve. Each of those
collective referents mediates the relation between the state and
society, transforming its underlying reality; hence their role in
achieving consensus and, correspondingly, in legitimating the power
exercised by the state institutions.

On the other hand, these mediations are the means through
which the social subject, as a member of society, rises above his
private life. Identifying himself in the symbols of the nation, exercising the rights of citizenship, and eventually making demands for
substantive justice as part of the *pueblo*, the social subject transcends his daily life and recognizes himself as part of a "we" which
is, from another perspective, the referent evoked by the state institutions. Hence, these institutions do not usually appear as the organizers and guarantors of social domination, but rather as agents of
the general interests expressed through those mediations. This fact
tends to result in a consensus which expresses the belief that what
the state institutions do and do not do—even though systematically
biased by the underlying system of social domination—is the consequence of the rights derived from being a citizen, as well as a member of the nation and *lo popular*. This tension between the underlying reality of the state as guarantor and organizer of social
domination, on the one hand, and as agent of a general interest
which, though partialized and limited, is not fictitious, on the other,
is characteristic of any state. This tension is the key to the theoretical analysis of the state. We cannot attempt such an analysis here.
Yet by examining certain characteristics of the BA [Bureaucratic-
Authoritarian] state we will be able to see, in a context in which

the above-mentioned mediations are largely missing, their crucial importance in facilitating what is fundamental for any system of social and political domination: to mask the reality of domination and to appear to be the expression of a general, encompassing interest.

Before turning to the main topic of this chapter, I must present other observations indispensable for understanding both the situation prior to the installation of BA and its subsequent impact once installed.

1. In Latin America the formation of the nation was accomplished much more through the mediation of *lo popular* than through that of citizenship. Whether or not it occurred through so-called "populisms," the political activation of the previously marginal popular sectors occurred through political relationships in which they were treated much more as a *pueblo,* as a carrier of demands for substantive justice, than as citizens.

2. This same process of constituting the nation involved the postulation of a "we" that defined itself as an adversary of an "antinational" social order whose most conspicuous components involved the role of transnational capital in the exportation of primary products and the dominant national classes that were more intimately tied to transnational capital.

3. This process contributed to the downfall of the system of oligarchic domination and its replacement by a system of bourgeois domination supported by the expansion of the institutional system of the state which opened the way for the supremacy of transnational capital in the urban productive structure.

4. In the periods preceding the installation of BA, the great advance in the transnationalization of the productive structure led to a fundamental alteration in the nature of civil society in relation to the territorial scope of the authority exercised by the state. That is, many of the principal centers of economic decision making in society, the final destination and criteria for the distribution of the capital generated in the local market, and many aspects of the social relations (not only economic ones) extended beyond the state's capacity for control within the scope of its territorial authority. This "denationalization" was added onto that which had occurred earlier in connection with the exportation of primary products, and now came to affect the most dynamic components of the urban productive and class structure.[3] Other factors that came into play prior to the implantation of the BA state, such as the different

---

[3] The most enlightening contribution on this and related topics continues to be that of Fernando Henrique Cardoso and Enzo Faletto in *Dependencia y desarrollo en América Latina* (Mexico City: Siglo Veintiuno Editores, 1969).

levels of "threat," the interaction between the pattern of economic growth that followed the transnationalization of the urban productive structure and the growing popular political activation, and the severity of the crisis that preceded it, have already been treated elsewhere.[4]

We can now delineate the most important features of the BA state as a starting point for analyzing the contradictory dynamic that is set in motion by its implantation.

THE BUREAUCRATIC-AUTHORITARIAN STATE

BA is a type of authoritarian state whose principal characteristics are:

1. It is, first and foremost, guarantor and organizer of the domination exercised through a class structure subordinated to the upper fractions of a highly oligopolized and transnationalized bourgeoisie. In other words, the principal social base of the BA state is this upper bourgeoisie.

2. In institutional terms, it is comprised of organizations in which specialists in coercion have decisive weight, as well as those whose aim it is to achieve "normalization" of the economy.[5] The special role played by these two groups represents the institutional expression of the identification, by its own actors, of the two great tasks that the BA state is committed to accomplish: the restoration of "order" in society by means of the political deactivation of the popular sector, on the one hand, and the normalization of the economy, on the other.

3. It is a system of political exclusion of a previously activated popular sector which is subjected to strict controls in an effort to eliminate its earlier active role in the national political arena. This political exclusion is achieved by destroying or capturing the resources (especially those embodied in class organizations and political movements) which supported this activation. In addition, this exclusion is guided by a determination to impose a particular type of "order" on society and guarantee its future viability. This order is seen as a necessary condition for the consolidation of the social domination that BA guarantees and, after achieving the normalization of the economy, for reinitiating a highly transnationalized pattern of economic growth characterized by a skewed distribution of resources.

---

[4] Here again, see "Reflections" and the references cited in that article.

[5] I use this phrase to refer to the tasks undertaken by the civilian technocrats in charge of the economic apparatus of BA, whose aim is to stabilize certain crucial variables (such as the rate of inflation and the balance of payments) in a manner that will gain the confidence of major capitalist interests—above all, in the first stage of BA, of transnational finance capital.

4.   This exclusion involves the suppression of citizenship, in the twofold sense defined above. In particular, this suppression includes the liquidation of the institutions of political democracy. It also involves a denial of *lo popular:* it prohibits (enforcing the prohibition with coercion) any appeals to the population as *pueblo* and, of course, as class. The suppression of the institutional roles and channels of access to the government characteristic of political democracy is in large measure oriented toward eliminating roles and organizations (political parties among them) that have served as a channel for appeals for substantive justice that are considered incompatible with the restoration of order and with the normalization of the economy. In addition, BA appears as if placed before a sick nation—as expressed in the rhetoric that derived from the severity of the crisis that preceded its implantation—whose general interest must be invoked; yet, because of the depth of the crisis, BA cannot claim to be the representative of that sick nation, which is seen as contaminated by innumerable internal enemies. Thus, BA is based on the suppression of two fundamental mediations—citizenship and *lo popular.* In an ambiguous way it may evoke the other mediation—the nation—but only as a "project" (and not as an actual reality) which it proposes to carry out through drastic surgical measures.

5.   BA is also a system of economic exclusion of the popular sector, inasmuch as it promotes a pattern of capital accumulation which is highly skewed toward benefiting the large oligopolistic units of private capital and some state institutions. The preexisting inequities in the distribution of societal resources are thus sharply increased.

6.   It corresponds to, and promotes, an increasing transnationalization of the productive structure, resulting in a further denationalization of society in terms of the degree to which it is in fact contained within the scope of the territorial authority which the state claims to exercise.

7.   Through its institutions it endeavors to "depoliticize" social issues by dealing with them in terms of the supposedly neutral and objective criteria of technical rationality. This depoliticization complements the prohibition against invoking issues of substantive justice as they relate to *lo popular* (and, of course, class), which allegedly introduces "irrationalities" and "premature" demands that interfere with the restoration of order and the normalization of the economy.

8.   In the first stage that we are considering here, the political regime of the BA state—which, while not formalized, is clearly identifiable—involves closing the democratic channels of access to the government. More generally, it involves closing the channels of access for the representation of popular and class interests. Such

access is limited to those who stand at the apex of large organizations (both public and private), especially the armed forces and large oligopolistic enterprises.

The characteristics that I have just enumerated permit us to distinguish the BA state from other authoritarian states and to identify shared traits among various cases of BA. These traits in turn interact with other features of BA that differ from case to case. These similarities and differences represent the terrain in which we will place ourselves starting in the next section, which explores some of the basic tensions of BA.

AMBIGUITIES IN THE SYSTEM OF DOMINATION

What goes on behind the imposing facade of power of the BA state? In what way is the imposing rhetoric of its institutions, directed at an ailing nation which the state is determined to save even against its will, a sign of uncertainties and weaknesses inherent in this state? I hope that the discussion of the state presented above will aid us in exploring a reality that is more complex than is suggested by these appearances.

Fundamentally, BA is a type of state which encompasses sharply contradictory tendencies. On the one hand, BA involves the further denationalization of civil society noted above that occurs first as a consequence of the urgent search for the transnational capital which is a requisite for the normalization of the economy, and later due to the necessity of maintaining a "favorable investment climate" in order to sustain the inflow of such capital. At the same time, BA entails a drastic contraction of the nation, the suppression of citizenship, and the prohibition of appeals to the *pueblo* and to social class as a basis for making demands for substantive justice. This contraction derives from the defeat of the popular sector and its allies; from the reaction triggered by the threat that the political activation of this sector seemed to pose for the survival of the basic parameters of capitalist society; and, once BA is implanted, from the aim of imposing a particular social "order" based on the political and economic exclusion of the popular sector.

Such exclusion appears as a necessary condition for healing the body of the nation, an organism with infected parts upon which, for its own good, it is necessary to perform the surgery of excluding the popular sector and its allies. This exclusion involves redefining the scope of the nation, to which neither the agents that promoted this illness nor the parts that have become infected can belong. They are the enemy within the body of the nation,[6] the "not-we"

---

[6] This organic image is, of course, reinforced by the doctrines of "national security."

of the new nation that is to be constructed by the institutions of BA. When the leaders of these institutions speak of the nation, the referent has been restricted, by the very logic of their discourse, to a far less comprehensive "we" than in the past; only those can belong who fit into their design—socially harmonious and technocratic—of the future nation.

On the other hand, like all states, BA claims to be a national state. Lacking the referent of the nation as a universally comprehensive idea that encompasses the entire population, the rhetoric of the institutions of BA must "statize" the meaning of the nation—at the same time that, in relation to the normalization of the economy, the same rhetoric defends an intense privatization. Such statizing of the idea of the nation implies that its general interest be identified with the success of the state institutions in their quest to establish a particular order in society and to normalize the economy. As a result, the state institutions no longer appear to play the role through which they usually legitimate themselves, that of serving an interest superior and external to themselves—i.e., the interests of the nation as a community that encompasses the totality of, or at least most of, the population. On the contrary, when the state institutions attempt to redefine the nation in terms of exclusion and of national infirmity, the power they exercise no longer has an external basis of legitimation and cannot but appear as its own foundation. In other words, domination becomes naked and dilutes its consensual mediations; it manifests itself in the form of overt physical and economic coercion. In addition, the suppression of citizenship, together with the prohibition against invoking *lo popular,* not merely dilutes but radically eliminates other legitimating mediations between the state and society.

Why are these costs incurred, which ultimately involve the prior renunciation not only of the basis of legitimation of the state, but also of the possibility that the system of domination that BA supports and organizes could ever achieve hegemony? To answer this question we must understand that the implantation of BA is the result of a frightened reaction to what is perceived as a grave threat to the survival of the basic capitalist parameters of society. The overarching network of solidarities of the nation has been shattered by a multitude of conflicts. Acute antagonisms have appeared in civil society, involving the emergence of "sectoral egotism" and of the threatening symbolism of class identifications. As a result, the leaders of the BA are not, nor can they see themselves as, the representatives either of this embattled nation or of the antagonisms of civil society. By contrast, their mission is to transform society profoundly in such a way that, in some distant future, the "we" of the nation will be sustained by a utopia of social integration. I have already suggested that the often repeated organic image of the infirm body, which still does not realize that radical surgery is in its own best interest, is also the radical denial of the role of the state as representative of the nation (and society). In turn, the suppression of *lo popular* and of citizenship, along with the elimination of the institutions of political democracy, are the tourniquet that impedes the spread of the poison and gives time for healing. As a result, BA cannot help but abandon the usual referents of legitimation and presents itself instead as the basis of its own power. It thus abandons the mediations which partially, yet effectively, transform the private life of civil society into the shared existence of collective identities through which social actors recognize themselves as members of the nation, as citizens, eventually as part of the *pueblo,* and as being included in a state to which they normally grant the right to rule and coerce.

The institutions of the BA state attempt to fill the void thus created through an intensive use of the martial and patriotic symbols of the nation. But these symbols must be anchored in some of the aforementioned referents if they are not to be merely grandiloquent rhetoric. The BA leaders attempt to recreate mediations with society by inviting "participation"; but the state's denial of its own role as representative of the nation and the elimination of the ideas of *pueblo* and citizenship mean that such participation can only involve a passively approving observation of the tasks that the state institutions undertake.

Under these conditions, the best that can be hoped for is a "tacit consensus," i.e., depoliticization, apathy, and a retreat into a completely privatized daily existence. And fear. Fear on the part of the losers and the opponents of BA, which results from BA's conspicuous capacity for coercion. And fear on the part of the winners, who face the specter of a return to the situation that preceded the implantation of BA. There is also the fear, on the part of those who carry out the physical coercion, of any "political solution" that could possibly lead to such a return; this last fear at times appears to drive them down a path of coercion that knows no limits.

Tacit consensus is a foundation too tenuous to sustain the state. Fear, together with the upper bourgeoisie and the "modern" sectors of the middle class more closely tied to it, are the major social supports of the BA state. But fear hardly serves as an adequate mediation between the state and society. Moreover, the fear on the part of the winners tends to diminish with the passage of time (in spite of efforts to refresh their memory) and with an awareness of the costs imposed on many of them by the continuation of BA.

In reality, the surgery that the higher institutions of the BA state attempt to perform upon the nation inflicts heavy costs on many of those who supported the implantation of BA. The imposition of "order" of course severely punishes the political and class organizations that served as channels for the political activation of the popular sector. The economic exclusion of this sector and the prohibition against raising issues of substantive justice around the symbols of *pueblo* and class make it clear that whatever the BA state may proclaim the nation to be, it does not include the popular sector. Those who were until recently an active political presence are ostracized from their own nation through their political and economic exclusion. On the other hand, the attempts to normalize the economy through a close alliance with the upper bourgeoisie (in the first stage of BA, above all with transnational and domestic finance capital) inflict serious hardships on a good portion of the middle sectors and the weakest (and more indisputably national) fractions of the bourgeoisie. As a result, a rapid contraction of the alliance that supported its implantation takes place in the initial period of BA. The supporters who withdraw from the alliance enter into the "tacit consensus" and engage in a disillusioned defense of their specific interests in the interstices of state institutions. Depending on the lesser or greater degree of previous threat, those who withdraw their support because of the policies of economic normalization may or may not, respectively, combine with the excluded sectors and participate, as in Argentina in 1969, in a decisive challenge to the BA state.[7] In cases of a high level of previous threat in which they do not withdraw, these sectors reinforce the silence and opacity of civil society.

The withdrawal of these initial supporters underscores the fact that the principal (and at that moment virtually the only) base of social support of BA is the upper bourgeoisie—i.e., the upper fractions of the local bourgeoisie and of transnational capitalism. But this is—ostensibly—the principal economic beneficiary of the new situation and the most transnationalized and, therefore, the least national component of society. In light of the economic and political exclusion of the popular sector, the economic hardships suffered by an important portion of the original alliance, the contraction of the nation, and the suppression of the mediations of citizenship and *pueblo*, the BA state remains—and overtly appears to be—sustained basically by the oligopolistic and transnationalized fractions of the bourgeoisie, along with—in its own institutional system—the armed forces and the technocrats who attempt the normalization of the economy. These oligopolistic and transnationalized fractions of the bourgeoisie serve poorly as a legitimating referent for the state because they are the antithesis of *lo popular* and of

---

[7] This and other arguments to which I will refer in the following pages have been presented in greater detail in "Reflections."

the symbolism of the nation defined as a "we" that stands in contrast to the "they" of other nations. On the other hand, the local bourgeoisie hardly provides an adequate legitimating referent for the state either. Though the BA economic policies have variegated impacts on different economic activities, they further weaken the already weak local bourgeoisie, placing part of it among those who are part of the "tacit consensus" and hardly leaving this class in an appropriate position to fill the role of a dominant class whose interests can plausibly be argued by the state institutions to be coequal with the general interests of the nation.

Thus, BA is the negation of the usual legitimating mediations of the state—the nation contracts, *pueblo* and citizenship are suppressed, and the state cannot sustain itself through the hegemonic potential of an unquestionably *national* dominant class. As a consequence, the ultimate basis of the state—coercion—is starkly revealed. In addition, it is evident that BA bestows immense advantages on the most oligopolistic and least national fractions of the bourgeoisie. The effort to saturate the mass media with symbols of the nation therefore fails because it falls into the abyss created by the further denationalization of civil society and the contraction of the nation.

In the face of these dilemmas, one escape might lie in the possibility that the state can convert itself, not only in its discourse but in the reality of its activities, into the institutional center of a national development project which could be invoked as representing the paramount general interest. That is to say, the state institutions themselves would become the economic and social center of such a project, emerging as the leaders of "development" and taking the place of the absent bourgeois leadership. This approach would lead toward state capitalism. Yet this alternative conflicts with the high degree of transnationalization of the productive structure and with the crucial role that private capital, especially the upper bourgeoisie, must play if BA is to endure. It generates ambiguities and tensions, both within BA and with its principal social base, which we will consider below.

On another level, the institutional system of BA reflects the priorities that its own actors set for themselves. The institutions specialized in the use of coercion occupy the apex of this system by virtue of having themselves ended the crisis that preceded BA and because they remain in charge of imposing order and, no less important, of guaranteeing the future effectiveness of this order. At the same time, the task of normalizing the economy is assigned to civilian technocrats closely identified with the upper bourgeoisie and with transnational financial institutions. The technocrats believe in the rationality of economic orthodoxy, know how to apply it, and are

trusted by the local and transnational elements of the upper bourgeoisie. The policies and institutions of the first phase of BA are
organized around these two concerns. The two great tasks of imposing order (with its organizational agent, the armed forces) and of
normalizing the economy (with its social base in the upper bourgeoisie, and its agents in the technocrats who direct it) are institution-
ally inserted into the BA state. As a result, BA cannot but appear
as the transparent conjunction of coercion and economic domination.

These priorities reflect something fundamental which has already
been mentioned, but which I hope we may now understand better.
The implantation of BA is an attempt to salvage a society whose
continuity as a capitalist system was perceived as threatened. This
goal can only be achieved, given the magnitude of this threat, by,
on the one hand, severely imposing "order," and, on the other, by
carefully obeying the rules of orthodoxy upon which the support
of transnational capital and of the most dynamic and economically
powerful fractions of these societies is contingent. These measures,
together with the suppression of mediations and the resulting exposure of the underlying system of domination, are the immense hom-
age which is rendered to the reproduction of society *qua* capitalist.
In the face of the alternative posed by the depth of the crisis that
preceded BA and the accompanying threat, the state is first and
foremost a capitalist state, rather than a national, a popular, or a
citizens' state. Yet the implementation of these measures entails
the immense risk of implanting a state that is incapable of converting itself into the foundation of its own legitimacy. The state must
rely instead on tacit consensus, coercion, fear, and the support of
the least national fractions of its society.

There cannot be consensus unless the connection between coercion and economic domination is veiled. Yet the opposite occurs
in BA. Moreover, in BA the proximity of coercion and economic
domination juxtaposes two social actors—the armed forces and the
upper bourgeoisie—who usually are separated, on a political level,
by the mediations mentioned above and, on the institutional level
of the state, by other institutions of civilian bureaucracy and democratic representation. That is to say, the social basis of BA in
the upper bourgeoisie, their ostensible support for BA, and their
"bridgehead" in the institutional system of the state in the form
of the economic technocrats intersect directly and visibly with the
armed forces. The upper bourgeoisie and the technocrats have a
strongly transnational orientation, both in their beliefs and in
their economic behavior. For them, the political boundaries of the
nation are basically a useless constraint on the movement of the
factors of production, on the free circulation of capital, and on

considerations of efficiency at the transnational level. They also
interfere with the efforts to reintegrate these economies into the
world market in the aftermath of the pre-BA crisis. All of these
aims clash with what is perceived by these actors as the narrow-
ness of the nation and of "nationalism." On the other hand, these
actors are the most fully and dynamically capitalistic members of
these societies. Hence, they are unabashedly motivated by profit,
the driving force behind an accumulation of capital which is
sanctioned by an ideology which claims that the maximization of
profit will, in the long run, contribute to the general welfare.

But a great problem within BA is that the other central actor
in its institutional system—the armed forces—tends to be the most
nationalistic and least capitalistic of the state institutions. With
their sense of mission, the martial values with which they socialize
their members, and their doctrines of national security which pre-
suppose the existence of a nation characterized by a high degree
of homogeneity in the orientations and actions of all civilians, the
armed forces are the state institution most predisposed to define
the nation as that which is *not* foreign, and to define appropriate
behavior as that which is inspired by an introverted and exclusivist
vision of the nation. In addition, the profit motive appears to them
to be of secondary importance, at most, and sordid in comparison
with the larger concerns and ideals that derive from their own
orientations. Profit may be necessary, but in any case it should
not become "excessive" or work against the mission of homogenizing
the totality of the nation.[8]

How is it possible that social actors with such different orientations and values can join together as the principal actors within
the institutions of BA? The answer is that with the legitimating
mediations suppressed—and, of course, pending always the problem
of maintaining the deactivation of the popular sector and the prohibition against evoking *pueblo* and class—economic domination and
coercion tend to become transparently close and mutually support-

---

[8] After closely examining the orientations of the armed forces in the countries
in which BA has emerged, I am convinced that this is a valid generalization. However,
this generalization does not preclude the possibility that in some cases the upper
echelon of the armed forces might be controlled by groups more favorably disposed
toward the orientations of the upper bourgeoisie. This greater affinity would doubtless
mitigate the problems which I analyze below—but it does not eliminate them, since
it seems to mean that the control over the armed forces exercised by this military
leadership will be more precarious. The most important case of such congruence
between the attitudes of high level military leaders and the upper bourgeoisie and
the officials in the economic team of the BA state is that of Castelo Branco and
his group in Brazil, from 1964 to 1967. Another case is that of the Lanusse presidency
in Argentina, from 1971 to 1973. However, in this case it was not the consolidation
of BA that was being attempted, but rather the negotiation of the conditions for
its liquidation.

ive. Particularly after many of the original supporters of BA with-draw to "tacit consensus" (in addition to the initial exclusion of the popular sector), the upper bourgeoisie needs coercion as a guar-antee of present and future social "order," without which it could neither reinitiate accumulation for its own principal benefit nor place its confidence in the future of the economy.[9] On the other hand, without this support and the resulting confidence, a BA state whose alliances have narrowed to such an extent could not even attempt economic normalization and would soon crumble.

In the BA state, economic domination and coercion, along with their social carriers, are mutually indispensable. But this mutual indispensability does not prevent the alliance forged in this way from being marked, on both sides, by numerous tensions. Nor does it prevent the emergence of a desire to reconstitute a system of domination which would again separate these two components by interposing the lacking mediations.

---

[9] These points, including that regarding the importance of the guarantee that both order and the rationality of the management of the economy (from the perspec-tive of the upper bourgeoisie) will be maintained in the future, are dealt with in my "Reflections."

CHAPTER FOUR

Communist Systems

— 11 —

Change in the Soviet Political System

Robert F. Byrnes

Every political system possesses strengths and weaknesses, some inherent in the nature of man, some reflecting the character and traditions of the society, some structural, some temporary and minor, some the price of progress as achievements strain old institutions and practices, some the consequence of reluctance to revise hallowed procedures, some the results of developments beyond the boundaries of the society.

Every political system, whatever its strengths and weaknesses, also undergoes change, some obviously and some imperceptibly, some from deliberate actions and others reluctantly, some because of progress and others because of failure, some through growth and others through decay, some rapidly and some slowly, some at different speeds and often at different directions at different times. In any case, change is everywhere the law of life, in ancient times and in 1984, in capitalism and in socialism, in dictatorship and in anarchy.

One of the principal problems that individuals as well as rulers of a state face is perceiving the need for transformation and directing the pressures for change along directions they consider useful and fruitful, in the short as well as the long run. No one for long

Source: Robert F. Byrnes, "Change in the Soviet Political System: Limits and Likelihoods," *The Review of Politics,* October 1984, pp. 502–15. With permission of *The Review of Politics,* University of Notre Dame. Article abridged by the editors.

can resist forces requiring change without creating the hazard of crisis or of revolution. Similarly, allowing or stimulating over-rapid innovation can damage or even destroy an individual or a society. Intelligent rulers and individuals therefore seek so to accommodate tradition and change as to avoid the need to choose between the disagreeable and the intolerable.

In an open, democratic society, change is constant, even permanent. It ordinarily occurs peacefully and gradually, although often not easily. In a dictatorship or an authoritarian system, some changes bubble from the bottom and percolate throughout the society, but the system restricts and seeks to direct the flow of information and innovation, and major changes require the assent and even the decision of the leader. Introducing change in a controlled society is therefore difficult and complicated. As de Tocqueville noted, "The most perilous moment for a bad government is when it seeks to mend its ways."

The 20th century has produced changes of every kind throughout the world of a magnitude and rapidity never before witnessed. Values, ideas, institutions, traditions, political and social systems, "ways of life," definitions of time and space, relations between the sexes and among the races, even diets have undergone continuous transformation. The most visible and most carefully studied of these changes, but perhaps not the most important, have been the products of political revolution. However, the most enduring have been the consequence of developments such as the spread of education, the rapid rise of population, discoveries in medicine, the revolutions in communication and in transportation, the weakening of some established creeds and the fundamental revival of others, the enormous growth of agricultural production, the waves of the scientific-technical-industrial revolution, and the growing awareness throughout the world of the political freedoms and economic opportunities peoples in the West enjoy.

Every rational person appreciates changes as they affect his daily life and his future role and therefore makes conscious and unconscious accommodations to the innovating factors that concern him. Similarly, every political system must adjust to the often profound problems that changes within its own society and throughout the world create. Some individuals, states, and social systems have not been alert at recognizing the emerging new forces and at introducing changes and have therefore succumbed. Others struggle painfully, tortuously, and successfully to preserve the best and the soundest of the past and to adapt to the future. The effort is and must be constant: revising and expanding an educational system to reflect new values and requirements and then providing interesting opportunities for graduates; establishing a social security system that will meet the demands of a changing population structure without bankrupting the economy or mortgaging the future; revising an economy because of a new product or a competitor in a distant part of the world; developing weapons to ensure security against a frightening challenge; adapting to pressures from hitherto neglected or oppressed minority groups for increased opportunities and greater access to political power. In short, change is everywhere. It is more than ever the law of life. Every individual, every government must respond to new situations, often confronting a need for innovation because successful policies have produced totally different situations.

THE NECESSITY FOR CHANGE IN THE SOVIET UNION

The Soviet Union in the 1980s and beyond as well faces requirements to introduce innovations throughout Soviet society to resolve issues as critical as those Lenin faced in 1921 when Soviet leaders discussed the policies they should adopt when first in power. The eternal pressures for modifying and altering are greater than usual, in part because the second half of the 20th century is an era of such uninterrupted change. The shrinking world of which the Soviet Union is ever more clearly a component part is changing rapidly in many ways, and the Soviet government must to some degree accommodate to these differences if the USSR is to remain a world power. For example, the West does not stand still economically. New industries, new techniques, new combinations of technological advances have revised the competition and require that the Soviet Union modify its economy if it is to remain an effective super power.

Paradoxically, the Soviet Union confronts the need for a number of systemic revisions because its successes in the past two or three decades have created new situations and new challenges. The rapid growth of the economy, the steady rise of the Soviet standard of living, the enormous expansion of every aspect of Soviet military power, the additions to the Soviet empire of territories in Southeast Asia, Central America and Africa, and the unquestioned emergence of the Soviet Union as a global power are remarkable achievements. However, these triumphs have so transformed the Soviet Union and so revised its role in the world that Soviet leaders in the 1980s confront the perils of prosperity or problems that progress itself has caused.

Third, the Soviet government faces a series of cumulative, converging, and interrelated problems, all coming to a point at about the same time and so intertwined that any effort to revise, or any failure to introduce innovation, will reverberate throughout the entire system and at the same time directly affect the Soviet position in world politics. The most important of these are the slowing down of Soviet economic growth and the appearance of systemic problems in the economy; the neglect of the visible and invisible infrastructures, from transportation and housing and education to health care and alcoholism; the collapse of the Communist party in Poland and the inherent instability of communist rule throughout Eastern Europe; and the growing gap in science and technology between the Soviet Union and the West, especially as the West moves into a quite different kind of economy just as the Soviet Union had closed the gap or even assumed the lead in industries now no longer so crucial for a modern state.

A further, increasingly important need is Soviet acceptance of and joining the age of information, which would threaten vital party control over access to information, undermine the foundations of the Soviet system, and greatly revise the Soviet Union's relationships with the outside world. Louis XIV declared that nations touch only at the top, but this century's revolutions in transportation and communications have destroyed that truism, even in an age of censorship and jamming. The Soviet government is struggling, as the tsars did, with the eternal problem of Western influence, trying to borrow on one hand and to keep infection away with the other. It seeks a fire that will not burn. It wishes to be in the world, but not of it.

The age of information, or the "Scientific-Technical Revolution" in Soviet terms, is transforming the West even more rapidly than did the steam and jet engines. Knowledge is becoming the world's most important resource, as agricultural research, atomic weapons and energy, medical science, and discoveries affecting every aspect of life demonstrate. The age of the university, miniature electronics, automatic machinery, computers, and satellites is inevitably a worldwide age. The production of information and the development and manufacture of equipment which creates and distributes knowledge quickly are transforming all Western societies, especially with the advent and use of microcomputers and personal computers. Those states that take advantage of this are becoming stronger. They also open themselves up to ideas from other countries, export their political systems and values and import those of others, develop closer relations with other states, and become increasingly interdependent. A country that maintains a wall with carefully monitored turnstiles, controls the number and use of Xerox machines, prevents or restricts automatic dial telephoning between its own cities, and tries to isolate itself inevitably slips toward decline. It forces itself into an eternally unsuccessful effort at "catching up," against restraints it creates for itself.

Finally, the capacity of the Soviet political system to respond to the demands economic, technical, social, demographic, and political developments place upon it must increase rapidly. Authoritarianism, like all forms of government, possesses some special great strengths. At the same time, it suffers from certain handicaps. One of these is slowness to respond to modifications in a world in which change has paradoxically become the one constant.

In short, the need for innovation, for change is visible: Soviet professional journals and the party press both recognize this. In fact, Western observers of the Soviet system acquire their knowledge of the system's problems as much from the Soviet criticisms as from their own analyses. In addition, Soviet publications abound with remedies for the problems the system faces, except those that affect the political system. The troubles lie in the limitations upon change, some inherent in the Soviet system and the ruling ideology, some reflecting the character and interrelatedness of the problems, and some depending upon the international situation and the way in which the Soviet rulers view this.

THE LIMITATIONS UPON CHANGE

1. One of the most powerful impediments to significant transformation is the primacy Soviet leaders grant to the military forces and to foreign policy that together provide the system its legitimacy and are the main instruments of Soviet power and prestige. This primacy is reinforced by Soviet concern to help prevent a nuclear war by maintaining and strengthening its powerful forces, by demonstrating vigor and resolution, and by using fear of war outside the Soviet Union to weaken the determination of other societies to defend themselves.

The Soviet leaders govern a self-isolated state without free allies in a shrinking world in which most Western European states are allied with the United States and Japan against it and in which the People's Republic of China and its policies play upon the irrational Russian fear of the Chinese. The most vivid nightmare is that the United States, Japan, China, and possibly a unified Western Europe will one day encircle the Soviet Union.

At the same time, Soviet leaders continue to assert the primacy of foreign policy and of military strength because of the bright opportunities the Soviet Union possesses for advantage through meddling or scavenging and through reliance upon its military strength and demonstrated skill in expanding Soviet leverage and influence. Thus, Western Europe lacks the confidence and will for political unity which would make it a world power and transform international politics. It has lost faith in Western superiority and in the American guarantee of peace and security and is vulnerable to outside pressures. This provides the Soviet Union a splendid opportunity for skillful diplomatic and psychological use of their military authority. Areas further afield than Western Europe also offer attractive opportunities. The more than one hundred new countries and some older Third World countries, especially in the Middle East and Latin America, vary greatly, but they are fragile constructs, they suffer from serious maladies, and even with outside assistance they will continue to encounter complicated difficulties in trying to master threats Soviet covert actions raise.

In short, for a variety of fundamental reasons, strong military forces and foreign policy will retain primacy for the Soviet Union, making international innovations of any magnitude almost impossible. The hazards and the opportunities combine to strengthen the view powerful throughout the Soviet leadership that this is not the time to create turmoil within Soviet society by experimenting with significant innovations.

2.   It is difficult to determine the impact of ideology upon those who lead the Soviet Union, but ideological restrictions upon internal change appear powerful. The Soviet leaders remain convinced that the party alone, as the vanguard of the proletariat, has the right and the capacity to define policies and to direct society along the chosen paths. For them, change can proceed only through the party and its central control of planning and management. Reform of or changes within the political system are therefore philosophically unthinkable. In addition, most of the economic changes proposed within the Soviet Union or that Western observers think would be effective would affront and embarrass the ideological foundations of communism by creating some unemployment, inflation, and visible sharp disparities in income and would increase social tensions in a society in which such strains are philosophically impossible.

So far as world politics are concerned, the power of ideology is such that Soviet leaders apparently believe that conflict between capitalism and socialism remains ineluctable, whether the Soviet Union and the United States term the relationship confrontation, containment, detente, peaceful coexistence, or whatever. Ambassador Charles Bohlen foresaw continued tension and hostility so long as Soviet leaders did not determine whether they led a cause or a country. His analysis remains correct.

3.   The third limitation upon change is the character of the domestic issues the Soviet Union confronts and the intricate way in which they are interrelated, as problems are in all advanced industrial societies. These difficulties have deep roots and long histories. Soviet leaders made sporadic and ineffective efforts to resolve them, or at least to reduce their significance, on numerous occasions, espe-

cially late in the 1960s, but reluctance and inability to act then has made them more intractable in the 1980s. In fact, the massive program under Brezhnev to modernize the Soviet economy by importing Western science and technology was in part an effort to evade domestic innovation. It reduced the need, delayed serious efforts to confront it, and contributed to making the concerns far more grave in the 1980s than they were in the 1960s. Unfortunately for Soviet leaders, these cumulative issues have all become critical at the same time and are so closely related to each other that any action to affect one would deeply influence the others and reverberate throughout the entire system.

The most important domestic concern is the slowing rate of growth of the highly centralized, complex economy and the stringencies and difficult decisions this raises concerning the allocation of resources, choices which affect the other issues and influence every part of the political system. Briefly, the Soviet Union now faces a period in which the annual rate of growth of the economy will probably average 2 or 2.5 percent (it was about 2 percent from 1978 through 1982) and may decline to 1 percent and virtual stagnation. The basic reason for the slowdown in industry is overcentralized planning and control: the system's mobilization approach gives little responsibility to managers and even less effective attention to consumers, produces frequent misallocations of resources, encourages inefficiency, makes initiative and innovation hazardous, and neglects incentives. In addition, the growth of the labor supply will continue to decelerate and labor productivity to decline because of insufficient capital investment, poor organization, failure to innovate, restrictions on labor mobility, and, above all, the state's continued inability to provide sufficient consumer goods for an apathetic working class that possesses large savings accounts but nothing to purchase. Most embarrassingly, Soviet agriculture proves less and less capable of meeting consumer demands. It suffers bouts of poor weather, but its problems lie deep in the system, in collectivization and the dead hand of centralized urban control of planning and management. The basic backwardness of rural life, from mud roads to dreadful housing and poor schools to inadequate consumer goods, the exodus of the young to the cities, and the aging of the agricultural labor force have all contributed to low productivity of farm labor.

A second crucial domestic concern is the need to repair the infrastructure of the social system, which resembles that which Russia's greatest historian ascribed to an earlier era, when the state had reached great power through policies that exhausted society. Thus, housing has not yet reached the standard for cities that the Soviet government established in 1928. The government has so neglected

health care that the infant mortality rate is now triple that in
the United States and is among the highest in the world. The mortality rate for males between the ages of 20 and 44 is so high that
the average life expectancy of males has declined from 66 in 1966
to 62 in 1982. The society emphasizes science and education, but
higher education is expanding so slowly that only one of seven who
are qualified is allowed to enter that coveted avenue to upward
mobility.

Unfavorable demographic trends have also become a serious issue. The state's reduced ability to achieve economic growth by inject-
ing new millions of laborers into the industrial system combines
with other demographic and political factors to create annoying
and potentially critical problems. Thus, the birth rate among non-
Russians in central Asia is two and one half times that of the peoples
in the Baltic and Slavic republic. This affects the determination
of investment priorities and constitutes a sensitive political subject.

Soviet culture remains formal, rigid and intolerant. Many distinguished artists and writers now live abroad, and Soviet culture
still suffers from the silence Isaiah Berlin noted more than 25 years
ago. The growing influence of the outside world has deepened awareness of this and created a malaise evident everywhere, in party
programs, the media, pulp literature and popular culture.

Social controls of all kinds have weakened, and civic morale has
declined. Abundant evidence demonstrates a loss of faith in the
system, the growth of cynicism at every level of society, nostalgia
about the heroic past and pessimism about the future, disinterest
in Marxism-Leninism and approved social values, emphasis upon
personal concerns, alcoholism, widespread corruption, and the vast
spread of a second economy, another form of corruption.

Another internal need is the inherent, growing instability of Eastern Europe, which the Soviet rulers consider an essential part of
their system. Much of this instability derives from a history that
30 or 40 years cannot overcome, but communist rule, anti-Soviet
nationalism, ineffective policies, food shortages, glaring corruption,
and political incompetence have enlarged it. The social and cultural
tensions which have developed in the Soviet Union have bubbled
in Eastern Europe too, only with greater visibility and effect. In
this critical area, Poland plays the central role it has often played.
The collapse of the Polish communist organization, except for the
central apparatus, and the conditions of the Polish economy illustrate the instabilities which wrack this explosive area. Poland constitutes a cancer that the Soviets may freeze into temporary remis-
sion but one for which even a miraculous economic renaissance
would provide no solution.

In short, a series of critical, interrelated domestic problems face the Soviet leaders. Every considered solution to one problem creates other issues which delay or prevent a decision. Thus, few problems receive greater attention in the media than alcoholism, yet the government has reduced the price of vodka, and the social and medical costs of this "opiate of the proletariat" continue to rise. The state's monopoly of the production and sale of vodka and state income from the tax on hard beverages produce about ten percent of the government's income. Moreover, drinking does serve a political purpose in a boring society by stupifying men and women who might otherwise demand more social activities or become interested in the need for change, even in the political system.

Increasing investment in the consumer goods industries to stimulate industrial productivity would directly affect the resources available for the military and investment, while increasing investment to stimulate growth, unleash new energy resources, develop new territorial complexes, and restore neglected infrastructures would force the leaders to reduce or freeze military spending or consumer goods production or both. Similarly, Soviet approval of some modification of the structure of Polish industry through decentralization of controls and some liberalization in the production and sale of consumer goods would increase pressures for sweeping changes in Poland, elsewhere in Eastern Europe, and perhaps in the Soviet Union itself. Allowing the Polish government to honor its 1980 agreements concerning trade union and other rights would unleash popular forces in Poland and would threaten Soviet control over Poland, its main approach to Germany and to Europe. Indeed, the Czechoslovak "spring" of 1968 and developments in Poland in the last decade have clearly hindered efforts at innovation within the Soviet Union because of the manner in which they alarmed Soviet rulers about the probable consequences of innovation, once launched in even the most innocent and responsible way.

4. Another limitation upon introducing change or innovation in the Soviet Union, one that most observers neglect, is the character of Soviet society, one of the principal goals and achievements of more than 60 years of communist rule. After generations of indoctrination and control, of centralized decision-making and management, of rewards for conformity and harsh penalties for inventiveness or independence, energizing such a society and encouraging initiative and individuality is a most difficult task, even though thousands of Soviet citizens are bursting with ideas and eager to help resolve the problems they recognize. No authoritarian government can expect to overcome years of encouraged inertia and passive acceptance of authority by encouraging its people to respond quickly to permission or even to an order to innovate. Moreover, it could hardly expect its thousands of officials suddenly to abandon their

beloved authority. Moreover, everyone knows, or at least suspects, that the hundred flowers that would bloom after such an opportunity or injunction would soon face wintry blasts from those in power fearful of all change and frightened by its first appearance.

5. The principal and abiding opponent of innovation is the system itself, the most conservative one in the world and the one least tolerant of change: the party sees innovation as a potential challenge to its ideology and control, and *control* remains the most vital word in the communist vocabulary. Basically, those in power are committed by their concern for personal security and power, by their essential philosophy or ideology, and by their view of the world situation to defend their preceptorial role and to oppose any innovation that might challenge their absolute authority. The system is immobile, frozen, and resistant to change. It lacks a reform mechanism that those who seek innovation can utilize. In fact, the way in which influence groups and bureaucracies instinctively unite to preserve their vested interests is the exact reverse of a reform mechanism. In addition, the leaders, planners, managers, workers, intellectuals, the subsidized, the fearful—all the millions who benefit from communist rule—are not only reluctant to accept new policies but are positioned to hamper even the most skilled and resolute rulers who seek change.

THE POSSIBILITIES FOR POLITICAL CHANGE

The Soviet leaders in the 1980s and 1990s, and sooner rather than later, must decide whether and how they can alter the political order in ways necessary to make the established society work effectively under greatly changing national and international conditions. The major questions are simple. Can a narrowly constituted political elite comfortable in the security of its achievements and power and reluctant to face the hazards of change move innovatively to meet potential threats of stagnation, instability and decline? Can it preserve the system and at the same time satisfy the apparently inexorable flowering of forces that seek change? Can it choose wisely between the disagreeable and the intolerable?

On one hand, the concatenation of these questions and the requirement to transfer power from the Brezhnev-Andropov-Chernenko generation to a new man and a new generation provide the Soviet party a splendid opportunity to introduce revisions into the system. On the other hand, dislocations at the top and the new uncertainties make innovations more difficult than even ordinarily.

The Soviet press provides abundant evidence that the leaders are aware of the character of the central issues facing them, particularly the economic and social ones. It also indicates that suggestions for changes, particularly within the economy, flow freely among Soviet specialists on the economy and that the leaders are aware both of the need for change and of the limitations against innovation. They need only agreement, will, and skill in enforcing their orders to jolt the system into a number of new approaches.

*   *   *   *   *

However, the thorny nature and interrelatedness of the problems, the primacy of foreign policy and of military authority (which is likely to grow), the effect of years of communist rule upon Soviet society, and the character of the system, suggest that far-reaching innovations within a decade are unlikely. Chernenko and his successors will almost certainly talk a great deal about the need for dramatic change and about specific experimental innovations, reshuffle administrative agencies, and use public relations abroad to persuade some foreign observers that the Soviet system is slowly accommodating itself to the problems their successes and their failures have created. However, the power of the system is such that they are likely to concentrate upon law and order, labor discipline, Soviet nationalism (and the threat foreign enemies pose), negative incentives, and cultural isolation. In short, corrections, not major changes, muddling through, or muddling down, are most probable, with somewhat more effective increased repression.

I think modification of the political system most unlikely. The most probable changes are those that affect the economy but do not threaten ideology or the political controls communists consider crucial. In some ways, the Soviet Union in the 1980s confronts a situation like that in 1921. Chernenko or his successors might therefore adopt Lenin's New Economic Policy of that time, with Lenin's mantle enveloping it, maintaining control of the "commanding heights" and encouraging experiments in those parts of the economy most important for the consumer, by encouraging private service shops in the cities, retail trade in some light consumer goods, family units and links and larger private plots in the countryside, especially near the cities, and increased foreign trade. The party would retain absolute control of the heights, especially over access to information, heavy and military industry, foreign policy, foreign trade, and the entire political apparatus. Such an approach would reduce the most acute pressures, impress foreign opinion, which the Soviet leaders must see as eager to believe in the system's mellowing and moderating, and provide time for continued study of other approaches that would somehow preserve the communist system and at the same time eliminate both the problems all advanced industrial countries and those that authoritarian states in particular confront.

In sum, the Soviet Union's need to restructure its economy and its political system increases constantly. The visible signs of life beneath the crust are coming to the surface, but resistance to change is powerful and determined. Corrections and minor repairs in the economy are likely, in part because they are relatively easy to manage without affecting the structure and the political system and in part because the benefits would accrue quickly. The likelihood that the Soviet leaders will rejuvenate and restructure the political system is remote, because such change threatens the establishment, its values, and its control in the short run and because the long-term hazards to the core of the system are so great. Developments in Poland in recent years demonstrate that a communist leadership can adamantly refuse to adapt, even when the situation is desperate.

The longer the leaders delay basic changes, the more difficult such changes will become. Continued inaction would ensure stagnation in the Soviet economy, but not in military power. This would not lead to deterioration or collapse, because the Soviet Union has strong foundations and both the system and the people are stubborn and adaptable. But the Soviet Union in the 1990s would survive as a strong state with ever declining economic power and attraction.

Outside actors can exercise little or no direct influence upon how the Soviet government chooses to manage its internal affairs. The United States and its allies should at least recognize the character of the challenge the Soviet Union presents as well as those that it faces and should remain prepared to use their considerable strengths at appropriate times to contain Soviet power. If the world outside the Soviet empire should descend further into economic and political disarray, the incentives for the Soviet leaders to modify their internal system and to moderate their ambitions abroad would correspondingly decline. On the other hand, if the Western allies should succeed in improving the quality of life in their societies and in establishing consistency and coordination in their foreign policies, they might be able to nudge the Soviet Union into policies that make the system more tolerable for its citizens and less threatening to the world.

12

China's Political Evolution

Michel Oksenberg and Richard Bush

In the past decade, but especially since Mao Zedong's death in 1976, the Chinese political system has experienced a spectacular sequence of events: the arrest of Mao's wife Jiang Qing and her associates in the "gang of four," one month after his death; the return to political power of Deng Xiaoping in mid-1977, a reversal of fate after his removal but 15 months earlier; the proclamation by Premier and party Chairman Hua Guofeng in early 1978 of the ambitious goal of transforming China into a modern state by the year 2000; the quiet abandonment of these unrealistic targets 10 months later, although the leaders still remained committed to rapid economic growth and openness to the outside world; the normalization of relations with the United States in late 1978; the incursion into Vietnam in late February 1979; the political experimentation epitomized by the "democracy wall" movement in the spring of 1979; the sharpening tension between Hua Guofeng and Deng Xiaoping; the erosion of Hua's position as well as the purge of Politburo members who had advanced during the Cultural Revolution; the proclamation of sharp economic retrenchment and the postponement of several multimillion-dollar import purchases in December 1980; the major reassessment of Mao Zedong in June 1981, which enumerated his many policy errors while reaffirming the essential wisdom of

Source: Michel Oksenberg and Richard Bush, "China's Political Evolution: 1972–82," *Problems of Communism* (September–October 1982), pp. 1–19. Reprinted by permission. Article and footnotes abridged by the editors.

his beliefs; the replacement of Hua as party chairman by Hu Yao-bang and as premier by Zhao Ziyang in 1980–81, thereby marking Hu and Zhao as Deng's chosen successors; a major shake-up of personnel in the party and state structure in early 1982; and finally, the 12th Congress of the Chinese Communist Party, in September 1982, which consolidated the gains of the previous three years in establishing a more durable political order.

Quieter developments have also occurred. Seven deserve to be specially emphasized:

- The strategy of economic development was changed. The leaders have cut the rate of capital accumulation sharply and allowed the nation's wage bill to increase. Furthermore, they have sought to alter the balance among heavy industry, light industry, and agriculture, moving away from the Stalinist emphasis upon heavy industry toward light industry. Within agriculture, cropping patterns have been changed to boost production of crops used in light industry.

- The methods of organizing agricultural production have undergone sweeping change. The incomes of peasant households in many regions are now based on the crops raised on specific plots of land assigned to the households. The institutions which directed peasant activity (commune, production brigade, and production team) have had their powers significantly curtailed. Changes of equal magnitude are being attempted in industrial management, although the obstacles in this area may be greater.

- The country has been opened to foreign commerce and foreign influence. Special economic zones now exist as a means of encouraging investment in China, and foreign firms enjoy special privileges. Foreign books in translation, classical and popular music, films, and clothing styles—all controlled and in limited scope, to be sure—are now available.

- Class labels and other terms of opprobrium (e.g., "landlord," "reactionary," "rightist") are being removed from several million Chinese. The government has promised to restore these people to their previous positions and, in some cases, has offered restitution for the damages they suffered.

- A major corpus of laws and regulations has been enacted which offers some promise of making life for Chinese more just and predictable. This includes criminal, civil, marriage, and tax laws.

- The government has vigorously encouraged family planning. Major programs have been enacted to achieve the goal of the one-child family.

- A growing energy problem has arisen due to a levelling-off in coal and petroleum production. Energy shortages now constitute a major brake on rapid industrial expansion.

Without denigrating the importance of these developments, this essay eschews a focus on either the factional power struggles or the specific economic and legal reforms. Instead, we wish to step back and to ask questions about the decade 1972–82, from the eve of Mao's decline to the arrangement of an initial succession after Deng. How does the Chinese political system today differ from that of a decade ago? What remains the same? More important, why the changes? Has the system reached an equilibrium point? Are aspects of the Maoist system that have been abandoned likely to be restored? Is the political evolution of the past 10 years likely to continue?

Our core argument can be summarized succinctly. During the decade under scrutiny, China passed a watershed. In 1972, totalitarian revolutionaries ruled the nation; by 1982, China's rulers had become authoritarian reformers. The totalitarian revolutionaries had acted upon their belief that rapid, violent, and comprehensive transformation of elites and institutions was the most effective mode of change. The leaders had unleashed upon society and themselves a reign of terror. They had constructed a totalitarian regime which sought to deny privacy or cultivation of individuality in society. They expected all citizens, especially those in urban areas, to express their belief in the integrating ideology of the regime, to participate in political life, and to surrender their individuality to a collective identity.

By contrast, in 1982, the top Chinese leadership appears to be committed to gradual and peaceful change within a framework of continuity of elites and institutions. The leaders have shifted their emphasis in implementing policy from mobilization of the populace to action through the bureaucracy. They have also sought to end the terror. While seeking orthodoxy to which all intellectuals and creative artists are expected to adhere, the authoritarians do permit individual silence and a limited withdrawal or distancing from politics. Also, orthodoxy is less well defined and broader in scope.

Being authoritarian, to be sure, China's leaders today maintain extensive surveillance over the population and tolerate no organized opposition or challenges to their rule. They value hierarchy and discipline and are not hesitant to employ force in ordering their realm. Yet, individuals may cultivate personal pursuits and are encouraged to plan their careers. The current leaders no longer measure their own performance by their progress in nurturing a new "socialist man" or in creating a classless society. Instead, they wish their performance to be judged by their ability to improve the material well-being of the populace.

This evolution can be attributed to several interrelated factors. The passing of Mao and the advent of a leadership group who had suffered during the Cultural Revolution is a key factor. More than personnel changes at the top are involved, however. The developments in China bear a great resemblance to trends in other societies after sustained periods of terror and politically induced social change. The case of the post-Stalin Soviet Union and the Khrushchev era comes immediately to mind. Yet, societies can manifest different types of Thermidor, and China's post-Mao moderation reveals the reassertion of certain deeply rooted traditions which the Maoist system had challenged. China's evolution since Mao's death represents the continued adaptation of Communist revolution to the Chinese cultural context.

We note that the process of domesticization has not yet ended. In some respects, the present reforms are not fully congruent with some aspects of the cultural heritage. Furthermore, certain bureaucracies of the Maoist era remain strong and resistant to change, while power is still vested as much in people as in institutions. Finally, China is undergoing massive economic changes, and the exposure to the outside world will also have its impact. For all these reasons, we conclude that the Chinese political system has yet to reach an equilibrium, and further evolution can be anticipated.

THE MAOIST SYSTEM BEFORE ITS DECAY

. . . As its principal architect, Mao had designed a system that supported not only his power needs but also his larger goals for China in the late 1960s, and his strategy for attaining those goals. Put in its best light, the policy process which Mao shaped through 1972, when for the last time it escaped his control, had this rationale.[1] It was meant to downplay economic interdependence among regions, the national use of material rewards, and the regular, formal promotion system as the best means of preserving China's unity. Instead, Mao relied on coercion and the propagation of a single ideology as his principal instruments for integrating his heterogeneous nation. To be sure, the central economic agencies retained a role in redistributing resources from the more developed

---

[1] See Stuart Schram, "Introduction: The Cultural Revolution in Historical Perspective," in *Authority, Participation and Cultural Change in China,* ed. Schram (Cambridge, Cambridge University Press, 1973), pp. 1–108; and John Bryan Starr, *Continuing the Revolution: The Political Thought of Mao* (Princeton: Princeton University Press, 1979).

to the less developed regions of the country, a process which may have reduced interprovince tensions and promoted unity. Nonetheless, in terms of allocating power among the organizational hierarchies in China, Mao assigned primacy in integrating the society to the propaganda apparatus, the public security forces, and the military. With Mao's proxy, those who presided over these hierarchies wielded great power.

The emphasis on the inculcation of values was related to the diagnosis of the major impediments to China's modernization made by Mao in his later years. Mao always had been sensitive to certain deeply ingrained cultural attributes which seemed to him inimical to China's modernization. These were fatalism, passivity, familialism, a preference for harmony and the avoidance of conflict, and a disdain for physical labor. But after achieving power in 1949, Mao chose to give more emphasis to the establishment of an economic infrastructure as the prerequisite for China's growth. Hence, he embraced the Stalinist development model, with its emphasis on steel, machine-building industries, and energy production. Then, in the late 1950s and early 1960s, Mao increasingly concentrated on institutional issues: the role of the party, the creation of rural communes, and the refinement of campaigns as a technique for implementation of policy. But from the early 1960s until the end of his life, Mao considered the attitudes of Chinese bureaucrats and the populace generally to be the major impediment to China's modernization. Hence he launched a *cultural* revolution. Mao had concluded that a new culture would emerge only through the deliberate fostering of class struggle, pitting portions of the populace against his own bureaucracy. By the mid-1960s, Mao had also decided that many of his associates and their subordinates were beyond salvation and were unworthy of succeeding him. Not only a cultural revolution but a massive purge of the unredeemable was necessary in his view to keep China on his path to modernity.

Similarly, Mao came to view the organizational web of party, government, and armed forces as an inherently conservative repository of the values he was seeking to eradicate. Distrustful of bureaucracy, he sought ways of administration which minimized its role. Hence, his attraction to campaigns *(yun-dong)* as an alternative mechanism of policy implementation. With the encouragement of his more radical supporters, especially Zhang Chunqiao, Mao deliberately promoted a primitive economy. His demand for maximum local self-sufficiency, the restrictions on the number of commodities that could be traded on the regulated free market, and his simultaneous curtailment of the capacity of planning agencies to allocate goods according to plan—all sought to minimize commerce and the division of labor in society. To bring about such an unstratified social and economic structure, Mao realized, would require enormous change. Thus, instead of the incremental, inherently cautious, fragmented decision making which a bureaucratic policy process tends to yield, Mao sought sweeping, bold, utopian policies that a mobilization system is more likely to engender.

Mao sought a system in perpetual change. According to his dialectic and idealist vision of history, thesis could be turned into antithesis, which in turn would become synthesis. What appeared irreconcilable today could be reconciled tomorrow. To name Mao's three favorite polarities—discipline and freedom, centralism and democracy, a general will and the individual spirit—they were viewed by him as equally desirable but contradictory qualities at this stage in history. However, Mao thought that wise leaders could drive their society forward, raising the material standard of living and altering the consciousness of the populace. Ultimately, the polarities could be reconciled in a classless, abundant society, provided that the greatest threat to the attainment of this vision—the calcification of the social structure—was overcome.

This brings us to the core of Mao and the policy process he structured. As noted earlier, he was to the end of his life a revolutionary and a totalitarian ruler. He believed that the only way to transform China was rapidly, violently, comprehensively; its elites and institutions would have to be subjected to continual change. China's problems were so vast that efforts to attain peaceful, gradual change could not be sustained and would eventually be lost in the morass of bureaucracy. In his view, to transform China required vision and extraordinary confidence that a politically involved Chinese populace—given no respite to cultivate individual pursuits—could overcome its plight of poverty and weakness. To unleash portions of the populace in all their fury required leaders capable of interacting directly with the forces in society without mediation by intervening bureaucracies. Mao saw little intrinsic value in institutions like the party, government, or army. They were to serve as instruments whose credibility and authority could be expended in his larger effort to transform China into a strong, prosperous, socialist nation.

EVOLUTION OF THE SYSTEM, 1972–82

Since early 1972, the Chinese system has evolved through several stages: (1) a concerted effort to restore order and to rebuild institutions based on an amalgam of pre-1966 and Cultural Revolution values, a period lasting until late 1973; (2) an unbridled struggle for political survival and succession to Mao, from late 1973 to October 1976, when the "gang of four" were arrested; (3) a period of uncertainty lasting until mid-1978, with some of the leaders seeking to establish a neo-Maoist system; (4) introduction of broad institutional reforms and a moderation and rationalization of economic goals, a stage that began with the emergence of Deng Xiaoping as the dominant political leader in mid-1978; (5) from late 1980 to mid-1982, the appearance of resistance to reforms and the resultant efforts by Deng and his associates to weaken and remove the points of resistance.

September 1971–August 1973. Mao sought to preserve his rule and surmount the Lin Biao affair by incorporating the two principal factional groupings—led by Zhou Enlai and Jiang Qing respectively—that had supported him in the attack on Lin. Mao turned to Zhou to create order out of the economic chaos, but he gave preeminence to the "radicals" in the cultural domain to preserve his ideological gains of the previous five years. As the military's role in civilian institutions declined, the rebuilding of the state and party apparatuses began, and a number of supposedly chastened "capitalist roaders" returned to help staff them (the most prominent returnee was Deng Xiaoping, who first reappeared in public in April 1973). They began to work with officials who had come to the fore during the Cultural Revolution.

This modus vivendi in personnel was accompanied by an attempt in a range of policy areas to introduce more pragmatic methods while retaining Cultural Revolution values. In industry, for example, limited material incentives were introduced, although mobilization continued to be used to stimulate output. In the educational sphere, examinations were reintroduced to judge the academic competence of students, even though ideological considerations remained important in the admissions process. In design, the policy process remained Mao-centered; in fact, the physically declining Chairman was unable to achieve the coherence he sought or to control the conflict he had built into the system.

September 1973–October 1976. In the wake of the Tenth CCP Congress in August 1973, struggle between the Zhou-Deng and Jiang factions intensified, each side trying to secure advantage for the day that Mao died. (The military and public security factions maneuvered on the sidelines.) Each faction offered competing programs for China's development. Each tried to put through its policy in various sectors. And each seemed to enjoy moments of political ascendancy: the Jiang forces during the first half of 1974 (the "Criticize Confucius-Criticize Lin Biao" campaign); the Deng forces from late 1974 to late 1975 (under the slogan of the "four modernizations"); and the radicals again from late 1975 until Mao's death in September 1976 (a period in which the more pragmatic policies were again set aside). The three years of unabated conflict left behind a weak and largely ineffective political system that had come to rely very heavily on coercion.

October 1976–October 1978.   After the euphoria that ensued from the arrest of the "gang of four" had somewhat abated, a long list of neglected economic problems came to attention. It became clear that, without major changes in the policy process, the nation would meet with disaster. The disparate groups that had combined to oust the radicals attempted to work together (as had been the case after the Lin Biao affair). Neo-Maoists, led by Hua Guofeng, and the pragmatists who supported the newly rehabilitated Deng Xiaoping could agree on the priority of economic growth and the need for some ideological liberalization in the fields of science, education, and culture. Material incentives and the purchase of foreign technology were again deemed acceptable. A mere 18 months after Mao's death, this leadership presented an ambitious program in pursuit of the "four modernizations" (in agriculture, industry, national defense, and science and technology).

However, the coalition was inherently unstable. The neo-Maoists were willing to accept modernization, especially when described as "a new leap forward." But they were less prepared to accept dilution of Maoist values or methods of rule. With Hua Guofeng as their principal spokesman, the neo-Maoists essentially advocated continuing the mobilization process, sustaining class struggle, propagating Mao's ideology, and implementing policy through campaigns. The pragmatist camp believed that Maoist values and Mao's style of rule were at the root of China's problems. They also judged that nothing less than an open attack on Mao was necessary to regain popular support. Also, some of Deng's followers came to question whether the leadership had the resources, institutional capacity, and popular support to pursue a policy of forced-draft industrialization. After some fencing over these issues during the spring and summer of 1978, the leadership dispute came to a head in December at the Third Plenum of the CCP Central Committee. In the streets of Beijing, an increasingly bold public began writing posters which attacked the Cultural Revolution and Mao.

November 1978–November 1980.   Both in China and abroad, the Third Plenum is now regarded as the crucial watershed of the post-Mao era. It was at that session (and the central work conference preceding it) that Deng Xiaoping unquestionably gained the upper hand in China's leadership. His colleagues living (Chen Yun and Peng Zhen, for example) and dead (Peng Dehuai, Tao Zhu) were rehabilitated. The case of Liu Shaoqi was reopened, and he was rehabilitated in February 1980. The neo-Maoists came under attack, historical verdicts on such issues as the Tiananmen Incident were reversed, and an evaluation of Mao was promised.

Equally important were the new directions charted for the country's institutional life. In law, politics, and economics, liberalization would, it was predicted, have a positive, energizing effect and engender popular support for the regime. In this spirit, the Third Plenum promised that "socialist modernization" was China's long-term priority, and that mass political campaigns and all that came with them were no longer appropriate. In order to promote "socialist legality" and limit police abuses, the criminal justice system was reformed, and economic laws were drafted. To promote "socialist democracy," direct popular vote was mandated for the election of delegates to county-level people's congresses, and plans to end the rubber-stamp nature of the National People's Congress were circulated. Life tenure in office, perceived to be the root of many of the problems of the late-Mao era, came under attack. Even the closing of Democracy Wall and the later ban on wall posters constrained but did not reverse this democratizing trend.

In addition, a major shift in economic policy became apparent especially after Chen Yun, an economic specialist and a top party official in the 1940s, joined the Politburo Standing Committee in December 1978. This "readjustment" entailed the abandonment of the investment policy stressing high rates of accumulation and development of heavy industry. It also entailed a "restructuring" in the Soviet-style system of central control, in the direction of allowing greater play of market mechanisms.

December 1980–Spring 1982. By late 1982, the institutional reforms and related policies had achieved success in some areas (for example, boosting agricultural production and peasant income), but fostered difficulties on other fronts (for example, generating inflation and a large government deficit). These economic difficulties prompted the declaration of a policy of economic retrenchment in 1980. Perhaps equally unsettling for the leadership, however, were the political and ideological repercussions of reforms. In 1979, elements of the public began to question the necessity for one-party rule and the socialist system itself, while in 1980, the leadership began to perceive a disruptive Western impact upon Chinese thought and behavior.

Indeed, Deng Xiaoping and Chen Yun themselves concluded that reform of institutions without a workable national consensus on ideology would not succeed. The issue was widely discussed during 1981, in the context of an evaluation of the filmscript "Unrequited Love," written by Bai Hua, who worked in the military's large cultural establishment. The film's sympathetic portrayal of a Chinese intellectual victimized during the Maoist era epitomized for the more orthodox party officials the damaging effects of cultural freedom. The leadership tried to disarm the critics with a rebuke of Bai Hua and a general attack on "bourgeois liberalism." In this context, the official verdict on Mao, adopted at the Sixth Plenum in June 1981, was less condemnatory than it might otherwise have been. In the absence of a clearcut ideological alternative to Mao's thought, the Deng regime had to soft-pedal its criticism of Mao the man in order to be able to espouse elements of his thought.

Writers and artists were not the only group affected by the new stress on values and ideology. Focusing on poor preparation of the party cadres, Chen Yun termed the problem of party work-style a "life-and-death matter," and a drive against economic crimes by officials began in early 1982. Young people were told more and more frequently that a "spiritual civilization" must accompany material progress. Fearing "the corrosive influence of capitalist ideas," the regime tightened restrictions on contacts between Chinese and foreigners.

In short, the parameters of institutional reform were more clearly etched. The Chinese system would remain highly centralized and authoritarian. The Communist party would retain its monopoly of power and be revitalized in order to perform well its distinctive role. The instruments of totalitarian rule—the public security forces and the propaganda apparatus—would be curbed but not dismantled. The economy would remain largely under state plan; the role of the market would be secondary. Within these constraints, the Maoist system would be significantly altered.

THE SYSTEM IN 1982

The tortuous path of development from 1972 to 1982 reveals that no single vision of rule—and certainly not Mao's—guided China during the entire decade. Differences existed among the leaders on many issues. Moreover, the twists and turns in policy suggest that the same leaders, even Deng Xiaoping, changed policy positions as they confronted new problems, learned new lessons, and faced shifting constellations of opponents. . . . In spite of all this, one can say that since 1978 an effective consensus has existed among the top leaders concerning broad political and economic objectives and the major methods to achieve them.

The dedication of the leadership to the attainment of a strong and prosperous China is as firm as that of Mao. However, their appraisal of the disastrous consequences of the Great Leap Forward and the Cultural Revolution, as well as their sensitivity to the excesses of the anti-rightist and rectification campaigns of 1957—which Deng himself had helped direct—caused them to depart sharply from Mao's view of the way to achieve the goal.

Instead of seeking to unite China primarily through coercion and propaganda, they encouraged unity through increased economic interdependence among regions, through reliance on effective, planned allocation of material goods and capital, and through a regularized promotion and personnel management system. The immediate bureaucratic beneficiaries of this emphasis were the leading economic agencies—the State Planning Commission, the Ministry of Finance, the People's Bank of China—and the central agency responsible for managing a regular personnel system, the Organization Department of the Chinese Communist Party (CCP). The losers were the Propaganda Department of the CCP, the Ministry of Public Security, and the military. Billboards that once displayed Mao's sayings now advertise various merchandise. Tens of thousands were released from the labor camps of the public security apparatus, while millions more lost their "labels" and ceased being under continual supervision by the public security forces. The military lost many of its privileges and suffered a reduced budget. Abandoning Mao's totalitarian demand for the positive involvement of everyone in politics, Deng has been willing to permit individuals to withdraw from politics and to pursue their private interests, be it careers or avocations, and to create works of art, provided these do not exhibit opposition to the rule of the party.

Deng and Chen saw the need for regularity and predictability. Their pledge has been: no more campaigns, no more Maoist dialectical swings between periods of mobilization and stability. The goal has been steady rule through a professional bureaucracy, untainted by corruption and personal ties. The object has been to eliminate the immobilism, the factionalism, and the reliance on personal ties (guan-xi) in the bureaucracy which had thrived during the Cultural Revolution. The establishment of the Academy of Social Sciences and the reestablishment of professional associations are intended to generate a more empirical policy process and to encourage greater communication among professionals working in different units or systems (xi-tong).

To guard against bureaucratism in the pejorative sense, the leaders have reestablished the disciplinary control commissions within the party that existed in the 1950s and again during the post-Great Leap Forward recovery. They have sought more vigorous monitoring of the bureaucracy through elected congresses. For a brief span in 1978–79, they encouraged open petitioning over accumulated grievances, in mid-1979 permitting petitioners to assemble at the entrance to Zhongnanhai (the state and party headquarters) and in late 1978 and the spring of 1979 sponsoring the Democracy Wall. They assigned close aides to high positions on newspapers and gave them a mandate to undertake investigative journalism. They saw expansion of the marketplace as a further check on bureaucratic slothfulness. There was even discussion in those heady days of 1979 about establishing a bicameral legislative system, with invigorated minor democratic parties playing a serious political role in the revitalized Chinese People's Political Consultative Conference. They have given considerable publicity to many cases of corruption and abuse of power and have punished the offending bureaucrats.

The major immediate objective domestically has been to improve the standard of living of the populace. Deng, Chen, and their associates clearly felt that the justification of party dictatorship and socialist rule in China rested on the party's ability to improve the welfare of the people. In this regard, performance in the past has been lackluster: the average income, diet, or availability of material goods in 1977 were hardly better than in 1957. Without improvement in the quality of life, the leaders believe, the Chinese people would not embrace more advanced socialist or collectivist forms of social organization. Deng and his associates also have envisioned a more lively, diversified cultural life than the narrow range of theater, literature, and movies offered in Mao's last years. In short, the reformers have staked their popular standing on improving the material and cultural quality of life in China now and have promised a more abundant tomorrow. Mao had avoided basing his legitimacy on such tangible promises and, except in 1955 and 1958, tried not to arouse expectations about a more abundant life in the near future. Deng and his associates have felt it necessary to do so in order to restore morale in the country and reestablish the confidence of the populace in the efficacy of their government. Only in this way, they believe, can China's major problems of productivity and modernization be solved.

When one looks at the program of reform espoused by the present leadership and at their strategy for implementing it, one has to conclude that the leadership has already succeeded in changing the system significantly from what it had been in 1972. First, China has begun to recover from the trauma of the Cultural Revolution and its aftermath. Though this is very difficult to judge, it does seem that the totally benumbed quality of much of the populace has begun to disappear. To be sure, cynicism and apathy are widespread, especially in urban areas. Some of the enthusiasm and optimism for the "four modernizations" generated among the urban intellectuals in 1978–79 appear to have dissipated. Nonetheless, the current leaders seem to have inspired some popular confidence in their capacity to steer a steadier course toward gradual economic growth. The fears of a return to the excesses of the Cultural Revolution so prevalent in 1976–78 appear to be subsiding. The leaders probably have done much to restore their ability to rule effectively, though they have yet to regain the power and authority which the system enjoyed in the 1950s.

China today has collective rule, in contrast to Mao's one-man rule. To be sure, Deng has enjoyed periods where the initiative was almost totally his; nonetheless, no one ruler can bend the entire system to his will, as Mao was able to do on many occasions. One cannot envision Deng, Chen, or any ruler at this stage being able to launch a Great Leap Forward or a Cultural Revolution as Mao did. The legitimacy of the regime is not rooted in the thought and writings of a single leader, as in the Maoist era. Most major decisions in China today appear to be based on the building of a consensus within the Politburo and Secretariat, and—in a formal sense—even minor decisions frequently require the approval of several members of the State Council's Standing Committee.

Power still appears rooted more in people than in institutions, and indications remain of factional alignments at the top. Nonetheless, factional strife has been dampened; it is no longer a Hobbesian struggle for survival. Progress has been made in rebuilding institutions. The streamlining of the State Council in early 1982, the drafting of the 1982 state constitution, and the restructuring of the apex of the party apparatus at the 12th CCP Congress represent major steps in this process. Appointment of Zhao Ziyang as premier and Hu Yaobang as party general secretary, as well as the anticipated naming of a head of state—i.e., a chairman of the People's Republic—will also contribute to the institutional revival. A smoother succession can now be anticipated following the deaths of Deng and Chen than occurred in 1976 when Zhou and Mao died. The leaders have begun to reveal how their policy process actually works—how documents are drafted and issued, how leaders live and work, how meetings are convened. Furthermore, they have begun to obey the rules governing the stages through which discussion of policy ought to proceed before a policy is formally promulgated.

Yet, certain aspects of the system remain the same. Different factional groupings on the Politburo and Secretariat still have their distinctive sources of power in the capital, based in different organizational hierarchies. *Guan-xi* networks of people still link leaders in Beijing to provinces, counties, and primary units. The power of middle-level bureaucrats remains intertwined with the waxing or waning influence of their bosses and protectors. Many bureaucrats continue to believe that the single most important factor determining their fate is the political strength and interest of the State Council Standing Committee member responsible for their agency.

Yet, in terms of the principal mechanisms for integrating the country, major changes have occurred since 1972. In Mao's last years, China's essential unity, severely tested to be sure, was retained primarily through coercion, the propagation of ideology, and the personal ties linking individual leaders in Beijing to leaders in different parts of the country. By 1982, the economic planning apparatus had been substantially reestablished, fiscal and monetary controls had been revitalized, and a national personnel management system, with promotions and dismissals based on merit, had begun to be restored. Meanwhile, the range of responsibilities of both the military and the public security forces has contracted. In particular, the public security forces have lost their direct control over millions of people previously in labor camps or under surveillance because they were charged with being one of the "five black elements." The establishment of a judicial system and procuracy and the proclamation of legal codes offer hope that some checks would eventually exist on the powers of the police. With the acknowledgment that Mao's body of writings was germane to his time, had to be reinterpreted to suit new conditions, and contained flaws in any case, no identifiable, authoritative, current doctrine prevails on which behavior has to be firmly based. . . .

Three additional developments have accompanied and undergirded the reemergence of the economic bureaucracies. First, campaigns as an alternative mode of policy implementation have been essentially abandoned. Since the death of Mao, the Chinese have not been subjected to one hallmark of the Chairman's rule: the designating of a particular task or set of tasks as central; the organization of ad hoc committees to direct the campaign, staffed by bureaucrats seconded to the committee; the supply of study documents to enlighten the populace about the campaign's objectives; and the struggle against people whom the ad hoc committees identified as obstacles to the campaign—all done in an atmosphere of frenzy. The campaigns totally disrupted bureaucratic routine, as budgets and personnel were altered. Perhaps no other development so clearly accounts for the reassertion of bureaucratic rule as does the abandonment of campaigns.

A second development has been some progress in rebuilding the state statistical network. . . .

The third development was the amelioration of tensions within the bureaucracies. From 1972 to 1976, the "cultural revolutionaries" and the rehabilitated "capitalist roaders"—the tormenters and the tormented—worked side by side in the various agencies. Since 1978, those officials who had risen during the Cultural Revolution have

TABLE 1
Evolution of the Chinese Political System, 1972–82

Attribute of the System	In 1972	In 1982
Method of change preferred by leader(s)	Revolution	Reform
How leader(s) view process of change	Dialectical	Linear
Preferred method of policy implementation	Mobilization of populace; class struggle	Rule by bureaucracy; regularity
Intrusiveness of state	Total	Pursuit of some private interests and withdrawal tolerated
Main tasks of governance	Restoration of order; attitudinal change; elimination of lingering bourgeois influences	Raising economic production and living standards
Mechanisms for integrating the policy	Networks of personal relations; coercion; ideology	Networks of personal relations; regularized personnel system; planned allocation of material goods and capital, coercion
Techniques for controlling "bureaucratism"	Campaigns	Experimentation with numerous techniques, none successful
Extent of "institutionalization"	Low; rule of men rather than institutions	Low; major efforts under way to rebuild institutions
Nature of politics at top level	Unbridled factionalism below top leader	Struggle among factions and opinion groups governed by unwritten rules
Rule at top	One-man rule	Collective leadership
Empirical bases of decisions	Prior preferences demonstrated in model units	Investigation; statistical compilation; model units
Popular confidence in political system	Low	Somewhat improved
Dominant organizational hierarchies	People's Liberation Army, public security forces, party Propaganda Department	Party committee chain of command, party Organization Department, State Planning Commission, Ministry of Finance, army, public security forces

been gradually weeded out, while more of the officials who had been purged have returned to office. Of course, a renewal of fragmentation among the top leaders could revive intra-agency strife around Cultural Revolution cleavages. However, personnel changes, new issues, and somewhat dimmed memories, as well as greater leadership cohesion at higher levels seem to have dampened animosities within agencies. This generalization does not apply to all agencies. Bureaucracies which were at the vortex of the Cultural Revolution—for example, the ministries of Culture and Education—manifested more evident scars than those which were either totally destroyed and had to be rebuilt (e.g., the Statistical Bureau), or which had been somewhat isolated from the turmoil (e.g., some of the machine-building ministries).

The developments from 1972 to 1982 we have sketched can be summarized in tabular form (see Table 1). Though the table is oversimplified, it vividly underscores the considerable change over the decade. The extent of the changes immediately raises two questions: Why did the changes occur? Will they endure?

CAUSES OF CHANGE AND ITS DURABILITY

Three interrelated factors help to explain the evolution of the system: the change in the top leaders, the course of revolution, and China's specific development problems. The human factor is the passing of Mao and the rise of Deng and Chen. Many of the changes only took place after Mao's death, the arrest of his principal allies in revolution, and the subsequent eclipse of his lingering beneficiaries (e.g., Hua Guofeng). The Chinese system remains one which reflects the aspirations and techniques of rule of the top officials. To that extent, the system will continue to evolve and take on the coloration of Deng's and Chen's successors.

A second, more systemic factor is also at work, namely, the course of any totalitarian revolution.[2] The reform-oriented, institutionalized polity which had begun to emerge by 1982 bears a great resemblance to the Chinese system which was making its appearance in the mid-1950s and then again in the early 1960s, after the Great Leap Forward campaign (1958–60). By launching the Cultural Revolution in 1966, Mao sought to postpone in China the inevitable aftermath of revolutions—be they in France, Russia, Germany, Cuba, or Vietnam—that is to say, the strengthened grip of bureaucracy over society. Mao deliberately sought mechanisms to keep

---

[2] On this topic, see Crane Brinton, *The Anatomy of Revolution* (Englewood Cliffs, N.J.: Prentice-Hall, 1965). See also Robert Tucker, *Marxian Revolutionary Idea* (Princeton: Princeton University Press, 1969), pp. 172–214.

society in constant turmoil so as to prevent a bureaucratic domination in China.

Nevertheless, it appears as though societies reach a limit beyond which they do not welcome turmoil and become exhausted by it. Problems of legitimacy and compliance come to the fore as the leaders must grapple with a cynical, disenchanted population which has been coerced for too long. Yet, upon closer examination, no revolutionary or totalitarian regime has followed exactly the same path. What is common among totalitarian regimes, as Richard Lowenthal has noted, is their

> call for mobilization to be directed toward development of one sector [of the nation], while totalitarian instruments of control and repression are used to demobilize the other sectors. . . . Herein lies the dilemma of the totalitarian regime that has successfully mobilized its system's assets to attain a single developmental objective. . . . Its very success has led to mounting pressures to bring the system into balance, to allow development in the hitherto unauthorized areas; yet, if it does so, it will be sanctioning the end of the revolution from above, the end of the movement toward the goal culture.[3]

Lowenthal's insight implies that the post-totalitarian phase in each case will be a specific reaction to the particular emphases of the mobilization effort. In sum, since each revolutionary effort to transform a society has its own emphasis, it will leave its own particular legacy. For this reason, while focusing on the post-Mao era, this essay laid initial stress on Mao's goals and techniques of rule. To an extraordinary extent, the pressing problems now, even six years after Mao's death, are precisely the ones Mao neglected as he directed the nation's energies elsewhere. The contours of the 1982 political system are, to a considerable degree, a reaction to the Maoist system. The political institutions and process Deng and his associates have called into being have been designed to cope with the particular set of problems Mao had neglected and thus bequeathed to his successors:

- Lagging agricultural production.
- An inefficient industrial system.
- High unemployment among youth.
- A low standard of living.
- Widespread apathy and cynicism.

---

[3] Richard Lowenthal, "Development vs. Utopia in Communist Policy," in *Change in Communist Systems,* ed. Chalmers Johnson. (Stanford: Stanford University Press, 1970), p. 14. See also David E. Apter, *The Politics of Modernization* (Chicago: University of Chicago Press, 1965), esp. chap. 10, and Seweryn Bialer, *Stalin's Successors* (New York: Cambridge University Press, 1980), especially pp. 5–62.

- An inadequate scientific and technological manpower base.
- Specific bottlenecks in transportation, communications, and energy.
- An unacceptably high rate of population increase.

So pressing are these problems and so seemingly supportive to their solution is the political system Deng, Chen, and their associates have designed, that the observer might be tempted to assume that rationality has prevailed and an equilibrium may have been reached. Such a conclusion is unwarranted on several grounds.

To begin with, the major instruments of totalitarian rule have been weakened but not eliminated. The military, the public security forces, and the propaganda apparatus have yet to acquire roles in domestic affairs commensurate with the objective resources under their command. They are potentially destabilizing institutions and focal points of resistance to the system which Deng and Chen have forged.

In addition, the current system and set of policies generate their own, new set of problems, and it is not yet clear that the Deng-Chen system is capable of handling these problems. . . .

Another potential source of instability stems from the promise the leadership has made to raise the standard of living of the populace. From 1978 to 1982, real income has gone up dramatically for many, particularly in the countryside, and moderately for others, especially in the cities. Not only have wages gone up, but construction of housing has increased significantly, as has the production of many consumer durables (watches, bicycles, portable radios, television sets, etc.). The slightly more affluent urban Chinese populace is beginning to press upon scarce leisure-time facilities, such as theaters, parks, and sports grounds. Therefore, questions remain. Are expectations rising more rapidly than the expansion of consumer goods industries? Is it in fact wise to stimulate support for the regime through such a heavy reliance on material incentives? What might happen if the economic strategy does not succeed, the growth rate falters, and standards of living stagnate? In that case, the fundamental stability of the Chinese regime would not necessarily be at stake, but many of the changes made since 1972 would be threatened, particularly in the relative importance of various bureaucracies and the mechanisms for integrating the society.

In addition to the leadership, the natural course of totalitarian revolutions, and the concrete problems facing the Chinese leaders, another consideration bears mention in explaining the change from 1972 to 1982 and in assessing the future: Chinese cultural traditions. One way of looking at the last years of Mao and the post-Mao era is in the light of China's cultural heritage. In many respects, what has transpired is a reassertion of certain dominant strands in the Chinese tradition. In particular, as W. Theodore deBary has argued, the two dominant models of rule in China have been harsh dictatorship or benevolent but still authoritarian bureaucracy, with the latter being more common through the centuries.[4] Ironically, the Cultural Revolution helped revive the traditional culture it had been intended to destroy. The harsh dictatorship under Mao strengthened people's desire to confide in those whom they trusted, i.e., those with whom they shared ties. Thus, the immediate family in many ways became more important; school, native place, or early career connections became tickets to survival. The disillusionment with the formal Maoist ideology led to increased interest in traditional religion, especially Buddhism and Taoism. Thus, what makes current China at least superficially resemble the imperial system is the twin reassertion of formal bureaucracy and the informal means (especially use of *guan-xi* and the prevalence of factions) for coping with the state.

The present leadership swiftly jettisoned those aspects of the Maoist system which ran especially counter to the dominant strands in the Chinese tradition. These were its denial of the cultivation of individual pursuits, its emphasis on class struggle, and its extreme denigration of bureaucracy and hierarchy. To be sure, such concepts as "privacy" and "individualism," so central to Western political thought, were not well developed in the Chinese tradition; on the other hand, notions of "withdrawal," "quietude," and particularly, "self-cultivation" were quite well developed. Not privacy but scholarship, meditation, and detachment were esteemed values, and rule which prevented cultivation of talent—poetry, painting, carving of seals—was threatening to culture and the attainment of virtue. Mao's fostering of struggle also ran counter to a deeply ingrained preference for harmony. Campaigns and the brawling that accompanied them brought disorder instead of the preferred regularity and order.[5]

To the extent that the Deng-Chen system represents a reassertion of "Chineseness," several exceptions must also be noted: collective leadership, the idea of linear progress, the downplaying of ideology, and the empirical basis of policy choice. Let us briefly identify each

---

[4] See DeBary's contribution to *China's Future and Its Implications for U.S.-China Relations,* Occasional Paper No. 2, Washington, D.C. East Asian Program, The Wilson Center, August 1980, pp. 1–11.

[5] On these points see Donald J. Munro, *The Concept of Man in Contemporary China,* (Ann Arbor: University of Michigan Press, 1977); and Richard H. Solomon, *Mao's Revolution and the Chinese Political Culture,* (Los Angeles: University of California Press, 1971).

of these very complicated matters. When unified, China always has had a single, discernible ruler. It remains to be seen if a system of shared power will work. The traditional Chinese view of history being cyclical has more in common with Mao's dialectic conceptions than with the current leadership's notions that progress can be gradual and evolutionary. As to ideology, in the absence of extensive, formal religion, the state always played a major role in the inculcation of morality; this had a major role in helping unify the country. The current system would seem to leave a vacuum in the propagation of a unifying, coherent set of beliefs.

Turning to epistemological matters, the current leaders are trying to build methods of research and analysis derived from Western social sciences into the empirical procedures of the bureaucracy. Many students of China would argue that these methods are antithetical to dominant Confucian precepts: the view that most facts are infused with values and hence that truly "neutral" social and policy sciences cannot be developed; the preference to learn through the emulation of models rather than through the understanding of scientific principles. It remains open to question, therefore, whether the current effort to develop an empirically based policy process will really succeed.

Deng and his associates seem to have rekindled the century-old debate over how best to root the quest for modernity in the nation's intellectual heritage. In fact, as Benjamin Schwartz has stressed, it is incorrect to speak of a single or even dominant Chinese intellectual tradition.[6] Rather, aspects of Confucianism, legalism, Buddhism, and various popular religions offered China's rulers a diversity of traditions upon which to draw. The real question was which of these diverse strands should be combined with which Western ideas to create an ideological amalgam suited to Chinese needs. China's rulers and their thinkers were confronted by a series of dualities each of which was sustained by an eclectic mixture of Chinese and Western thought. Among these polarities spurring debate were:

- The notion that societies can be egalitarian versus the notion of a hierarchical natural order.

- The notion that hierarchy is inevitably oppressive versus the idea that hierarchy is essential for order and the attainment of morality.

---

[6] Benjamin Schwartz, *In Search of Wealth and Power: Yen Fu and the West*, (Cambridge, Mass.: Harvard University Press, 1964), and his "Some Polarities in Confucian Thought," in *Confucianism in Action*, ed., David Nivison and Arthur Wright (Stanford: Stanford University Press, 1959), pp. 50–62.

- The view that only external controls can order a society versus the idea that fostering of virtue in each person is the requisite for order.

- The notion that China can attain modernity through self-reliance and exclusion of the outside world versus the belief that the West and Japan have much to offer.

- The belief that mankind can swiftly create a utopian community if properly motivated versus the view that economic conditions basically shape the social structure and that economic conditions can be changed only gradually.

- The belief that theory—abstract knowledge—is acquired in practice versus the notion that theory can arise from reflection.

The distinctive and complex response to each of these polarities which was provided by Mao became the official ideology of the nation.

The reassertion of "Chineseness" in post-1976 China has meant a partial return to examining these polarities in ways which had absorbed Chinese intellectuals before 1949. To be sure, the precise terminology and the centers of gravity have changed in the intervening years, thus revealing the impact of Marxism-Leninism and Maoism. But the polarities that are being explored and the syntheses that are being sought echo the debates of an earlier period.

As we have already noted, Deng and his associates have exhibited an ambivalent attitude toward renewed intellectual ferment. On the one hand, they acknowledge its necessity since Mao's prescriptions seem inadequate for dealing with China's current problems. On the other hand, they fear that the ferment will escape their control—with unpredictable consequences. No matter what the ideological proclivities of the leaders, they are unlikely to be able to provide the same continuity and coherence in ideology that Mao had achieved. Until a consensus on ideology exists, it is improbable that China's political system will be fully stable.

13

Communist Political Cultures

Gabriel A. Almond

A TEST OF POLITICAL CULTURE THEORY

The success or failure of communist regimes in transforming the attitudes and behavior of populations may constitute a test of the explanatory power of political culture theory.[1] We may view communist regimes as "natural experiments" in attitude change. Such regimes seek and usually succeed in establishing organization and communication media monopolies, as well as penetrative police and internal intelligence systems. Ideological conformity is rewarded; deviation is heavily penalized. Communities and neighborhoods come under the surveillance of party activists. Children of all ages are organized in party-related formations, and school instruction places emphasis on appropriate ideological indoctrination. In addition to this powerful array of institutional and communication controls, the communist movement has a clear-cut, explicit set of attitudes, beliefs, values, and feelings that it seeks to inculcate.

Political culture theory imputes some importance to political atti-

Source: Gabriel A. Almond, "Communism and Political Culture Theory," *Comparative Politics* 15 (January 1983), pp. 127–38. Permission to reprint by *Comparative Politics,* © The City University of New York. Article and footnotes abridged by the editors.

[1] This is a position argued by a number of British specialists on communist countries. See Archie Brown and Jack Gray, *Political Culture and Political Change in Communist States* (New York: Holmes & Meier, 1977); also, Stephen White, *Political Culture and Soviet Politics* (New York: Macmillan, 1979). We have benefited greatly from these studies and conclusions.

tudes, beliefs, values, and emotions in the explanation of political, structural, and behavioral phenomena—national cohesion, patterns of political cleavage, modes of dealing with political conflict, the extent and the character of participation in politics, and compliance with authority. Political culture has never seriously been advanced as the unidirectional "cause" of political structure and behavior, although political culture theorists have been represented as taking such a position by some critics.[2] The relaxed version of political culture theory—the one presented by most of its advocates—is that the relation between political structure and culture is interactive, that one cannot explain cultural propensities without reference to historical experience and contemporary structural constraints and opportunities, and that, in turn, a prior set of attitudinal patterns will tend to persist in some form and degree and for a significant period of time, despite efforts to transform it. All these qualifications and claims are parts of political culture theory. The argument would be that however powerful the effort, however repressive the structure, however monopolistic and persuasive the media, however tempting the incentive system, political culture would impose significant constraints on effective behavioral and structural change because underlying attitudes would tend to persist to a significant degree and for a significant period of time. This is all that we need to demonstrate in order to make a place for political culture theory in the pantheon of the explanatory variables of politics.

The communist experience is particularly important as an approach to testing political culture theory because from one point of view it represents a genuine effort to "falsify" it. The attitudes that communist movements encounter in countries where they take power are viewed as false consciousness—whether they be nationalism, religious beliefs, liberal-pluralistic views, ethnic subcultural propensities, or attitudes toward economic interests. These attitudes are viewed as the consequences of preexisting class structure and the underlying mode of production, as transmitted by associated agents of indoctrination. Communist movements either eliminate or seek to undermine the legitimacy of these preexisting structures and processes and replace them with a quite new and thoroughly penetrative set. If they succeed in some reasonable length of time— let us say, a generation—in transforming attitudes in the desired direction, we might conclude that political culture theory has been falsified, that it is a weak variable at best.

---

[2] See Brian M. Barry, *Sociologists, Economists, and Democracy* (London: Collier-Macmillan, 1970), pp. 48ff.; Carole Pateman, "The Civic Culture: A Philosophical Critique" in *The Civic Culture Revisited*, ed. Almond and Verba (Boston: Little, Brown, 1980); and Ronald Rogowski, *A Rational Theory of Legitimacy* (Princeton: Princeton University Press, 1976).

Surely communist takeovers are the best historical experiments we have for these purposes. In addition, there are quite a few of them; they have occurred in different cultural-developmental settings; and most of them have been in operation for a generation. The principal problem with this approach to testing theory is that it leaves much to be desired as an experimental test. The "laboratories" are not open to investigators; the data are spotty and in large part inferential. And finally the scale and the intensity of the efforts undertaken to change attitudes have varied from one country to another. The experiences of Poland, Hungary, and Czechoslovakia are quite different from those of the Soviet Union, Cuba, and Yugoslavia.

One further intriguing point about this topic is that it represents a good illustration of a payoff for theory derived from area case studies. From this point of view the reader should not expect a contribution to the depth of knowledge about an area but an exploitation of findings in an effort to develop theory.

POLITICAL CULTURE THEORY IN MARXISM AND LENINISM

This utilization of communist experience to test political culture theory fits congenially into the great themes of Marxist and Leninist ideology. . . .

. . . The phenomena of political culture have been accorded an important place in communist theory, although the terms employed by Marx, Lenin, and contemporary communist scholars are ideology, consciousness, spontaneity, economism, and the like. In the works of Marx and Engels, political culture phenomena are important intervening variables; in Lenin's political culture—in particular, elite political culture—is the independent variable. Indeed, an elite possessed of a particular political culture in the sense of an indoctrinated communist party and an "objective revolutionary situation" very broadly defined are the necessary and sufficient conditions of communist revolution. No one can read Lenin's organizational text, *What Is to Be Done,* without becoming aware of how much importance he attached to the proper indoctrination of the communist party, the unambiguous explication of beliefs, procedures, and appropriate affective modalities.

For Marx, a changed political consciousness was a consequence of underlying structural alterations—it developed gradually at first and changed its cognitive content and affective tone as the means of production and class characteristics and relations changed. Marx predicted that at certain points in the historical process, for example, at the point of extreme proletarian "immiseration," the cultural transformation would be more rapid. Although the concepts of political socialization and elite political culture are present in Marxism, they are not well developed. According to Marx, capitalist ideology gradually loses its force as its deviation from reality becomes increasingly plain. Men are rational actors; the leaders "catch on" first, the followers soon after. The transformation of political culture occurs in bursts and is congruent with major structural changes—the dictatorship of the proletariat, the introduction of socialism and of communism. The learning process may be slow, but it is sure.

Marxism is thus a structural theory. Marx would probably have sided with Brian Barry, Carole Pateman, and Ronald Rogowski about the priority of structure in the causal interaction with attitude, belief, and feeling. Changes in culture follow inevitably from changes in structure; cultural properties have a consequential relation to structure. Attitudinal variables explain *lead* and *lag* in the processes of historical change and hence may be viewed as intervening rather than independent variables.

It is clear from the Leninist strategy of elite and mass political socialization that Lenin understood the interactive character of structural-cultural relationships. He believed in the possibility of indoctrinating a revolutionary elite, in other words, transforming its political culture. But he did not believe that the revolutionary indoctrination of the masses was possible. Ordinary workers and peasants had to be manipulated into revolution by appealing to their immediate values and interests; that is, the revolutionary elite would have to adapt their revolutionary tactics to the cultures of the masses. Lenin expected that once a revolution had been attained these subcultural tendencies among the workers, peasants, ethnic, and religious groups would persist for some unknown length of time until the communist millennium, which would be brought about by fundamental structural changes. . . .

POLITICAL CULTURE IN COMMUNIST REALITY

If we turn from ideological formulations to the political reality of Eastern Europe, the picture we get of political attitudes and values is a complex and varied one. We may perhaps distinguish three versions of political culture in communist countries: (1) the official or ideological political culture that is a mix of exhortation and imputation, (2) the operational political culture or what the regime is prepared to tolerate and believes it has succeeded in attaining, and (3) the real political culture based on evidence such as opinion surveys and other kinds of research or on inferences drawn from the media or official statements. The distinctions among these three versions of political culture need to be elaborated. All communist regimes have some version of the Leninist ideological culture, although in those countries that made their own revolutions (e.g., Yugoslavia, China, and Cuba), the political culture may deviate from the ideal model, from the Soviet version, and from the versions in those countries dominated by the Soviet Union. The operational political culture consists of values, attitudes, and feelings that the regime is prepared to tolerate at least in the short run, given the universal shortfall from the ideological model in all communist countries. This operational model may encompass the extreme of Hungary, where Kadar's slogan of the 1960s, "He who is not against us is with us," represents a substantial admission of defeat in efforts undertaken to produce positive culture transformation, to the situation in the Soviet Union, where the operational expectations are a good deal more positive and are in part supported by reality.

The difference between what is sometimes called the operational political culture and the real political culture is defined in a sense by the battleground between the regimes' immediate campaigns and efforts to change attitudes, behavior, beliefs, and the affective tone of the population. From this point of view we can argue that Kadar's slogan is an acknowledgement that the Communist party of Hungary had failed to falsify political culture theory or that the "Czech Spring" is dramatic evidence of a similar sort that a score of years of organizational and media monopoly, repression and terror, and powerful incentives had failed to alter in any significant degree the civic propensities of the Czechoslovak population. Insofar as the operational political culture itself acknowledges the resistance it is encountering and in the degree that it has lowered its sights from some reasonable approximation of a Marxist-Leninist culture, we can argue that political culture theory survives unfalsified. If in addition evidence of a direct sort points to the fact that attitudes and beliefs among the population fall significantly short of this official operational political culture, then we have even stronger confirmation of the validity of political culture theory.

The ideological political culture in every communist country posits an ideal communist man who is both the builder of the new society and a product of its institutions and practices. The fullest elaboration of the qualities of this ideal communist man is to be found in the Program of the Communist party of the Soviet Union adopted by the 22d Congress in 1961, in a section entitled "The Moral Code of the Builder of Communism." Some version of this moral code (or something very similar in the values and qualities stressed) is to be found in a central place in the most important ideological formulations, training manuals, school books, and the like of all the communist countries. The qualities stressed include "dedication to the Communist cause; love for the socialist motherland and other socialist countries; conscientious labor for the good of society; a high consciousness of social duty; collectivism and comradely mutual assistance and respect; moral integrity in public and private life; intolerance of injustice, dishonesty or careerism; friendship and brotherhood with the other peoples of the USSR, and solidarity with the workers and peoples of other countries; and firm opposition to the enemies of communism, peace and freedom."

The evidence does not suggest that any of the communist regimes has succeeded in inculcating these values among significant parts of the population. Even in the Soviet Union, where the regime has been in substantial control of the population for two full generations and where the revolution was led by an indigenous elite, the extent of success in remodeling man has been relatively modest. Samuel Huntington's claim that the Soviet Union is a dramatically successful case of planned political culture change would seem to be exaggerated.[3] This is not to argue that there have been no positive accomplishments in culture change. The Soviet regime has widespread legitimacy; its centralized, penetrating, and relatively unlimited institutions are accepted. A diffuse notion of socialism has widespread validity, and the acceptance of the obligation of sociopolitical activism in the sense of participating in campaigns has strong and widespread support. But these limited successes in the center of the communist world hardly extend into the countryside, into the blue-collar, relatively uneducated working class, or into the non-European parts of Russia. It can be argued that particularly in Asiatic Russia, where traditional-religious attitudes and ethnic nationalism display considerable staying power, Soviet indoctrinators have had to come to terms with stubborn traditionalism of various kinds.[4] Much of the legitimacy of the Soviet regime, one writer argues, results from the fact that the structure of the Soviet system is very much like the preexisting tsarist one in the sense of centralization, the extensive scope of government, and its arbitrariness. The acceptance of socialism as well as the obligation of sociopolitical activism is the success story of communist political socialization, but these attitudes tend to be concentrated in the European center and among the educated, professional, and white-collar strata of the population.[5] Political activism in this context should not be confused with civic and political participation; instead, it takes the

---

[3] See White, *Political Culture and Soviet Politics*, pp. 114 ff.

[4] Ibid., p. 95; See also Gregory J. Massell, *The Surrogate Proletariat: Moslem Women and Revolutionary Strategies in Soviet Central Asia, 1919–1929* (Princeton: Princeton University Press, 1974), pp. 322 ff.

[5] White, *Political Culture and Soviet Politics*, chaps. 3 and 4. For a detailed analysis of participation in the Soviet Union, see Theodore H. Friedgut, *Political Participation in the USSR* (Princeton: Princeton University Press, 1979), chap. 1 and pp. 307 ff.

form of mobilized activity and voluntary public service. One writer has described Soviet participation in the following terms: "The many political and administrative activities in which Soviet citizens participate take place within a dual framework of control. The hierarchical structure of the Soviets, and of the Soviet political system in general, serves to coordinate the agenda and priorities of the participatory organs at any given moment, concentrating them on centrally determined goals, while the supervision of Communist party organs provides control of staffing, leadership selection, and auditing of the quality of activities."[6]

This contrast between the ideological and the operational political culture creates a certain tension among communist ideologists and students of public opinion and the media of communication. With the introduction of public opinion research in the Soviet Union and Eastern Europe in the 1960s, the problem of opinion and attitude differences had to be confronted, for it produced a polemic of modest proportions among "monists" and "pluralists." A. K. Uledov, a Soviet interpreter of public opinion who presents a monist point of view, argued that deviations in opinion from the ideological model reflect a lag between the old and the new, between progressive and backward forces. Proponents of a pluralist point of view, reflected in the writing of Grushin and to a much greater extent in the work of Polish, Czechoslovak, and Yugoslav scholars, argue that under socialism, nonconforming opinion may contribute to social progress. Thus the pluralist attempt to legitimate oppositional and critical tendencies, thereby reducing the tensions between the ideological, the operational, and the real political culture, tends to reduce the ideological model to that of a credo by adopting an operative normative model more reconcilable with reality. This treatment of pluralism as legitimate, however, is distinctly a minor theme in the more conservative communist regimes, having surfaced primarily in such countries as Poland, Czechoslovakia, and Yugoslavia.[7]

In testing political culture theory in communist countries it is useful to sort them into three categories: (1) the Soviet Union itself where the communist "experiment" began and was carried through by an indigenous communist elite; (2) other countries such as Yugoslavia, China, Cuba, and Vietnam where the communist revolution

---

[6] Ibid., p. 49. The Soviet regime has succeeded in inculcating a sense of "participatory-subject competence" particularly among the educated strata of the society. See G.A. Almond and S. Verba, *The Civic Culture* (Princeton: Princeton University Press, 1963), and citations and discussions in Friedgut, *Political Participation*, pp. 319 ff.

[7] Walter D. Connor and Zvi Gitelman, *Public Opinion in European Socialist Systems* (New York: Praeger Publishers, 1977), chap. 1.

was imported and carried out by indigenous elites; and (3) countries such as Poland, Hungary, Czechoslovakia, Romania, and East Germany where communist regimes were imposed from the outside. For our purposes in this paper we will examine briefly the experience of (1) the Soviet Union, (2) Yugoslavia and Cuba, and (3) Poland, Hungary, and Czechoslovakia. If political culture theory is to be falsified, we would expect to see major change in political culture in the desired direction in all three categories and to a larger degree in the case of the Soviet Union because its revolution was indigenous and has been in operation more than 60 years; to a substantial degree in Yugoslavia and Cuba because their revolutions were made by indigenous elites; and to a lesser degree in Poland, Hungary, and Czechoslovakia because their communist regimes, which have been in existence for only a single generation, were imposed on them from the outside and have been maintained by the threat or the actuality of Soviet military occupation.

POLITICAL CULTURE IN YUGOSLAVIA AND CUBA

In the case of Yugoslavia it may be inappropriate to speak of three versions of political culture. The Leninist ideological version is not seriously propagated. The operational version is a relatively loosely formulated set of norms and expectations that on the basis of empirical evidence are not too far from the reality of opinion and attitude. These norms include an acceptance of ethnic identity and of political autonomy of the various ethnic components, an acceptance of private land ownership among the peasantry, and of religious freedom. The two new elements in Yugoslav political culture are political activism and participation and enterprise self-management, which ideologically is supposed to represent the fulfillment of the ideal of participation and the essence of Yugoslav democratic socialism. Here one can distinguish a difference between the official political culture and the real political culture. The official political culture sanctions "classlessness" in participatory patterns; but much evidence that has been gathered from studies of political recruitment and opinion surveys demonstrates that political participation in the sense of officeholding and other forms of activism is biased toward the upper social and economic groupings in the population and is dominated by members of the League of Communists. Enterprise self-management appears to be effective. It involves all levels of workers in matters having to do with wages, hours, conditions of labor, and similar trade union issues but not in production and other management decisions. Thus the political leadership of Yugoslavia has settled for a set of operational political cultural norms that accommodate prerevolutionary ethnic, religious, and economic propensities and the socialization agencies that tend to perpetuate them. The novel elements of participation and decentralized socialism have been accepted in a limited way, particularly among the educated, advantaged, and politically mobilized strata of the population.

In contrast to Yugoslavia, another country that made its own revolution—Cuba—has been subjected to concentrated indoctrination designed to produce a new "Cuban socialist man." This ideological political culture differs from the Leninist one in its lack of emphasis on the "party" and its greater emphasis on heroism, selflessness, *personalismo,* and the propaganda of the deed. It appears to draw on a Latin American revolutionary tradition as much as on specifically Leninist ideological norms. In two decades of Cuban communism, these ideals have been propagated in connection with major campaigns of mobilization for purposes of defense, literacy, sugar cane harvesting, and revolutionary-military activities abroad. Such evidence as we have from reports and surveys of one kind or another suggests that these campaigns have had moderate success in creating regime legitimacy, the acceptance of the norm of activism in the implementation of goals, and the acceptance of socialism in the diffuse sense of that term. In recent years there is evidence of growing bureaucratization, less stress on utopian ideals and mass mobilization, and more stress on efficiency and regimentation. A pattern similar to that in the Soviet Union, in which the utopian culture of the socialist man takes on the proportions of an eschatology and the operational political culture stresses compliance with the regime's policies and programs, may emerge. Real popular values and attitudes may increasingly take the form of adaptions to constraints and incentives as well as according legitimacy to the new institutions.[8]

Thus our three cases of indigenous communist revolutions—the Soviet Union, Yugoslavia, and Cuba—fail to falsify political culture theory. The revolutionary aims of creating a "socialist man" have been practically given up in the Soviet Union and Cuba and were never seriously pursued in Yugoslavia. The Soviet Union has settled for popular legitimacy, a general belief in socialism, and a willingness to participate in campaigns initiated by the regime. The Yugoslav political elite has tended to accommodate itself to powerful ethnic commitments, peasant proprietary values, and religious be-

---

[8] See Richard R. Fagen, *The Transformation of Political Culture in Cuba* (Stanford: Stanford University Press, 1969); Jorge I. Dominguez, *Cuba: Order and Revolution* (Cambridge, Mass.: Harvard University Press, Belknap Press, 1978), chap. 12; Francis Lambert, "Cuba: Communist State in Personal Dictatorship" in Brown and Gray, *Political Culture and Political Change,* chap. 8.

liefs and has successfully inculcated a sense of legitimacy, an acceptance of decentralized socialism, and an obligation to participate.

In the case of Cuba, a personalist version of Leninism seems to be giving way to a more bureaucratic, apathetic relationship between elite and mass, with positive culture changes taking such forms as regime legitimacy, a belief in "socialism," and an acceptance in some sense of the obligation to take part in campaigns.

The changes that have taken place under these relatively favorable circumstances are of a limited sort, not of sufficient magnitude and character to falsify political culture theory and accord validity to a structural one.

THE CASES OF POLAND, HUNGARY, AND CZECHOSLOVAKIA

The communist experiences in Poland, Hungary, and Czechoslovakia offer even stronger supports for political culture theory. Communist parties have been in control in all three countries for over 30 years, and Soviet troop deployments and the Brezhnev Doctrine impose constraints on their policies. Despite these penetrative pressures and external threats and constraints, prerevolutionary nationalist, religious, economic, and political attitudes have persisted and have resulted in the renunciation of sanguine expectations of fundamental attitude change. Were the Soviet threat to be neutralized, there is little doubt that liberal regimes, even ones initiated by the communist parties (as was the case in Czechoslovakia in 1967–68), would be established. Communist efforts at resocialization might have been counterproductive in the sense of having created strong liberal propensities in countries such as Poland and Hungary where those orientations were relatively weak in the prerevolutionary era.

In Poland after 30 years of revolutionary experience, something like a legitimate pluralist regime emerged in 1981, which allowed the new Solidarity union, the Catholic church, and the army to engage in bargaining relations with the Communist party. As of this writing it is not clear which arrangements will survive the martial law regime. On the positive side, there is evidence of an acceptance of a diffuse egalitarian socialism among a large proportion of the Polish population. But the evidence is overwhelming that the Polish working class continues to be passionately Polish, Catholic, and "bread and butter" oriented.

In Hungary, peasant proprietary attitudes, reflected in surveys showing that private garden plots and household improvements are the preoccupations of most of the agricultural population, remain strong. Similarly, religious attitudes remain strong even among young people. Hungarian nationalism shows no signs of abating. One writer described the legitimacy of the communist regime in Hungary in the following terms: "The current standoff in Hungary between elites and potential publics is tenuous, but it appears as if everyone fears the hazards of questioning the situation too closely."[9] Although most Hungarians accept an egalitarian socialism, there is little acceptance of Marxism-Leninism among the population. In Hungary, the reaction to ideological indoctrination takes the form of a thoroughgoing depoliticization.

Of all the communist cases, that of Czechoslovakia presents the strongest support for political culture theory. As one writer observed of the period after 1948, "Neither the new economic base nor the new institutional structures succeeded in changing the political cultures of Czechs and Slovaks in the direction which the holders of institutional power desired. If anything, the opposite happened. The old values and beliefs were reinforced. . . . If a Czech 'new man' had been created by 1968, he was, ironically, one more firmly devoted to social democratic and libertarian values than the Czech of 1946. In the interactions between structures and cultures it would appear that the dominant Czech political culture came much closer to changing Czechoslovak Communism than Czechoslovak Communism came to procuring acceptance of its official political culture."[10]

What the scholarship of comparative communism has been telling us is that political cultures are not easily transformed. A sophisticated political movement ready to manipulate, penetrate, organize, indoctrinate, and coerce and given an opportunity to do so for a generation or longer ends up as much or more transformed than transforming. But we have to be clear about what kind of a case we are making for political culture theory. We are not arguing at all that political structure, historical experience, and deliberate efforts to change attitudes have no effect on political culture. Such an argument would be manifest foolishness. Major scholarly efforts such as those of Alex Inkeles and David H. Smith and Herbert Hyman demonstrate the powerful and homogenizing effects of education, the introduction of the mass media, and factory employment in very different cultural contexts.[11] There is a major literature of experimental studies on some of the conditions and possibilities

---

[9] Zvi Gitelman in Connor and Gitelman, *Public Opinion*, p. 161.

[10] Archie Brown and Gordon Wightman, "Czechoslovakia: Revival and Retreat," in Brown and Gray, *Political Culture and Political Change*, p. 189; see also Connor and Gitelman, *Public Opinion*, p. 178.

[11] Alex Inkeles and David H. Smith, *Becoming Modern: Individual Change in Six Developing Countries* (Cambridge, Mass.: Harvard University Press, 1974); and Herbert Hyman, *The Enduring Effects of Education* (Chicago: University of Chicago Press, 1975).

of attitude change. What all this seems to demonstrate is that man is a complex animal who is tractable in some respects and intractable in others. Both the successes and the failures of our communist cases suggest that there is a pattern to this tractability-intractability behavior, that liberty once experienced is not quickly forgotten, and that equity and equality of some kind resonate in the human spirit.

14

The Post-Revolutionary Phase in China and Russia

Richard Lowenthal

The death of Mao Zedong in 1976 was, as everybody felt at once, the end of an epoch in the evolution of Communist China—and that in more senses than one. It was the death of the leader of the long drawn-out revolutionary struggle that had established communist rule in China, and of the man who, by breaking up the alliance with the Soviet Union he had signed from a less than equal position, had destroyed the last of the unequal treaties in China's modern history. It also marked the end of the same man's failed attempt, in the last decade of his life, to establish despotic personal rule over the party's institutions, and potentially opened the way to restoration of institutional party rule. But it could not be foreseen with certainty at once that this restoration of party institutions would also coincide with the end of the effort to continue the "institutionalized revolution" of which Mao had been the unbending exponent.

It is the thesis of this paper that both the tendency to institutionalize revolution as a recurrent phenomenon due to the utopian impulses of communist ideology, and the necessity for the revolutionary process finally to exhaust itself due to the requirements of economic modernization, are inherent in communist party re-

Source: Richard Lowenthal, "The Post-Revolutionary Phase in China and Russia," *Studies in Comparative Communism* 16, no. 3 (Autumn 1983), pp. 191–201. By permission. Footnotes abridged by the editors.

gimes—at least if they are created by the victory of a revolutionary mass movement and not imposed by a great power from outside. The tendency for a personal despotism to paralyze or replace institutional party control in the course of this long-drawn out revolutionary process, but for "normal" party control eventually to be restored after the death of the despot or would-be despot, is not equally general for communist regimes, but is typical enough to have manifested itself in the two leading communist powers—Russia and China. It is my intention to discuss the general phenomenon of the exhaustion of the revolutionary process from the angle of its interaction with the post-despotic normalization in Russia and China.

INSTITUTIONALIZED REVOLUTION

Permit me first to explain briefly what I mean by the process of institutionalized revolution and by the need for its eventual exhaustion. . . . Communist revolutionary movements are motivated by visions of a society of perfect equality excluding all social conflict, which are utopian in the strict sense of being impossible to achieve among human beings. In the real world, all their power cannot prevent that every step forward in the planned revolutionary destruction of formerly or potentially "ruling classes" is followed by unplanned, spontaneous processes of new social differentiation— as in the rise of a class of prosperous peasants after the expropriation of the landowners in Russia, or in the rise of a new privileged bureaucracy in Soviet industry with its growth under Stalin's five-year plans. Hence new "revolutions from above" were undertaken first against the "kulaks" in the form of Stalin's forced collectivization, and later against important parts of the bureaucratic, industrial and military elites in the form of his notorious blood purge, and were projected by him still in the final year of his life in the form of replacing the right of the collective farms to sell their produce to the state by some kind of centrally controlled barter. You can easily draw the parallel first to Chinese agricultural collectivization, then to the tightening of party control over the industrial managers in the course of the "Great Leap Forward" and to the creation of the "People's Communes" by Mao, finally to his desperate struggle against differentiated material incentives as a form of "Capitalism" and his attempt to uproot, by the "Cultural Revolution," the underlying mentality in the masses and the inclination of the party and state bureaucracy to make concessions to it.

Yet communist revolutions have only taken place in underdeveloped countries under the pressure of their economic problems: hence all communist regimes have faced the need to combine the struggle for equality with the struggle for economic modernization, which necessarily requires social differentiation and material incentives—thus striving to reconcile the irreconcilable. Accordingly, a tendency to restrict, stop or finally reverse the extreme egalitarian measures has arisen both from the more productive part of the working classes and from the administrative elites responsible for economic success, and has found at different times and in different places more or less of a hearing among the leadership. Stalin, for instance, while destroying the more prosperous peasants by his mass deportation of "kulaks" with disastrous economic consequences and severely holding down the general wage level under his first five-year-plan, took a stand early in favor of differentiated incentive wages, and in his great purge favored the well-trained industrial managers and technicians without a revolutionary past over the "Red Directors" with a party tradition but poor technical knowledge—and after the purge of the "Reds" opened the party ranks wide to the "experts." Mao Zedong, on the other hand, the more he freed himself from the Soviet model after Khrushchev's de-Stalinization, became more and more critical of differentiated material incentives as spoiling the people's chances of developing a true socialist consciousness, and while originally coining the slogan that managers and technicians should be both "red and expert," in practice became increasingly determined to favor non-expert reds over not-so-red experts: this was true during the Great Leap, and central to the Cultural Revolution.

However, the more a country has already begun to overcome primitive economic conditions, to develop industrial technology and train technicians, the higher becomes the cost of insisting, in the name of the ideological imperative of egalitarianism, on continuing the institutionalized revolution at the expense of the economic imperative of modernization. Over time, then, the tendency is bound to grow for the dynamics of the revolutionary process to run down and the dynamics of the pressure for modernization to gather momentum. We have long known that it is impossible to invent a *perpetuum mobile* in the physical world; the communists, first in Russia and later in China, have had to learn that no *perpetuum mobile* exists in the world of political revolution either.

THE RUNNING DOWN OF INSTITUTIONALIZED REVOLUTION IN RUSSIA AND CHINA

Let me now try to recall in somewhat more detail how the running down of the institutionalized revolution occurred first in Russia and then in China. It has often been said that Stalin turned essentially conservative in the course of World War II, if he had not already in his Great Purge; above all, those people who are convinced that a revolution must be something humane and beautiful, naturally consider the Great Purge a counter-revolution rather than a revolution. But the Great Purge was no attempt to restore a previous state of affairs: apart from inaugurating Stalin's personal despotism above the party institutions, it largely destroyed the traditional revolutionary elite, but replaced it by a new one by no means averse to further revolutionary upheavals. The bureaucrats, technicians and army officers trained since the end of the civil war eagerly entered the gates of the party now widely opened for them by Stalin; and the party, though now subject to the despot's every whim, had not abandoned its program of social transformation: there had been no "Thermidor," as Trotsky believed.

It is true that during the war, Stalin made important concessions both to the material demands of the peasants and to the ideological traditions of Great Russian nationalism and orthodoxy—but from necessity, not from conviction. The concessions to the peasants and to non-communist ideologies and literature were revoked as soon as the war was over. By 1950, planned social transformation restarted with the merging of the collective farms to greater units: this reduced their number to little more than one-third within two years, thus making sure at last that there should be a party unit in most collective farms. A year later, Nikita Khrushchev, then responsible for agriculture in Stalin's Politburo, suggested the next step: the peasants should be uprooted from their villages and rehoused in one central "agrotown" for each of the new merged farms, losing access to their former private plots and getting much smaller gardens in the process. But this met opposition within the leadership, both because of the risk of a disincentive effect on the peasant's work and of the lack of the needed masses of building materials. Stalin did not back Khrushchev, and the project was cancelled.

Yet in 1952, Stalin himself came forward with a far more revolutionary project. In a series of essays published as a pamphlet on the eve of the 19th Party Congress–the first since the war and the last in his lifetime—he proposed a plan for replacing all trade between the cities and the countryside by centrally organized barter! The idea was that as long as the peasants owned their produce, even collectively, there was a danger of a return to capitalism. The new plan was aimed to cut out market and money altogether from the relations between town and country—and Stalin's final essay on the subject urged that first steps toward this gigantic revolutionary change should be taken at once. But strangely, the plan was not discussed, let alone approved at the party congress: for the first time in years, there seems to have been resistance in the Politburo against the despot's idea, which would have made any

comparison of the collective farms' income and expenditure, difficult
as it was anyhow, completely impossible. At any rate, at the end
of the Congress Stalin replaced the Politburo by a much larger
Presidium, and Khrushchev later told us that Stalin planned a
purge of some of its members and that the "doctor's plot" affair,
announced in January 1953 but planned at the time of the congress,
was his preparation for that. But by 5 March 1953, the despot was
dead.

Clearly, while institutionalized revolution had not been abandoned by Stalin, its continuation had become increasingly difficult
in his later years. During the struggle for his succession, which
ended with the restoration of party primacy under Khrushchev,
the rival leaders were indeed more interested in initiating popular
reforms than unpopular revolutionary upheavals. But by 1959, the
victorious Khrushchev unveiled at the 21st Party Congress his plan
for another turn of the revolutionary screw, though this time a
nonviolent one: he resumed his campaign for the resettlement of
the peasants in "agrotowns," now combined with a drive for the
"voluntary" sale of the peasants' private cattle to the collective
farms. Yet early successes of the campaign announced in the press
soon turned out either to have been faked by the local officials or
to have been achieved with so much pressure that the peasants
slaughtered most of their cattle rather than sell them—and within
less than two years the campaign was abandoned. It was the Soviet
communist party's last attempt to continue the institutionalized
revolution: the new party program presented by Khrushchev to
the 22d Party Congress in October 1961 treated further changes
in the direction of "the higher stage of communism" no longer as
a task for the revolutionary transformation of the social structure,
but as an expected by-product of the party's concentration on the
increase in productivity and the improvement of the general standard of living. Modernization had finally won over utopianism, and
the post-revolutionary period had definitely begun in Russia.

However, it turned out that Khrushchev, with his dynamic urge
for innovating changes, was not the right kind of leader for a post-
revolutionary communist party regime. The party's bureaucratic
oligarchy, consolidated in their physical security by Khrushchev's
denunciation of Stalin's purges, now wanted the security of regular
procedures of decision within their circle, without a dynamic leader
inclined to appeal over their heads to "public opinion." It was their
discontent with Khrushchev's uncontrollable improvizations that
finally led to his overthrow by a central committee formed under
his primacy and led by men of his choice—drawing the final conclusion of his transition to the post-revolutionary phase which he had
failed to draw himself. As the 18 years of the Brezhnev era have
shown, that conclusion was oligarchic rule bringing to the Soviet

Union stable procedures of decision for the first time in its history—
with the advantages of unprecedented stability, and the setbacks
of unprecedented stagnation.

In China, the struggle for or against continuing the institutionalized revolution started at the time of the Great Leap Forward and
the inauguration of the People's Communes: it formed the core of
what Mao Zedong and his followers came to call "the struggle between two lines." Its beginning coincided with the beginning of
Mao's political estrangement from post-Stalin Russia, which sharpened as the Chinese leader came to attribute the—in his view—
insufficiently militant character of Soviet foreign policy to an abandonment of revolutionary principles inside the Soviet Union itself;
he saw this symbolized by the statement in the Soviet party program
of 1961 that, owing to the disappearance of hostile classes in the
Soviet Union, it could no longer be described as a "dictatorship of
the proletariat." Mao correctly perceived that this formula was an
expression of Russia's entrance into a post-revolutionary period.

You will recall that the policies of the Great Leap and the People's
Communes were explicitly justified by the doctrine of "uninterrupted revolution," and that this doctrine was not abandoned by
Mao when the early illusions that the Communes would make possible a quick transition to communism faded by the end of 1958,
and when a number of adjustments to harsh economic realities
had to be made in the policies based on the doctrine, particularly
between 1960 and 1962. In 1964, parallel to his twin campaigns
for "socialist education" and for "learning from the army," Mao
further developed the doctrine in his famous reply to "Khrushchev's
Phoney Communism," laying down that the danger of a capitalist
restoration, such as had allegedly taken place in Russia, would persist in China throughout the period preceding the achievement of
full communism, which he now expected to last for "5 to 10 generations or one or several centuries," and to require new revolutionary
struggles throughout this period. It was in the context of this vision
that he came to prepare the "Cultural Revolution" as a struggle
not only against non-revolutionary thought, but against "people
in authority walking the capitalist road"—in other words, against
all members of the party leadership who opposed his priority for
institutionalized revolution in the name of a priority for economic
modernization—and that he launched it, probably without the support of a majority of the Central Committee, in 1966.

I do not have to retell here the phases of the Cultural Revolution,
nor the lasting damage it did both to the party regime and to the
Chinese economy. What matters in our context is that even after
Mao decided in 1968 to end the chaos caused by the Red Guards
and restore the paralyzed party with the help of the same armed
forces on which he had previously relied to back the Red Guards

against the institutions of party rule, he still expected the army under the leadership of Lin Biao (from 1969 his deputy and designated successor) to pursue a course of continuing revolution if by different means. After Lin Biao's death following an alleged plot, the "struggle between the two lines" continued in a divided leadership, with Mao's authority visibly fading and Zhou Enlai, who had in the past both supported Mao against his opponents and tried to moderate his policies, now assuming the leadership in the struggle for a turn towards modernization (and rehabilitation of surviving victims of the Cultural Revolution), but being attacked by the Maoist diehards in an abstruse campaign allegedly directed "against Lin Biao and Confucius." As Zhou succumbed to an illness a few months before the death of Mao, those diehards got a final opportunity to resume their struggle for uninterrupted revolution.

The death of Mao in September 1976 was thus the precondition for China's entry into a post-revolutionary period, but that entry did not take place immediately. While Hua Guo-feng, who now assumed power, was able to arrest Mao's widow and his most extremist followers, and was unwilling to continue "revolutionary" measures, he was equally unwilling to break openly with the late-Maoist doctrine and continued to mouth the formulas of continuing revolution and class struggle used by the "infallible" leader. It took two years until a decision of the Central Committee in late 1978 actually opened the post-revolutionary period by disavowing those formulas as absurd in the absence of hostile classes and giving priority to a policy of modernization, and another two years and a half until another Central Committee meeting in mid-1981 demonstrated the finality of the turn by passing a resolution on the history of Communist China which recognized the lasting merits of the early Mao on the road to communist power and in the building of the new society, but clearly condemned the doctrinal and political errors of the late Mao and admitted the damage they had done both to the nation and to its communist regime. The same meeting also replaced Hua Guo-feng as leader of the party. The new leader, not in title but in fact, had been already for some time Deng Xiaoping, once ousted as general secretary of the party and banished during the Cultural Revolution, then rehabilitated by Zhou Enlai but banished once more by the Maoist extremists after Zhou's death, and finally rehabilitated a second time as the party moved towards a post-revolutionary priority for modernization.

DESPOTISM IN RUSSIA AND CHINA

So far, this rapid survey has shown that both in Russian and in Chinese communism, the conflict between the tendency to institutionalized, recurrent revolution and the tendency to give priority to modernization has in some way been intertwined with another drama—the rise of a despotic or would-be despotic leader paralyzing or even temporarily destroying the institutions of party rule for a period, and the restoration of the normal functioning of party institutions after the death of the despot or would-be despot. I shall now attempt to suggest some reasons for the appearance of this type of drama in some major communist party regimes, and to ask just how it has affected the struggle between revolutionary and post-revolutionary forces which is my main theme.

I should like to start from a difference between communist party regimes and fascist regimes, with which the rules of Stalin and of Mao have been frequently compared.[1] The fascist regimes of Mussolini and Hitler were based from the start on the *Führerprinzip*, the principle of one-man leadership. Legitimacy in those regimes was attached primarily to the person of the leader rather than to the institution of the party. Hence a conflict of authority in those regimes could only arise in case of a crisis of succession—and neither regime lasted long enough for this to happen.

Communist regimes, being run by highly centralized parties organized from the top downward, also depend for their functioning on a single leader; but their ideology does not proclaim that. Legitimacy is not primarily attached to the person of the leader but to the institution of the party, which is supposed to be governed by a principle called "democratic centralism." Under this principle, the leadership is elected by a party congress, but the leadership also "proposes" the candidates for leading the party's regional and local units who, in turn, "propose" delegates to the party congress; hence a united leadership can always be sure both to perpetuate itself with minor changes and to get its policies approved "democratically." The system works as smoothly as the fascist one—on condition of unity in the leadership. But this unity can only be assured, amidst the crucial policy issues that have to be decided in the course of a revolutionary process, if there happens to be a leader who enjoys virtually uncontested authority. That was the case with Lenin, who had led the Bolsheviks to power; and it also applied to Mao, who had led the Chinese communists to victory, for many years. But it was not the case with any of the candidates for Lenin's succession, and it no longer applied to the aging Mao from 1958 onwards.

---

[1] Cf. above all the description of Stalin's and Mao's rule as a system of "Führerism" essentially similar to that of Hitler and Mussolini and sharply distinct from the "Bolshevism" of Lenin in Leonard Schapiro and John Wilson Lewis, "The Role of the Monolithic Party Under the Totalitarian Leader," in *Party Leadership and Revolutionary Power in China*, ed. John Wilson Lewis (London: Cambridge University Press, 1970). The same argument is also used for a *definition* of totalitarianism by this type of leader in Leonard Schapiro, *Totalitarianism* (New York: Macmillan, 1972).

Yet if the leadership of a ruling communist party is not united, it turns out that there is also no generally accepted procedure for decision making. There is, originally, no duty for a communist that he must follow the leader, as there is for a fascist. But neither is there a clear duty that he must follow the majority in all conditions. For Lenin, in building his party and leading it to power, taught that the majority can err, and that the true revolutionary must not submit to an erring majority, but rather split or refound the party, as he did repeatedly himself before he was in power. But the same Lenin, when later leading a party that ruled a dictatorial state and that therefore could not tolerate a split, taught that "factional" opposition to decisions once passed by the highest party organs was a danger to the party's monopolistic rule—hence potentially counter-revolutionary. Thus well-trained communists grow up with two contradictory lessons going back to Lenin—that it is better to fight an erring majority than to submit to it, and that it is better to submit to the ruling majority than to endanger the unity of a ruling party.

As I said before, those problems do not become acute while the party leadership is united behind a generally respected leader. But if there is no longer such a leader, and if policy disputes arise about the "correct" solution, on which the fate of the revolution may depend, minorities may feel authorized by the "early" Lenin to oppose majority decisions on vital issues and found factions, and majorities will feel authorized by the "later" Lenin to suppress them. It is from such factional struggles on vital issues of the revolutionary road to take, that an internal power struggle in the ruling party may arise—and may end in personal despotism.

The rise of personal despotism, or of attempts at personal despotism, is thus an inherent *possibility,* though not, as far as we can observe, an inherent *necessity* in communist regimes. An all-powerful leader is not demanded by their ideology. But the fact that ideology neither forces all communists to submit to the leader whatever he does, nor forces them to submit to a majority whatever it decides, means that communist ideology offers no clear system of rules for the procedures of decision within the party; and this lack of procedural clarity may lead to inner-party conflicts sharpening to a point where a despot seeks to achieve general submission no longer based on ideologically motivated discipline, but on force. Clearly, such conflicts are most likely to arise on the need for another phase of the institutionalized revolution.

Lenin had been unable to designate a successor enjoying his unique authority, and none was available at his death. In the factional quarrels now arising within the "collective leadership," Stalin enjoyed the double advantage that as general secretary he had the decisive influence on appointments, and that he saw more clearly than his rivals that as the share of members who had joined the party after the seizure of power increased with the lapse of time, the late-Leninist stress on the need for party unity was bound to seem more convincing to the rank and file than the early-Leninist argument for the right to defy an erring majority. Accordingly, he used in each conflict the tactics of presenting his policies from the start as those of "the party," and his critics as a "factional" opposition. It worked successively first against Trotsky, then against the "left opposition" of Zinoviev and Kamenev, and finally, after some initial difficulty, also against Bukharin and his supporters once Stalin had maneuvered them into the role of a "right opposition."

By 1929, when Stalin had defeated all inner-party opposition and initiated a new "revolution from above" by the "dekulakization" and forced collectivization of Soviet agriculture and the first five-year plan for forced industrialization, he had become the effective single leader of the party, but still by the use and abuse of his statutory powers—not yet by the use of despotic force inside the party. The massive use of force against the peasants and the resulting widespread misery and discontent, by seeming to endanger the survival of the regime, even increased the feeling in the party that Stalin's strong arm was indispensable for saving it. Yet as late as 1932 the Politburo, by rejecting Stalin's demand that a communist who had secretly circulated a pamphlet calling for Stalin's replacement by the party, should be tried and executed for allegedly calling for his assassination, showed that Stalin was not yet a despot above the party institutions; and when the crisis was over, the Seventeenth Party Congress of 1934, as part of an effort to restore a more normal atmosphere, apparently made an attempt to reduce his powers: it renamed him "First Secretary" instead of "General Secretary," sought to strengthen the collective character of the party secretariat by electing the popular Leningrad secretary Kirov to become his colleague, and in a secret ballot is said to have given Stalin the lowest vote of all Central Committee members.

It was this apparent threat to Stalin's institutional power that evidently decided him to move towards establishing despotic power above the party institutions. He put men beholden to him into key positions in the secret police, the prosecutor's office and the judiciary; he at the very least did nothing to make the secret police prevent a second and successful attempt on Kirov's life in December 1935 after a first attempt by the same man had failed; and he used Kirov's assassination to start the Great Purge, which began with measures against former oppositionists, culminating in the notorious show trials, and extended quickly to his own former supporters who had shown doubts about his new methods: the victims finally included the majority of members both of the 1934 Party Congress and of the Central Committee elected there, as well as the most outstanding army leaders and a large part of the industrial leadership. With that purge, Stalin had assumed the full powers of a despot; the party remained the bearer of legitimacy in name, but henceforth was no more than one of the instruments of the *Vozhd*— less important than the secret police, and no more important than the government bureaucracy and the army during the war.

From the 18th Party Congress in March 1939 which announced the end of the mass purge to the 19th Party Congress in the fall of 1952, the Central Committee met only rarely and the Politburo mostly in *ad hoc* groups selected by Stalin's whim; during the war, the highest collective organ under Stalin, who had become head of government as well, was not a party organ at all, but the "State Defense Committee." Smaller purges in the post-war period affected particularly the party organizations of Leningrad and the Caucasus as well as prominent Jewish communists. But the party was never dissolved, and after Stalin's death in 1953, Khrushchev's struggle for the succession was at the same time a struggle for the restoration of the primacy of the party over the other machines of power, of which the overthrow of Beria and the subordination of the secret police, the replacement of Malenkov as head of the government, the "de-Stalinization" started by the disclosure of Stalin's crimes at the 20th Party Congress, the partial decentralization of the economic bureaucracy and the defeat of the "anti-party group," i.e., the Politburo majority which tried to oppose it, and finally the demotion of Marshal Zhukov for excessive independence as head of the Soviet armed forces were the principal stages. By late 1957, Khrushchev in his capacity as first secretary of the party was the unmistakable political leader of the Soviet Union—without attempting or indeed needing to become a despot; and as we have seen, it was under him that the decision to end the process of institutionalized revolution was taken in 1960–61.

When Khrushchev's method of leadership, while far from despotic, proved too irregular and incalculable for a post-revolutionary period, he was overthrown in 1964—without serious resistance, and without another succession crisis. In the post-revolutionary phase, disagreements within the leadership, while no more absent than in Western governments, were now fought without the revolutionary fervor that could have justified a refusal to submit to the majority, in a new type of communist "cabinet discipline"—and the post-revolutionary phase in Russia, as I said before, became a period of generally accepted, clear procedures of decision making and of oligarchic normality and stability.

China, as you know, went through the early stages of institutionalized revolution without major leadership conflicts, thanks largely to the unique authority of Mao Zedong as the leader of the original struggle for power. But that authority, somewhat diminished by the failed experiment of the "Hundred Flowers" campaign in 1957, was seriously shaken by the results of the "Great Leap Forward" in 1958 and after. Despite Mao's willingness to retire from day-to-day decisions to the "second line," his stubbornness in defending and extending the principle of the "uninterrupted revolution" led to a sharpening "struggle between two lines." It was the increasing difficulties Mao encountered in trying to win this struggle by normal inner-party methods which caused him to launch the Cultural Revolution by seeking once more to make inner-party power grow out of the barrel of the gun—as he had done in Tsunyi in 1935. The Cultural Revolution, carried out by mobilizing the Red Guards of university and high school students with the help of the army and intimidating and paralyzing the regular party organs with their help, was Mao's attempt to establish a form of personal despotism.

This attempt differed from Stalin's in its aims, its means and the degree of its success. It was motivated by a determination to continue the institutionalized revolution regardless of the damage this might do to economic modernization, while Stalin had long tried to combine new revolutionary transformations in particular fields with such concessions to economic needs as differentiated material incentives and authority for technical and managerial experts. It was based on temporarily mobilizing not the secret police, but the armed forces and an ideologically inspired youth movement against the party bureaucracy. And while succeeding temporarily in breaking the party's resistance and dissolving the communist youth organization as well as the trade unions, it failed to create a *stable* despotism. Stalin, while for a time primarily relying on the secret police, had been able repeatedly to depose and execute their heads. Mao became dependent on the army for taming the anarchic youth movement he had mobilized with its help, and reorganizing the near-dissolved party with the cooperation of a mixture of old cadres and young rebels selected as supposedly reliable. Even after the fall of Lin Biao, Mao remained to his death dependent on an uneasy and unstable balance of military leaders, surviving party "moderates" around Zhou and Deng and unrepentant revolutionary ultras around his wife—not only not a despot, but not even any longer an effective leader with a clear line of policy.

The death of Mao was followed with remarkable speed by the restoration of the primacy of the weakened party—mainly from lack of serious rivals, as the army little had proud memories of its intervention in the domestic power struggle. But within the party, the struggle for or against continuing the institutionalized revolution went on for at least two more years, and only its end with a clear victory of the modernizers around Deng created the conditions for the kind of oligarchic stability with regular procedures of decision making suitable to a post-revolutionary phase.

CONCLUSION

It is time to attempt to draw some conclusions from the facts of the conflict, inherent in communist systems, between the needs of institutionalized revolution and the requirements of modernization, and of the less inherent, but not atypical conflict between a tendency to establish a personal despotism above the party institutions and the counter-tendency to restore the primacy of those institutions after the death of the despot. Can we say anything general about the causal connection or interaction of the two processes? I think we can.

First of all, it seems clear that the major obstacle to disciplined acceptance of majority decisions in communist political systems is the ideological passion connected with the struggle for new stages of the institutionalized revolution. It follows that despotism, or an attempt at despotism, is likely to arise in communist systems only as long as the belief in an institutionalized revolution has not been finally abandoned. To put it more bluntly, the turn to despotism remains likely only while utopianism is still alive.

Second, and to some extent conversely, the abandonment of the institutionalized revolution has occurred both in Russia and China only after the death of the despot or would-be despot. In both cases, the liberation from his terror has made it easier for the desire for a more normal life to come to the surface, particularly among the party oligarchy; and the security of an oligarchy is best assured by the renunciation of further revolutionary change.

Third, and turning now to the present and future consequences, we are now dealing in the Soviet Union and the Chinese People's Republic with two communist party regimes that are both in their post-revolutionary and post-despotic phase. That means that both are governed by bureaucratic oligarchies with more or less generally accepted procedural rules of decision making, whose domestic policies are no longer marked by ideological conflicts, but by the conflict between the goal of economic modernization and the tendency towards bureaucratic stagnation. Both oligarchies stick to their party monopoly, and both are firmly opposed to political liberalization; but neither tends to return to the experiments in mass annihilation of the revolutionary period.

Fourth, a vital *difference* between the two countries concerns the stage of development at which the revolutionary process was stopped. When Khrushchev announced his 1961 program, the Soviet Union, for all its structural weaknesses, had become one of the major industrial countries of the world. China at the present time is still far from that stage, and her difficulties in reaching it are still tremendous—for reasons of lack of capital compared to the pressure of the population, of lack of scientific and technical cadres proportionate to the size of the problems, and perhaps also of the repercussions of the absurdities of the period of the Cultural Revolution on working morale and general confidence. But this last must be a tentative judgment.

Finally, the fact that China, almost two decades after Russia, has entered her post-revolutionary phase, has one major international consequence: the power conflict between those two neighbors has lost its ideological component. The Chinese communists can no longer accuse the Russians of having abandoned their revolutionary principles, and the Russians can no longer blame the Chinese for utopianism and adventurism in domestic affairs. The fact that both sides are aware of that post-revolutionary change has made it easier for them to discuss a possible normalization of their relations. But that does not and cannot mean that those relations will, at some future date, be characterized by an apparent ideological community, as they were a long time ago, instead of of by ideological conflict. They will be determined, like other relations between great powers, by their interests—and that means important conflicting interests, but potentially some common interests as well.

PART THREE

Political Dynamics and Processes

In every political system, we have noted, individuals and groups seek to influence the state and thereby translate their interests into authoritative political decisions. An indispensable condition for the efficient functioning of political systems is widespread acceptance of the decision-making process—which we shall call "consensus." Wherever this kind of consensus exists, the state itself becomes legitimized. Legitimacy and consensus are key indicators of the effectiveness and performance of the system and conversely of the existence of basic instabilities that may undermine it. Ultimately, the phenomenon of government—what Mosca calls "the political fact"—is a matter of will as well as force; that is, political relations are willed relations.

POLITICAL AUTHORITY

One aspect of legitimacy is the use of the power of the state by officials in accordance with prearranged and agreed upon rules. A legitimate act is also legal, but a lawful command is not always legitimate. For example, the commands issued by the Nazi government in Germany were legal, and presumably subordinate officials down to the private soldier or individual citizen had to obey them. But at the same time, these orders violated a code of civilized behavior and morality that brought into question their legitimacy. Legality refers to the letter of the law as decreed by a state organ, while legitimacy involves the very character of the state and the substance and purpose of a legal enactment. But who will decide when there is a difference between legality and legitimacy? No clear answer can be given. On the one hand, the state always claims legitimacy for its legal commands. "What is pleasing to the prince has the force of law," according to an old axiom of the Romans. On the other hand, many individuals see a higher law beyond the formal law of the state. Ultimately, they obey their own conscience and consider some acts of the state as illegitimate. This is the justification of civil disobedience, as advocated by Thoreau, Tolstoy, and Gandhi.

But these extreme formulations are hypothetical. In actual political life, legality, legitimacy, and consent *tend* to converge. Consensus is more than agreement; it denotes acceptance of a given political system. Acceptance may be due to individual consent stemming from recognition of the beneficent purposes of the state; acceptance is also the product of tradition and habit. Consensus is generally addressed to the basic rules that establish, define, limit, and channel political power—that is, to the constitution. It is not limited to specific laws or specific acts of the government, or even to governmental forms. Consensus transforms power into authority, and the legal enactments emanating from the government into legitimate orders.

Democratic theory postulates canons of legitimacy that clarify the distinctions we are trying to make. Force can be used only in accordance with certain previously agreed upon procedures. There is an elaborate setting of limitations upon the exercise of power, which can be used only by persons elevated to office through elections. Individuals agree to the basic rules so long as they are not violated. The government derives its authority from these basic rules; whenever disagreements about the government and its policies erupt, they are resolved through popular choice. The substance of political life, therefore, is the consensus—or "agreement on fundamentals"—that binds the citizens into an organized common political life.

The contract theory as developed by John Locke is a classic formulation of this consensual model. According to it, the formation of a political community is an act of will embodying the cardinal rule that the majority of the people, acting through their legislature, govern. However, property rights and individual freedoms may not be infringed upon by the majority, and there must be periodic free elections of the legislative body. In such a political community, a minority can be coerced only in order to implement the basic agreement entered into by the whole community. But such coercion cannot be used to destroy or silence the minority. The consensus on a free and open society gives the majority the right to act, while allowing the minority the right to protest peacefully and ultimately to appeal to the community at large in favor of its positions—in other words, the right to become the majority. This model, then, incorporates the obligation to obey and the right to protest, criticize, and oppose. It allows the force of the state to be transformed into authority, deriving its legitimacy from the basic agreement. Individual dissent is expressed not in disobedience, but through organized opposition seeking to present alternative policies. Thus, opposition in the democratic scheme is harnessed to the total political system, which is strengthened, not weakened, by dissent.

The model helps us to see clearly the distinctions between force and authority, consensus and legitimacy. It also has analytic value in calling our attention to the conditions under which consensus is likely to emerge, or be disrupted. But most political systems at present are not based on the Lockean model. Force rather than authority is frequently the rule, and this is an indication of a lack of consensus binding the citizens together. More important, values other than free elections, including national or ethnic identity, may serve to legitimize the state. Political decisions may be accepted by a population for a variety of reasons. Freely given consent is only one basis of legitimacy, and in the modern world is becoming increasingly precarious.

Consensus Building

The contract theory that Locke used to illustrate the formation of a political community—all citizens agreeing to form it through a solemn compact—is at best a fiction or simply an illustration with no historical foundation. It holds that, under certain conditions, a state of mind develops among a given people to establish a set of fundamental rules about the manner in which they would cooperate and live peacefully together. But what accounts for such a state of mind? And why was it reached in some societies and not in others? When and under what conditions does a community become a political one accepting a common agreement?

There are no simple answers to these questions, but some general indications may be given. First, there must be a fairly extensive acceptance of common norms of social conduct. Customs must begin to develop—even everyday habits—before we can begin to talk of a community. Second, social behavior must be predictable, at least to the extent that makes human intercourse possible. If all parishioners spied upon one another, while celebrating mass, for fear that each might carry a gun, a functioning community would hardly be likely. Third, a political community requires common expectations of material benefits for all members. The utilitarian argument was put forward by Thomas Hobbes and, later, more persuasively by James Mill and John Stuart Mill. Put simply, this means that the chances for achieving consensus are greater in political communities that enjoy economic prosperity.

Finally, the role of elites is crucial in the formation of consensus.

It is axiomatic that leadership is always lodged in the hands of a few. In all countries that have experienced the Industrial Revolution, rule by a relatively small traditional elite was challenged by new groups, in particular the bourgeoisie and the working class. This was a momentous period in the evolution of political systems, since claims to political leadership had to be subordinated to the requirements of popular participation and support. Two developments can be discerned. In some cases, the ruling groups became restrictive and negative, attempting to thwart participation and to maintain themselves in a position of control and leadership through the use of repressive measures. In other cases, they became permissive and supportive, allowing their claims to leadership to be qualified and indeed ultimately subverted by new symbols, forms, and practices deriving from popular participation. The greater the degree of permissiveness on the part of the traditional elites, the smoother was the transition to a consensual and participant society; the greater their tendency to reject newcomers, the more difficult and the less likely was the emergence of consensus.

In Britain, for example, ever increasing participation and influence was offered to the citizenry at large throughout the 19th century. But in Russia, despite some half-hearted reforms, autocratic rule was maintained. The result was that in Britain the people began to value and accept their system as an instrument for the satisfaction of their wants, while the rising groups in Russia either rejected their government or remained apathetic to it. In the one case, consensus was built; in the other, its very preconditions were denied. Thus, we may postulate that the congruence between mass demands for participation and influence and a positive elite response to these demands is a fundamental condition for the development of consensus.

This hypothesis is equally relevant for the developing societies today. Throughout Asia, Latin America, and Africa many of the preconditions of consensus—the sense of national identity, compatibility of values, and predictability of behavior—are lacking. In all these societies demands for material progress have been stimulated through exposure to more advanced societies. The role of the elites then becomes critical for the development of political consensus. Rejection of new groups may lead to sharp conflict between the few and the many, and a state of virtual civil war. Complete permissiveness, on the other hand, may thrust unprepared and unqualified groups into power prematurely. Inability to forward industrialization produces popular disenchantment and apathy.

In the last analysis, it is the interplay between a great number of factors that accounts for the development of a consensual society, or for the failure of consensus to emerge. We have emphasized the relationship between mass and elite under conditions of economic modernization in order to illustrate the complexity of the phenomenon rather than to identify it as a single causal factor. For the very attitude of the elite—whether it is permissive and open or restrictive and negative—in turn depends upon many other historical and social factors. Common linguistic or religious bonds; prolonged community life behind natural barriers that deter attack or invasion; feelings of ethnic or racial identity; continuing economic progress; and the impact of technology and science upon the society are all factors that we subsumed earlier under the general terms of common values, predictability of behavior, and perception of common material benefits. It is only when these factors materialize at the proper time that the conditions for consensus also emerge, and that the Lockean model is relevant.

Consensus is always under stress, even in systems with a long tradition of legitimacy. Efforts to create an independent Quebec, the conflict between the Flemish and Walloons in Belgium, the appearance of a black power movement in the United States, and Scottish nationalism in the United Kingdom, are all threats to the basic consensus in previously stable systems. In these cases, dissidence stems from the conditions we have discussed—repressive or rejective measures by the elite and a relative inability to fulfill the demands for economic well-being aroused by the elites themselves and the ideology prevalent in the whole system. A theory of consensus therefore can be used to assess and to measure degrees of alienation, including the emergence of revolutionary situations.

The processes of socialization and politicization—whereby individuals are conditioned to accept their society and government— are of special importance in consensus building. No society can exist for long unless its norms are transmitted to the young. In early childhood the pattern of transmission is sheer habit. The young simply accept the behavior of their parents, on pain of discipline, identifying with their symbols and values. There can be no rational inquiry into the fundamental rules of the system. Within the entire educational establishment an overt effort is made to inculcate favorable attitudes toward the state. Through ceremony, ritual, and outright indoctrination, the young learn to cherish their national community and their political system. The manner in which national history is taught and the emphasis upon the unique and superior traits of the national culture are calculated to create an emotional acceptance of the political system.

Generally, the young begin to assume a critical attitude toward authority in secondary schools and universities. In many societies there is a tradition of unrest and political alienation among university students, though frequently radical students of middle class backgrounds tend to be absorbed readily into the system once they complete their studies and enter the job market. But revolutions can rarely, if ever, be traced to intergenerational strife. They stem rather from discontinuities in historical development, and basic divisions within the society that split the generations internally. In revolutionary situations consensus is already undermined. Disagreement about norms and symbols of authority is sharp, and the young are inducted into a system that is embroiled in conflict. The agencies of socialization, including the family, school, and church, speak with different tongues and cultivate contradictory ideas, involving the very nature and character of the system itself.

Effectiveness and Performance

All social groups have goals or purposes in terms of which their discipline is justified. The effectiveness of the organization—be it church, trade union, corporation, or state—must be appraised in relation to its success in achieving stated goals. An army, for example, has well-defined goals: the application of superior firepower at a given point or, more broadly, defense of the country. An army is disciplined—command and obedience relations are established in unequivocal fashion, and criticism of its code is severely limited. It is an organization geared to performance, so that an order by a single chief moves masses of men and equipment. The efficiency of the "army model" accounts for widespread admiration of autocratic and authoritarian political systems, and constantly feeds the antidemocratic schools of thought. Lenin fashioned his theory of the Communist party after the army model, calling for rigorous discipline and total commitment of its members. Many of the symbols of fascist and other authoritarian parties are borrowed from the military. Order, discipline, and unquestioning obedience are equated with performance and effectiveness.

The army is a single or limited purpose organization. Politics, on the other hand, entails regulation and control of a society that contains many organizations, each striving to attain unique and frequently divergent goals. The family, school, church, corporation, and university are concerned with such distinctly different activities as reproduction of the species, rearing of the young, education, religion, industrial production, and the acquisition of scientific knowledge. The state is not only a relationship of command and obedience; it also involves conciliation and supports. For example, throughout Europe in the 19th century new groups were being created in the course of industrialization, and sought entry into the political system. Complex societies are participant societies. The "army model" is relevant only to the coercive aspect of a political system.

As Karl Deutsch suggests, in his *Nerves of Government,* [1] a political system may be viewed as complex sets of messages with a communication system that has been learned and internalized by all members of the society. A structured and learned communication system makes the government a sensitive instrument for the satisfaction of demands and interests of the citizens, and also makes the citizens receptive to the needs and directives of the government. The government and citizens are mutually supportive.

The "communications model" is useful in analyzing performance. It points to the following: that obedience to commands is learned and willed; that the government is constantly listening to the messages that come from all social groups and individuals; that so long as official directives are generally consonant with demands and expectations they are likely to be obeyed—indeed, obedience is taken for granted; that if such a pattern of relations is established over a period of time the relationship between government and citizens will become intimate and positive, characterized by marked interdependence and mutual trust. The capabilities of the government to act are immense since it can count on popular support. It can mobilize the citizenry for common purposes.

But what are these common purposes? In terms of what criteria is the effectiveness of a political system to be appraised? Every political society sets for itself varying goals, both specific (such as the creation of the infrastructure of a modern economy) and broad (the realization of values like equality or freedom). Comparison of political systems in terms of performance is difficult. What is considered success in one society may be failure in another, since the goals or values may be entirely different. There are, however, some generally accepted ends to which all political systems are committed—the survival of their societies in a hostile world; the maintenance of order; the resolution of conflicting demands and the allocation of goods in a manner that provides maximum satisfaction for all. The system must be able to maintain itself as it adjusts to constantly changing environmental factors. It must resolve problems as they arise and provide mechanisms for settling them.

A consensual democratic system derives its strength from the open communication between state and society. It contains a responsive mechanism that permits the articulation of interests and

---

[1] Karl Deutsch, *Nerves of Government,* rev. ed., (New York: Free Press, 1966).

demands on the part of the governed, gears its decisions to those demands, and, by so doing, elicits supports that can again be converted into a resource for the achievement of common ends. Emerging conflicts engage the attention of government and citizens so that the way is paved for their resolution. Broad participation in the system and the open nature of communications guarantee acceptance of policy, and help legitimize the state. A consensual system does not hesitate to arm the citizens, to draft them into the army, and to decree stringent measures calling for individual restraints in order to safeguard collective ends.

But, as we noted earlier, consensus is never universal in complex societies. The very openness of communications in democratic regimes permits dissident elements ample opportunity to clash with each other, and with the government. Indeed, dissidence may be so widespread that no majority can form, and the ability of the political system to formulate public policy is reduced. Nonconsensual democracies will tend to be ineffective in achieving socially accepted goals, or may even collapse altogether—as in Russia in October, 1917, Italy in 1922, and Germany in 1933.

Authoritarian regimes do not enjoy the advantages of an open communication system between leaders and the people. Since the citizens do not have the right to express their criticism, it is difficult for those in power to understand the nature of popular expectations, and to assess the effectiveness of policy. There is always a danger of solving political problems by violence, which includes popular uprisings as well as repression by the state. But some dictatorships have demonstrated a remarkable ability to mobilize popular energies and resources, and to promulgate effective policy. This requires exceptional dynamism and perspicacity on the part of the leaders, who in effect give the people what they want without going through the bother of inquiring beforehand or afterward. The citizens may be reasonably content, even if they have no opportunity to criticize, under conditions of full employment and material progress, and especially if the regime succeeds in embodying nationalistic sentiment. Military victory is also a good way of arousing popular enthusiasm for any regime, democratic or authoritarian. Popular support for authoritarian regimes is most likely in countries which have been governed previously by ineffective parliamentary democracies. It is noteworthy that the most important dictatorships in modern Europe—Bolshevism in Russia, fascism in Italy, and Nazism in Germany—all replaced nonconsensual and ineffective democracies.

The student will find that analysis of any aspect of a given political system—such as the interest groups, parties, political institutions, administration, and ideologies—always leads back to the critical question of consensus.

POLITICAL DYNAMICS

The pursuit of power—the capacity to command the actions of others—by individuals and groups is a universal phenomenon. Individuals and groups are organized through specialized associations representing their interests; they also promulgate or associate themselves with ideological orientations. By *political dynamics* we mean the interplay of social groups, organized interests, and ideologies, generally taking place through political parties and institutions in order to shape public policy.

The process whereby groups compete for positions and advantage takes place in all political systems, and hence can be studied functionally and comparatively. In some political systems, groups press their demands and claims mainly through "interest" or "pressure" groups; in others, through the parties or administration. Comparative analysis can be conducted by studying the diverse patterns of interest articulation. Interest groups can be considered in terms of their size, membership, leadership, organization, relations with political parties, and means used to mobilize public opinion, gain access to the state, and influence decisions. Group analysis has the merit of bringing the student directly into the heart of the political process—social conflict and its resolution. By studying the "interest group universe" in a given political system, we gain a good insight into the distribution of power in that society and the manner in which interests are organized and expressed.

One of the striking features of industrialized societies is the development and proliferation of specialized groups. In a modern society they represent every conceivable social, economic, religious, and professional interest. The largest and most powerful groups, speaking on behalf of the major social classes, are the business, labor, and agricultural organizations. Every modern political system must provide these associations or interest groups with the opportunity to gain access to the policy makers and make known their proposals or demands.

Reconciliation of the demands of interest groups and, broadly speaking, of social forces, is perhaps the most serious single challenge confronting any political system. We are not referring here to the demands, say, of trade unions and management for a minimum wage fixed at a particular level, though this kind of conflict is quite intense. We refer rather to the attitude of social groups toward the political process itself, the acceptance of the "rules of the game" by all the players. For example, there is a complex network of specialized associations in both Great Britain and France. In both countries we find powerful trade unions, business groups, churches, and associations of farmers, veterans, teachers, and so on. Some French groups are more powerful than their opposite numbers in Britain (for example, farmers, small merchants, lay Catholics) and vice versa (British trade unions and business groups are more highly organized than their counterparts in France). Yet the basic attitudes of the groups are significantly different. In spite of their political rivalry, expressed through support of the Labor and Conservative Parties, the trade unions and management groups in Great Britain accept a commitment to parliamentary institutions. With a few exceptions (such as the Irish nationalists), they are willing to work within the existing system in order to realize their goals, and do not turn against it when they lose. The habits of compromise are solidly established in British society. The actors abide by fundamental rules that are embodied in the constitutional system.

In France, however, the same economic or social interests are *not* in agreement upon the values of the state or on political procedures to be used in the resolution of group conflicts. The labor and business groups are fundamentally hostile to each other, and constantly strive to change the rules of the game or the system itself so as to secure a more advantageous position. The most powerful trade union in France, the General Confederation of Labor, is Communist controlled and Communist oriented. That is, the industrial proletariat in France largely expresses its demands through a union and a party that reject the system. Important elements of the business community, on the other hand, not only distrust the workers, but wish to introduce a "strong" state to deal with them. The parliamentary system is held in low repute by other important interests as well. Political debates and meetings are marked by verbal and physical violence. In practice the disaffected groups are generally unable to overthrow the system, and accept it provisionally. Compromise is difficult to achieve and breaks down altogether during political crises. There is a distinct tendency to change the rules of the game (usually by promulgating a new constitution) whenever the balance shifts and one constellation of groups or forces gains the upper hand. Thus, one of the most important questions to pose about a political system is the attitude of the principal organized groups toward each other and toward the system itself.

Political Parties

Max Weber's definition of party is useful for placing the subject in broad social and historical perspective. "The term political party," he suggested, "will be employed to designate an associative type of social relationship, membership in which rests on formally free recruitment. The end to which its activity is devoted is to secure power within a corporate group for its leaders in order to attain ideal or material advantages for its active members. These advantages may consist in the realization of certain objective policies or the attainment of personal advantages or both."[2] As Weber uses the term, a "party" can exist in any corporate group—unions, fraternal orders, churches, university faculties, and corporations. It can be oriented toward personal interest or toward broad policy. When the rules of the corporate group provide for campaigns and elections, the parties coalesce around interests. Political victory in party terms means that its adherents, in assuming direction of the state, can realize party proposals. Political parties thus tend to be complex social institutions holding together those who have a common program and those who strive for power and personal advantage. In a sense they are specialized associations *within* specialized associations and become more complex, organized, and bureaucratic as a society approaches the "modern" type.

It is therefore understandable that political parties were not studied systematically until the modern period, when they were fully developed. John Stuart Mill's treatise *On Representative Government,* written in 1861, contained an extensive plea for proportional representation but no analysis of parties. Insofar as parties were brought under scrutiny, they were generally denounced as expressions of factionalism. In a classic criticism of political parties, James Bryce expressed his fear that insofar as parties are permitted to run the government a community falls below the level of ideal democracy. "In the ideal democracy every citizen is intelligent, patriotic, disinterested. His sole wish is to discover the right side in each contested issue, and to fix upon the best man among competing candidates. His common sense, aided by a knowledge of the constitution of his country, enables him to judge easily between the arguments submitted to him while his own zeal is sufficient to carry him to the polling booth." But, Bryce continues, the electorate is *not* informed or interested. Hence, politicians discover the advantages of organization. "Organization and discipline mean the command of the leaders, the subordination and obedience of the rank and file; and they mean also the growth of a party spirit which is in itself irrational, impelling men to vote from considerations which have little to do with a love of truth or a sense of justice."[3]

Most students of political parties at the turn of the century, like

---

[2] See Max Weber, *The Theory of Social and Economic Organization* (London: Oxford University Press, 1947), pp. 407–12.

[3] From James Bryce's preface to M. Ostrogorski, *Democracy and the Organization of Political Parties* (New York: Macmillan, 1902).

Bryce, were concerned with the shortcomings and deficiencies of the political parties: with bossism, corruption, and the inability of the parties to put forward coherent programs and implement them once in power. M. I. Ostrogorski's classic treatise on *Democracy and the Organization of Political Parties* emphasized especially the sordid side of politics—above all, the politicians' craving for spoils. The thesis argued by Bryce and Ostrogorski concerning American parties was strengthened by Robert Michels' study of the German Social Democratic party, *Political Parties*. From the viewpoint of comparative analysis Michels' work marked an advance, since his "iron law of oligarchy" could be construed as a general theory in the light of which all political parties may be examined. Bryce, Ostrogorski, and Michels, taken together, offered a full-fledged theory of parties and their role in democracies. They fully documented the growth of mass political parties with complex structures in the United States, Britain, and Germany. They assumed that democracy somehow involves meaningful participation by the masses in the making of important decisions. They agreed that parties were controlled by a handful of politicians and leaders. Democracy therefore becomes less and less feasible as parties become more and more complex.

Theory regarding the role of parties in a democracy has undergone sweeping change since then. The widespread view of parties as destructive of democracy has given way to an almost equally widespread view that parties are indispensable to the operation of democratic institutions. American political scientists were especially affected by the New Deal, which seemed to demonstrate the potential utility of political parties in mobilizing public support for a program of social reform. Also, the hostile reaction to the Nazi regime included searching appraisal of the one-party system. In defense of Western democracy against the challenge of fascism and communism, it was discerned that democracy was bound up somehow with the existence of at least two parties. The previously despised parties were elevated to positions of great prestige by political philosophers and researchers.

Stress was laid upon the role of parties in the democratic process by such writers as A. D. Lindsay, R. M. MacIver, C. J. Friedrich, Joseph Schumpeter, and Walter Lippmann, to name but a few.[4] They argued that a distinct element of democracy, as contrasted

---

[4] See A. D. Lindsay, *The Modern Democratic State* (New York, 1947); R. M. MacIver, *The Web of Government* (New York, 1947); Carl J. Friedrich, *Constitutional Government and Democracy* (Boston, 1946); Joseph Schumpeter, *Capitalism, Socialism and Democracy* (New York, 1947); and Walter Lippmann, *Public Opinion* (New York, 1945).

two-party, and multiparty systems tend to correspond to the major types of contemporary regimes. Thus, dictatorships are characterized by the single party, and democracies by either a two- or multiparty system. The two-party system is frequently held up as a model form, permitting the majority to govern and the minority to criticize. Multiparty systems are usually considered less stable, but offer the voter a greater choice of alternatives. However, this classification has come under attack. Some observers have suggested that one-party systems may serve as transitional forms, making possible the creation of a more democratic regime at a later time. Mexico is frequently cited as an instance where one-party rule is compatible with democracy because debate can take place within the dominant party.

The customary distinction between two- and multiparty systems has also been questioned, particularly with regard to France and Scandinavia. French political scientists have called attention to the agreements (electoral alliances and cabinet coalitions) between parties of the same political family, which provide a measure of coherence. Thus, François Goguel speaks of the "party of order" and the "party of movement" in interpreting the conflict among the various parties of the Third Republic, in his *La Politique des partis sous la IIIᵉ République* (1946). In run-off elections under the Third and Fifth Republics the French voter has frequently been presented with a choice between only two or three serious candidates. Similarly, students of Scandinavia have pointed out that these multiparty systems are capable of sustaining dynamic and stable governments. The parties form coalitions in the same way that wings of a major party in Britain or the United States come to agreement on a common policy or leader. It may be more fruitful to view party systems in terms of the nature of the national consensus, that is, whether or not the major parties (within either a two- or multiparty system) and in turn the major social groups on which they are based, share the same attitudes toward basic values and goals and the means by which they are to be attained.

In recent years party systems have been reappraised in the context of the general process of modernization. As a traditional society breaks up and takes on the characteristics of "modernity," it goes through a series of political crises. The first is a crisis of *legitimacy*. Values sanctioning rule by a traditional monarchy or aristocracy are called into question, and are eventually replaced by values such as parliamentary democracy or nationalism that are more consonant with mass participation in the political system. This goes hand-in-hand with a crisis of *participation*. New social groups, in particular an industrial middle class and a working class, make their appearance and demand entry into the political system. In mature industrial societies there is a continuing crisis of *conflict management*. The political system is confronted by the need to facilitate economic growth, reconcile the claims of powerful social groups for a greater share of wealth and power, and ensure the continued adherence of these groups to the system itself.

Political parties, it may be argued, have gone through stages of development that correspond to the successive crises of legitimacy, participation, and conflict management. Parties throughout Europe in the early part of the 19th century were primarily concerned with new principles of legitimacy and the representation of fairly narrow interests. With the extension of the suffrage in the course of the 19th century the parties created mass organizations outside of parliament. Mass parties, like the German Social Democrat, British Liberal, and, later, Labor parties sought to defend the interests of the new middle and working classes, and to mobilize popular support for their policies. At this stage the parties tended to reflect sharp ideological orientations. The "parties of participation" had to make adjustments in order to cope with the demands of late industrialization, when problems became more complex and less susceptible to ideological solutions. They became more concerned with the management of conflict and tensions when in power, and more pragmatic in their appeals to the electorate.

One of the most noticeable trends affecting parties at present is the development of plebiscitary government. Its main trait is the bypassing or the diminution of the powers of all representative bodies in favor of personalized leadership stemming from direct popular support in periodic elections. In France under the Gaullist constitution, the President, as the political leader and head of the executive, now derives his powers from direct election. This is also the case for the American president and the British cabinet under the leadership of the prime minister, who is head of the majority party. The political parties select and nominate a leader who then appeals directly to the public. Although the parties may set broad policy guidelines, the personal appeal of the leader and his ability to secure widespread support may, in the last analysis, be the decisive factor for victory or defeat at the polls.

In France, plebiscitary government has an old and venerable lineage that goes back to Bonapartism. In all countries it is a reflection of profound social changes that have led to an increasingly homogeneous body politic. Under these altered circumstances the parties can no longer sell their ideological or policy programs. Large national formations vie for support on the basis of broadly similar appeals to consumer interests. As a result, identification with the party becomes weaker, or, to put it another way, the personality of a leader becomes more important. Correspondingly, the ratio of party members to voters, for the whole community and for each party, goes down, while there are growing numbers of independents or "floaters."

In totalitarian systems the ruling party excludes competition and uses the election as a well-controlled plebiscitary instrument. The leader in a communist system is likely to emerge only after he has proven himself within the party, which remains a powerful recruitment and screening agency. In presidential democracies non-party people may, without any prior screening or testing, avail themselves of the plebiscitary character of the election. Even in Britain and other parliamentary democracies the struggle for leadership of the party, and certainly the general election itself, is greatly influenced by the personal qualities of the contending leaders. The logic of plebiscitary government applies to both Western democracies and totalitarian systems. The intermediary organs—including the parties and representative assemblies—are weakened, and power is concentrated in the political executive. A continuing problem in all modern political systems is to create institutions that might counterbalance the tremendous political and decision-making powers of plebiscitary leaders.

Interests

There are three basic models in terms of which the relationship between the state and interests can be viewed: pluralist, corporatist, and totalitarian. Each model, in turn, has versions reflecting the unique traditions and circumstances of individual nations.

In the pluralist (or democratic) model, interests (whether trade unions, business groups, professional associations, or churches) are autonomous and free to act. They make demands through publicity, electoral pressure, and direct or indirect action on the state. Their aim is to maximize their own interests at the expense of others, but in most cases there is accommodation and compromise. According to this model the state and its agencies respond to the constant demands of interest groups; and the public good is the sum total of particular interests. Under certain conditions pluralism may lead to stalemate—when competing interests are evenly matched. Some observers attribute recent indications of crisis in democracies to the inability of political institutions, including parties, to create a synthesis among competing and conflicting interests. The state becomes a captive of an interest universe that it cannot transcend.

In the corporatist model it is assumed that clashes among interests (especially labor and business) are prejudicial to the public good. It is therefore necessary to secure cooperation among interests

(and classes) under the overall direction and often control of the
state. Some specific powers are delegated to interests, for example,
to fix prices and wages, organize production in various sectors of
the economy, and assume responsibility for social and welfare services. But all interests and associations operate under state control.
Interest groups do not enjoy autonomy; their relations with other
groups are structured and supervised by public agencies. They are
not free to pressure the state, nor to communicate among themselves
in order to make compromises or strike bargains. They function
as part of the state structure, not as free agents acting upon the
state.

In the totalitarian model interests and professional associations
are taken over physically, or are absorbed by the state. This is
notably the case in communist systems where the means of production and virtually all economic and entrepreneurial activities are
run by the state and its agencies. The interest groups have no independent resources, no freedom to take their case to the public, and
no autonomy. The political elite dominates the interest universe
and infuses it with its own purpose and imperatives. How effectively
depends on a number of factors: the strength of the single political
party, the appeal of the official ideology, the tenacity of past political
culture, and the level and degree of economic modernization. The
Soviet Union, Rumania, China, and Vietnam differ markedly
though they all propose the same subordination of interests to an
official ideology and party.

These models rarely exist in a "pure" or ideal form. In most
democracies the pluralist model has been qualified by corporatist
practices whereby interest groups and professional associations
work closely with state agencies in the making and carrying out
of public policy. In communist systems interest groups have been
able to interact with the party and state agencies, and in some
cases have acquired a modicum of autonomy. Corporatist practices
have become current everywhere as groups assert their identity
and specificity even while the state seeks to maintain its position
of supremacy.

POLITICAL INSTITUTIONS

Interests and interest groups are the raw material of politics.
Through the political parties, or through other larger groupings,
they press their claims upon the governmental structures and the
decision-making organs of the political system. Policy is often the
result of such claims. The farmers wish protection; the workers
ask for wage increases; the military for special appropriations; the
church for subsidies; the business community for lower taxes. To

the uninitiated the striving for satisfaction by various interest groups, the multiplicity and the intensity of conflicts, the incompatibility of the interests involved, often make a political community seem something like a jungle where the survival of the fittest or the strongest appears to be the only rule.

Yet over and above interest and interest conflict there is a basic consensus on the fundamental rules of the game, that is, the acceptance of certain rules according to which conflict will be waged, interests articulated, and conflict resolved. All political systems are characterized by the existence of these rules—what A. D. Lindsay in his book *The Modern Democratic State* calls "operative ideals." That is, in every political society there is an organ that makes decisions according to certain procedures, and these decisions are accepted and obeyed. The state has authority and prestige, not only force.

Constitutions

The general organization and structure of authority is in essence a "constitution." Whether written or unwritten a constitution expresses the "fundamental agreement" of the political society on how it will be governed. It usually defines the scope of governmental authority, the way in which decisions are made, and the manner in which decision makers are selected and held accountable. It both creates and limits power. The legacy of the Middle Ages was to define what today we call rights that limit arbitrary power and narrow the scope of the state's authority. With the beginning of the 19th century most political systems began to establish responsibility of the governors to the governed through representative assemblies and periodic elections.

A system in which a constitution is widely accepted may be referred to as *consensual,* that is, the people in it agree on how they will resolve their differences. They do not "bicker about fundamentals." Political systems may well be classified, therefore, in terms of this criterion. In some systems the agreement on fundamentals is not widely shared or intensely felt—they have a *low degree of consensus or legitimacy.* In others, there is no such agreement— they are *highly divided or transitional systems.* In still others, the agreement is overtly manufactured through the control of the media of communication by a small group of political leaders—this is the case in authoritarian systems. But authoritarianism is not in itself evidence of low consensus, for in some cases leadership may bring about a high degree of unity and perhaps popular support.

The distinction between consensual and highly divided systems may be illustrated by the cases of Great Britain and France. In both countries the feudal scheme was disrupted, the traditional monarchy was severely restricted or overthrown, and parliamentary democracy was introduced. The British monarchy during the 17th century proved to be less adaptable than the French. The loss of its prerogatives was registered in the Declaration and Bill of Rights of 1689. That is, by the end of the 17th century parliamentary sovereignty was enunciated as the basic principle of the British consitution. Political conflict did not disappear, and the monarch continued to exert great influence upon his ministers and the Parliament. With the extension of the suffrage in the 19th century, the political base of the House of Commons was transformed. Its legitimacy now derived from the people, whose will was expressed and shaped by mass political parties. These new forces accepted the venerable principle of parliamentary sovereignty, and the practice of parliamentary government.

The new interests and classes created by the Industrial Revolution thus found a ready-made instrument for the resolution of their conflicts. Slowly the system absorbed, or rather integrated, the new groups, notably the industrial middle class and the workers. But in so doing the political institutions were themselves greatly modified. The country was governed not by an independent and narrowly based House of Commons, but rather by disciplined parties, the cabinet, and the civil service. The need for strong leadership and the increasing importance of the personality of the leader strengthened the position of the prime minister; on the other hand, the growing complexity of administration made it difficult for the cabinet to function as a collective agency. The trend in the modern era has been toward the concentration of power in the prime minister, who dominates the cabinet much as the cabinet previously dominated Parliament.

In France, and other countries of the continent, a radically different situation prevailed. Parliaments in these countries knew an uneasy and eventful life, becoming the source of unresolved opposition to the powers of the king or the nobility. The French representative assemblies were not allowed to meet for over a century and a half. When finally they met in 1789, they set aside the powers of the king and ushered in a period of turmoil. A democratic constitution was accepted only by a part of the population. The 19th century was a period of conflict and struggle in which sometimes democracy and sometimes monarchy or personal government (Bonapartism) triumphed. The working classes found it impossible to accommodate themselves to one or the other form and developed a utopian or revolutionary outlook. Thus by the end of the 19th century there was no widespread agreement in France about any constitution; sizable fractions of the population had not been integrated into the system; and people remained divided not only about interests and aspirations but also on how they should resolve their conflicts. The French found it difficult to "agree on how they were to disagree."

Throughout the 19th and 20th centuries, constitutional instability was also the rule in most other European countries where sharp incompatibilities and ideological divisions were very much in evidence. The threat of revolutionary uprising by the underprivileged groups that had never been fully integrated into the system was ever present. The Bolshevik Revolution of 1917 gave sharpness and meaning to their demands. The Nazi system in Germany and, to a lesser degree, the Fascist system in Italy, gave hope to the wealthier groups, to the military, some of the conservative elements of the Church, and to the many lower-middle-class groups that a "strong" government, based on one-party rule, could provide stability and unity. Both the Bolshevik and Fascist movements imperiled democratic constitutionalism and provided their followers with an armed vision that undermined the tolerance and agreement on which democracy rests.

Governmental Institutions

The decision-making functions of all political societies have been distinguished traditionally into three separate types: the executive, the legislative, and the judicial. However, this threefold division is not a realistic guide to the exercise of political power. In some systems the legislature assumed the totality of decision-making power, with the executive simply executing the will of the lawmakers and the judiciary applying and interpreting the law in case of litigation. In other instances, a precarious balance between the executive and the legislature was established, with the executive slowly assuming increased powers and independence of action. In other systems—notably those with a federal organization of power—the judiciary emerged as a genuinely independent organ with wide latitude to interpret the constitution and in so doing to limit the powers of the legislature and the executive.

The 19th century was the period of legislative supremacy in most of the Western constitutional democracies. Walter Bagehot, writing in the latter part of the century, pointed out that the Parliament nominated the members of the executive, passed laws, prepared and voted the budget, supervised the cabinet and finally aired grievances and ventilated issues, thus helping to mold and shape public opinion. It was primarily a body of people who represented the upper and middle classes of the community, fundamentally in agreement about the policies to be pursued, unharried, embodying the complacency and stability of the Victorian period. They usually debated broad political problems—educational reform, extension of the franchise, the rights of associations and individuals, and international treaties. Controversy was resolved in compromise that could be spelled out in general parliamentary enactments. This was also the case in some other systems where parliamentary democracy developed—Sweden, Holland, Norway, and Denmark. In the United States the pendulum swung between "presidential" government, especially in times of crisis, and "congressional" government.

On the continent representative assemblies were often regarded as the instruments of popular rule against the privileged groups. They claimed on behalf of the people the totality of political power, and relegated the executive to the role of an agent. This was notably the case of France, where the legislative assemblies reduced the cabinet to a subservient role.

Outside of Western Europe, North America, and the British Dominions, representative government in the 19th century was virtually unknown. In the Balkans and Latin America, constitutions and parliamentary institutions were provided on paper, but the practice belied the constitutional forms. Most of these systems were oligarchies where political power, irrespective of the forms, was in the hands of the landowners, the military, or the church. Others were traditional societies, in which political rule was hereditary. They had not experienced the conflicts and modernization, associated with the French Revolution and industrialization, that led to progressive political emancipation of the masses in Europe. Their political systems were encrusted in tradition and immemorial custom.

With the beginning of the 20th century, an important change in the organization and functioning of democratic institutions can be discerned. The internal balance of power between the three organs—executive, legislative, and judicial—began to shift in favor of the executive. This trend reflects profound modifications in the social and political structures of modern societies.

Representative institutions operated well when the pressure upon them to make decisions was light. The free-market system provided an automatic mechanism of decision making. Matters of wages, hours of work, employment, social security, education, technological improvement, investment, and economic development were to remain outside of the province of the state. The increasing complexity of the industrial society called, however, for regulation of economic activity. The need for state intervention grew, and demanded special knowledge and skill. The legislature proved singularly unfit to perform these tasks. The legislature was cumbersome;

its members had neither technical knowledge, nor expertise, nor time. Slowly the burden of decision making shifted to the political executive and the civil service.

Political reasons also accounted for this shift. Most significant were the extension of suffrage and the growth of large national parties. The two phenomena are historically associated. Elections became increasingly confrontations between two or more parties appealing to a mass electorate on specific issues or on a general program for action. Thus the legislature was bypassed, since victory at the polls meant that the leadership of the majority party would form a government to carry out its pledges. Wherever party discipline was strong, therefore, popular elections were equivalent to the selection of the "government," i.e., the executive.

Political and technical trends reinforced each other and during the interwar years the executive assumed more and more powers. Representative assemblies have lost virtually all of the functions attributed to them by Walter Bagehot in the 19th century. The vast majority of legislative projects emanate from the executive; the preparation of the budget has become an executive function in which the cabinet, in association with the top civil service or independent executive bodies, drafts the specifications involving public expenditures and revenue. Parliament has even virtually lost the power to nominate the cabinet. Finally, the very scope of lawmaking has changed. Special laws or regulations are needed that can best be made by those in touch with the problems of developed industrial societies—that is to say, by the executive departments and the civil service. Thus the legislature has fallen into the habit of drafting general laws in which regulatory powers are generously delegated to the executive. For all practical purposes such delegation is so broad as to invest the executive and civil service with virtual lawmaking powers.

In modern political systems, then, leadership has shifted to the executive, with the legislature acting mainly as a forum for the airing of grievances. The executive has taken the initiative as regards general lawmaking, foreign and defense policy, and direction of the economy. Assumption of these responsibilities and the concentration of these functions in the executive branch have led to a proliferation of new agencies and bureaus. The political executive has become "bureaucratized." It initiates policy, coordinates policy decisions, and is responsible for their implementation and execution. Institutions have developed within the executive corresponding to these three phases of the policy-making process.

In both presidential and parliamentary systems, a small group of political leaders is in charge of overall policy initiation and formulation. They are the president, or the prime minister, and his or her immediate advisers. To assist the top leaders in the formulation of policy there are a number of "adjunct" administrative staff organizations. They draft policy papers on economic planning, foreign policy, defense, and the budget. In the United States, the Office of Management and the Budget, the National Security Council, and the Council of Economic Advisers perform important deliberative and policy-initiation functions. In Britain and France, cabinet committees are responsible for similar activities. Thus deliberation is institutionalized at the executive level.

Policy proposals put forward by various executive agencies must then be coordinated. Suggestions and countersuggestions are thrashed out in the cabinet, or in small ministerial committees made up of top civil servants, the chiefs of staff, and the personal advisers to the president or prime minister. Reconciliation of conflicting proposals may require the ultimate personal intervention of the president or prime minister. The interdependence of military, economic, and foreign policy has called increasingly for such interdepartmental coordination.

Finally, it is necessary to execute decisions. This is the task of the vast majority of civil servants—to inspect, repair, perform, and check. They do what the employees of any large corporation do— they perform on the basis of orders and regulations decided by their superiors.

THE BUREAUCRACY

It is one of the characteristics of industrial societies, irrespective of their form of government, to develop a civil service recruited on the basis of specific technical requirements. "Bureaucratic administration means fundamentally the exercise of control on the basis of knowledge," observed Max Weber. It is above all a rational organization characterized by: (1) a clearly defined sphere of competence subject to impersonal rules: (2) a hierarchy that determines in an orderly fashion relations of superiors and subordinates; (3) a regular system of appointments and promotions on the basis of free contract; (4) recruitment on the basis of skills, knowledge, or technical training; and (5) fixed salaries.

The Prussian civil service was an early example of a professional service with clear-cut demarcation of spheres of competence, rigid rules of recruitment, and allocation of posts on the basis of skills. It reflected the high degree of military organization and centralization of that country. After the unification of Germany the same standards were made applicable to the whole German bureaucracy.

In Great Britain professionalization was introduced officially in 1853 by the Northcote-Trevelyan Report on the "Organization of the Permanent Civil Service," which opened the civil service to talent through competitive examinations. Until then civil service appointments were made on political considerations and were, by and large, restricted to the nobility. The civil service was divided into three "classes," each corresponding to a distinct function: (1) the administrative class, which is the highest policy-making group within the departments; (2) the executive class, whose main task is the execution of policies; and (3) the clerical or manipulative class, whose work is primarily clerical and manual.

In France it was only after the Liberation in 1944 that drastic reforms—inspired in large measure by the organization of the civil service in Britain—were made. First, a general entrance examination has been established for all candidates. Previously each department did its own recruiting. The examination stresses law, political science, economics, and social sciences in general. Secondly, the civil service was broadly divided into two classes: (1) civil administrators (approximating the British administrative class) and (2) "secretaries of administration" (corresponding to the executive class). Thirdly, the *Ecole Nationale d'Administration* has been founded to serve as the training school for all prospective civil administrators. Students are considered public officials from the moment they enter, receive a stipend, and after successful completion of their studies and the passing of the final examinations, are assigned to an executive department. Throughout their training, which is jointly offered by civil servants and academicians, an effort is made to depart from the formalistic and legalistic approach so typical of the past and to create a self-reliant and imaginative civil servant.

The American civil service has also been "professionalized," beginning with the Pendleton Act of 1883. Recruitment is by competitive examinations, but the emphasis tends to be on specialized knowledge rather than a broad, liberal education. There is no clear-cut division between an administrative and executive class, in terms of rigidly separate educational requirements and examinations, though of course those who occupy the highest "general classes" within the hierarchy in effect perform the policymaking function. The American civil service thus is not as homogeneous as its European counterparts. American top-level administrators are graduates of universities all over the nation and are drawn from a wider range of social classes. There is also considerable movement of individuals between the civil service and private life (business, universities, and law practice, for example)—which is rare in Europe. The undoubted advantage of the European system is to create a corps of administrators who have demonstrated brilliance in academic studies during their youth, and who have shared common experiences. The result is a remarkable *esprit de corps*. In the United

States, on the other hand, it is easier to invigorate the administrative establishment by providing new recruits from private life, and also to make use of talented individuals who may not have distinguished themselves as college undergraduates.

Traditionally "bureaucracy" has been viewed as an instrument of enforcement and execution of the law. Impartial and neutral—at least in theory—it was also remote, incarnating the authority and majesty of the state. It emphasized legality rather than equity, application of rules rather than innovation, continuity rather than change. The civil servant (or "mandarin," as called by the French) remained aloof from everyday affairs, saw more files than citizens, and made decisions of a quasi-judicial character.

But in some respects modern bureaucracy has departed from the Weberian model of a legal-rational organization. The increase in sheer numbers and the expansion of functions produced profound changes. The civil servant became ubiquitous, and as a result, less aloof and remote from the society that was governed. By taking on new responsibilities, bureaucrats were transformed from guardians of the law into quasi legislators. Their powers became increasingly political, and had immediate consequences for those affected by their decisions and for the whole society. The bureaucrats' world was expanded, and they began to view their constituency not as a host of individual plaintiffs who sought redress in accordance with the law, but as groups and interests pressing for decisions affecting the very nature of social relations. They found themselves confronted with conflicts among interests that called for political analysis and choice among alternatives. While still clinging to the tradition of statism and neutrality, the bureaucrat and the bureaucracy as a whole became integral parts of the policy-making process.

The civil servants' mentality inevitably changed when they entered the realm of direct action in the world of commerce and industry. The skills required to set regulations for, let us say, credit, are different from those needed to apply laws in individual cases. The people responsible for the use of atomic energy to produce electricity, for construction of new cities, for settlement of labor disputes, or for maintenance of full employment, no longer resemble their 19th-century counterparts. The requisites of bureaucratic decision making are knowledge, expertise, originality, inventiveness, and an ability to gain cooperation and support from the interests involved. Civil servants who participate in the drafting of an economic plan must not only know their own jobs, but must be in touch with the interest groups that are affected by the plan.

Consultation with the organized interests and mutual interpenetration of interests and the civil service has become general. The old bureaucracy based on "imperative coordination" has become a "consultative" bureaucracy making decisions that affect the whole society, thoroughly permeated by the interests it serves. While links have always existed between organized interests and bureaucracy, the open consultative process is a central feature of modern political systems. Interest groups in the past have attempted to colonize, influence, or neutralize the bureaucracy, and usually tried to maintain anonymity while doing so. Now the dialogue is open, the anonymity has been shed, and decisions engage the responsibility of the civil servants who make them. The bureaucracy thus takes on some of the characteristics of political parties in seeking close ties with specific interests (like business or labor) and broad popular support from all consumers and citizens. The "mandarin" has become a manager and a politician, while the spokesmen of interest groups and executives of private corporations are directly involved in the decision-making process. A "new corporatism" seems to be emerging in all modern political systems.

The executive has thus become in all contemporary industrialized societies a huge bureaucracy in which millions of people work, performing thousands of interrelated tasks. A small group of persons are ultimately responsible for the policies made and the manner in which they are implemented. They alone have to confront the public in periodic elections and give an account of their activities. They have to answer questions raised in the representative assemblies and reply to criticism. They have the burden of political responsibility—and this applies to authoritarian and democratic systems alike, though the forms of enforcement may differ.

But political responsibility, even where enforced through periodic elections and accountability to legislative assemblies, is not enough. The magnitude and the complexity of modern government are so great that no legislature (not even through its committees) can take full cognizance of them. Legislative control has often proven inadequate for effective supervision of the operations of nationalized industries, the performance of regulatory actions, and many other technical decisions.

The crucial problem facing all democratic systems today is to devise other forms and techniques of executive accountability. One possibility is the development of a sense of "internal responsibility" within the civil service itself. This can be inculcated by education and the development of strict rules of performance and rules of accountability of subordinate to superior. Another technique often suggested is the creation of specialized legislative committees to deal with specific areas of executive activity—nationalized industries, delegated legislation, defense, and the budget. A third one is the establishment of advisory bodies in which the major interests affected by policy decisions may participate. Recently there has been considerable discussion concerning the parliamentary Ombudsman (or Grievance Man) in Scandinavia, and the possibility of transplanting this office in other parts of the world. None of these techniques, however, appear to be fully successful and the truth of the matter is that they cannot be. The notion of "political responsibility" appears to be increasingly anachronistic in an era of massive technological development. The leaders of any modern society—democratic or authoritarian—confront the challenge of implementing common aspirations. Success or failure depends mainly upon the technical competence and skill of the political leadership.

The growth of the executive and its assumption of policy-making functions, the tremendous expansion of public services coupled with the ineffectiveness of political controls over the bureaucracy, pose serious threats to individual freedom. A highly complex bureaucratized apparatus geared to performance is potentially an ever-present danger to the individual, even when it claims to serve his or her interests. To the old "reason of state" may be added a new, perhaps even more dangerous, "reason of service." Managerialism or *technocratie,* as the French call it, may finish by exalting efficiency, skill, and organization over criticism, freedom, and individualism. It may encourage conformity rather than eccentricity, unity rather than pluralism, action rather than thought, discipline rather than freedom. An astute author writing some 40 years ago predicted that managerialism would be the political form of the future in all contemporary industrialized societies—democratic or not.[8]

The rise of the large bureaucratized state as well as the example of totalitarianism have aroused widespread concern for the protection of individual rights and freedoms. In some post–World War II constitutions, higher courts were given power to scrutinize legislative acts and see to it that the legislative and executive branches remained strictly within the confines of the constitution. In Western Germany, Italy, Austria, and recently in France, constitutional courts were established for this purpose. In both Britain and the United States administrative courts have been created to try cases involving litigation between the state and individuals. "Administrative law," long misunderstood by American and British observers of the French scene, has developed slowly as a guarantee of the rights of individuals in their dealings with the administrative and regulatory agencies of the state.

Other safeguards have also been sought. Federalism, for instance, has as a major purpose internal limitation upon the omnicompetence of the state. Even in unitary states, like Britain and France, efforts have been made to revitalize local governments in order to

---

[8] J. Burnham, *The Managerial Revolution* (New York: John Day, 1941).

stimulate experimentation and avert uniformity and rigidity of centralized control.

However, the techniques of judicial review, administrative courts and federalism have not proved capable of bringing central bureaucracies under effective political or legal control. The problems of modern society are so complex and far ranging that protecting the governed by enforcing responsibility of the governors remains a central political problem.

CHAPTER FIVE

Groups, Parties, and Elections

———— 15 ————

Groups and Group Theory

Roy C. Macridis

Without attempting to enter into a detailed discussion it would seem to me that group analysis is (epistemological labels may be used without implying any guilt by association) a crude form of determinism. Interest is the primary propelling force and every action is based upon sharing of interest. Power configuration is basically the configuration of competing and struggling interests organized into groups. Ideology, values, the state, the formal organization of political decision making, and the content of decisions are determined by the parallelogram of group forces. Perhaps this may be an oversimplification, but I do not think that it does violence to the scheme of group analysis. It is interesting, for instance, that not only concern with the state recedes into the background in the writings of all proponents of the group theory, but also the role of ideology, of extra-economic and non-rational motivational patterns, and of the political system as an independent factor influencing group behavior.

But while Marx with his class theory and its deterministic underpinnings provided a broad theory of history and development through which man would ultimately be able to shed interest in order to attain freedom—that is, while Marxist determinism led progressively to higher stages of consciousness and perception of the environment, group theorists anchor man's life into the

Source: Roy C. Macridis, "Interest Groups in Comparative Analysis," *The Journal of Politics* 23, no. 1 (February 1961). By permission.

perennial group conflict which by their very nature groups can never transcend. Not only our lives remain intolerably and unredeemably "nasty and brutish," but our theoretical universe in terms of which we can explain behavior becomes unduly restricted. Interest is the propelling force and man is forever destined to live in an environment that mirrors interest. It may be argued that group theory is "realistic" and, furthermore, that the "group" is a far more useful concept analytically than "class." I doubt it very much—first, because group analysis as I have noted has normative implications and second and more important, because the concepts of "interest" and "group" are fuzzy analytically, perhaps just as much as that of the "class."

But the above criticisms involve philosophic questions that are highly controversial. What is more important for our discussion is that group theory puts exaggerated demands upon empirical research and data collection. If an understanding of a political system at a given moment depends upon the study of the total configuration of interests the task of the political scientist becomes stupendous. We have to study every and all interest groups, index them and measure carefully and constantly the increments of power and influence they generate before we can make any statements about the most meaningful aspects of politics—the resolution of conflict and policy making, including foreign policy. We would have to elaborate precise units of power in order to assess and reassess continuously group power. But such a measurement would involve so many variables that meaningful measurement and quantification would become hopeless. . . . Where then do we start and even more important where do we stop indexing and measuring group power and interaction: business interests, economic interests, labor interests, religious interests, local interests, bureaucratic interests, organized interests, to say nothing of potential groups that hide in their bosom potential interests that are ready to blossom forth? How many of them do we study and exactly for what purpose? The index of power at any given moment would be inaccurate unless we measure the potential counter-power that can be generated by the potential groups. How can we tell exactly under what conditions groups will compromise? What can we learn about the perception that groups have of other groups or the total group configuration? How can we measure the adherence of groups to the "rules of the game" that in all political systems curb, limit, and often shape group action? What I am saying, of course, is that group analysis may prove to be both self-defeating and misleading. We cannot know the power configuration in a society unless we have studied all groups as they interact, and when we do so we still do not know why groups interact in one manner rather than another.

Finally, group analysis seems to beg rather than answer the very question it purports to ask—to give us an explanatory frame of reference in terms of which we can account for differences and uniformities in political behavior and action. This is the central problem of comparative analysis. Group theory assumes the existence of organized groups or interests that can be defined in objective terms; labor, business, and agriculture are some of the more obvious and frequently studied ones. It is further assumed that their members have a common perception of the interest involved which accounts for the very formation of the group and its organization and articulation. So far so good. Descriptive and comparative study immediately presents us with extreme variations in the organization, cohesiveness, membership strength, forms of action, and patterns of interaction among these groups. It reveals some striking differences in the manner in which interest groups in various political systems relate to the political parties and the political processes.

To attempt to explain such differences in terms of a group theory is impossible. Why are, for instance, agricultural groups so well organized under the National Farmers Union in England, to which more than 90 percent of the farmers belong, but dispersed and relatively unorganized in the United States and France? Why are more than 85 percent of all manufacturing concerns in England represented in their national association while not more than 6 percent are so represented in the United States? Why do more than 50 percent of the British workers belong to trade unions which are almost all represented in their peak organization, the TUC, while in France membership remains low and articulation of labor interest dispersed in at least four trade union organizations? Why is it that in England interest groups avoid large publicity campaigns and center their attention on the party and the cabinet, while in the United States interest groups perform important publicity and propaganda functions through the media of communications and center their efforts on the electorate and the legislature, primarily, while French interest groups shy publicity and center their activities upon the legislature and the administration?

A number of answers can be given to these questions in the form of propositions to be carefully investigated, but I submit none of them are researchable in terms of group analysis. The answers are often given (without adequate evidence, to be sure) in terms of other categories: the American political system *with multiple foci* of decision making, for instance, makes the legislature and more particularly individual legislators more susceptible to pressure either directly or indirectly; *the diffusion of power* in the political party in the United States makes any effort to control or influence the party unrewarding for pressure groups; the same applies for

France, where it is often pointed out that "interest" and "interest groups" are divided and sub-divided and lose their "objective" or "real" interest *because of political reasons.* The workers, the farmers, the teachers have no spokesmen and no cohesive and disciplined interest articulation because they are divided into a number of "political" or "ideological" families. As for group interaction, again the differences are striking: in some cases, groups interact within a given political party and compromise their differences; in other cases, compromise is made outside of the political parties, or is not made at all, leading to immobility; elsewhere compromise is made impossible by virtue of the fact that interests are "colonized" by ideological parties so that interest groups mirror the ideological divisions of the society instead of causing them.

In all cases the reasons advanced for a given pattern of group organization, action and interaction derive from categories other than group analysis would suggest: the formal organization of power; the cohesiveness or dispersal of political power; the two-party or multiparty configuration; the "climate of public opinion"; the intensity of consensus or lack of same in given political systems. . . .

Let me further illustrate the shortcomings of group analysis as an explanatory theory by borrowing from the conclusions of authors interested in comparative study or who did field work in foreign political systems. Professor Ehrmann writes in his introduction to *Interest Groups on Four Continents:* "The political system, as well as the social structure, will often decide whether claims raised in the name of special interests will be successful or not; it may determine the "style" used by pressure groups when raising their demands."[1] Professor Lavau, after indicating in detail the fragmentation of many French interests because of ideological reasons, points out that "This hostile ideological and moral climate surrounding pressure groups in France reacts in turn upon their behavior." He indicates that some pressure groups if *not politicized* play an aggregative and integrative role that the French political parties do not play. This is, for instance, the case with some peak organizations that include a variety of professional groups. "Since it is [their] function to arbitrate or mediate possible conflicts between different member organizations, this role confers upon [them], in the eyes of the administration and the politicians, a considerable dignity."[2] In fact one of the most pervasive efforts of the French interest groups is to liberate themselves from a divided political culture

---

[1] Henry Ehrmann, ed. *Interest Groups on Four Continents* (Pittsburgh: University of Pittsburgh Press, 1959), p. 1.

[2] Ibid., pp. 61 and 78.

and be able to organize their membership on the basis of interest alone. That they fail more often than they succeed is an indication of the importance, and what is more, the independence, of political and ideological factors. Professor Sam Finer accepts Beer's emphasis upon the British "consensus" and the general agreement of the British leadership on a number of policy issues as a factor that shapes and structures group action. He adds that such beliefs are brought together in English political life by the myth of "public interest" which provides a yardstick in terms of which interest claims are judged. The image of the national interest acts as a cohesive force. Professor Beer in an excellent analysis points to the parallel development in Great Britain of well organized and integrated political parties with well organized national interest groups.[3] For the purpose of our discussion this parallelism between interest organization and party organization is striking and one cannot avoid the impression that British interests gradually evolved a pattern of organization and cohesiveness *that corresponds* to and *parallels* the highly centralized and cohesive political system; that perhaps their "style" of action was conditioned by the cohesiveness of the political culture and the organization of political parties very much as the dispersion of the French interest groups may well have been shaped by the diversity of the French political culture and multipartism. Joseph LaPalombara[4] points out bluntly that many interest groups in Italy (and the same applies to France) operate within the political sub-cultures of the system (communist, catholic, socialist, etc.) resulting in an enormous proliferation (and the same applies to France) of pressure groups. Writing for the Swedish pressure groups Gunnar Heckscher points out that "there is hardly any point at which this term (politics of compromise) seems more definitely warranted than with regard to interest organizations: an equilibrium is maintained chiefly through the willingness of each of them to make concessions in order to achieve important results." But why? Because "the pluralistic character of the Swedish society is openly accepted on all sides."[5] Back we come to the general values of the community in terms of which the role of pressure groups and pressure group action and interaction can be explained. Jean Meynaud, in his comprehensive study of French pressure groups in France comes very close to a very important theoretical

[3] Samuel Beer, "Group Representation in Britain and the United States," *The Annals,* September 1958.

[4] "The Utility and Limitations of Interest Group Theory in Non-American Field Situations," *Journal of Politics,* February 1960.

[5] Gunnar Heckscher, "Interest Groups in Sweden," in Ehrmann, *Interest Groups on Four Continents,* p. 170.

insight, when he points out that the fragmentation of parties like the fragmentation of the groups has its origin in the divisions in the public mind.[6] Political ideologies and religious considerations destroy the unity that would result from objective professional and interest considerations. A number of organizations mushroom *within the same* professional sector because of ideological reasons. One might hypothesize indeed that this parallelism between the political system and the interest configuration is true everywhere. *Whenever the political governmental organization is cohesive and power is concentrated in certain well-established centers the pressure groups become well organized with a similar concentration of power and vice versa.*

Despite the reputed advantage of concreteness, groups appear to be as elusive as some of the much criticized terms used in the past—such as the state, consensus, social structure, national character, or class; implicitly accepting the power theory, group analysts tend to embrace a theory of group determinism in which interest groups appear to be the most significant actors within a system with the individual, on the one hand, and the state on the other, receding in the background; from the standpoint of research in a political system group analysis compels the student, if he is to gain a solid view of a system, to study all groups and all patterns of group interaction—no clear-cut discrimination of what is relevant and what is not being offered. Indeed, when David Truman brings the potential groups into the picture any discriminating feature that group analysis might offer goes to the winds; finally, and what is very revealing, researchers who start with a group orientation finish by admitting the inadequacy of their approach—they tell us that in order to understand how groups behave and how they interact, we must study the political system, the overall behavior patterns, the values and beliefs held by the actors, the formal organization of authority, the degree of legitimacy, etc., etc. Without realizing it, they reverse their theoretical position. They start with the groups only to admit the primacy of the political phenomenon and suggest that in order to explain group behavior we must start with what group behavior purported to explain—the political system!

*   *   *   *   *

The road to theory in comparative politics is a long one. Group theory claims that it is more "comprehensive" and "operational" in that it directs the student to the study of concrete and observable entities—the groups—and leads him immediately to the promised

---

[6] Jean Meynaud, *Les Groupes de Pression en France* (Paris: Armand Colin, 1959), particularly chaps. 1 and 5.

heaven of data-accumulation and explanation. When the real test of the utility of the theory comes, however—field work—groups prove to be just as stubborn in yielding their secrets as other structures and units of a system. Their pulsating reality often proves to be nothing but a ghost that haunts the field worker from one interest group office and organization to another, from one interest group publication to another. In some cases, especially in the underdeveloped systems where interest articulation is weak, the office may be vacant. Even where interest articulation and interest groups pulsate with life and vigor the student soon discovers that the "interest universe" overlaps with the political universe; that it is indeed enmeshed with the political universe in which tradition, values, habits, styles, and patterns of leadership and the governmental organization must be carefully studied before we begin to understand the system as a whole. The dichotomy between "interest" and "government" appears increasingly tenuous and the student has often to study the latter in order to understand better not only the manifestations and actions but also the motivation and organization of the former. He is soon forced to the conclusion that "interest" like any other activity in a system is conditioned by secular forces that have shaped the political culture of the community and that the best way to a theory of comparative politics is at this stage a comprehensive comparative look at the main features of a political system—political culture, social configuration, leadership, and governmental institutions. It is only such an approach, which requires a good understanding of the historical dimension of any and all political systems, that may help us differentiate between political systems and isolate those factors that may account for the diversities and similarities we observe.

16

Interest Groups and Political Parties

Howard J. Wiarda and Harvey F. Kline

The Latin American political tradition differs in many ways from that of the United States and West Europe. The distinct political tradition of Latin America is reflected in the composition and inter-relationships of political groups in the area.

There is considerable disagreement whether Latin America has a politics of interest-group struggle comparable to that of the United States. Of course there is competition among various groups and factions throughout Latin America. But whereas in the United States group politics is looked upon as a natural, generally whole-some aspect of the political system, in Latin America the emphasis is often on creating an administrative state above party and interest-group politics. Another difference has to do with the fact that al-though in the United States the major groups, religious agencies, and the like are assumed to be independent from the government, in Latin America such agencies as the Church, the army, the univer-sity, and perhaps even the trade unions are often more than mere interest groups: They are a part of the state system and inseparable from it. Of course there are degrees of government control over these groups, ranging from almost complete control to almost com-plete freedom as under liberalism. But the usual pattern involves

Source: Howard J. Wiarda and Harvey F. Kline, eds., *Latin American Politics and Development,* 2d ed. (Boulder, Colo.: Westview Press, 1985) pp. 52–75. By per-mission.

considerably more state control over interest groups than in the United States, and this helps put interest- (or what some have preferred to call corporate-) group behavior in Latin America in a different framework than is the case in the United States.

Latin America, as Charles Anderson has suggested, never experienced a definitive democratic revolution—that is, a struggle resulting in agreement that mobilization of votes would be the only legitimate way to obtain public power. In the absence of such a consensus, political groups do not necessarily work for political power by seeking votes, support of political parties, or contacts with elected representatives. The groups might seek power through any number of other strategies. Other resources used include coercion (the military), economic might (upper-class groups and foreign enterprises), technical expertise (bureaucrats), and controlled violence (labor unions, peasants, and students). Any group that can mobilize votes is likely to do so for an election. Since that is not the only legitimated route to power, the result of any election is tentative. The duration of any government is uncertain, given the varying power of the competing groups and the incomplete legitimacy of the government itself.

Further, group behavior in Latin America is conditioned by a set of unwritten rules, leading to what Anderson has called the "living museum" effect. Before a new group can participate in the political system, it must tacitly demonstrate both that it has a power resource and that it will respect the rights of already existent groups. Until a new group has demonstrated that it has some capacity to challenge or even overthrow a government, there is little reason for the established groups to take it seriously. Equally important, this potential participant in the political process must give assurances that it will not use its power to harm or eliminate those groups that already exist. The result is the gradual addition of new groups under the two conditions but seldom the elimination of the old ones. The newest, most modern groups coexist with the oldest, most traditionalist ones.

A related factor is the tradition of *co-optation or repression.* As new groups emerge as potential politically relevant actors, already established actors (particularly political parties or strong national leaders) sometimes offer to assist them in their new political activities. The deal struck is one mutually beneficial to both: The new group gains acceptance, prestige, and some of its original goals, and the established group or leader gains new support and increased political resources. The co-opted group drops some of its original goals, leading many observers to be critical of the system. But those leaders and observers who prefer stability to change see the co-optation system as beneficial to the political system.

In some circumstances, new groups refuse to be co-opted and fail to accept the rules of the game. Instead, they take steps indicating to established groups and leaders that they might act against the interests of the established elites. In the case of a group that violates the ground rules by employing mass violence, for example, an effort is made by the established interests to repress the new group, either legally by refusing it legal standing or in some cases through the use of violence. The army or hired thugs are employed to suppress the group that ventures outside the system. Most commonly, such repression has proved successful, and the new group, at least for the time being, disappears or atrophies, accomplishing none of its goals. The general success of repression makes co-optation seem more desirable to new groups, since obtaining some of their goals through co-optation is preferable to being repressed.

In a few cases, the result is quite different. The established political groups fail to repress the emergent groups, and the latter come to power through revolutionary means, proceeding to eliminate the traditional power contenders. These are known as the "true," genuine, or social revolutions in Latin America and include only the Mexican Revolution of 1910–1920, the Bolivian Revolution of 1952, the Cuban Revolution of 1959, and the Nicaraguan Revolution of 1979. Examples of the reverse process—utilization of violence and repression to eliminate the newer challenging groups and to secure in power the more traditional system—are Brazil in 1964 and Chile in 1973. Both led to the elimination of independent political parties, student associations, and labor and peasant unions as power groups.

It is in this context of often patrimonial, corporative tradition, now overlain with the trappings of liberalism (and in some countries more than mere trappings), and of a set of elaborate though unwritten rules of the game that we should view the politically relevant groups of Latin America. After independence three groups, often referred to as the "19th-century oligarchy," were predominant: the military, the Roman Catholic Church, and the large landholders. These groups were once staunch defenders of the status quo; now they are more heterogeneous. Through the process of economic growth and change new groups emerged: first commercial elites; later industrial elites, students, and middle-income sectors; most recently industrial labor unions and peasants. Throughout the process, political parties have existed. Particularly since the end of the 19th century, the United States has been a politically relevant force in the domestic politics of the Latin American countries, in both its governmental and its private business incarnations. The U.S. Embassy is a leading actor, not only in terms of Latin America's trade and diplomatic relations but in internal affairs, comparable in importance to such major forces as the Church, the oligarchy, and the army.

THE ARMED FORCES

During the wars for independence, the Spanish American countries developed armies led by a great variety of individuals, including well-born *criollos*, priests, and people of more humble background. The officers did not come from military academies but were self-selected or chosen by other leaders. Few of the officers had previous military training, and the armies were much less professional than the armies we know today.

Following independence, the military element continued as one of the first important power groups. The national army was supposed to be preeminent, and in some countries national military academies were founded in the first quarter century of independence. Yet the national military was challenged by other armies. The early 19th century was a period of limited national integration, with the *patrias chicas* or regional subdivisions of the countries often dominated by local landowners or caudillos—men on horseback who had their own private armies. One aspect of the development of Latin America was the struggle between the central government and its army on the one hand and the *patrias chicas* and local caudillos on the other, with the eventual success of the former.

The development of Brazil varied somewhat from the norm because of the different colonizing power and because of the lack of a struggle for independence. The military first gained preeminence in the Paraguayan War (1864–1870). Until 1930, the Brazilian states had powerful militias, in some cases of comparable strength to the national army.

Although Latin American militaries varied in the 19th century, a study of them reveals two general themes. First, various militaries, including the national one, became active in politics. At given times they were regional or personal organizations; at others, they were parts of political parties that were the participants in the civil wars frequently waged between rival factions. But, second, the national military often played the role of a moderating power—staying above factional struggles, preferring that civilians govern, but taking over power temporarily when the civilians could not effectively rule. Although this moderating power did not emerge in all countries, it is seen in most, especially in Brazil, where, with the abdication of the emperor in 1889, the military became the chief moderator in the system.

As early as the 1830s and 1840s in Argentina and Mexico, and later in the other Latin American countries, national military academies were established. Their goal was to introduce professionalism into the military, requiring graduation for officer status. Aided in the first decades of the 20th century by military missions from Germany and France, and later by Chilean missions, these academies were for the most part successful in making entry and promotion in the officer corps proceed in a routinized manner. No longer did individuals become generals overnight; rather, they were trained in military tactics and procedure. By the 1950s a Latin American officer was named a general, with potential political power, only after a career of some twenty years.

Through professionalization, the military career was designed to be a highly specialized one that taught the skills for warfare but eschewed interest in political matters. Officership would absorb all the energy of its members, and this functional expertise would be distinct from that of politicians. Civilians were theoretically to have complete control of the military, which would stay out of politics. Yet this model of professionalism, imported from West Europe and the United States, never took complete root in the Latin American political culture. The military continued to play politics and to exercise its moderating power, and coups d'état continued.

By the late 1950s and early 1960s, a change occurred in the nature of the role of the military in Latin America and in the developed countries of the West. The success of guerrilla revolutions in China, Indochina, Algeria, and Cuba led to a new emphasis on the military's role in counterinsurgency and internal defense functions. In addition, Latin American militaries—encouraged by U.S. military aid—began to assume responsibility for civic-action programs, which assisted civilians in the construction of roads, schools, and other public projects. This led to a broader responsibility for the military in nation building.

The new professionalism of the past two decades is more in keeping with the Latin American political culture than the old professionalism was. Military skills are no longer viewed as separate or different from civilian skills—management, administration, nation building. The military was to acquire the ability to help solve those national problems that might lead to insurgency—which is, in its very essence, a political rather than apolitical task. The implication of the new professionalism is that, besides combating active guerrilla factions, the military will take care that social and economic reforms necessary to prevent insurgency are adopted if the civilians prove incapable of doing so. Although the new professionalism has also been seen in the developed Western world and in other parts of the Third World, it has been particularly prevalent in Latin America, where it coincided with the moderating power tradition. Professionalism in Latin America therefore has led to more military intervention in politics, not less.

It is difficult to compare the Latin American militaries cross-nationally. Trying to distinguish "civilian" from "military" regimes is also a meaningless task sometimes or at best a difficult one. Often military personnel temporarily resign their commissions to take leadership positions in civilian bureaucracies. Frequently they hold military and civilian positions at the same time. In some cases, an officer might resign his commission, be elected president, and then govern with strong military backing. In almost all instances, coups d'état are not just simply military affairs but are supported by civilians as well. It is not unheard of for civilians to take a significant part in the ensuing governments. In short, Latin American governments are usually coalitions made between certain factions of the militaries with certain factions of civilians in an attempt to control the pinnacles of power of the system.

Few would argue that all Latin American governments are exactly alike in the degree of military influence. Various attempts have been made to categorize military intervention in politics. Although this is not the place to present a definitive classification, we suggest that several dimensions be considered . . .

1. How often does the military forcefully remove chief executives, either elected ones or the victors in previous military coups? Colombia, for example, has had only two successful coups in this century. Ecuador has had many more. Bolivia has had more than 200 in 160 years of independent life.

2. How often are military men elected to the presidency? And if they are elected, to what extent are they "Dwight D. Eisenhower civilians" and to what extent is this a way to bring the military to power and yet remain "democratic"?

3. To what degree do military officers occupy key positions in the civilian bureaucracy, having resigned their commissions but fully expecting to be recommissioned at the same level without losing seniority when their civilian days are over?

4. To what extent do the leaders of the military have a say in nonmilitary matters, issues other than the size of the military budget and the nature of defense?

5. In what way does the moderating power of the military obligate it to step in and unseat an incompetent president or one who has violated the rules of the game?

Besides the degree of military influence in the political system, several other interrelated questions should be kept in mind . . .

1. Why is the military active in politics? Is this normal behavior in the country, or does it occur only in times of severe crisis?

2. Whom does the military represent? Is it acting in its own corporate interests, for the perceived good of the entire nation, or in the interests of the middle class, from whose ranks most members of the officer corps come?

3. Is the result of military rule conservative, maintaining or returning to the status quo, or is the military the handmaiden of social change?

4. How is the military divided? In no country does it seem to

be a monolithic entity. Splits have occurred between branches of service (the more upper-class navy against the middle-class army), between age groups of officers (the young colonels against the old generals), between factions with different perceptions of the military's role in society (officers preferring civilian rule versus those who like military governments), and between groups with various ideologies (the traditionalists versus the radicals).

The military is one of the traditional pillars of Latin American society, with rights *(fueros)*, responsibilities, and legal standing that can be traced back to colonial times. This means the military will and must play a different role than it does in the United States. Hence, it is advisable to look at the military's role in any country in the context of the interaction of these traditions with the problems that the individual countries face. Little is gained from blanket condemnation or blanket approval of military intervention.

THE ROMAN CATHOLIC CHURCH

All Latin American countries are nominally Catholic, although the form of that religion varies from country to country. The Spanish and Portuguese came to "Christianize the heathens" as well as to seek precious metals. In areas of large Amerindian concentrations, religion became a mixture of pre-Columbian and Roman Catholic beliefs. To a lesser degree, Catholicism later blended with African religions, which also exist on their own in certain areas, especially in Brazil and Cuba. In contrast, religion in the large cities of Latin America is similar to that in the urban centers of the United States and West Europe. But in the more isolated small towns, Roman Catholicism is still of 15th century vintage.

The power of the Church hierarchy in politics also varies. Traditionally the Church was one of the main sectors of Spanish and Portuguese corporate society, with rights and responsibilities in such areas as care for orphans, education, and public morals. During the 19th century, the Church was one of the three major groups in politics, along with the military and the landed interests. Yet during the same century, some lay people wanted to strip the Church of all its temporal power, including its lands. Generally speaking, the conflict over the role of the Church had ended by the first part of the present century, with some exceptions.

Today the Church is changing—expecially if by *Church* we mean the top levels of the hierarchy that control the religious and political fortunes of the institution. These transformations were occasioned by the new theologies of the past hundred years, as expressed through various papal encyclicals, Vatican II, and the conferences of the Latin American bishops at Medellín, Colombia, in 1968 and

Puebla, Mexico, in 1979. There are significant numbers of bishops (and many more parish priests and members of the various orders) who subscribe to what is commonly called liberation theology. This new theology stresses that the Church is of and for this world and should take stands against repression and violence, including the "institutionalized violence"—the life-demeaning and -threatening violence—experienced by the poor of the area. Liberation theology also stresses the equality of all believers—lay people as well as clerics and bishops—as opposed to the former stress on hierarchy. The end result has been, in some parts of the area, new People's Churches, with lay leadership and only minimal involvement of priests.

It would be a mistake, however, to assume that all, or even most, members of the Latin American clergy subscribe to liberation theology. Many believe that the new social doctrine has taken the Church more into politics than it should be. Some are concerned with the loss of traditional authority that the erosion of hierarchy has brought. . . .

The result of the changes is a clergy that is no longer uniformly conservative, but rather one whose members differ on the role that the Church should play in socioeconomic reform and on the nature of hierarchical relations within the Church. At one extreme of this conflict is the traditional Church elite, usually with social origins in the upper class or aspirations to be accepted by it, still very conservative, and with close connections to other supporters of the status quo. At the other end of this intraclergy conflict are those priests, of various social backgrounds, who see the major objective of the Church as assisting the masses to obtain social justice. In some cases (the most notable of which was Camilo Torres in Colombia, who left the clergy to fight in the guerrilla wars), these priests are openly revolutionary. Other priests fall between these two extremes of political ideology, and still others favor a relaxing of the rigid hierarchy, giving more discretion to local parish priests.

The Church still participates in politics to defend its material interests, although in most cases its wealth is no longer in land. Certain Church interests are still the traditional ones: giving religious instruction in schools and running parochial high schools and universities, the cost of which has traditionally made higher education possible only for people of middle income or higher; and occasional attempts to prevent divorce legislation and to make purely civil marriage difficult. At times, the Church has been a major proponent of human rights, especially when military governments deny them. A touchier issue is that of birth control, and in most cases the Latin American hierarchies have fought artificial methods. However, in the face of the population explosion, many Church officials have assisted in family-planning clinics, turned their heads when governments have promoted artificial methods of birth control, and occasionally even assisted in those governmental efforts.

Nominally Latin America is the most Catholic area of the world, although many individuals are not active communicants. The general religious ethos that permeates some of the Latin American countries gives the Church an indirect power, making it unnecessary for the archbishop or the clergy actively to lobby for or against legislation or to state the formal position of the Church on a traditional issue. Decision makers usually have been exposed to religious education at some point and know perfectly well the Church's position.

Some analysts feel the Church is no longer a major power contender. They argue that on certain issues its sway is still considerable, but that the Church is no longer as influential politically as the army, the wealthy elites, or the U.S. Embassy. Other analysts, pointing to the liberation theology People's Churches, argue, on the contrary, that the Church or individual clerics connected to it are powerful as never before. . . .

LARGE LANDOWNERS

In all the countries of Latin America, save Costa Rica and Paraguay, the colonial period led to the establishment of a group of large landowners who had received their lands as royal grants. With the coming of independence, these *latifundistas* (owners of large land tracts called *latifundios*) were more powerful than before and developed into one of the three major groups of 19th century politics. This is not to say that they operated monolithically; in some cases they were divided against each other.

In recent times, these rifts have remained among the large landowners, usually along the lines of crop production. They might disagree on a governmental policy favoring livestock raising to the detriment of crop planting. However, the major conflict has been between those who have large tracts of land and the many landless peasants. In those circumstances the various groups of large landowners tend to coalesce, burying their differences. In some cases, there is an umbrella organization to bring all of the various producer organizations together formally; in other cases, the coalition is much more informal.

In the 1960s, the pressures for land reform were considerable, both from landless peasants and from foreign and domestic groups who saw this reform as a way to avoid Castro-like revolutions. In some countries, such as Mexico, land reform had previously come by revolution; in others, such as Venezuela, a good bit of land had been distributed to the landless; in still others, the power of the landed, in coalition with other status quo groups, led to the appearance of land reform rather than the reality. More and more of the landless moved to the cities. In many of the Latin American countries, especially those in which the amount of arable land is limited and where the population explosion has led to higher person-land ratios, the issue of breaking up large estates will continue for the foreseeable future. Given the power of the landed, such change is likely to be slow in the absence of something approaching a social revolution.

One failure of the land reforms of the 1960s was not achieving the vision, about which U.S. Agency for International Development (AID) officials and sociologists waxed poetic, of countries of middle-class farmers reflecting all of the Jeffersonian virtues of tilling the land and encouraging liberal democracy. Only three countries in Latin America have significant numbers of these family farms— Costa Rica, Colombia, and Mexico—and these predated the 1960s. In the absence of wholesale land reform (and even with it, if the policymakers decide that the economies of scale call for collective or state ownership of land), a middle-class farmer group seems very unlikely for the future.

COMMERCIAL AND INDUSTRIAL ELITES

Commercial elites have existed in Latin America since independence; one of the early political conflicts was between those who wanted free trade (the commercial elites and allied landed interests producing crops for export) and those who wanted protection of nascent industry (industrial elites with allied landed groups not producing for export).

Although the early industrial elites were important in this conflict, the real push for industrialization in Latin America did not come until the Great Depression and World War II, when Latin America was cut off from trade with the industrialized world. Before those crises, industrial goods from England and the United States were cheaper, even with transportation costs and import duties, than locally produced goods. The one exception to this generalization was the textile industry.

Over the past forty years, the Latin American countries have experienced industrialization of the import-substitution type—that is, producing goods that formerly were imported from the industrialized countries. This has been the case in light consumer goods— in some consumer durables—including assembly plants for North American and European automobiles, and in some other heavy industries such as cement and steel. Because import substitution necessitates increased foreign trade in order to import capital goods, there no longer is much conflict between commercial and industrial elites: Expanded trade and industrialization go together.

Much of the industry that exists in Latin America today is of a subsidiary nature—parts of large multinational corporations based in the United States, West Europe, and Japan. This detracts from the industrial elite's status as an independent power contender in the political process, although the multinationals have their own power. Likewise, private industry is not as strong a group as it might be, since Latin American governments themselves have developed or nationalized many of the industries that traditionally are private in the United States: steel, railroads, and petroleum, among others.

Another complicating factor in the consideration of the industrial elite is its relationship with the landed elite. In some countries, such as Argentina, the early industrialists were linked to the landed groups; later, individuals who began as industrialists invested in land. The result was two intertwined groups, a marriage of older landed and newer moneyed wealth, with only vague boundaries separating them and some families and individuals straddling the line. Although this might not be true of all Latin American countries, the interrelationship between the two has been offered as a reason for industrialist opposition to land reform. The land to be received by the *campesinos* (those living on the land) was that of the industrialist, his family, or his friends!

Industrialists and commercial elites are highly organized in various chambers of commerce, industrial associations, and the like; they are strategically located in major cities of Latin America; and generally they favor a status quo that profits themselves. They are seen as the driving forces in Latin American economic development and for these reasons and because they are frequently represented in high official circles no matter what government is in control, they are very powerful.

STUDENTS

Student activism in politics is a long-standing tradition in Latin America, not only at the university level, but at high school levels too. University students are an elite group in Latin America in that they have the leisure to study rather than work. Although the figure varies from country to country, it is estimated that only about 3 percent of the university-aged population at any time has the opportunity to pursue post-secondary education.

University students tend to have power beyond their numbers. They are a highly prestigious group, traditionally held in high regard in Spanish and Portuguese culture and seen as the leaders of the coming generation. They are often looked to by workers and peasants as their natural leaders. Major universities are located in the capital and other large cities. Since much of Latin American politics is urban politics, students are in the right place to have maximum input with street demonstrations and, sometimes, urban guerrilla activities. The traditional autonomy of university campuses means the military and police cannot enter to make an arrest, even in hot pursuit of urban guerrillas.

Although most students are of various leftist persuasions, political parties of all ideologies have attempted to include the students in their ranks. Each party tends to have its own student branch. The parties also sponsor "professional students," who dedicate more of their time to organizing than to studying. This attempt to organize students is based on their proven ability in politics, although students tend to be more successful opposing than supporting groups in the government.

Yet students are not so strong a group as those discussed in the preceding sections. Deep political divisions among the students militate against their exercising greater power, as does the fact that students are a transitory group, with nearly 100 percent turnover every five or six years. This is a disadvantage for a group, as recruitment to political activity and training must be constant. Finally, students have less influence than they might since some are much more concerned with education as a method of social mobility or of preserving their social status than they are with politics.

Students can be expected to remain a politically relevant group, especially if economic growth is slow or nonexistent. In alliance with workers or a faction of the military, they can play an important role in making or breaking a government. Latin American universities, although they train a relatively small percentage of the population, are producing more potential white-collar workers than there are places for in government bureaucracy and private enterprise. Students who see slight possibilities of a professional career after college are likely to be drawn into politics because of frustration and insecurity.

THE MIDDLE SECTORS

Although the Latin American countries began independence with a basically two-class system that still exists today, there have always been individuals who fell statistically into the middle ranges, neither very rich nor abjectly poor. These few individuals during the 19th century were primarily artisans and shopkeepers and, later, doctors and lawyers. More recently, the number of these middle elements has significantly grown.

The emergence of a larger middle sector was a 20th-century

phenomenon, associated with urbanization, technological advances, industrialization, and the expansion of public education and the role of the government. All of these changes necessitated a large number of white-collar, managerial workers. New teachers and government bureaucrats constituted part of this sector, as did office workers in private businesses. In addition, small businesses grew, particularly in the service sector of the economy. Many of these new nonmanual professions have been organized—teachers' associations, small-business associations, lawyers' associations, organizations of governmental bureaucrats, and so forth. Frequently these and such other new groups as organized labor and the students have taken up liberal and socialist values at odds with the older hierarchical, Thomistic notions.

The people who filled the new middle-sector jobs were the product of social mobility. Some came from the lower class; others were "fallen aristocrats" from the upper classes. They lacked a prolonged, common historical experience. This, together with their numerous and heterogeneous occupations, temporarily impeded the formation of a sense of common identity as members of a middle class. Indeed, in some of the countries of Latin America this identification has yet to emerge—and may not emerge. In the United States, there has always been an idealization of the middle class; in Latin America, in contrast, the ideal is to be a part of "society," preferably high society.

In those countries of Latin America in which a large middle-sector group has emerged, certain generalizations about its political behavior can be made. In the early stages of political activities, coalitions tended to be formed with groups from the lower classes against the more traditional and oligarchic groups in power. Major goals included expanded suffrage, the promotion of urban growth and economic development, a greater role for public education, increased industrialization, and social-welfare programs. The principal means of accomplishing these goals was through state intervention.

In the later political evolution of the middle sectors, the tendency has been to side with the established order. In some cases the middle-class movements allied with landowners, industrialists, and the Church against their working-class partners of earlier years; in other cases, when the more numerous lower class seemed ready to take power on its own, the middle sectors were instrumental in fomenting a middle-class military coup, to prevent "premature democratization." Over the years, then, middle-class movements changed dramatically.

Yet this transformation was sometimes more apparent than real. All the original goals of the middle-sector movements had as their effect, if not their intention, the creation of new white-collar, non-manual jobs for teachers, government bureaucrats, and private bureaucrats in industry. Further, when the middle-sector movements took political control, they did not completely replace the traditional elite; they came to terms with that elite, entered into compromises with the members of it, and, in the process, came to be identified with the very elite institutions that they had planned to take over.

This general introduction, based largely on the more industrially advanced countries of the southern cone of South America should raise a number of questions that students should consider . . .

1.   How large are the middle-income sectors of the country?

2.   To what extent do the middle sectors tend to act together politically? Do they tend to work in one or several political parties, or are they split between parties on loyalties predating the emergence of the middle class?

3.   To what degree do the members of the middle sectors identify themselves as such? Is there a perceived commonality of interests? Or alternatively, although objectively they have the same class interests, do they fail to see them?

Many publications dealing with Latin America used to assume that there was a kind of progressive spirit inherent in the individual members of the middle class and that this spirit would be defined in terms of a desire for economic development and political democracy. This assumption was based on an idealized vision of what the middle classes had done in the United States and West Europe. The evidence now suggests that in some, but surely not all cases, the growth of middle-class movements in Latin America might retard economic development and impede liberal democracy, encouraging instead military rule.

LABOR UNIONS

From its inception, organized labor in Latin America has been highly political. Virtually all important trade-union groups of the area have been closely associated with a political party, strong leader, or government. On some occasions, labor unions have grown independently until they were co-opted or repressed. In other cases, labor unions have owed their origins directly to the efforts of a party, leader, or government.

Two characteristics of the Latin American economies have favored partisan unionism. First, Latin American unions came relatively early in the economic development of the countries, in most cases earlier than in the United States and West Europe. In Latin America the labor pool of employables has been much larger than the number who can get the relatively well-paid jobs in industry.

An employer in that situation can almost always find people to replace striking workers unless they are protected by a party or by the government. Further, inflation has been a problem in Latin America in recent decades, making it important for unions to win the support of political groups in the continual renegotiation of contracts to obtain higher salaries, which often need governmental approval.

The Latin American legal tradition requires that unions be officially recognized by the government before they can collectively bargain. If a group cannot obtain or retain this legal standing, it has little power. Further, close attention must be paid to labor legislation. In some countries, labor codes have made it mandatory that labor organizers be employed full time by the industry that they are organizing, limiting the power of unions lacking leaders who are paid full salary to spend part of the working day in union activities. This is only one of the many governmental restrictions placed on labor unions.

Labor groups of some kind have long existed in Latin American industry. Before the early years of this century, they tended to be mutual benefit societies, a collective insurance and Catholic charity agency formed in the absence of governmental social-security programs. Labor movements moved to the next stage with the arrival of large numbers of Europeans in the early years of this century, especially in Argentina, Uruguay, Brazil, and Cuba. Anarcho-syndicalism was the dominant philosophy of the period, with Marxism as its main competition. From these original countries the labor movement and its competing ideologies spread to other countries of Latin America.

The influence of anarcho-syndicalism waned after World War I, when factory industry grew and with it the need for collective bargaining, which the anarcho-syndicalists did not accept as a tactic. Various national parties entered into the labor field, as well as the socialists and Communists with their international connections. Since World War II, the older, international-type organizations have lost influence, and in most countries of Latin America the major labor federations have had few international ties, although some have belonged to Catholic associations and others have received support from the American Federation of Labor–Congress of Industrial Organizations (AFL-CIO). Attempts to convert Latin American labor unions into something more like unionism in the United States have failed.

Yet the co-optation–and–repression system has by no means taken over the labor unions of Latin America. Some union organizations have been co-opted; others remain outside the system. For [individual countries] certain questions are relevant.

1.   To what extent are industrial (and middle-class) workers organized?

2.   How is the labor code used to prevent or facilitate labor organization?

3.   What is the nature of the relationships between labor and political parties, or between labor and government? Who has gained what from these associations?

4.   To what extent are there labor unions that have not been co-opted or repressed? Is there a potential for new labor federations with new leaders outside of the unions themselves?

5.   When labor allied with political parties, did it do so with one single party or are there various co-optive relationships with several parties?

PEASANTS

The term *peasants* refers to many different kinds of people in Latin America. Some prefer the Spanish term *campesinos* rather than the English term with its European-based connotations. The major groups of *campesinos,* who vary in importance from country to country, include the following:

1.   Amerindian groups, who speak only their native language or who are bilingual in that language and Spanish;

2.   workers on the traditional hacienda, tilling the fields in return for wages or part of the crops, with the owner as a *patrón* to care for the family or, more frequently, a manager-patron who represents the absentee owner;

3.   workers on modern plantations, receiving wages but remaining outside of the older patron-client relationship;

4.   persons with a small landholding *(minifundio),* legally held, of such a size that a bare existence is possible;

5.   persons who cultivate small plots, with no legal claim, perhaps moving every few years after the slash-and-burn method and the lack of crop rotation deplete the soil;

6.   persons who are given a small plot of land to work by a landowner in exchange for work on the large estate.

What all of these *campesinos* have in common, in the context of the extremely inequitable distribution of arable lands in Latin America, is a marginal existence due to their small amount of land or income and a high degree of insecurity due to their uncertain claims to the lands they cultivate. It was estimated in 1961 that over 5 million very small farms (below 30 acres—74 hectares) occupied only 3.7 percent of the land, while, at the other extreme, 100,000 holdings of more than 1,500 acres (3,706 hectares) took up some 65 percent of the land. Two decades later, the situation had changed little. At least 80 million people still live on small landholdings with insufficient land to earn a minimum subsistence, or they work as agricultural laborers with no land at all. For many of these rural masses, their only real chance of breaking out of this circle of poverty is by moving to an urban area, where they face another—in some ways even worse—culture of poverty. For those who remain on the land, unless there is a dramatic restructuring of ownership, the present subhuman existence is likely to continue.

Rural peasant elements have long been active in politics. The traditional political structure of the countryside was one in which participation in national politics meant taking part in the patronage system. The local *patrones*, besides expecting work on the estate from the *campesino*, expected certain political behavior. In some countries, this meant that the *campesino* belonged to the same political party as the *patrón*, voted for that party on election day, and, if necessary, served as cannon fodder in its civil wars. In other countries, the national party organizations never reached the local levels, and restrictive suffrage laws prevented the peasants from participation in elections. In both patterns, there was no such thing as national politics, only local politics, which might or might not have national party labels attached to the local person or groups in power.

This traditional system still exists in many areas of Latin America. But since the 1950s, signs of agrarian unrest and political mobilization have been more and more evident. In many cases, major agrarian movements have been organized by urban interests—political parties, especially those of the Marxist left. Some of these peasant movements have been openly revolutionary, seeking to reform and improve the land tenure system and to reform significantly the entire power structure of the nation. They have employed strategies that include the illegal seizure of land, the elimination of landowners, and armed defense of the gains thus achieved. We could call these movements ones of revolutionary agrarianism. Less radical are the movements that seek to reform the social order partially, through the elimination of a few of the most oppressive effects of the existing power structure that weighs on the peasant subculture, but without threatening the power structure as such.

The peasants, numerically the largest group in Latin America, remain politically weak. That is so chiefly because the peasant sector is largely unorganized—a situation that those of wealth and power have a vested interest in maintaining. Because of the diversity of land and labor patterns, the dispersed nature of the countryside, and high illiteracy, it is difficult to mobilize a strong peasant movement. Their distance from the urban centers of power also makes it hard for peasants to effect change. Hence, they remain subjects of the political system rather than participants in it, despite the activities of revolutionary agrarianism.

[There is] a wide spectrum of peasant organizations and a wide variation of peasant success in Latin America. In some countries, one or two political parties have been instrumental in the organization of peasants, who have received a fair degree of land as a result. In other cases, governments have facilitated the organization of peasants, who for reasons of economy of scale do not receive private land titles. In still other instances, the landed elites have been successful in preventing significant agrarian reform. . . .

THE UNITED STATES

Another important power element in Latin American politics is the United States. This influence has been seen in at least three interrelated ways: U.S. governmental representatives, U.S.-based private business, and U.S.-dominated international agencies. Some people would deny the validity of this separation. The United States, they would argue, presents a common front either by design or by effect. Their position is party substantiated by the following quote from Maj. Gen. Smedley D. Butler, U.S. Marine Corps:

> I helped make Mexico and especially Tampico safe for American oil interests in 1914. I helped make Haiti and Cuba a decent place for the National City Bank boys to collect revenue in. . . . I helped purify Nicaragua for the international banking house of Brown Brothers in 1909–1912. I brought light to the Dominican Republic for American sugar interests in 1916. I helped make Honduras "right" for American fruit companies in 1903.[1]

The general concern of this section is the activities of various U.S. groups in the Latin American political process. At times these groups work in harmony, and at times they operate at cross-purposes.

The U.S. government has been interested in the area since Latin America's independence. Its first concern, that the new nations not fall under the control of European powers, led to the Monroe Doctrine in 1823. Originally a defensive statement, the doctrine was later changed through various corollaries to a more aggressive one, telling the Latin Americans that they could not sell lands to non-hemispheric governments or businesses (if the locations were strategic) and that the United States would intervene in Latin America to collect debts owed to nonhemispheric powers (the Roosevelt

---

[1] Quoted in John Gerassi, *The Great Fear in Latin America* (New York: Collier Books, 1965) p. 231.

Corollary). At various times, the U.S. government has set standards that must be met before full diplomatic recognition is accorded to a Latin American nation. This de jure recognition policy, most memorable in the Wilson, early Kennedy, and Carter administrations, favors elected democratic governments, exclusion of the military from government, and a vision of human rights that should be applied in Latin America. At other times the United States has pursued a de facto recognition policy, according full diplomatic standing to any government with effective control of its nation's territory.

Whatever recognition policy is followed, the U.S. ambassador to a Latin American country has impressive powers. One ambassador to pre-Castro Cuba testified that he was the most influential individual in the country, second only to the president. This ambassadorial power has typically been used to support or defeat governments, to focus governmental policy of the Latin American countries in certain directions, and often to assist U.S.-based corporations in the countries. In Central America recently a number of U.S. ambassadors have played this strong proconsular role.

From their early beginnings, particularly in agribusiness (especially sugar and bananas), U.S.-based corporations in Latin America have grown dramatically. In addition to agribusiness, corporations have now entered the extractive field (petroleum, copper, iron ore), retailing (Sears, Roebuck, among others), the services industry (accounting firms, computer outfits), and communications (telephones, telegraphs). The most recent kind of U.S. corporation introduced to Latin America is the export-platform variety—that is, a company that takes advantage of the low wages in Latin America to produce pocket calculators in Mexico or baseballs in Haiti, mainly for export to the industrialized world.

U.S. corporations in Latin America often enter into the politics of their host countries. Some of the instances are flagrant: bribing public officials to keep taxes low or threatening to cut off a country's products if certain policies are approved by its government. But most political activities of the gringo corporations are probably much less dramatic. Almost always Latin Americans in the host countries buy stock in the U.S. corporations and hold high managerial positions in them. In many cases, U.S. corporations purchase Latin corporations, the leaders of which then work for the new owners. The result is that the U.S. corporation develops contacts and obligations like those powers possessed by Latin American industrialists and commercial interests. But there are now indications that the era of large U.S. corporate holdings and hence influence in Latin America may be in decline. Many U.S. corporations are pulling up stakes in Latin America, withdrawing their capital, and moving on to more profitable and stable areas.

Most foreign-aid and international lending organizations are dominated by the United States. These agencies, especially active since the early 1960s, when aid to Latin America began in large quantities, include the U.S. Agency for International Development, which administers most of our foreign aid, the World Bank, the International Monetary Fund (IMF), and a variety of others. The World Bank and the IMF are international agencies, results of post–World War II agreements between the countries of the West. However, the representation of the United States on the governing boards of both is so large (based on the amount of money donated to the agencies) and the convergence of interests of the two with those of the U.S. government is so great that they can be considered U.S.-oriented groups. Since economic development has been a central goal of the Latin American states for the past 20 years, since loans for that development have come predominantly from AID and the World Bank, and since those loans are contingent many times on a monetary policy judged as healthy by the IMF, the officials of these three groups have much influence in the day-to-day policies of the governments of the area.

This power of the lending agencies was probably greatest during the 1960s. AID had most leverage or "conditionality" during the Alliance for Progress. This foreign-aid program, initiated by the Kennedy administration, attempted to change Latin America dramatically in a decade. Even though it failed, it did lead to large loans from the U.S. government, substantial progress in some fields, and along with it much influence for the local AID head in the domestic politics of some Latin American countries. Some AID representatives sat in on cabinet meetings and wrote speeches for and gave advice to the local officials with whom they worked, and others largely ran the agencies or even ministries of the host government to which they were assigned.

The Alliance for Progress was terminated by the Nixon administration. Further, the power of the World Bank has waned in the wake of the crisis of the industrialized economies of the West following the Arab oil embargo of 1973–1974 and with the growing power of OPEC. Many leaders of the industrialized nations are searching for a new international system of monetary and trade stabilization. In the meantime, the economies of Latin America are undergoing crisis while in the importing nations protectionist measures have risen. The Latin American nations are clamoring for access to U.S. markets, and they are likely to be partially successful in that quest. The U.S. government has also proposed a new massive assistance program for Central America and the Caribbean designed to restore solvency and preserve stability.

The influence of U.S.-directed and -oriented groups—diplomatic, business, foreign-assistance—in Latin America is considerable. This does not mean that the power is equal in all the Latin American countries. One might venture the hypothesis that U.S. influence is greater for security reasons in those countries nearer the continental United States and/or where U.S. private investments are larger. When a Latin American country is important strategically to the United States and when U.S. private investors have established a large investment in the economy (Cuba before Castro), U.S. elements are extremely powerful in domestic Latin politics. This does not mean that the United States cannot have considerable influence in domestic politics in distant countries with relatively little private investment by U.S. corporations, as the example of Allende's Chile has shown.

POLITICAL PARTIES

In Latin America, political parties are oftentimes only one set of groups among several, probably no more (and perhaps less) important than the army or the economic oligarchy. Elections are not the only legitimated route to power, nor are the parties themselves particularly strong or well organized. We do not want to denigrate the place of parties in Latin America, for they are important actors in the political process and in some of the more democratic countries they represent the chief means to gain high office. But neither do we want to give parties a significance they do not have, since frequently the parties are peripheral to the main focal points of power and the electoral arena is considered only one arena among several.

General elements of the groups just discussed have combined in political parties in their pursuit of governmental power. One must be careful with the term *political party,* as the term *partido* has a much more general application than the English equivalent. For example, *el partido militar* is used in the press of the Dominican Republic and other countries to refer to the military, although clearly the officers do not use electoral tactics such as those normally associated with a U.S. political party. Further, some civilians belonging to political parties have been known to plot with factions of the military to take power in a coup d'état.

There have been a myriad of political parties in the history of Latin America; indeed, someone once quipped that to form a political party, all you needed was a president, vice president, secretary-treasurer, and rubber stamp. (If times were bad, you could do without the vice president and the secretary-treasurer!) Nevertheless, there have been certain characteristics common to parties . . .

Groups calling themselves political parties have existed from the early years of independence. The first parties were usually founded by elite groups in competition with other factions of the elite. Mass demands played only a small role, although *campesinos* were mobilized by the party leaders, often to serve as cannon fodder. In many cases, the first cleavage was between individuals in favor of free trade, federalism, and anticlericalism (the Liberals) and those for protectionism for nascent industry, centralism, and clericalism (the Conservatives). In some countries these original party divisions have long since disappeared, replaced by other cleavages; in other countries they are still very much alive.

With social and economic change in some countries of Latin America, the emergence of new social strata led to the founding of new political parties. A portion of these attracted those in the growing middle sectors who were quite reformist in the early years but later changed as they became part of the system. In other cases, new parties were more radical, calling for a basic restructuring of society and including elements from the working classes. Some of these originally radical parties were of international inspiration; most of the countries have had Communist and socialist parties of differing effectiveness and legality. Other, more radical parties were primarily national ones, albeit with ideological inspiration traceable to Marxism.

One such party, founded in 1923 by the Peruvian Victor Raúl Haya de la Torre while in exile in Mexico, was the American Popular Revolutionary Alliance (APRA). Although APRA purported to be the beginning of a new international of like-minded democratic-left individuals in Latin America, this goal was never fully reached. An inter-American organization was established, but it never had great importance. At the same time, inspired by Haya and APRA, a number of national parties were founded by young Latin Americans. The most successful Aprista-like party has been Democratic Action (AD) in Venezuela, but the same programs have been advocated by numerous other parties of this group, including the Party of National Liberation in Costa Rica and the National Revolutionary Movement in Bolivia, as well as parties in Puerto Rico, Paraguay, the Dominican Republic, Guatemala, Honduras, and Argentina. Only in Venezuela and Costa Rica did the APRA-like parties come to power more than temporarily, and by that time, 20 years after the founding of APRA, they were no longer extremely radical. They favored liberal democracy, rapid reform, and economic growth. In most cases, the APRA-like parties were led by members of the middle sectors, and they received much of their electoral support from middle- and lower-class ranks.

A newer group of political parties are the Christian-Democratic ones, particularly successful in Chile and Venezuela. These parties call for fundamental reforms but are guided by Church teachings and papal encyclicals rather than Marx or Engels, even though they are nondenominational and open to all. The nature of the ideology of these parties varies from country to country.

Other parties in Latin America have been based on the leadership of one or few persons, and hence do not fit into the neat party spectrum just described. Quite often the "man on horseback" is more important than the program of a party. This tradition of the caudillo is seen in the case of Brazil, where Getúlio Vargas founded not one but two official political parties; in Ecuador, where personalistic parties have been strong contenders for the presidency; and in Communist Cuba, where in the 1960s the party was more Castroist than Communist.

The system of co-optation further complicates the attempt at classification. How is one to classify a political party traditional in origin that includes at the same time large landowners and the peasants tied to them, as well as trade-union members organized by the party with the assistance of parts of the clergy? How does one classify a party such as the Mexican Institutional Revolutionary party (PRI), which has made a conscious effort to co-opt and include all politically relevant sectors of the society?

Even further complicating the picture is the question of party systems—that is, how many parties are there in a country and how often does power pass from party to party (or for that matter, from party to military)? All parties are coalitions; but is a party still only a single party if it offers more than one candidate for president or more than one list of candidates for congressional seats? Both have occurred in recent years in the only two-party systems of Latin America—Colombia's and (formerly) Uruguay's. These kinds of things do not happen by accident; they are the results of electoral laws drawn up by political elites with various goals in mind.

As in the case of the military, the literature on parties in Latin America is replete with contradictions, misleading classifications, and misunderstandings. We suggest . . . keeping in mind these questions:

1. How many major parties are there? What are their historical origins, their formal programs as enunciated by candidates and platforms, and their policies when in power?

2. How is the electoral law written, favoring or impeding parties? Since proportional representation, with countless variations, is most common, is this a reflection of societal circumstances when electoral laws are written, or rather does unwitting legislation change party systems?

3. What is the electoral behavior in the countries? Do voting patterns show regionalism, urban-rural dichotomies, class voting, or some combination of the three?

4. What kinds of contacts are there between the political parties and the military? Are they friendly and cooperative or hostile? The military is still the ultimate arbiter of the nation's politics, and mere political parties must take care not to go beyond the "dikes of military opinion," to paraphrase Harvard professor V. O. Key's statement about U.S. politics.

5. How often in national history have civilian political parties been in power? If they are weak, is it because the military institution so quickly monopolized power after independence, or did the military do so because the parties were weak? No matter which is the chicken and which the egg, is this a situation that can be changed by Latin America or is the area to follow the historical patterns in the near future?

6. What roles do parties play and how do they vary from country to country? Is their function to devise platforms and run candidates in elections? Or are they really just another giant patronage agency? Are they independent of government or simply mechanisms of the state? Do they serve a public interest or are they merely a means by which the ambitious may gain status and a following?

On two notable occasions in the past three decades, students of Latin America have been told to study political parties. Perhaps the time has now come to change this advice, to urge not just a study of parties per se but, more importantly, of the relations of parties to the military, to the state, and to the system as a whole.

CONCLUSIONS AND IMPLICATIONS

The preceding discussion has indicated that there are many politically relevant groups in Latin America and that they use various means to secure and retain political power. Yet at least two other themes should be introduced that tend to complicate the picture.

First, it should be noted that the urban and rural poor—outside the labor unions—have not been included in the discussion. This shows one of the biases of the system. Preceding the first step in attaining political relevance is another—being organized. This means that potential groups, especially poorly educated and geographically dispersed ones like the peasants and the urban poor, face difficulties in becoming politically relevant since they have difficulties in organizing themselves or being organized from the outside. Peasants have become increasingly organized. The same is not the case of the urban poor, working in cottage industries, as street vendors, or not at all. Their numbers are swelling rapidly, with the growing exodus from the countryside to the cities. Although to this point the urban poor have not been organized, political party leaders are increasingly aware of their large numbers and are beginning organizational attempts that employ, not surprisingly, co-optation or repression tactics common to the Latin American practice. As *campesinos* were increasingly organized in the 1960s, perhaps the urban poor will be the next addition to the "living museum" in the 1980s.

Second, not all politically relevant groups fall into the neat categories of this chapter (which, of course, are familiar to both liberals and Marxists of the European and North American traditions). Anthony Leed's research in Brazil has shown (at least in small towns, probably larger cities, and even perhaps the whole nation) a politically more relevant series of groups to be the *panelinhas* ("little saucepans").[2] These are composed of individuals of common interest but different occupations—say, a doctor, a large landowner, surely a lawyer, and a governmental official. The *panelinha* at the local level controls and endeavors to establish contacts with the *panelinha* at the state level, which might have contacts with a national *panelinha*. Of course, at the local level there are rival *panelinhas*, which contacts with rival ones at the state level, with contacts. . . . As is generally the case with such patrimonial-type relations, all interactions (except those within the *panelinhas* themselves) are vertical, and one level of *panelinha* must take care to ally with the winning one at the next higher level if it wants to have political power.

Similar research in other countries has revealed a parallel pattern of informal, elitist, patronage politics. Whether called the *panelinha* system in Brazil or the *camarilla* system in Mexico, the process and dynamics are the same. The aspiring politician (almost always a man) connects himself with an aspiring politician at a higher level, who is connected with an aspiring . . . and so forth on up to an aspiring candidate for the presidency. If the person in question becomes president, the various levels of *camarillas* prosper; if he remains powerful without becoming president, the *camarillas* continue functioning in expectation of what will take place in six years (in Mexico, the next presidential election); but if the aspiring candidate is disgraced, dismissed from the official party, or dies, the whole system of various levels of *camarillas* connected with him disintegrates. Although this *camarilla* phenomenon is also known in the United States and the Soviet Union, it is more common in the personalistic politics of Latin America. The *camarilla* system operates outside, while overlapping with the formal structure of groups and parties described here.

This discussion of *panelinhas* and *camarillas* raises the question

---

[2] Anthony Leeds, "Brazilian Careers and Social Structure: A Case History and Model," *American Anthropologist* 66 (1964), pp. 1321–47.

again of whether U.S.-style interest groups and political parties are operating and are important in Latin America. The answer is: They are and they aren't. In the larger and better-institutionalized systems, the parties and interest groups are often important and function not unlike their North American or European counterparts. But in the less-institutionalized, personalistic countries of Central America (and even behind the scenes in the larger ones), it is frequently family groups, cliques, clan alliances, and patronage networks that are more important—often disguised behind the appearance of partisan or ideological dispute. One must be careful therefore in some countries not to minimize the importance of a functional, operational party and interest-group system, while recognizing that in others it is the less formal network through which politics is carried out.

17

Political Participation

Norman H. Nie and Sidney Verba

WHAT IS POLITICAL PARTICIPATION?

Political participation is one of those terms that can have so many meanings that it ultimately loses its usefulness. The term is applied to the activities of people from all levels of the political system: the voter *participates* by casting his or her vote; the secretary of state *participates* in the making of foreign policy. Sometimes the term is applied to political orientations rather than activities: the citizen *participates* by being interested in politics. And sometimes the term applies to participation outside of politics as we usually think of that term: citizens *participate* in the family, the school, etc.

It is not for us to determine what the term really means. But the wide range of meanings suggests that it is best to begin by indicating how we will delimit the term in this essay, for when one uses the more limited notion we shall describe, political participation can represent an interesting and coherent field of study.

By political participation we refer to those legal activities by private citizens which are more or less directly aimed at influencing the selection of governmental personnel and/or the actions they take. The definition is rough but adequate for delimiting our sphere of interest. It indicates that we are basically interested in *political*

Source: Norman H. Nie and Sidney Verba, "Political Participation," in *Handbook of Political Science,* vol. 4, ed. Greenstein and Polsby (Reading, Mass.: Addison-Wesley Publishing, 1975) (pp. 1–3; 5–12; 38–53). References abridged by the editors.

participation, that is, in acts that aim at influencing *governmental* decisions. Actually, we are interested more abstractly in attempts to influence "the authoritative allocations of values for a society," which may or may not take place through governmental decisions. . . .

* * * * *

HOW ACTIVE ARE CITIZENS?

The four modes of political participation provide a framework within which we can present some data on how active citizens are. While these data are descriptively interesting and help us understand the place of participation in politics, the reader ought to be warned about the comparability of such data. The measurement across nations of amounts of political activity is subject to a number of limitations inherent in cross-national comparisons.

To compare the frequency with which citizens in one nation report that they are active in a particular way with the frequency of such reports elsewhere is to assume that one has something equivalent to compare. But the validity of a comparison of such frequencies can be questioned in two ways. In the first place the measurements are quite dependent on the techniques used to elicit the information. Second, the meaningfulness of comparisons of frequencies of political activities depends on certain assumptions as to the equivalence of these activities within the respective societies. Acts that appear to be similar may differ in their impact on policies. And political acts that appear the same may differ in how difficult they are from nation to nation and may, therefore, indicate different levels of active involvement. Voting is a prime example: the lower turnout rate in the United States compared with some other countries is probably due less to political passivity among Americans than to differences in the methods of voter registration. Furthermore, the social circumstances surrounding political participation may differ such that an act in one country represents a greater commitment than a similar act elsewhere. Voting is again an example. In India voting is a much more passive act than in the United States; Indian citizens are mobilized by parties and leaders rather than by their personal involvement in political matters.

The reader should keep all these qualifications in mind in considering the data in Table 1. Despite their limitations they have enough intrinsic interest to be worth consideration. We report the proportions of the population active in the various ways we have been discussing based on data from seven nations. The data reported are the proportions of the sample who indicated that they

TABLE 1
Percentages of Citizens Active in Various Ways in Seven Countries

	Austria	India	Japan	Netherlands	Nigeria	United States	Yugoslavia
Voting							
Regular voters[b]	85	48	93	77	56	63	82
Campaign activity							
Members of a party or political organization[c]	28	5	4	13	a	8	15
Worked for a party[d]	10	6	25	10	a	25	45
Attended a political rally[e]	27	14	50	9	a	19	45
Communal activity							
Active members in a community action organization[f]	9	7	11	15	34	32	39
Worked with a local group on a community problem[g]	3	18	15	16	35	30	22
Helped form a local group on a community problem[h]	6	5	5	a	26	14	a
Contacted an official in the community on some social problem[i]	5	4	11	6	2	13	11
Contacted an official outside the community on a social problem	3	2	5	7	3	11	a

Particularized contacting						
Contacted a local official on a personal problem[j]	15	12	7	38	2	6	20
Contacted an official outside the community on a personal problem	10	6	3	10	1	6	[a]
Number of cases	1,769	2,637	2,657	1,746	1,799	2,544	2,995

[a] Not asked.

[b] Vote regularly in both local and national elections.

[c] Formal membership in political parties in Austria, India, and the Netherlands; in political clubs in the United States and Japan; in the League of Communists in Yugoslavia. Item not asked in Nigeria.

[d] Worked for a political party in an election. In the Netherlands refers to displaying or distributing posters or leaflets. In Yugoslavia refers to any electoral activity.

[e] Refers to attending an election meeting or rally. In Yugoslavia refers to attending a voters' meeting.

[f] Active member of an organization that is in turn active in community affairs. In Yugoslavia refers to taking part in a formally organized community action.

[g] Refers to working with an informal group on some community matter. In Yugoslavia refers to taking part in an informal community action. In Austria refers to cooperating with others to bring community problems to the attention of officials.

[h] Helped form a group such as mentioned in [g] above.

[i] In Yugoslavia this item contains contacts both in and out of the community.

[j] In Yugoslavia this item contains contacts both in and out of the community.

participated in various activities about which they were questioned. (Citizens were questioned about other activities as well, more specific to each nation, but for our purposes here we have limited ourselves to the set of activities that have the greatest face similarity.) In each case a citizen is considered as active in relation to a particular act if he or she reported having ever engaged in it, except for voting, for which only those who can be considered fairly regular voters are reported as active. (A more precise definition is in the footnotes to Table 1.)

Voting rates do vary widely across the countries, with the European nations and Japan outvoting the others. When it comes to the three campaign activities one finds a fair degree of similarity across the three more industrialized nations—Austria, Japan, and the United States. A very high proportion in Japan reports attendance at a political rally (though the extent to which such an item really measures active involvement in the political process is unclear). Otherwise the figures on activity range from fairly small percentages up to about one fourth of the sample. The ways in which citizens become involved in partisan activity differ. In Austria and to a lesser extent the Netherlands citizens are more likely to belong to a political organization than actually to work for a candidate or party. In Japan and the United States formal membership is much rarer, but about one fourth of the sample indicates it has worked for a party. The rates of party membership and campaign activity in India, on the other hand, are somewhat smaller.

The patterns vis-à-vis communal activities offer some interesting contrasts. The first three items of communal activity involve cooperation with one's fellow citizens—the first via a formal organization, the other two in more informal groups. This seems most widespread in Yugoslavia, Nigeria, and the United States, with India, the Netherlands, and Japan having some moderate frequency of informal group activity and Austria the least (though in the latter case the comparison is uncertain due to a substantial difference in the measure used). One finds individual activity—for example, a citizen contacting an official on a civic problem—occurring most frequently in the United States, similarly frequently (with regard to local officials) in Japan and Yugoslavia, but relatively infrequently elsewhere.

Finally, we can consider the proportion of the citizens which reports having brought a personal problem to a government official, either within the community or on a higher level. This takes place most frequently in the Netherlands and Yugoslavia, followed by Austria, India, the United States, Japan, and Nigeria.

A few conclusions do emerge clearly from the table, perhaps the most obvious having to do with the diversity of patterns displayed. It is by no means clear how one would rank the nations in terms of frequency of political activity. On voting one finds Japan displaying greatest frequency; on membership in a political organization, Austria; on cooperative activity, Yugoslavia, Nigeria, and the United States; on contacting on a personal matter, the Netherlands.

Nor does the amount of participation vary clearly with level of affluence or economic development. India does tend to have fewer participants than the other countries, but Nigerians report a high frequency of participation of certain kinds. If one expands one's view of participation beyond the electoral process one finds a richer and more variegated pattern of participation than if one sticks to voting and campaign activity.

Voting is the only political act that a large part of the citizenry engages in. No other political act (with the exception of the large proportion that has attended a political meeting in Japan) is engaged in by more than one half of the citizens in any country. In India no political act other than voting is engaged in by more than 18 percent of the citizenry. In short, only a minority of citizens takes part in any of the specific acts listed on Table 1. Widespread activity—that is, activity engaged in by close to or more than half of the population—is found largely for those acts that are relatively easy. The main characteristic of voting and attendance at a political rally is that the citizen does not have to take the initiative in choosing when and how to be active. The occasion for the activity (the election, the campaign meeting) is provided by others.

The conclusion is simple: citizens in each country have a wide repertory of ways in which they can participate (and, of course, our questions do not exhaust that repertory). In different countries citizens will choose different ways to take part. Such a conclusion hardly contributes to a generalized understanding of political change and development, if by such understanding we mean the formation and testing of general hypotheses about political participation. But it does warn against overly simple generalizations linking political participation to social change without taking into account the wide range of ways in which citizens can and do participate.

Protests and Other Such Activities

The above discussion paid no attention to protest activities—marches, demonstrations, and more direct actions—even though many of these clearly fit into the scope of our concern, being both legal and aimed at influencing the government. It is difficult to obtain accurate figures, but it is likely that relatively few citizens have taken part in such activities. One study, conducted in the United States during the height of the Vietnam War protests, found only eight citizens (out of 1,500 interviewed) who had ever taken part in a demonstration about Vietnam—about one half of 1 percent. And another study of a city in upstate New York found that about 2 to 3 percent of the white citizens had ever attended a protest demonstration, and 4 percent said that they had attended a protest meeting. And Lipsky's study of rent strikes in New York shows that the participation by renters was not nearly as widespread as one might have been led to believe by the media.

But two points should be made about such activity. Only a small percentage of the citizenry as a whole may take part in demonstrations, but large proportions of particular groups with high visibility may be involved. Thus the same study that found that only 2 to 3 percent of whites had taken part in a street demonstration found that 11 percent of blacks had. And one does not know the proportion of college students that has taken part in antiwar demonstrations, but it is certainly likely to be larger than the minuscule percentage of the population as a whole that has done so. One study of France at the time of the May 1968 crisis found 8 percent had taken part in some demonstration.

The second point is more important. One goal of political participation is to communicate to political leaders. Protest activities, even when engaged in by a small percentage of the population, speak very loudly indeed. The main point to be made about the New York rent strikes is not that so few took part but that such a small number could make such a big splash, in part by appearing to be more in number than they actually were. Furthermore, a small percentage of the population is still a substantial number of people. If one extrapolates from the one half of 1 percent estimate of Vietnam War protesters, one gets close to a million protesters. The very fact that the activity goes outside usual channels increases its salience, as does the penchant of the mass media for reporting such activities. . . .

The Concentration of Participation

The data presented in Table 1 above are consistent with one of the more widely accepted findings of recent research on political activity: only a small minority of the citizenry is active beyond the act of voting. This generalization is usually supplemented by the generalization that political acts form a structured hierarchy such that those who engage in the more difficult acts (i.e., the least frequent acts) are likely to engage in all more frequent ones.

However, if, as our factor analysis suggests, political activity is multi-dimensional, then acts may not form a clear hierarchy and more people may be active—some in one way, others in other ways—than one would expect if acts formed such a hierarchy. Consider the data in Table 1. On the basis of the fact that the proportion engaging in any particular political activity beyond the vote rarely exceeds one third of the population, one is tempted to conclude that only about a third of the citizenry ever engages in any political activity beyond voting. Such a result is possible given the data in Table 1, but it is by no means necessary. If 28 percent of our Austrian sample belongs to a political organization, and belonging to a political organization is the act (beyond the vote) performed most frequently in Austria, it would be compatible with such data to conclude that the proportion of citizens that participates beyond the vote is no more than 28 percent. But this would be the case only if political activities formed a hierarchy whereby those who performed less frequent acts also performed the more frequent ones.

To put it another way, if political activities formed a perfect Guttman scale, the 28 percent that belongs to political organizations in Austria would contain all those citizens who engaged in less frequent acts; the degree of concentration of participation could be simply inferred from the marginals on a table such as Table 1.

That the participatory acts should form a Guttman scale accords with the general view of participation as an essentially unidimensional phenomenon. Under such circumstances the citizen who performed the relatively difficult (i.e., infrequent) acts of contacting an official would be certain to engage in the easier act of attending a rally. But our analysis above indicates that participation is not a unidimensional phenomenon. The alternative modes of activity are useful for different purposes and are engaged in by citizens who have different attitudes toward politics. If this is the case, the citizen who contacts an official may not attend a political rally—even if that act is easier—simply because he or she is not interested in that kind of activity. Some citizens might specialize in partisan, others in nonpartisan, activity. Under such circumstances the more difficult political acts would be more dispersed throughout the population than the assumption of a Guttman-scale hierarchy would imply.

In Figure 1 we present the proportion of citizens in each of six countries that is active beyond the vote, that is, engages in one

FIGURE 1
Proportions Active beyond the Vote in Five Countries
(actual and hypothetical data)

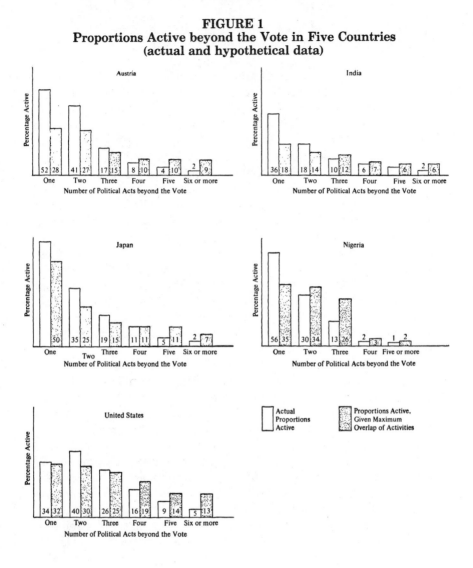

or more of the other political activities, aside from voting, listed
in Table 1. In Figure 1 we also indicate the proportions that engage
in at least one of the acts beyond the vote, in at least two acts,
and so forth up to those who engage in at least six or more acts.
Note that we say *at least* one and *at least* two, etc., indicating
that the groups partially overlap: the proportions listed as engaging
in at least one act contain those who engage in at least two, and
so on. And we also compare the *actual proportions* active beyond

the vote with the proportions that *one would find,* given the marginal distributions in Table 1, if political activity were maximally concentrated, that is, if the acts formed a perfect Guttman scale, in which those performing the less frequent acts always performed the more frequent acts.

The pattern is essentially the same in each nation. The assumption of maximum concentration of activities predicts fewer citizens active in at least one activity beyond the vote than is in fact the case and predicts more citizens in the most active category, performing six or more political acts, than is in fact the case. In Austria, for instance, the most frequent act beyond voting is membership in a political organization and is performed by 28 percent of the sample. Were political activity maximally concentrated, only 28 percent of the citizenry would be active beyond the vote. In fact, 52 percent engages in some activity beyond voting. The point is that many citizens who are not members of political organizations obviously engage in other kinds of activities which are less frequent than such membership; these citizens may contact officials, belong to community organizations, and so forth.

Or consider the other end of the graph for Austria. If participation were maximally concentrated, one would expect to find a much larger group of "superactivists"—people who engage in six or more activities beyond the vote—than one finds in fact. Maximum concentration of political activity predicts that 9 percent of the citizenry will fall in this supercategory; in fact, 2 percent does.

These graphs make a substantive point: participation does not form a fully hierarchical set of activities in which those who engage in one type of activity are certain to engage in other less costly and time consuming activities. If that were the case and participation were maximally concentrated, one would have the situation in each country reflected in the data in the shaded bars: in general, only a minority of the population would be active beyond voting, ranging from 50 percent in Japan down to 18 percent in India and averaging about 33 percent of the population across the five nations. A small but substantial proportion would be superactivists—an average of 7 percent across the nations. In fact, the proportions that are at least moderately active are larger—over 50 percent of the population in each nation. The exception is India, but there the proportion is still twice as large as the 18 percent predicted by maximum concentration. And the proportion that is superactivist averages about 2 percent. Thus, participation is more dispersed than the marginals might lead one to expect: a large proportion of the populace in each case is at least moderately active and a smaller proportion intensely active.

But one ought not to exaggerate our argument in the other

direction. The various political acts do not maximally overlap, but they are, nevertheless, positively correlated. Thus, though one finds fewer superactivists than one would expect if activity were maximally concentrated, one finds more such activists than if there were no underlying participation dimension.

*   *   *   *   *

18

The Transformation of the
Western European Party Systems

Otto Kirchheimer

[Editors' Note. *Mention is made in this excerpt of parties of "individual representation" and "mass integration." Professor Kirchheimer explains earlier that parties of individual representation,
such as the bourgeois parties of the Third French Republic, are based
on "the local parish pump and the operation of the parliamentary
factions." These parties are unable to function as transmission belts
between the population and the government. By political integration
he means "the capacity of a political system to make groups and
their members previously outside the official fold full-fledged participants in the political process." A mass integration party is one that
helps perform this function.*]

THE POSTWAR CATCH-ALL PARTY

Following the Second World War, the old-style bourgeois party of
individual representation became the exception. While some of the
species continue to survive, they do not determine the nature of
the party system any longer. By the same token, the mass integration party, product of an age with harder class lines and more

Source: Otto Kirchheimer, "The Transformation of the Western European Party
System," in *Political Parties and Political Development,* ed. Jospeh LaPalombara
and Myron Weiner, Copyright © 1966 by Princeton University Press: Princeton
Paperback, 1968, pp. 184–200. Reprinted by permission of Princeton University Press.
Article and footnotes abridged by the editors.

sharply protruding denominational structures, is transforming itself into a catch-all "people's" party. Abandoning attempts at the
intellectual and moral *encadrement* of the masses, it is turning
more fully to the electoral scene, trying to exchange effectiveness
in depth for a wider audience and more immediate electoral success.
The narrowed political task and the immediate electoral goal differ
sharply from the former all-embracing concerns; today the latter
are seen as counter-productive since they deter segments of a potential nationwide clientele.

For the class-mass parties we may roughly distinguish three
stages in this process of transformation. There is first the period
of gathering strength lasting to the beginning of the First World
War; then comes their first governmental experience in the 1920s
and 1930s (MacDonald, Weimar Republic, *Front Populaire*), unsatisfactory if measured both against the expectations of the class-mass
party followers or leaders and suggesting the need for a broader
basis of consensus in the political system. This period is followed
by the present more or less advanced stages in the catch-all group-
ing, with some of the parties still trying to hold their special working-class clientele and at the same time embracing a variety of
other clienteles.

Can we find some rules according to which this transformation
is taking place, singling out factors which advance or delay or arrest
it? We might think of the current rate of economic development
as the most important determinant; but if it were so important,
France would certainly be ahead of Great Britain and, for that
matter, also of the United States, still the classical example of an
all-pervasive catch-all party system. What about the impact of the
continuity or discontinuity of the political system? If this were so
important, Germany and Great Britain would appear at opposite
ends of the spectrum rather than showing a similar speed of transformation. We must then be satisfied to make some comments on
the general trend and to note special limiting factors.

In some instances the catch-all performance meets definite limits
in the traditional framework of society. The all-pervasive denominational background of the Italian *Democrazia Cristiana* means from
the outset that the party cannot successfully appeal to the anticleri-
cal elements of the population. Otherwise nothing prevents the
party from phrasing its appeals so as to maximize its chances of
catching more of those numerous elements which are not disturbed
by the party's clerical ties. The solidarity element of its doctrinal
core has long been successfully employed to attract a socially diversified clientele.

Or take the case of two other major European parties, the German
SPD (Social Democratic Party) and the British Labour party. It is

unlikely that either of them is able to make any concession to the specific desires of real estate interests or independent operators of agricultural properties while at the same time maintaining credibility with the masses of the urban population. Fortunately, however, there is enough community of interest between wage-and-salary earning urban or suburban white- and blue-collar workers and civil servants to designate them all as strategic objects of simultaneous appeals. Thus tradition and the pattern of social and professional stratification may set limits and offer potential audiences to the party's appeal.

If the party cannot hope to catch all categories of voters, it may have a reasonable expectation of catching more voters in all those categories whose interests do not adamantly conflict. Minor differences between group claims, such as between white-collar and manual labor groups, might be smoothed over by vigorous emphasis on programs which benefit both sections alike, for example, some cushioning against the shocks of automation.

Even more important is the heavy concentration on issues which are scarcely liable to meet resistance in the community. National societal goals transcending group interests offer the best sales prospect for a party intent on establishing or enlarging an appeal previously limited to specific sections of the population. The party which propagates most aggressively, for example, enlarged educational facilities may hear faint rumblings over the excessive cost or the danger to the quality of education from elites previously enjoying educational privileges. Yet the party's stock with any other family may be influenced only by how much more quickly and aggressively it took up the new national priority than its major competitor and how well its propaganda linked the individual family's future with the enlarged educational structures. To that extent its potential clientele is almost limitless. The catch-all of a given category performance turns virtually into an unlimited catch-all performance.

The last remark already transcends the group-interest confines. On the one hand, in such developed societies as I am dealing with, thanks to general levels of economic well-being and security and to existing welfare schemes universalized by the state or enshrined in collective bargaining, many individuals no longer need such protection as they once sought from the state. On the other hand, many have become aware of the number and complexity of the general factors on which their future well-being depends. This change of priorities and preoccupation may lead them to examine political offerings less under the aspect of their own particular claims than under that of the political leader's ability to meet general future contingencies. Among the major present-day parties, it is the French UNR . . . [Union for the New Republic] a late-comer, that speculates most clearly on the possibility of its channeling such less specialized needs to which its patron saint De Gaulle constantly appeals into its own version of the catch-all party. Its assumed asset would rest in a doctrine of national purpose and unity vague and flexible enough to allow the most variegated interpretation and yet—at least as long as the General continues to function—attractive enough to serve as a convenient rallying point for many groups and isolated individuals.

While the UNR thus manipulates ideology for maximum general appeal, we have noted that ideology in the case of the *Democrazia Cristiana* is a slightly limiting factor. The UNR ideology in principle excludes no one. The Christian Democratic ideology by definition excludes the nonbeliever, or at least the seriously nonbelieving voter. It pays for the ties of religious solidarity and the advantages of supporting organizations by repelling some millions of voters. The catch-all parties in Europe appear at a time of de-ideologization which has substantially contributed to their rise and spread. De-ideologization in the political field involves the transfer of ideology from partnership in a clearly visible political goal structure into one of many sufficient but by no means necessary motivational forces operative in the voters' choice. The German and Austrian Social Democratic parties in the last two decades most clearly exhibit the politics of de-ideologization. The example of the German Christian Democratic Union (CDU) is less clear only because there was less to deideologize. In the CDU, ideology was from the outset only a general background atmosphere, both all-embracing and conveniently vague enough to allow recruiting among Catholic and Protestant denominations.

As a rule, only major parties can become successful catch-all parties. Neither a small, strictly regional party such as the South Tyrolian Peoples' party nor a party built around the espousal of harsh and limited ideological claims, like the Dutch Calvinists; or transitory group claims, such as the German Refugees; or a specific professional category's claims, such as the Swedish Agrarians; or a limited-action program, such as the Danish single-tax Justice party can aspire to a catch-all performance. Its raison d'être is the defense of a specific clientele or the lobbying for a limited reform clearly delineated to allow for a restricted appeal, perhaps intense, but excluding a wider impact or—once the original job is terminated—excluding a life-saving transformation.

Nor is the catch-all performance in vogue or even sought among the majority of the larger parties in small democracies. Securely entrenched, often enjoying majority status for decades—as the Norwegian and Swedish Social Democratic parties—and accustomed to a large amount of interparty cooperation,[1] such parties have no incentive to change their form of recruitment or their appeal to well-defined social groups. With fewer factors intervening and therefore more clearly foreseeable results of political actions and decisions, it seems easier to stabilize political relations on the basis of strictly circumscribed competition (Switzerland, for instance) than to change over to the more aleatory form of catch-all competition.

Conversion to catch-all parties constitutes a competitive phenomenon. A party is apt to accommodate to its competitor's successful style because of hope of benefits or fear of losses on election day. Conversely, the more a party convinces itself that a competitor's favorable results were due only to some nonrepetitive circumstances, and that the competitor's capacity of overcoming internal dissension is a temporary phenomenon, the smaller the overall conversion chance and the greater the inclination to hold fast to a loyal—though limited—clientele.

To evaluate the impact of these changes I have found it useful to list the functions which European parties exercised during earlier decades (late in the 19th and early in the 20th centuries) and to compare them with the present situation. Parties have functioned as channels for integrating individuals and groups into the existing political order, or as instruments for modifying or altogether replacing that order (integration-disintegration). Parties have attempted to determine political-action preferences and influence other participants in the political process into accepting them. Parties have nominated public officeholders and presented them to the public at large for confirmation.

The so-called expressive function of the party, if not belonging to a category by itself, nevertheless warrants a special word. Its high tide belongs to the era of the 19th century constitutionalism when a more clear-cut separation existed between opinion formation-and-expression and the business of government. At that time the internally created parliamentary parties expressed opinions and criticism widely shared among the educated minority of the population. They pressed these opinions on their governments. But as the governments largely rested on an independent social and

---

[1] . . . For both weighty historical and contemporary reasons the Austrian Social-Democratic party forms a partial exception to the rule of less clear-cut transformation tendencies among major class-mass parties in smaller countries. It is becoming an eager and rather successful member of the catch-all club. For the most adequate treatment see K. L. Shell, *The Transformation of Austrian Socialism* (Albany, N.Y.: State University of New York, 1962).

constitutional basis, they could if necessary hold out against the promptings of parliamentary factions and clubs. Full democratization merged the opinion-expressing and the governmental business in the same political parties and put them in the seat either of government or an alternative government. But it has left the expressive function of the party in a more ambiguous state. For electoral reasons, the democratic catch-all party, intent on spreading as wide as possible a net over a potential clientele, must continue to express widely felt popular concerns. Yet, bent on continuing in power or moving into governmental power, it performs this expressive function subject to manifold restrictions and changing tactical considerations. The party would atrophy if it were no longer able to function as a relay between the population and governmental structure, taking up grievances, ideas, and problems developed in a more searching and systematic fashion elsewhere in the body politic. Yet the caution it must give its present or prospective governmental role requires modulation and restraint. The very nature of today's catch-all party forbids an option between these two performances. It requires a constant shift between the party's critical role and its role as establishment support, a shift hard to perform but still harder to avoid.

In order to leave a maximum imprint on the polity a party has to exercise all of the first three functions. Without the ability to integrate people into the community the party could not compel other powerholders to listen to its clarions. The party influences other power centers to the extent that people are willing to follow its leadership. Conversely, people are willing to listen to the party because the party is the carrier of messages—here called action preferences—that are at least partially in accord with the images, desires, hopes, and fears of the electorate. Nominations for public office serve to tie together all these purposes; they may further the realization of action preferences if they elicit positive response from voters or from other powerholders. The nominations concretize the party's image with the public at large, on whose confidence the party's effective functioning depends.

Now we can discuss the presence or absence of these three functions in Western society today. Under present conditions of spreading secular and mass consumer-goods orientation, with shifting and less obtrusive class lines, the former class-mass parties and denominational mass parties are both under pressure to become catch-all peoples' parties. The same applies to those few remnants of former bourgeois parties of individual representation which aspire to a secure future as political organizations independent of the vagaries of electoral laws and the tactical moves of their mass-party competitors.[2] This change involves: *(a)* Drastic reduction of the party's ideological baggage. In France's SFIO, for example, ideological remnants serve at best as scant cover for what has become known as *"Molletisme,"* the absolute reign of short-term tactical considerations. *(b)* Further strengthening of top leadership groups, whose actions and omissions are now judged from the viewpoint of their contribution to the efficiency of the entire social system rather than identification with the goals of their particular organization. *(c)* Downgrading of the role of the individual party member, a role considered a historical relic which may obscure the newly built-up catch-all party image. *(d)* Deemphasis of the *classe gardée,* specific social-class or denominational clientele, in favor of recruiting voters among the population at large. *(e)* Securing access to a variety of interest groups. The financial reasons are obvious, but they are not the most important where official financing is available, as in Germany, or where access to the most important media of communication is fairly open, as in England and Germany. The chief reason is to secure electoral support via interest-group intercession.

From this fairly universal development the sometimes considerable remnants of two old class-mass parties, the French and the Italian Communist parties, are excluding themselves. These parties are in part ossified, in part solidified by a combination of official rejection and legitimate sectional grievances. In this situation the ceremonial invocation of the rapidly fading background of a remote and inapplicable revolutionary experience has not yet been completely abandoned as a part of political strategy. What is the position of such opposition parties of the older class-mass type, which still jealously try to hold an exclusive loyalty of their members, while not admitted nor fully ready to share in the hostile state power? Such parties face the same difficulties in recruiting and holding intensity of membership interest as other political organizations. Yet, in contrast to their competitors working within the confines of the existing political order, they cannot make a virtue out of necessity and adapt themselves fully to the new style of catch-all peoples' party.[3] This conservatism does not cost them the confidence

---

[2] Liberal parties without sharply profiled program or clientele may, however, make such conversion attempts. Val Lorwin draws my attention to the excellent example of a former bourgeois party, the Belgian Liberal party, which became in 1961 the "Party of Liberty and Progress," deemphasizing anticlericalism and appealing to the right wing of the Social Christian party, worried about this party's governmental alliance with the Socialists.

[3] However, even in France—not to speak of Italy—Communist policies are under pressure to accommodate to the new style. For a concrete recent example see W. G. Andrews, "Evreux 1962: Referendum and Elections in a Norman

of their regular corps of voters. On the other hand, the continued renewal of confidence on election day does not involve an intimate enough bond to utilize as a basis for major political operations.

The attitudes of regular voters—in contrast to those of members and activists—attest to the extent of incongruency between full-fledged participation in the social processes of a consumer-goods oriented society and the old political style which rested on the primordial need for sweeping political change. The latter option has gone out of fashion in Western countries and has been carefully eliminated from the expectations, calculations, and symbols of the catch-all mass party. The incongruency may rest on the total absence of any connection between general social-cultural behavior and political style. In this sense electoral choice may rest on family tradition or empathy with the political underdog without thereby becoming part of a coherent personality structure. Or the choice may be made in the expectation that it will have no influence on the course of political development; it is then an act of either adjusting to or, as the case may be, signing out of the existing political system rather than a manifestation of signing up somewhere else.

THE CATCH-ALL PARTY, THE INTEREST GROUP, AND THE VOTER: LIMITED INTEGRATION

The integration potential of the catch-all mass party rests on a combination of factors whose visible end result is attraction of the maximum number of voters on election day. For that result the catch-all party must have entered into millions of minds as a familiar object fulfilling in politics a role analogous to that of a major brand in the marketing of a universally needed and highly standardized article of mass consumption. Whatever the particularities of the line to which a party leader owes his intraparty success, he must, once he is selected for leadership, rapidly suit his behavior to standard requirements. There is need for enough brand differentiation to make the article plainly recognizable, but the degree of differentiation must never be so great as to make the potential customer fear he will be out on a limb.

Like the brand whose name has become a household word, the catch-all mass party that has presided over the fortunes of a country

Constituency," in *Political Studies* 11 (October 1963), pp. 308–26. Most recently, Maurice Duverger, "L'Eternel Marais, Essai sur le Centrisme Français," in *Revue Française de Science Politique* 14 (February 1964), pp. 33 and 49.

for some time, and whose leaders the voter has therefore come to know on his television set and in his newspaper columns, enjoys a great advantage. But only up to a certain point. Through circumstances possibly outside the control of the party or even of the opposition—a scandal in the ranks of government, an economic slump—office-holding may suddenly turn into a negative symbol encouraging the voter to switch to another party as a consumer switches to a competitive brand.

The rules deciding the outcome of catch-all mass party competition are extremely aleatory. When a party has or seeks an almost nationwide potential constituency, its majority composed of individuals whose relation to politics is both tangential and discontinuous, the factors which may decide the eventual electoral outcome are almost infinite in number and often quite unrelated to the party's performance. The style and looks of the leader, the impact of a recent event entirely dictated from without, vacation schedules, the weather as it affects crops—factors such as these all enter into the results.

The very catch-all character of the party makes membership loyalty far more difficult to expect and at best never sufficient to swing results. The outcome of a television contest is dubious, or the contest itself may constitute too fleeting an exposure to make an impression that will last into the election. Thus the catch-all mass party too is driven back to look out for a more permanent clientele. Only the interest group, whether ideological or economic in nature or a combination of the two, can provide mass reservoirs of readily accessible voters. It has a more constant line of communication and higher acceptance for its messages than the catch-all party, which is removed from direct contact with the public except for the comparatively small number intensively concerned about the brand of politics a party has to offer these days—or about their own careers in or through the party.

All the same, the climate of relations between catch-all party and interest groups has definitely changed since the heyday of the class-mass or denominational integration party. Both party and interest group have gained a greater independence from each other. Whether they are still joined in the same organization (like British Labour and the TUC [Trades Union Congress]) or formally enjoy complete independence from each other (like the German SPD and the DGB [Workers' Federation]), what matters most is the change of roles.[4] Instead of a joint strategy toward a common goal there

---

[4] See the conclusions of Martin Harrison, *Trade Unions and the Labour Party Since 1945* (London: Allen and Unwin, 1960).

appears an appreciation of limited if still mutually helpful services to be rendered.

The party bent on attracting a maximum of voters must modulate its interest-group relations in such a way so as not to discourage potential voters who identify themselves with other interests. The interest group, in its turn, must never put all its eggs in one basket. That might offend the sensibilities of some members with different political connections. More important, the interest group would not want to stifle feelings of hope in another catch-all party that some moves in its direction might bring electoral rewards. Both party and interest group modulate their behavior, acting as if the possible contingency has already arrived, namely that the party has captured the government—or an important share in it—and has moved from the position of friend or counsellor to that of umpire or arbitrator. Suddenly entrusted with the confidence of the community as a whole, the government-party arbitrator does best when able to redefine the whole problem and discover solutions which would work, at least in the long run, in the favor of all interest claimants concerned.

Here there emerges a crucial question: What then is the proper role of the catch-all party in the arbitration of interest conflicts? Does not every government try to achieve the best tactical position for exercising an effective arbitration between contending group claims? Is the catch-all party even needed in this connection? Or— from the interest viewpoint—can a society dispense with parties' services, as France now does?

A party is more than a collector of interest-group claims. It functions at the same time as advocate, protector, or at least as addressee of the demands of all those who are not able to make their voices felt as effectively as those represented by well organized interest groups: those who do not yet have positions in the process of production or those who no longer hold such positions, the too young and the too old, and those whose family status aligns them with consumer rather than producer interests.

Can we explain this phenomenon simply as another facet of the party's aggregative function? But functionalist phraseology restates rather than explains. The unorganized and often unorganizable make their appearance only on election day or in suddenly sprouting pre-election committees and party activities arranged for their benefit. Will the party be able and willing to take their interests into its own hands? Will it be able, playing on their availability in electoral terms, not only to check the more extreme demands of organized groups but also to transcend the present level of intergroup relations and by political reforms redefining the whole political situation? No easy formula will tell us what leader's skill, what amount of pressure from objective situations has to intervene to produce such a change in the political configuration.

In this job of transcending group interests and creating general confidence the catch-all party enjoys advantages, but by the same token it suffers from an infirmity. Steering clear of sectarianism enhances its recruiting chances in electoral terms but inevitably limits the intensity of commitment it may expect. The party's transformation from an organization combining the defense of social position, the quality of spiritual shelter, and the vision of things to come into that of a vehicle for shortrange and interstitial political choice exposes the party to the hazards of all purveyors of nondurable consumer goods: competition with a more attractively packaged brand of a nearly identical merchandise.

LIMITED PARTICIPATION IN ACTION PREFERENCE

This brings us to the determination of action preferences and their chances of realization. In Anthony Down's well-known model, action preference simply results from the party's interest in the proximate goal, the winning of the next election. In consequence the party will arrange its policies in such a way that the benefits accruing to the individual members of the community are greater than the losses resulting from its policy.[5] Downs's illustrations are frequently, though not exclusively, taken from fields such as taxation where the cash equation of political action is feasible. Yet Downs himself has occasionally noted that psychological satisfactions or dissatisfactions, fears or hopes, are elements in voters' decisions as frequently as calculations of immediate short-terms benefits or deprivations. Were it different, the long-lasting loyalty of huge blocks of voters to class-mass integration parties in the absence of any immediate benefits from such affiliation could scarcely be explained. But can it be said that such short-term calculations correspond much more closely to the attitudes connected with the present-day catch-all mass party with its widely ranging clientele? Can the short-term benefit approach, for example, be utilized in military or foreign-policy issues?

In some countries in the last decade it has become the rule for catch-all parties out of office simply to lay the most recent shortcomings or apparent deterioration of the country's military or

---

[5] "It always organizes its action so as to focus on a single quantity: its vote margin over the opposition is the test at the end of the current election period." In A. Downs, *An Economic Theory of Democracy* (New York: Harper & Row, 1957), p. 174.

international position at the doorstep of the incumbent government, especially during election campaigns; thus in the United States the Republican party in 1952 with regard to the long-lasting indecisive Korean War, or in Germany more recently the Social Democrats with regard to Adenauer's apparent passivity in the face of the Berlin Wall. In other instances, however, the opposition plays down foreign or military issues or treats them in generalities vague enough to evoke the image of itself as a competitor who will be able to handle them as well as the incumbent government.

To the extent that the party system still includes "unreformed" or—as in the case of the Italian Socialist party—only "half-reformed" class-mass integration parties, foreign or military issues enter election campaigns as policy differences. Yet even here the major interest has shifted away from areas where the electorate could exercise only an illusory choice. The electorate senses that in the concrete situation, based in considerable part on geography and history, the international bloc affiliation of the country rather than any policy preference will form the basis of decision. It senses too that such decisions rest only partially, or at times nominally, with the political leadership. Even if the impact of the political leader on the decision may have been decisive, more often than not election time-tables in democracies are such that the decision, once carried out, is no longer contested or even relevant to voter choices. As likely as not, new events crowd it out of the focus of voters' attention. Few voters still thought of Mendès-France's 1954 "abandonment" of Indo-China when Edgar Faure suddenly dissolved the Assembly in December 1955. While a party may benefit from its adversary's unpopular decisions, such benefits are more often an accidental by-product than the outcome of a government-opposition duel with clearly distributed roles and decisions.

A party may put up reasonably coherent, even if vague, foreign or military policies for election purposes. It may criticize the inept handling of such problems by the government of the day, and more and more intensively as it gets closer to election day. But in neither case is there a guarantee of the party's ability to act as a coherent body in parliament when specific action preferences are to be determined. Illustrative of this dilemma are the history of EDC in the French Parliament and the more recent battles within the British parties in regard to entrance into the Common Market (although the latter case remains inconclusive because of De Gaulle's settling the issue in his own way, for the time being). Fortuitous election timetables and the hopes, fears, and expectations of the public do not intermesh sufficiently with the parliamentary representatives' disjointed action on concrete issues before them to add up to the elaboration of clear-cut party action preference.

The catch-all party contributes general programs in the elaboration of domestic action preferences. These programs may be of a prognostic variety, informing the public about likely specific developments and general trends. Yet prognostics and desirability blur into each other in this type of futurology, in which rosy glasses offer previews of happy days for all and sundry among the party's prospective customers. These programs may lead to or be joined with action proposals in various stages of concretization. Concrete proposals, however, always risk implying promises which may be too specific. Concretizations must remain general enough so that they cannot be turned from electoral weapons to engines of assault against the party which first mounted them.

This indeterminacy allows the catch-all party to function as a meeting ground for the elaboration of concrete action for a multiplicity of interest groups. All the party may require from those who obtain its services is that they make a maximal attempt to arrive at compromises within the framework of the party and that they avoid coalescing with forces hostile to the party. The compromises thus elaborated must be acceptable to major interest groups even if these groups, for historical or traditional reasons, happen not to be represented in the governing party. Marginal differences may be submitted to the voter at elections or, as older class-mass parties do on occasion, via referenda (Switzerland and Sweden). But expected policy mutations are in the nature of increments rather than major changes in intergroup relations.

It is here that the difference between the catch-all and the older form of integration party becomes most clearly visible. The catch-all party will do its utmost to establish consensus to avoid party realignment. The integration party may count on majority political mechanisms to implement its programs only to find that hostile interests frustrate the majority decision by the economic and social mechanisms at their disposal. They may call strikes (by labor or farmers or storekeepers or investors), they may withdraw capital to safe haven outside the country, they may undermine that often hypocritically invoked but real factor known as the "confidence of the business community."

INTEGRATION THROUGH PARTICIPATION IN LEADERSHIP SELECTION—THE FUTURE OF THE POLITICAL PARTY

What then remains the real share of the catch-all party in the elaboration of action preferences? Its foremost contribution lies in the mobilization of the voters for whatever concrete action preferences leaders are able to establish rather than a priori selections of their own. It is for this reason that the catch-all party prefers to visualize action in the light of the contingencies, threats, and promises of concrete historical situations rather than of general social goals. It is the hoped-for or already established role in the dynamics of action, in which the voters' vicarious participation is invited, that is most in evidence. Therefore the attention of both party and public at large focuses most clearly on problems of leadership selection.

Nomination means the prospect of political office. Political office involves a chance to make an impact via official action. The competition between those striving to influence official action puts into evidence the political advantage of those in a position to act before their political adversaries can do so. The privilege of first action is all the more precious in a new and non-repetitive situation where the political actor can avoid getting enmeshed in directives deriving from party action preferences. Much as the actor welcomes party support on the basis of revered (but elastic) principles, he shuns specific direction and supervision. In this respect the catch-all party furnishes an ideal background for political action. Where obtaining office becomes an almost exclusive preoccupation of a party, issues of personnel are reduced to search for the simplest effective means to put up winning combinations. The search is especially effective wherever the party becomes a channel by which representatives of hitherto excluded or neglected minorities may join in the existing political elite.

The nomination of candidates for popular legitimation as officeholders thus emerges as the most important function of the present-day catch-all party. Concentration on the selection of candidates for office is in line with an increasing role differentiation in industrial society. Once certain levels of education and material welfare are reached, both intellectual and material needs are taken care of by specialized purveyors of communications and economic products. Likewise the party, which in less advanced societies or in those intent on rapid change directly interferes with the performance of societal jobs, remains in Western industrial society twice removed—through government and bureaucracy—from the field of direct action. To this state of affairs correspond now prevailing popular images and expectations in regard to the reduced role of the party. Expectations previously set on the performance of a political organization are now flowing into different channels.

At the same time, the role of the political party as a factor in the continued integration of the individual into the national life now has to be visualized in a different light. Compared to his connection with interest organizations and voluntary associations of a non-political nature and to his frequent encounters with the state bureaucracy, the citizen's relations with the political party are becoming more intermittent and of more limited scope.

To the older party of integration the citizen, if he so desired, could be closer. Then it was a less differentiated organization, part channel of protest, part source of protection, part purveyor of visions of the future. Now, in its linear descendant in a transfigured world, the catch-all party, the citizen finds a relatively remote, at times quasi-official and alien structure. Democratic society assumes that the citizen is finally an integral and conscious participant in the affairs of both the polity and the economy; it further assumes that as such he will work through the party as one of the many interrelated structures by which he achieves a rational participation in his surrounding world.

Should he ever live up to these assumptions, the individual and society may indeed find the catch-all party—non-utopian, non-oppressive, and ever so flexible—an ingenious and useful political instrument.

What about the attitude toward the modern catch-all party of functional powerholders in army, bureaucracy, industry, and labor? Released from their previous unnecessary fears as to the ideological propensities and future intentions of the class-mass party, functional powerholders have come to recognize the catch-all party's role as consensus purveyor. In exchange for its ability to provide a clear-cut basis of legitimacy, functional powerholders are, up to a point, willing to recognize the political leadership claims of the party. They expect it to exercise certain arbitration functions in intergroup relations and to initiate limited political innovations. The less clear-cut electoral basis of the party's leadership claim and the closer the next election date, the smaller the credit which functional powerholders will extend to unsolicited and non-routine activities of the political powerholders impinging on their own positions. This lack of credit then sets the stage for conflicts between functional and political leadership groups. How does the catch-all party in governmental positions treat such conflicts? Will it be satisfied to exercise pressure via the mass media, or will it try to re-create a militant mass basis beyond the evanescent electoral and publicity levels? But the very structure of the catch-all party, the looseness of its clientele, may from the outset exclude such more far-reaching action. To that extent the political party's role in Western industrial society today is more limited than would appear from its position of formal preeminence. Via its governmental role it functions as coordinator of and arbitrator between functional power groups. Via its electoral role it produces that limited amount of popular participation and integration required from the popular masses for the functioning of official political institutions.

Will this limited participation which the catch-all party offers the population at large, this call to rational and dispassionate participation in the political process via officially sanctioned channels, work?

The instrument, the catch-all party, cannot be much more rational than its nominal master, the individual voter. No longer subject to the discipline of the party of integration—or, as in the United States, never subject to this discipline—the voters may, by their shifting moods and their apathy, transform the sensitive instrument of the catch-all party into something too blunt to serve as a link with the functional powerholders of society. Then we may yet come to regret the passing—even if it was inevitable—of the class-mass party and the denominational party, as we already regret the passing of other features in yesterday's stage of Western civilization.

19

Democratic Theory and
Neocorporatist Practice

Philippe C. Schmitter

NEOCORPORATISM

The concept of corporatism, usually accompanied by some prefix such as "societal-," "liberal-," "bargained-," or, more recently, "neo-," burst upon the social-science scene in 1974[1] and has since grown in prominence to the point that it has been described by one author as "a growth industry."[2] Confused in political discourse with fascism and authoritarian rule—not to mention with the French-Italian polemic usage which identifies it with the pursuit of narrow and immediate sectoral interests—and confounded in academic discussion by competing definitions and theoretical approaches, it has become a controversial subject, an "essentially contested" concept. Neocorporatism (the *neo* is intended both to separate it from its historical predecessors—whether medieval or

---

Source: Philippe C. Schmitter, "Democratic Theory and Neocorporatist Practice," *Social Research* 50, no. 4 (Winter 1983), pp. 885–928. By permission. Article and footnotes abridged by the editors.

[1] Gerhard Lehmbruch, "Consociational Democracy, Class Conflict and the New Corporatism," in *Trends Toward Corporatist Intermediation*, ed. Schmitter and Lehmbruch (Beverly Hills, Calif.: Sage, 1979). pp. 53–62. Philippe C. Schmitter, "Still the Century of Corporatism?" *Review of Politics* 36 (January 1974), pp. 85–131; R. E. Pahl and J. T. Winkler, "The Coming Corporatism," *New Society* 10 October 1974.

[2] Leo Panitch, "Recent Theorizations of Corporatism: Reflections on a Growth Industry," *British Journal of Sociology* 31 (June 1980), pp. 159–87.

interwar—and to indicate its relative novelty) has been found everywhere—and nowhere. It has been credited with producing all sorts of goods—and charged with promoting all manner of evils. It has been described as an inexorable political trend—and called a passing academic fancy. Most of all, it has been difficult to define neocorporatism clearly and consensually. One of its strengths has been its ability to speak to the concerns of scholars from different disciplines and orientations—each of whom, however, has tended to give his or her own twist to the concept. It has become virtually impossible to tell whether all of the contributors to this growth industry are talking about related, much less identical, phenomena.

For purposes of this essay, neocorporatism refers to a recently emergent *political* arrangement—not to a new way of running the economy or ordering the entire society. It is concerned primarily with the activities of permanently organized and specialized *associations*—not units of production (firms, enterprises, corporations, etc.), not units of consumption (individuals, families, cooperatives, etc.), not units of status or affect (corps, colleagues, cliques, etc.), and not units of public authority (state agencies, ministries, parliaments, local governments, etc.). These associations seek to advance or defend interests by influencing and contesting collective choices. And they do this by intermediating between members and various interlocutors (mostly the State) without presenting candidates for electoral approval or accepting direct responsibility for the formation of governments (i.e., they are not parties, caucuses, coalitions, etc.). Any or all of the other above-mentioned units of political action may have a significant effect on the emergence or viability of neocorporatism by supporting, opposing, or circumventing it, but they are not an integral part of its defining properties. Indeed, it is arguable that neocorporatist practices have proven compatible with a rather wide range of surrounding units.

However, neocorporatist arrangements are not the only way in which intermediation between interest associations and authoritative interlocutors can be institutionalized. Indeed, if one leaves aside medieval precedents and the short period of state-enforced corporatization under interwar dictatorships, they are relatively recent and rare. For a considerable period, the predominant way of conceptualizing interest intermediation was "pluralism," and a very substantial and impressive literature on that topic was devoted to demonstrating that its arrangements were not just compatible with but actively promotive of democracy. Much of the "cloud of suspicion" which hangs over neocorporatism is due, not just to the objections of those "utopians" who reject organized intermediation and incorporation of partial interests into policymaking on the grounds that it is destructive of the direct citizen role in public affairs and of government by popular assembly, but to the suspicions of "realists" that these new arrangements represent a serious distortion and perversion of "proven" pluralist processes. . . .

NEOCORPORATIST PRACTICES AND THE CITIZENSHIP PRINCIPLE

In our effort to develop normative standards for evaluating its performance, we defined modern, representative democracy as a general principle in search of a certain qualitative relationship between rulers and ruled. Connecting the two are decision rules, procedural norms, and political institutions which have varied considerably over time—no matter how established and definitive they may appear at a given moment. Except in instances of dramatic refounding after the collapse of an authoritarian regime or in periods of deliberate reform in the face of manifest crisis, these specific rules, procedures, and institutions tend to change slowly, often imperceptibly, and usually by consensus under the pressure of opportunistic situations, internal diffusion, or evolutionary trends.

Neocorporatism is a good example of such a transformation within democratic polities in which the "procedural minimum" has been respected but substantial changes in such things as majority rule, parliamentary sovereignty, public deliberation, etc. have occurred. Perhaps precisely because these contemporary trends in the organizational structure of interests and in their relation to policymaking have not been backed by an explicit ideology—again in contrast to interwar state or authoritarian corporatism—and because they evolved in such a piecemeal, uneven, and almost surreptitious manner within distinct policy arenas, they have largely escaped evaluative scrutiny. Only once they have accumulated over time, so to speak, and are manifestly affecting a wide range of producer and consumer—as well as citizen—behaviors is the question of their compatibility with democracy likely to arise and to attract the attention of scholars as well as activists.

Our first and most diffuse evaluative standard is whether these arrangements violate the principle of citizenship. Do they diminish the extent to which individuals have equal opportunities to act as citizens and to be treated as equals by their fellow citizens? Do they reduce the extent to which citizens feel obligated to respect choices made by collective deliberation among equals (or their representatives)?

If one equates the opportunity to act as citizen only with voting and the obligation to conform only to laws which have been certified by a sovereign legislature, then neocorporatism is manifestly contrary to the citizenship principle. It introduces elements of "weighted" calculation and consensual bargaining with privileged minorities which clearly violate the sacred norms of "one man, one vote" and "the most votes win." It generates binding commitments which either are never subject to parliamentary approval or involve a mere officializing of package deals hammered out elsewhere. However, if one broadens the notion of equal political opportunity and treatment to include intraelectoral periods and extraelectoral processes, then neocorporatism can be interpreted as extending the citizenship principle.

Basically, what it does is to resolve "the paradox of liberal associability," the fact that where the freedom to associate is equally accorded but the capacity to exercise this freedom is unequally distributed, those that most need to act collectively in defense of their interests are the least likely to be able to do so. Small, compact, and privileged groups who are already better able to advance their interests through existing economic and social exchanges than larger, more dispersed, and equally endowed ones, will find it easier to recruit members and extract contributions for a further defense of their interests in the political realm—if and when such a response is required. Hence comes the theme of the "institutionalization of bias" in pressure politics which has been decried by so many critics of pluralism.[3] What neocorporatism does is shift the basis of associability from a predominantly voluntaristic and individualistic calculus to one where contributions become more generally binding on all members of a relevant category (or more difficult to avoid), and mutual recognition and official certification protect the role of specific collectivities at the expense of competing fragments or individual actors. In short, as "free riding" and "freebooting" became increasingly difficult under such arrangements, virtually everyone can be made to contribute and conform to associative action. This can have the effect of evening out considerably the organizational capacity of competing groups, particularly capital and labor. In addition, most neocorporatist forums are based on highly formalized systems of parity in representation and, not infrequently, produce policies which make the participating "social partners" co-responsible for their implementation. Under such conditions, organized socioeconomic interests may never be equally counted, but they are likely to be more equally weighed than they would be if citizens invested voluntarily and individually their own disparate resources and personal intensities in the liberal "art of association."

The normative problem with applying this "science of organization" to interest intermediation is that it may make more equal

---

[3] Peter Bachrach and Morton S. Baratz, *Power and Poverty: Theory and Practice* (New York: Oxford University Press, 1970), esp. pp. 3–66.

the capacities for exerting influence of incorporated collectivities at the same time that it purposively excludes others which may be affected by their deliberations. So far, neocorporatism has privileged interests organized along functional lines of production within a capitalist economy—classes, sectors, and professions. Its relative success has depended on restricting the number and identity of participants and passing on the costs to those not directly represented in its deliberations: consumers, taxpayers, youths, feminists, irregular workers, foreigners, cultural minorities, nature lovers, pedestrians, prohibitionists, etc. Granted that the more comprehensive scope of the associations engaged in neocorporatist bargaining may encourage them to take into account some of these "marginal" interests—for example, when a comprehensive trade union calculates the effect of its demands on its member interests as consumers or when a national business association agrees to moderate its position in deference to the need for environmental protection[4]—but this is a tenuous and contingent relationship, hardly reliable enough in the long run to lead to an effective equalization of influence for such categories of citizens. Existing corporatist associations which defer too much to such interests risk a paralysis of their own internal decision structures and/or a defection of their own core supporters.

One "democratic" answer would be to extend the process of corporatization to cover interests structured along distributional lines or causes generated by cultural and ideological diversity, but that hardly seems feasible. Establishing monopolistic, hierarchically coordinated, and topically differentiated national associations for, say, consumers, taxpayers, youths, environmentalists, and foreign residents would likely involve such extensive state intervention and subsidization that it would be difficult to avoid the appearance, not to mention the reality, of manipulation and cooptation from above. The officially recognized associations would be simply disavowed by their nominal members and lose all credibility for contracting in their names. In addition to which, many of these groups define their very existence in ways that defy professionalized representation and bureaucratic *encadrement*. To be organized corporatistically would destroy the very basis of their collective identity. Finally, even if the organizational problem could be solved, bringing such a quantity and variety of recognized interlocutors into the policy-making process on a coequal basis would destroy the properties of small-group interaction, specialized competence, reciprocal

---

[4] Mancur Olson, *The Rise and Decline of Nations: Economic Growth, Stagflation and Social Rigidities* (New Haven: Yale University Press, 1982), attempts to elevate this contingent point into a major explanatory factor.

trust, and propensity for compromise which have contributed so much to the viability of existing neocorporatist arrangements.

In summary, a pattern of more equalized and formally structured exchange among associations has emerged in some democratic countries—a sort of corporatism for the functionally privileged—which could be defended as a direct extension of the citizenship principle outside the electoral-parliamentary arena in ways that go beyond the formalistic opportunities afforded by pluralist associability. Moreover, its operation has undoubtedly had the indirect effect of promoting policies which have extended citizen rights to protection against unemployment, to more extensive welfare services, and to representation within institutions previously governed by other authority principles, especially business firms and state agencies. Citizens of pluralistically structured polities have suffered significantly greater inequalities in all these domains. Its unintended consequence, however, has been to consolidate a disparity between these more equally *competent* and privileged class, sectoral, and professional interests and less equally *competent* and organized ones— leaving a sort of residual pluralism for the distributionally disadvantaged and the culturally underprivileged. Since there appear to be serious impediments to extending neocorporatist practices to these latter interest domains and since at least some of these appear to be of genuine concern to the citizenry of contemporary democracies, neocorporatism is neither fully compatible with the citizenship principle nor are decisions made under its auspices likely to go unchallenged by those who are expected to obey them. However, like so many of its forerunners in the history of democratic development, its norms and institutions may long be tolerated as a second-best compromise: "a better system than those that preceded it and those that have hitherto followed it."[5]

A SHIFT IN THE QUALITY OF DEMOCRACY?

. . . Neocorporatist arrangements shift performance away from a concern with *participation* and *accessibility* toward a greater emphasis on *accountability* and *responsiveness*. Individual citizens become less intensely and directly involved in political life; at the same time, organizations active in their interests became increasingly integral components of the policy process. The number and type of interlocutors with equivalent and effective access to authorities decrease considerably due to the recognition of monopolies, the creation of associational hierarchies, and the formalization of

---

[5] Norberto Bobbio, "Are There Alternatives to Representative Democracy?" *Telos*, no. 35 (Spring 1978), p. 29.

functional systems of representation; at the same time those that are able to obtain such privileged status acquire more resources and become more indispensable to the management of public affairs so that arbitrary (and often self-serving) actions by state officials become less likely. Subjects of collective choice which were highly politicized—that is, subject to intense citizen concern, public debate, group mobilization, and extensive pressure—become less so, at the same time as institutions of administrative and market allocation which were previously defined as outside the realm of democratic polities become subject to greater scrutiny by political associations.

In the midst of this shift from participation/accessibility to accountability/responsiveness lies a phenomenon which modern democratic theory has been ill prepared to analyze or even to recognize, namely, the development of "private" or "class governance." Perhaps one major reason for this stems from its historical roots in liberalism. Democratic theory was originally closely identified with the liberal struggle against the constraints that obligatory associability had placed on the economic and social behavior of individuals: guild restrictions, state-chartered monopolies, licensing provisions, etc. It continued to regard all associations which subsequently grew up under its tolerance and encouragement as purely voluntary and autonomous, an embodiment of that original resistance to regimentation and loss of individual freedom.

Neocorporatism changes not merely the resources of associations and the nature of policymaking. It can also radically alter the relationship between interest groups and their members. Instead of merely aggregating independently formed preferences and articulating them before authorities, its associations acquire an enhanced capacity for defining the interests of members and controlling their behavior. In the pluralist idiom, *information* is the key resource involved in interest exchange; in the corporatist mode, it becomes *compliance*. Associations do not just inform policymakers about the intensities of preference and likely reactions of their members, expecting officials to react accordingly; they also agree—for a price— to deliver member compliance to contracts negotiated with the approval of public authorities. All this presumes, of course, that it will be to the long-term benefit of members to be forced to cooperate irrespective of their individualistic, short-term preferences. Occasionally and always reluctantly, neocorporatist organizations may even have to wield directly the coercive powers necessary to keep dissident members (and even nonmembers where contracts are extended to cover a whole category) in line: fines, expulsions, refusal to provide services, loss of license, etc. Whether this authority is generated consensually from within or devolved legally upon it from without, the net result is the same. The society acquires a set of parallel institutions of semiprivate and semipublic governance capable of coordinating the behavior of some large social aggregates—classes, sectors, professions—without directly burdening or involving state authorities. This may provide one element for explaining why the more neocorporatist polities have proven demonstrably more "governable" in recent decades than pluralist ones at a similar level of capitalist development and organizational complexity.

This leaves us with competitiveness, the quality of democracy which putatively ties all the others together. What happens to it under the auspices of neocorporatism? Obviously, some forms are eliminated altogether or reduced to insignificance. Groups with overlapping domains no longer compete for members or for access to public authorities on the same issues. Factions within associations are less likely to risk investing their resources in founding alternative organizations, if only because other public and private interlocutors will persist in recognizing only the officially monopolistic one. Under a general process of incorporation, highly specialized or very particularistic "maverick groups" will find it increasingly prudent to merge with larger and more established units or to accept coordination from overarching "peak associations" if they do not wish to suffer a progressive margination from the policy process.

It is not clear whether the politics *within* neocorporatist organizations is likely to become more competitive as that between them diminishes. Certainly the rewards for winning office become more substantial with the increase in associational resources and semipublic functions, but that may only encourage entrenched oligarchies to defend their positions more assiduously and tempt state and party officials to intervene in order to ensure that interest interlocutors will continue to play the responsible and respectful role assigned to them. At the level of national peak associations, executive leaders become highly visible and influential figures who can count on help from "outsiders" provided they agree to stay within the rules of the corporatist game.

But this does not mean that competitiveness disappears altogether under such arrangements. Rather its effect tends to become more implicit than explicit, more potential than observable. One must never forget that neocorporatism is a chosen, not an imposed, strategy for the promotion and defense of interests and that it is not the only mode of intermediation between citizens and authorities. Associations can withdraw from negotiations patterned this way—and they can survive, even prosper, by engaging in classic pressure politics. Specific issues can be taken to other arenas—and they can be articulated through single-issue movements or spontaneous protest actions. Association members are also voting citizens—and they can express their dissatisfaction by switching allegiance among existing parties or by supporting new ones. Parties which have promoted corporatist arrangements can lose elections— and their successors in government may choose to dismantle or ignore those arrangements. Parliaments can assert their legal sovereignty—and they can refuse to ratify the social contracts which are put before them. Members can refuse to obey the directives of their associations—and the sanctions available may be so weak or difficult to wield that they can get away with such defections. The fact that such occurrences have been relatively rare in neocorporatist polities does not alter the latent role that competitiveness continues to play in setting boundaries upon such arrangements. Participants in them are forced to anticipate that such reactions could occur and to adjust their bargaining behavior accordingly. They cannot act as if neocorporatism were the only game in town. Observers, however, who predicted its imminent demise after each wildcat strike or electoral failure of Social Democracy have been generally disappointed. It even appears to be surviving under the conditions of increased national and international competitiveness induced by protracted recession and consequent failure to meet such performance goals as full employment and economic growth. Nevertheless, the politics of these countries has not settled into some "postproblematic" consensus. Controversial items still manage to get on their agenda for collective deliberation; citizens continue to be offered real choices; associational leaders know they must be accountable to member preferences—just as they know they must be responsive to system imperatives.

Moreover, one cannot ignore the fact that many of the polities where neocorporatist practices have become most firmly entrenched have either inherited (e.g., Switzerland) or experimented with (e.g., Sweden, Norway, Denmark, Austria, West Germany) a wide range of institutional innovations which have extended the equal rights of individual citizens in their direct interaction with public officials and partisan representatives: referenda, proportional representation, ombudsman systems, subsidies for political parties and citizen groups, elections to works councils, public-disclosure laws, decentralized administration, protection of personal data, profit-sharing arrangements, and so forth. One can argue that not all of these have had that much of an impact (and some have been very selectively implemented), but one can hardly fault these systems for not trying. It is at least plausible that discussion of them and their eventual presence in political life has effectively compensated for some of the more insidious and less positive effects that creeping neocorporatism has had upon the other democratic qualities of participation, accessibility, and competitiveness.

Finally, one must acknowledge the almost complete absence of

popular resistance to neocorporatist trends in those countries. This
is all the more remarkable since they have rarely been defended
explicitly and globally. Ordinarily they have been sanctioned only
pragmatically on a case-by-case basis. No one confesses to being a
"corporatist," or even to some euphemism thereof. There exists no
explicit justification of its practice in terms of its conformity to
democratic principles or procedures. And yet citizens have by and
large accepted it upon reflection. They might recognize that its emergence has altered their rights and obligations, and they might occasionally grumble to survey researchers that "organized business,"
"organized labor," or "organized professions" seem to have too much
influence, but few if any seem to feel that they have lost more
than they have gained by entrusting the management of their interest politics to such intermediaries. Ironically, it is in those countries
whose interest associations have been least corporatized that one
hears the epithet "corporatist" thrown most often at opponents
and that intellectuals denounce all signs of its prospective emergence as a threat to traditional freedoms and democratic institutions.

THE SPECTER OF VICARIOUS DEMOCRACY?

So does this mean that the more neocorporatist polities are already
headed toward some new form of postindividualistic, vicarious democracy, with other advanced industrial/capitalist societies soon
to follow? That the famous myth of the rational, well informed,
and active citizen has finally been put to rest and been replaced
by the specter of the reasonable, well staffed, and recognized association as the basic unit of democracy? That the notion of a civil society
composed of natural groups voluntarily entering into exchanges
in the pursuit of their own autonomously defined preferences and
capable of reproducing itself without the constant intromission of
the state has given way to a vision of a semipublic society composed
of artifactual organizations compulsorily negotiating compromises
in the pursuit of their members' imputed interests and capable of
sustaining itself only by symbiotic interdependence with public authorities?

Let us leave aside the probability that neocorporatism and vicarious democracy may well be a solution to the problem of modern
interest conflict confined to particular countries and national circumstances. Small size, high international vulnerability, well-established state legitimacy, centralized administrative structures, clear
preponderance of class cleavage over other bases of social and cultural conflict, ideological hegemony of social democratic over bourgeois values are all factors which seem to have contributed to the

emergence of such a pattern, although they may not all necessarily be prerequisites for such an outcome in the future.

I suspect that the answer to the "paradox of corporatist associability"—to its ambiguous impact on the *practice* of democracy—eventually lies in the truth of what is one of the most central tenets of the *theory* of democracy, namely, that for a polity to be really responsive to the needs and concerns of its citizens, these citizens must *participate* actively and freely in the definition of those needs and the expression of those concerns. They must not only have the "enlightened understanding" of their interests which Robert Dahl so rightly stressed, but they must also have the resources *and* the desire to engage in the political struggle necessary to make sure their preferences are taken into consideration by those who govern or by seeking themselves to govern. Specialized experts, organic intellectuals, designated spokespersons, professional intermediaries, benevolent rulers, etc. may, in some contexts and for some period of time, be better informed and more capable of interpreting the interests of social groups, but unless they are kept accountable by an active citizenry, their theories and suppositions about what is good for their members, clients, followers, etc. are likely to prove erroneous in the long run. What is more, the organizational and political "rents" which these intermediaries extract for the service they perform will systematically distort the very content of demands made upon the polity.

The progressive assertion of interest politics, its conversion from an "art of association" into a "science of organization," may have greatly changed the identity of relevant actors. It may have expanded the resources and extended the range of such intermediaries. The emergence of a neocorporatist mode may have increased the immediate governability, improved the aggregate economic performance, and equalized access to policymaking in advanced capitalist societies, but the "vicarious democracy" which has accompanied these transformations may not prove so satisfying and in the long run so governable. *Rulers may become more accountable under such arrangements, but to the wrong collectivities*—not necessarily to the units with which persons voluntarily identify and from which they naturally derive a sense of shared existence, but to those which struggle, convenience, connivance, and luck have allowed to become formally organized, often at levels of aggregation far above that which would have been spontaneously forthcoming. *Governments may also be more responsive, but to the wrong needs*—not necessarily to those which individuals would themselves feel and become concerned about, but to those which professional intermediaries have defined and promoted as the "real" interests of their respective memberships or clienteles—often while including substantial side payments for themselves and the organizations which they control.

Whatever impact the organization of interest politics has had upon political performance, whatever has been the relationship between neocorporatism and governability, whatever both have done to growth, equality, and democracy, it is difficult to imagine that these changes have completely voided the old liberal adage that "each individual person is the best judge of his or her own interests." Ultimately, if not immediately, the polity will be judged by its ability to satisfy *these* interests—not just *those* which have been identified, given generic labels, and packaged collectively by intermediaries and to which authorities have presumably been dutifully accountable and responsive. Moreover, if among these "really felt" interests of individual citizens are distinctively political needs for active participation and close access to rulers, then one would have even more grounds for suspecting that the sort of "vicarious democracy" promoted by neocorporatism will prove to be but a passing phase—hopefully, an appropriate and proportionate (if temporary) adjustment in the "art of association" that Tocqueville thought was so necessary to keeping our collective existence "civilized" while our individual conditions were becoming "equalized."

CHAPTER SIX

Political Institutions and Performance

——— 20 ———

Princes, Parliaments, and the Public Service

Samuel E. Finer

The bureaucracy is the armature of the modern state; and the modern state has, everywhere, been patterned on the European model. This armature is (supposedly at least) powered by the ruler. It is also to a greater or less extent (sometimes not at all) checked and balanced by organs of popular control. Between the three elements—rulers, bureaucrats and popular organs—there is a perpetual tension. A shift in the balance is tantamount to a shift in the regime. Where the organs of popular control over the ruler and his bureaucracy are strong enough to make them answerable to the public, this is the necessary though not the sufficient condition for a democracy. Where these organs are feeble or absent, and the ruler effectively leads and commands his bureaucracy, the regime is authoritarian, possibly absolutist. Where, however, the ruler is lazy or inept and the organs of popular control equally weak, there we find bureaucracy in its original pejorative sense: the impersonal rule of anonymous and faceless officials.

It may be that the officials who head such a bureaucracy are themselves men of genius and imagination, far different from their juniors who are the more circumscribed and routine-ridden the

Source: Samuel E. Finer, "Princes, Parliaments, and the Public Service," *Parliamentary Affairs,* Autumn 1980, pp. 353–72. By permission. This article was originally published in Alan Bullock, ed., *The Faces of Europe* (Oxford, Engl.: Phaidon Press, 1980). Article and footnotes abridged by the editors.

lower their rank. The top bureaucrats may, in these circumstances, innovate in ways which their skill and dedication put beyond the capacity of the nominal rulers and in directions unhindered by the harrying of representative assemblies or the courts of law. Such an ideal—founded at present on an enthusiasm for what supposedly passes in France—is clearly desired by a number of present-day students of politics. Their view leads straight into the inescapable central dilemma of bureaucratised polities: the more the bureaucrats enjoy discretion, the less are they accountable, and the more accountable, the less they enjoy discretion. In a word—the bureaucrat can be either creative or formalistic, but never both at once. This inner tension in the bureaucratic role is an ever-recurrent theme in its long march through European history. . . .

Within the last half-century what were often untidy and unsystematised aggregates of public servants have become self-governing, self-regulating professional organisations largely insulated from outside interference, whether popular or partisan. Recruitment had previously been made by patronage, often by party patronage, and while this still holds good for the upper echelons in some countries (Belgium, for instance), the overwhelming bulk of civil servants have for as much as a century past in certain countries (in Britain, for example) been recruited only if they possessed publicly defined qualifications. Thus in Britain, France, Belgium and Italy today the upper civil servant is recruited by competitive examinations; and in Scandinavia, Holland, Switzerland and West Germany on the basis of specified paper qualifications. In France the recruit receives a special training if he is to be retained; in Germany he will proceed to in-service training and must then pass a state examination; elsewhere recruits become probationers and are set to "learn on the job." But in all cases, qualifications are needed and an impartial board, insulated from party and personal pressures, is the body that recruits the candidates. By the same token the civil servant everywhere today enjoys an almost perfect security of tenure. This was true of most countries even in the 19th century, where only Spain, Italy and Belgium provided exceptions. Today there are no exceptions: if dismissal is to take place, it must be decided by a special and highly circumscribed disciplinary procedure. True, the security is not absolute; but whatever the reason for a dismissal—national security, impropriety or rank incompetence—it will require in some form or another the active participation and acquiescence of other members of the civil service.

In short the bureaucracy has become a professionally qualified meritocracy recruited by impersonal standards and guaranteed tenure: this insulates it from political, personal and public pressures and so do arrangements for pay and promotion. It is true that the regulations governing these can be fiddled somewhat for party advantages, but the general conditions of pay and service are usually established by a central department or council: the Civil Service Department in Britain, the *Direction de la fonction publique* in France, the *Secretariat permanent de recrutement* in Belgium, the *Consiglio superiore della pubblica amministrazione* in Italy. Additionally, in many European states the rights and duties of the civil servant are formulated in a document like the *Statut des fonctionnaires* in France, with similar codes in Germany, Belgium or Italy. Furthermore in most West European countries—Britain and the Irish Republic being the major exceptions, since they are common-law countries—such statutes or codes are adjudicated by the administrative courts.

The obverse of such insulation is the political neutrality of the civil servant. Since he is appointed and removed on the basis of his technical capacity to serve the state, he is expected to serve it without regard to persons or to the party complexion of the government of the day. Consequently all states impose some kinds of restrictions on the political activities of civil servants. Little difficulty arises in assimilating the rights of the junior civil servants to those of the general electorate, for these are concerned in routine functions. The problem only arises for the upper 2,000 or 3,000 "higher" civil servants who occupy that sensitive hinge area where policy and administration merge. Britain perhaps imposes the severest limitations on the rights of the civil servant to campaign for a political party or to stand for election to Parliament, and Germany perhaps the least. In similar ways higher civil servants are usually debarred for a certain time from taking posts in private business after they have resigned or retired from the service. The degree of insulation from active politics or private business varies, as one would expect, from country to country but the general tenor is plain enough: the career is to be self-sufficient and full-time and dedicated to the impersonal "state". In practice the general rule is breached in individual cases, particularly in the sensitive highest echelon: in most of the states of the continent, some posts are regarded as "posts of confidence" where the political leanings of a civil servant are held to be relevant, as will be seen later. But, except for a few such posts at the very top, the bureaucracy in contemporary Europe is not only intended to be but is a non-partisan corps expected to serve all and any ruling parties.

The industrialisation of Europe and World Wars I and II generated consequences which together pushed for a vast bureaucratic explosion after 1918. Industrialism engendered a new self-conscious, industrial, working class, soon canalised into socialist parties demanding universal suffrage. The economic system was liable to massive boom and slump, prone to occupational and health hazards: all of these invited government attention. All such consequences pressed the aristocratic and upper-middle-class governments of Europe into "preventive modernisation": that is to say, into measures of social amelioration self-consciously taken from on high to ward off threats of socialism, unrest, perhaps even revolution. Bismarck's social insurance laws of the 1880s are only a blatant example of this tendency. The influence of the wars pressed in the same direction. They were qualitatively quite different from all previous wars in involving entire civil populations. The sacrifices demanded were made by everyone out of nationalistic fervour. But it is in the logic of nationalism that, if all members of the nation offer equal and perhaps fatal sacrifices for the sake of the nation, then they are likewise entitled to equal rewards and opportunities inside it. The taxation, the direction of labour, the conscription of materials and property that were imposed to win a war, could, it was plausibly argued, continue to be imposed in order to equalise social benefits and opportunities. This is why in all the belligerent countries the level of non-military spending makes a quantum jump immediately after the close of hostilities, and stays at or above that level thereafter. All the elements mentioned so far were absorbed into a third, namely the emergence of mass parties. Nowadays every parliamentary democracy in Europe is powered by the competitive outbidding of parties, and in this the all-out collectivisers—the Communist and Socialist parties—naturally set the pace.

The effect of these factors is to be found in the scope, the scale and the direction taken by every bureaucracy in Europe. As to scope, in 1849 the main expenditures of states were on sine qua non activities (defence and foreign affairs, justice and public order, taxation and post office to service all these) and the distribution is not markedly different in 1914. The new departments and agencies that have been added since then relate to the control or even the direction of industries and to social and educational provision. An admittedly crude estimate of the division between defence and public order expenditure on the one hand and social service expenditure on the other, expressed as a percentage of the national budgets, gives the following figures for 1973:

	Defence/Public Order	Social Services
Britain	12.6	46.3
Sweden	18.0	34.0
W. Germany	21.0	31.0
Netherlands	10.7	27.0

The scale of government has expanded accordingly, perhaps more than accordingly, even. Realistic comparison between the various states is impossible because each country classifies its civil servants in a different way. The best figure for France (1970) is some 1,317,913 officials in the central services, and some 650,000 in the municipalities: a ratio of 1:25 for the population as a whole. In Germany a somewhat comparable count, including the federal, land and municipal officers, yields 2,108,124 persons or 1:29 for the total population. For Italy, in 1970, the number of centrally employed officials (this omits the overstaffed provincial administrations and the local authorities) stood at 1,697,020, which is 1:31 to the total population. The figures become more significant if they are expressed as ratios of the total *working* population, however, in which case they stand at France 1:10.7, Germany 1:11, Italy 1:11. A better indicator, because it is strictly comparable in the countries concerned, is the total employed in "the public sector" in all capacities, excepting only the armed services, as a percentage of the labour force. These figures can be estimated at: Britain (1975) 27.8, France (1968) 22.0, Germany (1968) 12.0. The public sector in Britain employs just under seven million persons of whom 1,197,000 are in central employ, 3,024,000 in local employ and 2,008,000 in the nationalised industries. Had we taken the comparable figure for 1961, however, the figures would have been much lower; only 5,369,000 or 22.3 percent of the labour force.

Finally, it is important to notice the directions into which this new bureaucratic activity has flowed. This complicates the problem of ensuring public control and accountability. Briefly it has moved into three new areas—that of the previously voluntary agency, that formerly occupied by the private firm and that formerly occupied by the elected local authority. In so doing, the advantages of large scale and universality may well be gained; but it is possible and indeed likely that there will be corresponding losses. This will be discussed later.

For the moment, however, we may sum up the position thus: in the last half-century there has occurred throughout Europe a bureaucratic expansion of enormous proportions. In every state the administration has become a self-contained and self-regulated profession, organised in a pyramid of authority, with a dominant tendency to universalise and centralise.

At the apex of the bureaucratic pyramid the civil servant comes into direct contact with his masters, the politicians, and therefore the top 2,000 or 3,000 bureaucrats in any country demand special attention. All Western European political systems, with a quirky qualification for the Fifth French Republic, have proceeded along

English lines in relating the bureaucracy to the legislature, which is purportedly the repository of the national will and purpose, and therefore the ultimate directing and controlling authority over the bureaucracy. It would be possible to arrange for the bureaucracy-legislature relationship along the pattern of a British local authority: that is to say by establishing committees of the legislature to which senior civil servants would work and from whom they would take direction. Instead, all the states of Europe have adopted the British practice of heading the departments by a politician—a minister—of the ruling political party, and making this minister accountable to the legislature for all acts of omission and commission by the civil servants of his department: these being deemed to be his servants and assistants, under his direction and control. This formula of "the individual responsibility of the minister for his department" is carried to greater lengths in Britain than on the continent where legislative committees have greater contact with individual civil servants who play a more open role in policy formulation. For all that, modal relationship is that the minister is the conduit between the legislature and the bureaucracy.

The top bureaucrats who come into immediate and personal contact with ministers—and with legislative committees—are wholly unrepresentative of the social make-up of their countries, even more so than the legislatures which are themselves far from being a representative cross-section. The "administrative élites in Britain, Germany and Italy are", we are told, "mostly middle-aged, mostly long-time civil servants, mostly university-educated, mostly from middle- and upper-class backgrounds, and mostly male."[1] As for France, they "all belong to the *bourgeoisie* or to those social groups which hope to enter the *bourgeoisie* . . . they come almost entirely from urban backgrounds . . ."[2] The introduction of the *École Nationale d'Administration* has in no wise democratised the social base; indeed, the most recent inquiry suggests that it has narrowed it.

The academic training of these administrative élites differs from country to country. The British have studied in mostly literary fields—history, classics and so forth. On the continent the largest proportion of higher civil servants will have graduated in law, and a high proportion of the remainder in economics. This is to leave out also the higher technical staffs, particularly influential in

---

[1] R. D. Putnam, "The Political Attitudes of Senior Civil Servants in Britain, Germany and Italy," in *The Mandarins of Western Europe,* ed. M. Dogan (London: Sage, 1976).

[2] B. Gournay, "Higher Civil Servants in France," in *European Politics: a Reader,* ed. M. Dogan and R. Rose (Boston: Little, Brown, 1971).

France where they represent the Napoleonic tradition of the *Polytechnique*, the *École des Mines* and the *Ponts et Chaussées.*

A cross-national survey of their attitude towards their political masters shows that in Germany, Britain and Holland (Italy is a strong exception) only a minority considered that technical considerations should be given more weight than political ones, and even smaller minorities thought that the so-called interference of politicians with what was "properly the affair of civil servants" was "disturbing." Even the inter-party struggle was regarded benignly by half the British and some two-thirds of the German respondents. Only the Italian higher bureaucracy displayed, on the whole, technocratic and anti-politician bias. The reason is idiosyncratic to Italy; for one thing the polarisation and fractionalisation of the political parties there are such as to make an anti-politician stance justifiable. More significantly, however, the bulk of the higher civil service were first appointed under the Fascist regime and, it would seem, reflect some of its values.

In Britain the doctrine of individual ministerial responsibility for the department operates nowadays as a highly impenetrable screen between the legislature and the civil service. At the same time, it is in Britain that movement between the top positions in the bureaucracy and Parliament is less, apparently, than in any other country except Denmark. Certainly in France and Germany and Norway there is a good deal of movement between the two. In the Fifth French Republic, for instance, over half the cabinet members have been selected from the higher bureaucracy and no fewer than six presidents or prime ministers have been ex-bureaucrats also. In Germany, too, the movement is easy: in the 1961–65 *Bundestag* no less than 22.3 percent of the deputies had previously been officials and state employees.

Furthermore, the top bureaucratic posts are more highly politicised in continental Europe than in Britain. The role and influence of the senior administrator are more overt: in France, for instance, it is not uncommon for such men to write highly polemical books about their policies. Correspondingly, some of these countries have developed usages for making the top echelon of the bureaucracy more politically sympathetic to the ministers. In Germany, for instance, the head of the Chancellor's office is such a key figure that it has become the practice to move him to another place in the service, replacing him by a more politically compatible bureaucrat, when a change of government makes this seem desirable. France has developed the ministerial *cabinet*, which nowadays is mostly composed of career civil servants (and is no longer merely the personal entourage of the minister as it once was), but they are personally selected by the minister himself. (This device, sadly misunderstood, is advocated by members of the Labour Party in Britain but got no further when Labour was in power than provision for the appointment of two dozen "personal advisers" among the various ministries.)

Such politicisation is not a mere matter of "jobs for the boys" as cynics might affirm. It is a mechanism for making the bureaucracy follow the lead of the ruling political parties. For, it is argued, if the political party is the expression of public opinion and if the bureaucracy is responsive to the political party, the end result will be a bureaucracy that is responsive and accountable to public opinion. And how to achieve this precise result is, today, the central dilemma of big government and big bureaucracy.

The large-scale bureaucratisation of western societies has created a set of problems concerning public accountability and control which are inherent and, it would seem, intractable. These problems stem from three root causes: the nature of the bureaucracy, the mutual incompatibility of the qualities popularly sought for in government and the nature of the social losses incurred by substituting the bureaucratic order for its predecessors. To begin with, the politician and the bureaucrat are very dissimilar animals: they have different outlooks, time-scales and constituencies. As an elected representative the politician is partisan, passionate, responsive: as an officer appointed on merit, the civil servant is critical, remote and neutral. The first serves a cause, the second pursues a career. The time perspectives of the politicians tend to be short—MPs and, nowadays, ministers move in and out of office and, more markedly still, in and out of any particular department; the civil servant, however, looks forward to perhaps half a century in the service, and perhaps in the same department. Furthermore, in entering the service he is made to feel that he is part of a permanent and continuing corporation which will be left to pick up the pieces long after the politicians have moved out of office. Irrespective of their technical and intellectual qualifications (which are nowadays often considerable), the sufficient condition for politicians being selected is popularity. In contrast, the civil servant is chosen on the basis of publicly established criteria of intellectual or technical skill.

The bureaucracy, therefore, is regarded as the "ballast" of the democratic state, counterpoising the volatility of politicians and electorates. The combination of these two elements via the Parliament-cum-cabinet system is regarded as the supreme achievement of the modern democratic state, blending the organ of popular direction and control with the organs of permanency and impersonality embodied in the bureaucracy.

Unfortunately this view is too bland. There is a basic inconsistency in the qualities which the public expect in their government. The most canvassed requirement is that it shall give the public what the public say they want—the representative principle. But citizens, at the same time, do not like their governments to be always chopping and changing. They demand a measure of consistency, predictability and stability in policies: this is the stability principle. Finally, they will not pardon a government which, it turns out, has lacked elementary foresight and failed to provide, in the past, for needs that have become pressing in the present; this is the futurity principle. The last two principles clash with the first. For the representative principle demands that as soon as public opinion alters, the policy should alter also, whereas the stability principle requires that it stays the same. Representativeness requires a turnover of rulers; order and stability require their permanence. Representativeness demands that these rulers respond to expressed preferences: care for the common welfare and especially for the future welfare may well require the opposite. Between the three attributes of representativeness, stability and futurity, any number of mixes is possible, but it is unlikely that any single one will satisfy all the public all the time.

Finally, the bureaucracy's product is qualitatively quite different from most others. It offers a service that is public and therefore inherently wholesale, unpriced and (usually) monopolistic. It is impersonal and universalised, treating all in the same category with a scrupulous impartiality. It is precisely to afford this kind of service, in contrast to one that differs from locality to locality, or from one purse to another, that its provision is taken over by the state—in short, bureaucratised. But when this happens, losses are made as well as gains and these stem from those three salient dimensions of the bureaucratic breakthrough which we mentioned earlier: increased scope, increased scale and diverse direction.

In widening its scope, government finds itself in the area of techniques, science and technology; for instance nuclear policy, underwater technology, managerial techniques and the like. The decisions in these fields are no longer made by corporations competing for private gain, whose profit is presumably bound up with getting the right answers. They have to be made by ministers, who have to rely on the second-hand opinions of their expert officials, and manifestly are no more likely to get the right answers than private consortia. Hence the introduction into modern bureaucratisation of substitutes for these losses in knowledge: public inquiries like the Windscale inquiry into uranium reprocessing, or tolerated and often publicly financed "counter-information" units like the American Brookings Institute or the British NIESR, or a host of advisory

committees consisting of civil servants, trade unionists and interested business men who, in France and Britain, are brought in to
assist the ministries.

The second new dimension—large scale—creates at least three
separate kinds of losses which again must be made good as well
as possible by some kind of substitutes. The first loss stems from
the increasing differentiation of an organisation as it grows larger
and, with it, the widening spans of control and the lengthening of
the hierarchical chain of authority. These consequences will occur
in any organisation as its size increases, whether private or public;
but the public organisation, in this case the modern bureaucracy,
is, as we have seen, very large indeed. As spans of control grow
wider and the chains of command longer, the spatial and the time
distance between the citizen and the official who will finally decide
on his case both become bigger and bigger. Hence a dilemma: if
special consideration is to be given to the case it will take a long
time to decide it; if, on the other hand, it is to be decided quickly,
then the decision will have to be a routine one.

A second loss from the increased differentiation of the organisation is the tendency for the specialised subunits to pursue their
own narrow goals, losing sight of those of the organisation as a
whole. The efforts of the Crown Agents' Office in Britain to give
itself an independent financial base, ignoring the cautions, queries
and complaints of its controlling bodies (the Treasury, the Bank
of England, the Comptroller and Auditor General's Department),
provide a grotesque illustration of this point.

Finally, large-scale bureaucracy has made the traditional control
mechanism—viz. ministerial responsibility to Parliament—more
and more nugatory. Whereas the numbers of MPs and ministers
have increased very slowly over the last 75 years, those of the bureaucracy have exploded. The much-cited figure for Britain, taken
from the Royal Commission on the Constitution (Kilbrandon), illustrates a general West European trend: in 1900 29 ministers and
31 junior ministers controlled some 50,000 civil servants, whereas
in 1969 48 ministers and 58 junior ministers were supposed to control over 500,000 civil servants. In short, the number of all ministers
doubled, but those of the bureaucracy increased tenfold. In no country in Western Europe can ministers, or for that matter committees
of the legislature, supervise their officers on anything other than
a "spot check" basis.

An immediate consequence is to throw a heavier burden on the
other traditional organ of public control, the courts of law. Here
the civil-law countries of the continent, which possessed administrative courts, were better off than the common-law countries, Britain
and Ireland. In these, the courts have had difficulty in grappling

with many classes of cases involving the citizens' complaints against the civil service; in particular in reviewing the substantive merits of rules, orders and regulations made by the bureaucracy under the authority of parliamentary statute and, for that matter, the adjudications made by a civil servant in pursuance of one of his innumerable new powers of intervention entailed by the ever-expanding scope of governmental activity. But even the administrative law courts of the continent of Europe are in many respects inadequate for the task of public control. For one thing, they can ensure strict conformity with the law—but cannot offer relief from the official's insensitivity or unfairness. Again, they are formalised and very slow. Furthermore, some governments set aside unwelcome rulings by enacting new legislation. The French government habitually does so in respect to income tax appeals which its servants have lost in the administrative courts.

As legislatures and courts cannot offer sufficient remedy, substitutes and ancillaries have had to be invented. For instance, to allow appeal against the flood of bureaucratic decisions in such matters as social security payments, fair rents, planning decisions, value-added tax and the like, more or less informal tribunals have been established where the citizen enjoys the right to a hearing and the right to appeal upwards—often, indeed, the right to appeal to the ordinary courts of law, if a matter of law is involved. The bureaucracy has, in short, "judicialised" a number of its processes. Another substitute is the *ombudsman*. For well over a century this institution was active in Sweden alone. In little more than a decade it has been seen as an answer to the complaints, not of illegality on the part of the bureaucracy, which is a matter the traditional courts can look into, but to unfairness and sheer bad administration. Hence a rash of adaptations including the Parliamentary Commissioner in Britain and the *mediateur* in France.

Such devices do indeed mitigate or, if one wishes, palliate the impersonality, inflexibility and remoteness of large-scale government with greater or less (on the whole, considerably less) success. For none of them can excise the root problem of all bureaucracy, large or small, which is this: the more effective is public control, the greater are bureaucratic routine, legalism and inertia. For, if such devices keep the civil servant up to the mark, in the same process they keep him down to the mark also.

Finally come the social losses that can be put down to the new directions of this bureaucratic activity—the take-over of the voluntary society, or the local authority services, or those of private firms and enterprises. These had each possessed certain qualities—local or technical knowledge, incentives or dedication, proximity to the consumer and, above all, flexibility. The voluntary society could and did tailor its service to the individual need; the private economic enterprise was subject, to some extent at least, to the pressures of the market. Once again governments have tried to provide substitutes. For what previously was local self-government they offer devolution or regionalism. For the competitive discipline of the market, they offer consumer councils. For the intimacy of voluntary service, they provide advisory councils in the social security services. Unfortunately, such devices are among the very least successful of the entire catalogue we have outlined.

All such mechanisms are designed to achieve what may be styled the "objective control" of the bureaucracy. By this term it is implied that the bureaucracy is, or at least may be, dissimilar to the public in its attitudes, methods and goals, and that it can only be made to conform to these by devices which in various ways make it accountable to the public. All that need be added is, to the extent that this strategy is successful, farewell creativity, innovation and even flexibility on the part of the administrators.

There is, however, another strategy for making the bureaucracy accountable, and it is claimed that it is superior to the former in that it will also permit of bureaucratic creativity. This arrangement may be described as "subjective control." It means that the bureaucracy is to be made so similar to the general public that their attitudes, methods and goals will coincide. If this were achieved, a bureaucracy could be allowed to innovate to its heart's content, since, by definition, its innovations would all be what the public desired. To bring this happy state of affairs into being requires that the bureaucracy be made representative—either socially representative or politically representative, or both. As to the first alternative, the higher bureaucracy are, as we have seen, wholly unrepresentative of the societies which they conduct and it is for this reason that radicals of all persuasions seek to extend the narrow basis of recruitment.

The second alternative is to politicise the higher civil service until it reflects the specific policy commitment of the elected parliamentary majority. We have already seen how in some countries, like Germany and France and Belgium, certain key positions in the higher bureaucracy are regarded as politically sensitive and are treated accordingly. In Britain such politicisation has not occurred, and it is not surprising that it is in this country that elements in the Labour movement have called over the years for politicisation of the higher civil service, which, they continuously reiterate, is socially and politically inimical to their goals. The Sedgemoor Report (a minority report attached to the Report of the House of Commons Expenditure Committee on the Civil Service, 1977) is an admirable illustration of the entire rationale of "subjective control."

The basis of recruitment is to be widened, much larger numbers of ministerial advisers are to be introduced at the top of each departmental hierarchy and the permanent officers of that echelon are to be subordinated to the minister much more strictly than at present. Then the minister, now (it is supposed) in full control of his department, will in turn be subject to the supervision and control of select committees of the Commons—which in plain language means the backbenchers, and indeed, in still plainer language, means the ruling party's backbenchers. In this way the ruling parliamentary party will control and direct the minister who, in his turn, will direct and control the bureaucracy. Thus the political programme of the party will be transmitted via the electoral process into the higher reaches of the administration.

Unfortunately, all such plans for establishing "subjective control" of the bureaucracy suffer the same fatal drawback: the more socially and politically "representative" the bureaucracy becomes, the less will be its skills, its professionalism and its objectivity. Moreover, in those countries where major parties rotate in and out of office, such as Germany, Britain and potentially France, such political representativeness would require a large-scale reshuffling or replacement of senior civil servants each time the government changed hands.

Yet all public opinion polls attest that the peoples of Western Europe all feel they are overgoverned and incapable of controlling what is being done in their name. Nowhere is the mix between representativeness, stability and futurity thought to be right. The truth is that there is no ideal "mix". Some problems, for instance those arising from the sheer size of the bureaucracy, can be solved only by reducing its size, or not at all. Others flow from the now ambiguous nature of the chief organ of public control—the legislature. Beginning . . . as an anti-prince to control the prince and his bureaucracy, it has in the last 50 years absorbed the prince's sovereignty by making the cabinet dependent on itself—while continuing nonetheless to pretend to itself that it is still the anti-prince. The reason is, as already stated, that both it and the prince are nowadays dependants of the true prince of modern times, the political party. This party will go to extreme lengths to perpetuate the rule of "its" cabinet; and so it will and it does, at the end of the day, abandon its critical role. This is the mechanism that has turned anti-prince into the prince's poodle. And this is the reason why efforts are being made to control the bureaucracy outside the parliamentary arena, in such things as entrenched bills of rights or institutionalised critics like the Ombudsman, or by a drastic decentralisation that would multiply the number and variety of elected critics and at the same time reduce the workload of the central legislature.

But the one impossible expectation is that the bureaucracy shall at one and the same time be both creative and controlled. If the French higher civil service is to be admired for its creativity—as in many quarters it is—then it must also be remembered that this is only possible because the countervailing forces of trade unions, employers' organisations and political parties themselves are much weaker than they are in Britain, while the principal organ of popular control—the French Parliament—has been lopped of most of its former powers of criticism and control to the benefit of a vastly strengthened executive branch. Such creativity is not possible in Britain where there still exists the widespread, even if naive, belief that creativity is the job of the elected politicians, not the appointed bureaucracy. In this country there still survives from the 17th century the tradition that the bureaucracy must be subject to popular control, just as in France there survives the 17th-century tradition of Louvois, Le Tellier and Colbert and the authoritarian state. That the bureaucracy has been not just coeval with the formation of the modern state but is its essential core has been the burden of this essay. Whoever says state, says bureaucracy. The benefits it has brought to populations are incalculable. To paraphrase William James, it is "the enormous flywheel of the state, its most precious conservative agent."[3] But for every gain it brings, there are attendant and inescapable losses. To permit it to create freely entails that one must forgo control. To impose tight control entails that it may not innovate freely. One is the obverse of the other. As the late Levi Eshkol said, though on a different matter: "You've got the dowry—the trouble is you've got the bride as well."

---

[3] William H. James, *Selected Papers on Philosophy* (London: J.M. Dent, 1969), p. 59.

21

Legitimation Crisis

Jürgen Habermas

THREE DEVELOPING CRISES

The rapid growth processes of late-capitalist societies have confronted the system of world society with new problems. These problems cannot be regarded as crisis phenomena specific to the system, even though the possibilities of coping with the crises *are* specific to the system and therefore limited. I am thinking of the disturbance of the ecological balance, the violation of the personality system (alienation), and the explosive strain on international relations.

The Ecological Balance. If physically economic growth can be traced back to the technologically sophisticated use of more energy to increase the productivity of human labor, then the societal formation of capitalism is remarkable for impressively solving the problem of economic growth. To be sure, capital accumulation originally pushes economic growth ahead, so there is no option for the conscious steering of this process. The growth imperatives originally followed by capitalism have meanwhile achieved a global validity by way of system competition and worldwide diffusion (despite the stagnation or even retrogressive trends in some Third World countries).

The mechanisms of growth are forcing an increase of both

Source: Jürgen Habermas, "What Does a Crisis Mean Today? Legitimation Problems in Late Capitalism," *Social Research* 40, no. 4 (Winter 1973), pp. 643–67. By permission. Article abridged by the editors.

population and production on a worldwide scale. The economic needs of a growing population and the productive exploitation of nature are faced with material restrictions: on the one hand, finite resources (cultivable and inhabitable land, fresh water, metals, minerals, etc.); on the other hand, irreplaceable ecological systems that absorb pollutants such as fallout, carbon dioxide, and waste heat. Forrester and others have estimated the limits of the exponential growth of population, industrial production, exploitation of natural resources, and environmental pollution. To be sure, their estimates have rather weak empirical foundations. The mechanisms of population growth are as little known as the maximum limits of the earth's potential for absorbing even the major pollutants. Moreover, we cannot forecast technological development accurately enough to know which raw materials will be replaced or renovated by future technology.

However, despite any optimistic assurances, we are able to indicate (if not precisely determine) *one* absolute limitation on growth: the thermal strain on the environment due to consumption of energy. If economic growth is necessarily coupled with increasing consumption of energy, and if all natural energy that is transformed into economically useful energy is ultimately released as heat, it will eventually raise the temperature of the atmosphere. Again, determining the deadline is not easy. Nevertheless, these reflections show that an exponential growth of population and production—i.e., an expanded control over external nature—will some day run up against the limits of the biological capacity of the environment.

This is not limited to complex societal systems. Specific to these systems are the possibilities of warding off dangers to the ecology. Late-capitalist societies would have a very hard time limiting growth without abandoning their principle of organization, because an overall shift from spontaneous capitalist growth to qualitative growth would require production planning in terms of use-values.

The Anthropological Balance.   While the disturbance of the ecological balance points out the negative aspect of the exploitation of natural resources, there are no sure signals for the capacity limits of personality systems. I doubt whether it is possible to identify such things as psychological constants of human nature that inwardly limit the socialization process. I do, however, see a limitation in the kind of socializing that societal systems have been using to create motives for action. Our behavior is oriented by norms requiring justification and by interpretative systems guaranteeing identity. Such a communicative organization of behavior can become an obstacle in complex societies for a simple reason. The adaptive capacity in organizations increases proportionately as the administrative authorities become independent of the particular motivations of the members. The choice and achievement of organization goals in systems of high intrinsic complexity have to be independent of the influx of narrowly delimited motives. This requires a generalized willingness to comply (in political systems, such willingness has the form of legitimation). As long as socialization brings inner nature into a communicative behavioral organization, no legitimation for norms of action could conceivably secure an unmotivated acceptance of decisions. In regard to decisions whose contents are still undetermined, people will comply if convinced that those decisions are based on a legitimate norm of action. If the motives for acting were no longer to pass through norms requiring justification, and if the personality structures no longer had to find their unity under interpretative systems guaranteeing identity, then (and only then) the unmotivated acceptance of decisions would become an irreproachable routine, and the readiness to comply could thus be produced to any desirable degree.

The International Balance. The dangers of destroying the world system with thermonuclear weapons are on a different level. The accumulated potential for annihilation is a result of the advanced stage of productive forces. Its basis is technologically neutral, and so the productive forces can also take the form of destructive forces (which has happened because international communication is still undeveloped). Today, mortal damage to the natural substratum of global society is quite possible. International communication is therefore governed by a historically new imperative of self-limitation. Once again, this is not limited to all highly militarized societal systems, but the possibilities of tackling this problem have limits specific to the systems. An actual disarmament may be unlikely because of the forces behind capitalist and postcapitalist class societies. Yet regulating the arms race is not basically incompatible with the structure of late-capitalist societies if it is possible to increase technologically the use-value of capital to the degree that the capacity effect of the government's demand for unproductive consumer goods can be balanced. . . .

DISTURBANCES SPECIFIC TO THE SYSTEM

. . . In my opinion, the late-capitalist state can be properly understood neither as the unconscious executive organ of economic laws nor as a systematic agent of the united monopoly capitalists. Instead, I would join Claus Offe in advocating the theory that late-capitalist societies are faced with two difficulties caused by the state's having to intervene in the growing functional gaps of the market. We can regard the state as a system that uses legitimate power. Its output consists in sovereignly executing administrative decisions. To this end, it needs an input of mass loyalty that is as unspecific as possible. Both directions can lead to crisislike disturbances. Output crises have the form of the efficiency crisis. The administrative system fails to fulfill the steering imperative that it has taken over from the economic system. This results in the disorganization of different areas of life. Input crises have the form of the legitimation crisis. The legitimation system fails to maintain the necessary level of mass loyalty. We can clarify this with the example of the acute difficulties in public finances, with which all late-capitalist societies are now struggling.

The government budget, as I have said, is burdened with the public expenses of an increasingly socialized production. It bears the costs of international competition and of the demand for unproductive consumer goods (armament and space travel). It bears the costs for the infrastructural output (transportation and communication, scientific and technological progress, vocational training). It bears the costs of the social consumption indirectly concerned with production (housing, transportation, health, leisure, general education, social security). It bears the costs of providing for the unemployed. And finally, it bears the externalized costs of environmental damage caused by private production. Ultimately, these expenses have to be met by taxes. The state apparatus thus has two simultaneous tasks. It has to levy the necessary taxes from profits and income and employ them so efficiently as to prevent any crises from disturbing growth. In addition the selective raising of taxes, the recognizable priority model of their utilization, and the administrative performance have to function in such a way as to satisfy the resulting need for legitimation. If the state fails in the former task, the result is a deficit in administrative efficiency. If it fails in the latter task, the result is a deficit in legitimation.

THEOREMS OF THE LEGITIMATION CRISIS

I would like to restrict myself to the legitimation problem. There is nothing mysterious about its genesis. Legitimate power has to be available for administrative planning. The functions accruing to the state apparatus in late capitalism and the expansion of social areas treated by administration increase the need for legitimation. Liberal capitalism constituted itself in the forms of bourgeois democracy, which is easy to explain in terms of the bourgeois revolution. As a result, the growing need for legitimation now has to work with the means of political democracy (on the basis of universal suffrage). The formal democratic means, however, are expensive.

After all, the state apparatus does not just see itself in the role of the supreme capitalist facing the conflicting interests of the various capital factions. It also has to consider the generalizable interests of the population as far as necessary to retain mass loyalty and prevent a conflict-ridden withdrawal of legitimation. The state has to gauge these three interest areas (individual capitalism, state capitalism, and generalizable interests), in order to find a compromise for competing demands. A theorem of crisis has to explain not only why the state apparatus encounters difficulties but also why certain problems remain unsolved in the long run.

First, an obvious objection. The state can avoid legitimation problems to the extent that it can manage to make the administrative system independent of the formation of legitimating will. To that end, it can, say, separate expressive symbols (which create a universal willingness to follow) from the instrumental functions of administration. Well known strategies of this sort are: the personalizing of objective issues, the symbolic use of inquiries, expert opinions, legal incantations, etc. Advertising techniques, borrowed from oligopolistic competition, both confirm and exploit current structures of prejudice. By resorting to emotional appeals, they arouse unconscious motives, occupy certain contents positively, and devalue others. The public, which is engineered for purposes of legitimation, primarily has the function of structuring attention by means of areas of themes and thereby of pushing uncomfortable themes, problems, and arguments below the threshold of attention. As Niklas Luhmann put it: The political system takes over tasks of *ideology planning*.

The scope for manipulation, however, is narrowly delimited, for the cultural system remains peculiarly resistant to administrative control. There is no administrative creation of meaning; there is at best an ideological erosion of cultural values. The acquisition of legitimation is self-destructive as soon as the mode of acquisition is exposed. Thus, there is a systematic limit for attempts at making up for legitimation deficits by means of well aimed manipulation. This limit is the structural dissimilarity between areas of administrative action and cultural tradition.

A crisis argument, to be sure, can be constructed out of these considerations only with the viewpoint that the expansion of state activity has the side effect of disproportionately increasing the need for legitimation. I regard such an overproportionate increase as likely because things that are taken for granted culturally, and have so far been external conditions of the political systems, are now being drawn into the planning area of administration. This process thematizes traditions which previously were not part of public programming, much less of practical discourse. An example of such direct administrative processing of cultural tradition is educational planning, especially the planning of the curriculum. Hitherto, the school administration merely had to codify a given naturally evolved canon. But now the planning of the curriculum is based on the premise that the tradition models can also be different. Administrative planning creates a universal compulsion for justification toward a sphere that was actually distinguished by the power of self-legitimation.

In regard to the direct disturbance of things that were culturally taken for granted, there are further examples in regional and urban planning (private ownership of land), health planning ("classless hospital"), and family planning and marriage-law planning (which are shaking sexual taboos and facilitating emancipation).

An awareness of contingency is created not just for contents of tradition but also for the techniques of tradition—i.e., socialization. Among preschool children, formal schooling is already competing with family upbringing. The new problems afflicting the educational routine, and the widespread awareness of these problems, are reflected by, among other indications, a new type of pedagogical and psychological writing addressed to the general public.

On all these levels, administrative planning has unintentional effects of disquieting and publicizing. These effects weaken the justification potential of traditions that have been forced out of their natural condition. Once they are no longer indisputable, their demands for validity can be stabilized only by way of discourse. Thus, the forcible shift of things that have been culturally taken for granted further politicizes areas of life that previously could be assigned to the private domain. However, this spells danger for bourgeois privatism, which is informally assured by the structures of the public. I see signs of this danger in strivings for participation and in models for alternatives, such as have developed particularly in secondary and primary schools, in the press, the church, theaters, publishing, etc.

These arguments support the contention that late-capitalist societies are afflicted with serious problems of legitimation. But do these arguments suffice to explain why these problems cannot be solved? Do they explain the prediction of a crisis in legitimation? Let us assume the state apparatus could succeed in making labor more productive and in distributing the gains in productivity in such a way as to assure an economic growth free of crises (if not disturbances). Such growth would nevertheless proceed in terms of priorities independent of the generalizable interests of the population. The priority models that Galbraith has analyzed from the viewpoint of "private wealth vs. public poverty" result from a class structure which, as always, is still being kept latent. This structure is ultimately the cause of the legitimation deficit.

We have seen that the state cannot simply take over the cultural system and that, in fact, the expansion of areas for state planning creates problems for things that are culturally taken for granted. "Meaning" is an increasingly scarce resource. Which is why those expectations that are governed by concrete and identifiable needs—i.e., that can be checked by their success—keep mounting in the civil population. The rising level of aspirations is proportionate to the growing need for legitimation. The resource of "value," siphoned off by the tax office, has to make up for the scanty resource of "meaning." Missing legitimations have to be replaced by social rewards such as money, time, and security. A crisis of legitimation arises as soon as the demands for these rewards mount more rapidly than the available mass of values, or if expectations come about that are different and cannot be satisfied by those categories of rewards conforming with the present system.

Why, then, should not the level of demands keep within operable limits? As long as the welfare state's programming in connection with a widespread technocratic consciousness (which makes uninfluenceable system-restraints responsible for bottlenecks) maintains a sufficient amount of civil privatism, then the legitimation emergencies do not have to turn into crises. To be sure, the democratic form of legitimation could cause expenses that cannot be covered if that form drives the competing parties to outdo one another in their platforms and thereby raise the expectations of the population higher and higher. Granted, this argument could be amply demonstrated empirically. But we would still have to explain why late-capitalist societies even bother to retain formal democracy. Merely in terms of the administrative system, formal democracy could just as easily be replaced by a variant—a conservative, authoritarian welfare state that reduces the political participation of the citizens to a harmless level; or a Fascist authoritarian state that keeps the population toeing the mark on a relatively high level of permanent mobilization. Evidently, both variants are in the long run less compatible with developed capitalism than a party state based on mass democracy. The sociocultural system creates demands that cannot be satisfied in authoritarian systems.

This reflection leads me to the following thesis: Only a rigid sociocultural system, incapable of being randomly functionalized for the needs of the administrative system, could explain how legitimation difficulties result in a legitimation crisis. This development must therefore be based on a *motivation crisis*—i.e., a discrepancy between the need for motives that the state and the occupational system announce and the supply of motivation offered by the socio-cultural system.

THEOREMS OF THE MOTIVATION CRISIS

The most important motivation contributed by the sociocultural system in late-capitalist societies consists in syndromes of civil and family/vocational privatism. Civil privatism means strong interests in the administrative system's output and minor participation in the process of will-formation (high-output orientation vs. low-input orientation). Civil privatism thus corresponds to the structures of a depoliticized public. Family and vocational privatism complements civil privatism. It consists of a family orientation with consumer and leisure interests, and of a career orientation consistent with status competition. This privatism thus corresponds to the structures of educational and occupational systems regulated by competitive performance.

The motivational syndromes mentioned are vital to the political and economic system. However, bourgeois ideologies have components directly relevant to privatistic orientations, and social changes deprive those components of their basis. A brief outline may clarify this.

Performance Ideology.   According to bourgeois notions which have remained constant from the beginnings of modern natural law to contemporary election speeches, social rewards should be distributed on the basis of individual achievement. The distribution of gratifications should correlate to every individual's performance. A basic condition is equal opportunity to participate in a competition which is regulated in such a way that external influences can be neutralized. One such allocation mechanism was the market. But ever since the general public realized that social violence is practiced in the forms of exchange, the market has been losing its credibility as a mechanism for distributing rewards based on performance. Thus, in the more recent versions of performance ideology, market success is being replaced by the professional success mediated by formal schooling. However, *this* version can claim credibility only when the following conditions have been fulfilled:

- Equal opportunity of access to higher schools.
- Nondiscriminatory evaluation standards for school performance.
- Synchronic developments of the educational and occupational systems.

- Work processes whose objective structure permits evaluation according to performances that can be ascribed to individuals.

"School justice" in terms of opportunity of access and standards of evaluation has increased in all advanced capitalist societies at least to some degree. But a countertrend can be observed in the two other dimensions. The expansion of the educational system is becoming more and more independent of changes in the occupational system, so that ultimately the connection between formal schooling and professional success will most likely loosen. At the same time, there are more and more areas in which production structures and work dynamics make it increasingly difficult to evaluate individual performance. Instead, the extrafunctional elements of occupational roles are becoming more and more important for conferring occupational status.

Moreover, fragmented and monotonous work processes are increasingly entering sectors in which previously a personal identity could be developed through the vocational role. An intrinsic motivation for performance is getting less and less support from the structure of the work process in market-dependent work areas. An instrumentalist attitude toward work is spreading even in the traditionally bourgeois professions (white-collar workers, professionals). A performance motivation coming from outside can, however, be sufficiently stimulated by wage income only:

- If the reserve army on the labor market exercises an effective competitive pressure.
- If a sufficient income differential exists between the lower wage groups and the inactive work population.

Both conditions are not necessarily met today. Even in capitalist countries with chronic unemployment (such as the United States), the division of the labor market (into organized and competitive sectors) interferes with the natural mechanism of competition. With a mounting poverty line (recognized by the welfare state), the living standards of the lower income groups and the groups temporarily released from the labor process are mutually assimilating on the other side in the subproletarian strata.

Possessive Individualism. Bourgeois society sees itself as an instrumental group that accumulates social wealth only by way of private wealth—i.e., guarantees economic growth and general welfare through competition between strategically acting private persons. Collective goals, under such circumstances, can be achieved only by way of individual utility orientations. This preference system, of course, presupposes:

- That the private economic subjects can with subjective unambiguity recognize and calculate needs that remain constant over given time periods.

- That this need can be satisfied by individually demandable goods (normally, by way of monetary decisions that conform to the system).

Both presuppositions are no longer fulfilled as a matter of course in the developed capitalist societies. These societies have reached a level of societal wealth far beyond warding off a few fundamental hazards to life and the satisfying of basic needs. This is why the individualistic system of preference is becoming vague. The steady interpreting and reinterpreting of needs is becoming a matter of the collective formation of the will, a fact which opens the alternatives of either free and quasi-political communication among consumers as citizens or massive manipulation—i.e., strong indirect steering. The greater the degree of freedom for the preference system of the demanders, the more urgent the problem of sales policies for the suppliers—at least if they are to maintain the illusion that the consumers can make private and autonomous decisions. Opportunistic adjustment of the consumers to market strategies is the ironical form of every consumer autonomy, which is to be maintained as the facade of possessive individualism. In addition, with increasing socialization of production, the quota of collective commodities among the consumer goods keeps growing. The urban living conditions in complex societies are more and more dependent on an infrastructure (transportation, leisure, health, education, etc.) that is withdrawing further and further from the forms of differential demand and private appropriation.

Exchange-Value Orientation.   Here I have to mention the tendencies that weaken the socialization effects of the market, especially the increase of those parts of the population that do not reproduce their lives through income from work (students, welfare recipients, social-security recipients, invalids, criminals, soldiers, etc.) as well as the expansion of areas of activity in which, as in civil service or in teaching, abstract work is replaced by concrete work. In addition, the relevance that leisure acquires with fewer working hours (and higher real income), compared with the relevance of issues within the occupational sphere of life, does not in the long run privilege those needs that can be satisfied monetarily.

The erosion of bourgeois tradition brings out normative structures that are no longer appropriate to reproducing civil and family and professional privatism. The now dominant components of cultural heritage crystalize around a faith in science, a "postauratic"

art, and universalistic values. Irreversible developments have occurred in each of these areas. As a result, functional inequalities
of the economic and the political systems are blocked by cultural
barriers, and they can be broken down only at the psychological
cost of regressions—i.e., with extraordinary motivational damage.
German Fascism was an example of the wasteful attempt at a collectively organized regression of consciousness below the thresholds
of fundamental scientistic convictions, modern art, and universalistic law and morals.

Scientism. The political consequences of the authority enjoyed
by the scientific system in developed societies are ambivalent. The
rise of modern science established a demand for discursive justification, and traditionalistic attitudes cannot hold out against that demand. On the other hand, short-lived popular syntheses of scientific
data (which have replaced global interpretations) guarantee the
authority of science *in the abstract.* The authority known as "science" can thus cover both things: the broadly effective criticism
of any prejudice, as well as the new esoterics of specialized knowledge and expertise. A self-affirmation of the sciences can further
a positivistic common sense on the part of the depoliticized public.
Yet scientism establishes standards by which it can also be criticized
itself and found guilty of residual dogmatism. Theories of tech-
nocracy and of democratic elitism, asserting the necessity of an institutionalized civic privatism, come forth with the presumption of
theories. But this does not make them immune to criticism.

Postauratic Art. The consequences of modern art are somewhat
less ambivalent. The modern age has radicalized the autonomy of
bourgeois art in regard to the external purposes for which art could
be used. For the first time, bourgeois society itself produced a counterculture against the bourgeois life style of possessive individualism, performance, and practicality. The *Bohème,* first established
in Paris, the capital of the 19th century, embodies a critical demand
that had arisen, unpolemically still, in the aura of the bourgeois
artwork. The alter ego of the businessman, the "human being,"
whom the bourgeois used to encounter in the lonesome contemplation of the artwork, soon split away from him. In the shape of
the artistic avant-garde, it confronted him as a hostile, at best seduc-
tive force. In artistic beauty, the bourgeoisie had been able to experience its own ideals and the (as always) fictitious redemption of the
promise of happiness which was merely suspended in everyday life.
In radicalized art, however, the bourgeois soon had to recognize
the negation of social practice as its complement.

Modern art is the outer covering in which the transformation of bourgeois art into a counterculture was prepared. Surrealism marks the historical moment when modern art programmatically destroyed the outer covering of no-longer-beautiful illusion in order to enter life desublimated. The leveling of the different reality degrees of art and life was accelerated (although not, as Walter Benjamin assumed, introduced) by the new techniques of mass reproduction and mass reception. Modern art had already sloughed off the aura of classical bourgeois art in that the art work made the production process visible and presented itself as a made product. But art enters the ensemble of utility values only when abandoning its autonomous status. The process is certainly ambivalent. It can signify the degeneration of art into a propagandistic mass art or commercialized mass culture, or else its transformation into a subversive counterculture.

Universalist Morality.   The blockage which bourgeois ideologies, stripped of their functional components, create for developing the political and economic system, is even clearer in the moral system than in the authority of science and the self-disintegration of modern art. The moment traditional societies enter a process of modernization, the growing complexity results in steering problems that necessitate an accelerated change of social norms. The tempo inherent in natural cultural tradition has to be heightened. This leads to bourgeois formal law which permits releasing the norm contents from the dogmatic structure of mere tradition and defining them in terms of intention. The legal norms are uncoupled from the corps of privatized moral norms. In addition, they need to be created (and justified) according to principles. Abstract law counts only for that area pacified by state power. But the morality of bourgeois private persons, a morality likewise raised to the level of universal principles, encounters no barrier in the continuing natural condition between the states. Since principled morality is sanctioned only by the purely inward authority of the conscience, its claim to universality conflicts with public morality, which is still bound to a concrete state-subject. This is the conflict between the cosmopolitanism of the human being and the loyalties of the citizen.

If we follow the developmental logic of overall societal systems of norms (leaving the area of historical examples), we can settle that conflict. But its resolution is conceivable only under certain conditions. The dichotomy between inner and outer morality has to disappear. The contrast between morally and legally regulated areas has to be relativized. And the validity of *all* norms has to be tied to the discursive formation of the will of the people potentially affected.

Competitive capitalism for the first time gave a binding force to strictly universalistic value systems. This occurred because the system of exchange had to be regulated universalistically and because the exchange of equivalents offered a basic ideology effective in the bourgeois class. In organized capitalism, the bottom drops out of this legitimation model. At the same time, new and increased demands for legitimation arise. However, the system of science cannot intentionally fall behind an attained stage of cumulative knowledge. Similarly, the moral system, once practical discourse has been admitted, cannot simply make us forget a collectively attained stage of moral consciousness.

I would like to conclude with a final reflection.

If no sufficient concordance exists between the normative structures that still have some power today and the politicoeconomic system, then we can still avoid motivation crises by uncoupling the cultural system. Culture would then become a nonobligatory leisure occupation or the object of professional knowledge. This solution would be blocked if the basic convictions of a communicative ethics and the experience complexes of countercultures (in which postauratic art is embodied) acquired a motive-forming power determining typical socialization processes. Such a conjecture is supported by several behavior syndromes spreading more and more among young people—either retreat as a reaction to an exorbitant claim on the personality-resources; or protest as a result of an autonomous ego organization that cannot be stabilized without conflicts under given conditions. On the activist side we find: the student movement, revolts by high-school students and apprentices, pacifists, women's lib. The retreatist side is represented by hippies, Jesus people, the drug subculture, phenomena of undermotivation in schools, etc. These are the primary areas for checking our hypothesis that late-capitalist societies are endangered by a collapse of legitimation.

22

On the Governability
of Democracies

Ralf Dahrendorf

These are times when we are forcefully reminded of the basic functions of government—law and order, and external defence. These are by the same token bad times for liberty. Liberty flourishes when reforms of the criminal justice system and reductions in defence expenditure are possible without any threat to people's safety at home and security abroad. Safety and security are never a sufficient condition of liberty; but they are a necessary condition. And today there is a smell of war in the air.

Chancellor Schmidt of West Germany tells us that 1980 is one long July 1914. We remember: when Archduke Ferdinand was assassinated at Sarajevo on June 28, 1914, everyone commiserated with the Austrian Emperor (never mind the unpopularity of the Archduke), and most gave the Austrian Government to understand that they would tolerate certain reprisals against Serbia. A month, endless diplomatic contacts, and quiet military preparations later, the world had changed out of recognition. One word, above all, was heard in the capitals of Europe, the word "inevitability": war, it was said, was now "inevitable"; and so it began. In his recent article in *Foreign Affairs,* Professor Miles Kahler has taken the analogy

Source: Ralf Dahrendorf, "Effectiveness and Legitimacy: On the 'Governability' of Democracies," *The Political Quarterly,* October–December 1980, pp. 393–410. By permission.

further.[1] He sees Russia today in the position of Germany 1914, the United States in the position of Britain, the Middle East as the Balkans of 1980, and above all once again the unwilling slide into inevitability everywhere.

There is, however, at least one major difference. It may be that once again there are those who believe that war can be "localised." One might even argue that John Hackett in his book on the *Third World War* has done us a disservice by suggesting that once Birmingham and Minsk have been wiped out by nuclear devices, all will be over, so that those of us who are lucky enough not to live in these doomed cities will be all right (provided, of course, we let NATO arm to the hilt).[2] In fact, the doctrine of limited war in the nuclear age is infinitely more dangerous than the equally mistaken doctrine of localised war was in 1914. The fact is that today mankind can destroy itself, or rather, can be destroyed by the decisions of a small number of governments. Never has there been as dramatic a mismatch between the potential of destruction and the frailty of men, including those who command the potential. Neither red telephones nor double-check command systems nor the fantasy of a monastic order of moral physicists who guard the dangerous material can bridge the mismatch. The fact is—to quote one of those responsible for these dangers, though one who has since given much thought to coping with them, the physicist-philosopher Carl Friedrich von Weizsäcker—that "the Third World War is probable," because nothing has changed in the hegemonial contest which leads to war; indeed "the Third World War will take place once it can be won."[3]

This is a gloomy beginning. It might even be called somewhat melodramatic, were it not for the fact that either the hegemonial contest, or the proliferation of nuclear weapons to nations threatened for survival, or a mere accident might well lead to widespread destruction. And if it is true that it is unlikely that there is any government which can be counted on to control the ultimate threat, then this presents clearly also the ultimate problem of governability: it appears that we have created technical possibilities of destruction which no conceivable human government can contain. We have reached limits of governability. I shall return to this point at the end of my lecture. For the moment, let me take refuge in a statement

---

[1] Miles Kahler, "Rumours of War: the 1914 Anthology," *Foreign Affairs*, New York, Winter 1979–80, pp. 374–96.

[2] Sir John Hackett, *Third World War* (London: Sidgwick & Jackson, 1978).

[3] Carl Friedrich von Weizsäcker, *Wege in der Gefahr* (Munich: DTV, 1979), pp. 110, 118.

by the philosopher of desperate optimism, Karl Jaspers, in his book
on *The Atom Bomb and the Future of Man:* "Reason tells us: it
shows little courage to make statements on the end and the inevitable downfall. It shows courage to do what is possible, given our
knowledge and our ignorance, and not to abandon hope as long
as one lives."[4] Let us leave the dark cloud of war in the distant,
or even not-so-distant sky then and turn to areas of life which are
more obviously within the orbit of government action, or would
seem to be so. Inflation is a topical and important example. One
of the many things which seem to have gone wrong with the economies of OECD countries in the 1970s, is the apparent inability to
contain inflation. Several recipes have been tried. First, there was
the stimulation of growth, in order to catch up with inflation, as
it were; but for a variety of reasons, growth itself has become more
difficult and never did catch up, quite apart from the fact that it
is doubtful whether it contains or generates inflation. Then, there
were tricks designed to cushion the effects of inflation, and perhaps
to expose its absurdity, such as indexation; but examples like Israel
show that while this may expose the absurdity it does not remove
it. Then, there was the "social contract," an agreement to hold
down expectations on the wages front, and sometimes on that of
prices as well; but whether "contract," "policy" or even "law," it
does not seem to work for any length of time. Finally, there is
the control of the money supply (whatever that is), by high interest
rates, cuts in public expenditure, growing unemployment, and the
like; but the more technical the policy is, the less does it come to
grips with the real problem of people's expectations. Those who
have tried a mix of the various policies have been most successful;
though even their success is limited, and may have been achieved
for different reasons, a strong industrial base, favourable terms of
trade, and other comparative advantages. Thus, inflation, one of
the banes of the OECD world, seems to have escaped the ability
of governments to cope. It is clearly a test of governability.

THE SCHIZOPHRENIA BETWEEN PERSONAL
AND POLITICAL WELL-BEING

James Alt has recently looked at what might be called the subjective
side of the story, people's perceptions (in Britain since 1964), in
his book, *The Politics of Economic Decline.*[5] His findings are a gold-
mine for analysis. For instance, he can show that people's inflation-

---

[4] Karl Jaspers, *Die Atombombe und die Zukunft des Menschen* (Munich, 1968).

[5] James E. Alt, *The Politics of Economic Decline* (Cambridge: Cambridge University Press, 1979).

ary expectations exaggerate existing trends considerably, thus making the monetarist remedy even less effective.[6] He also shows that wage controls are the most popular remedy,[7] though he does not tell us whether people want to see the wages of others controlled, or their own. But in our context, another of his findings is the most important. For a long time, Alt tells us (in line with Butler and Stoke, and others),[8] people have distinguished quite clearly between their personal well-being and that of their country. And with a curious schizophrenia, they did not associate their personal well-being with politics, but took it for granted that by and large they have never had it so good. On the well-being of the country, on the other hand, views varied, and changed, and these changes and variations determined the electoral success of the parties. Then comes inflation; and suddenly personal and national well-being merge. Not only the country, but people themselves are doing badly if inflation rates run into two figures. So naturally, people expect government to do something about it. However, governments, successive governments of different parties, fail. "In 1970," James Alt reports, "nearly 60 percent felt that 'a government can do a lot to check rising prices.' In early 1974, only a quarter of the electorate felt that way."[9] Alt's conclusions may be far reaching, but they are not implausible: people have ceased to expect government to deliver the goods:

> In large measure, then, the story of the mid 1970s is the story of a politics of declining expectations. People attached a great deal of importance to economic problems, people saw clearly the developments that were taking place, and people expected developments in advance and thus were able to discount the impact of the worst of them. However, in unprecedented numbers, people also ceased to expect the election of their party to make them better off, largely because they also ceased to expect it to be able to do very much about what they identified as the principal economic problems of the time. The result of this . . . was not a politics of protest, but a politics of quiet disillusion, a politics in which lack of involvement or indifference to organised party politics was the most important feature.[10]

If there is a problem of governability—and the examples given leave little doubt that there is—most of its elements are probably assembled in this illustration. However, before examples are taken

---

[6] Ibid. chap. 7.

[7] Ibid. p. 206.

[8] *Cf.* D. Butler and D. Stokes, *Political Change in Britain* (New York: Macmillan, 1975).

[9] Alt, *The Politics of Economic Decline,* p. 157.

[10] Ibid. p. 270.

further, there is a case for making sure that it is clear what we are talking about. Our concern is with governments, and essentially with national governments, or perhaps I should say with central governments of the units which we have come to recognise as countries, or states. For them to work—or so I shall argue without any claim to originality—two things have to be present: effectiveness and legitimacy. Effectiveness is a technical concept. It simply means that governments have to be able to do things which they claim they can do, as well as those which they are expected to do; they have to work. Legitimacy, on the other hand, is a moral concept. It means that what governments do has to be right. This takes us straight into the confusions of moral philosophy, of course.

Suffice it to say here that what is "right" in the sense of giving legitimacy to governments has at least two aspects. One is that of absolute moral imperatives, or, slightly less ambitiously put, that of values which may be assumed to apply to all human societies. What we call human rights, even, in the most general sense, the rule of law, belongs in this category. Then there are values which, while still of long-term validity, are culturally determined; they vary, and they change. We have to assume that democracy belongs in this category, that is the institutions which, by enabling all citizens to express their views, make change possible without revolution. The category also includes Max Weber's patterns of legitimation, at any rate those of "traditional" and of "legal" or "rational authority." A government is legitimate if what it does is right both in the sense of complying with certain fundamental principles, and in that of being in line with prevailing cultural values. Written constitutions, where they exist, usually begin by spelling out the values which make the actions of the state legitimate, and then proceed to describe the institutions which are intended to guarantee effectiveness. A Bill of Rights has to do with legitimacy, electoral reform has to do with effectiveness in this sense.

How do we measure effectiveness, and legitimacy? The temptation has always been great to be too idealistic in this respect. Political education has tended to emphasise general consent and participation as a condition of effectiveness; in fact, it would seem that the absence of effective protest is good enough. People are not political beings except as political "fleets in being"; in the normal course of events, participation is nice, but not indispensable. What is important, is the possibility of participation in order to veto developments, to express dissent. (Admittedly, to mention this practical point in passing, it is difficult to assess how much of James Alt's "lack of involvement or indifference" is normal disinterest, and how much is dissent or opposition by abstention.) Legitimacy, similarly, should be measured not in terms of the active will of all, or even some

fictitious general will, but in terms of doubt, of a perceived dissociation of government action and basic as well as cultural values.
Again, the distinction is important. When governments violate
values which apply to all societies, they may not meet with doubts
by the majority. This is where minorities have a crucial function:
dissidents, human rights groups, underground publications, "flying"
universities. By contrast any dissociation of government action and
prevailing cultural values, be it due to the imposition of an alien
government, the alienation of an indigenous government or changes
in cultural values, is bound to find expression in widespread doubts
of one kind or another. In our context, the important question is
whether changes in prevailing values are taking place which, while
barely perceptible as yet, may well in due course expose the alienation of traditional democratic governments. I do not want to take
the conceptual discussion too far, but one further point is indispensable for the following argument. I said that a Bill of Rights has
to do with legitimacy, and electoral reform with effectiveness. Could
it not be the other way round? Is not electoral reform intended to
re-establish belief in the fundamental fairness of the political system, whereas a Bill of Rights merely regulates effective relations
between politics and the judiciary? Conceptual sophistry apart, it
is clear that effectiveness and legitimacy are related. The relationship is asymmetrical. Unfortunately, governments can be effective
without being legitimate. Totalitarian rule offers the main example.
Hitler's rule was certainly effective, but it was not legitimate in
that it violated the rule of law deliberately and systematically. It
is more difficult to imagine governments which are legitimate without being effective. One is tempted to think of Weimar Germany
which has so often been described as the purest democracy of them
all; though "pure democracy," like "inner freedom," has a suspicious
ring of deception. Over time, ineffectiveness will probably erode
legitimacy. A government which cannot do its job, and seems systematically unable to do so, will not only be shown up by protest
and dissent, but in the end also by spreading doubt in the name
of underlying values, whether they be universal like the rule of
law, or culturally specific like the rational or traditional exercise
of power.

WHAT IS UNGOVERNABILITY?

The notion of governability has to do with the effectiveness of government. In the first instance, it tells us whether governments can
cope with what they have on their plate. There is a useful definition
of the concept by the historian, Theodor Schieder, who says that
"ungovernability" is given if:

1. there is a weakness or complete absence of the expression of a uniform political will because political consensus is lacking,

2. the process of political decision making is thereby seriously endangered or made impossible,

3. existing institutions based on written or traditional constitutional law and functioning accordingly prove insufficient or completely unsuitable, and

4. thus the function of self-preservation of a political unit—internal and external security, satisfaction of needs in the context of the prevailing, at present steadily growing level of expectations, adaptability to historical change in its different forms as social change, change of values— is put in jeopardy.[11]

This is a tall order. According to Schieder the statement that a society is ungovernable means that it can no longer preserve itself as a polity because it is unable to protect its integrity, to satisfy the needs and expectations of its citizens, and to accommodate change. This in turn reflects on the usefulness of institutions.

Schieder's definition appears in a German collection of essays on our subject, entitled *Regierbarkeit* (governability). Its publisher, eager to raise the appeal of the book, printed a laconic statement on the title page: "*The problem:* A horrifying slogan has for some time come to articulate the growing political defeatism of the West: ungovernability of democracies. *The solution:* we must counter technocratic megalomania and the political pusillanimity of the slogan 'ungovernability' by enlightenment about the conditions of reasonable government and the limits of what politics can do."[12] A splendid project—or is it perhaps "reasonable government" itself which has brought about the ineffectiveness of government in the democracies of the OECD countries? And is it "enlightenment" that we need, or are there requirements for tangible institutional reform? Leaving the "horrifying slogan" on one side for the moment, it appears from the (vast) literature as well as from immediate observation that there are three main processes which begin to impair the effectiveness of democratic governments.

The first of these is what has come to be called "overloading." This is, of course, Michael Crozier's great preoccupation; but in his or in other words it has been observed by many.[13] It has been

---

[11] Theodor Schieder, "Einmaligkeit oder Wiederkehr," in *Regierbarkeit. Studien zu ihrer Problematisierung,* ed. Wilhelm Hennis, Peter Graf Kielmannsegg, and Ulrich Matz (Stuttgart: Klett-Cotta, 1977), p. 31.

[12] Hennis, *Regierbarkeit.*

[13] *Cf.* M. Crozier's contribution to *The Crisis of Democracy* by Michael J. Crozier, Samuel P. Huntington, Joji Watanuki (New York: New York University Press, 1975).

argued that this is not so much an overloading with new objectives of the state (Staatsziele) that is at issue as one with new tasks within traditional objectives (Staatsaufgaben). [14] Either way, there are few today who would doubt that modern governments have taken on more than they can cope with, and in doing so have partly responded to, and partly generated expectations which were bound to be disappointed. Such disappointments need not be as extreme as those of the gambler who, as he was losing all his savings in a casino, told himself that surely the State, which had given the casino its licence, would not wish him to be impoverished to the point of destitution. He actually wrote a book about his experience which contains the ringing—and telling—accusation: "What kind of State is it that does not prevent people who have been caught by the gambling passion from falling into the certain abyss and which then leaves them miserably alone?"[15] What kind of State indeed? One begins to understand why Milton Friedman not only opposes the licensing of casinos, but even the banning of marijuana, indeed of heroin, so that the state is not involved at all in people's misery.

More seriously (though the example is not to be dismissed lightly), there are two areas in particular in which the State has taken on responsibilities, and has come to be expected to deliver, in which it is now apparent that its limits are closer than many expected: economic policy, and social policy. In the field of economic policy, governments appear to have come up against human values, and the difficulties of manipulating them. There is no simple answer to the problem of inflation; and Alt may well be right that it is bound to lead to further estrangement from the political system. But this much is clear that there is no endemic inflation as long as people's expectations of their standard of living, and their ability to produce coincide. The ability to produce—productivity—can, of course, be raised. But if it is not raised enough, expectations will have to come down to cope with the problem. Yet there is relatively little that government can do to dampen expectations. In the field of social policy, at least two restrictions of the effectiveness of government are apparent today. One is financial. The systems of social policy built into most welfare states involve an automaticity almost like the Common Agricultural Policy of the European Community. This means that they reach ceilings of taxability, especially if demographic changes take place which tilt the balance further towards recipients of help and against contributors.

---

[14] Thus by Ulrich Matz, "Der überforderte Staat," in Hennis, *Regierbarkeit*.

[15] Frank Hordan, *Die Banken des Satans* (Tirschenreuth: Hordan-Verlag, 1980).

THE PRICE OF BUREAUCRATISATION

The other limit of social policy has to do with the clumsiness of planning, and the price of bureaucratisation. It is probably an impermissible extrapolation to predict that by the year 2000 there will be, in the National Health Service, one administrator for every patient; but there is a trend not only towards larger but towards less effective organisation.

The first problem of governability, then, is that of "overloading." The second process which has begun to impair the effectiveness of modern government has to do with the space in which it operates. Few institutions seem more jealous of their position than the nation-state. Government and Parliament make a great song and dance about "sovereignty" whenever the question of a redistribution of powers arises. But of course they cannot prevent it. Issues are stronger than institutions; and the "productive forces" of the time tend away from national governments to two opposing directions. One is, decentralisation. Most European societies have been through a paradoxical period of institutional change. On the one hand, people were promised more rights of participation at all levels, and were encouraged to become active citizens. On the other hand, "rationalisation" was the order of the day; in the name of this suspicious slogan, local government was all but destroyed in many places. Whether it can be re-established is uncertain. But it is certain that today the pendulum is swinging towards participation rather than rationalisation. It may be that "small is beautiful"; certainly it is more effective in many respects. We have somehow gone over the top of all economies of scale, in human terms, but also in technical terms. Thus, government, industry and organisations alike are re-discovering the smaller dimension; and I have little doubt that in democratic countries the battle for devolving authority will in the end be won.

But, of course, not everything can be devolved. Scotland alone cannot guarantee an international monetary system. Small firms need access to wider markets. In an age of Super Powers, even Middle Powers are too weak to defend themselves. No one country can hope to win the fight against poverty in the world. Monetary stability, trade rules, defence organisations, and development are but four examples of subjects which have irreversibly emigrated from the political units to which we have grown accustomed. There is a case for European co-operation, even if the European Communities sadly fail to live up to its requirements. There is a case for a Western alliance. There is a case for joint action on the part of the rich to make sure that at the very least people's basic needs are met everywhere. There is a case for world-wide rules of monetary stability, free trade and a number of other fields. Whoever resists such needs will find himself poorer, weaker, less responsible and, before long, less secure.

But governments resist both the forces for devolution and those for international co-operation. We have noted already that such resistance does not quench the forces themselves; or put differently, governments are not all-important. There is in fact a revival of local politics. Many groupings have emerged in recent years around specific concerns at the local level. The "black economy" at least provides many an example of the success of small businesses. If this is not too far-fetched a comment: people want to belong, which they do neither as cogs in the wheel of a big organisation nor as men and women in the street nor as inhabitants of a high-rise monster. Thus they build their own ligatures where they live and work and play. At the other end, the forces of change have pushed their way through a less popular though equally effective fashion. In the absence of flexible governmental arrangements transcending nations and continents, private organisations have stepped into the breach. Whatever issues the accountability of transnational companies, or its absence, may raise, there can be no doubt that they have discovered and exploited the potential of wider spaces for action. They demonstrate beyond doubt that ineffective government and effective private action can exist side by side. Suspicions of transnational companies may be well-founded in some respects. It is irresponsible to make fortunes out of the production and sale of cheap tobacco in developing countries. Windfall profits as well as currency manipulations and the sudden closure of factories for reasons of corporate convenience raise many a question. But when all is said and done, there is a case for acknowledging that transnationals have been more effective in recognising the need for wider spaces of action than our rigid and tired governments.

Is there a lesson here? Is it possible that ungovernability, at least with respect to overloading and the stubborn defence of a useless political space, will be overcome by autonomous development? Is there a case for assuming that the hidden hand of new social forces will in the end correct the arrogance of traditional structures of power? The point is worth bearing in mind, though before we pursue it we have to consider the third and most serious process contributing to the declining effectiveness of government.

THE BRITISH EXAMPLE

If one wants to give it a name, one could call it the arteriosclerosis of government, though there are more familiar descriptions, such as corporatism, group politics, even collectivism. Britain has provided the preferred subject of the study of this phenomenon which has to do with Schieder's fourth point, the ability of political communities to absorb new forces and change. The first stage of the process was the gradual dissipation of the Westminster Model which John Mackintosh has described so vividly in his *Government and Politics of Britain*. [16] He shows, above all, "how the executive gained control over parliament," and how government thus became identified with the executive. But the executive did not remain suspended in mid-air. It was soon surrounded by a number of groups, of which political parties are only one, with which arrangements had to be made. At least some of these groups, such as the TUC and the CBI, gradually became "governing institutions." This is Keith Middlemas's term who uses it to describe the development of a "corporate bias" in Britain in the 1920s and 1930s.[17] By the 1950s, a system had come to full bloom which engaged in a veritable "cult of the equilibrium." Decisions were taken, not by adversary politics growing out of the class struggle, but by an organised consensus between government and governing institutions. More extreme analysts of this development have argued that there is a sense in which the end government came to be but one group among others, indeed several groups if one considers the bargains between government departments.[18] These analysts may be right in the world of effectiveness, as it were: this is how things happen. But they are wrong in the world of legitimacy: without government, decisions lack two crucial ingredients, authority and money. Nevertheless, there remains the central point that the Westminster Model has been turned into a bargain process between government and important organisations the result of which is a more-or-less harmony in place of strife.

This is the British example. Others, who have never followed the Westminster Model, have reached the same destination by different routes. In the United States, quite contrary to its constitutional assumptions, there is no simple notion of "the executive"; parts of congress are involved in the great consensus. In continental countries, the state itself has been regarded as an instrument of consensus, if not as the "reality of the moral ideal," and non-adversary consensus is backed up by legal systems of the Roman Law tradition. Everywhere, however, the terms in which Keith Middle-

---

[16] John Mackintosh, *The Government and Politics of Britain* (London: Hutchinson, 1977).

[17] Keith Middlemas, *Politics in Industrial Society* (London: Andre Deutsch, 1979).

[18] *Cf.* J. J. Richardson and A. G. Jordan, *Governing Under Pressure* (Oxford: Martin Robertson, 1979).

mas, in his *Politics in Industrial Society,* describes the way in which the great consensus has gone sour, are applicable. From the "high aspirations" which accompanied the consensus when it was built, it has now sunk to being "the lowest common denominator of policies designed to avoid trouble."[19] And this does not work for very long. The "stagnant mediocrity" of an inflexible system of consensus has revived, or generated for the first time, doubts and conflicts with which the system itself cannot cope. The consensus was meant to bring about massive social changes, the new deal of a just society; but in the end it became a thoughtless administration of the past. In the 1970s, the rigidity of the system became fully exposed. "Like an overloaded electrical circuit, the system began to blow more fuses than electricians could cope with in that dismal decade."[20]

There is a danger in metaphorical language. It evokes images, and plays on preconceptions without proving anything. However, there are quite fundamental issues which support the point that the "corporate bias" creates new problems without necessarily solving old ones. Such a bias was an appropriate response to a condition in which overriding class interests had dissolved into multiple interests of a more specific character. It could be assumed that there would be, for each of the major concerns of people, an organised group which had access to, or formed itself, "governing institutions." All seemed well, because the bargaining system reflected, or was capable of reflecting, the relative weight of different interests at different times. New concerns could always be absorbed into the system. But then, a new kind of interest emerged. It is the desire of individuals to check the power of large organisations, and to be free of their domination. The concern is paradoxical; the same people feel represented by, say, trade unions and resent their bigness and power. Thus the question is not how to weaken the unions, but how to have them strong and yet safeguard individual liberty. However, the corporate bias cannot make any provisions for this. There cannot be an anti-group group which becomes one of the "governing institutions." Even political parties fail to play this role. As a result, an important concern remains unexpressed in official politics, and that means, it is expressed in unofficial and unpredictable ways, by massive abstention, by votes for parties and candidates outside the consensus, by situational protest, ecological, fiscal or otherwise. This is where the corporate system blows its fuses.

---

[19] Middlemas, *Politics in Industrial Society,* p. 429.

[20] Ibid, p. 459.

WHY IS ECONOMIC GROWTH DIFFICULT?

The example provides a partial answer to the question of whether the processes which have impaired effective government are important. They are. Their symptoms are everywhere, and there is little reason to believe that they will go away. This becomes even more clearly evident if we ask ourselves why it is that we have reached this position.

There are at least two answers to this question, one conjectural and one structural. Samuel Huntington was the first to argue that the "crisis of democracy" is a reflection of changing economic circumstances.[21] Democracy worked as long as the contest for higher expectations built into its structures promised some success. As long as a governing party could deliver at least some of the goods, all was well. But once economic growth—the necessary condition of the ability of governments to respond to expectations the increase of which they themselves had to stimulate—became more difficult, democratic governments were in trouble. If there is, say, the beginning of a Kondratieff cycle which means a quarter-century of low growth or even decline, democratic politics has no way of coping. It is only—thus Huntington's conclusion—by introducing elements of authoritarianism that we can survive the long slump. Leaving this conclusion on one side, there is much that seems persuasive in the argument. Yet in a crucial sense it begs the question: why is it that economic growth has become more difficult?

The point can be made in a different way. Britain has a great deal of experience with the politics of economic decline. Yet a century of low, at times "negative" growth has in fact not led to the decadence of political democracy. On the contrary, Britain is one of a mere handful of countries in the world in which democracy has survived the ups and downs of this century. Economic growth is in fact no more than one symptom of a much deeper process. Growth, too, has become difficult for reasons which have to do with its own assumptions; unmanageable size and the accompanying cost of research, development and investment, provide but one significant example; changes in values (from a "protestant" to a hedonist ethic) and satiation if not of markets then of human capacity to absorb innovation are others. The same principle applies to the processes of government as well: the very assumptions on which modern, "reasonable" government is based have created the problems to which we have spoken.

John Mackintosh has seen this clearly: "Thus while the Westmin-

---

[21] Cf. Samuel Huntington's contribution to Michel Crozier et al., *The Crisis of Democracy*.

ster Model was never reconstructed or revised, the continuation of trends such as the extension of the right to vote, the consequent growth of parties, the new demands of the electorate and the complex administration required to fulfil these demands all affected it, introducing new elements and finally altering the balance between institutions."[22] By developing its own assumptions, parliamentary democracy turned into corporate democracy. The machine of corporate democracy in turn has run hot and is about to crank to a halt. Similarly, the assumptions of a community of citizens whose rights extended from the legal to the political and the social sphere led of necessity to an increase in government activity, to big government, until in the end its very bigness prevents government from moving ahead. And the vested interests, that go with big government and the "governing institutions" which surround it, are such that a change in relevant spaces of action goes unnoticed, or rather is resisted in the hope that no one will notice. In the end, as we have seen, government itself wears the Emperor's new clothes. The declining effectiveness of democratic government is, in other words, endemic, or structural. It is a result of its own assumptions; it is one of the contradictions of modernity. The central point is not that too many fuses have been blown for electricians to cope; the point is that we need a different system of fuses and retrained electricians to cope.

It has become fashionable to make proposals for change. Not only is the boundary between description and prescription, analytical and normative statements no longer respected, there is in fact an expectation that the academic lecturer will come up with remedies, the more radical, even outrageous, the better. I shall disappoint those who expect such a conclusion. There are, to be sure, important proposals to discuss. In passing at least, I have mentioned some of them: a Bill of Rights, electoral reform, the devolution of powers, a new internationalism. But in a sense, programmes are easy to come by, whereas analysis is not. At the risk of appearing unduly gloomy, I propose to take my argument a last step further without pretending to have answers.

There are today serious limitations of the effectiveness of democratic government. They concern (to return to Theodor Schieder's definition yet again) both the ability of governments to satisfy rising expectations and their ability to absorb changes in values and social structure. Such limitations are serious. They mean that governments are weak at a time at which it could be argued that we can ill afford such weakness. They also mean that reforms are necessary without it being evident where the ideas of the future should

---

[22] Mackintosh, *The Government and Politics of Britain,* p. 28.

come from. For the moment, not only political parties, but intellectuals, too, seem to have run out of ideas. Keith Middlemas involuntarily sums up the problem when at the end of a critical tirade about the ills of democracy, he admits that while change is necessary "the form it will take cannot be seen."[23] We need thought and discussion, publications and even policy research institutes, but they are merely the shell of thought and designs of the future.

Yet there is no reason to think that the dearth of ideas about the future and the resistance of institutions to necessary change must be fatal. In the end, as transnationals, or the "black economy" show, the imagination of reality is greater than that of professors or ministers. For this seems beyond doubt: Neither the "unloading" of functions nor recognition of appropriate spaces nor the acknowledgment of individual rights in a group society are in principle outside the orbit of democratic governments. Changes are likely to be painful, but they are not impossible. Robert Heilbroner has made this point with respect to inflation. Inflation is, in his analysis, the latest malady of capitalism. But capitalism has coped before: with poverty, with trusts and cartels, with depressions. In every case, coping was costly. Again with inflation, major cataclysmic events are likely before the obvious solution is implemented: "permanent wage and price controls" and "a sufficiently heavy and well-directed structure of taxation [to] prevent a buildup of purchasing power."[24] But, Heilbroner adds: "in the end, I believe that capitalism will again evidence its extraordinary institutional and ideological flexibility and will accept the necessary text 'socialistic' steps as the only means by which it can extend its nervous, expansionary life." It is not just capitalism which has this ability to adjust, but even more so the open society and its political institutions which are, after all, designed to accommodate change without revolution.

Yet, when this is said, and even done, one wonders: is this all? What about the famous "crisis of legitimacy" of modern, late capitalist, democratic corporatist societies? Are we not faced with a deeper malady? Are there not endemic threats greater than the challenges of reform of which we have spoken? Has the declining effectiveness of government not begun to affect its legitimacy in the democratic countries of the world?

There is evidently a great temptation to deduce the answer from one's political preconceptions. Habermas, for example—and Middlemas tends to follow him—would like to think that we are faced, if not with a proletarian revolution, then with some other great

---

[23] Middlemas, *Politics in Industrial Society*, p. 463.

[24] Robert Heilbroner, "Inflationary Capitalism," *The New Yorker*, October 8, 1979, pp. 121–41.

historical earthquake; and as a result he tends to introduce the notion of a "crisis of legitimacy" first and then seek material to support it.[25] Heilbroner, on the other hand, allows his social democratic pragmatism to reject the notion of a crisis of legitimacy out of hand; he assumes that somehow or other problems will be worked out, or will work themselves out. If one is neither a critical theorist nor a dogmatic pragmatist, the answer is less easy. It is really that we do not know for sure, but that there are signs which point to more serious cataclysms than a mere crisis of effectiveness would suggest. There are in particular threats to liberty which arise from the unpredictability—dare one say, the predictable unpredictability?—of governments which are alienated from people's values, worried about self-preservation, and faced with the ultimate threats to governability and to survival.

I have hinted once or twice at a condition which I have described as the alienation of government. What this means is quite simple. On the one hand, a certain system and practice of government produces problems, endemic problems like, say, the inability to satisfy expectations which the process of government has raised or implied. On the other hand, people's expectations turn away from government. While government desperately, and vainly, attempts to live up to its self-imposed aims, people have long decided to look for other ways to safeguard their life chances. It is as if the carpet is pulled away from underneath government. But government tries to resist: a situation in which it is not surprising that Samuel Huntington and others demand a return to authority, if not authoritarianism.

This is most dramatically evident if we consider the basic functions of government. It seems that today the conflict between the prevailing social democratic consensus which informs the ineffectual actions of government, and the values which haltingly and tentatively, but no less clearly inform people's actions, has reached the social contract itself (Thomas Hobbes's social contract, not Jack Jones's, to be sure). Government is still very largely, and understandably, about increasing people's options, about what has come to be called, somewhat misleadingly, "liberalisation." People, on the other hand, begin to wonder what these options are for. They find that options make little sense if one is not anchored in a framework of social ties, ligatures. So they look for ligatures, often desperately, as in Jonestown, or perversely, as in drug abuse, or in criminal gangs. There is, in other words, a real problem of holding society together, of social control, and it could be argued that few things

---

[25] Cf. Jürgen Habermas, *Legitimationsprobleme im Spätkapitalismus* (Frankfurt: Suhrkamp, 1979). See also Middlemas, *Politics in Industrial Society*, chap. 15.

are clearer indices of declining legitimacy than problems of the fundamental social contract. The return of a war of all against all documents doubt in the ability of governments to do what they were initially set up to do. Governments are not unaware of this dilemma. So they translate the social contract into "law and order," and this in turn into the "short, sharp treatment" of offenders, only to find that it makes matters worse. Once again, there is a great danger that the response to a crisis of legitimacy will be authoritarianism and illiberty.

This, then, takes us back to the frightening question with which I began this lecture. Who will save us from disaster? Karl Jaspers's recommendation, not to lose hope, is fine but hardly enough. Raymond Aron—not, to be sure, a Hegelian, despite his somewhat abstract terminology—gave what is the only possible answer: "In the nuclear age, the only chance that mankind will be saved from itself is that the intelligence of the personified state will bring armaments under control."[26] The "intelligence of the personified state," that is the capacity of governments to comprehend and to do the right thing. But does it exist? The potential of destruction, so we said, takes us to the limits of governability; it is too great for the moral and intellectual weaknesses of man. These weaknesses need, of course, not be tempted. The intelligence of the personified state can be such at least that the ultimate threat remains remote and unlikely. This is where the effectiveness, and above all, the legitimacy of governments comes in. Illegitimate governments are worried governments. The new authoritarianism documents their worries with respect to security within societies. Outside, with respect to external security, worried governments are liable to make every mistake in the book. This is why the danger is so great that widespread doubts in the effectiveness of governments turn into doubts in their legitimacy. A free society does not need a strong government.

It may indeed fare better if government is fairly inactive and quiet. But a free society needs an unworried government, and that means one which is effective where necessary and legitimate throughout.

---

[26] Raymond Aron, *Penser la Guerre, Clausewitz* (Paris: Gallimard, 1978), vol. 2.

23

Preferential Policies

Myron Weiner

Do preferential policies—or affirmative action programs as they are called in the United States—have similar political consequences in very different social and cultural settings? The object of this paper is to suggest that they do.[1]

The governments of India, Malaysia, Sri Lanka and the United States have adopted policies intended to give preferences in employment and in education to selected disadvantaged ethnic groups. The effects of these policies on the education, occupation, and income of the intended beneficiaries vary within and among these countries. But the political effects are remarkably similar, suggesting that there is a political and policy logic to such policies shared by very diverse societies and polities.

One way to study the effects of policies is to use what John Stuart Mill called the "method of difference" in comparative analysis. According to this method, if we wish to examine the effects of, say, tariff policies, we should compare at least two countries "whose habits, usages, opinions, laws and institutions are the same in all

Source: Myron Weiner, "The Political Consequences of Preferential Policies: A Comparative Perspective," *Comparative Politics* 16 (October 1983), pp. 35–52. Permission to reprint by *Comparative Politics,* © The City University of New York.

[1] . . . Many of the arguments presented here were initially developed in a book I wrote with Mary Fainsod Katzenstein, *India's Preferential Policies: Migrants, the Middle Classes and Ethnic Equality* (Chicago: University of Chicago Press, 1981).

respects, except that one of them has a more protective tariff."[2] Clearly this standard is so demanding that it makes comparative analysis impossible.

An alternative method is to look at the effects of the same policy on at least two countries "whose habits, usages, opinions, laws and institutions" are *different*. No conclusions can be drawn if the effects are different, but if the effects are similar then a causal relationship has been established.

To test our hypothesis that preferential policies produce similar political consequences in widely different social and cultural settings we shall draw our evidence from India and the United States, two countries that are very different but which have adopted similar policies to deal with the issue of inequalities among ethnic groups.

First, it is necessary to clarify the conceptual language.

Preferential policies refers to laws, regulations, administrative rules, courts orders, and other public interventions to provide certain public and private goods, such as admission into schools and colleges, jobs, promotions, business loans, and rights to buy and sell land on the basis of membership in a particular ethnic group.[3]

By *ethnicity*, I mean the way individuals and groups characterize themselves on the basis of their language, race, religion, place of origin, shared culture, values, and history. Ethnicity is generally, but not always, a matter of birth. Many people collectively may redefine their identity: government policies often are important in shaping the identity of an ethnic group and determining who is a member.

Ethnic equality can refer to *equality of opportunity, equality of results, or equality of treatment*. By *equality of opportunity* I mean that individuals, irrespective of the ethnic group they belong to, are considered for education and employment as well as other public and private goods on the basis of their ability and skills or their needs. When there is equality of opportunity, individuals are neither discriminated against nor given benefits because of their language, religion, race, place of origin, caste, or any other ethnic category.

Equality of results, as it relates to ethnicity, means that the distribution of income, wealth, and occupations among individuals

---

[2] John Stuart Mill, *Logic,* (quoted by Denis Thompson), *John Stuart Mill and Representative Government* (Princeton: Princeton University Press, 1976), p. 22.

[3] In the United States these policies are called "affirmative action" or "compensatory" policies by supporters and "reverse discrimination" by detractors, while in India these policies are called "protective discrimination" or simply, "reservations." The terminology often reveals the writer's point of view. No term is completely neutral but I have used the word "preferences" as the least value-loaded term not specifically tied to either country.

is in proportion to the population of each ethnic group in the country.

Equality of treatment suggests that individuals, regardless of the ethnic group they belong to, are treated alike, that people with more money are entitled to more material goods but are not entitled to degrade others because of their lower income or ethnic group.

THE ARGUMENTS FOR PREFERENTIAL POLICIES

Virtually everywhere in the world there is now a demand for greater equality among ethnic groups. Whether it is India or the United States, Sri Lanka or Belgium, Malaysia or Canada, educationally and economically disadvantaged ethnic groups are demanding governmental intervention on their behalf. Most governments have responded either out of a concern for social justice or to mitigate political conflict. Preferential policies—or affirmative action programs, reservations, or compensatory discrimination, as these policies are variously called—are one such government response.

There is a universality to ethnic inequality. All multi-ethnic societies exhibit a tendency for ethnic groups to engage in different occupations, have different levels and often types of education, receive different incomes, and occupy different places in the social hierarchy. In some instances this ethnic division of labor reflects domination by one ethnic group over another through the imposition of its economic powers, control over the state, and assertion of central legitimizing principles and symbols intended to justify the domination. In other instances the ethnic division of labor may be the consequence of different values, preferences, and ambitions of ethnic groups. One group, for example, may have little regard for education where another values education highly. One group may prefer entrepreneurial activities, another the professions, and still another physical labor. One group consists of high achievers who seek to move up to whatever occupations are most valued or best paid, while members of another group are less ambitious, prefer to live as they have in the past, and are less willing to venture forth from their community or into new occupations.

Which explanation is "true," is often a matter of debate. The debate within a country between those who see differences as a result of societal constraints and those who see them as a result of individual or group cultures, values, and preferences—between the socio-political determinists and cultural/individual behavioralists—is often at the root of different policy perspectives. The policy lever one pulls depends in part on how one explains ethnic differences. In fact both sets of factors can be at work within the same society. Groups may be the victims of societal discrimination and lack initiative and drive; there may be barriers to education as well as indifference to education; groups kept out of certain occupations may also have occupational preferences.

Whatever the cause or explanation, what is striking is the growing contemporary concern for the removal of these differences. Until recently, however, most societies did not view these differences as a problem. That particular religions, castes, or linguistic groups in India predominated in the military, the bureaucracy, trade, and commerce, as landowners, tenants-cultivators, landless laborers, or artisans, seemed to many to be a "natural" order reflecting, if not innate differences in ability, at least innate differences in culture. And in the United States it struck no one as a problem that in New York City the Irish dominated the police and the Jews the school system and that municipal garbage collectors, postal workers, textile workers, and, for that matter, corporate, university, and foundation presidents tended to come disproportionately from particular ethnic groups.

Why there is a growing world-wide concern with reducing inequalities among ethnic groups, need not concern us here in any detail. Fundamentally, it is related to the broader concern with income and social inequalities among classes. But there are at least two reasons why many consider ethnic inequality more unacceptable than class inequality. One is that differences among ethnic groups are often seen as an indication of differences in opportunity, proof that society has allocated access to education and employment unfairly, and that dominant groups are using their position to restrict others from moving upward. In contrast, class differences are not necessarily viewed as an indication of inequality of opportunity. To the contrary, they may be the result of equality of opportunity. A society that provides equal opportunity is one in which the results are uneven and where the unequal results are considered legitimate. Winners believe they deserve more, losers that they deserve less, in a competitive race in which all have an equal opportunity to move up. If one has succeeded and another has failed, presumably differences in ability, skill, hard work, and ambition are reflected. If the outcome is stratified by ethnic group, however, the presumption is made that the results may have been fixed, that is, that some groups were discriminated against while others were favored. Thus, in both India and the United States the low status and the low income of ex-untouchables and blacks are widely viewed as the result of discrimination by dominant ethnic groups, whereas poverty among Brahmins and Protestant Whites is ordinarily not seen as a result of prejudice.

The second reason why ethnic inequality is often of greater social and political concern than class differences is that when ethnic differences lead to ethnic conflict the result often is more disruptive to the social order than class conflicts. On a global basis more people have been killed in this century because of the ethnic group to which they belonged than to their class. Forceful expulsion of populations, genocide, civil wars, and a variety of internal upheavals linked to ethnic conflicts have marked social and political life in the advanced industrial countries no less than in the newly independent states of Asia and Africa. Ties of blood (whether real or a social invention) have driven mankind to commit acts that exceed the brutalities committed on behalf of class.

It is this concern for both distributive justice and the minimizing of ethnic conflict that has led some governments to turn their attention to the question of how to reduce inequalities among ethnic groups.

Various policies aimed at increasing the income and occupational equality of ethnic groups are available to governments; preferential treatment is only one of several such alternatives. Among the others are regional and urban development programs where disadvantaged ethnic groups are geographically concentrated; government aid for selected sectors of the economy where disadvantaged ethnic groups are concentrated in agriculture, fishing, forestry, or particular industries; social service programs for improving the health, education, and housing of low-income groups; wealth and income distribution policies, such as land reform, tenancy reform, and minimum wages, which differentially benefit one ethnic group in relation to another; and a variety of policies that increase the political power of selected ethnic groups, such as the devolution of authority, the redrawing of administrative boundaries, and electoral reform.

Such policies, though intended to benefit particular ethnic groups, do not use ethnic criteria as their basis. Preferential policies do. Under preferential policies individuals are given special benefits, not because they live in poor regions, work in lagging sectors of the economy, or are educationally and economically disadvantaged, but because they belong to a particular ethnic category—a caste, race, tribe, religion, linguistic or cultural group which, on the average, is less educated, earns less, and has lower status employment than other ethnic groups. The advantage of such explicit policies is that only the targeted group benefits: it is also argued that the benefits accrue faster; most important, the policies are politically attractive to the leadership and to the more advanced elements of the ethnic group, for they are the major gainers.

Preferential policies have been adopted in the United States, India, Malaysia, and Sri Lanka. They have been advocated in several European countries (particularly Holland and the United Kingdom) and in Israel. In each instance there is a controversy not only over the efficacy of such policies, but also over the deeper philosophical question of the justice of employing ethnic criteria as the basis for the distribution of benefits, that is, whether the characteristics of the group rather than of the individuals who belong to the group should be the basis for the receipt of entitlements and preferences. At the heart of the controversy is the question of individual versus group rights. India and the United States have approached the issue of preferential policies from quite different philosophical traditions; yet, as we shall try to argue, similar (though by no means the same) policies have produced remarkably similar political consequences.

Our account of the American debate will be highly condensed, since we shall assume that the reader is broadly familiar with the issues, while our account of the debate—and the assumptions that underlie that debate—in India will be presented in greater detail. We shall then turn our attention to the political consequences of preferential policies in India and suggest similarities in the American experience.

PREFERENTIAL POLICIES IN THE UNITED STATES

In the United States, advocates of ethnic equality initially directed their attention to eliminating discrimination in education, employment, housing, and civil rights. A series of Supreme Court decisions—particularly *Brown* v. *Board of Education* (1954)—and legislative decisions—especially the 1964 Civil Rights Act—attempted to break the barriers to equality of opportunity and equality of treatment. A prime target of reform was school segregation. American civil rights supporters argued that the integration of whites and blacks in the schools, combined with the elimination of discrimination in employment and housing, would enable disadvantaged blacks to compete with whites, and that in time most of the disparities would disappear. Others argued that, since the effects of past discrimination were reflected in current individual capabilities, equal opportunity would result in unequal outcomes. They argued that the assumption that the removal of discrimination in education would equalize opportunity and bring about more equal results was false. Holders of this view rejected the classic liberal view that the educational system could even out class barriers and that subsequent differences in income or productivity could then be explained by examining the personal deficiencies of workers. Moreover, if cultural differences affected the ability of groups to compete, under conditions of perfect competition some ethnic groups would win a disproportionate share of the higher occupations and incomes.

Perhaps the strongest argument against a color-blind policy came from those who questioned whether there could be real equality of opportunity in a society where prejudice and discrimination were so widespread. Neither school integration nor legal measures to counter discrimination would, therefore, be sufficient to create equality of opportunity between the races.

Affirmative action programs were proposed as a way to equalize the races, but there was division between those who saw such programs as a goal and those who saw them as a system of quotas or preferences. For some, *affirmative action* meant programs of training and recruitment in support of a national commitment to equal *opportunity* in education and employment. Others stressed reserving a certain percentage of positions for exclusive use by blacks, Hispanics, and other targeted groups. The line between goals and actual quotas is difficult to draw in practice; to many non-Americans it probably is an arcane distinction with no significant difference of outcomes. Nonetheless, the issue calls attention to the widespread American belief in equality of opportunity, but not necessarily equality of results, and more fundamentally to the American preference for individual rights as opposed to group rights.

These issues were drawn in the Bakke case, a case involving a white male who argued that he was denied admission to the University of California Medical School at Davis because 16 out of 100 places in the entering class had been reserved for minorities. Supporters of affirmative action argued that the unequal distribution of benefits among races with respect to the number of doctors reflected discrimination against minorities and that group performance was a way to determine whether equal opportunities existed. Most supporters of the Davis Medical School also subscribed to the notion that it was individual performance that counted; they argued that affirmative action in education would lead to equal opportunity in employment, which ultimately would bring equal results. This classic liberal position was articulated by Archibald Cox, professor of law at Harvard and the lawyer for Davis. In fact, he said, if the Davis program were to "give rise to some notion of group entitlement regardless either of the ability of . . . individuals or of their potential contribution to society . . . I would first, as a faculty member, criticize and oppose it; as a constitutional lawyer, the further it went the more doubts I would have."[4]

Some observers interpreted the Bakke case as a classic clash between the principle of meritocracy and the goal of racial equality, but defenders of meritocracy argued that merit was the only way

[4] Timothy J. O'Neill, "The Language of Equality in a Constitutional Order," *American Political Science Review* 75 (September 1981), p. 627.

to guarantee equal opportunity. Some saw the case as a test of the principle of compensatory justice, while others argued that nothing was more unfair than to measure individuals by their race. There were also arguments about the need for role models, analogies between proportionality in politics and proportionality in education, and a controversy over whether there had to be prior discrimination on the part of the Davis Medical School to justify a compensatory admissions policy. At the heart of the debate, however, lay the question, are constitutional rights for individuals or for groups? To supporters of the doctrine of individual rights the meaning of the 14th Amendment was clear and decisive: "No state shall . . . deny to any *person* within its jurisdiction the equal protection of the laws."

Many advocates of affirmative action policies see them not as group preferences but as an attempt by government to stop discrimination. From this perspective, Executive Orders 11246 and 11375, which required federal contractors to establish affirmative action plans, were the means by which the federal government sought compliance with Title VII of the 1964 Civil Rights Act outlawing employer discrimination. While some civil rights advocates distinguished between anti-discriminatory policies (which they support) and numerical goals or quotas (which they oppose), others argued that "without numerical goals Title VII is virtually unenforceable" since it is nearly impossible to prove that racial bias affects individual hiring decisions.[5]

Supporters of quotas argue that there is a "pool" of potentially qualified applicants among minorities and that if an employer consistently hires a smaller percentage than those in the available pool there is a pattern of discrimination. One must therefore define what the appropriate qualifications are for a particular job or admission into an educational institution, develop appropriate measures for determining the number and percentage of qualified minorities, and then monitor employers and educational institutions to assure that hiring or admission of minorities is proportionate to the number in the qualified pool of applicants.

This view of quotas is conceptually different from one which em-

---

[5] Christopher Jencks, "Special Treatment for Blacks?" *The New York Review* (March 17, 1973), p. 14. For other views on these issues see Nijole V. Benokaitis and Joe R. Feagin, *Affirmative Action and Equal Opportunity: Action, Inaction, Reaction* (Colorado: Westview Press, 1978); "Evaluating the Impact of Affirmative Action: A Look at the Federal Compliance Program: A Symposium," *ILR Review* 29 (July 1976), pp. 485–584; Nathan Glazer, *Affirmative Discrimination: Ethnic Equality and Public Policy* (New York: Basic Books, 1975); Richard A. Lester, *Reasoning about Discrimination* (Princeton: Princeton University Press, 1980); John E. Fleming, Gerald R. Gill, and David E. Swinton, *The Case for Affirmative Action for Blacks in Higher Education* (Washington: Howard University Press, 1978); Thomas Sowell, *Markets and Minorities* (New York: Basic Books, 1982).

phasizes hiring and admissions in proportion to the size of the ethnic group within the society. Its advocates argue that it is a policy intended ultimately to create color-blind hiring and hence is consistent with an individual rather than a group rights position. But its critics argue that while goals can be consistent with an individual rights position, in practice efforts to define "qualifications," "pools," and "numerical goals," particularly when these are defined and set by government bureaucrats, can easily become quotas and group rights.

The case for moving from one position to the other is forcefully articulated by Franklin Thomas, President of the Ford Foundation, who argues that anti-discrimination policies in the United States have moved through three ascending stages. Stage 1 is "racial neutrality," that is, anti-discriminatory laws intended to create color-blind behavior. Stage 2 is an active anti-discriminatory policy requiring equal opportunity policies by employers, programs to enlarge the pool of qualified persons, and a degree of "special treatment" for blacks. Stage 3, he writes, "advances affirmative action by a giant's leap" to what Thomas calls a "federally-mandated race-conscious policy."[6] Thomas agrees that mandated numerical remedies change the relationship between the individual and the group, but he supports these remedies on the grounds that "affirmative action in all its forms serves the most profound goal of a democratic society—equality and justice for everyone regardless of color, ethnicity, or sex. All of the sophisticated tools of regulation, enforcement and litigation are only instruments toward that end."[7]

In any discussion of preferences it is also useful to distinguish between *procedural* and *substantive* preferences. Procedural preferences are intended to increase the access of a group to political power, education, and employment, but unlike substantive preferences do not necessarily guarantee equal results. Government policies that force employers to look at a larger pool than the known work force, define job-related standards that do not impose higher educational or physical strength qualifications than required by the job, and set equal opportunity requirements to replace the traditional "old boy" network are examples of procedural "preferences." Such procedures are generally less contentious than substantive preferences intended to assure equal results. The reason is that these procedures can also be described as ways of eliminating discriminatory practices and thus are consistent with the individual rights/equal access position.

---

[6] Franklin A. Thomas, *Reflections on a Multi-Racial Society* (London: Granada Publishing, 1983), pp. 12–13.

[7] Ibid. p. 18.

According to public opinion polls, most Americans object to the notion of group rights and quotas but support other measures to advance greater ethnic equality. Congress and, with some important exceptions, the courts have held to the individual rights position, while in effect sanctioning goals and timetables designed to achieve equality for disadvantaged groups. But some civil rights organizations and many government agencies charged with implementing affirmative action programs have tended to operate on the basis of group rights and goals. As with many political debates, code words became a shorthand way of expressing deeper philosophical positions. *Quotas* has come to mean a group rights position, while for many liberals *goals* is a device for preserving the commitment to individual rights while advocating steps to reduce inequalities among ethnic groups.

PREFERENTIAL POLICIES IN INDIA

The Indian position is more explicit in support of group than individual rights, though both positions have a place in the country's constitution. Indeed, imbedded in the Indian constitution are two conflicting notions of equality, each derived from an opposing philosophical tradition.[8]

Article 15 of the Indian constitution states: "The state shall not discriminate against any citizens on grounds only of religion, race, caste, sex or place of birth." Similarly, Article 16 (2) states that no citizen "shall on grounds only of religion, race, caste, sex, descent, place of birth, residence or any of them be ineligible for or discriminated against in state employment." This is the standard liberal position on individual rights.

---

[8] See Weiner and Katzenstein, *India's Preferential Policies*, for a more detailed historical account of how the policies were adopted in India and how they affected employment and education in selected regions of the country. See also Barbara R. Joshi, *Democracy in Search of Equality* (Delhi: Hindustan Publishing Corporation, 1982); Suma Chitnis, *A Long Way to Go* (New Delhi: Allied Publishers, 1981); Parta C. Aggarwal and Mohammed Siddig Ashraf, *Equality Through Privilege: A Study of Special Privileges for Scheduled Castes in Haryana* (New Delhi: Shri Ram Center for Industrial Relations and Human Resources, 1976); G. P. Verma, *Caste Reservations in India: Law and the Constitution* (Allahabad: Chugh Publications, 1980); Karuna Ahmad, "Towards Equality: Consequences of Protective Discrimination," *Economic and Political Weekly*, January 14, 1978, pp. 69–72; Marc Galanter, "Equality and Protective Discrimination in India," *Rutgers Law Review* 16 (1961), pp. 42–74; Marc Galanter, "Group Membership and Group Preferences in India," *Journal of Asian and African Studies* 2 (1967), pp. 91–124; Alan Gledhill, "Constitutional Protection of Indian Minorities," *Journal of the Indian Law Institute* 1 (1959), pp. 403–15; Raj Kumar Gupta, "Justice: Equal but Inseparate," *Journal of the Indian Law Institute* 11 (1969), pp. 57–86; Mohammed Imam, "Reservations of Seats for Backward Classes in Public Services and Educational Institutions," *Journal of the Indian Law Institute* 8 (1966), pp. 411–66.

But Article 15 (4), an amendment adopted in 1951, modifies Article 15 with a clause that states: "Nothing in this article. . . . shall prevent the state from making any special provision for the advancement of any socially and educationally backward classes of citizens or for the scheduled castes and the scheduled tribes." Similarly, Article 16 (4) modifies Article 16: "Nothing in this article shall prevent the state from making any provision for the reservation of appointments or posts in favour of any backward class of citizens." This is the standard group rights principle.

Thus, after boldly reconfirming the 19th-century liberal conception of the rights of citizens, the Indian constitution then asserts the principle of collective rights of classes of citizens based upon religion, race, caste, sex, descent, place of birth, or residence when the claims are made on behalf of classes "socially and educationally backward." Other provisions of the constitution go beyond enabling the government to give preference to specified classes of citizens by *requiring* the government to do so. Article 335, for example, provides for reservations of appointments of scheduled castes and scheduled tribes to the administrative services, and other provisions provide for reservations in parliament and the state assemblies.

Thus, the Indian government in its constitution and in subsequent legislative and administrative decisions, confirmed in court rulings, established the policy that the government can and should allocate seats in legislative bodies, admit students into educational institutions, grant scholarships, provide employment in government services, and make available various other entitlements to individuals on the basis of membership in a group. Once this principle was established the political controversies then centered on two ancillary questions: What groups should be entitled to preferences? What particular preferences should be provided?

An earlier legislative history largely settled the identity of the scheduled castes and scheduled tribes. These groups are widely known and locally accepted and are often specified in the census as well as various other administrative and legislative acts. The only significant controversy concerned whether ex-untouchables who had opted out of Hinduism by converting to Christianity or Buddhism qualified as members of scheduled castes since the latter were initially defined as castes within the Hindu religious framework. The controversy was ultimately settled by broadening rather than narrowing the definition of scheduled castes. Similarly, a legislative effort to exclude Christian tribals from the reservations provided scheduled tribes was rejected by the Indian parliament.

The issue of giving other "backward classes" benefits and of the way these classes should be chosen was more controversial. The "backward class" category is an especially elastic one since the criteria for inclusion are left to the political arena. As Ambedkar, India's law minister at the time when the constitutional provision for backward classes was written, said: "A backward community is a community which is backward in the opinion of the government." And T. T. Krishnamachari, another member of the Constituent Assembly, described Article 16 (4) as a "paradise for lawyers."[9]

The debate over the choice of criteria for including particular communities has been indecisive. Some government commissions argued that objective measures of "backwardness," such as average education or income levels, be employed. Other commissions emphasized position in the social hierarchy: a caste should be included as "backward" on the basis of its low status or the inferior treatment of its members by other communities. Whether the test for inclusion is an economic or a caste one, the consensus was that the criteria should be applied to groups, not individuals.

Some states were highly selective, but others chose to define as "backward" virtually any non-Brahmin caste. Efforts by the central government to develop a uniform set of criteria, if not a uniform list, were rejected by parliament and the courts, with the result that each state government has its own criteria and its own list. One consequence is that, while members of scheduled castes and scheduled tribes are given reservations in the central services and in centrally-run educational institutions as well as at the state level, reservations for the backward classes are confined to state and locally-run institutions and administrative services.

Although virtually all states provide benefits to some backward classes, several states have aggressively incorporated a substantial number of castes with large populations in their list. It is not unusual for 20 or 25 percent of the population of a state to appear on lists of backward classes, in addition to the 15 percent of the Indian population classified as scheduled caste, and another 7 percent as scheduled tribe.

In addition, most states have extended preferences to *residents* of the state, particularly in educational admissions and in employment for the state government. Although the laws and administrative rulings are usually explicit in specifying a time period as a definition of residence, it is not uncommon for residence to be used as a surrogate for ethnicity. The widely used term is "sons of the soil," referring to populations indigenous to a particular area, as distinct from migrants. Thus, in Assam "sons of the soil" rules specify residence, but both private and public employers understand that the intention of these policies is to give employment preferences

---

[9] Marc Galanter, "Who Are the Other Backward Classes? An Introduction to a Constitutional Puzzle." *Economic and Political Weekly* 13 (October 28, 1978), 1814.

to Assamese over Bengalis. Similar policies in Bombay are intended to benefit those who speak the Maharashtrian language over Tamils and other migrant communities, irrespective of the duration of their residence.

The main argument for extending reservations to "sons of the soil" is that they, too, are "socially and educationally backward" in relation to some migrant communities. In many regions of India an ethnic division of labor has developed, involving migrants and natives, with migrants holding positions in the state and central administrative services, the professions, the colleges and universities, and business and trade. The demand for preferential policies to protect the native middle classes over the migrant middle classes is an old one: preference was given to residents of the state in Hyderabad in the 1920s and in Bihar in the 1930s. In the 1960s and early 1970s, similar policies were adopted in Assam (against Bengalis), in Maharashtra (against Tamils), and within the Telengana region of Andhra (against people from the delta).

An interesting feature of Andhra's policies that may foreshadow developments elsewhere is that "local" was defined not in terms of residence in the state but as residence in regions and districts of the state. Demands for the "regionalization" of preferences have already been made in other states.

There was thus a progression in the application of the principle of reservations: from scheduled caste and scheduled tribe minorities that were lowest on the social scale, to the more numerous and somewhat better-off backward castes, to autochthonous populations, a majority diverse in its social and economic characteristics yet backward in relation to its migrant competitors.

These extensions have not been without controversy, however. In some states both scheduled castes and forward castes have opposed extension of preferences to backward castes—most notably in Bihar, where a recommendation by the state government was accompanied by massive demonstrations in the colleges. "Sons of the soil" preferences have been opposed, not only by migrant communities, but often by the governments of the states migrants came from, along with warnings of reprisals if state governments became too restrictive.

Some critics of reservations for backward castes and for "sons of the soil" urged the state governments to put aside all benefits for castes and linguistic groups, proposing instead that benefits go only to individuals from families that lacked education or adequate income. But this proposal for replacing group characteristics with individual characteristics was uniformly rejected by policymakers.

Objections notwithstanding, the extension of preferences to communities previously not receiving preferences has over the past three decades moved inexorably forward. The only limitation imposed by the courts is that, with respect to scheduled castes, scheduled tribes, and backward castes, the total number of reservations for admission to colleges and for positions in the administrative services must be below 50 percent. No such numerical restriction, however, was placed on preferences for "sons of the soil."

There has also been a progression in the kind of reservations provided. Initially, reservations were provided for admission to schools and colleges, including engineering and medical schools. They were provided for appointments to the state administrative services and, in the case of scheduled castes and tribes, to the central administrative services. Reservations were then extended to the entire public sector, though not to private employment. Private employers, however, are under pressure from state and central governments to provide reservations for scheduled castes and tribes and for "sons of the soil."

The system of reservations was originally intended for admission to educational institutions and for government employment. In some instances, preferences were also extended to promotions. More recently, there have been demands that preferences in educational admissions to medical schools be "held over"; that is, seats not filled one year must be added to reservations for the next.

The Indian policy, then, is to create a new kind of labor market in which each ethnic group is given a share commensurate with its population. Shares are first apportioned in educational institutions, then in various categories of employment in the public sector, and ultimately in private employment.

From this perspective, the model society is not a socialist one in which all individuals have, if not equal levels of education, at least equal incomes and wealth. Nor is it the liberal capitalist model of a society based upon equal opportunity in which individuals compete for higher education and higher incomes. Rather, it is a society in which each of the *upper* levels of education, income, and occupation are proportionately made up of persons from all the country's ethnic groups. This objective is to be achieved, not by an open competitive market, but by a government-regulated educational and labor market that ensures an appropriate place for each group. Social justice, according to this view, thus requires a public policy that guarantees individual mobility by means of group allocation.

THE POLITICAL CONSEQUENCES OF PREFERENTIAL POLICIES

To view policy options, policy choices, and program implementation simply in rational, cost-benefit terms based upon an assessment of policy outcomes, its gainers and losers, is to ignore the political dimension of the policy process. On the other hand, to reduce the system of reservations to a struggle by various groups for economic position, or by one group for mastery over another, is to miss the deeper conceptual issues which underlie political struggles. Neither approach provides a satisfactory answer to the question of why two countries, the United States and India, both committed to ethnic equality, both employing similar policy instruments, nonetheless continue to deal with the question of ethnic equality in different ways. Behind such words as *ethnicity, equality, integration,* and even *preferences* lie fundamentally different beliefs.

But at another level there is a convergence among countries that chose to follow the path of preferential policies, a convergence dictated by the *political logic* of preferential policies. This logic is especially clear in the Indian case precisely because India has so explicitly made a policy commitment to ethnic-group preferences. By "political logic" I mean a policy decision that creates a political space, shaping the terms of subsequent policy debates and substantially influencing political responses and new policy choices. In the Indian case, the political logic of preferential policies worked as follows:

1. Group Preferences.   There has been a progression from one group to another in the allocation of preferences. As we have seen, a policy initially intended to benefit scheduled castes and tribes was extended to backward castes and to autochthonous populations.[10] There have been pressures to expand the list of backward castes and to define autochthonous in an increasingly localized manner, as well as demands that reservations be extended to Muslims, to the families and children of immigrants overseas, and to various other groups.

2. Kinds of Preference.   The Indian constitution asserts that government can make provisions for the "reservations of appointments or posts" but leaves to the legislature the determination of what precise reservations should be provided. The result has been a

---

[10] The extension of preferences to autochthonous majorities has brought to the fore the question of when preferences are merely a rationale for discriminatory policies. In India, as elsewhere, the argument that the "native" population has a more authentic claim to land, education, and employment than people of migrant origin has raised the issue of whether there are two classes of citizens with different rights. This issue has been raised in Sri Lanka where the Sinhalesse are given preferences over the Tamils, in Malaysia where the Malays ("bhumiputra" or native population) are given preferences over Chinese and Indians, and in Kenya where the prime minister recently proposed that businessmen of Asian origin who broke the law would be expelled, while "African" businessmen would be fined or jailed.

debate over whether reservations should be provided in engineering and medical schools as well as in colleges, in public sector companies as well as in government services, and for privately as well as publicly owned firms. Controversy has arisen over what categories of employment to impose quotas on, and whether promotions as well as initial appointments should be by quota.

Determining which groups should be given preferences and what kind are not matters that can readily be resolved by some principle, especially since other widely held principles conflict with preferences. The principle, for example, that preferences should be given to local people conflicts with the principle of national citizenship. "This is a matter," said Mrs. Gandhi, "in which one has to have a certain balance. While we stand for the principle that any Indian should be able to work in any part of India, at the same time it is true that if a large number of people came from outside to seek employment . . . that is bound to create tension in that area. Therefore, while I do not like the idea of having such a rule, one has to have some balance and see that the local people are not deprived of employment."[11]

Similarly, the notion of making appointments on the basis of ethnic membership is seen as conflicting with the goal of institutional efficiency and the notion of individual merit. Heads of public sector firms, for example, have pressed for the exclusion of certain categories of employment (by skill level or rank) from reservations, but what is an acceptable "balance" to a manager is often not an acceptable balance to the leaders of ethnic communities.

Thus, what preferences and for whom are political matters, resolved not by legal doctrines or general principles but in the political arena, with struggles in the streets, at the polls, within the government bureaucracy, and in the state legislatures. Concessions granted to one group then become the basis of demands by another.

3. Mobilization. Because the question of what groups are to be given preferences is constitutionally and politically open, the demand for preferences has become a devise for political mobilization. Politicians can mobilize members of their caste, religious, or linguistic community around the demand for inclusion on the list of those to be given preferences. Leaders of ethnic groups and their supporters have demanded preferences either on the grounds that they are economically backward or that they have suffered from discrimination as a result of their low status in the caste hierarchy, or both.

As an issue around which to organize ethnic groups, the demand

---

[11] Weiner and Katzenstein, *India's Preferential Policies,* p. 25.

for reservations has been highly effective. This is particularly true in the case of the backward classes—a variety of castes diverse in their occupations, income, education, and size who (especially in northern India) have banded together politically around the claim for preferential treatment. Similarly, it has been a unifying demand for autochthonous groups (of many castes and religious affiliations) united in their opposition to "outsiders."

4. Backlash. As preferences were extended to backward castes and as more benefits were given to scheduled castes and scheduled tribes, the "forward" castes have mobilized in opposition. In the state of Gujarat, for example, upper caste students launched a movement to end preferences for the scheduled castes when benefits were extended. In Bihar, upper castes, with the support of the scheduled castes, opposed giving reservations to the backward castes. Increasingly, political groups are now organizing either to resist the further expansion of preferences or to oppose those in place.

One reason for the backlash is an awareness that some individuals receiving preferences are not themselves from educationally backward or economically deprived families. The more successful reservations are in producing a middle class within the backward community, the more such cases increase and the more resentful are members of communities denied reservations.[12]

5. Supernumerary Positions. As the number of reservations increases, categories are expanded, and a backlash emerges, governments seek to reduce ethnic conflict by creating supernumerary positions, both in education and in employment. In Andhra, for example, when the state government agreed to reserve admissions to Osmania University in proportion to the number of people residing in each district of the state (a policy intended to increase the proportion of students from the backward western districts and to reduce the number from the more advanced eastern districts), the government mollified the losers by creating another university, one that would be open to everyone in the state without regard to place of birth or residence. Similarly, when the state government agreed to establish regional representation in appointments to the

---

[12] The acceptability of a preferential policy is also often based upon its rationale. It makes a difference if a policy is intended to overcome previous discrimination, is a remedy for backwardness, or is a benefit given to "natives" because it is asserted that an indigenous population has greater rights. The same policies may be acceptable to those who are excluded if they are adopted on one principle, but rejected on another. In Malaysia, for example, Chinese acceptance of preferences for Malays was substantially higher when preferences were justified on the grounds that Malays were backward than when the government announced that Malays were entitled to special benefits because they were "bhumiputra" or "sons of the soil."

administrative services it created supernumerary positions in order not to fire those who came from "overrepresented" districts. In Gujarat, when the forward castes agitated against reservations for scheduled castes and tribes in the medical schools, the state government agreed to expand admissions in proportion to the number of reservations, so the forward castes would not feel deprived by the admission of scheduled castes and tribes.

6. Institutional Opposition. The need by institutions—private and public firms, government departments, hospitals, universities, and research organizations—for individuals of particular skills and motivation is sometimes at variance with the requirement that appointments and promotions be based on membership in an ethnic group. Institutions may fight for the exclusion of certain categories from the system of reservations or resist the allocation of a particular position to a less qualified member of a scheduled caste, tribe, or backward caste. Alternatively, heads of institutions may take the supernumerary route and make more appointments than are needed so that double appointments can be made, one for the reserved candidate and the second for a more skilled person who can do the work and exercise genuine authority. The result is often bitterness on the part of those holding the reserved slot that they have been given rank without actual responsibility and resentfulness on the part of others that they have been given responsibility without commensurate rank and salary.

7. Intra-Group Conflict. Preferences may lead to conflicts within ethnic groups as to whether reservations are allocated fairly. Since the ethnic category to which preferences have been given is often a composite of numerous ethnic groups, tension develops when one ethnic group receives more benefits than another. If the winners in the competition for reserved positions come predominantly from one identifiable ethnic group (say, Christian tribals as against non-Christian, or the Oraon tribe as against the Mundas, or the Mahar caste of ex-untouchables as against the Chamars), then demands may be made for subdividing preferences or for dropping one or more groups from the list. As we have noted, some Hindu tribals want to exclude Christian tribals, and some scheduled castes want to exclude those converted to Christianity, Buddhism, or Islam. Some critics have called for the application of socioeconomic criteria to individuals so as to exclude from benefits the children of prosperous members of the community. Understandably, the advanced sections of the targeted community resist proposals that deprive them of benefits, by emphasizing the demands that unite their ethnic group. For this reason, it is not uncommon for the advanced sections to be among the most militant in their espousal of ethnic group rights.

8. Social Marking. The policies strengthen ethnic group membership by establishing a new form of social marking: individuals are labeled in the occupational structure in terms of the community from which they come. This marking may ensure greater access to education, employment, and promotion, but it makes social mobility contingent upon membership in an ethnic group. Individuals are what they are because of the group they belong to—a statement that once described an individual's subordinate status but which now explains and even facilitates mobility. There is a kind of justice; the same principle that prevented mobility has become an instrument for mobility.

For example, an Oraon tribesman, a college graduate now employed in a government department, told me that he is looked down upon because the community to which he belongs is regarded by caste Hindus as primitive. He concluded that he could only raise his social status when the social status of his entire tribe was raised. A hierarchical system based upon caste ranking does not easily permit individuals to escape their status. Individuals are treated with condescension or deference, as impure or pure, because of the community to which they belong. This powerful linkage of individual status to community status makes the system of preferences based upon group membership as acceptable as it is. For lower castes, reservations facilitate educational and occupational mobility, but they do not remove the stigma of social rank. An ex-untouchable remains an ex-untouchable although he and 3.5 percent of his colleagues in the senior administrative services are ex-untouchables.[13] The preferential system thus helps preserve caste membership. Individuals are members of scheduled castes, scheduled tribes, or backward castes no matter what level of education they possess, what income they earn, what occupation they practice, or what authority they exercise.

Supporters of the system argue that in a hierarchical society based upon inequality, the introduction of the merit principle would worsen inequalities, that equality among ethnic groups can take place only when individuals are accorded education and employment on the basis of the ascriptive group they belong to. Preferential policies may deepen ethnic attachments, but they can also be viewed as an adaptation to the demand for equality in a society which

---

[13] The phenomenon of stigma is generally associated with higher-level jobs where one looks for the maximum, not minimum, qualifications.

has a tradition of hierarchy, where status and benefits historically have been allocated on the basis of group membership and group relationships.

9. Termination.   The politics of termination may yet prove to be one of the most explosive issues. Advocates of preferential policies see them as temporary measures to enable groups to catch up— similar to a tariff policy for infant industries—but in practice it has proven politically difficult to find ways to terminate such policies. Proposals in India to substitute individual for group characteristics and for descheduling groups that have successfully moved up the educational and occupational hierarchy have been rejected by the government and by all major political parties. Political leaders seek to woo segments of the electorate by promising preferential benefits; there are no political advantages to be gained by proposing to terminate benefits.

Theoretically, one could conceive of "anticipatory" termination measures, that is, policies that set conditions now for future termination. Distinctions could also be drawn between procedural and substantive preferences with provision for the future termination of the latter, but not the former. But given the political forces at work, it is most unlikely that the government and legislative bodies are likely to be farsighted enough to consider anticipatory termination policies.

CONCLUSION: COMPARATIVE IMPLICATIONS

The Indian experience suggests that preferential policies facilitate the mobilization of groups to demand preferences or their extension, creating political struggles over how the state should allocate benefits to ethnic groups, generating a backlash on the part of those ethnic groups excluded from benefits, intensifying the militancy of the beneficiaries, and reinforcing the importance of ascription as the principle of choice in allocating social benefits and facilitating mobility. A major consequence of preferential policies, therefore, is that they create a political process influencing the ways in which groups organize, the demands they make, the issues over which policies are debated, and the coalitions that are formed. From a political perspective, it is the impact of preferences on ethnic group cohesion, group status, and political mobilization that is significant. Preferential policies are intended, not to destroy the system of ethnic hierarchy, but to improve the position of groups within the hierarchy. The purpose of such policies is not only to facilitate the movement of some individuals upward but to move an entire group within the hierarchy. Positional change, not individual mobility, is the aim.

Integration thus has a quite different meaning in a hierarchical social order than it does in a society concerned with equality of opportunity and treatment. The mixing of children in schools and of families in neighborhoods, so central to the American concept of integration, is not a goal in India, where it is assumed that linguistic and caste groups may attend their own schools and live in their own quarters. The proponents of integration in India envisage a social order in which each group has a proportional share of benefits and statuses, but in which they do not necessarily mix together socially.

By now it should be self-evident that the political process set in motion by the adoption of preferential policies in India is not confined to India. Even though American courts have abjured quotas, in practice policy skirts close to the principle of group rights, and many of the same questions raised in India have been raised in the U.S. as well.

—To what groups should preferences be given—blacks, native Indians, Hispanics, Orientals, women?

—What ethnic groups should be classified under each category? Are Portuguese and Brazilians to be classified as Hispanics? Should well-educated Chilean and Argentinian refugees be included along with less educated Chicanos and Puerto Ricans? Should African students who recently settled in the United States be included among "blacks"? Should recent migrants from Taiwan, Vietnam, South Korea, or India be included among "Orientals"?

—What constitutes group membership? What degree of consanguinity makes one an Indian or a black or an Oriental? What is an Hispanic? A surname? Can one become Hispanic through marriage?

—What preferences should be granted? Promotions as well as hiring? Membership on the law school journal as well as admission to law school?

—Should individuals be given preferences even when they do not come from disadvantaged families and have themselves never personally been disadvantaged?

—How far should an institution modify its admissions, employment, or promotion criteria to meet group quotas?

—With respect to what kinds of positions might reservations undermine efficiency by the appointment of less qualified individuals?

—At what point do appointments based upon affirmative action goals or quotas become discriminatory against others?

These issues affect not only the courts, legislatures, and administrative agencies, but each institution engaged in the process of recruitment, hiring, and promotion. Thus, both "mini-political processes" and a national political process are created around these issues.

The many similarities between the Indian and the American experience suggest that there is a political logic to preferential policies. However great the differences between the social systems of the two countries and however different the effects of preferential policies on group equality, there is a convergence with respect to the kind of political process produced by preferential policies. It is this convergence that leads us to pose three questions for those who argue for the use of preferential policies, ethnic group rights, and equality of results:

1. Is the kind of society produced by a system of ethnic group preferences more just than the society that might be produced by other kinds of policies intended to reduce ethnic differences?

2. If a policy of ethnic group preferences is put in place, is it politically possible to place limits on who receives preferences and what kind?

3. If preferential policies are adopted, how, if at all, can they ever be terminated?

Supporters of preferential policies may well reply that what ultimately matters is whether the policies work. Are these policies better able than other policies to reduce the gap separating the well-being of one ethnic group from another? Opponents of preferential policies must, in turn, demonstrate that alternative policies are available—within their framework of individual rights and a commitment to the goal of equal opportunity—that will bring about a more equitable distribution of society's benefits among ethnic groups. They must show that other policies to bring about a more equitable distribution of income within society without *explicit* regard for race, religion, or ethnic group—policies centering around sectoral and regional investments, incomes policies, tax policies, social welfare programs, land reforms, etc.—are at least as efficacious.

The position one takes in this debate may ultimately depend upon whether one believes it is possible to create a social order in which the significance of ethnic group membership in gaining equal access to education and employment can be substantially reduced, or even eliminated. Those who think it can be reduced or eliminated will prefer ethnic-blind social policies and oppose preferences as a policy that will merely reinforce ethnic differences. Those who believe that an ethnic-blind society is not possible, and that people will in practice be educated, hired, and promoted on the basis of their group membership, will advocate preferences as the most feasible way of reducing ethnic inequalities. They will see the political consequences discussed in this paper as an acceptable cost.

On one point, at least, both sides agree. No democratic political system can long tolerate a social order in which the major educational, income, and occupational divisions are along ethnic lines. The question is not whether, but how these divisions can be bridged.

PART FOUR

Political Change

One of the most important historical developments of the 20th century has been the achievement of independence by peoples who had been brought under the political control of European states in the course of the preceding two centuries. At least one third of the population of the world is involved in this surge toward national independence. The Europeans were able to conquer and administer vast areas of Asia, Africa, and the Middle East because of their crushing superiority in military technology, in turn based on a vastly more developed economy. The Indonesians, Indochinese, Indians, and Africans simply were unable to resist the comparatively small but modern armed forces of the European powers intent upon expanding their influence in the world. The epoch of imperialism registered European advance and domination in all areas of human activity—economic, military, and even cultural. During the era of imperialism, political analysts confined their attention mainly to Europe and North America. Little attention was paid to other parts of the world, except by students of colonial administration.

Colonialism collapsed in the wake of World War II. The chief colonial powers—Great Britain, France, and Holland—were exhausted by the conflict and unable to engage in any new military ventures. Their rule over possessions in Asia and southeast Asia had been shattered by Japanese armies, which demonstrated to the world that the Europeans were not invincible. In order to gain the loyalty of India in the face of a threatened Japanese invasion, the British were compelled to promise independence. France and Holland were unable to reimpose their sovereignty in Indochina and Indonesia by arms. The countries of Western Europe lost their predominant position in 1945. Power shifted to two non-European states: the United States and the Soviet Union, both of whom began to court the support of former colonial peoples. The European

powers were thus at a severe disadvantage in relation to their former colonies. They were not permitted by the new dominant world
powers to attempt reconquest, and in any case they were no longer
capable of doing so.

The new relationship among the principal areas of the world is
comparable in importance to the French Revolution, the industrialization of Europe and North America, and the triumph of Communism in Russia. Each of these historical events changed the social
and cultural environment, and led to new forms of political power
and organization. The resurgence of the formerly subjugated peoples
of Asia and Africa symbolizes a new kind of world crisis and requires
a new focus of interest in our study of comparative politics.

But political change is not confined to the developing nations.
All political systems are undergoing a rapid evolution, including
those of the advanced industrial societies. Change is inherent in
the political process. We have already seen that in all political
systems there must be institutions through which claims and demands are translated into decisions. Existing conditions are then
inevitably modified. New groups assume a position of power and
influence while others lose their prerogatives; new rights are proclaimed and new services provided. Throughout the 19th century,
for example, there was a continuing struggle for the attainment
of political rights on the part of the social groups brought into
being by the industrial revolution. The 20th century is witnessing
a similar struggle for political emancipation in the rest of the world
and assumption of collective responsibility for economic development and social welfare.

The nature of change, the rate at which change takes place and
the specific correlates of change are not yet fully understood. Nor
is it easy to tell in advance the direction change is likely to take.
According to the Marxists, societies evolve through clearly defined
stages, from feudalism through capitalism to socialism, as a result
of economic pressures. Under certain conditions change is wrought
by violence and revolution since the groups and classes that wield
power are unwilling or unable to adapt to new conditions. Innovation may also bring about sweeping changes in social and political
institutions. All societies that have undergone the technological
and scientific revolutions of the past two centuries have been transformed, regardless of their particular cultures and political systems.
At the present time economic, social, and political change is occurring at an accelerated rate throughout the world. Political leaders
almost everywhere are now committed to a drastic overhaul of their
societies. They are attempting to popularize new values and norms,
and create new attitudes in order to achieve industrialization, prosperity, and equality. There is an unparalleled urgency in this move-

ment, which is taking place in a variety of ways and through a number of political forms. A major challenge confronting students of comparative politics is the development of analytic categories in terms of which the component elements of change can be understood and societies undergoing rapid change fruitfully compared.

TRADITIONAL AND MODERN SOCIETIES

It will be useful for analytic purposes to distinguish between two "ideal types" or models of societies: the *traditional* and the *modern*. These terms do not imply any value judgment. A traditional society may include a large number of highly educated persons whose level of culture and social grace is higher than that of the mass of inhabitants of any modern society. Furthermore, these terms refer only to abstract "constructs"; they do not describe any existing societies. For example, the United States is a predominantly modern society, but one with many traditionally oriented groups in its population.

The distinction here suggested is a familiar one in the literature of the social sciences. Similar classificatory schemes have been suggested by such eminent theoreticians as Sir Henry Maine, Ferdinand Tönnies, and especially Max Weber. Thus, Weber suggested that claims to legitimacy may be based on:

1. Rational grounds—resting on a belief in the "legality" of patterns of normative rules and the right of those elevated to authority under such rules to issue commands (legal authority).

2. Traditional grounds—resting on an established belief in the sanctity of immemorial traditions and the legitimacy of the status of those exercising authority under them (traditional authority); or finally,

3. Charismatic grounds—resting on devotion to the specific and exceptional sanctity, heroism or exemplary character of an individual person, and of the normative patterns or order revealed or ordained by him (charismatic authority).[1]

One implication which may be drawn from Weber's scheme is that the three types correspond to historical development from simple to more complex societies. In the former, obedience is to the person of the chief, and the values of the family permeate the whole social system. A society breaks out of this stage usually under the leadership of a charismatic chief, who is obeyed because of his personal or heroic qualities. In modern societies obedience is to the legal order. It is associated with the office more than with the person who occupies it.

---

[1] Max Weber, *The Theory of Social and Economic Organization* (New York: Oxford University Press, 1947), p. 328.

In both traditional and modern societies the individual participates in the political process through groups or associations, but there are fundamental differences as regards their nature and importance. Traditional societies are characterized by the predominance of the family and family-type groups (that is, primary organizations) in which the members are in a face-to-face relationship. An individual's status in the society is determined by his or her family's status. He or she is nurtured, cared for, educated, and protected by the family, which tends to be a self-sufficient economic as well as social unit. The dominant economic activity is agriculture, which requires the participation of the family as a cohesive group. Virtually the entire population (and not 1 in 10, as in modern societies) is engaged in agriculture, the hunt, or fishing in order to provide sustenance. There is little knowledge of science or technology, no opportunity to accumulate reserves of food, no leisure class able to devote itself to the arts and culture. The people live close to nature, even as part of nature. They are almost completely at the mercy of the seasons, storms, droughts, and rains. Superstition and magic permeate the society. People seek to relate events in their own lives with external occurrences, the stars, or the seasons.

Family values—personal loyalty, authority, reverence—pervade the whole social structure. The state tends to resemble the family, with the king or chief of state in the role of father, whose paternal authority derives from a superhuman source. The various families gathered together in clans or tribes are his children, bound to obey for the same reason that each elder in the tribe is obeyed by the younger leaders. Insofar as a bureaucracy comes into existence to administer the will of the chief, it is like a huge household—with nepotism an expected practice.

There have been, historically, a wide range of types *within* the general category of "traditional societies," from the subsistence agriculture and pastoral societies of primitive tribes in Africa, to the military structure of Egypt, the land empires of Asia Minor and China, the island civilization of the Aegean, Ancient Greece and Rome, and the feudal age. All of these societies, however, preceded the technological and industrial breakthrough of the 18th century.

Technical and scientific progress brought in their wake far-reaching change in social and political organization. The old agricultural subsistence economy was replaced by an industrial market-place economy. In the model modern society, individuals gain their livelihood not within the family but in a factory, commercial enterprise, or office. Population concentrates in the great urban centers, creating a host of administrative problems (sanitation, transportation, education, etc.). Modern societies are characterized by the predominance of *secondary organizations,* that is, large specialized and im-

personal associations like labor unions, corporations, farm cooperatives, political parties, universities, and churches. Unlike the family,
the secondary organizations have large numbers of members who
need not be in a face-to-face relationship, are joined by a voluntary
action of the prospective members, and carry on highly specialized
activities. Most of the former functions of the family are assumed
by the new associations (education by the schools, charity by the
state, religious instruction by the church, and exchange of produce
by the banks and market place). The state itself tends to take on
the character of these secondary organizations. It becomes large,
complex, impersonal, and increasingly rational. Old ideas of divine
right fall into disrepute, and more rational themes of legitimacy
(for example, popular sovereignty) come into vogue. The family itself
is grievously weakened and is based more and more on consent
and mutual interest.

After a period of evolution, the state expands to meet the needs
of an industrialized economy. The civil service, for example, cannot
fulfill its obligations as the closed preserve of a single family or
clan, but must recruit able people from all layers of society. As
Max Weber has pointed out, a modern bureaucracy is "rational,"
that is, recruits universally, boasts a system of tenure, grade classifications, and fixed salaries. Political conflict resembles the market
place itself: Each specialized group puts forth its offers and demands,
with the state acting as a broker. Individuals express their interests
primarily through the secondary organizations to which they belong.

Let us briefly summarize the differences between the two ideal
types. *Traditional* societies are characterized by: subsistence economies; face-to-face social structures in which the family predominates; cultural systems that emphasize heredity, devotion, and
mystery; and a highly personalized political system that is virtually
an extension of the joint family. *Modern* societies are the exact
opposite in all these respects. They are characterized by industrial
economies; complex and impersonal social structures; a culture that
emphasizes the values of science, knowledge, and achievement; and
a highly bureaucratized political system, legitimized through rational processes, like elections.

Typological analysis is only a first step in the study of modernization. In effect, it constitutes a checklist for the observer, pointing
to relationships among social, economic, cultural, and political factors that might otherwise escape attention. It also makes possible
an assessment of the pace and extent of modernization in any given
society. But the explanatory power of typologies is limited. The
complexities of world history, the rise and decline of great powers
and of civilizations, and the shifting balance of international power

cannot be reduced to a handful of sociological concepts. Modernization provokes crises to which there are any number of possible
reactions or solutions within a political system. It is perhaps most
fruitful to consider modernization as a complex process that produces a series of challenges to both modern and traditional societies.
How these challenges are met is the major concern of the student
of political change.

COMPARATIVE ANALYSIS OF MODERN POLITICAL SYSTEMS

All nations on the modern side of the scale may be compared in
terms of their distinctive experience of modernization. Each of these
nations at one time was traditional; in each case the traditional
society was undermined, and eventually displaced by new forms
of organization. As we have pointed out in the earlier introductory
essays, the process of modernization inevitably causes a series of
political crises. Whatever the nature of the traditional society and
whatever the nature of the modern political institutions (whether
one-, two-, or multiparty, presidential or cabinet, democratic or authoritarian) at least three political crises must be surmounted in
the course of modernization: the crises of legitimacy, participation,
and conflict management. The way in which these crises occur and
are dealt with is of great consequence for the functioning of modern
political systems.

The crisis of legitimacy is inevitable because of the close link
between political values and the systems they serve to justify. The
kind of values that permeate a traditional society, such as divine
right or rule by a hereditary aristocracy, must undergo modification
as that society is transformed. Throughout Western Europe, for
example, the breakup of feudalism was accompanied by a shift in
the basis of political legitimacy. Everywhere the rights of monarchs
were circumscribed and the power of parliaments increased.
Whether monarchy continued to exist with reduced prerogatives
or was replaced by a republic, the political systems of Europe sought
to justify themselves in some way as the expression of popular will
and national sovereignty. The crisis of legitimacy also involved the
status of the church, which was generally a bulwark of the traditional ruling classes.

A new but related crisis comes into being with the rapid growth
of industry. Power continues to be wielded by a landed aristocracy,
the church, and the wealthier strata. But new social groups, above
all the industrial middle classes and the working class, enter upon
the political scene. These classes are officially excluded from power
in the traditional society; they demand entry into the political sys-

tem; they gain this entry by organizing themselves behind and through political parties. How this is accomplished—through slow and successful integration, or with violence and grudging acceptance—makes a deep mark upon the political life of the country. In some cases the working class is never fully incorporated into the political system, and in countries like France and Italy large communist parties constitute a permanent opposition of principle. In communist systems the problem of integration is solved by eliminating the aristocracy, small peasantry, and middle classes as autonomous political forces.

Whether in stable parliamentary democracies, unstable parliamentary democracies, or authoritarian regimes, mature industrial societies pose grave problems for the political system. Specialized groups proliferate within both the middle and working classes; the scientists, managers, bureaucrats, military, and intellectuals compete with party leaders for a share of decision-making power. The state must organize itself so as to cope with these strong interest groups, integrate them into the political system, and satisfy their minimal demands. As the technology becomes more complex, the task of the political leaders requires more and more technical knowledge and competence, as well as the ability to manage the distinctive political tensions of highly industrialized societies.

Comparative analysis of modern political systems requires broad knowledge of their historical evolution. The student should compare the way in which each of the crises of modernization was handled in individual systems, and the extent of "carry-over" from one crisis to another. Many observers have suggested that the *timing* of the crises of modernization is of critical importance. Did these crises occur one by one, with a considerable period elapsing between crises? In these cases the political system has a greater opportunity to resolve them singly and thus acquire stability. Or were the crises "telescoped"? Did the political system have to confront the crises of participation and conflict management while the controversy over its basic institutions and values continued? In such cases a much greater load is placed upon the system, and it requires an immense collective effort to create dynamic, effective, and stable government. Special attention should be paid to the problems of mature industrial societies. Are similar techniques being used in all modern political systems in dealing with massive technological development, urbanization, and the maintenance of individual creativity in mass societies? Or are there significant differences between democratic and authoritarian systems? Are there differences between such parliamentary democracies as the United States and the countries of Western Europe? Between the Soviet Union on the one hand and China and Cuba on the other? Modernization theory thus provides

the student with a framework for inquiry; it is the starting point
for the formulation of hypotheses concerning political life in all
industrialized societies.

COMPARATIVE ANALYSIS OF DEVELOPING NATIONS

Modernization theory can also be used for a study of contemporary
trends in the developing nations. There is a clear tendency for these
societies to move from the traditional category into a *transitional
period* during which they acquire many of the characteristics of
modern society while retaining some traditional features. But it
is impossible to foretell the exact development of any of these societies. For example, the so-called uncommitted nations are doubtless
on the way to modernization. But there are two chief prototypes
of advanced industrial states in the world: the Western countries
(especially the United States) and the Communist nations (notably
the Soviet Union). Developing countries could pattern themselves
after either model of modernity.

Comparative study could usefully be focused on the decision-making or political elite: their social origin, position with respect to
the masses, technical or educational qualifications for governing,
and relationship with the important social groups within the nation
(for example, landowners, army, church, civil service, and intellectuals), and their characteristic ideologies. At least four different leadership types can be distinguished in the developing nations: traditional, liberal, authoritarian, and radical.

The *traditional* leaders derive their authority from historical
status and prestige, and from one predominant form of property—
land. They constitute a self-perpetuating group in that recruitment
comes from a small circle (either royalty or landowning nobility)
by virtue of birth. Their values vary from one system to another,
but generally reflect a family structure—the emphasis is on kinship,
loyalty, devotion, duty, and courage. They are averse to changes
that will endanger their economic and social position. They are
apt to react unfavorably to any economic or technological innovations that might weaken the political system. They insist upon the
preservation of prevailing modes of political recruitment and hence
are hostile to popular participation in politics. They are opposed
to industrialization and to its political and social implications.

The *liberal* leaders are in favor of "reforming out of existence"
the traditionalist-oriented economy, society, and political system.
They welcome industrialization and mass participation in political
affairs. They accept both the goals and the methods of the Western
constitutional democracies. Thus, the liberals desire political reforms, establishment of a constitutional order with guarantees of

individual rights, the articulation of interests within an accepted legal order, and the gradual displacement of the traditionalist groups from positions of power. They wish to create the proper conditions within which meaningful political choices can be made by the whole people. Recruitment of the liberal elite is usually from the professional and middle classes, particularly among those who have attended European and American universities. The traditionalists and liberals tend to be allied in their respect for property rights but split over the question of democratic reforms and modernization.

Authoritarian leaders, like the liberals, tend to accept democracy as an ideal or goal. But they do not believe it can be achieved by indiscriminate adoption of all features of Western systems. They distinguish between "formal" or "procedural" democracy (elections, parliaments, organized opposition, etc.) and "real" or "substantive" democracy (equal opportunity, economic development, moral regeneration). An active opposition only obstructs the efforts of the government to bring about "real" democracy, and hence must be suppressed. The emphasis is therefore on national unity and the direction of the efforts of the masses by an educated, informed, morally responsible elite. Frequently the hope is held out that the people, one day in the future, after rapid economic progress has been accomplished, will be ready for representative government of the Western type. Authoritarian leaders, like the liberals, come mainly from the professional and middle classes, and occasionally from the landed aristocracy.

The fourth type of leadership is *radical*. Inspired by a revolutionary ideology, the radicals are committed to drastic and rapid change of the economic and social structure. They organize their followers in a manner that will enable them to take the system by assault. The classic pattern is the single mass party led by professional revolutionaries, along lines laid down by Lenin. Radical leadership comes from the "alienated" groups, particularly the intelligentsia, and it appeals to the disaffected elements of the population—the peasants, the students, and the city workers. They are in favor of industrialization, but at the expense of the liberal values—individual rights, political freedoms, and private property. Above all they impose collective goals upon the total society, and discipline the masses in order to achieve those goals. The main differences between the authoritarians and radicals are of degree and social origin: the latter want more change more rapidly, with greater social control and discipline, and tend to be drawn from less favored social classes. The radicals are also much more suspicious of the Western powers, and tend to seek aid as well as ideological inspiration from the Communist camp.

The "benefits" of modernization have been felt throughout the world in the form of manufactured goods, moving pictures, radio broadcasts, and so on. All native populations have had their expectations aroused or modified as a consequence. The economic structure of traditional systems has been undermined. Land ownership is no longer a secure base for a political elite. New economic activities have created new social groups and stimulated others who view the traditional elite as a stumbling block on the road to further economic development.

Industrialization, however, is viewed only as a means for the attainment of economic goals and the satisfaction of wants. Its prerequisites—the development of skills, the training of the masses, the establishment of an orderly pattern of social intercourse, and particularly discipline and regular work in the factory—are understood only by a small group of political leaders. Industrialization is often equated with a vision of plenty in the foreseeable future and as such it becomes a potent political force. The discipline required for industrialization, however, is appreciated by very few, and perhaps only by the "radicals."

As the conflict develops over demands for industrialization, the political position of the traditional elite becomes precarious. Their legitimacy is brought into question. There follows a period of instability, overt defiance of authority, and sporadic uprisings. The new political leaders—liberal, authoritarian, and radical—vie for control. A limited number of alternatives for future political development present themselves.

One alternative is the maintenance of traditional social organization and leadership. This alternative, though always possible, is becoming anachronistic. Most of the traditional forces are fighting a losing battle for survival. The independence movement is associated with an ideology calling for social and economic reforms that are inconsistent with the interests of the traditional forces. Mobilization of the masses in the struggle for independence brings with it profound modifications in the economic and social structure. Change may be held off by a temporary alliance between the traditional and new leaderships and groups for the realization of independence, by the inability of one particular group to impose its ideology, or by foreign intervention. But the will for change in a society generally indicates that the emerging political elites will use every means available to eliminate the traditional leaders who are still desperately clinging to the last vestiges of their rule.

At a certain stage, the liberal elements come into sharp conflict with the authoritarian and radical elements. The liberals advocate a relatively slow pace of structural modifications and industrialization, technological improvements, a rising standard of living, the gradual training of managerial and labor groups, progressive land reforms, and involvement of the masses in politics through the extension of literacy and education. But these demands are made with little urgency and the envisaged manner of their implementation is permissive rather than coercive. Liberal elites attempt to create the conditions within which the individual can become capable of choice—always considered in the best tradition of liberalism as an individual act. The system should provide opportunities for the individual and only "hinder the hindrances."

The authoritarians and radicals, on the other hand, urge coercive and authoritarian practices in order to bring about quickly the same overall goals. Suspicious of the continuing strength of the traditionalist elements (particularly among the peasants), they insist on rapid mobilization of the masses in a manner that will wrench them from their former way of life. Distrustful of the colonial powers, they seek to industrialize rapidly by using their own human resources and by accepting aid from the Communist countries. This political leadership, therefore, uses force and not persuasion, seeks the outright organization of the masses rather than a gradual process of political education, stresses social discipline rather than general rules, norms, and guaranties of individual freedom.

In the contest for power, the liberal leaders are at a severe disadvantage. In relatively backward economies, the application of liberal economic doctrine does not result in rapid industrialization or structural change. Development of a market economy favors the merchant class and production of consumer goods, and fails to satisfy the pent-up demand of large social groups. Subordination of social goals to individual choice only increases the feeling of social injustice on the part of the masses. All too often, it leads to "private wealth and public poverty." Politically, liberalism has no slogan that can activate and mobilize the masses. Most important, liberalism as a social force fails to inculcate new social incentives for the purpose of industrialization. In brief, liberal elites are generally unable to reach the people, to capture their imagination, and to lead them into the modern era. On the other hand, the great advantage enjoyed by the authoritarian and especially the radical leaders is that they create a system of controls under which industrialization may take place.

Of course, it is impossible to predict the exact evolution of events in the developing nations. New forces may come to the fore, perhaps slowing down the tempo of modernization and permitting the traditional elite to rally. Industrialization may follow the Western historical experience and lead to the establishment of a legal order within which individual freedoms are guaranteed. The technician and the manager may win out over the party boss and the commissar—perhaps even in existing totalitarian systems! Indications are, however, that the new nations are departing from the norms and institutions of Western democracies. Liberal elites are finding it exceptionally difficult to attract mass support. Communism and Fascism seem to be models for the most dynamic leadership groups in the new nations, even though they may follow their own path.

Comparative study of change, revolution, and modernization obviously calls our attention to the dynamics of the political process. Are there any similarities in conditions that precede revolutions? Are the new nations in a "revolutionary" situation like that of France before 1789 or Russia before 1917? Comparative study may focus on specific social groups—the intellectuals, the working class, the peasantry—to see how they react to the traditional elite, and to what extent they are influenced by revolutionary ideas. Comparison should also be made of political evolution in the developing nations. Liberal elites are more successful in gaining mass support in such nations as the Philippines and the Ivory Coast than in Ceylon and Guinea. What factors account for these similarities and differences? Analysis of political change in both industrial and traditional societies is perhaps the most serious and challenging task of contemporary political science.

CHAPTER SEVEN

Modernization and Development

24

The Idea of Political Development

Harry Eckstein

From one point of view, the study of political development is a major area of achievement in recent political inquiry; from another, which matters more, it is a conspicuous failure.

What has been achieved is great and rapid growth. The study of political development, in contemporary form, started barely two decades ago.[1] In short order, an extraordinary boom occurred in publications on the subject. By 1975, a standard overview listed over two hundred pertinent works. Accretion became especially rapid after 1964, though it seems to have "peaked out" (at a high level of production) in 1970–71.[2]

The negative side is that the result is mostly muddle. The study of political development has all the traits of too-rapid, jerry-built

Source: Harry Eckstein, 'The Idea of Political Development: From Dignity to Efficiency," *World Politics,* July 1982, pp. 451–86. By permission. Article and footnotes abridged by the editors.

[1] The salient exploratory works are Rupert Emerson, *From Empire to Nation* (Boston: Beacon Press, 1960), and Gabriel Almond and James S. Coleman, eds., *The Politics of the Developing Areas* (Princeton: Princeton University Press, 1960). Among the pioneers, two others also stand out: Karl W. Deutsch, "Social Mobilization and Political Development," *Political Science Review* 55 (September 1961), pp. 493–514, and Lucian W. Pye, *Politics, Personality, and Nation Building* (New Haven: Yale University Press, 1962).

[2] Samuel P. Huntington and Juan I. Dominguez, "Political Development," in *Handbook of Political Science,* III, ed. Fred I. Greenstein and Nelson W. Polsby (Reading, Mass.: Addison-Wesley, 1975), pp. 98–114.

growth, and of its concomitant, "decay."[3] The muddle is especially pronounced where it does the most harm: in regard to the very meaning of political development. Even scholars who were conspicuous in pushing the boom along are now viewing the matter of definition with dismay. Thus, Huntington and Domínguez start their review of the literature with remarks about loaded and wishful definitions—an "alarming proliferation" of them—and the consequent "superfluity" of much work on political development.[4] It stands to reason that, if a concept is encumbered with many meanings, theories using it also will vary alarmingly, because they are not about the same thing.

The study of political development thus is at a critical juncture. One can let it decay further or, not much different, choose to abandon it—Frank Lloyd Wright's prescription for what to do about Pittsburgh (and, I think, Huntington's for political development). Or one can try a project in conceptual and, through it, theoretical renewal. In this essay, I develop a basis for renovation. Abandonment might, of course, be the wiser course. But the present conceptual muddle in studies of political development seems to me due to avoidable causes; the early explorers of the subject were getting at something worth getting at—if it was attainable.

. . . It should be obvious that the mysteries of modernity . . . still are very much with us. For a long time, in contemporary political inquiry, they were shifted to the Third World. But now, again, they arise in reference to ourselves: e.g., in the concerns with the nature and future of postindustrial societies, and their governability. Developmental thought was itself developed to deal with these puzzles. Surely, it is uniquely suited to do so; thus, it is sensible to take such thought seriously—that is, to try to construct developmental theory properly. Hence this section, as groundwork for the next.

The quintessential developmental theorist, Durkheim, best summarized the spirit of the developmental mode of thought:

> Every time we explain something human, taken at a given moment in history . . . it is necessary to go back to its primitive and simple form, to try to account for the characterization by which it was marked

---

[3] The term decay is used in Huntington's sense, as an antonym to "order." See Samuel P. Huntington, *Political Order in Changing Societies* (New Haven: Yale University Press, 1968), chap. I. Earlier, Huntington had used "decay" as an antonym to "development"; see "Political Development and Political Decay," *World Politics*, 17 (April 1965), 386–430.

[4] Huntington and Domínguez, "Political Development," p. 3.

at that time, and then to show how it developed and became complicated little by little, and how it became that which it is at the moment in question.[5]

I propose now to do this, in broad strokes, for the political aspect of human experience.

SKETCH FOR A REVISED THEORY OF POLITICAL DEVELOPMENT

The passage from Durkheim succinctly describes what is needed to renovate the idea of political development. A more detailed agenda of questions to be dealt with follows from the summary of the traits of developmental thought:

1. What conception of continuous growth can plausibly describe the long passage from primal to highly advanced polities?
2. What is the essential nature of polity in its "primitive and simple" form?
3. What forces make the "advancement" of primal polities toward "higher" forms ineluctable (or at least highly probable)?
4. What distinctive stages lie along the trajectory of political time? In what ways do these stages involve both quantitative growth and change in kind?
5. What forces move polities from stage to stage?
6. What do the answers to these questions imply for polities that are at present less developed, and for "advanced," modern polities?

1. What Conception of Continuous Growth Describes the Passage from Simple to Highly Advanced Politics?

I have argued that contemporary theories of political development are historically myopic. Even in Georgian England—hardly remote history—the traits now most widely associated with political development were still embryonic. Democratization was certainly not far advanced. The suffrage was severely restricted; leaders (e.g., M.P.s) either were nobles and gentry or their hand-picked clients, bound to serve their patrons' interests. In regard to

---

[5] Emile Durkheim, *The Elementary Forms of the Religious Life* (New York: Free Press, 1947), p. 3.

bureaucratization, administrative and judicial roles remained en-
tangled, nationally and locally; recruitment was highly ascriptive;
specialization and formalization were elementary. Among the more
familiar conceptions of political development, only the "clarification" of societal authority was mature, for the messiness of corporate jurisdictions had certainly been cleared up by the 18th century.

How, then, can one characterize a continuum of political time
on which the Georgian polity itself belongs to a rather advanced
period? Recall that such a continuum must involve quantitative
growth, and must be a "form" that can contain much variable content. Moreover, the dimension involved must be anchored in time
by minimal and maximal poles, one corresponding substantially
to rudimentary cases, the other a vision that links perceptions of
modernity to its remote and nearer past and, still more important,
to an approximated future.

I suggest that the most serviceable way to characterize such a
continuum is also the simplest: *what grows in political development
is politics as such*—the political domain of society. Through political
history, political authority and competition for politically allocated
values have continually increased. Using Durkheim's terminology,
we might regard this as growth in "political density," perhaps as
a special aspect of a growing "moral density." More and more political interactions occur, overall and in place of nonpolitical interactions.

To avoid confusion about what is being argued here, a conceptual
distinction must be made. One can think of "the political" as any
relations that involve, say, legitimate power, or conflict management, or the regulation of social conduct, and the like. In that case,
"politics" may simply exist throughout society and not be located
in any clearly defined social domain or institution. Or one can think
of "politics" as the functions and activities of such a concrete domain: that of the heads of societies, the princes, chiefs, or kings
(for, in its modern sense, politics is associated with government,
and government and social headship are synonymous). What I argue
is that, through political time, the "princely domain" has constantly
grown—increasingly penetrating society. And, in conjunction, political activities and relations in the less concrete sense have also
grown. Expropriation by "princes" and expansion of political activity occur in conjunction.

One pole of the dimension of political time thus might be called
the *social polity*. In the social polity, as a pure type, there exists
a "princely" domain: some institution of headship of society, chieftaincy, firstness. That domain, though, is little differentiated from
others, in the sense of having separate organizations and administrative staffs; it is anything but a subsociety—neither a "machine"

nor a "system" in itself. Above all, next to nothing is done by princes, at least as we understand political activity: there is almost no active princely management of society. The society is virtually all and the polity virtually nothing. Relations of power exist, regulations of conduct and of conflicts occur; but they do so throughout society, not in special relation to chieftaincy.

At the other pole is _political society._ In political society as a pure type, "private" relations have been wholly preempted by the "public" domain of the chiefs. The institutions of that domain are highly differentiated and separately organized; governmental officers and staffs constitute a large subsociety. That subsociety is a complex system in itself, while at the same time it permeates social life.

The passage from social polity to political society can be described summarily: The domain of princes, who at the outset do virtually nothing, has great, indeed irresistible, potential for growth: power resources. Over a long period, these power resources are gradually realized. The chiefs of society convert headship into primacy, and primacy into actual control—at first very slowly, then with gathering, ultimately runaway, momentum. The momentum results from the fact that, as power resources are converted, they are not used up, but in fact increase. As this process unfolds, growth in degree corresponds, at specifiable periods, to transmutations of type. In our own modern period, we approach a condition in which the distinction between polity and society has again become blurred—not because the public realm is minimal, but because it has virtually eliminated all privacy. This, though, is not an end, but itself a stage in a continuing process. The political society generates its own dynamics; and we should at least be able to discern the forces likely to move it, even if not yet where it is destined to go.

This conception of political time has been anticipated by other theorists. It parallels Durkheim's view of more general social development. The minimal pole of the continuum is grounded in the anthropologists' notion of "stateless" societies.[6] The conception of political development as expropriation is in Weber: the emergence of the modern state was, for Weber, a process of continuous expropriation by princes of "autonomous and 'private' bearers of executive power," resembling the expropriation by large capitalist enterprises of small, independent economic units. In his publicist essays written shortly after the Russian Revolution, Weber envisaged the further, accelerating, and continuous expropriation by the political domain

---

[6] See, for instance, Lucy Mair, _Primitive Government_ (Harmondsworth, Middlesex: Penguin Books, 1962), Part I—especially the chapter on "Minimal Government" (pp. 61–77).

of economic life, and then also of the more intimate, and the scientific and cultural, spheres—a remarkable prevision. The idea of "total" politics now also is a recurrent theme in works on modern democratic states. Sharkansky, for example, refers to runaway governmental growth "in response to incessant demands for more services," and repeatedly alludes to the erosion of the "margins" of formal government as a consequence.[7] The vision of political society informs especially the critiques of modern governments by perspective (if also hotheaded) "libertarians": Hayek, Oakeshott, Ellul, Nisbet, and others.[8]

2. What Is Polity in Its "Rudimentary" Form?

To sustain the thesis that what grows and changes in political development is the political domain *per se,* one must, first of all, characterize that domain in its "primitive and simple form," from which advancement proceeds. None of the many structural or functional notions that political scientists have used to define the essence of polity seem to make sense for its very early forms. What seems distinctive and universal to the princely realm in its simplest form is that its occupants and practices represent the very fact that society exists. Chiefs, khans, liegelords "embody" society. They are figures through whom societies personify themselves or sometimes (much the same) the ideal order of things imperfectly reflected in social order. They stand for the fact that a common, thus moral, life exists, and they celebrate the common life and make it compelling.

Surely that is fundamental in society, if anything is, because societies are nothing if not collective entities with which members identify—that is, define themselves. Thus, ceremony and symbolism—what Bagehot called the dignified parts of government—are not to be regarded as mere pretty trappings of power; nor are consummatory (expressive) and instrumental polities,[9] or "sacred" and "secular" ones, distinctive types at developmental stages. At the "simple" stage (thus, perhaps, always), symbolism is the very nature of the princely, not a guise. That is why, to us, the primal political domain seems empty. Primal "symbolic politics" does not stand for "real politics." It stands for society.

---

[7] Ira Sharkansky, *Whither the State?* (Chatham, N.J.: Chatham House, 1979), throughout.

[8] See, for example, Kenneth S. Templeton, Jr., ed., *The Politicization of Society* (Indianapolis: Liberty Press, 1979).

[9] These are Apter's terms; see David E. Apter, *The Politics of Modernization* (Chicago: University of Chicago Press, 1965), 24ff.

The evidence suggesting that primal politics is symbolic is considerable. For instance, in Schapera's study of sub-Saharan tribes[10] the following points emerge: The chiefs, as heads of societies, do not do much at all; they are simply marked out from others (e.g., in costume), exalted (in special rituals), subjects of rejoicing and of eulogies.[11] Tribes are often defined simply by identification with chiefs, not by territoriality or even kinship. Sometimes no abstract tribal name exists, only that of the chief. Often, tribal names are the inherited names of the ancestors of chiefs, and at times chiefs are named by the tribal name. In some cases, any injury done to a member of a tribe is regarded as an injury to the chief (as we talk about crimes against society). In short, the collective and the personal are thoroughly joined in the chief's personage. Much the same comes out in Lucy Mair's studies of primitive governments and African kingdoms.[12] Mair argues, indeed, that the substantive wielding of "power over the conduct of public affairs" generally is not so much the chief's or the court's function as that of lesser figures, for whom kings are mouthpieces. Lowie's work on North American Indian tribes makes a similar point.[13]

More important from the developmental point of view, we find this to be true also in the primitive condition of a prototypical advanced society—English society. (England may be considered as a good concrete approximation of an idealized case of continuous development: something close to an experimentally contrived universe—free of uncontrolled, deceiving contingencies—which any theory of sociopolitical development should fit closely.)

Anglo-Saxon society approaches the extreme of what I have called social polity.[14] If a "public sector" existed in that society, it could only have been that of king, *folkmoot*, and *Witan*. The king was principally a source of social identity, as were all lesser chiefs of

---

[10] I. Schapera, *Government and Politics in Tribal Societies* (London: Watts, 1956).

[11] *Ibid.*, chap. 4. Varying "powers" are associated with chiefliness (102ff.). I will refer to the most common below. But simply being "chiefly" is clearly the heart of the matter.

[12] Mair, *Primitive Government* (fn. 47), and *African Kingdoms* (Oxford: Clarendon Press, 1977).

[13] R. H. Lowie, "Political Organization among American Aborigines," *Journal of the Royal Anthropological Institute* 78 (February 1948), pp. 1–17.

[14] Dating poses difficulties here, but a sensible point in time for looking at the Anglo-Saxon polity surely is circa 900 A.D. A sense of an English society had crystallized out of the diverse identities of Teutonic tribal invaders and become personified in a single chief, Edward of Wessex. *Beowulf* remains the best primary source for understanding Anglo-Saxon life. See also J. E. A. Jolliffe, *Constitutional History of Medieval England* (New York: Norton, 1967), parts 1 and 2; Sir Frank Stenton, *Anglo-Saxon England* (Oxford: Oxford University Press, 1943); Dorothy Whitelock, *The Beginning of English Society* (Harmondsworth, Middlesex: Penguin Books, 1952).

the English tribes. His one significant activity was leadership in the common enterprise of making war, and practically no other common enterprise was engaged in. The *folkmoot* originally was not a council, but simply a local muster of warriors. By 900, local moots had pretty much been displaced by the *Witan*, a "national" council of "wise men." But the *Witan's* essential function simply was to advise the king on the nature of "unchanging custom." Here the primacy of society is especially evident: while the king embodied its consciousness of itself, the *Witan* kept him honest, as the guardian of its mores.

Much the most perceptive study of primal politics as I conceive it is Geertz's magnificent book on the 19th-century "theatre-state" in Bali, *Negara*.[15] Geertz alone seems to have grasped fully the critical significance of political ceremony and ritual: of the "poetics" of power as against its "mechanics"—as Bagehot alone discerned that the dignified parts of English government were not mere vestigial histrionics, but essential to its "efficiency." Geertz does temporize between regarding theatre as essential in polities as such and considering Bali an exotic alternative to politics as efficient power. But, at least in Bali, "power served pomp, not pomp power."

3. What Forces Make the Growth of Primal Polity Ineluctable?

Chieftaincy in primal polities is much indulged and rewarded, with awe and with goods. But that does not immunize chiefs (much less their retainers) against the appetite for mundane power; and, perhaps just because the chiefs are symbolic figures—awesome rather than powerful—power struggles are pervasive in primal societies. For the purpose of developmental theory, it is necessary to show next that in such struggles the princely domain has overwhelming resources for subduing rivals and enlarging its effective control over society. What, then, are its power resources?

By itself, the representation of societies is an essential resource for power—perhaps the one seed that is capable of growing into political society. Societies are requisites of personal identity, safety, the satisfaction of material needs. But, though necessary, they are highly intangible. They are complex even when they are rudimentary. Seeing them as networks, or complexes of roles, or fields of interaction, or patterns of exchange—these are major feats even for modern professionals. Even if the task of abstract understanding were less difficult, such understanding would hardly move affections,

---

[15] Clifford Geertz, *Negara: The Theatre-State in Nineteenth Century Bali* (Princeton: Princeton University Press, 1980).

which surely are needed for identification and legitimacy. So the personal symbols of society derive potential from the fact that they perform the most necessary of societal functions: making society appear "real."

It is true that there are other ways of making societies tangible. Primal societies, in fact, are always personified in their gods, through rites and magic. Thus, priests and magicians are the logical (and actual) main rivals of the chiefs for principal power. But the chiefs themselves are generally presumed to have special links to the supernatural, magical world—for instance, as rainmakers, healers, invokers of prosperity, possessors of sacred objects (fishing spears and the like), and as wielders of curses.

These links to the supernatural not only reinforce secular symbolism (or make it sacred), but also associate chiefliness and "potency," for the magical world is a world of fateful powers. Chiefs are also considered especially potent figures in the material sense of prowess. All societies have collective business of some sort—in primal societies, for instance, moving camp and herds. The function of making decisions about societal business naturally tends to be lodged in the locus of collectiveness. The one universal collective business of rudimentary societies is warfare: in defense against predatory others, for conquest (slaves, tribute, etc.), or, often, simply as a ritual. So chiefs, though they have rivals in heroes, generally are the main loci of potency as prowess. This accounts for the strange duty of chiefs in some tribal societies to be in good health, as well as for the use of wars of succession (in which the strongest survive), and for the frequent use of the phallus as a symbol of chieftaincy.

To exist, and to carry out collective enterprises, societies must, of course, be harmonious in some degree. Conflicts must be managed, quarrels mediated, crimes avenged. There is a universal social need for adjudication, and, again, a "natural" tendency to associate that necessary function with society's embodiments. The actual management of conflicts and deviance tends, in fact, to be decentralized and dispersed in primal societies—a matter of self-help in feuds, revenge, and exacting reparations. But the chief always has at least some vague special responsibility in regard to justice. For instance, we are told by Traill that a basic function of the Anglo-Saxon kings was to go about the kingdom putting down "evil customs." Traill's catalogue of judicial duties actually is a list of things kings could *not* do; and it seems evident that kings were little more than especially prestigious "oathhelpers.[16] Still, justice and chieftaincy had special, even if largely hortatory, links.

---

[16] H. D. Traill, ed., *Social England,* I (New York: Putnam, 1894), p. 134.

The moral, surely, is evident. The primal princely domain is ages removed from the monopoly of legitimate power. But where could there be greater potential for eventual monopoly than in a domain standing for society itself; for potency, military, and magic; and for justice? "Dignity" and "efficiency," granted, are obverse faces of politics—but also interchangeable resources.

4. What Are the Stages of Political Time?

The fact remains that in primal polities, whatever the chief's potential, one can barely detect an active public core. Our own political world could hardly differ more. At "our" location in political time, as stated, it is difficult to find anything that is clearly private. I am not referring to "totalitarian" polities, or only to those, but (less categorically) to the other typically modern form of polity: popular democracies. (Modern democracies, in historical perspective, simply are the gentler twins of totalitarian rule, mitigated by open competition, free communications, and a sense of rights and liberties—which, compared to earlier times, no longer really divides the public from the private, but is a sense of political decency.)

I have described the extraordinary pervasiveness of political authority in contemporary British society elsewhere, and need not dwell much on details.[17] To convey the flavor of the matter, suffice it to say the following: (1) The national government (as in other modern democracies) now directly controls about half of GNP, and indirectly plans, guides, and channels most of the remainder. (2) Parliamentary sessions, once convened only occasionally, fill up the whole available legislative work-year, and even this at the cost of large omissions—uncontrolled "executive legislation," and a severe decline in the role of private members. (3) The Cabinet has virtually disappeared; as I wrote in 1958:

> Cabinet functions have become dispersed to an almost unfathomably complex administrative and deliberative machinery. Decisions once made collectively in the Cabinet are now made by cabinet committees, by individual Ministers, bureaucrats, the Treasury, official committees, party machinery, and even private associations; and, most often, by interaction among all of these bodies. If power is concentrated anywhere in the British machinery of government it is concentrated not in the Cabinet but in this complex framework of decision-making.[18]

---

[17] See Samuel H. Beer and Adam Ulam, eds., *Patterns of Government*, 2d ed. (New York: Random House, 1962), chap. 10.

[18] *Ibid.*, p. 235.

One can argue that what mainly mitigates the darker aspects of fully politicalized society is the very inability to control such a concentration of functions, due to sheer diversity and overload. The gentle myths of liberal rule surely help, but perhaps not as much as the fact that monolithic authority itself is too large to manage. Privacy, in political society, is found in the interstices of authority; it is, perhaps, itself mainly a product of the structure of the public realm.

How did this transmutation to something close to "political society" come about? What lies beyond the primal polity's potential for growth? This is an enormous question, and we have not even the beginning of a plausible answer. As such a beginning, I suggest a six-stage process. The process is "logical" in that each stage manifestly is a condition for the next. The stages also make sense in the context of the English polity—our standard case for observing gradual, evolutionary "unfolding" (the literal meaning of *développer*) in politics. For this reason I will use English history—in gross summary—to exemplify the stages.

The Politics of Primacy.   I have already treated the first stage, primal polity, using Anglo-Saxon England to illustrate its nature. The second stage involves what might be called the struggle for, and achievement of, primacy. The forces that push polities to and through that stage (and later stages) will be discussed presently. Here, it must suffice to say that nothing in political development can possibly come before the clarification of a distinct public domain that, in regard to "efficient" functions, is minimally *primus inter pares*. Without this, there is nothing that may grow. One may suppose that the establishment of a realm of substantive primacy— one that involves more than symbolic headship—will not be a tranquil process, but will involve stubborn conflicts over domination and autonomy. Aside from chiefs, there are others who have politically convertible resources: religious, economic, and military. But, as we have seen, the chiefs generally have much weightier resources for providing political goods—not least, safety, in a context of continuous struggle among social domains: Hobbes's good, and no doubt the fundamental value.

This general stage fits, in England, the period of *feudal monarchy*, say of the 12th century. The feudal monarchy certainly was quite different from the Anglo-Saxon, despite the fact, generally agreed, that the Conquest caused no sharp break. The domain of the Angevin and early Plantagenet princes, to be sure, remained mainly on the level of symbol and pomp; its practical authoritative functions were sparse. What is most conspicuous about the period is struggle for "dominion" as such. The histories portray incessant turmoil. But the tumult was not about policy, in our sense. It involved competition about spheres of autonomy and subjection; and the fundamental source of that struggle was a lack of clarification and resolution of the functions of the great and small corporations of society— all authoritative in their own domains, and constantly striving to expand or protect them.

Corporate boundaries now, though, mattered for more than symbolic reasons. They mattered because the princely domain had begun to acquire a critical function: material extraction—a condition of all effective action, and thus an obsession in feudal monarchy. The Treasury preceded all other political institutions in development. The classic account of 12th-century royal "administration" is FitzNeal's *Dialogue on the Exchequer,* the exchequer being its one great administrative creation. It regularized the royal revenues, and the great pacification under Henry II was, at heart, a matter of reestablishing the central revenues in face of embezzlement by the barons. Extraction increased political "density," and the latter changed institutions.

Still, Henry's charter upon his coronation was little more than an assurance of liberties, grants, and customs. Petit-Dutaillis' study of feudal monarchy tells us that the King's *concilium* attended to "all sorts of business";[19] but, as to particulars, he lists only personal issues (e.g., marriages) and familiar matters of peace, war, loyalty, treason, and the administration of justice.

The last is important, however. Judicial activities now were much enlarged and wholly reorganized—coequal with pomp and war as the core of royal primacy. Indeed, aside from finance and war, the whole royal establishment now looked like a sort of national judiciary. The King's "prime minister" was the Chief Justiciar; the Curia had become a "normal court" for the kingdom, not just an occasional tribunal; the judicial circuits, administering Common Law, had been established; and central justice had largely expropriated the seignorial jurisdictions, of which only "a few islets" remained.

The feudal monarchy thus achieved, gradually, a considerable legal and extractive permeation of society, as a material basis for primacy. Contestation persisted for a long time, but in an increasingly muted, one-sided way. The nascent monopoly over extraction, the increasing practical responsibility for the management of conflicts, and the emergence of specialized institutions to handle these

---

[19] Ch. Petit-Dutaillis, *The Feudal Monarchy in England and France* (London: Adam & Charles Black, 1948), p. 128.

functions, realized a potential already present in the primal polity; but, more important, all this added to the growth potential of the prince's domain.

The "Prophylactic" Polity. Substantive primacy, especially when added to symbolic headship, is both gratifying in itself and a supremely valuable resource for acquiring additional resources. Once it is established, struggles for its possession inevitably occur. One of the fundamental tasks of politics is to institutionalize such struggles in order to defuse them—a basic function, for instance, of competition among political parties. But institutionalization is always gradual—a sort of subtheme of development. Early on, contestation for possession of the domain of primacy must involve— in greater or lesser degree—unregulated, brutal conflicts. Lacking institutionalization (or the transformation of real and deadly conflicts into ritualized competition) damage can be limited only by prevention: prophylaxis.

In the prophylactic polity, the overriding objective of the prince is to detect and disarm usurpation, while that of others is to seize or control principality. To protect principality, it is functional to place it in a tangible physical domain and to draw potential usurpers into that domain. Hence, the identification of primacy with the prince's court. It is there that the game of trying to get and keep primacy and its perquisites is played; politics turns inward.

To a degree, however, prophylactic politics must also reach out into society, further than before. Courtly politics cannot be wholly isolated, because the discontents of society might play into the hands of usurpers. Therefore—rather than for altruistic reasons—the princely domain begins to furnish something else that is valuable to society: a degree of controlled social order, as prophylaxis in everyday life against society's *misérables*. The result is both a qualitative change in the nature of politics and the increased penetration of society by its political domain.

In England, *the era of the Tudors* illustrates the stage. The late medieval and Renaissance political struggles in England increasingly had a flavor different from those of feudalism. They were epitomized, and pretty much ended, by Tudor rule, for which "absolutism" is an egregious misnomer. Nothing really was absolute. Rather, the Tudors—especially Elizabeth—successfully coped with conspiracies *within* the realm of princely authority. If anything authoritative was absolute it was courtly absolutism, which transformed Lords into mere courtiers. Concomitantly, political competition was courtly competition—scheming within the firm.

Nevertheless, one can discern a threshold in the permeation of society by authoritative policy. Outside of the royal palaces, authoritative regulation was still sparse; but before the Tudors (conflict management and extraction aside), authoritative space, outside its royal core, had been virtually empty. A good many histories refer to an abundance of "proclamations" by the Crown, and subservient parliaments and courts, in Tudor times. Elizabeth's parliaments did indeed pass 429 bills. The figure is often mentioned to impress. Actually, it brings out only the limitations of policy making. Elizabeth's reign lasted 45 years; nowadays, British legislative output runs to about a hundred bills a year. Much of Elizabethan "legislation" had to do with issues of diplomacy, foreign intrigues, war, and extraction. Some of the regime's authoritative activities, however, involved a novel extension of authority into society: the systematic maintenance of roads and bridges, the licensing of alehouses, controls over wages, the mobility of labor, entry into trades, dealings in commodities, interest rates, and—most familiar—a uniform law to care for the poor.

Growing political density surely is evident, especially since this reaching out into society supplemented unprecedented ceremonial activity (royal equipages and pageantry) and an even greater increase in foreign adventurism, war, and defense. The primacy of feudal monarchy clearly was now being put to use as a generalized resource. Perhaps this was a response to much-increased "social density": the manufacturing revolution in textiles, mining, ironmaking, and petty trades (perfumery, barbering, etc.)—a response, in general, to a busy society of promoters, speculators, patentees, dramatists, composers, astronomers, astrologers, physicians, surgeons, alchemists, sorcerers, explorers. What Black calls "the chaos of society,"[20] however, did not engender policy as an attempt to impose any sort of rational order. Rather, the point of authoritative "outputs" seems to have been an extension of the defusing of courtly intrigues: the prevention of social discontents and marginality that were potentially threatening to the security (and isolation) of the courtly domain. The increased permeation of society under Tudor rule aimed, above all, at prophylaxis: controlling vagabonds, dealing with food riots, limiting speculators, usurers, and drunkards. The Poor Law and the relentless pursuit of religious recusants are all of a piece in this effort. A valuable resource was now being hoarded—though not yet much used for additional gain.

The Polity of Interests. When principality no longer needs to be preoccupied with usurpation, but has been institutionalized at

---

[20] J. B. Black, *The Reign of Elizabeth: 1558–1603* (Oxford: Clarendon, 1936), p. 217.

least in accepted rules of succession, politics can turn outward for reasons other than prophylaxis. The primacy of a social domain above other domains and, even more, the "distancing" of courts from societies, inevitably lead to a conception of princely power and social order (not "orderliness") as being somehow unrelated. The initial extroversion of the princely domain thus can hardly be concerned with such matters as engineering social harmony or just distribution. In introverted politics, these are matters for natural order or divine ordination. When politics turns outward from the court, then, the purpose is initially not so much to manage society as to exploit primacy as a safe resource: the gainful use of primacy by privilege. In the polity of interests, competition overshadows majesty. Though it in no sense involves democratization, the arena of politics as competition becomes much enlarged and structurally altered. It still takes place in the court, but now also in institutions associated with the court (e.g., parliament) and, to a degree, in society. Through the "outputs" sought by patrons and their clients, the polity, as Durkheim would say, markedly "condenses." Royal administrative and judicial institutions become a rather complex "machinery" government.

In England, such acquisitive exploitation of established primacy—and through it the much enlarged penetration of society—is the essence of the Georgian period. [21] One sees the scope of the 18th-century British polity best in the activities of its local officials. The Justices of the Peace were broadly charged with collecting and delivering revenues; assuring the proper practice and flow of trade; looking after the poor, the food supply, prices, and wages; licensing brewers and drinking-houses; supervising goals; establishing asylums and confining lunatics; seeing to the lighting of streets, their paving, policing, and cleaning. All this required at least an embryonic differentiation of political labor—though bureaucratization had hardly yet begun. There were now distinct judicial and administrative sessions, distinct highway and licensing councils, as well as individual specialists, like road surveyors and constables. Late in the century, new statutory authorities, with special duties, appeared: for instance, turnpike trusts, corporations for administering relief to the poor, and, above all, a growing number and variety of improvement commissions.

This expansion of activities, and of organizations for performing

---

[21] The great work on the Georgian polity is Sir Lewis Namier, *The Structure of Politics at the Accession of George III* (New York: Macmillan, 1957); the standard history is J. Steven Watson, *The Reign of George III: 1750–1815* (Oxford: Clarendon, 1960); and the best concise political perspective on the period is provided by Samuel H. Beer, *British Politics in the Collectivist Age* (New York: Alfred A. Knopf, 1965).

them, was not intended to manage society. The overriding trait of the Georgian polity was that it was a marketplace of influence and spoils. The central level did not really manage society, yet there was extraordinary jockeying among parliamentarians and, as a result, ministerial instability. According to Namier, men went into parliament partly out of a sort of "predestination" (men of "political families"), but even more as clients looking after patrons' interests: as placemen and as purveyors and receivers of favors (there was, says Namier, a "universal . . . plaguing of Ministers on behalf of friends and relations");[22] to advance themselves in the military and administrative services or reap rewards from service; to obtain contracts, jobs, subscriptions, loans, and remittances. The Enclosure Acts and what Beer calls "canal politics" epitomize this extraordinary politics of interests.

The Politics of Incorporation and of Incumbency. When the domain of politics is used chiefly for acquisitive purposes by privileged groups, other groups will try to become incorporated into the game as players, rather than be excluded from it as passive victims. As the stakes grow (that is, the spoils increase) so, one may suppose, does the appetite for shares. Certainly the pervasive theme of early modern (19th-century) British politics is democratization. Tilly depicts the process as one in which excluded subjects first become "challengers," and then, through challenge, incorporated "members" of the polity:[23] voters, of course, and eligible to hold office. The transformation of challenge into membership occurs because the challengers have resources of their own that can be effectively mobilized—such as strikes, violence, and the like.

As the polity's membership expands, and thus becomes more diverse in interest, the political penetration of society necessarily grows rapidly in scope; when "civic incorporation" is virtually total, so is the politicization of social life—but not just in the sense of universal citizenship. Two other processes occur that rapidly transform social into political space. One is familiar: as new members are incorporated, the volume of political demands grows, and with it, the volume of outputs; with outputs, the network of committees, agencies, departments, boards, to define and deliver them; and, with such organizations, their own demands: "withinputs," as David Easton calls them.

Perhaps this chain reaction sufficiently explains the rapid devel-

---

[22] Namier, *The Structure of Politics,* p. 76.

[23] Charles Tilly, *From Mobilization to Revolution* (Reading, Mass.: Addison-Wesley Publishing, 1978).

opment of political society out of acquisitive politics. I would suggest, though, that a second process supplements the demand-response relation, and perhaps is more consequential. It bears at least a vague resemblance to the Tudor preoccupation with political prophylaxis. To put it starkly: political primacy in the modern polity clearly is more than ever worth possessing and keeping in possession; however great the resources of princes before, they were puny compared to the fully realized monopoly over legitimate power. The theater of political struggle, though, is no longer confined to the small stage of the court; it comprises society as such. Thus, the modern counterpart of coping with conspiracy in order to retain control over the princely domain is either mass suppression or the search for mass support (plus the special support of the more powerful, better organized interests). Mass support is elicited, at least in part, by going *beyond* responsiveness: by "redistributive" policies that make large public groups into clients—collective placemen. The unparalleled scale both of repression in authoritarian modern polities and of the political provision of all sorts of goods in welfare states serves the maintenance of incumbency. No doubt welfare policies and other distributions of benefits result from good intentions; but surely, they also provide benefits, in the form of political support, for their providers. At any rate, here is a parsimonious explanation of the substantial consensus on social policy in the contemporary British welfare state. The politics of incorporation leads logically to that of incumbency.

"Political density" during these stages grows rapidly toward its maximal pole. The vastness of the business done by the machine of government requires, as Durkheim realized, more and more internal complexity of structure, in large part just for keeping things sorted and coordinated; it requires the development of a political "system,"[24] which is not at all the same as a machinery of government. Structures of political competition also become highly organized and institutionalized networks of organizations. In gist, the pomp of primal chiefliness virtually disappears within the systems and networks of the polity.[25]

Two important questions should be raised about the abstracted

---

[24] I use "system" here in the manner of general and political systems theorists; the latter seem to me pertinent only—or anyway, chiefly—to "modern" polities. See, for instance, James G. Miller, "Living Systems: Basic Concepts," *Behavioral Science*, 10 (July 1965), pp. 193–237; David Easton, *A Systems Analysis of Political Life* (New York: John Wiley & Sons, 1965).

[25] The elevation of the leader in totalitarian polities can certainly be regarded as a reaction against the fathomless sobriety of typical modern political systems. It is, of course, more satanic than sacred. And surely the "system" uses the leader, perhaps more than vice versa.

stages to determine whether they indeed constitute a general developmental sequence. First: Do the stages occur, *mutatis mutandis,* in other longitudinal political processes, and do they furnish a good typology for the "cross-sectional" classification of polities in the present? If so, we can assert (in the manner of early exponents of the "comparative method"—Ferguson, Comte, Tylor, Morgan)[26] that typological differences among polities are basically developmental: viz., that there is history, not just histories. Second: Would a schematic treatment of political functions, goals, and structures by stages indeed show qualitative distinctions in each class, along with the quantitative growth of the political domain? These questions cannot be treated briefly; they are posed here as items on an agenda to follow up this essay.

5.   What Forces Move Polities from Stage to Stage?

In the preceding section, I have tried to show sequential connections between stages of political development: how the earlier stages are preconditions for those that follow, and how these, in turn, are latent in preceding stages. (An important, familiar issue for *praxis*— too large to be tackled here—is raised by the question whether stages can be skipped, without the occurrence of pathologies, and without regression.) This demonstration, though, says nothing about the forces that propel polities from stage to stage. We need at least a summary answer to complete our sketch for a theory of political development.

In developmental theory, one wants, ideally, to identify a general motive force that operates throughout developmental time (akin to physical inertia) and also special forces, generated in each earlier stage, which similarly lead to each later stage.

The general motive force at work in the sequence of stages I have described is surely the drive for the direct and indirect benefits of "efficient" primacy in and over society—the direct benefit of social elevation and indirect perquisites, such as material goods. That drive characterizes most directly the transformation of primal, ceremonial polity. The maintenance of primacy for getting other values follows in the polity of interests, and leads to the challenges that incorporate excluded groups in the domain of primacy. The possession of higher positions—primacy in the domain of primacy—animates political motion in the most advanced stage.

Although primacy-seeking is the essence of the initial developmental transformation of polities, it is clear that struggles for estab-

---

[26] Robert A. Nisbet, *Social Change and History: Aspects of the Western Theory of Development* (New York: Oxford University Press, 1969).

lishing an "efficient" principal domain are only resolved when an urgent societal need for such resolution arises. In the West, that need arose from the differentiation of society into distinct but overlapping "corporations" in virtually continuous collision. One may surmise, more generally, that an initial locus of efficient primacy will emerge when it is functionally critical to social integration that this occur—that is, when the integrative force of "mechanical solidarity" no longer works. The theatrical chiefs are destined to win struggles to perform the integrative function, and to reap its benefits.

If there is such a thing as "pure" power politics, it occurs when struggles for primacy have been resolved. Pure power politics is about possessing primacy, not about establishing it. Once the domain of the prince itself is safe, a different propulsive force emerges; we might call it resource conversion.

The results of converting political into other goods now come to pose a quite different, but again functionally critical problem of integration: not of society but of the political domain itself, for the sake of its effective operation. The need for political integration has two facets. As new groups are incorporated into the polity, the plethora of interests and demands they generate must be coordinated: in Almond's terminology, a need exists to aggregate interests, so that demands may be effectively pressed and responded to. More important, as society is greatly politicized through processes of civic incorporation, the machinery of government grows into a complex system; as a result, efficient management of the system itself must increasingly become a *sine qua non* of political goals, even exploitative ones. Without efficient political management, social life itself is imperiled, precisely because the polity pervades it; and, without such management, power itself is a chimera. In this way, we can see in political development a diminution, if not a metamorphosis, of pure power politics—and still avoid the "fault" of tender-mindedness.

Thus, while struggles for primacy propel politics throughout developmental time, at each stage they take different forms and are reinforced by special forces: forces of greed and, more important, forces generated by collective functional needs. These themes of politics—primacy-seeking, power-seeking, greed, and integration—are familiar. What is not familiar is the special roles they play at different stages of political development.

The process of political development moved by these forces is monotonic in two senses. I have stressed one—the politicalization of society. The long trajectory from social polity to political society can also be considered a modulation from "dignity" to "efficiency" (the most fundamental qualitative social change conceivable), and each stage of the process can be treated as a changing balance between the two. In parallel, polities change structurally from personage to court, to machine, to system.

CONCLUSION

The idea of political development, then, seems to me capable of renovation along the lines sketched. What I have tried to present is a design along proper "developmental" lines. The design is, and must continue to be, far from a completed theoretical structure. But if it proves to have merit, it helps to answer the final question raised above. It has important implications precisely for the issue that a developmental theory should illuminate: the puzzle of our own modernity. I will mention one such implication for a critical problem in modern political life.

We have lately heard much about a crisis of authority in highly advanced societies. The evidence is overwhelming that there is at least a malaise about authority. Strangely, that malaise seems to exist concurrently with the progressive growth of what people supposedly (and no doubt actually) want authority to be: decent, down to earth, participant, lenient, concordant, open to achievement. Might not the solution of this riddle lie in the "disenchantment" of theatrical politics (which moves affections), by rationally effective but too-drab systems? After all, society and polity remain intangible mysteries; the social sciences are devoted to their understanding. They have become all the more mystifying as they have grown in scale, density, and differentiation. At the same time, dignity has waned in relation to efficiency. More and more, our representative figures are capable but plain, managers but not princes: Fords, Carters, Wilsons, Heaths; in our families, schools, and workplaces, authority increasingly also has derogated rank. We want this, and it seems good; but can we live with it?

Perhaps that is what Weber saw when he forecast a political "polar night of icy darkness and hardness." Perhaps, too, the tension between the needs for what Weber called matter-of-factness and devotion is the force propelling us into the future of political time.

25

The Creation of Knowledge and Technique

David Landes

The heart of the whole process of industrialization and economic development is intellectual: it consists in the acquisition and application of a corpus of knowledge concerning technique, that is, ways of doing things. It is customary for economists to think of this corpus of knowledge as a common property of mankind, a pool into which any and all can dip at will. This assumption of general accessibility is subject, to be sure, to a significant constraint: the existence of secrets, which may or may not be protected by patent. The existence of such secrets is inherent in the character of knowledge, for knowledge is not given, it is created, and there is always a lag between the creation of knowledge or the exclusive application thereof by the creator and its communication or diffusion to others. Such secrets, however, are assumed by economists to be short-lived. Given the fact that the scientific knowledge from which technology is commonly derived is almost always published and widely disseminated, any attempt to keep a superior technique secret is bound to fail. If the technique yields a product, the object itself will almost invariably yield up its secrets to the expert eye. If the technique concerns a way of making the product (if it is what the economist calls a

Source: David Landes, "The Creation of Knowledge and Technique: Today's Task and Yesterday's Experience," *Daedalus* 109, no. 1 (Winter 1980), pp. 111–20. Special issue on "Modern Technology: Problem or Opportunity?" Reprinted by permission of *Daedalus,* Journal of the American Academy of Arts and Sciences. Footnotes abridged by the editors.

process innovation), imitators will either learn it (sometimes by illicit means) or find an equivalent or better substitute (there is more than one way to skin a cat).

All of these theses concerning the nature and accessibility of knowledge are based on the experience of what the economist calls advanced economies. These are those few industrial nations that not only possess technologies on the frontier of human knowledge and performance, but are capable of training new scientists and technicians to work in the context of that technology and push back that frontier. Short of that happy state, however, the great majority of the people in this world are barred from access to much of this knowledge and seriously hampered in the application of such knowledge as they have. They are barred by their lack of appropriate education and training, the inadequacy of their resources, and their inability to mobilize and organize such resources as they have. Small wonder that a demand for technological parity constitutes a key plank of the platform of the so-called New Economic Order.

The advanced nations have not been unmindful of the handicap imposed on less developed countries by their ignorance of, and inability to apply, more efficient techniques. Insofar as those who possess this knowledge and enjoy the fruits thereof feel a moral obligation to reduce the gap between rich and poor, or perhaps have a prudential interest in doing so, they have been especially sympathetic to projects for the dissemination of technology. For one thing, if I may be permitted a materialist observation, knowledge is the one commodity that can be given away without impoverishing the giver. For another, it is far cheaper to teach people how to do or make things than to give them the things or, even more expensive, give them the means to make things without really showing them how.

These projects for the dissemination of knowledge have thus far had only moderate success. To the extent that advanced nations have received students from less developed countries and offered schooling and training, they have often succeeded only in adding to their own pool of scientists and technicians. American hospitals are filled with foreign interns who find the practice of medicine more remunerative and satisfying in this country than in their own poor countries. This and other examples of "brain drain" have been the subject of much moralizing and hand-wringing; but it is hard for free societies to exclude those who have in a matter of years set down roots and have acquired skills and talents that are of value not only to society at large, but to hospital administrators and laboratory directors trying to balance their budgets.

Those who return home, moreover, are as much unprepared by

their experience as prepared. They know much more than when they left, but often it is the wrong knowledge—agricultural techniques, for example, that make sense in temperate climates but not in tropical. Even when they know what they need, they may lack the opportunity to apply their knowledge: equipment may be inadequate; collaborators, few and deficient; complementary services (especially governmental), wanting or maddeningly incompetent. Sometimes it may be easier to know less and try less than to know more and not be able to try or do.

As for those trained in the poor countries, they may be less surprised by the impediments to postgraduate application and achievement, but they are no less frustrated. For all the limitations of their training, they have been sorted out by it and raised beyond the knowledge, comprehension, and even sympathy of their compatriots. They, often along with those trained abroad, constitute a small elite in a sea of conservative custom, fearful self-interest, and ideological suspicion. The private sector is weak; the public, ineffective, if not corrupt and malign.

Finally, there are the foreign experts, many of them idealistic volunteers ready to accept unaccustomed hardships and difficulties in order to do something for those less fortunate. Their efforts are often rewarded by small and big successes, by the introduction of new and better crops, by a reduction in infant mortality, and by the adoption of more productive techniques. At their best, though, they are not the remedy for technological backwardness. History shows that foreign craftsmen and technicians can do wonders in teaching new ways to a less skilled population. Indeed, there is hardly an advanced country that has not benefited enormously from the migration of knowledge—the English, from the Flemish weavers of the so-called new draperies (16th century); the French, Belgians, and Germans, from British mechanics during their industrial revolution (19th century); the Americans, from a steady stream of skilled (as well as unskilled) settlers; the Japanese, from European technicians hired on during their drive to modernize under Meiji (post-1868).

The same record, however, tells us something of the conditions of effective absorption of foreign knowledge and techniques. Most of these countries kept their visitors, who constituted a permanent addition to the stock of human capital; and to the extent they did not or did not want to keep them (Japan is the best example here), made it a point to get from them whatever they had to teach before sending them on their way.

Now, this is surely the kind of task that confronts the less developed countries of our day. They will not hold their visitors, nor is it clear that they want to; and this means that they must learn these techniques and—much harder—learn to generate new techniques themselves. Outsiders may help, but unless the seeds of knowledge and invention take root, there will be a one-time increase in yield and then a return to the *status quo ante*.

This brings me to the key question: What does it take to learn and domesticate new knowledge and ways, to the point not only of doing things differently and better, but of finding new ways of one's own?

I shall not pretend to be able to answer that. (If I could, I would not be writing this article; I'd be changing the world.) But I think that history can give us clues as to what is *not* the answer. In particular, I think it shows conclusively that knowledge and skills are not disembodied things that can be propagated and received at will, like radio waves or light. Let me tell a story on that point.

In the 16th century European sailors began for the first time to undertake oceanic voyages on a continuing, regular basis.[1] They did so in spite of the fact that, once on the high seas, they could know their location only approximately, and that mistakes on this score could cost them their lives. Of the two coordinates that defined their position, they could calculate only the latitude with any precision. Longitude had to be more or less guessed at by a procedure known as dead reckoning: the officers would keep track of the ship's course and speed, and work out its presumed location at the end of each day's sailing. Since estimates of speed were made only every two hours or so, and then with gross margins of error (a floating object was thrown overboard, and the time it took to pass from one observation point to another was measured by the recital of some standard bit of prayer or verse),[2] dead reckoning could be seriously misleading. Sailors making for small targets in wide seas learned to play safe by aiming for points well to the east or west of their mark and then running the latitude to their destination. Even that was not enough, and the annals of sailing are dotted with tales of ships lost because their crews were lost.

For maritime powers of Europe, this was a costly weakness.

---

[1] Oceanic navigation goes back earlier, of course. But these voyages were the product of accident or feats of derring-do, with the exception of the Norse leaps to Iceland and Greenland and archipelagic travel in the Pacific. It was only with the establishment of normal trading and administrative connections to Asia and America that one can speak of oceanic sailing as a continuing, regular activity.

[2] Later, this technique was much improved by making use of a log and sand clock. The log was thrown astern and unwound a rope tied with knots at regular intervals. At the end of the time marked by the sand clock (far more accurate, obviously, than some verbal formula), the knots run out were counted and converted to speed, that is, distance over time. To this day the knot continues as a measure of nautical speed.

Ocean-sailing ships were immensely valuable, in themselves, for the crew that manned them, for the cargoes they carried. Small wonder that Philip of Spain offered in 1598 a fabulous fortune to the person who would discover a way of determining longitude: a prize of 6,000 gold ducats, a life pension of 2,000, and a further gratuity of 1,000—the equivalent of millions of today's dollars. No one won the prize, though the scientific principle on which such a method might be based was well known. The rotating earth, after all, is a clock, so that differences in longitude translate into differences in time and vice versa—as Gemma Frisius had pointed out a half-century before. Since the time where one was could be determined by astronomic observation—the sun's passage of the meridian, for example—one needed only to have a clock precise enough to keep the time at another place of known longitude, and to convert the difference in time into a difference of distance.

There was no one in Spain, however, or anywhere else at the time, capable of building such a clock. The Spanish government paid smaller, but substantial, sums to numerous postulants who pretended to be well on the way to a solution, some of them cranks promising the navigational equivalent of the philosopher's stone. In the end Spain gave up: necessity may be the mother of invention, especially if backed by money, but there is no substitute for the kind of environment that generates novelty.

Over the next century and more these encouragements and enticements were imitated by the governments of Venice and Holland, in vain, and finally by those of England (Act 12 Queen Anne, 8 July 1714) and France (1716). The English prize was particularly generous: £20,000 (say $6 million today) for a method accurate to within half a degree of arc, or 30 nautical miles. By this time horology had made revolutionary advances. The invention of the pendulum clock (Huygens, 1660) had made possible time measurement to the fraction of a second, thereby enhancing enormously the effectiveness of astronomical observation. But because of the rolling motion of ships, pendulum clocks proved unusable for the determination of longitude at sea. A comparable advance in the production of smaller timepieces, the use of a coiled spring to govern the to-and-fro motion of the balance, whose beat is the heart of the timekeeping mechanism (Huygens, c. 1675), held out more promise as a controller or governor. But major sources of variation, hence imprecision, remained, so that some of the leading scientists of the time gave up hope of a horological solution. None less than Isaac Newton, commenting in 1721 on a proposal to solve the problem by "watch works of new construction," noted discouragingly: "It is not to be found at sea by any method by which it is not to be found at land. And it is not yet found at land by Watchwork."

The great pundits may have been skeptical, but some clockmakers and watchmakers were not. The challenge was accepted by a number of these in England and France, at least one of whom, Henry Sully, gave all else up to devote the rest of his life to the invention of an effective "sea clock." In the end, though, it was not a professional clockmaker who won the prize. Rather, it was an autodidact, a carpenter-son of a carpenter, John Harrison of Barrow, a tiny, isolated hamlet in north Lincolnshire, near the mouth of the Humber. Harrison, who was certainly a genius, taught himself to make clocks, using wood for plates and wheelwork, instead of the usual brass. He also so impressed one of the traveling clergymen who ministered at the local church on Sundays, that he lent him a manuscript copy of lectures on natural philosophy by Nicholas Saunderson, Lucasian Professor of Mathematics at Cambridge; and it is clear, from the careful copy Harrison made of text and diagrams, that he learned much from and was much guided by these in his further work in chronometry.

To make a long story short, Harrison succeeded over a period of some 30 years in building a timepiece accurate enough to satisfy the conditions of the prize (completed 1759, tested 1761). To do this, he had to solve a large number of difficult technical problems, which he did in the most ingenious but also the most idiosyncratic manner. His first three models were Rube Goldbergian in their size and complexity, far too cumbersome ever to serve at sea; but anyone who sees them working in the National Maritime Museum in Greenwich cannot but be awed by their craftsmanship and artistry. And then he brought out his No. 4, the clock with which he won the prize, a triumph of miniaturization, only five inches in diameter, with an entirely new array of solutions to these same problems.

Interestingly enough, these solutions never took with other makers. Harrison's devices were too difficult or costly to build, even when understood. But his contribution lay in showing that a marine chronometer was possible, that the job could be done. The most gifted horologists of both England and the Continent made it a point to examine his mechanisms and were inspired by them to undertake their own researches and experiments. They found other answers, which proved definitive; but the honor for the great breakthrough belongs to Harrison, the self-taught nonprofessional.

One last aspect of this story deserves notice. The principle of the escapement device that is at the heart of all mechanical marine chronometers was discovered by a Frenchman, Pierre Le Roy; but its improvement and application on a production basis was largely the work of Englishmen, in particular John Arnold and Thomas

Earnshaw. And although the French learned to make some of the finest chronometers to be found anywhere, it was the British who came to manufacture the great majority of these instruments. They had the largest market—the biggest navy, the biggest merchant marine. Invention may follow genius, but production follows demand.

I have told (retold) the story of John Harrison and the marine chronometer because it illustrates some of the circumstances that condition the diffusion and invention of knowledge. In particular, it emphasizes the close links among comprehension (the ability to understand and absorb), application, opportunity, and the larger cognitive and social environment. Spain, for all its priority in oceanic navigation, was in no position to experiment and invent in this sphere. It lacked the craftsmen, in part because intelligence and skill gravitated in Spain to other, more honorific occupations. It lacked a base of interest and experience in time measurement, which was far more important to merchants and manufacturers (as in England) than to conquistadores, encomenderos, and caballeros; also, for a variety of reasons, to Protestants than to Catholics.

To be sure, John Harrison was something of a sport; his achievements testify to the importance of the personal, accidental factor in history. But his career was made possible by contacts with the world of science even in his isolated Lincolnshire village; and when he went to London, he found the kind of comprehension and support that come only with sympathy and knowledge. He was fortunate enough to find in George Graham, the leading watch- and clockmaker of the day, a man of uncommon generosity, of spirit as well as pocket. But Graham was not so exceptional that he does not convey something of the openness and mutual awareness that characterized the scientific and technological community of the time and place.

All of this, in little, exemplifies the general characteristics of European technology from the Middle Ages. Away back then, in a time that historians had long portrayed as miserably poor and backward. Europeans were quick learners and improvers of techniques from any source. Building on a long-forgotten or neglected legacy of technique from classical antiquity, with additions imported by the so-called barbarians, or acquired from more advanced cultures to the east, they succeeded in developing by the 14th century— certainly by the 15th—a corpus of knowledge and skills that not only put them far ahead of their teachers, but conferred on them a decisive superiority of power. It is on this basis that Europe changed from a hapless victim to global aggressor, from a poor backwater, obliged to make its balance of payments in slaves for want of marketable exports, to the affluent workshop of the world.

The explanation of this extraordinary turnaround and the subsequent divergence of the West from the Rest is still a matter of inquiry and debate. The economic expansion and development in themselves have usually been accounted for in Smithian terms—as the natural consequence of restored order and security. Trade was advantageous, so the Europeans traded; the rest followed.

Even if this were enough to explain what Robert Lopez calls the commercial revolution of the Middle Ages, however, it will not tell whence this inventiveness, this growing interest in novelty, this cumulative emulation in ingenuity. Other societies have known moments of commercial prosperity and economic expansion, yet they have not taken this course of sustained technological advance.

Some of the answers to this question have stressed the special character of medieval political institutions. In *The Unbound Prometheus* I noted two of these. The first was the political fragmentation, which made for rivalry among competing units and led rulers to accept the alliance of the bourgeoisie, grant substantial autonomy to cities and towns (unknown anywhere else), and encourage and support those technicians, scientists, and artists whose work could redound to their prestige and advantage. Second, and related to the first, was the early recognition of rights of property, which afforded inventors and entrepreneurs security in the enjoyment of the fruits of their labor and wealth.[3] The contrast with other societies in this regard was striking. Listen to Sir Thomas Roe, ambassador of James I to the Mogul emperor in India (1615): "Lawes they have none written. The Kyngs judgement byndes. . . . His Governors of Provinces rule by his *Firmanes*. . . . They take life and goodes at pleasure."[4]

Yet such factors are surely only part of the story; and, indeed, one would not have to be a Marxist to turn some of this around and argue that it was the successful bourgeoisie that made the property rights and not the reverse.

Another significant element of the story was the role of the Christian church, particularly the monastic orders, which constituted highly productive agricultural and industrial communities organized not for absolute self-sufficiency but for economic autonomy. Their ranks included some of the best mechanics and architects of the time; their shops were schools for skill and technique; and

---

[3] The latter point has since been made by Douglass North and Robert P. Thomas, the keystone of their analysis of European economic development. See *The Rise of the Western World: A New Economic History* (Cambridge: Cambridge University Press, 1973).

[4] Wm. Foster, ed., *The Embassy of Sir Thomas Roe to the Court of the Great Mogul, 1615–1619*, 2 vols. (London: Hakluyt Society, 1899), vol. 1, p. 123.

their dispersion throughout Europe was a strong force for the diffusion of knowledge.

Once again, though, the existence of the institution is not in itself an explanation. The question remains: Why this behavior, which contrasts sharply with that of other religions and even with the Eastern branch of the Christian faith. Without attempting a process of endless regression, the answer to that lies in the realm of values and attitudes: the choice of activism over the contemplative life (Martha over Mary), the Benedictine equation of work to prayer (laborare est orare), a paradoxical concern to soften the pain of labor, the Judaic desacralization of nature, and others still to be explored.[5]

The values of the monastic orders were (became?) those of a creative minority of the population as a whole. Why this was so, I am not prepared to say: people learned from the Church; the Church learned from the people. Too many—the vast majority—of the inventors, innovators, and doers of the Middle Ages are unknown to us. But what has come down to us, largely as a result of recent research, is the sense of a growing community of savants and builders and mechanics (homo faber), communicating with one another, copying and improving, climbing by standing on the shoulders of those who came before, tingling with the excitement of achievement. Lynn White cites a sermon preached by the Dominican Fra Giordano of Pisa in 1306, singing the praises of invention:

> Not all the arts have been found; we shall never see an end of finding them. Every day one could discover a new art . . . indeed they are being found all the time. It is not 20 years since there was discovered the art of making spectacles, which help you to see well and which is one of the best and most necessary in the world. And that is such a short time ago that a new art, which never before existed, was invented. . . . I myself saw the man who discovered and practiced it, and I talked with him.[6]

It is this turn of mind, this excitement and pleasure, this Faustian passion even within the bosom of the Church that goes far to account for the peculiarity of European technological development. For better and worse: the same impulse that gave us eyeglasses, and added years of useful study and work to some of the best minds and most skilled hands of the age, also gave us gunpowder and firearms. (The Chinese used powder in their fireworks; the Europeans borrowed it, improved it to increase its explosive force, and used it in cannon.)

---

[5] See especially Lynn White, Jr., "Cultural Climates and Technological Advance in the Middle Ages," *Viator: Medieval and Renaissance Studies* 2 (1971), pp. 171–201.

[6] *Ibid.*, p. 174.

And it is this turn of mind—or some approximation to it—that I would argue is a prerequisite not only for the diffusion of technology, but the ability to generate technology in preindustrial societies.

What does that mean for the education in technology of the less developed countries, with which we began? I am afraid it may seem at first sight to imply a counsel of despair: if a society does not have the kind of spirit that generates technology, it will not absorb technique or knowledge. But social scientists, no less than natural scientists or engineers, do not like counsels of despair. They prefer to think that problems have solutions, that tasks are made to be done, hence, that the diffusion of technology is everywhere feasible. If the ability to assimilate and generate knowledge is linked to the value system of the society, why then, we must find ways to inculcate and nurture the right values.

Unfortunately, it has proved easier to transfer capital, materials, and labor than values or even knowledge. It is not hard to know what to teach; the questions are: How? To whom? On what level? Should we build a broad base? Concentrate on elites? Let me attempt some first approximations to answers on the basis of the Western experience.

1. There has been a shift from learning by doing to learning in school. The first centuries of European technological advance built on empirical experience. Apprentices learned at the bench, alongside trained workers and masters—the whole process often organized and regulated by craft guilds. Bench learning never disappeared—it is still important today—but from the 18th century on, it has been increasingly confined to skill-intensive branches of hand manufacture or to a complementary role, taking the products of school training and fitting them for the special demands of a given job.

The growing emphasis on school learning reflects, first, the changing content of technology: the newer branches of production especially (chemicals, say, or anything connected with electricity) use techniques more esoteric, less apprehensible by observation and common sense than the older branches (textiles, machine building, and so on). Second, schooling offers the possibility of training more people faster and for a wider range of activities. Bench learning tends to be job-specific; school learning can be adapted to a variety of applications. It is no wonder, then, that within Europe the so-called follower countries, those that wanted to emulate Britain in the course to industrialization, came to rely far more extensively than the British had on formal school instruction.

2. These educational programs have always been highly selective in character. They have built on a broad base of literacy and

numeracy, but elementary schooling as such has been important, not for its direct contribution to economic performance, but as training in citizenship and as a device for the recruitment of talent. Other things being equal, the bigger the pool one draws from, the better the chances of finding gifted and original scientists and technicians.

3. The European achievement has always rested on a close alliance between science and technology, between theory and application. Indeed, until fairly recent times it would have made little sense to distinguish between those two modes. The scientists (that is, those whom we would call scientists) were invariably engaged in applications; indeed, derived most of their theoretical thought by reflecting on observation and experience. The technicians drew on what they knew of the corpus of scientific knowledge and added to it by study (like Harrison) and personal consultation. Even after scientific training and procedure separated themselves from application and engineering, and so-called pure science was set aside (above?) as something special, the old ties remained important. Industry in advanced countries has continued to treat faculties of science as an intellectual resource; and these same faculties have given numerous gifted students and teachers to the ranks of industry and enterprise.

4. European performance owed much to an atmosphere of competition and emulation. There have always been multiple points of initiative, of creation, imitation, improvement. This was only partly due to the political fragmentation; it was also inextricably tied to a system of free enterprise.

5. This atmosphere of competition and emulation has been, in my opinion, a most powerful force for the sustained enthusiasm, even joy, of the European (Western, Japanese) research effort. Because of it, the pursuit of knowledge and its application have yielded great psychic as well as material rewards. We may still not be able to account for the origin of this *Neuerungsfreudigkeit,* this joy in novelty, but its persistence clearly owes much to its agonistic character.

What are the lessons in all this for the less developed countries of today? Their principal weakness lies in their inability to find the equivalents of competition and enthusiasm. The first three conditions are difficult enough, but at least one can see there the outline of an educational strategy. But the latter conditions are as much political as economic and fly in the face of all the prevailing trends and predilections. To be sure, it is not hard to postulate nonmarket (socialistic) substitutes for the stimuli and incentives of freedom and competition: loyalty to a social or national ideal (also present in a market economy such as Japan); bestowal of awards and rewards from above (the Legion of Honor or the numerous Soviet prizes and privileges); to say nothing of the power of a disinterested curiosity and creative energy.

But all of that is a promissory note without a maturity date. The historical record shows that, so far, the only nations that have generated an autonomous and creative technology have been those characterized by freedom of initiative and enterprise. The one apparent exception, the Soviet Union, was able to build on a substantial educational and industrial base inherited from the Old Regime. China may yet prove to be a second exception, though it too has had much more to work with than most of the less developed countries in Asia and Africa.[7]

These have their task cut out for them. We can help, but in the last analysis, this is one aspect of growth and development that each society has to accomplish by itself, from within.

---

[7] In this regard, note the recent Chinese development of the technology and manufacture of optical fibers, "virtually without outside help." "Jumping a Century," *The Economist* 273 (7107) (Nov. 17, 1979), pp. 105–6.

26

The Ethnocentrism of
Social Science

Howard J. Wiarda

The proposition advanced here is that the vast bulk of our social science findings, models, and literature, which purport to be universal, are in fact biased, ethnocentric, and not universal at all. They are based on the narrow and rather particular experiences of Western Europe (actually a much smaller nucleus of countries in central and northwest Europe) and the United States, and they may have little or no relevance to the rest of the world. A growing number of scholars, particularly those who have had long research experience in the so-called developing nations, have now come to recognize this fact; and among others new efforts are being made to reexamine the very "Western" experience on which so many of our social science "truths" and models have been based. Because these verities are still widely believed, however, by many scholars and policymakers alike, the ethnocentric biases and assumptions undergirding them need to be examined and their implications for research and policy explored.[1]

Source: Howard J. Wiarda, "The Ethnocentrism of the Social Science Implications for Research and Policy," *The Review of Politics,* April 1981, pp. 163–97. With permission of *The Review of Politics,* University of Notre Dame. Article and footnotes abridged by the editors.

[1] The themes treated here complement those developed in Reinhard Bendix, "Tradition and Modernity Reconsidered," *Comparative Studies in Society and History* 9 (April 1967), pp. 292–346; reprinted in Bendix, *Embattled Reason* (New York, 1970). The present essay goes considerably beyond Bendix's argument, however, develops some distinctive propositions, and elaborates more far-reaching conclusions.

* * * * *

THE NATURE OF THE WESTERN BIASES

To most of us a liberal arts education is something familiar, comfortable, an integral part of our intellectual upbringing. It shapes our thinking, our attitudes and our intellectual preconceptions. However much our liberal arts heritage is celebrated, nonetheless, we must also recognize the biases inherent in that approach. Indeed, it may be that it is the very nature of our liberal arts focus that lies at the heart of our present dilemma and of our incomprehension of Third World nations. For as presently structured liberal arts education is essentially *Western* education, the Greco-Roman and Judaeo-Christian traditions and European history, from which derive a set of concepts, ethics, and governing norms and experiences that have their bases in the Western background and that may have little reference to or applicability in other global areas. Although it is understandable that those who inhabit the West should structure their educational system as an appreciation of their own history and culture, we must also recognize such training for what it is: traditional liberal arts education is essentially the first "area study" program.

Our concepts of "justice," "fair play," "good government," "progress," and "development" are similarly Western concepts. The latter two terms imply a certain unilinearism and inevitability in the evolution of man's social and political institutions. The former three imply some shared expectations as to the social and political institutions and concomitants that are supposed to follow from industrialization and economic development. So long as we could divide the world into two parts, Western and non-Western, and so long as we assumed, à la Hegel, Marx, or W. W. Rostow, that the non-Western world would inevitably follow the same developmental path as the West ("the developed world shows to the less developed the mirror of its own future"), our social science assumptions rested easily and comfortably. By this point, however, it is abundantly clear that these conditions no longer, if they ever did, apply. The world cannot be so simply divided, and it seems obvious that the developmental experience of today's emerging nations cannot repeat or mirror the experience of Western Europe. Our social science assumptions, based so heavily on the European experience, therefore require close reexamination as well. . . .

It is one of the contentions of this essay that such concepts as "development" or "modernization" must be re-recognized for what they are: metaphors, poetic devices, shorthand tools, abstractions that have some importance in defining, outlining, or describing reality but that should not be mistaken for reality itself. Not only are they metaphorical devices with all the limitations for describing reality that implies, but they are *Western* metaphors which may or may not (most likely the latter) have relevance to the non-Western world. Let us examine these propositions in terms of three major disciplinary areas of particular importance, both to the study of development and to our understanding of the Western biases therein: political theory, political sociology, and political economy. . . .

Political Theory

. . . To assert that the great tradition of political thought with which we are familiar is of less than universal applicability and that there are major geographic and culture areas, including within the West, that are entirely neglected in our political and social theory courses is to imply that there *is* something worth studying in these other areas and traditions. That is a difficult proposition to demonstrate to those who have always thought in Eurocentric terms, and it helps explain why so many of those studying other areas spend much of their professional careers defensively seeking to justify to their colleagues why their areas may be just as profound and complex, with as many important research implications, as Britain, France, Germany, or the United States. It is a long, uphill battle which is still only partially won but seems to be gaining added momentum due to the relative decline of these core areas in recent years and the corresponding increase in importance of such previously neglected nations as Brazil, China, India, Iran, Mexico, Nigeria, and Tanzania. In my own research and writing I have tried to show the continued importance of Iberian and Latin American organic-corporatist thought and sociopolitical organization, to present this as a viable alternative to the usual liberal-pluralist models with which we look at these areas, to understand Latin America, in the words of novelist Carlos Fuentes, as a distinct *civilization* and not as a series of agreements about tomatoes (or coffee, sugar, or bananas). In other quite distinct cultural and national settings, comparable studies are now appearing or being rediscovered of traditions of thought, law, and social and political organization that were previously ignored and remain largely unknown but which are probably at least as important as the European ones for analyzing these nations' unique developmental processes. It is not our purpose here to describe these alternative traditions in any detail but merely to note that they exist and to point readers toward some of the literature.[2]

Political Sociology

Political sociology demonstrates many of the same biases as does political theory, and is probably more dangerous because sociology is taken more seriously than political theory. Indeed an entire generation and more grew up on the development sociology literature of the last three decades, a body of literature that is as narrow, particularistic, ethnocentric, and Western-biased as the theory just analyzed. .

I wish to suggest that the empirical evidence does not support the claims to universalism and inevitability put forth by the major Western theories of sociopolitical development concerning the impact of industrialization on the broader social system.[3] The transition from agraria to industria and such factors as increased population, urbanization, the separation of place of residence from place of work, coupled with rising occupational differentiation and specialization have tended *in the West* to have brought specific kinds of changes in familial, religious, political, and all other major areas of social organization. It is for this reason, and because at that time the sociologists and political economists who analyzed these changes were themselves exclusively from that area, that the specifically Western social and political concomitants of industrialization came to be incorporated into theoretical conceptualizations of the change process per se. Given the historical context (the mid-to-late 19th century), the fact that northwest Europe experienced these mammoth changes first, and particularly at that time the lack of any non-Western experience with the transition to an industrial society, one might well say that the Western social adaptations occurring then almost *had* to be closely associated with a more general and presumptively universal theory of development and modernization.

The Western bias pervades the work of the great figures in sociology. For example, Weber's and Tawney's work on the mutual influ-

---

[2] For starters see Paul E. Sigmund, ed., *The Ideologies of the Developing Nations* (New York: Praeger Publishers, 1972); W. A. Beling and G. O. Totten, eds., *Developing Nations: Quest for a Model* (New York: Van Nostrand Reinhold, 1970); Howard J. Wiarda, *Politics and Social Change in Latin America: The Distinct Tradition* (Amherst, Mass.: University of Massachusetts Press, 1974).

[3] The analysis here and in the next three paragraphs derives in large measure from Thomas O. Wilkinson, "Family Structure and Industrialization in Japan," *American Sociological Review* 28 (October 1962), pp. 678–82; and his *The Urbanization of Japanese Labor* (Amherst, Mass.: University of Massachusetts Press, 1965).

ence of religion and economics in the growth of rational capitalism, Toennies's *Gemeinschaft* and *Gesellschaft,* Durkheim's mechanical and organic solidarity, and the mass society concept developed by MacIver are major examples of analyses concerned with particular aspects of a particular *Western* cultural history. The development literature was largely grounded on this same set of concepts and understandings, generalizing unduly from what was a narrow and limited historical and cultural experience. There is no reason to assume that in other culture areas the same sociopolitical concomitants of industrialization must necessarily follow. Students of non-Western or partly Western areas, whose development is taking place in a quite different context, must face the more difficult task of distinguishing between the processes and dynamics of industrialization *and* the social and political changes accompanying these which may take quite different and varied directions from those of "the West."

Not only are the timing, sequences, and international context of development different, but non-Western societies have generally been quite selective in accepting what is useful from Western modernization while often rejecting the rest. Of course this is a mixed situation, for while some elements associated with Western modernization are kept out, other aspects enter regardless of the barriers erected. But the process itself is one of filtering and not simply of imitating and inevitably following. For example, Japanese modernization under the Meiji came about through the cooperation of government and powerful family groups. The tenacity of such traditional family elements and their persistence were not the result merely of nostalgic attachment to the past or to some vague tradition; rather there were valid economic reasons—Japan's abundance of manpower as opposed to capital, her traditional family handicraft industry which could be used to generate the needed capital—for their retention. The result has been the Japanese pattern of modernization indicates significant differences from that of the West (and it obviously continues to do so). The social and political concomitants that in the West followed from industrialization have not necessarily followed.

The Japanese evidence and parallel findings from other regions of the world suggest that the forms of Western social and political organization are not the inevitable consequence of the replacement of feudalism, traditionalism, and agriculturalism by a modern industrial technology. Instead the capitalistic individualism, secularism, the particular role of the middle classes and middle classness, the growth of liberalism and interest group pluralism, and a host of other features that are so much a part of the northwest European and United States religious, familial, social, and political system and order should be seen as only one of numerous possible alternatives in the urban-industrial transition, and not necessarily a more developed or ethically or morally superior one. Other, *alternative* routes to modernization also command our attention. . . .

In sociology as in political theory the models and metaphors used derived exclusively from the Euro-American experience. It is not necessary here to go into non-Western concepts of time and space, cyclical theories of history as opposed to the predominantly evolutionary ones of the West, notions of permanence and continuity as opposed to Western belief in perpetual change. Suffice it to say that the images, perceptions, and understandings used to depict development were all Western in origin, that we had no comprehension of societies based on presumptions other than that of constant progress. How arrogant that no consideration was given to non-Western concepts, except as these constituted traditional, dysfunctional "problems to be overcome." It is small wonder that theories purporting to be universal but actually quite particularistic should run up against major barriers or produce unexpected results when they were applied to societies where their major assumptions had no bases in local history, tradition, or understandings.

Especially presumptuous was the expectation of a single, unilinear path to development. There was only one acceptable route along with certain common signposts—all derived from the Western experience—along the path. "Traditional society" was seldom further differentiated, leaving the impression that all Third World nations had a common background, began at the same starting point, and, once started, embarked on a single path that led them to shed their traditional features and proceed irreversibly to modernization. Almost no thought was given to the fact that not only were the starting points, the nature of traditional societies, immensely different, but that the paths (plural!) to development and the end products were certain to be vastly dissimilar as well. The image that should have been used was not that of a single path or route to development but that of a much more complex *lattice*, with numerous, diverse beginnings and multiple, crisscrossing channels.[4]

A key reason developmental sociology went astray—and a major cause of its attractiveness—is that a close identification was made between development as a process and development as a moral and ethical good. Not only could we as social scientists analyze development but we could also identify with it, like apple pie and motherhood, as a desirable normative goal toward which all "right-

---

[4] The image is that of Philippe C. Schmitter, "Paths to Political Development in Latin America," in *Changing Latin America* (New York: Academy of Political Science, 1972), pp. 83–105.

thinking" people should surely work. Particularly as development was closely identified with the values that social scientists hold—secularism, rationalism, pluralism, and the like—and as it implied the destruction or replacement of the values and institutions social scientists tend not to like (authoritarian and traditional structures; religious beliefs and institutions; familial, tribal, or clan ties), it carried enormous appeal.

There is certainly something we can analyze as *change:* development and modernization are probably too Western, too loaded, to be of much use. But change should be regarded as a neutral process and not involve the intrusion of ethical, political, or moral judgments—unless we are willing to abandon all pretense to objectivity and assume that our private values are or ought to be everyone's values. How conceited and pretentious that is! Certainly it is difficult to be against development and modernization. The mistake was in social science presuming to *know* what a developed society looked like (liberal, pluralist, democratic: our idealized image of ourselves) and in assuming that the values of Western civilization were or had to become everyone's values. Hence, if traditional societies or institutions—African tribalism, Indian caste associations, a host of others—failed to develop in terms of prevailing social science theory, they had of necessity to be uprooted and obliterated in favor of new modernizing ones; and if in the process the modernizing institutions such as political parties and trade unions failed to develop, it was again the societies that were dysfunctional rather than the theory that needed reexamination. . . .

There are, certainly, universals in the development process and perhaps Western Europe and the United States provide us with a model of how this occurs. Economic development and industrialization *are* occurring in virtually all areas of the globe; class transformations are under way: people are being uprooted and mobilized; urbanization is accelerating; traditional institutions are changing and new ones are being created; specialization and differentiation are going forward. The mistake of the development literature was in ascribing specific social and political concomitants to these changes based on a model that was not universalistic, as it claimed, but particularistic and narrowly Euro-American. All economic and class transformations are, after all, filtered through and shaped by distinct, indigenous cultural, social, and political institutions, no less so in the Third World than in Western Europe; and the timing, sequences, and context of these changes are also quite varied. What the social sciences did, however, was to generalize inappropriately from the sociopolitical institutional concomitants of modernization in Western Europe, which they knew best and assumed to be desirable, to other nations which they knew less well and with whose traditional institutions they felt uncomfortable.

Generalization from a single unique case to the rest of the world
is not unusual among social scientists; in the case of the development
literature, however, the assumptions were widely shared, and the
results for developing nations have been particularly unfortunate.
The costs of this myopia we must now begin to pay.

Political Economy

. . . Non-Marxian developmental economics is as Eurocentric as
is the classical Marxian variety. The famous aeronautical stages
in the "non-Communist manifesto" of W. W. Rostow ("drive to take
off," "take off," etc.), which so strongly shaped—as did Parsons and
Lipset in sociology and the Almond and Coleman volume on "The
Politics of the Developing Areas" in political science—whole generations of development-minded economists, were based almost exclusively on the Western European and United States experiences.
The logic of the Rostow analysis (and of the Alliance for Progress
and U.S. foreign assistance, since as National Security Adviser Rostow was also the chief influence in shaping these programs) was
that if only the United States could pour in sufficient economic
aid, "take off" would occur and the following social and political
effects would be felt: organized labor would become less extremist
and revolutionary; more professional, and hence less political, armies and bureaucracies would grow; a large middle class would
emerge that would be a bulwark of stable, middle-of-the-road rule;
the peasants would become yeomen, middle-class family farmers;
and radical ideologies such as communism—a "disease of the transition," Rostow called it—would diminish in attractiveness. . . .

By this point it should be abundantly clear that the Rostowian
stages do not necessarily follow one another, that there is no unilinear and inevitable path to development, that with the oil crisis,
the internationalization of capital, and other features, the condition
of the Third World nations today is fundamentally different from
those prevailing a century or more ago, that the development process in these nations hence will not and cannot be a mirror of
the European experience, that there are numerous culturally conditioned routes to modernization and not just the European one, and
therefore that the social and political concomitants which, based
on the European experience, are supposed to follow from modernization may not, in these quite different temporal and spatial contexts,
follow at all.[5] Rather, development will take directions that reflect

---

[5] These considerations of "historical space-time," a concept that has often confused
U.S. observers, lay behind the efforts of Haya de la Torre and the Peruvian *Apristas*
to develop an indigenous ideology for Latin America.

indigenous traditions and institutions: and it is time that we recognize this fact rather than continue to dismiss these processes and institutions as dysfunctional or try to interpret them through a Western social science framework that has only limited relevance in non-Western areas. As David Apter reminded us some time ago, industrialization in the West is only one form of industrialization.[6] The dilemma for most developing nations is hence not westernization or even modernization but how to gain and employ Western capital and technology while preserving what they see as valuable in their own cultures and traditions.

CONSEQUENCES OF THE WESTERN BIASES

*   *   *   *   *

The theory and assumptions we have applied to the developing nations have often led us to expect certain trends to occur and institutions to develop that have, in fact, not consistently developed. We have expected, and perhaps hoped, that modernization would produce more pluralist and secular societies when, in fact, in Iran and elsewhere powerful religious revivals are taking place that are monistic and theocratic, that proclaim a single right-and-wrong way to do everything which seems appallingly oppressive to most Westerners. We celebrate democracy and pluralism in our theories in the political sphere as well, when the real question in virtually all developing nations is which form authoritarianism will take.[7] We have expected more universalist (our own?) criteria to take hold when in fact particularism seems everywhere on the rise. We applaud merit and have elevated it to a universal norm of modernity when the fact is ascriptive criteria seem ascendant, perhaps increasingly so even in our own society. Obviously, differentiation of labor, specialization of function, and rationalization and bureaucratization have occurred throughout the developing world, but rather than producing much democratization in countries where a strong imperious central state has been either the norm or the aspiration, these trends have chiefly produced more efficient and centralized forms of statism and even terror.[8]

---

[6] D. Apter, *The Politics of Modernization* (Chicago, University of Chicago Press, 1965).

[7] Anthony James Joes, *Fascism in the Contemporary World* (Boulder, Colo.: Westview, 1978); James Malloy, ed., *Authoritarianism and Corporatism in Latin America* (Pittsburgh: University of Pittsburgh Press, 1977).

[8] Claudio Veliz, *The Centralist Tradition of Latin America* (Princeton: Princeton University Press, 1979); A. James Gregor, *Italian Fascism and Developmental Dictatorship* (Princeton: Princeton University Press, 1979); David Collier, ed., *The New Authoritarianism in Latin America* (Princeton: Princeton University Press, 1979).

Our social science assumptions have also led us to look for the growth of an increasingly more prosperous working class and hence a more apolitical trade unionism when in fact, in Italy, Argentina, and elsewhere the latter does not seem necessarily to follow from the former; for an increasingly professional and thus apolitical military when in fact increased professionalism leads many militaries (Brazil, Chile, Peru, Portugal) to become more political rather than less; for stronger local government when in fact the dominant tendency even of our "community development" programs, has been toward greater concentration of state power; for mass-based political parties that perform the interest aggregation and articulation functions when actually most "parties" in the developing nations are that only in name and may not at all be inclined to perform the functions Western political science assigns to them; for a middle class that is moderate, democratic, and inclined to assist the less-favored elements in the society, when in fact the divided middle sectors in most Third World nations are inclined to ape upper-class ways and use the instruments of the state (armies, labor ministries, and the like) to keep their own lower classes subservient; for elites and businessmen who recognize their social responsibilities to the poor in a more pluralist setting when the real situation is that the elites are intent not on sharing but on getting more wealth and monopolizing it; for greater respect for civil liberties and democracy rather than the increased statism, authoritarianism, and corporatism that seems to be the real life situation virtually everywhere in the Third World. The list of misapplied theories and programs goes on and on. In short, few of the social and political concomitants of modernization that our Western experience would lead us to expect to see developing are in fact developing. The problem lies not in the developing areas since they are often merely continuing preferred and traditional practices; rather, the problem lies in the Western-based concepts and ofttimes wishful social science with which we have sought to interpret these nations.

At the same time that too much attention has been devoted to those institutions that, based on the Western experience, social scientists expected or hoped to develop, too little has been afforded those not in accord with these preferences. It seems obvious, for example, that in the Islamic world and elsewhere religious beliefs and institutions cannot simply be relegated to the ashcans of history under the "inevitable" onslaught of "secularism," nor can the former be dismissed as part of traditional society certain to be superseded. The same applies to tribal and caste associations: these are not just traditional institutions certain to give way under modernization's impact. Behind much of the ideological skirmishing in Africa, for instance, is a tribal context, one that should not be denied or wished away as much social science does but taken as a given and perhaps as a base for other kinds of social and political associations than the preferred Western ones. Similarly, India's caste associations, once consigned to the realm of the traditional, are now viewed as adaptable institutions capable of serving as modernizing agencies.[9] There is a refreshing degree of realism now on the part of political leaders and intellectuals in the Third World to take such institutions as givens and potential developmental building blocks rather than as symbols of "backwardness" that had to be destroyed. The functioning and changes in such institutions during epochs of transition ought also to be a primary focus of social scientists, rather than the easy dismissal of them.

With the strong social-democratic bias that undergirds much of the development literature, social scientists have disregarded a variety of other institutions either because we do not like them politically or because they do not fit our preferred models. Most social scientists, for instance, are uncomfortable with, and often quite hostile toward, the Catholic, elitist, and authoritarian assumptions of traditional Latin society. Because we do not like elite-structured societies, we have seldom studied the dynamics of elite strategies and elite networks, preferring to dismiss these out of hand or apply the familiar traditional label, which seemingly helps make the problem go away. There is abundant literature on labor and peasant movements but very little on elites, both because of practical research problems and because social scientists, like most Americans, are ill at ease with elitist assumptions. We do not like theocratic societies either and especially despise the Islamic mullahs for seeking to resurrect one, but our understanding of events in Iran and other nations will not be advanced by complete hostility or the dismissal of such popular movements as irrational.

Military coups provide another illustration of the familiar biases. Most Western social science, with its favoritism toward democratic and civilian government, treats coups as aberrations, irregular, dysfunctional, and unconstitutional, thus ignoring their normalcy, regularity, functionality, and ofttimes legal-constitutional basis, the reasons for them, their functional similarity to elections and the fact the former may be no more comic opera than the latter. Our antimilitary bias, however, often prevents us from seeing these events neutrally and scientifically.

The examples of such ethnocentrism are numerous in the areas

---

[9] Lloyd I. Rudolph and Susanne Hoeber Rudolph, *The Modernity of Tradition: Political Development in India* (Chicago: University of Chicago Press, 1967); Randall Stokes and Anthony Harris, "South African Development and the Paradox of Racial Particularism: Toward a Theory of Modernization from the Center," *Economic Development and Cultural Change* 26 (January 1978), pp. 245–69.

of both public policy and institutions. In President Carter's human rights campaign, for example, it was consistently the United States model and understanding that was imposed abroad; no consideration was given to the fact that other societies define terms like *rights, democracy,* or *justice* in different ways, that they see these differently or assign them a different priority. One pales also at the thought of how many countries and how many women and men in them have been called irrational because they desire larger families rather than smaller, a decision that in their circumstances may well be perfectly rational. Or, in another tradition, one wonders at the easy and widespread use of the term "false consciousness" to describe peasants and workers who may be uncomfortable with or suspicious toward revolutionary movements organized, so they claim, on the lower classes' behalf. The number of policy areas and institutions in which labels and slogans substitute for close examination, dismissal or relegance to the dustbins of history or to the ranks of traditionalism or dysfunctionality for hard analysis, seems almost endless. Even whole continents and regions, such as Latin America and Africa are often dismissed by social scientists as constituting areas without political culture and therefore unworthy of study. Such attitudes reflect not the true importance of these areas but the biases of the social sciences, the fact these areas seldom fit our favored models and because we are often vaguely antipathetic toward their underlying premises.

If these errors of both commission and omission by social scientists and policymakers were merely benignly neutral, there would be little to worry about; unfortunately, such errors and oversights are neither benign, neutral, nor harmless. The subject merits much fuller attention; here let it simply be said that: (1) based on the ethnocentric developmental assumptions of the social sciences, enormous amounts of money and effort have been wasted on a variety of misguided and misdirected programs; (2) confirmed in the modernity and hence superiority of our own institutions, we have continued patronizingly to dismiss or disparage as traditional or primitive a large number of beliefs, practices, and institutions in the Third World; (3) because our models and perspectives are so narrow and Eurocentric, our comprehension of the real dynamics of change and continuity in these nations remains woefully inadequate, based more on prejudice and/or romance than actuality; (4) grounded on this same particularistic and ethnocentric northwest European and United States experience, the policy measures we have sought to implement have produced hosts of backfires, unanticipated consequences, and sheer disasters; and (5) in the name of advancing modernity, we have helped undermine a great variety of quite viable traditional and transitional institutions, thus contributing by our policies to the breakdown, chaos, and ruination of many developing nations that we had ostensibly sought to avoid.

All these charges are serious but the last one may have the gravest long-term consequences. By helping destroy their traditional institutions and by erecting ephemeral modern ones cast in our own image to replace them but often entirely inappropriate in the societies where we have sought to locate them, we have left many developing nations with neither the traditional and indigenous institutions which might have helped them bridge the wrenching transition to modernity, nor with viable new ones that have any bases or hope of functioning effectively in the native soil. By forcing some wrong and falsely dichotomous choices on the developing nations ("traditional" *or* "modern", "democracy" *or* "dictatorship"), social scientists and policymakers have contributed strongly to the institutional vacuum that plagues these countries and to the "basket cases" that, in the absence of genuinely homegrown institutions, they are certain to become.[10]

CONCLUSIONS AND IMPLICATIONS

The development literature, whether in political science, sociology, or economics, assumes that the path to modernization in the Third World can be explained by reference to the past or present of the already industrialized nations. Development in Africa, Asia, Latin America, and the Middle East is seen in Glaucio Ary Dillon Soares's words, as specific instances of a general course of events already studied and fully comprehended in the experience of the Western European countries and the United States.[11] Such an approach assumes quite distinct culture areas and historical epochs can be understood using the same terms and concepts as in the West. It assumes a single unilinear path to development and also the universality of what is a far narrower and particular European or Western experience and set of institutions. The ethnocentrism of this interpretation and the absurdity of reducing a great variety of histories and sociopolitical formations to the single matrix of the Western European–United States experience are patent. This approach has stultified the creation of new concepts, prevented us from understanding the realities of the developing nations, wreaked positive harm upon them, and cast the developing nations and those

---

[10] For one such example see Howard J. Wiarda, *Dictatorship, Development, and Disintegration: Politics and Social Change in the Dominican Republic* (Ann Arbor: Xerox University Microfilms Monograph Series, 1975).

[11] Dillon Soares, "Latin American Studies in the United States: A Critique and a Proposal," *Latin American Research Review* 2 (1976), pp. 51–69.

who study them in an inferior position vis-à-vis both the developed countries and those who study them. . . .

The universals in the modernization process include economic growth and industrialization, class and societal changes, division of labor and increased specialization of functions, rationalization and bureaucratization of society and polity, and the impact of what Lucian Pye once called the "world culture" (not just jeans, Coke, and rock but also outside political ideologies and forces).[12] The difficulty is that the presumed more specific social and political concomitants of these changes—modern political parties, armies, etc.—have not in fact developed concomitantly. The problem is not just "lag" or "uneven development" but that we have failed to appreciate sufficiently the present era's changed circumstances and also the strength and functionality of many traditional institutions and how these may shape, mold, even determine the impact of these larger, more universal changes. We have dismissed as traditional the role of tribes, caste associations, mullahs, religious and fundamentalist movements, elites and family structures, patron-client systems transferred to the national level, and a host of other local and particularistic institutions, rather than seeing them as persistent, flexible, perhaps viable structures on which an indigenous process of development might be based. By now it is clear such institutions will not necessarily disappear or be superseded as modernization proceeds, nor should they be easily dismissed, as our social science literature is wont to do, as dysfunctional. We must recognize the diversity of societies and developmental experiences.

Social scientists must begin with a renewed awareness of their biases, societal likes and dislikes, the Eurocentric bases of so many of their theories, their particularistic rather than universalistic nature. This will require a fundamental reexamination of most of the truths social scientists, especially [North] American social scientists, hold to be self-evident. It will also require a new and stronger dose of cultural relativism. Cultural relativism need not be carried so far as to accept or remain neutral toward a Hitler or a Bokassa. But it does imply a much more empathetic than previously understanding of foreign cultures and institutions, an understanding of them in terms of their own cultural traditions and even language, rather than through the distorting, blinding prism of Western social science.[13] The social sciences have been guilty of over- and too-hasty generalization; hence, we require more modesty than before concern-

---

[12] In Lucian Pye and Sidney Verba, eds., *Political Culture and Political Development* (Princeton: Princeton University Press, 1965).

[13] For such a *verstahen* approach and its effect *both* on the region studied and the researchers, see Jean Duvignaud, *Change at Shebika: Report from a North African Village* (New York, 1970).

ing the universal applicability of our social science notions, greater uncertainty in our assertions of global social science wisdom, more reluctance to apply the social science findings (apples) of our culture to the realities (oranges) of another, where they neither fit nor add up.[14]

To say that much social science theory we took as universal is somewhat less than that implies that future theory ought probably to be formulated at a lower, culture-area level. We shall probably have to develop an African social science, an Islamic social science, a Latin American social science, and so on. It may be that such middle-range theory at the culture-area level will eventually yield again some more general, even universal findings about the development process, but this will be a long-term process and we may well find few universals on which to hang our social science hats. Many social scientists will be uncomfortable with this fact; a more useful approach may be to take the absence of such universals as a given and proceed from there. Some prominent social scientists are already saying that theory and research at the culture-area level, the examination of more particularistic, culturally unique, perhaps regionally specific institutions and processes, will probably be the focus of future comparative development studies. The necessity of analyzing indigenous institutions on their own terms and in their own cultural contexts rather than through Western social science frameworks seems particularly appropriate in the present circumstances, given both the assertion of indigenous ideologies and movements in many developing nations, and the corresponding rejection of European, American, and Western ones. In my own particular areas of special research interest, for example, Latin America and southern Europe, I have been fascinated both by the new literature on corporatism, dependency, patron-client relations, center-periphery relations, organic-statism, and the like, which have helped form the bases for a new Latin American, or perhaps Iberic-Latin, social science, *and* the way these concepts have now found their way into interpretations of other areas and into the general literature. It may be that the flow of ideas and concepts, historically from Europe and European studies out to the periphery, may be in the process of being reversed. It may be that Western social scientists will now have to learn from Africa, Asia, Latin America, and the Middle East instead of their always learning from us.[15]

The emergence and articulation of such distinctive Latin

[14] Peter Winch, *The Idea of a Social Science and Its Relations to Philosophy* (London: Routledge & Kegan Paul, 1960).

[15] Howard J. Wiarda, "Toward a Framework for the Study of Political change in the Iberic-Latin Tradition," *World Politics* 25 (1973); *Politics and Social Change;* "The Latin Americanization of the United States," *The New Scholar* 7 (1977), pp. 51–85; and *Corporatism and National Development in Latin America* (Boulder: Westview Press, 1981).

American, African, Islamic, and so forth sociologies and political sciences of development raise a host of intriguing issues for scholarship. Implied is that we now take the developing nations and their alternative civilizations seriously for the first time, and on their own terms rather than through the condescension and superiority of United States or Western European perspectives. It means that the rising sense of nationalism and independence throughout the Third World is likely also to be reflected in a new insistence on indigenous models and institutions of development. It requires the formulation or reformulation of a host of new concepts and interpretations. It also implies that if the West, particularly the United States, is no longer to be the world's policeman, it must also cease being its philosopher-king, in terms of its assertion of the universality of its particular developmental experience.

This essay has been something of a broadside. Its claims and criticisms are sweeping. Essentially it says the social sciences of development must start all over. Of course one purposely overstates the case in order more forcefully to make it. We have seen there are universals in the development process, and we need to sort out more carefully what non-Western developing societies allow in and what gets winnowed out. We need sharper distinctions between cultural definitions of concepts as implicitly influencing social science theory construction, ethnocentrism as a distortion of perception, lack of research in specific culture areas, simple analogy to the Western development experience instead of analysis of the respective dynamics of given cases, political shortsightedness and interest politics. We require qualification and refinement of other arguments. Nonetheless the criticisms leveled here are fundamental and far-reaching.

The policy implications of these comments are also major. They mean the reexamination and likely scrapping of most of our aid and foreign assistance programs directed toward developing nations. They imply the shortsightedness and impropriety of seeking to apply European and North American strategies and institutional paraphernalia to societies and cultures where they simply do not fit; hence, they mean also a drastic curtailing of the travel and consulting fees that all those presumably developmentalism experts have been enjoying. They imply that United States and international agency decision makers be much more circumspect in their assertion that they know best for the developing nations. Even more fundamental, these comments imply a virtually complete reeducation, in nonethnocentric understandings, of at least two generations of social scientists, policymakers, and the informed public, indeed of our educational focus, national ethos, and career system. One should not be optimistic.

CHAPTER EIGHT

Dependency

27

The Capitalist World-Economy

Immanuel Wallerstein

Words can be the enemy of understanding and analysis. We seek to capture a moving reality in our terminology. We thereby tend to forget that the reality changes as we encapsulate it, and by virtue of that fact. And we are even more likely to forget that others freeze reality in different ways, using however the very same words to do it. And still we cannot speak without words; indeed we cannot think without words.

Where then do we find the *via media,* the working compromise, the operational expression of a dialectical methodology? It seems to me it is most likely to be found by conceiving of provisional long-term, large-scale wholes within which concepts have meanings. These wholes must have some claim to relative space-time autonomy and integrity. They must be long enough and large enough to enable us to escape the Scylla of conceptual nominalism, but short enough and small enough to enable us to escape the Charybdis of ahistorical, universalizing abstraction. I would call such wholes "historical systems"—a name which captures their two essential qualities. It is a whole which is integrated, that is, composed of interrelated parts, therefore in some sense systematic and with comprehensible patterns. It is a system which has a history, that is, it has a genesis, an historical development, a close (a destruction, a disintegration, a transformation, an *Aufhebung*).

Source: Immanuel Wallerstein, "The States in the Institutional Vortex of the Capitalist World-Economy," *International Social Science Journal* vol. 32, no. 4 (1980), pp. 743–51. © Unesco 1980. Reproduced by permission of Unesco.

I contrast this concept of "historical system" with that of the more usual term of "society" (or of "social formation," which I believe is used more or less synonymously). Of course, one may use the term "society" in the same sense I am using "historical system," and then the issue is simply the choice of formal symbol. But in fact the standard use of "society" is one which is applied indiscriminately to refer to modern states (and quasi-states), to ancient empires, to supposedly autonomous "tribes," and to all manner of other *political* (or cultural-aspiring-to-be-political) structures. And this lumping together presumes what is to be demonstrated—that the political dimension is the one that unifies and delineates social action.

If boundaries drawn in every conceivable way—integrated production processes, exchange patterns, political jurisdiction, cultural coherence, ecology—were in fact always (or even usually) synonymous (or even highly overlapping), there would be little problem. But, as a matter of empirical fact, taking the last 10,000 years of human history, this is not at all the case. We must therefore choose among alternate criteria of defining our arenas of social action, our units of analysis. One can debate this in terms of philosophical *a priori* statements, and if so my own bias is a materialist one. But one can also approach this heuristically: which criterion will account for the largest percentage of social action, in the sense that changing its parameters will most immediately and most profoundly affect the operation of other parts of the whole?

I believe one can argue the case for integrated production processes as constituting this heuristic criterion, and I shall use it to draw the boundaries which circumscribe a concrete "historical system," by which I mean an empirical set of such production processes integrated according to some particular set of rules, the human agents of which interact in some "organic" way, such that changes in the functions of any group or changes in the boundaries of the historical system must follow certain rules if the entity's survival is not to be threatened. This is what we mean by such other terms as a social economy, or a specific social division of labour. To suggest that a historical system is organic is not to suggest that it is a frictionless machine. Quite the contrary: historical systems are beset by contradictions, and contain within them the seeds of processes that eventually destroy the system. But this, too, is very consonant with the "organic" metaphor.

This is a long preface to a coherent analysis of the role of states in the modern world. I think much of our collective discussion has been a prisoner of the word "state," which we have used transhistorically to mean any political structure which had some authority network (a leading person or group or groups, with intermediate cadres enforcing the will of this leading entity). Not only do we assume that what we are designating as "states" in the 20th century are in the same universe of discourse as what we designate as "states" in, say, the 10th century, but even more fantastically, we frequently attempt to draw lines of historical continuity between two such "states"—of the same name, or found in the same general location in terms of longitude and latitude—said to be continuous because scholars can argue affinities of the languages that are spoken, or the cosmologies that are professed, or the genes that are pooled.

The capitalist world-economy constitutes one such historical system. It came into existence, in my view, in Europe in the 16th century. The capitalist world-economy is a system based on the drive to accumulate capital, the political conditioning of price levels (of capital, commodities and labour), and the steady polarization of classes and regions (core/periphery) over time. This system has developed and expanded to englobe the whole earth in the subsequent centuries. It has today reached a point where, as a result of its contradictory developments, the system is a long crisis.[1]

The development of the capitalist world-economy has involved the creation of all the major institutions of the modern world: classes, ethnic/national groups, households—and the "states." All of these structures postdate, not antedate capitalism; all are consequence, not cause. Furthermore, these various institutions, in fact, create each other. Classes, ethnic/national groups, and households are defined by the state, through the state, in relation to the state, and in turn create the state, shape the state, and transform the state. It is a structured maelstrom of constant movement, whose parameters are measurable through the repetitive regularities, while the detailed constellations are always unique.

What does it mean to say that a state comes into existence? Within a capitalist world-economy, the state is an institution whose existence is defined by its relation to other "states." Its boundaries are more or less clearly defined. Its degree of juridical sovereignty ranges from total to nil. Its real power to control the flows of capital, commodities, and labour across its frontiers is greater or less. The real ability of the central authorities to enforce decisions on groups operating within state frontiers is greater or less. The ability of the state authorities to impose their will in zones outside state frontiers is greater or less.

Various groups located inside, outside, and across any given

---

[1] I have developed these theses at length in *The Modern World-System*, 2 vols. (New York, Academic Press, 1974 and 1980); and *The Capitalist World-Economy* (Cambridge: Cambridge University Press, 1979).

state's frontiers are constantly seeking to increase, maintain, or decrease the "power" of the state, in all the ways referred to above. These groups are seeking to change these power constellations because of some sense that such changes will improve the particular group's ability to profit, directly or indirectly, from the operations of the world market. The state is the most convenient institutional intermediary in the establishment of market constraints (quasi-monopolies, in the broadest sense of the term) in favour of particular groups.

The historical development of the capitalist world-economy is that, beginning with relatively amorphous entities, more and more "states" operating within the interstate system have been created. Their boundaries and the definitions of their formal rights have been defined with increasing clarity (culminating in the contemporary United Nations structure of international law). The modalities and limits of group pressures in state structures have also been increasingly defined (in the sense both of the legal limits placed on such pressures, and of the rational organization by groups to transcend these limits). None the less, despite what might be called the "honing" of this institutional network, it is probably safe to say that the relative power continuum of stronger and weaker states has remained relatively unchanged over 400-odd years. That is not to say that the same "states" have remained "strong" and "weak." Rather, there has been at all moments a power hierarchy of such states, but also at no moment has there been any one state whose hegemony was totally unchallenged (although relative hegemony has occurred for limited periods).

Various objections have been made to such a view of the modern state, its genesis and its mode of functioning. There are four criticisms which seem to be the most frequent and worthy of discussion.

First, it is argued that this view is too instrumental a view of the state, that it makes the states into a mere conscious instrument of acting groups with no life and integrity of their own, with no base of social support in and for themselves.

It seems to me this counter-argument is based on a confusion about social institutions in general. Once created, all social institutions, including the states, have lives of their own in the sense that many different groups will use them, support them, exploit them for various (and even contradictory) motives. Furthermore, institutions large and structured enough to have permanent staffs thereby generate a group of persons—the bureaucracies of these institutions—who have a direct socio-economic stake in the persistence and flourishing of the institution as such, quite independent of the ideological premises on which the institution was created and the interests of the major social forces that sustain it.

None the less, the issue is not who has some say in the ongoing decisions of a state-machinery but who has decisive or critical say, and what are the key issues that are fought about in terms of state policy. We believe that these key issues are: (1) the rules governing the social relations of production, which critically affect the allocation of surplus-value; and (2) the rules governing the flow within and across frontiers of the factors of production—capital, commodities and labour—which critically affect the price structures of markets. If one changes the allocation of surplus-value and the price structures of markets, one is changing the relative competitivity of particular producers, and therefore their profit-levels.

It is the states that make these rules, and it is primarily the states that intervene in the process of other (weaker) states when the latter attempt to make the rules as they prefer them.

The second objection to this mode of analysis is that it ignores the reality of traditional continuities, as ensconsed in the operative consciousnesses of groups. Such consciousnesses do indeed exist and are very powerful, but are the consciousnesses themselves continuous? I think not, and believe the merest glance at the empirical reality will confirm that. The history of nationalisms, which are one of the salient forms of such consciousnesses, shows that everywhere that nationalist movements emerge, they create consciousness, they revive (even partially invent) languages, they coin names and emphasize customary practices that come to distinguish their group from other groups. They do this in the name of what is claimed to have always been there, but frequently (if not usually) they must stretch the interpretation of the historical evidence in ways that disinterested observers would consider partisan. This is true not only of the so-called "new" nations of the 20th century[2] but of the "old" nations as well.[3]

It is also clear that the successive ideological statements about

---

[2] In 1956, Thomas Hodgkin wrote in a "Letter" to Saburi Biobaku *(Odù,* No. 4, 1957, p. 42): "I was struck by your statement that the use of the term 'Yoruba' to refer to the whole range of peoples who would nowadays describe themselves as Yoruba (as contrasted with the Oyo peoples simply) was due largely to the influence of the Anglican Mission at Abeokuta, and its work in evolving a standard 'Yoruba' language, based on Oyo speech. This seems to me an extremely interesting example of the way in which Western influences have helped to stimulate a new kind of national sentiment. Everyone recognizes that the notion of 'being a Nigerian' is a new kind of conception. But it would seem that the notion of 'being a Yoruba' is not very much older. I take it from what you say that there is no evidence that those who owed allegiance to the kingdom of Oyo—or to the earlier State system based upon Ife?—used any common name to describe themselves, although it is possible that they may have done so?"

[3] George Bernard Shaw has the Nobleman in *Saint Joan* exclaim: "A Frenchman! Where did you pick up that expression? Are these Burgundians and Bretons and Picards and Gascons beginning to call themselves Frenchmen, just as our fellows are beginning to call themselves Englishmen? They actually talk of France and England as their countries. Theirs, if you please! What is to become of me and you if that way of thinking comes into fashion?"

a given name—what it encompasses, what constitutes its "tradition"—are discontinuous and different. Each successive version can be explained in terms of the politics of its time, but the fact that these versions vary so widely is itself a piece of evidence against taking the assertion of continuity as more than a claim of an interested group. It surely is shifting sand on which to base an analysis of the political functioning of states.

The third argument against this form of analysis is that it is said to ignore the underlying centrality of the class struggle, which is implicitly asserted to exist within some fixed entity called a society or a social formation, and which in turn accounts for the structure of the state.

If, however, classes is the term we use for groups deriving from positions in relation to the mode of production, then it is to the realities of the set of integrated production processes that we must look to determine who constitute our classes. The boundaries of these integrated production processes are in fact, of course, far wider than the individual states, and even sub-sets of production processes do not correlate very often with state boundaries. There is consequently no a priori reason to assume that classes are in some objective sense circumscribed by state boundaries.

Now, it may fairly be argued that class consciousnesses have tended historically to be national in form. This is so, for good reasons we shall discuss below. But the fact that this is so is no evidence that the analytic perception is correct. On the contrary, this fact of the national form of consciousness for trans-state classes becomes itself a major explicandum of the modern world.

Finally, it is said that this mode of analysis ignores the fact that the wealthiest states are not the strongest states, but tend indeed to be relatively weak. But this is to misperceive what constitutes the strength of state machineries. It is once again to take ideology for analytic reality.

Some state machineries preach the line of a strong state. They seek to limit opposition; they seek to impose decisions on internal groups; they are bellicose vis-à-vis external groups. But what is important is the success of the assertion of power, not its loudness. Oppositions only need to be suppressed where they seriously exist. States that encompass relatively more homogeneous strata (because of the unevenness of allocation of class forces in the world economy) may achieve via consensus what others strive (and perhaps fail) to achieve via the iron hand. Entrepreneurs who are economically strong in the market do not need state assistance to create monopoly privileges, though they may need state aid to oppose the creation by others, in other states, of monopoly privileges which would hurt these market-strong entrepreneurs.

The states are thus, we are arguing, created institutions reflecting the needs of class forces operating in the world economy. They are not however created in a void, but within the framework of an interstate system. This interstate system is, in fact, the framework within which the states are defined. It is the fact that the states of the capitalist world economy exist within the framework of an interstate system that is the *differentia specifica* of the modern state, distinguishing it from other bureaucratic polities. This interstate system constitutes a set of constraints which limit the abilities of individual state machineries, even the strongest among them, to make decisions. The ideology of this system is sovereign equality, but the states are in fact neither sovereign nor equal. In particular, the states impose on each other—not only the strong on the weak, but the strong on the strong—limitations on their modes of political (and therefore military), behaviour, and even more strikingly limitations on their abilities to affect the law of value underlying capitalism. We are so used to observing all the things states do that constitute a defiance of other states that we do not stop to recognize how few these things are, rather than how many. We are so used to thinking of the interstate system as verging on anarchy that we fail to appreciate how rule-ridden it is. Of course, the "rules" are broken all the time, but we should look at the consequences—the mechanisms that come into play to force changes in the policies of the offending states. Again, we should look less at the obvious arena of political behaviour, and more at the less observed arena of economic behaviour. The story of states with communist parties in power in the 20th-century interstate system is striking evidence of the efficacities of such pressures.

The production processes of the capitalist world-economy are built on a central relationship or antinomy: that of capital and labour. The ongoing operations of the system have the effect of increasingly circumscribing individuals (or rather households), forcing them to participate in the work process in one capacity or the other, as contributors of surplus-value or as receivers.

The states have played a central role in the polarization of the population into those living off appropriated surplus, the bourgeoisie, and those whose surplus-value is appropriated from them, the proletariat. For one thing, the states created the legal mechanisms which not merely permitted or even facilitated the appropriation of surplus-value, but protected the results of the appropriation by enacting property rights. They created institutions which ensured the socialization of children into the appropriate roles.

As the classes came into objective existence, in relation to each other, they sought to alter (or to maintain) the unequal bargaining power between them. To do this, they had to create appropriate institutions to affect state decisions, which largely turned out to be over-time institutions created within the boundaries of the state, adding thereby to the world-wide definiteness of state structures.

This has led to deep ambivalences in their self-perception and consequently contradictory political behaviour. Both the bourgeoisie and the proletariat are classes formed in a world economy, and when we speak of objective class position, it is necessarily classes of this world economy to which we refer. As, however, the bourgeoisie first began to become class-conscious and only later the proletariat, both classes found disadvantages as well as advantages to defining themselves as world classes.

The bourgeoisie, in pursuit of its class interest, the maximization of profit in order to accumulate capital, sought to engage in its economic activities as it saw fit without constraints on geographic location or political considerations. Thus, for example, in the 16th or 17th centuries, it was frequent for Dutch, English or French entrepreneurs to "trade with the enemy" in wartime, even in armaments. And it was frequent for entrepreneurs to change place of domicile and citizenship in pursuit of optimizing gain. The bourgeoisie then (as now) reflected this self-perception in tendencies towards a "world" cultural style—in consumption, in language, etc. However, it was also true then, and now, that, however much the bourgeoisie chafed under limitations placed by particular state authorities for particular reasons at one or another moment, the bourgeoisies also needed to utilize state machineries to strengthen their position in the market vis-à-vis competitors and to protect them vis-à-vis the working classes. And this meant that the many fractions of the world bourgeoisie had an interest in defining themselves as "national" bourgeoisies.

The same pattern held for the proletariat. On the one hand, as it became class-conscious, it recognized that a prime organizational objective has to be the unity of proletarians in their struggle. It is no accident that the *Communist Manifesto* proclaimed: "Workers of the world, unite!" It was clear that precisely the fact that the bourgeoisie operated in the arena of a world-economy, and could (and would) transfer sites of production whenever it was to its advantage, meant that proletarian unity, if it were to be truly efficacious, could only be at the world level. And yet we know that world proletarian unity has never really been efficacious (most dramatically in the failure of the Second International to maintain an anti-nationalist stance during the First World War). This is so for a very simple reason. The mechanisms most readily available to improve the relative conditions of segments of the working classes are the state machineries, and the political organization of the proletariat has almost always taken the form of state-based organizations. Furthermore, this tendency has been reinforced, not weakened, by whatever successes these organizations have had in attaining partial or total state power.

We arrive thus at a curious anomaly: both the bourgeoisie and the proletariat express their consciousness at a level which does not reflect their objective economic role. Their interests are a function of the operations of a world-economy, and they seek to enhance their interests by affecting individual state machineries, which in fact have only limited power (albeit real power, none the less) to affect the operations of this world economy.

It is this anomaly that constantly presses bourgeoisies and proletariats to define their interests in status-group terms. The most efficacious status-group in the modern world is the nation, since the nation lays claim to the moral right to control a particular state structure. To the extent that a nation is not a state, we find the potential for a nationalist movement to arise and flourish. Of course, there is no essence that is a nation and that occasionally breeds a nationalist movement. Quite the contrary. It is a nationalist movement that creates an entity called a nation, or seeks to create it. Under the multiple circumstances in which nationalism is not available to serve class interests, status-group solidarities may crystallize around substitute poles: religion, race, language, or other particular cultural patterns.

Status-group solidarities remove the anomaly of national class organization or consciousness from the forefront of visibility and hence relax the strains inherent in contradictory structures. But, of course, they may also obfuscate the class struggle. To the extent that particular ethnic consciousnesses therefore lead to consequences which key groups find intolerable, we see re-emergence of overt class organizations, or if this creates too much strain, of redefined status-group solidarities (drawing the boundaries differently). That particular segments of the world bourgeoisie or world proletariat might flit from, say, pan-Turkic to pan-Islamic to national to class-based movements over a period of decades reflects not the inconsistency of the struggle but the difficulties of navigating a course that can bridge the antinomy: objective classes of the world economy/subjective classes of a state structure.

Finally the atoms of the classes (and of the status-groups), the income-pooling households, are shaped and constantly reshaped not only by the objective economic pressures of the ongoing dynamic of the world-economy but they also are regularly and deliberately manipulated by the states that seek to determine (to alter) their boundaries in terms of the needs of the labour-market, as well as to determine the flows and forms of income that may in fact be pooled. The households in turn may assert their own solidarities and priorities and resist the pressures, less effectively by passive means, more effectively, when possible, by creating the class and status-group solidarities we have just mentioned.

All these institutions together—the states, the classes, the ethnic/national/status-groups, the households—form an institutional vortex which is both the product and the moral life of the capitalist world-economy. Far from being primordial and pre-existing essences, they are dependent and coterminous existences. Far from being segregated and separable, they are indissociably intertwined in complex and contradictory ways. Far from one determining the other, they are in a sense avatars of each other.

28

Modernization and Dependency

J. Samuel Valenzuela and Arturo Valenzuela

The end of World War II marked the beginning of fundamental transformations in world affairs. The defeat of the Axis powers and the devastating toll which the war had exacted on Britain and the European allies propelled the United States into a position of economic and military preeminence. However, the United States' power did not go unchallenged. The Soviet Union was able to influence the accession of power of socialist regimes throughout Eastern Europe and Chinese Communists defeated their Western-backed adversaries to gain control of the most populous nation on earth. These events called for an urgent strategy to revitalize the economies of the Western nations. With massive U.S. public and private economic investment, Western Europe and Japan soon recovered from the ravages of war.

But World War II ushered in another important change whose global implications would not be felt for some years to come. The weakening of the European powers and the logic of a war effort aimed at preserving self-determination, marked the final collapse of the vast colonial empires of the 19th century and the establishment of a multiplicity of states each claiming sovereign and independent status. The "new nations" soon drew the attention of U.S.

Source: J. Samuel Valenzuela and Arturo Valenzuela, "Modernization and Dependency: Alternative Perspectives in the Study of Latin American Underdevelopment," *Comparative Politics* 10 (July 1978), pp. 535–57. Permission to reprint by *Comparative Politics,* © The City University of New York. Article and footnotes abridged by the editors.

policymakers concerned with the claim that Marxism presented the best and most logical road to full incorporation into the modern world. They also captured the attention and imagination of U.S. scholars who in the pursuit of knowledge, as well as the desire to influence government policy, began to produce a vast literature on the "developing" nations. For many economists the solution was another Marshall plan designed for the Third World. But other social scientists argued that fundamental differences between the developmental experience of Europe and the less-developed countries mitigated against the success of such a strategy. It was not simply a matter of reconstruction but one of development and, as such, a fundamental question needed answering before policy recommendations could be advanced: Why was there such a stark contrast in the developmental experience of a few Western countries and most of the rest of the world?

The answer to this question led to the development of the "modernization perspective." Elaborated by a few economists and by anthropologists, sociologists, and political scientists, this perspective argued that it was essential to consider the cultural characteristics of "new" nations in determining their potential for development. These "noneconomic" factors became the cornerstone of a conceptual framework which would influence the U.S. response to the Third World. Though "Latin Americanists" did not write the major theoretical or conceptual works of the modernization literature, that perspective soon became the dominant approach influencing the methodology and conclusions of the most important and trendsetting studies.

U.S. scholars, however, were not the only ones preoccupied with the difficulties of applying neoclassical economic assumptions to the developmental problems of Latin America. In international agencies, notably the United Nations Economic Commission for Latin America, and university research centers, Latin American social scientists tried to come to grips with the widespread economic stagnation which affected the region in the postwar period. Working separately, often with little communication, scholars in various disciplines soon turned to the broader and more basic question of the roots of Latin American underdevelopment. Many intellectual strands came together in the 1960s with the elaboration of a more general and comprehensive conceptual framework. The "dependency perspective" became the dominant approach in most Latin American intellectual circles by the mid to late 1960s.

* * * * *

Modernization and dependency are two sharply different perspectives seeking to explain the same reality. They originated in different areas, with different evaluative judgments, different assumptions, different methodologies, and different explanations. The purpose of this review essay is not to describe the origins of the two perspectives, their "extra scientific" elements, but to compare their conceptual approaches to the study of Latin America. As such, it will be necessary to consider the two perspectives as "ideal types," accentuating important characteristics of each framework in a manner not found in any particular author. There is a good deal of variety and several polemics (particularly in the dependency literature) stemming from disagreements over the emphasis given to key elements of the conceptual framework, the operationalization of concepts, and the way in which certain processes occur empirically. Though the essay will mention some of the controversies within each perspective, its purpose is to draw broad comparisons and to provide some judgment as to the relative utility of these competing frameworks in explaining Latin American underdevelopment.

THE MODERNIZATION PERSPECTIVE

Assumptions. The basic building blocks of the modernization perspective are parallel tradition-modernity ideal types of social organization and value systems, distinctions borrowed from 19th-century sociology.[1] Since societies are understood to move from tradition to modernity, the ideal typical dichotomy constitutes the polar ends of an evolutionary continuum, though at some point incremental changes give way to the qualitative jump into modernity. The location of this point is unclear; and yet, Third World countries, including those of Latin America, are perceived to be below the threshold of modernity, with a preponderance of traditional features.

The specific elements included in the two polarities vary substantially in the literature. The traditional society is variously understood as having a predominance of ascriptive, particularistic, diffuse, and affective patterns of action, an extended kinship structure with a multiplicity of functions, little spatial and social mobility, a deferential stratification system, mostly primary economic activities, a tendency toward autarchy of social units, an undifferentiated political structure, with traditional elitist and hierarchical sources of authority, etc. By contrast, the modern society is characterized by a predominance of achievement; universalistic, specific, and neutral orientations and patterns of action; a nuclear family structure serving limited functions; a complex and highly differentiated occupational system; high rates of spatial and social mobility; a

---

[1] For antecedents of the modernization literature, see the work of scholars such as Maine, Tonnies, Durkheim, Weber and Redfield.

predominance of secondary economic activities and production for exchange; the institutionalization of change and self-sustained growth; highly differentiated political structures with rational legal sources of authority; and so on.

The literature assumes that the values, institutions, and patterns of action of traditional society are both an expression and a cause of underdevelopment and constitute the main obstacles in the way of modernization. To enter the modern world, underdeveloped societies have to overcome traditional norms and structures opening the way for social, economic, and political transformations. For some authors modernization derives from a greater differentiation of societal functions, institutions, and roles and the development of new sources of integration. For others, modernization is based more on the actual transformation of individuals through their assimilation of modern values. But in general, the primary source of change is discussed in terms of innovations, that is, the rejection of procedures related to traditional institutions, together with the adoption of new ideas, techniques, values, and organizations. Innovations are pursued by innovators and the group that assumes this role inevitably clashes with defenders of the old order. The struggle is over two different ways of life.[2]

In describing the assumptions of the modernization literature, it is important to note that the modern pole of the parallel ideal types is the pivotal conceptual and analytical point because it best approximates the characteristics that societies must attain in order to develop. The traditional end of the dichotomy is largely a residual category, established by logical opposition to the modern end. In turn, the basic features of the modern pole are derived from characteristics attributed to those countries already considered modern. Moreover, since in the process of modernization all societies will undergo by and large similar changes, the history of the presently modern nations is taken as the source of universally useful conceptualization. Thus, as historian C. Black notes, "Although the problems raised by generalizations from a rather narrow base (the now modern countries) must be acknowledged, the definition of modernity takes the form of a set of characteristics believed to be applicable to all societies. This conception of modernity, when thought of as a model or ideal type, may be used as a yardstick with which to measure any society."[3] G. Almond adds that to study modernization in the non-Western areas the political scientist needs to "master the model of the modern, which in turn can only be derived from

---

[2] See Cyril Black, *The Dynamics of Modernization* (New York, 1966), pp. 68–75.

[3] Ibid., pp. 53–54.

the most careful empirical and formal analysis of the functions of the modern Western polities."[4]

These assumptions are logically consistent with the view that the impetus to modernize in the now developed countries was the result of endogenous cultural and institutional transformations, while change in the late developers results primarily from exogenous stimuli, that is, the diffusion of modern values and institutions from the early modernizers. Modernizing Third World elites are understood to be guided by the Western model adopting and adapting its technology; assimilating its values and patterns of action; importing its financial, industrial, and educational institutions; and so on. Western colonialism, foreign aid, foreign educational opportunities, overseas business investments, the mass media, etc., are all important channels for the transmission of modernity. For some writers this means that the world is converging toward a uniform and standardized culture resembling that of the United States and Western Europe.

Though, as will be noted below, there is disagreement on the extent to which traditional features will disappear, there is broad agreement on the notion that individual developing countries must in some way replicate the path followed by the early modernizers. The principal difference between already developed countries and developing ones is not in the nature of the process, but in the speed and intensity making it possible for the late modernizers to "skip stages" or "telescope time."[5] Despite the fact that the modernization perspective stresses the importance of the worldwide context in its analysis of social change, the basic historical setting for modernization is the nation state. As Black notes, "Societies in the process of modernization must . . . be considered both as *independent* entities, the traditional institutions of which are being adapted to modern functions, and also as societies under the influence of many *outside* forces."[6] The world is fragmented, and yet bound by intersocietal communication. It is, in the words of Dankwart Rustow, a "world of nations."[7]

---

[4] Gabriel Almond, "Introduction: A Functional Approach to Comparative Politics," in Almond and James S. Coleman, *The Politics of the Developing Areas* (Princeton, 1960) p. 64. Statements such as these have led to the criticism that modernization is an ethnocentric approach. But rather than pointing out their ethnocentricity, it is more important to indicate that they reflect an assumption which becomes a key methodological option, ethnocentric or otherwise.

[5] See Kalman H. Silvert, *The Conflict Society: Reaction and Revolution in Latin America* (New York, 1966), p. 261.

[6] Black, *The Dynamics of Modernization,* p. 50 (emphasis added).

[7] Dankwart A. Rustow, *A World of Nations: Problems of Political Modernization* (Washington: The Brookings Institution, 1967).

Finally, it is clear that the stress on the differences in values from one context to another has some important implications for the modernization perspective's concept of human nature. The characteristic of developed societies which has received the most attention in the literature is the presumed "rationality" of both leaders and followers. Indeed, W. Moore has recently argued that modernization is best understood as "the process of rationalization of social behavior and social organization." Rationalization, or the "institutionalization of rationality," is defined as the "normative expectation that objective information and rational calculus of procedures will be applied in pursuit or achievement of any utilitarian goal. . . . It is exemplified but not exhausted in the use of sophisticated technology in construction and production."[8] As such, modernization theorists agree with the assumption of economic rationality implicit in the economic growth models of traditional economic theory. But as Moore noted in a 1950s article, where they differ with traditional economics is in the assumption that rational behavior is a universal human characteristic. By contrast with the developed countries, attitudes and values in developing nations are such that individuals "behave in ways that are 'irrational' or 'nonrational' as judged on economic grounds."[9] This explains why Bolivian businessmen will not take risks with their capital, preferring to put money in Swiss banks. Or why Ecuadorians will study law rather than enter a more lucrative career in business or technology.

In concluding this section, it is necessary to note that from the very outset certain elements of the modernization perspective came into criticism from scholars who shared its basic assumptions. It is revealing that much of the criticism came from researchers who were experts in many of the features of individual "traditional" societies. They were uncomfortable with the arbitrary designation of a wide variety of phenomena as "traditional," with little concern for the rich, complex, and often strikingly different characteristics subsumed under that vague concept. They argued that many belief systems and institutional arrangements with no common referent in the United States or Western Europe could indeed have modernizing functions. J. Gusfield has summarized many of the relevant arguments adding that even in modern societies certain traditional characteristics may survive or gain renewed importance.[10] These

---

[8] Wilbert Moore "Modernization and Rationalization: Processes and Restraints," *Economic Development and Cultural Change*, 35 (1977, supplement), pp. 34–35.

[9] Moore, "Motivational Aspects of Development," in *Social Change*, ed. Amitai and Eva Etzioni, (New York, 1964), p. 292. See also his "Social Change" in the *International Encyclopedia of the Social Sciences* (1968).

[10] J. Gusfield, "Tradition and Modernity: Misplaced Polarities in the Study of Social Change," *American Journal of Sociology* 72 (January 1967).

arguments do not, however, constitute a rejection of the assumptions of the modernization perspective but an illustration of their use. Despite the title of his article, Gusfield does not argue that tradition and modernity are "misplaced polarities." Gusfield simply points to a confusion in the use of terms and their misapplication in concrete situations. He continues to accept the assumptions that tradition and modernity are valid theoretical polarities and that tradition in its many ramifications is the basic obstacle to modernization. If a particular society or region experiences significant economic growth, what was thought to be an other-worldly religion undermining rational economic behavior may in fact be a creed capable of promoting instrumental values conducive to modernization. There can be a "modernity of tradition."[11]

Recent amendments to the modernization perspective are extensions of the same internal critique. Reflecting the sobering reality of the 1970s with many studies pointing to an ever increasing gap between rich and poor nations, several modernization writers have questioned the earlier belief in an inevitable and uniform process leading to the convergence of societies on economic as well as social and political grounds.[12] Others, while not questioning the inevitability of the process, point more forcefully than before to its disruptive and negative effects which affect the "latecomers" much more seriously than the "survivors."[13] It still remains the case that to modernize, however good or inevitable that process may be, it is by definition necessary to overcome traditional values and institutions and substitute them for more modern ones.

Latin America and the Modernization Perspective. Mainstream U.S. scholarship on Latin America has implicitly or explicitly drawn on the modernization perspective to explain Latin American underdevelopment. Often contrasting the Latin American experience to that of the United States or Western Europe, it has argued that traditional attitudes and institutions stemming from the colonial past have proven to be serious, if not fatal, stumbling blocks to any indigenous effort to develop economically, socially, or politically. The values of Catholicism, of large Indian populations, or of aristocratic rural elites have contributed to "irrational" patterns of behavior highly detrimental to modernization.

One of the most influential statements is S.M. Lipset's "Values,

---

[11] Lloyd I. and Susanne H. Rudolph, *The Modernity of Traditional Development in India* (Chicago, 1967). Another work in this vein is Robert Ward and Rustow, eds. *Political Modernization in Japan and Turkey* (Princeton, 1964).

[12] S.N. Eisenstadt, *Tradition, Change and Modernity* (New York, 1973) and Moore, "Modernization and Rationalization."

[13] Marion Levy, Jr., *Modernization: Latecomers and Survivors* (New York, 1972).

Education and Entrepreneurship," the introductory essay to the best-selling text *Elites in Latin America.* Lipset draws directly from T. Parsons and D. McClelland in arguing that:

> The relative failure of Latin American countries to develop on a scale comparable to those of North America or Australasia has been seen as, in some part, a consequence of variations in value systems dominating these two areas. The overseas offspring of Great Britain seemingly had the advantage of values derivative in part from the Protestant Ethic and from the formation of "New Societies" in which feudal ascriptive elements were missing. Since Latin America, on the other hand is Catholic, it has been dominated for centuries by ruling elites who created a social structure congruent with feudal social values.[14]

In his article Lipset concentrates primarily on explaining economic underdevelopment as a function of the lack of adequate entrepreneurial activity. The lack of instrumental behavior, weak achievement orientations, and the disdain for the pragmatic and material have prevented the rise of a risk-taking business sector oriented toward rational competitive and bureaucratic enterprise. The educational system has only served to perpetuate the problem by continuing to socialize the population with inappropriate attitudes. "Even [in Argentina] the second most developed Latin American country . . . the traditional landed, aristocratic disdain for manual work, industry, and trading, continues to affect the educational orientations of many students."[15] Lipset cites a whole host of studies, many of which were based on survey research in Latin America, to conclude that "the comparative evidence from the various nations of the Americas sustains the generalization that cultural values are among the major factors which affect the potentiality for economic development."[16] Recent textbooks on Latin America have clearly been influenced by such observations. Thus, R. Adie and G.E. Poitras note that "there is in Latin America a social climate in which the very rewards which have spurred on the entrepreneurs in, for exam-

---

[14] Seymour Martin Lipset, "Values, Education and Entrepreneurship," in *Elites in Latin America,* ed. Lipset and Aldo Solari, (New York, 1963). For another study in which Lipset expresses similar views about Latin America, while extolling the opposite values in the United States, see his *The First New Nation* (New York, 1963).

[15] Lipset, "Values, Education and Entrepreneurship," p. 19.

[16] Ibid., p. 30. Some of the studies cited include T. C. Cohran, "Cultural Factors in Economic Growth," *Journal of Economic History* 20 (1974); T. R. Fillol, *Social Factors in Economic Development: The Argentine Case* (Cambridge, Mass., 1961); B.J. Siegel, "Social Structure and Economic Change in Brazil," in *Economic Growth: Brazil, India, Japan* ed. Simon Kuznets et al., (Durham, N.C., 1955); and W. P. Strassman, "The Industrialist," in *Continuity and Change in Latin America,* ed. John J. Johnson (Stanford, 1964).

ple, North America, are consistently deemphasised . . . socioeconomic change dependent on business activities . . . cannot necessarily be expected to follow the same path as it has elsewhere."[17]

*   *   *   *   *

THE DEPENDENCY PERSPECTIVE

Like the modernization perspective, the dependency perspective resulted from the work of many different scholars in different branches of the social sciences. . . .

In its emphasis on the expansive nature of capitalism and in its structural analysis of society, the dependency literature draws on Marxist insights and is related to the Marxist theory of imperialism. However, its examination of processes in Latin America imply important revisions in classical Leninist formulations, both historically and in light of recent trends. The focus is on explaining Latin American underdevelopment, and not on the functioning of capitalism, though some authors argue that their efforts will contribute to an understanding of capitalism and its contradictions.

Assumptions.   The dependency perspective rejects the assumption made by modernization writers that the unit of analysis in studying underdevelopment is the national society. The domestic cultural and institutional features of Latin America are in themselves simply not the key variables accounting for the relative backwardness of the area, though, as will be seen below, domestic structures are certainly critical intervening factors. The relative presence of traditional and modern features may, or may not, help to differentiate societies; but it does not in itself explain the origins of modernity in some contexts and the lack of modernity in others. As such, the tradition-modernity polarity is of little value as a fundamental working concept. The dependency perspective assumes that the development of a national or regional unit can only be understood in connection with its historical insertion into the worldwide political-economic system which emerged with the wave of European colonizations of the world. This global system is thought to be characterized by the unequal but combined development of its different components. As Sunkel and Paz put it:

> Both underdevelopment and development are aspects of the same phenomenon, both are historically simultaneous, both are linked

---

[17] R. Adie and G.E. Poitras, *Latin America: The Politics of Immobility* (Englewood Cliffs, N.J., 1974), pp. 73, 75. For similar views see pp. 252–53 and W.R. Duncan, *Latin American Politics: A Developmental Approach* (New York, 1976), p. 240.

functionally and, therefore, interact and condition each other mutually. This results. . . in the division of the world between industrial, advanced or "central" countries, and underdeveloped, backward or "peripheral" countries.[18]

The center is viewed as capable of dynamic development responsive to internal needs, and as the main beneficiary of the global links. On the other hand, the periphery is seen as having a reflex type of development; one which is both constrained by its incorporation into the global system and which results from its adaptation to the requirements of the expansion of the center. As Theotônio dos Santos indicates:

Dependency is a situation in which a certain number of countries have their economy conditioned by the development and expansion of another . . . placing the dependent countries in a backward position exploited by the dominant countries.[19]

It is important to stress that the process can be understood only by reference to its historical dimension and by focusing on the total network of social relations as they evolve in different contexts over time. For this reason dependence is characterized as "structural, historical and totalizing" or an "integral analysis of development."[20] It is meaningless to develop, as some social scientists have, a series of synchronic statistical indicators to establish relative levels of dependence or independence among different national units to test the "validity" of the model.[21] The unequal development of the world

---

[18] Osvaldo Sunkel and Pedro Paz, *El subdesarrollo latinoamericano y la teoria del desarrollo* (Mexico, 1970), p. 6.

[19] Theotônio dos Santos, "La crisis del desarrollo y las relaciones de dependencia en América Latina," in *La dependencia político-económica de América Latina,* ed. H. Jaguaribe et al. (Mexico, 1970), p. 180. See also his *Dependencia y cambio social* (Santiago, 1970) and *Socialismo o Fascismo: El nuevo carácter de la dependencia y el dilema latinoamericano* (Buenos Aires, 1972).

[20] Sunkel and Paz, *El subdesarrollo latinoamericano* p. 39; Fernando Henrique Cardoso and Enzo Faletto, *Dependencia y desarrollo en América Latina* (Mexico, 1969). chap. 2.

[21] This is the problem with the studies by Robert Kaufman et al., "A Preliminary Test of the Theory of Dependency," *Comparative Politics* 7 (April 1975), pp. 303–30, and C. Chase-Dunn, "The Effects of International Economic Dependence on Development and Inequality: A Cross National Study," *American Sociological Review* 40 (December 1975). It is interesting to note that Marxist scholars make the same mistake. They point to features in the dependency literature such as unemployment, marginalization etc., noting that they are not peculiar to peripheral countries but characterize capitalist countries in general. Thus "dependence" is said to have no explanatory value beyond a Marxist theory of capitalist society. See Sanyaya Lall, "Is Dependence a Useful Concept in Analyzing Underdevelopment?" *World Development* 3 (November 1975) and Theodore Weisscopf, "Dependence as an Explanation of Underdevelopment: A Critique." (Paper presented at the Sixth Annual Latin American Studies Association Meeting, Atlanta, Georgia, 1976). The point of dependency analysis is not the relative mix at one point in time of certain identifiable factors but the evolution over time of structural relations which help to explain

goes back to the 16th century with the formation of a capitalist world economy in which some countries in the center were able to specialize in industrial production of manufactured goods because the peripheral areas of the world which they colonized provided the necessary primary goods, agricultural and mineral, for consumption in the center. Contrary to some assumptions in economic theory the international division of labor did not lead to parallel development through comparative advantage. The center states gained at the expense of the periphery. But, just as significantly, the different functions of center and peripheral societies had a profound effect on the evolution of internal social and political structures. Those which evolved in the periphery reinforced economies with a narrow range of primary exports. The interdependent nature of the world capitalist system and the qualitative transformations in that system over time make it inconceivable to think that individual nations on the periphery could somehow replicate the evolutionary experience of the now developed nations.[22]

It follows from an emphasis on global structural processes and variations in internal structural arrangements that contextual variables, at least in the long run, shape and guide the behavior of groups and individuals. It is not inappropriate attitudes which

---

the differential development of capitalism in different parts of the world. As a historical model it cannot be tested with cross national data. For an attempt to differentiate conceptually contemporary capitalism of the core and peripheral countries, and thus more amenable to such criticism, see Samir Amin, *Accumulation on a World Scale* (New York, 1974).

[22] Some authors have criticized the focus of the literature on the evolution of the world capitalist system. David Ray, for example, has argued that "soviet satellites" are also in a dependent and unequal relationship vis-à-vis the Soviet Union and that the key variable should not be capitalism but "political power." Robert Packenham has also argued that the most important critique of the dependency literature is that it does not consider the implications of "power." See Ray, "The Dependency Model of Latin American Underdevelopment: Three Basic Fallacies," *Journal of Interamerican Studies and World Affairs* 15 (February 1973) and Packenham, "Latin American Dependency Theories: Strengths and Weaknesses." (Paper presented to the Harvard-MIT Joint Seminar on Political Development, February, 1974), especially pp. 16–17, 54. This criticism misses the point completely. It is not power relations today which cause underdevelopment, but the historical evolution of a world economic system which led to economic specialization more favorable to some than others. It is precisely this concern with the evolution of world capitalism which has led to the preoccupation in the dependency literature with rejecting interpretations stressing the "feudal" rather than "capitalist" nature of colonial and post colonial Latin American agriculture. On this point see Sergio Bagú, *Economía de la Sociedad Colonial* (Buenos Aires, 1949); Luis Vitale, "América Latina: Feudal o Capitalista?" *Revista Estrategia*, 3 (1966) and *Interpretación Marxista de la historia de Chile* (Santiago, 1967); and E. Laclau, "Feudalism and Capitalism in Latin America," *New Left Review* 67 (May–July 1971). A brilliant recent exposition of the importance of studying the evolution of the capitalist world system in order to understand underdevelopment which focuses more on the center states than on the periphery is Immanuel Wallerstein, *The Modern World System: Capitalist Agriculture and the Origins of the European World Economy in the Sixteenth Century* (New York, 1974).

contribute to the absence of entrepreneurial behavior or to institutional arrangements reinforcing underdevelopment. Dependent, peripheral development produces an opportunity structure such that personal gain for dominant groups and entrepreneurial elements is not conducive to the collective gain of balanced development. This is a fundamental difference with much of the modernization literature. It implies that dependence analysts, though they do not articulate the point explicitly, share the classical economic theorists' view of human nature. They assume that individuals in widely different societies are capable of pursuing rational patterns of behavior; able to assess information objectively in the pursuit of utilitarian goals. What varies is not the degree of rationality, but the structural foundations of the incentive systems which, in turn, produce different forms of behavior given the same process of rational calculus. It was not attitudinal transformations which generated the rapid industrialization which developed after the Great Depression, but the need to replace imports with domestic products. Or, as Cardoso points out in his studies of entrepreneurs, it is not values which condition their behavior as much as technological dependence, state intervention in the economy, and their political weakness vis-à-vis domestic and foreign actors.[23] What appear as anomalies in the modernization literature can be accounted for by a focus on contextual processes in the dependence literature.

It is necessary to underscore the fact that dependency writers stress the importance of the "way internal and external structural components are connected" in elaborating the structural context of underdevelopment. As such, underdevelopment is not simply the result of "external constraints" on peripheral societies, nor can dependency be operationalized solely with reference to clusters of external variables.[24] Dependency in any given society is a complex set of associations in which the external dimensions are determinative in varying degrees and, indeed, internal variables may very well reinforce the pattern of external linkages. Historically it has

---

[23] Cardoso, *Empresário industrial e desenvolvimento econômico no Brazil* (São Paulo, 1964) and *Ideologías de la burguesia industrial en sociedades dependientes* (Mexico, 1971).

[24] Cardoso and Faletto, *Dependencia y desarrollo*, p. 20. Indeed Cardoso argues that the distinction between external and internal is "metaphysical." See his "Teoría de la dependencia o análisis de situaciones concretas de dependencia?" *Revista Latinoamericana de Ciencia Política* (December 1970), p. 404. The ontology implicit in such an analysis is the one of "internal relations." See Bertell Ollman, *Alienation: Marx's Conception of Man in Capitalist Society* (London, 1971). This point is important because both Frank and the early ECLA literature was criticized for their almost mechanistic relationship between external and internal variables. Frank acknowledges this problem and tries to answer his critics in *Lumpenbourgeoisie and Lumpen-development* (New York, 1967). "Tests" of dependency theory also attribute an excessively mechanical dimension to the relationship. See Kaufman et al., "A Preliminary Test."

been rare for local interests to develop on the periphery which are capable of charting a successful policy of self-sustained development. Dominant local interests, given the nature of class arrangements emerging from the characteristics of peripheral economies, have tended to favor the preservation of rearticulation of patterns of dependency in their interests.

It is also important to note that while relations of dependency viewed historically help to explain underdevelopment, it does not follow that dependent relations today necessarily perpetuate across the board underdevelopment. With the evolution of the world system, the impact of dependent relations can change in particular contexts. This is why Cardoso, in studying contemporary Brazil, stresses the possibility of "associated-dependent development," and Sunkel and Fuenzalida are able to envision sharp economic growth among countries most tied into the contemporary transnational system.[25] Because external-internal relations are complex, and because changes in the world system over time introduce new realities, it is indispensable to study comparatively concrete national and historical situations. As Aníbal Quijano says, "The relationships of dependency . . . take on many forms. The national societies in Latin America are dependent, as is the case with the majority of the Asian, African and some European countries. However, each case does not present identical dependency relations."[26] The dependency perspective has thus concentrated on a careful historical evaluation of the similarities and differences in the "situations of dependency" of the various Latin American countries over time implying careful attention to "preexisting conditions" in different contexts.

The description of various phases in the world system and differing configurations of external-internal linkages, follow from this insistence on diachronic analysis and its application to concrete cases. The dependency perspective is primarily a historical model with no claim to "universal validity." This is why it has paid less attention to the formulation of precise theoretical constructs, such as those found in the modernization literature, and more attention to the specification of historical phases which are an integral part of the framework.

---

[25] Cardoso, "Associated Dependent Development: Theoretical Implications," in *Authoritarian Brazil*, ed. Alfred Stepan (New Haven, 1973), and Sunkel and Edmundo Fuenzalida, "Transnational Capitalism and National Development," in *Transnational Capitalism and National Development*, ed. José J. Villamil (London, forthcoming). It is thus incorrect to argue that dependency analysts ignore the evidence of certain kinds of economic growth. For fallacies in the dependency literature see Cardoso "Las contradicciones del desarrollo asociado," *Desarrollo Económico* 4 (April–June 1974).

[26] Anibal Quijano, "Dependencia, Cambio Social y Urbanización en América Latina," in *América Latina: Ensayos de interpretación sociológico político,* ed. Cardoso and F. Weffort (Santiago, 1970).

The dependency literature distinguishes between the "mercantilistic" colonial period (1500–1750), the period of "outward growth" dependent on primary exports (1750–1914), the period of the crisis of the "liberal model" (1914–1950), and the current period of "transnational capitalism."

As already noted, because of the need for raw materials and foodstuffs for the growing industrialization of England, Germany, the United States, and France, Latin American productive structures were aimed from the outset at the export market. During the colonial period, the economic specialization was imposed by the Iberian monarchies. As Bagú notes in his classic study, "Colonial production was not directed by the needs of national consumers, and not even by the interests of local producers. The lines of production were structured and transformed to conform to an order determined by the imperial metropolis. The colonial economy was consequently shaped by its complementary character. The products that did not compete with those of Spain or Portugal in the metropolitan, international or colonial markets, found tolerance or stimulus."[27] During the 19th century, exports were actively pursued by the politically dominant groups. The independence movement did not attempt to transform internal productive structures; it was aimed at eliminating Iberian interference in the commercialization of products to and from England and northern Europe. The logic of the productive system in this period of "outwardly directed development," in ECLA's terms, was not conducive to the creation of a large industrial sector. Economic rationality, not only of individual entrepreneurs but also of the system, dictated payments in kind and/or extremely low wages and/or the use of slavery, thus markedly limiting the internal market. At the same time, the accumulation of foreign exchange made relatively easy the acquisition of imported industrial products. Any expansion of exports was due more to political than economic factors and depended on a saleable export commodity, and plenty of land and labor, for its success.

There were, however, important differences between regions and countries. During the colonial period these are attributable to differences in colonial administrations, natural resources, and types of production. During the 19th century a key difference was the degree of local elite control over productive activities for export. Though in all countries elites controlled export production initially (external commercialization was mainly under foreign control), towards the end of the century in some countries control was largely relinquished to foreign exploitation. Where this occurred, the economic role of local elites was reduced considerably, though the importance

---

[27] Bagú, *Economía de la sociedad colonial,* pp. 122–23.

of this reduction varied depending both on the degree to which the foreign enclave displaced the local elite from the export sector and the extent to which its economic activities were diversified. Concurrently, the state bureaucracy expanded and acquired increasing importance through regulations and taxation of the enclave sector. The state thus became the principal intermediary between the local economy and the enclave, which generally had little *direct* internal secondary impact. Other differences, especially at the turn of the century, are the varying importance of incipient industrialization, the size and importance of middle- and working-class groups, variations in export products, natural resources, and so on.

The world wars and the depression produced a crisis in the export-oriented economies through the collapse of external demand, and therefore of the capacity to import. The adoption of fiscal and monetary policies aimed at supporting the internal market and avoiding the negative effects of the external disequilibrium produced a favorable climate for the growth of an industrial sector under national auspices. The available foreign exchange was employed to acquire capital goods to substitute imports of consumer articles. The early successes of the transition to what ECLA calls "inwardly directed development" depended to a large extent on the different political alliances which emerged in the various national settings, and on the characteristics of the social and political structures inherited from the precrisis period.

Thus, in the enclave situations the earliest developments were attained in Mexico and Chile, where middle- and lower-class groups allied in supporting state development policies, ultimately strengthening the urban bourgeoisie. The alliance was successful in Chile because of the importance of middle-class parties which emerged during the final period of export-oriented development, and the early consolidation of a trade union movement. The antecedents of the Mexican situation are to be found in the destruction of agricultural elites during the revolution. Such structural conditions were absent in other enclave situations (Bolivia, Perú, Venezuela, and Central America) where the internal development phase began later under new conditions of dependence, though in some cases with similar political alliances (Bolivia, Venezuela, Guatemala, Costa Rica). Throughout the crisis period agrarian-based and largely non-exporting groups were able to remain in power, appealing in some cases to military governments, and preserving the political scheme that characterized the export-oriented period.

In the nonenclave situations, considerable industrial growth was attained in Argentina and Brazil. In the former, export-oriented agrarian entrepreneurs had invested considerably in production for the internal market and the contraction of the export sector only accentuated this trend. In Brazil the export-oriented agrarian groups collapsed with the crisis and the state, as in Chile and Mexico, assumed a major developmental role with the support of a complex alliance of urban entrepreneurs, nonexport agrarian elites, popular sectors, and middle-class groups. In Colombia the export-oriented agrarian elites remained in power and did not foster significant internal industrialization until the fifties.

The import substituting industrialization attained greatest growth in Argentina, Brazil, and Mexico. It soon, however, reached its limits, given the parameters under which it was realized. Since capital goods for the establishment of industrial parks were acquired in the central nations, the success of the policy ultimately depended on adequate foreign exchange supplies. After reaching maximum growth through the accumulation of foreign exchange during the Second World War, the industrialization programs could only continue—given the available political options—on the basis of an increased external debt and further reliance on foreign investments. This accumulation of foreign reserves permitted the success of the national-populist alliances in Argentina and Brazil which gave the workers greater welfare while maintaining investments. The downfall of Perón and the suicide of Vargas symbolized the end of this easy period of import substitution.

But the final blow to "import substitution" industrialization came not from difficulties in the periphery but further transformations in the center which have led, in Sunkel's term, to the creation of a new "transnational" system. With rapid economic recovery the growing multinational corporations sought new markets and cheaper production sites for their increasingly technological manufacturing process. Dependency consequently acquired a "new character" as Dos Santos noted, which would have a profound effect on Latin America. Several processes were involved resulting in (1) the investment of centrally based corporations in manufactures within the periphery for sales in its internal market or, as Cardoso and Faletto note, the "internationalization of the internal market"; (2) a new international division of labor in which the periphery acquires capital goods, technology, and raw materials from the central nations, and export profits, along with its traditional raw materials and a few manufactured items produced by multinational subsidiaries; and (3) a denationalization of the older import substituting industries established originally.[28] Although the "new dependence"

---

[28] Sunkel "Capitalismo transnacional y desintegración nacional en América Latina," *Estudios Internacionales* 4 (January–March 1971) an "Big Business and Dependencia: A Latin American View," *Foreign Affairs* 50 (April 1972); Cardoso and Faletto, *Dependencia y desarrollo;* Dos Santos, El nuevo carácter de la dependencia (Santiago, 1966).

is in evidence throughout the continent, the process has asserted itself more clearly in the largest internal markets such as Brazil, where the weakness of the trade-union movement (the comparison with Argentina in this respect is instructive) coupled with authoritarian political structures has created a singularly favorable investment climate.

In subsequent and more recent works writers in the dependency framework have pursued different strategies of research. Generally speaking, the early phases of the historical process have received less attention, though the contribution of I. Wallerstein to an understanding of the origins of the world system is a major addition to the literature. Most writers have preferred to focus on the current "new situation" of dependence. Some have devoted more attention to an effort at elaborating the place of dependent capitalism as a contribution to the Marxist analysis of capitalist society. Scholars in this vein tend to argue more forcefully than others that dependent capitalism is impossible and that socialism provides the only historically viable alternative. Others have focused more on the analysis of concrete cases of dependence, elaborating in some detail the various interconnections between domestic and foreign forces, and noting the possibility of different kinds of dependent development.[29] Still others have turned their attention to characterizing the nature of the new capitalist system, with particular emphasis on the emergence of a "transnational system" which is rendering more complex and problematic the old distinctions of center and periphery. Particularly for the last two tendencies, the emphasis is on the design of new empirical studies while attempting to systematize

---

[29] Cardoso, "Teoría de la dependencia." A recent trend in dependency writings attempts to explain the current wave of authoritarianism in Latin America as a result of economic difficulties created by the exhaustion of the easy import substituting industrialization. The new situation leads to a process of development led by the state and the multinational corporations, which concentrates income toward the top, increases the levels of capital accumulation and expands heavy industry; the old populist alliances can therefore no longer be maintained. See Dos Santos, *Socialismo o fascismo: el nuevo carácter de la dependencia y el dilema latinoamericano* (Buenos Aires, 1972): Guillermo O'Donnell, *Modernization and Bureaucratic-Authoritarianism: Studies in Latin American Politics* (Berkeley: University of California 1973); Atilio Borón, "El fascismo como categoría histórica: en torno al problema de las dictaduras en América Latina," *Revista Mexicana de Sociología* 34 (April–June 1977); the effects of this situation on labor are explored in Kenneth P. Erickson and Patrick Peppe, "Dependent Capitalist Development, U.S. Foreign Policy, and Repression of the Working Class in Chile and Brazil," *Latin American Perspectives* 3 (Winter 1976). However, in the postscript to their 1968 book, Cardoso and Faletto caution against adopting an excessively mechanistic view on this point, against letting "economism kill history": Cardoso and Faletto. "Estado y proceso político en América Latina," *Revista Mexicana de Sociología* 34 (April–June 1977), p. 383. Articles with dependency perspective appear frequently in the *Revista Mexicana de Sociología* as well as in *Latin American Perspectives*.

further some of the propositions implicit in the conceptual framework.

SUMMARY AND CONCLUSIONS

Modernization and dependency are two different perspectives each
claiming to provide conceptual and analytical tools capable of explaining the relative underdevelopment of Latin America. The object of inquiry is practically the only thing that these two competing
"visions" have in common, as they differ substantially not only
on fundamental assumptions, but also on methodological implications and strategies for research.

Though there are variations in the literature, the *level of analysis*
of a substantial tradition in the modernization perspective, and
the one which informs most reflections on Latin America, is behavioral or microsociological. The primary focus is on individuals or
aggregates of individuals, their values, attitudes, and beliefs. The
dependency perspective, by contrast, is structural or macrosociological. Its focus is on the mode of production, patterns of international
trade, political and economic linkages between elites in peripheral
and central countries, group and class alliances and conflicts, and
so on. Both perspectives are concerned with the process of development in national societies. However, for the modernizaton writer
the national society is the basic *unit of analysis,* while the writer
in a dependence framework considers the global system and its
various forms of interaction with national societies as the primary
object of inquiry.

For the dependency perspective, the *time dimension* is a crucial
aspect of what is fundamentally a historical model. Individual societies cannot be presumed to be able to replicate the evolution of other
societies because the very transformation of an interrelated world
system may preclude such an option. The modernization potential
of individual societies must be seen in light of changes over time
in the interactions between external and internal variables. The
modernization perspective is obviously concerned about the origins
of traditional and modern values; but, the time dimension is not
fundamental to the explanatory pretensions of a model which claims
"universal validity." Without knowing the source of modernity inhibiting characteristics, it is still possible to identify them by reference to their counterparts in developing contexts.

At the root of the differences between the two perspectives is a
fundamentally different *perception of human nature.* Dependency
assumes that human behavior in economic matters is a "constant."
Individuals will behave differently in different contexts not because
they are different but because the contexts are different. The insis-

tence on structures and, in the final analysis, on the broadest structural category of all, the world system, follows logically from the view that opportunity structures condition human behavior. Modernizationists, on the other hand, attribute the lack of certain behavioral patterns to the "relativity" of human behavior; to the fact that cultural values and beliefs, regardless of opportunity structures, underlie the patterns of economic action. Thus, the *conception of change* in the modernization perspective is a product of innovations which result from the adoption of modern attitudes among elites, and eventually followers. Though some modernization theorists are now more pessimistic about the development potential of such changes, modernizing beliefs are a prerequisite for development. For dependency analysts the conception of change is different. Change results from the realignment of dependency relations over time. Whether or not development occurs and how it occurs is subject to controversy. Given the rapid evolution of the world system, dependent development is possible in certain contexts, not in others. Autonomy, through a break in relations of dependency, may not lead to development of the kind already arrived at in the developed countries because of the inability to recreate the same historical conditions, but it might lead to a different kind of development stressing different values. Thus, the *prescription for change* varies substantially in the dependency perspective depending on the ideological outlook of particular authors. It is not a logical consequence of the historical model. In the modernization perspective the prescription for change follows more automatically from the assumptions of the model, implying greater consensus.

From a methodological point of view the modernization perspective is much more parsimonious than its counterpart. And the focus of much of the literature on the microsociological level makes it amenable to the elaboration of precise explanatory propositions such as those of D. McClelland or E. Hagen. Dependency, by contrast, is more descriptive and its macrosociological formulations are much less subject to translation into a simple set of explanatory propositions. Many aspects of dependency, and particularly the linkages between external phenomena and internal class and power relations are unclear and need to be studied with more precision and care. For this reason the dependency perspective is an "approach" to the study of underdevelopment rather than a "theory." And yet, precisely because modernization theory relies on a simple conceptual framework and a reductionist approach, it is far less useful for the study of a complex phenomenon such as development or underdevelopment.

But the strengths of the dependency perspective lie not only in its consideration of a richer body of evidence and a broader range of phenomena, it is also more promising from a methodological point of view. The modernization perspective has fundamental flaws which make it difficult to provide for a fair test of its own assumptions. It will be recalled that the modernization perspective draws on a model with "universal validity" which assumes that traditional values are not conducive to modern behavioral patterns of action. Given that underdevelopment, on the basis of various economic and social indicators, is an objective datum, the research task becomes one of identifying modernizing values and searching for their opposites in underdeveloped contexts.

In actual research efforts, the modernity inhibiting characteristics are often "deduced" from impressionistic observation. This is the case with much of the political science literature on Latin America. However, more "rigorous" methods, such as survey research, have also been employed, particularly in studies of entrepreneurial activity. Invariably, whether through deduction or survey research, less appropriate values for modernization such as "arielismo" (a concern for transcendental as opposed to material values) or "low-achievement" (lack of risk-taking attitudes) have been identified thus "confirming" the hypothesis that traditional values contribute to underdevelopment. If by chance the use of control groups should establish little or no difference in attitudes in a developed and underdeveloped context, the research instrument can be considered to be either faulty or the characteristics tapped not the appropriate ones for identifying traditional attitudes. The latter alternative might lead to the "discovery" of a new "modernity of tradition" literature or of greater flexibility than anticipated in traditional norms or of traditional residuals in the developed country.

The problem with the model and its behavioral level of analysis is that the explanation for underdevelopment is part of the preestablished conceptual framework. It is already "known" that in backward areas the modernity inhibiting characteristics play the dominant role, otherwise the areas would not be backward. As such, the test of the hypothesis involves a priori acceptance of the very hypothesis up for verification, with empirical evidence gathered solely in an illustrative manner. The focus on individuals simply does not permit consideration of a broader range of contextual variables which might lead to invalidating the assumptions. Indeed, the modernity of tradition literature, which has pointed to anomalies in the use of the tradition modernity "polarities," is evidence of how such a perspective can fall victim to the "and so" fallacy. Discrepancies are accounted for not by a reformulation, but by adding a new definition or a new corollary to the preexisting conceptual framework.

Much work needs to be done within a dependency perspective

to clarify its concepts and causal interrelationships, as well as to assess its capacity to explain social processes in various parts of peripheral societies. And yet the dependency approach appears to have a fundamental advantage over the modernization perspective: It is open to historically grounded conceptualization in underdeveloped contexts, while modernization is locked into an illustrative methodological style by virtue of its very assumptions.

29

The Underdevelopment of Dependency Theory

Tony Smith

In the midst of the turbulent 70s, when the ascendancy of the "South," or noncommunist industrializing countries, is everywhere in evidence, it is a bit difficult to remember back to the 60s when the social science establishment in the United States apparently dominated world literature on the topic of political and economic modernization in Africa, Asia, and Latin America. The end of colonialism and the expansion of this country's global power into the "vacuums" open to revolutionary activity were largely responsible for calling forth much of this scholarly effort; and, thanks to a growing interest in model building and to well-financed opportunities in area studies, solid professional careers were built in relatively short order. Some of this work has stood the test of time: monographs on delimited problems or, more rarely, theoretical explorations of general patterns of development. For the most part, however, standards of historical scholarship were not high, and to reread the methodological sections of these works with their jargon and their models is often a tedious affair, tempered only by amazement at the poverty of it all. Nor did this literature do much apparent good in influencing political judgment in Washington, if the last two decades of American policy in South-

Source: Tony Smith, "The Underdevelopment of Development Literature: The Case of Dependency Theory," *World Politics,* January 1979, pp. 247–88. By permission. Article and footnotes abridged by the editors.

east Asia or Latin America are any standard by which to measure.

Today a rival literature has appeared on the scene which might be called dependency theory. North Americans figure in its ranks, but the writers are more likely to bear African, Asian, or Latin American surnames. The term "dependency" originated with writings on Latin America; previously, work of this sort was better known for speaking of "neocolonialism," thereby betraying its African or Asian origins. As the different nomenclature suggests, the *dependencistas*, if we may use their Latin American name, are no monolithic group. Their general outlook has been in evidence for some time in a variety of places, so that substantial disagreements exist within this "school." Nevertheless, it is useful to distinguish the *dependencistas* as a group, since in important respects these writers share an identity of outlook.

Probably the chief feature of the dependency school is its insistence that it is not internal characteristics of particular countries so much as the structure of the international system—particularly in its economy aspects—that is the key variable to be studied in order to understand the form that development has taken in non-communist industralizing countries. Such an emphasis is not the only distinguishing mark of dependency literature, of course: it tends to put more weight on the interaction of political and economic forces than does its developmentalist rival, and it often identifies itself as being unambiguously on the side of change in the South in order to benefit the poorest and more oppressed members of society there. But, as its name implies, dependency theory's most distinctive point is its insistence that the logic of contemporary southern development can only be grasped by placing this process firmly within a globally defined historical context. That is, contemporary political and economic change in the South must be understood as aspects of imperialism today and yesterday. From this perspective alone—from the standpoint of local histories globally understood—can the logic of the development process be comprehended correctly.

As a result, dependency literature has emerged as a powerful ideological vehicle joining southern nationalists and Marxists (together with their northern supporters) within the confines of a generally agreed-upon form of historical analysis. The importance of this union, whatever the tensions existing within it, should not be underestimated: dependency theory is not simply an academic exercise. For the most part, *dependencistas* are committed by their ideas to a form of political action (as they would maintain their developmentalist opponents in the United States to be, however much the latter might deny it). The literature stands out, therefore, because it is something more than a movement in the intellectual history of our day; it is an ideology as well—a form of discourse able to motivate significant political activity. That is, dependency theory represents far more than the intellectual association of Marxism and southern nationalism. It also represents an effort at the practical, concrete unification of two of the most important historical forces of our century, with potentially significant consequences for both local and world history.

This essay is an attempt to investigate what I believe to be a major historiographic failure of dependency theory. It is not intended to assess the relevance of this theory to concrete historical change, nor is it meant as a comprehensive review of the literature (needed as both of these studies are). My argument is simply that dependency theory in general substantially overestimates the power of the international system—or imperialism—in southern affairs today. This is not to deny that northern power is real in the South, nor to dispute that its effect may be to reinforce the established order of rank and privilege there, nor to suggest that imperialism is a term altogether lacking in meaning today. But it is to assert that dependency theory has systematically underestimated the real influence of the South over its own affairs, and to point out the irony of nationalists who have forgotten their own national histories. I hope to suggest not only a critical flaw in dependency theory as it is now written, but an alternative approach to the study of subordinate states in the international system.

I

*   *   *   *   *

There is no doubt that the international system under the expansionist force of European and American capitalism has had an impact on the internal development of technologically backward areas of the world over the last two centuries. Dependency theorists make us aware how intense and complex these interactions were (and still are), and there is substance to their criticism that development literature as it is currently written in the United States tends to mask these linkages for its own ideological reasons. Nor is my objection to the simple omission of evidence relevant to the construction of an historical argument. Selective judgment in the presentation of material is an inevitable part of the study of history. Rather, the objection is to a certain style of thinking which—to use two of the dependency school's favorite words—is biased and ideological, distorting evidence as much in its fashion as the "bourgeois science" that it claims to debunk.

. . . The chief methodological error of this kind of writing is to deprive local histories of their integrity and specificity, thereby making local actors little more than the pawns of outside forces. Feudalism as a force in Latin America? Nonsense, says Frank (to be applauded by Wallerstein); since capitalism has penetrated every nook and cranny of the world system, the concept of feudal relations of production cannot be validly used. Destroy the particular, exalt the general in order to explain everything. Cite Hegel: "The Truth is the Whole." Tribalism as a force in Africa? Colin Leys cannot even bring himself to use the word without putting it in quotation marks, asserting that "among Africanists [this] point . . . perhaps no longer needs arguing." " 'Tribalism,' " Leys maintains, "is a creation of colonialism. It has little or nothing to do with pre-colonial relations between tribes. . . . In neo-colonial Africa, class formation and the development of tribalism accompany each other."[1] Why? Because the logic of the whole (capitalist colonialism) has found it expedient to work its will in the part (Africa) through creating, virtually *ex nihilo,* the divisive force of "tribalism." By such reckoning, all the social structures in history after a certain low level of development in the division of labor could be dissolved—feudal and bureaucratic estates, castes and clans, as well as tribes—in favor of class analysis, the only "real" social formation.

Because this approach is formulistic and reductionist, it is bad historiography. It is formulistic in the sense that it seeks to specify universal laws or processes in blatant disregard of the singular or the idiosyncratic. By the same token it is reductionist, since it forces the particular case to express its identity solely in the terms provided by the general category. The error of this approach is not that it draws attention to the interconnectedness of economic and political processes and events in a global manner, but that it refuses to grant the part *any* autonomy, *any* specificity, *any* particularity independent of its membership in the whole. Such writing is tyrannical. And it has its ties, I suspect, with other ways in which these writers view history. Thus, as late as 1962, in the preface to the second edition of *The Political Economy of Growth* (much lauded by dependency theorists), Paul Baran gives his *nihil obstat* to Stalin's forced industrialization of the Soviet Union in terms that depend for their authority on the author's ability to "totalize," to grasp the logic of the whole.

The problem of the relationship of the whole to the parts is, of course, a recurrent one in the social sciences. The only key to understanding their interaction, so far as I am aware, is to recognize that, while the whole does have a logic undiscernible from analysis

---

[1] Colin Leys, *Underdevelopment in Kenya: The Political Economy of Neo-Colonialism, 1964–1971* (Berkeley: University of California Press, 1974), pp. 198–99.

of the parts considered separately, the parts too have an identity that no amount of understanding of the whole will adequately reveal. In his monumental *Critique de la raison dialectique,* Jean-Paul Sartre makes a telling criticism of Marxists who make "a fetish of totalizing." He illustrates it with an example of the problem of relating an individual biography to a social milieu: "Valéry is a petit bourgeois intellectual, no doubt about it. But not every petit bourgeois intellectual is Valéry. The heuristic inadequacy of contemporary Marxism is contained in these two sentences."[2] Part and whole must be comprehended at the same time as an aspect of each other and as analytically autonomous—although the degree of relative independence will obviously be more or less complete depending on the historical moment. The theoretical consequences are clear: systems composed of complex parts may expect change to come not only from the evolution of the whole (considered dialectically or otherwise), or from outside influences in the form of the impingement of other systems, but also from developments *within the parts* whose movements are endogenously determined. Therefore, in studying the changing configurations of power in North-South relations over the past several decades, we must be aware not only of the way the system is changing overall (for example, in terms of the growing role of the multinational corporation), or of the way the system is being challenged from outside itself (such as in the arms race with the Soviet Union), but also of the manner in which the units within it (both North and South) are evolving in response to locally determined forces whose ultimate development may have profound effects on the greater system outside. Historical analyses that hold to these premises may be difficult to write, since lines of movement tend to become more numerous and more difficult to see synthetically. But only such a form of writing can hope to portray at all adequately the complexity that history actually is.

II

At the risk of sounding hopelessly old-fashioned, I would suggest that, in order to understand the nature of their specificity apart from the international system, the primary single structure of southern countries to be studied is the organization of the state. Even in colonial situations, where the apparatus of the state was under foreign control at the highest levels, the natives invariably

---

[2] Sartre, *Critique de la raison dialectique* (Paris: Gallimard, 1960), p. 44. For a criticism of Sartre on precisely the grounds that he also rides roughshod over the individual case on occasion, see Tony Smith, "Idealism and People's War: Sartre on Algeria," *Political Theory* 1 (November 1973).

wielded significant power at lower levels of the government and in a variety of informal ways. Indeed, it was precisely these constellations of interests accommodating or opposing foreign rule that made for many of the significant differences in the pattern of postwar decolonization. For the colonial regimes themselves had never amounted to more than a thin crust of European officials and officers atop complex networks of local collaborating groups. In the case of India, for example, Mahatma Gandhi tirelessly pointed out to his fellow countrymen that, in the 1930s, a mere 4,000 British civil servants assisted by 60,000 soldiers and 90,000 civilians (businessmen and clergy for the most part) had billeted themselves upon a country of three hundred million persons. The British had constructed a delicately balanced network through which they gained the support of certain favored economic groups (the zamindars acting as landed tax collectors in Bengal, for example), different traditional power holders (especially the native princes after the Great Mutiny of 1857), warrior tribes (such as the Sikhs of the Punjab), and aroused minority groups like the Muslims. Such a brokerage system was to be found in every colonial territory. In some there was a foreign economic presence: the Chinese in Vietnam, Malaya, and Indonesia; the Asians in East Africa; the Levantines in West Africa; the European settlers in Kenya and Algeria. In other cases, there were alliances with traditional ruling groups: the Native Authorities in Nigeria, the Princely States in Malaya, the imperial bureaucracies in Tunisia and Morocco, the Hashemite family in the Fertile Crescent, the ruling cliques in Cochin China and Tonkin which were interested in acting independently of Hue. Still another source of support came from the oppressed groups who found their rights protected and their interests secured by foreigners: Muslim sects in the Levant, Jews in Algeria, Christians in many parts of Asia and Africa. Simple rivalries also played their part: the *politique des races* practiced by Gallieni in Madagascar, or the support of competing religious brotherhoods in the British Sudan and French North Africa. There also were the agents of Western ways: caids in North Africa, native schoolteachers in West Africa, and economic middlemen (compradors). The latter entered into important collaboration with European overseas expansion when a rich Hindu merchant failed to bring his army to the support of his Muslim overlord, the Nabob of Bengal, thereby assuring Robert Clive's great victory at Plassey in 1757. This description should not give the illusion of a system of permanent alliances: old friends could become new enemies and old enemies new friends on the shifting grounds of political competition; ultimately, the collaborative networks found themselves superseded by indigenous forces determined to achieve independence. Thus, even when they failed to control the heights of the state, native political forces played a fairly powerful role

in the colonies; it was their character and structure that profoundly
influenced the process of decolonization.

Just as the variety of local political structures working for or against
colonial rule must be understood in order to make sense of the
intricate pattern of decolonization, so the range of state structures
in the South in the 19th and 20th centuries is the best general
organizational feature for sorting through the wide number of cases
involved and for making sense of their experience. The spectrum
of state structures extends from those that are clearly the paramount power within their society (monopolizing the means of violence and thereby enforcing a complete set of rules ranging from
property ownership to the way political participation is permitted)
to those that are states in little more than name, lacking either
the party or the bureaucratic structures that would give them the
scope of local control properly incumbent upon a state. Yet even
in these latter cases (except perhaps for a few extreme examples
among the sheikdoms of the Arabian Peninsula or in the poorest
parts of Africa) the existence of an indigenously controlled state
does insulate the local society from the international system in a
manner greater than was true under direct colonial rule. Short
of military intervention, the leverage of the outside is significantly
reduced, since foreign ties with local groups are in general restricted
to certain economic interests and occasional religious bodies. Foreigners have neither the scope nor the intensity of ties within the
independent southern country which they had under colonialism.
Moreover, the power capacity of local interests and the state tends
to grow as bureaucrats in the government and the army, jealous
of their positions, show themselves likely to act on behalf of foreigners only when such behavior coincides with their own interests.
Thus, no matter how great the diversity among southern countries,
they almost all have a state apparatus that depends on the aggregation of at least some local interests and is possessed of the ability
to take at least some initiatives in regard to domestic and international issues. In this respect, the use of the word "neocolonial" is
misleading to the extent that it suggests—as it apparently does
to many—that the political distinctions between independent and
colonial status are trivial. Surely Kwame Nkrumah overstated the
case when he wrote in 1965, "The essence of neo-colonialism is
that the State which is subject to it is, in theory, independent and
has all the outward trappings of international sovereignty. In reality
its economic system and thus its political policy is directed from
outside."[3]

---

[3] Kwame Nkrumah, *Neo-Colonialism: The Last State of Imperialism* (New York:
International Publishers, 1966), p. 9.

Many dependency theorists, seemingly persuaded of the correctness of the traditional Marxist reduction of the state to an administrative body of the ruling class, either overlook the function of the state entirely, or dismiss it as historically insignificant, or recognize its importance only to reduce it forthwith to a product of the international system. Thus, writing on the fate of independent Africa in relation to the world order, Frantz Fanon calls for a strong state, able to protect the nation from imperialist designs and improve the quality of life for the mass of the population; what he actually sees are weak governmental bodies, the servants of a new African bourgeoisie which itself has entirely sold out to foreign interests:

> The national middle-class which takes over power at the end of the colonial regime is an under-developed middle-class. It has practically no economic power, and in any case it is in no way commensurate with the bourgeoisie of the mother country which it hopes to replace. . . . Since the middle-class has neither sufficient material nor intellectual resources . . . it limits its claims to the taking-over of business offices and commercial houses formerly occupied by the settlers. From now on it will insist that all the big foreign companies should pass through its hands, whether these companies wish to keep their connections with the country, or to open it up. The national middle-class discovers its historic mission: that of intermediary.[4]

In this descriptive account of a number of post-independence African regimes, Fanon is undoubtedly correct. But as an analytical principle for the study of Third World countries past, present, and future, his point is surely inadequate.

Nevertheless, it is precisely as an analytical point that Immanuel Wallerstein means to press the issue. He writes:

> the world-economy develops a pattern where state structures are relatively strong in the core areas and relatively weak in the periphery. . . . What is necessary is that in some areas the state machinery be far stronger than in others. What do we mean by a strong state-machinery? We mean strength vis-à-vis other states within the world-economy including other core-states, and strong vis-à-vis local political units within the boundaries of the state.[5]

Apparently not even these strong states can compare with the real mover of international affairs—the dynamic of economic forces: "It is the social achievement of the modern world, if you will, to have invented the technology that makes it possible to increase the flow

---

[4] Frantz Fanon, *The Wretched of the Earth* (New York: Grove Press, 1966), p. 122.

[5] Wallerstein, *The Modern World-System* (New York: Academic Press, 1974), p. 355.

of surplus from the lower strata to the upper strata, from the periphery to the center, from the majority to the minority, by eliminating
the 'waste' of too cumbersome a political superstructure."[6] Thus,
Charles V was the last to make the impossible attempt of putting
the entire economic apparatus of the West under a single political
authority. The present eclipse of the United States, Wallerstein
believes, should in no way endanger the system: "such a decline
in United States state hegemony has actually *increased* the freedom
of action of capitalist enterprises, the larger of which have now
taken the form of multinational corporations." Indeed, he minimizes
the role of the state to such an extent that he can say: "There
are today no socialist systems in the world economy any more than
there are feudal systems because there is one world system. It is
a world-economy and it is by definition capitalist in form." But
history does not move blindly, free of human agency. If not states,
then what social force coordinates this activity, fights its battles,
projects it into the future? The obvious answer is class:

> We must maintain our eye on the central ball. The capitalist world
> economy as a totality—its structure, its historic evolution, its contradic-
> tions—is the arena of social action. The fundamental political reality
> of that world-economy is a class struggle which, however, takes con-
> stantly changing forms: class-consciousness versus ethno-nationalist con-
> sciousness, classes within nations versus classes across nations.[7]

As we have seen, this set of assumptions is somewhat similar to
that of many dependency theorists who make little reference to
the state and hold that the international system has established
its interests locally through the medium of an alliance with the
dependent classes of the Third World.

Although there may be many instances when state action is not
important, Wallerstein's abrupt dismissal of the potential significance of the state is in error. I have recited his argument at some
length in order to illustrate the theoretical importance of correctly
understanding what a strong state may be able to accomplish. For
even on his home ground, the 16th century, Wallerstein is surely
wrong in his discussion of state power. As Theda Skocpol has pointed
out, the strong states of the 16th century were not at the core (in
England and Holland), but on the periphery (in Spain and Sweden).
Holland was ruled by a federation of merchant oligarchs while the
English crown, deficient in terms of a bureaucracy or a standing

---

[6] Ibid., pp. 15–16.

[7] Wallerstein, "The Rise and Future Demise of the World Capitalist System,"
Comparative Studies in Society and History 16 (Sept. 1974), pp. 412, 415; Wallerstein,
"Class Formation in the Capitalist World-Economy," *Politics and Society* 5, no. 3,
1975, p. 375.

army, was beholden to merchants and local notables.[8] Later history substantiates Wallerstein's position no better. Alexander Gerschenkron has demonstrated that the "late industrializers" in every case were successful because of exceptionally strong state structures that were determined to modernize. One-time peripheral countries like Russia, Germany, and Japan could not possibly have developed as they did without the vigorous leadership of the state.[9] Nor is it clear today that the state structure of the United States corresponds to the Leviathan one might expect of the "core country of the world-economy" any more than that many governments on the periphery are the weak structures which Wallerstein declares them to be.

Granted, some of the literature associated with dependency does recognize the importance of southern states. But in its discussion, these governments sound more like products of the international system than of local circumstances; thus it loses by one set of assumptions part of what it has gained from another set. A large number of essays and books appearing in recent years on Latin America have maintained that the "bureaucratic-authoritarian" or "authoritarian-corporatist" regimes so prevalent there since the mid-1960s are the most recent result, in the words of Philippe Schmitter, of situations of "delayed, dependent capitalist development and non-hegemonic class relations."[10] In an essay on authoritarian government in Brazil, Argentina, and Mexico, Robert R. Kaufman, drawing heavily on the work of Guillermo O'Donnell, comes to much the same conclusion: "such regimes are linked to a particular phase (or crisis) of capital accumulation encountered in the maturation of dependent industrializing economies"; he points out that their advent is related to increasing local investments by multinational corporations.[11] And several contributors to an anthology of essays on Latin American authoritarianism observe that since this kind of regime occurs not only in South America, but in other parts

---

[8] Theda Skocpol, "Wallerstein's World Capitalist System: A Theoretical and Historical Critique," *American Journal of Sociology* 82 (March 1977), 1083ff.

[9] Alexander Gerschenkron, "Economic Backwardness in Historical Perspective," in *Economic Backwardness in Historical Perspective* (Cambridge, Mass.: Harvard University Press, 1963).

[10] Schmitter, "Still the Century of Corporatism?" *Review of Politics,* 36 (January 1974), p. 108.

[11] See Kaufman, "Mexico and Latin American Authoritarianism," in *Authoritarianism in Mexico,* ed. José Luis Reyna and Richard S. Weinert, (Philadelphia: Institute for the Study of Human Issues, 1977), p. 195, and the chart derived from O'Donnell, p. 197. Nevertheless, neither Kaufman nor Schmitter should be classified as dependency theorists: see Kaufman and Schmitter, "Desarrollo retrasado, dependencia externa y cambio político en America Latina," *Foro Internacional* 12 (December 1971).

of the Third World, what they all have in common is their dependent status internationally. *Ergo,* the character of the world system is said to be the factor that is basic to the genesis of all authoritarian Third-World regimes. O'Donnell asserts that the focus of his work is on Latin America "only in a trivial sense; the pertinent historical context is provided by the political economy of nations that were originally exporters of primary materials and were industrialized late, but extensively, in a position of dependency upon the great centers of world capitalism."[12]

It should be emphasized that these authors do not intend to provide a simplistic explanation of how the dependent status of these countries engendered authoritarian regimes. From their perspective, the fact that the United States reacted to Castro's coming to power by increasing aid to the militaries of Latin America, thereby encouraging them to topple civilian governments, is only incidental to the process. They point to the long-term evolution of South America's social structure, insisting that the strains and tensions that were the product of dependent development set the stage for the wave of authoritarian regimes of the past 15 years. The indirect molding power that the North exercised through the international economic system did more to cause these developments than direct political intervention alone could have accomplished.

But the obvious question is by what line of reasoning we are brought to see that authoritarianism grew out of dependency; that in assigning relative weights of importance to domestic and external factors in such developments, it is the latter that emerge as decisive. Is there not historical evidence—provided, for example, by Germany and Japan—to suggest that authoritarian regimes do not reflect dependency but the effort to avoid subordination? And does the case of India not suggest that at times dependency has contributed to liberal forms of government outside Europe? More to the point, there are reasons to link authoritarian governments in Latin America to domestic rather than to foreign causes. One internal factor (usually conceded by dependency theorists themselves) is that 300 years of rule by Catholic Spain and Portugal left Latin America a legacy of authoritarian government complete with a corporatist ideology. The vertical ties of patron-client relations for which the continent is well known, especially in its agrarian structures, and the traditions of regional caudillo rule must have made their contribution to the form of governments we see today.

---

[12] Guillermo O'Donnell, "Corporatism and the Question of the State," in *Authoritarianism and Corporatism in Latin America,* ed. James M. Malloy (Pittsburgh: University of Pittsburgh Press, 1977), p. 54. For similar observations in the same volume, see Silvio Duncan Baretta and Helen E. Douglass, "Authoritarianism and Corporatism in Latin America: A Review Essay."

Or we could move forward in time, pointing out that the political heritage of the last hundred years set the pattern for authoritarian government in more recent years. For example, both Lorenzo Meyer and Roger Hansen see more continuity than change in style between the Porfiriato (1876–1910) and present-day government in Mexico.[13] An even better line of reasoning linking Latin American authoritarianism to domestic factors would be to maintain that it is the fruit of unsuccessfully resolved problems born of the populist nationalism common to most of the continent after 1930. World War I and especially the Great Depression brought populist leaders such as Vargas and Perón to the fore in Latin America; they were opposed to foreign influence and its local collaborators (chiefly the landed oligarchs of the export sector), and committed to developing their countries through import substitution industries. In this sense, Latin America "decolonized" in the 1930s; populist nationalism appeared triumphant. By the 1950s, import substitution had exhausted itself as a means of domestic economic expansion; at the same time, the market for Latin exports weakened, thus beginning a period of decline in the terms of trade for these commodities. The result was economic crisis.

The civilian governments in power proved unable either to correct the situation or to muster enough support to ensure stability. The drastic inflation rates of the period were symptoms of the government's trying to please rival sectors of the polity. Ultimately, the situation was exacerbated to the point that the populist alliance disintegrated, with the middle and upper classes choosing authoritarian military governments over their quasi-democratic republican predecessors. This choice provided stability, but it did not ensure growth. Only when the authoritarian governments enlisted the multinational corporate community in their development drives could the Latin American economies once again experience expansion at a significant pace. In this (admittedly schematic) account, it is unquestionably the domestic factors that emerge as the predominant force behind the creation of authoritarian states—however much one may wish to blame external influences for making the failure of populist ambitions inevitable and for supplying aid to military dictatorships once the crisis had come. For populism *itself* bred corporatist government, albeit of the kind that initially included significant mass participation. As the governing structure

---

[13] Meyer, "Historical Roots of the Authoritarian State in Mexico," in Reyna and Weinert, *Authoritarianism in Mexico.* Meyer speaks of Díaz's "inability to transform an authoritarian situation into an authoritarian system" and states that "the Mexican Revolution did not destroy the authoritarian nature of Mexican political life, it modernized it" (pp. 9, 4); Roger Hansen, *The Politics of Mexican Development* (Baltimore: The Johns Hopkins Press, 1971), p. 149.

was elaborated, however, it became fairly easy to exclude this same political membership. Argentina and Brazil certainly fit this pattern, but the case of Mexico is especially clear-cut: the Partido Revolucionario Institucional which has ruled Mexico since the Revolution (under various appellations) took its most important steps toward institutionalizing itself in its present corporatist form around 1938, at the very time the Cárdenas Government was dramatically bearding Washington with its expropriations of American utility and oil companies in Mexico. The chief explanation for the contemporary spread of authoritarianism through the continent is not the dependent status of Latin America internationally, but the internal evolution of its social and political forces.

* * * * *

Certainly the ability of Japan to industrialize and to become in its turn an important member of the international community cannot be understood apart from the actions of the state. For in the aftermath of the Meiji Restoration (1868), it was the state, acting on behalf of the nation and not at the behest (although in the interests) of any particular group or class, that undertook a fundamental reordering of the Japanese government and economy. It was the state that insisted on agrarian reform in order to accelerate industrial development; it was the state that invested in a whole range of industrial enterprises where merchant capital at first feared to enter; it was the state that absorbed as many samurai as it could into its bureaucracies and broke the resistance of the rest; it was the state that began modern systems of banking, taxation, and education in Japan. To be sure, these dramatic developments cannot be isolated from the assault Japan correctly feared from the international system, nor from the advantages given the state in its social and economic heritage from the Tokugawa period. But to underestimate the independent role of the state—to see developments in Japan as the product either of international factors alone or as the reflection of no more than domestic class interests—is to miss the central feature of Japan's exceptional economic performance.

By the middle of the 19th century, it was only in Latin America that a group of states had escaped direct colonial control and had also managed, in contrast to Peking and Constantinople, to expand their capacity to rule. A good part of the explanation surely has to do with the continent's geographic remoteness from the centers of geopolitical rivalry, and with the Monroe Doctrine which had a real, if limited, influence on keeping the area free of competitive annexations. But a more basic reason for the success of these states in establishing themselves locally had to do with the strength they drew from participation in the international system. In China, the

Ottoman Empire, and Africa, the international connection functioned mainly *to undermine* the local political systems (however much the Europeans may have hoped to do otherwise); in Latin America, these same linkages worked instead *to reinforce* the position of the ruling elite. *Not so much designs formulated at the center, but rather conditions among the states on the periphery were the fundamental factors determining the impact of European economic power abroad.*

*   *   *   *   *

. . . It may be maintained that because Latin America did not grow economically along the lines of what is today called "basic human needs," its development was "delayed" and "distorted." For example, Rene Villarreal refuses to speak of "development"—as do many other dependency theorists—unless it involves full employment, equal income distribution, and external economic independence.[14] Ethically speaking, this concern with words may be commendable; but when matters of definition become the key issue, as they frequently do, it is fairly obvious that major issues of structural analysis are being lost sight of. That is not to say that moral concerns should not make themselves felt in the study of history, but rather that their pursuit should not interfere with our appreciation of structural historical development. To cite but one example, Bradford Burns describes early 19th century Latin American economic development in the ambiguous language one finds recurrent in the literature:

> The elite proudly regarded the new railroads, steamships, telegraph lines, and renovated ports as ample physical evidence of the progressive course on which their nations had embarked. In their satisfaction, they seemed oblivious to another aspect of modernization: that those very steamships, railroads, and ports tied them and their nations ever more tightly to a handful of industrialized nations in Western Europe and North America. . . . They failed to take note of the significance that many of their railroads did not link the principal cities of their nations but rather ran from plantations or mines directly to the ports, subordinating the goal of national unification to the demands of the industrial nations for agricultural products and minerals. As foreign investment rose, the voices of foreign investors and bankers spoke with greater authority in making economic decisions for the host countries. Local economic options diminished. In short, modernization magnified Latin America's dependency.[15]

---

[14] Villarreal, "The Policy of Import-Substitution Industrialization, 1929–1975," in Reyna and Weinert, *Authoritarianism in Mexico* (fn. 11).

[15] Burns, *Latin America: A Concise Interpretive History* (Englewood Cliffs, N.J.: Prentice-Hall, 1972), pp. 130–31.

The clear inference to be drawn from such writing is that the process victimized Latin America and that some alternative form of economic development was possible. But the author defends neither allegation. Was an alternate path available? In his own account Burns gives evidence aplenty that, following the struggle against Spain, national populations were small, the agrarian structures of the countries were rigid, political instability was rampant, and capital for investment simply did not exist in any quantity. Men can hardly be blamed for being "oblivious" to options that did not exist. Nor is it so apparent that the choices made victimized Latin America as a whole. Díaz writes that the rapidity of growth in Argentina from 1860 to 1930 "has few parallels in economic history," it was so rapid, and he points out the compelling logic of reliance on the international system:

> Pre-1930 growth can be said to have been "export-led" [because] . . . exports and capital inflows led to an allocation of resources far more efficient than the one which would have resulted from autarkic policies. In particular, the domestic cost of capital goods, which would have been astronomical under autarky, say in 1880, was reduced to a low level by exports of commodities produced by the generous use of an input—land—whose economic value under autarky would have been quite small.[16]

With very good reason one may of course object that the social form economic development has taken in Latin America is ethically objectionable (and has been for some time). But to suggest—as many influenced by dependency theory appear to do—that because the social form is objectionable, growth itself was "delayed" and "distorted" is to mix the arguments, to draw empirical conclusions from normative premises in an unacceptable manner.

During the 19th century, world trade grew tremendously under the impetus of the Industrial Revolution, and European and American investments abroad grew apace. In 1820, world trade was valued at 341 million pounds sterling; by 1880, its value topped 3 billion pounds. In 1810, British investments abroad were approximately 10 million pounds sterling; by 1890, they approached 200 million and probably represented about half the European and American investments abroad.[17] How could this dramatic increase fail to have

---

[16] Carlos F. Díaz Alejandro, *Essays on the Economic History of The Argentine Republic* (New Haven: Yale University Press, 1970), pp. 2, 11. For a similar argument on Brazil, see Carlos Manuel Peláez, "The Theory and Reality of Imperialism in the Coffee Economy of Nineteenth-Century Brazil," *Economic History Review* 29 (May 1976).

[17] For trade figures, see E. J. Hobsbawm, *Industry and Empire* (London: Pelican, 1969), p. 139, and J. Forbes Munro, *Africa and the International Economy, 1800–1960* (London: Rowman and Littlefield, 1976), p. 40; for investment figures, see Michael Barrett-Brown, *After Imperialism* (New York: Humanities Press, 1970), 93.

repercussions on the pre-industrial countries of the globe as the industrial leaders sought primary materials and markets as well as strategic vantage points in their competitive race? Indeed, any specific southern area *looked at in isolation* will show clear signs of the impact. But when the range of southern countries is *placed side by side,* what also emerges is the *variety* of responses to this global experience of the expansion of the Industrial Revolution. The Ottoman Empire disintegrated while Japan modernized successfully; Africa was partitioned while Latin American governments were more effectively expanding and consolidating their rule. Although the study of the international system as such may suggest some reasons for these differences, it is by no means able to substitute for an inspection of each specific case.

The key variable to be analyzed in order to explain these significant differences lies in the abilities and behavior of the various southern states as they encountered the technologically superior force of Europe and the United States over the last century-and-a-half. Some states, such as the kingdoms of West Africa which had been built up partly through a preceding period of trade with the North, were taken by assault; others, like the Ottoman Empire and the Manchu Dynasty, collapsed—for reasons fundamentally caused more by internal factors than by the overwhelming power of the North; Japan managed to mount a rival industrial establishment; and the Latin American states drew strength from the international connection—albeit of a sort that made them satellites of the economic dynamism of the North. Both Theda Skocpol and Ellen Kay Trimberger have suggested that the key to whether a 19th century agrarian order could preserve itself in the face of internal and external threats may lie in whether the state was functionally independent enough of the economic elite to take initiatives despite the opposition of this class. Skocpol writes of governmental responsiveness to the threat of revolution:

> The adaptiveness of the earlier modernizing agrarian bureaucracies was significantly determined by the degree to which the upper and middle ranks of the state administrative bureaucracies were staffed by large landholders. Only state machineries significantly differentiated from traditional landed upper classes could undertake modernizing reforms which almost invariably had to encroach upon the property or privileges of the landed upper class.[18]

Trimberger makes the same general point with reference to the ability of the Meiji State and Kemalist Turkey to undertake economic modernization, and she goes on to link these experiences with contemporary developments in Latin America. The central

---

[18] Theda Skocpol, "France, Russia, China: A Structural Theory of Social Revolution," *Comparative Studies in Society and History* 18 no. 2, 1976, p. 185.

characteristic of a strong state, she argues, is that its bureaucracy—
and particularly the military officer corps—be neither recruited
from nor responsible to the classes economically dominant in
society.[19] The autonomy from vested reactionary interests allows
such a state to undertake the necessary (and always, to some, unpopular), reforms necessary for modernization. At the same time,
however, it is well not to overemphasize the autonomy of the state:
any ruling apparatus must have some allies, potential or actual,
in the population at large. For all the usefulness of Skocpol's and
Trimberger's distinctions, Bill Warren's point on the multiple forms
that vigorous state rule may take calls attention to the danger of
defining the issue too narrowly:

> Significant capitalist industrialization may be initiated and directed by
> a variety of ruling classes and combinations of such classes or their
> representatives, ranging from semi-feudal ruling groups (northern Nige-
> ria) and including large landowners (Ethiopia, Brazil, Thailand), to bu-
> reaucratic-military elites, petty bourgeoisies and professional and state
> functionaries (especially in Africa and the Middle East). These "industri-
> alizers" may themselves become industrial bourgeoisies or may be dis-
> placed by the industrial Frankensteins they have erected. . . . the crucial
> point is this—that it is the characteristic of the post-war period through-
> out the underdeveloped world that the social forces compelling industri-
> alization have developed with more massive impetus and greater rapidity
> than ever before in history. . . . This partly explains the importance
> of the state in most underdeveloped countries where it often assumes
> the role of a bourgeois ruling class prior to the substantial development
> of that class.[20]

The style of state action will thus vary with time and place.
Alexander Gerschenkron has described not only what is common
to "late industrializers"—the speed of industrial growth and its
concentration in large enterprises favoring capital goods production,
for example—but also how different countries use different structures to further the same functional end of growth—England used
accumulated capital, Germany the investment banks, and Russia
the state budget.[21] Barrington Moore makes the same general point
when he insists that historical timing is a crucial factor in the
style of state action:

---

[19] E. K. Trimberger, *Revolution From Above* (Edison, N.J.: Transaction Books,
1977); Trimberger and Irving Louis Horowitz, "State Power and Military Nationalism
in Latin America," *Comparative Politics* 8 (January 1976).

[20] Warren, "Imperialism and Capitalist Industrialization," *New Left Review* 81
(September–October 1973), pp. 42–43.

[21] Gerschenkron, *Europe in the Russian Mirror: Four Lectures in Economic History*
(New York: Cambridge University Press, 1970) 99, pp. 102–3. See also Rondo Cam-
eron, ed., *Banking and Economic Development: Some Lessons of History* (New York:
Oxford University Press, 1972).

To a very limited extent these three types—bourgeois revolutions culminating in the Western form of democracy, conservative revolutions from above ending in fascism, and peasant revolutions leading to communism—may constitute alternative routes and choices. They are much more clearly successive historical stages. . . . The methods of modernization chosen in one country change the dimensions of the problem for the next countries who take the step, as Veblen recognized when he coined the now fashionable term "the advantages of backwardness." Without the prior democratic modernization of England, the reactionary methods adopted in Germany and Japan would scarcely have been possible. Without both the capitalist and reactionary experiences, the communist method would have been something entirely different, if it had come into existence at all. . . . Although there have been certain common problems in the construction of industrial society, the task remains a continually changing one.[22]

III

Whether industrializing countries today will imitate any of the historical models of growth, or will find new forms of development, or indeed will succeed at all in their ambition to become autonomous centers of technological advance is a key question. Albert O. Hirschman notes that "late, late industrializers" seem unable to move as decisively as their historical predecessors.[23] Dependency theorists would link this to the role that external forces have played in the growth of southern countries, and insist that the impetus for forward movement does not yet come from inside. A strong state would seem to be an indispensable prerequisite for success. And few of the states of the Third World today have developed governing institutions appropriate to the social forces they must integrate and control. Regional, ethnic, and class demands are not effectively aggregated through party structures (if, indeed, they are capably articulated at all), while bureaucracies, which determine the ability of governments to act, are frequently incompetent and corrupt. In a strong polity, party and bureaucratic structures parallel and reinforce one another. But in a weak state, the shortcomings of each system feed the vices of the other.[24] Some governments are obviously

---

[22] Barrington Moore, Jr., *Social Origins of Dictatorship and Democracy* (Boston: Beacon Press, 1966), pp. 112–14. See also David Collier, "Timing of Economic Growth and Regime Characteristics in Latin America," *Comparative Politics* 7 (April 1975) . . .

[23] Hirschman, "The Political Economy of Import-Substituting Industrializing in Latin America," in *A Bias for Hope: Essays on Development and Latin America* (New Haven: Yale University Press, 1971).

[24] Samuel P. Huntington, *Political Order in Changing Societies* (New Haven: Yale University Press, 1968); Fred W. Riggs, *Administrative Reform and Political Responsiveness* (Beverly Hills, Calif.: Sage Publications, 1970).

stronger than others on the same continent—India in Asia, Tanzania in Africa, Mexico in Latin America; meanwhile, military regimes converting themselves into civilian governments, or popular
parties with roots in a variety of social groups may yet succeed
in institutionalizing political authority. Few are as weak as some
of the former French territories of Black Africa, where Europeans
continue to staff many of the important government positions and
the presence (or absence) of a metropolitan paratrooper company
or two determines political stability. And few are as corrupt as
Zaire, where one apparently informed source reports the disappearance in 1971 of 60 percent of the state's revenues (not counting
under-the-table transfers).[25]

For most southern countries, the Algerian dilemma seems familiar: the failure of the party system engenders the failure of the
bureaucracy—which in turn makes the eventual success of the party
all the more difficult. Thus the present attempt in Algeria to bring
about wide-scale land reform is every bit as much a political as
an economic effort. What the Boumédienne regime requires to
achieve modern stability is power dispersion; that is, the creation
of institutional linkages throughout the country by means of a party
structure and organized interest groups. Of course a risk is involved.
An increasingly participant peasantry may challenge well-designed
programs as well as inefficiency and corruption in government.
Thus, increased mass participation is at once a possible salvation
for the regime and a real threat to it. The result has been to temporize. Now the Peasant Unions, like the Communal Assemblies, will
be participatory in form but carefully controlled in practice. The
attempt may succeed; or again, it may not. Since the summer of
1972, the idea of the Agrarian Revolution has been broadcast to
every corner of Algeria in an official campaign quite without prece-
dent in the country's history. The media have long and actively
promoted it, thousands of students have been mobilized to come
to its assistance, and religious as well as military and political authorities have pronounced favorably on its ambitions. One thing
is becoming evident: Algeria must somehow institutionalize the participation of its peasantry if its political order is to find strength
and stability and its economic order is to create prosperity. The
peasantry has a genuine interest in participation. The overriding
question is whether the state, through its party and bureaucratic
structures, can acquire a mature form in the process. The task is
not unique to Algeria. Throughout the Third World, similar prob-

---

[25] J. P. Peemans, "The Social and Economic Development of Zaire since Independence," *African Affairs* 74 (April 1975), p. 102.

lems of political development are being confronted by equally bold programs of reform.

The job of the modernizing state in contemporary domestic terms therefore appears paradoxical: it must have autonomy, yet it must sink roots. It must have the autonomy of a unitary actor if it is to make long-term plans and to implement them despite some opposition (and on occasion those who object will eventually benefit more than those who truly pay the price). Particularistic interests of every variety must be weaker than the state, which is competent to act on behalf of what it will call the collective good. At the same time, the state must sink roots, both as a precondition and as a result of this very effort at change. If some interests must be checked or broken, others must be mobilized and controlled if the state is to attain its ends. In Samuel Huntington's terms, state power must be both concentrated and expanded in a complex process that will depend in each case on specific configurations of social forces.[26] Different regimes will choose to promote different sectors of their populations, and a variety of political structures may be used to the same functional end. But the final product must be a state apparatus that can effectively knit together the social forces under its jurisdiction, and provide for future growth.

Is a state that is strong domestically also a state that is strong internationally? No obvious direct relationship holds. For a society may be possessed of a strong state in the sense that governmental structures have a demonstrated capacity to integrate the social forces of the land, while at the same time it may lack military strength and hence be weak on the world scale. Or else, a state may be strong internally while its economic system is highly dependent on world trade over whose rules it has no power. As a result, this state is weak internationally, since the coalition of domestic forces on which it depends would be upset if the world economy failed to perform in certain necessary ways. On the other hand, internal strength would seem a precondition of strength internationally. For a globally powerful state must be possessed of an ability to extract resources from its citizenry and coordinate them in a fashion that suggests that its government is strong internally as well.

It is thus legitimate to say that an aspect of the growing international power of southern states is their ability to grow strong internally. As their economies become more diversified and their societies are better organized politically, the probability is that they will gain in international strength. It would be a mistake to think that

---

[26] Huntington, *Political Order*, chap. 2.

this process is unidimensional, however: a society may over time vary in its dependence on outside influences. In Mexico, for example, the Porfiriato (1876–1910) signified one type of incorporation to the hegemony of the United States, only to be ended when Mexico [was] in effect "decolonized" by the Revolution of 1910–1917, and by the subsequent economic Mexicanization of the country until 1945. Subsequently, however, Mexico once again became more closely involved with the United States, although in ways significantly different from the pattern that ended nearly 70 years ago. The complexity of the modern Mexican economy and the demonstrated ability of the state to control the social forces under its jurisdiction make the Mexican state today stronger domestically than it was before the Revolution; but how do we describe its international position?

One recent event confirms the growing power of the South in striking fashion. More clearly than the defeat of the Italians at Adua in 1896 and the Japanese victory over Russia in 1904, the ultimate triumph of nationalist communism in Vietnam stands as an historical benchmark of the first order in the process of reversing nearly 500 years of European overseas expansion. Direct leverage over the political and bureaucratic institutions in the South may have ended with colonialism, but the North could retain the belief that if a southern state failed to respect basic northern interests (defined not only economically and strategically, but in some cases ideologically or symbolically), it ran the risk of military intervention. So at least it had been in Asia and the Middle East since the time of the First Opium War in 1840. We are witness to the failure of the United States to continue the tradition.

*   *   *   *   *

It was under the shadow of America's military reversal in Vietnam that the rise in petroleum prices occurred. In 1972, the OPEC states received $29.2 billion for their exports, which constituted 7 percent of world trade by value; by 1975, the value of their exports reached $114 billion and represented some 13 percent of world commerce (down from 16 percent in 1974). Nor is the success of OPEC the only sign of strength in southern economic development. Statistics on manufacturing output in the Third World show this sector to have been the pacesetter in most Third-World economies for approximately the past two decades. Even during the recession of 1974, so called "middle income" countries, those with per capita incomes of $200 to $700 a year, managed to expand their manufacturing output by 8 percent, while the OECD countries registered a zero growth rate. . . .

One must be careful not to push this point too far and thereby fail to recognize the substantial power that the North still retains over the South. In my opinion, dependency theory is certainly correct when it maintains that northern power is not only preponderant, but that its effects significantly influence the course of economic, social, and political development in southern countries. Nor would I dispute the use of the word "imperialism" to characterize this relationship. But I would repeat that it is essential not to assume that the power of this interaction between North and South is so great as to mold single-handedly all aspects of social life in the South. Not for a moment should the strength and independence of local factors be forgotten. In the case of Mexican industrialization, to take but one example, the role of northern multinational investment is indisputable in providing capital and technology for development. But much more important were changes within Mexico itself, chief of which was the Revolution of 1910. Here the groundwork was laid, as William Glade recounts it, for the economic, social, and political infrastructure basic to industrialization. And the Revolution was achieved not *because* of the international system, but *against* it and its local allies.[27] Nor should it be assumed that southern leaders, even when heavily dependent on the North, are mere puppets of the international system. It was Porfirio Díaz, after all, who not only opened Mexico to American economic penetration on an enormous scale at the close of the 19th century, but who also coined the phrase still dear to Mexicans, "Pobre México, tan lejos de Dios, tan cerca de los Estados Unidos" (Poor Mexico, so far from God, so close to the United States). In short, the system is far more fluid than dependency theory allows. It is fluid in the sense that it has weaknesses permitting important actors to escape its direct influence, in the sense that it contains contradictory movements within it (American support for Israel has been no way to run an imperial system, for example), and in the sense that in many respects the very success of the system prepares the ground for its own displacement.

Let us look at this last point more closely. Even if the North were to advance a blueprint for North-South economic relations more comprehensive than anything suggested to date, are we to suppose that it would unquestionably succeed in perpetuating the present international distribution of power? Such might be the short-term consequences, which for a generation or two might perhaps be able to improve the mechanisms of northern control; but what about the longer term? Marxist and southern nationalist rhetoric notwithstanding, where is the evidence that the system is

---

[27] Glade, "Revolution and Economic Development: A Mexican Reprise," in *The Political Economy of Mexico*, eds. William Glade and Charles W. Anderson (Madison: University of Wisconsin Press, 1963).

operating to make the Third World perpetual "hewers of wood and drawers of water" as the now standard cliché has it? If that were the northern intention—and I have never seen it seriously alleged that the countries of the OECD or the United States alone have the cunning or the organization to be able to draw up such a scheme—then the attempt would be a notable failure. Where is the whole-hearted effort to prevent southern industrialization, monopolize southern raw materials, break up domestically integrated southern markets, oppose southern regional integration schemes, and develop a greater degree of international specialization that would heighten southern reliance on northern goods and markets? Neither the OECD nor the United States gets high marks for imperialist strategy: plans are neither clear nor resolute in purpose; the means whereby to gain the ends have not been specified; interests at home have not been harmonized so that such a strategy would seem enticing. Unlike the influence of Britain in Egypt, India, and Latin America at the end of the 19th century, and unlike Nazi policy toward Southeastern Europe, the impact of the North today would seem to accelerate rather than retard southern industrialization.

The standard reply in the dependency literature is to maintain that foreign enterprise holds the commanding heights in Third World industrialization, thereby "decapitalizing" and "denationalizing" southern industry. It is held that whatever gains are being made would be greater and less vulnerable without this presence. The favored way to document the alleged decapitalization is to present figures of capital inflow and outflow over time to show that foreign investment is taking more out of southern countries than it is bringing in. For instance, in the case of Latin America, Dale Johnson repeats the standard charge, declaring that "between 1950 and 1961, $2,962 million of U.S. private capital flowed into the seven principal countries of Latin America, while the return flow was $6,875 million."[28] Although this state of affairs might suggest that northern investment is no assistance in terms of southern balance-of-payments problems, it is obvious that these figures, cited by themselves, cannot establish the case for southern exploitation. For unless we know what this surplus in favor of the United States amounting to $4 billion means in relation either to American investment in Latin America or to the output of American firms there, the sum says very little. The available statistics suggest that "decapitalization" is a nationalist/Marxist myth, at least in the

---

[28] Johnson, "Dependence and the International System," in *Dependence and Underdevelopment*, ed. James D. Cockcroft et al. (New York: Anchor Books, 1972), 75n.; repeated with other dates, 94n.

terms in which it is usually presented. For example, in 1975, Latin America received $178 million from the United States to be invested in private manufacturing there. At the same time, American corporations remitted $359 million in profits and $211 million in fees and royalties from this sector to the United States. Apparently, therefore, United States private investments "decapitalized" Latin America of $392 million that year in terms of manufacturing alone. Yet, if we compare this to United States manufacturing investments in Latin America of $8.6 *billion,* the sum repatriated to the North amounted to a mere 4.6 percent, hardly an extortionist outflow. The sum of $392 million is all the more insignificant when we compare it to the total sales of United States manufacturing affiliates in Latin America in 1974, which amounted to $20.9 billion. In other words, if we consider the $392 million as return either on investment or on volume of business generated, it can scarcely be maintained that Latin America is being "decapitalized."

It is more difficult to refute unambiguously the charge that Third World economies are being "denationalized"—a term that refers to the tendency of northern industries to buy out successful local businesses and to control local capital through encouraging its minority participation in northern ventures there. For example, the Department of Commerce provides figures showing that from 1968 to 1972, Latin Americans provided from 33 to 54 percent of the capital called for by United States companies in the region. Should that be interpreted as southerners financing the takeover of their own countries? Similarly, Richard J. Barnet and Ronald E. Müller cite a study by the Harvard Business School for the years 1958–1967 to underscore the familiar allegation of *dependencistas* that Americans are buying up able southern firms and are thereby stifling southern entrepreneurs: "About 46 percent of all manufacturing operations established in the period were takeovers of existing domestic industry."[29] A closer inspection of this argument suggests that once again the dependency school is presenting its statistics selectively. For if we look more thoroughly through the material assembled by the Harvard Business School survey, it appears that through liquidations or expropriations, or sales of an entire affiliate or a substantial part thereof, American interests had divested themselves of nearly as many manufacturing concerns as they had acquired: 332 lost as compared with 337 gained.[30] Nor do sheer

---

[29] Barnet and Müller, *Global Reach: The Power of the Multinational Corporation* (New York: Simon and Schuster, 1974), pp. 154–55.

[30] James W. Vaupel and Joan P. Curhan, *The Making of Multinational Enterprise* (Cambridge, Mass.: Graduate School of Business Administration, Harvard University Press, 1969), pp. 240–41 for expansion; pp. 376–77, 505 for losses.

numbers of firms present the most interesting statistics; it is the *value* of affiliates bought or sold that may be more important. And, so far as the figures for 1975 and 1976 are concerned, Department of Commerce statistics show that United States firms sold off about as much in value of their manufacturing affiliates in the South as they acquired through takeovers. Moreover, there seems to be unanimous agreement that as a percentage of gross business volume, the multinational corporations are declining in importance in the South: it is only in terms of their control over certain of the leading sectors of the economy that their presence is dominant. Even in these sectors, the emerging pattern seems to be for the southern governments to restrict foreign investment to those areas of the economy where local abilities cannot yet provide adequate capital or skills, and to push the foreigners out once conditions warrant it. To be sure, in many instances foreigners continue to operate behind the scenes: the custom of *prestanombres* (borrowed names), whereby locals act as figurehead directors and owners of establishments that are actually controlled from abroad is by no means restricted to Latin America, as the Spanish term might suggest. However, as the state and domestic interests gain in strength, there is little reason to think the letter of the law will not be increasingly applied. In the process of the "nationalization" of these foreign concerns, might not the investors in such enterprises, those who hold minority shares as reflected in the Commerce Department survey cited above, be considered the logical next majority owners? "Denationalization" of southern industry has as little substance to it as "decapitalization."

The moral of these considerations is that the system of North-South relations is not only too weak to determine all aspects of change in the South—a fundamental point bearing reiteration—but that even in those areas where its influence is real, its long-run effect may well be to hasten the end of the international predominance of the North. For example, Algeria had managed to run up an external public debt of over $9 billion as of the end of 1975, and the United States had moved into position as the country's largest trading partner and substantial creditor. Yet, one would mistake this involvement with the outside world if one were to see it as anything other than an Algerian effort to practice that skill of the martial arts whereby the strength of the opponent is used against himself. The same point of view has predominated in the Soviet Union since 1920, when Lenin actively sought to recruit capitalist trade and investment in his effort to build up his country's economic base. It is the unhistorical dogmatist, a familiar fellow in dependency literature, who asserts solely on the basis of certain grand ideas that, whatever the situation, the international system is a "trap," and that "self-reliance" through socialism is the only road to economic development.[31]

In this essay I have attempted to deal only with a major historiographic shortcoming common to most of dependency theory. I have made no claim to review the literature in full, to deny its genuine insights, or to analyze the ideological "united front" the theory is sponsoring between southern nationalists and Marxists. Instead, I have tried to encourage skepticism about propositions alleging the all-pervasive and self-perpetuating character of northern power with respect to the South, and to establish some measure of the relative autonomy of the various Third-World countries which comes from the real strength of local traditions and institutions.

---

[31] Johan Galtung, "The Lomé Convention and Neo-Capitalism," *African Review* 6, no. 1, 1976.

CHAPTER NINE

Revolution

30

The Anatomy of Revolution

Crane Brinton

SOME TENTATIVE UNIFORMITIES

When all necessary concessions are made to those who insist that events in history are unique, it remains true that the four revolutions we have studied (English, American, French, and Russian) do display some striking uniformities. Our conceptual scheme of the fever can be worked out so as to bring these uniformities clearly to mind. We shall find it worth while, in attempting to summarize the work of these revolutions, to recapitulate briefly the main points of comparison on which our uniformities are based.

We must be very tentative about the prodromal symptoms of revolution. Even retrospectively, diagnosis of the four societies we studied was very difficult, and there is little ground for belief that anyone today has enough knowledge and skill to apply formal methods of diagnosis to a contemporary society and say, in this case revolution will or will not occur shortly. But some uniformities do emerge from a study of the old regimes in England, America, France, and Russia.

First, these were all societies on the whole on the upgrade economically before the revolution came, and the revolutionary movements seem to originate in the discontents of not unprosperous people who feel restraint, cramp, annoyance, rather than downright

---

Source: Crane Brinton, *The Anatomy of Revolution* (Englewood Cliffs, N.J.: Prentice-Hall, 1952). Reprinted with Permission of Prentice-Hall, Inc., © 1952 by Prentice-Hall, Inc.

crushing oppression. Certainly these revolutions are not started by down-and-outers, by starving, miserable people. These revolutionists are not worms turning, not children of despair. These revolutions are born of hope, and their philosophies are formally optimistic.

Second, we find in our prerevolutionary society definite and indeed very bitter class antagonisms, though these antagonisms seem rather more complicated than the cruder Marxists will allow. It is not a case of feudal nobility against bourgeoisie in 1640, 1776, and 1789, or of bourgeoisie against proletariat in 1917. The strongest feelings seem generated in the bosoms of men—and women—who have made money, or at least who have enough to live on, and who contemplate bitterly the imperfections of a socially privileged aristocracy. Revolutions seem more likely when social classes are fairly close together than when they are far apart. "Untouchables" very rarely revolt against a God-given aristocracy, and Haiti gives one of the few examples of successful slave revolutions. But rich merchants whose daughters can marry aristocrats are likely to feel that God is at least as interested in merchants as in aristocrats. It is difficult to say why the bitterness of feeling between classes *almost* equal socially seems so much stronger in some societies than others—why, for instance, a Marie Antoinette should be so much more hated in 18th century France than a rich, idle, much publicized heiress in contemporary America; but at any rate the existence of such bitterness can be observed in our prerevolutionary societies, which is, clinically speaking, enough for the moment.

Third, there is what we have called the desertion of the intellectuals. This is in some respects the most reliable of the symptoms we are likely to meet. Here again we need not try to explain all the hows and whys, need not try to tie up the desertion of the intellectuals with a grand and complete sociology of revolutions. We need state simply that it can be observed in all four of our societies.

Fourth, the governmental machinery is clearly inefficient, partly through neglect, through a failure to make changes in old institutions, partly because new conditions—in the societies we have studied, pretty specifically conditions attendant on economic expansion and the growth of new monied classes, new ways of transportation, new business methods—these new conditions laid an intolerable strain on governmental machinery adapted to simpler, more primitive, conditions.

Fifth, the old ruling class—or rather, many individuals of the old ruling class—come to distrust themselves, or lose faith in the traditions and habits of their class, grow intellectual, humanitarian, or go over to the attacking groups. Perhaps a larger number of them than usual lead lives we shall have to call immoral, dissolute, though one cannot by any means be as sure about this as a symptom as about the loss of habits and traditions of command effective among a ruling class. At any rate, the ruling class becomes politically inept.

The dramatic events that start things moving, that bring on the fever of revolution, are in three of our four revolutions intimately connected with the financial administration of the state. In the fourth, Russia, the breakdown of administration under the burdens of an unsuccessful war is only in part financial. But in all our societies the inefficiency and inadequacy of the governmental structure of the society come out clearly in the very first stages of the revolution. There is a time—the first few weeks or months—when it looks as if a determined use of force on the part of the government might prevent the mounting excitement from culminating in an overthrow of the government. These governments attempted such a use of force in all four instances, and in all four their attempt was a failure. This failure indeed proved a turning point during the first stages, and set up the revolutionists in power.

Yet one is impressed in all four instances more with the ineptitude of the governments' use of force than with the skill of their opponents' use of force. We are here speaking of the situation wholly from a military and police point of view. It may be that the majority of the people are discontented, loathe the existing government, wish it overthrown. Nobody knows. They don't take plebiscites *before* revolutions. In the actual clash—even Bastille Day, Concord, or the February Days in Petrograd—only a minority of the people is actively engaged. But the government hold over its own troops is poor, its troops fight half-heartedly or desert, its commanders are stupid, its enemies acquire a nucleus of the deserting troops or of a previous militia, and the old gives place to the new. Yet, such is the conservative and routine-loving nature of the bulk of human beings, so strong are habits of obedience in most of them, that it is almost safe to say that no government is likely to be overthrown until it loses the ability to make adequate use of its military and police powers. That loss of ability may show itself in the actual desertion of soldiers and police to the revolutionists, or in the stupidity with which the government manages its soldiers and police, or in both ways.

The events we have grouped under the names of first stages do not of course unroll themselves in exactly the same order in time, or with exactly the same content, in all four of our revolutions. But we have listed the major elements—and they fall into a pattern of uniformities—financial breakdown, organization of the discontented to remedy this breakdown (or threatened breakdown), revolutionary demands on the part of these organized discontented, demands which if granted would mean the virtual abdication of those governing, attempted use of force by the government, its failure, and the attainment of power by the revolutionists. These revolutionists have hitherto been acting as an organized and nearly unanimous group, but with the attainment of power it is clear that they are not united. The group which dominates these first stages we call the moderates. They are not always in a numerical majority in this stage—indeed it is pretty clear that if you limit the moderates to the Kadets they were not in a majority in Russia in February, 1917. But they seem the natural heirs of the old government, and they have their chance. In three of our revolutions they are sooner or later driven from office to death or exile. Certainly there is to be seen in England, France, and Russia a process in which a series of crises—some involving violence, street fighting, and the like—deposes one set of men and puts in power another and more radical set. In these revolutions power passes by violent or at least extralegal methods from Right to Left, until at the crisis period the extreme radicals, the complete revolutionists, are in power. There are, as a matter of fact, usually a few even wilder and more lunatic fringes of the triumphant extremists—but these are not numerous or strong and are usually suppressed or otherwise made harmless by the dominant radicals. It is therefore approximately true to say that power passes on from Right to Left until it reaches the extreme Left.

The rule of the extremists we have called the crisis period. This period was not reached in the American Revolution, though in the treatment of Loyalists, in the pressure to support the army, in some of the phases of social life, you can discern in America many of the phenomena of the Terror as it is seen in our three other societies. We cannot here attempt to go into the complicated question as to why the American Revolution stopped short of a true crisis period, why the moderates were never ousted in this country. We must repeat that we are simply trying to establish certain uniformities of description, and are not attempting a complete sociology of revolutions.

The extremists are helped to power no doubt by the existence of a powerful pressure toward centralized strong government, something which in general the moderates are not capable of providing, while the extremists, with their discipline, their contempt for half measures, their willingness to make firm decisions, their freedom from libertarian qualms, are quite able and willing to centralize. Especially in France and Russia, where powerful foreign enemies threatened the very existence of the nation, the machinery of government during the crisis period was in part constructed to serve as a government of national defense. Yet though modern wars, as we know in this country, demand a centralization of authority, war alone does not seem to account for all that happened in the crisis period in those countries.

What does happen may be a bit oversimply summarized as follows: emergency centralization of power in an administration, usually a council or commission, and more or less dominated by a "strong man"—Cromwell, Robespierre, Lenin; government without any effective protection for the normal civil rights of the individual—or if this sounds unrealistic, especially for Russia, let us say the normal private life of the individual; setting up of extraordinary courts and a special revolutionary police to carry out the decrees of the government and to suppress all dissenting individuals or groups; all this machinery ultimately built up from a relatively small group—Independents, Jacobins, Bolsheviks—which has a monopoly on all governmental action. Finally, governmental action becomes a much greater part of all human action than in these societies in their normal condition: this apparatus of government is set to work indifferently on the mountains and molehills of human life—it is used to pry into and poke about corners normally reserved for priest or physician, or friend, and it is used to regulate, control, plan, the production and distribution of economic wealth on a national scale.

This pervasiveness of the Reign of Terror in the crisis period is partly explicable in terms of the pressure of war necessities and of economic struggles as well as of other variables: but it must probably also be explained as in part the manifestation of an effort to achieve intensely religious ends here on earth. The little band of violent revolutionists who form the nucleus of all action during the Terror behave as men have been observed to behave before when under the influence of active religious faith. Independents, Jacobins, Bolsheviks, all sought to make all human activity here on earth conform to an ideal pattern, which, like all such patterns, seems deeply rooted in their sentiments. A striking uniformity in all these patterns is their asceticism, or if you prefer, their condemnation of what we may call the minor as well as the major vices. Essentially, however, these patterns are a good deal alike, and all resemble closely what we may call conventional Christian ethics. Independents, Jacobins, and Bolsheviks, at least during the crisis period, really make an effort to enforce behavior in literal conformity with these codes or patterns. Such an effort means stern repression of much that many men have been used to regarding as normal; it means a kind of universal tension in which the ordinary individual can never feel protected by the humble routines to which he has been formed: it means that the intricate network of interactions among individuals—a network which is still to the few men devoted to its intelligent study almost a complete mystery—this network is temporarily all torn apart. John Jones, the man in the street, the ordinary man, is left floundering.

We are almost at the point of being carried away into the belief that our conceptual scheme is something more than a mere convenience, that it does somehow describe "reality." At the crisis, the collective patient does seem helpless, thrashing his way through a delirium. But we must try to avoid the emotional, metaphorical appeal, and concentrate on making clear what seems to be the really important point here. Most of us are familiar with the favorite old Tory metaphor: the violent revolutionist tears down the noble edifice society lives in, or burns it down, and then fails to build up another, and poor human beings are left naked to the skies. That is not a good metaphor, save perhaps for purposes of Tory propaganda. Even at the height of a revolutionary crisis period, more of the old building is left standing than is destroyed. But the whole metaphor of the building is bad. We may take instead an analogy from the human nervous system, or think of an immensely complicated gridwork of electrical communications. Society then appears as a kind of a network of interactions among individuals, interactions for the most part fixed by habit, hardened and perhaps adorned as ritual, dignified into meaning and beauty by the elaborately interwoven strands of interaction we know as law, theology, metaphysics, and similar noble beliefs. Now sometimes many of these interwoven strands of noble beliefs, some even of those of habit and tradition, can be cut out, and others inserted. During the crisis period of our revolutions some such process seems to have taken place; but the whole network itself seems so far never to have been altered suddenly and radically, and even the noble beliefs tend to fit into the network in the same places. If you kill off *all* the people who live within the network, you don't so much change the network of course as destroy it. And in spite of our prophets of doom, this type of destruction is rare in human history. Certainly in none of our revolutions was there even a very close approach to it.

What did happen, under the pressure of class struggle, war, religious idealism, and a lot more, was that the hidden and obscure courses which many of the interactions in the network follow were suddenly exposed, and passage along them made difficult in the unusual publicity and, so to speak, self-consciousness. The courses of other interactions were blocked, and the interactions went on with the greatest of difficulties by all sorts of detours. The courses of still other interactions were confused, short-circuited, paired off in strange ways. Finally, the pretensions of the fanatical leaders of the revolution involved the attempted creation of a vast number of new interactions. Now though for the most part these new interactions affected chiefly those strands we have called the noble beliefs—law, theology, metaphysics, mythology, folklore, high-power abstractions in general—still some of them did penetrate at an experimental level into the obscurer and less dignified part of the network of interactions among human beings and put a further strain on it. Surely it is no wonder that under these conditions men and women in the crisis period should behave as they would not normally behave, that in the crisis period nothing should seem as it used to seem. . . .

Certainly none of our revolutions quite ended in the death of civilization and culture. The network was stronger than the forces trying to destroy or alter it, and in all of our societies the crisis period was followed by a convalescence, by a return to most of the simpler and more fundamental courses taken by interactions in the old network. More especially, the religious lust for perfection, the crusade for the Republic of Virtue, died out, save among a tiny minority whose actions could no longer take place directly in politics. An active, proselyting, intolerant, ascetic, chiliastic faith became fairly rapidly an inactive, indifferent, worldly ritualistic faith.

The equilibrium has been restored and the revolution is over. But this does not mean that nothing has been changed. Some new and useful tracks or courses in the network of interactions that makes society have been established, some old and inconvenient ones—you may call them unjust if you like—have been eliminated. There is something heartless in saying that it took the French Revolution to produce the metric system and to destroy *lods et ventes* and similar feudal inconveniences, or the Russian Revolution to bring Russia to use the modern calendar and to eliminate a few useless letters in the Russian alphabet. These tangible and useful results look rather petty as measured by the brotherhood of man and the achievement of justice on this earth. The blood of the martyrs seems hardly necessary to establish decimal coinage.

Yet those who feel that revolution is heroic need not despair. The revolutionary tradition is an heroic one, and the noble beliefs which seem necessary to all societies are in our Western democracies in part a product of the revolutions we have been studying. Our revolutions made tremendous and valuable additions to those strands in the network of human interactions which can be isolated as law, theology, metaphysics and, in the abstract sense, ethics. Had these revolutions never occurred, you and I might still beat our wives or cheat at cards or avoid walking under ladders, but we might not be able to rejoice in our possession of certain inalienable rights to life, liberty, and the pursuit of happiness, or in the comforting assurance that one more push will bring the classless society.

When one compares the whole course of these revolutions, certain tentative uniformities suggest themselves. If the Russian Revolution at the end of our series is compared with the English at its beginning, there seems to be a development of conscious revolutionary technique. This is of course especially clear since Marx made the history of revolutionary movements of the past a necessary preparation for revolutionists of the present. Lenin and his collaborators had a training in the technique of insurrection which Independents and Jacobins lacked. Robespierre seems almost a political innocent when his revolutionary training is compared with that of any good Bolshevik leaders. Sam Adams, it must be admitted, seems a good deal less innocent. All in all, it is probable that this difference in the explicitness of self-conscious preparation for revolution, this growth of a copious literature of revolution, this increasing familiarity of revolutionary ideas, is not one of the very important uniformities we have to record. It is a conspicuous uniformity, but not an important one. Revolutions are still not a form of logical action. The Bolsheviks do not seem to have guided their actions by the "scientific" study of revolutions to an appreciably greater degree than the Independents or the Jacobins. They simply adapted an old technique to the days of the telegraph and railroad trains.

This last suggests another conspicuous but not very important tendency in our four revolutions. They took place in societies increasingly influenced by the "Industrial Revolution," increasingly subject to those changes in scale which our modern conquests of time and space have brought to societies. Thus the Russian Revolution directly affected more people and more square miles of territory than any previous revolution; its sequence of events compresses into a few months what in England in the 17th century had taken years to achieve; in its use of the printing press, telegraph, radio, airplanes and the rest it seems, as compared with our other revolutions, definitely a streamlined affair. But again we may well doubt whether such changes of scale are in themselves really important factors. Men's desires are the same, whether they ride toward their achievement in airplanes or on horseback. Revolutions may be bigger nowadays, but surely not better. Our prophets of doom to the contrary notwithstanding, the loudspeaker does not change the words.

Finally, at the risk of being tedious, we must come back to some of the problems of methods in the social sciences which were suggested in our first chapter. We must admit that the theorems, the uniformities, which we have been able to put forward in terms of our conceptual scheme, are vague and undramatic. They are by no means as interesting or as alarming as the ideas of revolution held by the late George Orwell, who really believed that totalitarian revolutionary leaders have learned how to change human beings into something wholly different from their immediate predecessors. They cannot be stated in quantitative terms, cannot be used for purposes of prediction or control. But at the very outset we warned the reader not to expect too much. Even such vague theorems as that of the desertion of the intellectuals, that of the role of force in the first stages of revolution, that of the part played by "religious" enthusiasm in the period of crisis, that of the pursuit of pleasure during Thermidor, are, one hopes, not without value for the study of men in society. In themselves they amount to little, but they suggest certain possibilities in further work.

In the first place, by their very inadequacies they point to the necessity for a more rigorous treatment of the problems involved, challenging those who find them incomplete and unsatisfactory to do a better job. In the second place, they will serve the purpose of all first approximations in scientific work—they will suggest further study of the *facts*, especially in those fields where the attempt to make first approximations has uncovered an insufficient supply of the necessary facts. Notably here the facts for a study of class antagonisms are woefully inadequate. So, too, are the facts for a study of the circulation of the elite in prerevolutionary societies. But there are a hundred such holes, some of which can surely be filled. Our first approximations will then lead the way to another's second approximations. No scientist should ask more, even though the public does.

A PARADOX OF REVOLUTION

Wider uniformities will, to judge by the past of science, someday emerge from more complete studies of the sociology of revolutions. Here we dare not hazard much that we have not already brought out in the course of our analysis of four specific revolutions. After all, these are but four revolutions of what seems to be the same type, revolutions in what may be not too uncritically called the democratic tradition. So precious a word is "revolution" to many in that tradition, and especially to Marxists, that they indignantly refuse to apply it to such movements as the relatively bloodless but certainly violent and illegal assumption of power by Mussolini or Hitler. These movements, we are told, were not revolutions because they did not take power from one class and give it to another. Obviously with a word in some ways as imprecise as "revolution" you can play all sorts of tricks like this. But for the scientific study of social change it seems wise to apply the word revolution to the

overthrow of an established and legal parliamentary government
by Fascists. If this is so, then our four revolutions are but one kind
of revolution, and we must not attempt to make them bear the
strain of generalizations meant to apply to all revolutions.

It is even more tempting to try to fit these revolutions into something like a philosophy of history. But the philosophy of history
is almost bound to lead into the kind of prophetic activity we have
already firmly forsworn. It may be that mankind is now in the
midst of a universal "time of troubles" from which it will emerge
into some kind of universal authoritarian order. It may be that
the democratic revolutionary tradition is no longer a living and
effective one. It may be that the revolutions we have studied could
only have taken place in societies in which "progress" was made
a concrete thing by opportunities for economic expansion which
cannot recur in our contemporary world, with no more frontiers
and no more big families. It may even be that the Marxists are
right, and that imperialistic capitalism is now digging its own grave,
preparing the inevitable if long-delayed world revolution of the proletariat. There are many possibilities, as to which it is almost true
that one man's guess is as good as another's. Certainly a conscientious effort to study four great revolutions in the modern world
as a scientist might cannot end in anything as ambitious and as
unscientific as social prognosis.

We need not, however, end on a note of blank skepticism. It
would seem that there are, from the study of these revolutions,
three major conclusions to be drawn: first, that, in spite of their
undeniable and dramatic differences, they do present certain simple
uniformities of the kind we have tried to bring together under our
conceptual scheme of the fever; second, that they point sharply to
the necessity of studying men's deeds and men's words without
assuming that there is always a simple and logical connection between the two, since throughout their courses, and especially at
their crises, they frequently exhibit men saying one thing and doing
another; third, that they indicate that in general many things men
do, many human habits, sentiments, dispositions, cannot be changed
at all rapidly, that the attempt made by the extremists to change
them by law, terror, and exhortation fails, that the convalescence
brings them back not greatly altered.

Yet one hesitant major generalization binding all four of these
revolutions together may here be made from many anticipations
earlier in this book. These four revolutions exhibit an increasing
scale of promises to the "common man"—promises as vague as that
of complete "happiness" and as concrete as that of full satisfaction
of all material wants, with all sorts of pleasant revenges on the
way. Communism is but the present limit of this increasing set of

promises. It is not for us here to rail or protest, but simply to record. So far, these promises in their extreme form have been fulfilled nowhere. That they are made at all offends the traditional Christian, the humanist, perhaps even the man of common sense. But they are made, more vigorously perhaps today in China, in Southeast Asia, in the Near East, wherever Communism is still a young, fresh, and active faith. It is not enough for us Americans to repeat that the promises are impossible of fulfillment, and ought not to be made. It would be folly for us to tell the world that we Americans can fill these promises, especially since we have not filled them at home. Revolution is not a fever that will yield to such innocent and deceptive remedies. For a time, at least, we must accept it as being as incurable as cancer.

As to what the experience of a great revolution does to the society that experiences it, we cannot conclude here too widely without trespassing on wider fields of history and sociology. Yet it does seem that the patient emerges stronger in some respects from the conquered fever, immunized in this way and that from attacks that might be more serious. It is an observable fact that in all our societies there was a flourishing, a peak of varied cultural achievements, after the revolutions. Certainly we may not moralize too much about the stupidities and cruelties of revolutions, may not lift up our hands in horror. It is quite possible that wider study would show that feeble and decadent societies do not undergo revolutions, that revolutions are, perversely, a sign of strength and youth in societies.

One quiet person emerges from his study, not indeed untouched by a good deal of horror and disgust, but moved also with admiration for a deep and unfathomable strength in men which, because of the softer connotations of the word, he is reluctant to call spiritual. Montaigne saw and felt it long ago:

> I see not one action, or three, or a hundred, but a commonly accepted state of morality so unnatural, especially as regards inhumanity and treachery, which are to me the worst of all sins, that I have not the heart to think of them without horror; and they excite my wonder almost as much as my detestation. *The practice of these egregious villainies has as much the mark of strength and vigor of soul as of error and disorder.*

Berkman the anarchist, who loathed the Russian Revolution, tells a story which may represent merely his own bias, but which may nonetheless serve as a brief symbolical epilogue to this study. Berkman says he asked a good Bolshevik acquaintance during the period of attempted complete communization under Lenin why the famous Moscow cabmen, the *izvoschiks,* who continued in diminished numbers to flit about Moscow and to get enormous sums in paper roubles for their services, were not nationalized like practically everything else. The Bolshevik replied, "We found that if you don't feed human beings they continue to live somehow. But if you don't feed the horses, the stupid beasts die. That's why we don't nationalize the cabmen." That is not an altogether cheerful story, and in some ways one may regret the human capacity to live without eating. But clearly if we were as stupid—or as sensible—as horses we should have no revolutions.

31

Radicalism or Reformism

Seymour Martin Lipset

From my work on my doctoral dissertation down to the present, I
have been interested in the problem of "American exceptionalism."
That curious phrase emerged from the debate in the international
Communist movement in the 1920s concerning the sources of the
weakness of left-wing radical movements in the United States. The
key question repeatedly raised in this context has been, is America
qualitatively different from other industrial capitalist countries?
Or, to use Sombart's words, "Why is there no Socialism in the United
States?"

In a forthcoming book, I evaluate the hypotheses advanced by
various writers from Karl Marx onward to explain the absence of
an effective socialist party on the American political scene. (For a
preliminary formulation, see Lipset 1977b, pp. 31–149, 346–63.) If
any of the hypotheses are valid, they should also help to account
for the variation among working-class movements in other parts
of the world. In this article, therefore, I shall reverse the emphasis
from that in my book and look at socialist and working-class movements comparatively, applying elsewhere some of the propositions
that have been advanced to explain the American situation.

A comparative analysis of working-class movements in western

Source: Seymour Martin Lipset, "Radicalism or Reformism: The Sources of Working-Class Politics," *The American Political Science Review* 77, No. 1 (March 1983),
pp. 1–18. By permission. From a presidential address to the American Political
Science Association, Denver, Colo., 1982. Article and references abridged by the
editors.

society is limited by an obvious methodological problem: too many variables and too few cases. The causal factors that have been cited as relevant literally approach two dozen. Among them are economic variables, such as the timing of industrialization, the pace of economic growth, the concentration of industry, the occupational structure, the nature of the division of labor, and the wealth of the country; sociological factors, such as the value system (collectivist versus individualist orientations), the status systems (open or rigid), social mobility, religious differences, ethnic variations, rates of immigration, and urbanization; and political variables, such as the timing of universal suffrage, of political rights, and of freedom of organization, the electoral systems, the extent of centralization, the size of the country, orientations of conservative parties, and the nature of the welfare systems in the country concerned.

Obviously, it would be well nigh hopeless to compare systematically western countries on all of the relevant variables. To limit the task to manageable proportions, I will concentrate on variations in national environments that determined what Stein Rokkan called "the structure of political alternatives" for the working class in different western countries before the First World War. Although much has changed since then, the nature of working-class politics has been profoundly influenced by the variations in the historic conditions under which the proletariat entered the political arena. Experiences antedating the First World War affected whether workers formed class-based parties and, where such parties developed, whether they were revolutionary or reformist.

Of the factors that shaped the character of working-class movements, two are particularly important: first, the nature of the social-class system before industrialization; second, the way in which the economic and political elites responded to the demands of workers for the right to participate in the polity and the economy.

With respect to the first, the following general proposition is advanced: the more rigid the status demarcation lines in a country, the more likely the emergence of radical working-class-based parties. Where industrial capitalism emerged from a feudal society, with its emphasis on strong status lines and barriers, the growing working class was viewed as a *Stand*, a recognizable social entity. As Max Weber emphasized, *Staende*, or "*status groups* are normally communities" defined by particular lifestyles, claims to social honor, and social intercourse among their members; as such they provide the direct basis for collective activity. In this respect, they differ from economic classes whose members share a common market situation, for " 'classes' are not communities, they merely represent possible, and frequent, bases for communal action." Nations characterized by an elaborate, highly institutionalized status structure, *combined* with the economic class tensions usually found in industrial societies, were more likely to exhibit class-conscious politics than those in which status lines were imprecise and not formally recognized. In contrast, in nations that were "born modern" and lacked a feudal and aristocratic past, class position was less likely to confer a sense of shared corporate identity.

The second proposition maintains that the ways in which the dominant strata reacted to the nascent working-class movements conditioned their orientations. Where the working class was denied full political and economic citizenship, strong revolutionary movements developed. Conversely, the more readily working-class organizations were accepted into the economic and political order, the less radical their initial and subsequent ideologies.

This proposition subsumes a number of subpropositions: (1) The denial of political rights in a situation in which a social stratum is led to claim such rights will increase its feelings of deprivation and increase the likelihood of a favorable response to revolutionary and extremist doctrines. (2) The existence of political rights will tend to lead governments and conservative political forces to conciliate the lower classes, thus enhancing the latter's sense of self-respect, status, and efficacy. (3) The development of political parties, trade unions, and other workers' organizations permits the most politically active members of the working class to increase their income, status, and power and in the process to become a privileged group within society and a force for political moderation. (4) A capable lower-class stratum that has been allowed to develop legitimate economic and political organizations, through which it can achieve some share of power in the society and improve its social situation, is potentially less radical in a crisis situation than a comparable stratum that has been unable to develop institutionalized mechanisms for accommodating political demands.

In the remainder of this article, I will present the evidence that substantiates these generalizations, beginning with variations in social status.

STATUS SYSTEMS

The proposition that rigid status systems are conducive to the emergence of radical working-class movements may be illustrated by contrasting the development of workers' parties in North America and Europe. In countries such as the United States and Canada, which did not inherit a fixed pattern of distinct status groups from feudalism, the development of working-class political consciousness, the notion of belonging to a common "class" with unique interests, required an act of intellectual imagination. In Europe, however, workers were placed in a common class by the stratification system. In a sense, workers absorbed a "consciousness of kind" from their ascribed position in the social structure. As Val Lorwin notes: "Social inequality was as provoking as economic injustice. Citizens of a country that has not passed through a feudal age cannot easily imagine how long its heritage conditions social attitudes" (Lorwin 1954, p. 37; Sturmthal 1953, p. 18).

The early socialists were aware of the problem that the lack of a feudal tradition in the United States posed for them. In 1890, Friedrich Engels argued that Americans are "born conservatives— just because America is so purely bourgeois, so entirely without a feudal past" (Engels 1936, p. 467, see also p. 501). The Austrian-born American socialist leader, Victor Berger, also accounted for the weakness of socialism as a result of the fact that "the feeling of class distinction in America . . . has not the same historic foundation that it has in Germany, France, or England. There the people were accustomed for over a thousand years to have distinct classes and castes fixed by law" (quoted in Friedberg 1974, p. 351). In 1906, H. G. Wells, then a Fabian, explained the absence in America of two English parties, Conservative and Labour, in terms of the absence of a "medieval heritage" of socially dominant and inferior strata (Wells 1906, pp. 72–76; Hartz 1955, pp. 50–64).

The absence of feudalism in the United States and Canada, as well as in Australia and New Zealand, sharply differentiated the working-class movements in these countries from those on the European continent. In North America, socialist parties were either very weak (the United States) or emerged late and remained small (Canada), while in Australia and New Zealand, working-class labor parties have always been much less radical than most of the socialist parties of continental Europe.

Still, the early existence of a powerful Labor party in Australia may seem to challenge the hypothesis that the absence of feudalism and aristocracy undermines class-conscious politics on the part of workers. The pattern of politics in Australia, however, was profoundly influenced by the fact that it was largely settled by 19th-century working-class immigrants from industrial Britain, who brought the strong class awareness of the mother country with them.

Many Australian immigrants had been involved in Chartist and similar working-class movements in Britain. Hence, Australia imported the class values of the working class of the mother country. The emergence of class politics in Australia, in contrast with the North American pattern, also reflects the fact that the rural frontier in the Antipodes was highly stratified with sharp divisions between the owners of large farms and a numerous farm labor population.

But despite strong class feelings, which facilitated the emergence of a powerful labor party, it was not Marxist, and hardly socialist or otherwise radical.

The case of New Zealand was somewhat different. Less urbanized than Australia, with a larger proportion of small, family-owned farms, its early British-derived two-party system of Liberals and Conservatives resembled that of the United States. The Liberals appealed to the small holders and the workers. The Labour party was weak until the post–World War I period. As in Britain, anti-union legislation induced the unions to try to elect Labour candidates. After having achieved the position of a strong third party in the 1920s, the New Zealand Labour party won power in 1935, capitalizing on the discontents of the Depression. Its electoral program in that year was characterized "by the omission of socialism and the substitution of measures which revived the old Liberal tradition" (Lipson 1948, p. 230).

In Europe, on the other hand, as Friedrich Engels noted, throughout the 19th century "the political order remained feudal." Writing in 1892, he emphasized: "It seems a law of historical development that the bourgeoisie can in no European country get hold of political power—at least for any length of time. . . . A durable reign of the bourgeoisie has been possible only in countries, like America, where feudalism was unknown" (Engels 1968a, p. 394).

As Joseph Schumpeter pointed out, in much of Europe, the nobility "functioned as a *classe dirigeante*. . . . The aristocratic element continued to rule the roost *right to the end of the period of intact and vital capitalism*" (Schumpeter 1950, pp. 136–37, emphasis in original). More recently, Arno Mayer has brilliantly detailed the ways in which "the feudal elements retained a formidable place in Europe's authority systems," down to World War II (Mayer 1981, p. 135; Bell 1973, pp. 371–72).

Although from the perspective of this article, the sharpest contrast in the political impact of varying status systems lies in the differences between the working-class movements of the English-speaking settler societies and those of continental Europe, there was great variation in the political behavior of the working classes within Europe that also may be related to differences in status systems.

Germany, whose socialist party was the largest in Europe before World War I, has frequently been cited as the prime example of an industrial society deeply influenced by the continuation of feudal and aristocratic values. Writing in the late 1880s, Engels stressed that Germany was "still haunted by the ghosts of the feudal Junker" and that it was "too late in Germany for a secure and firmly founded domination of the bourgeoisie" (Engels 1968b, p. 97). Max Weber pointed to the continued emphasis on "feudal prestige" in Imperial Germany in explaining the behavior of its social classes (Dahrendorf 1967, p. 50). As Dahrendorf has noted: "If one wants to give the social structure of Imperial Germany a name, it would be a paradoxical one of an industrial feudal society" (Dahrendorf 1967, p. 58; Parsons 1969, p. 71).

Many historians and social analysts have placed considerable emphasis on status differentiation in explaining the existence in Germany of numerous parties, each representing a particular status group and having a distinct ideology. Skilled German workers and socialist leaders exhibited a stronger hostility to the lowest segments of the population than occurred in other western countries. For most European socialist parties, all depressed workers, whether urban or rural, were a latent source of support. But for the German socialists, the lowest stratum was a potential enemy. Writing in 1892, in a major theoretical work, Karl Kautsky, the leading Social Democratic theorist, described the "slum proletariat" as "cowardly and unprincipled, . . . ready to fish in troubled waters . . . exploiting every revolution that has broken out, only to betray it at the earliest opportunity" (Kautsky 1910, p. 196).

The Austrian part of the Hapsburg Empire also retained major postfeudal elements into the 20th century, as reflected in its electoral system, similar to that of Hohenzollern Prussia. Until 1895, the Austrian electorate was divided into separate entities—the aristocracy, chambers of commerce, cities, and rural districts, with the latter two being limited by property franchise. In 1895, a fifth class, all others, was added to give the poorer strata some limited form of representation. And, as in Germany, the socialist movement was radical and Marxist.

The strong support obtained by the Social Democrats in Sweden, culminating in the formation of the most durable majority socialist government in Europe, was deeply influenced by the strength of *Staendestaat* elements in the most status-bound society of northern Europe. Comparing the three Scandinavian countries at the end of the 19th century, Herbert Tingsten noted that "the Swedish nobility . . . still enjoyed considerable social prestige and acted partly as a rural aristocracy, partly as a factor in the bureaucratic machinery and officers' corps, [and] was far more numerous than the Danish. . . . [while] in Norway there was no indigenous nobility" (Tingsten 1973, p. 11; Rokken 1981, pp. 60–61). The social structure of Sweden in this respect resembled that of Wilhelmine Germany. Class position has correlated more strongly with party choice in Sweden than in any other European country, a phenomenon that helped generate majority support for the Social Democrats.

The strength of the Finnish Socialists, who in 1916 formed the first majority labor-based government in Europe, also can be linked to the character of the class system. The Finns were exposed to the strong emphasis on status and aristocracy that characterized both Russian and Swedish culture. Finland was a Grand Duchy under the Czar from 1809 on, and a small Swedish minority was predominant within the social and economic upper classes. Before 1905, the Finnish Parliament was divided "into Four Estates or Houses: the Nobility, the Clergy, the Burghers, and the Peasantry. . . . Major cleavages formed along these status dimensions and tended to co-align and reinforce each other" (Martin and Hopkins 1980, p. 186).

The political history of Great Britain, however, would seem to contradict the hypothesis that radical class consciousness was encouraged by sharp status differentiation derived from a feudal past and the continued influence of aristocracy. Marxists, such as Friedrich Engels, emphasized the importance of status factors in accounting for the fact that in England, the major capitalist nation of the 19th century, "the bourgeoisie never held undivided sway." As he noted, the "English bourgeoisie are, up to the present day [1892] . . . deeply penetrated by a sense of their social inferiority . . . ; and they consider themselves highly honoured whenever one of themselves is found worthy of admission into this select and privileged body" of the titled nobility (Engels 1968a, pp. 394–95).

The emphasis on status clearly has had an impact on British working-class politics from the outset of the Industrial Revolution down to the post–World War II period. E. P. Thompson has stressed that in the early 19th century, "there was a consciousness of the identity of interests of the working class or 'productive classes,' as against those of other classes; and within this was maturing the claim for an alternative *system*" (Thompson 1968, pp. 887–88). Such consciousness presumably facilitated the emergence of Chartism, the strongest working-class movement in the first half of the 19th century, which mobilized workers in a militant class-conscious struggle for the suffrage and ultimately may have helped to create the strong correlation between class position and electoral choice that has characterized British politics since World War I. As Peter Pulzer put it: "Class is the basis of British party politics; all else is embellishment and detail" (Pulzer 1967, p. 98).

But socialist movements were much weaker in Britain than in most Continental countries in the late 19th and early 20th centuries. The Labour Party, allied to the Liberals, did not become a factor in British politics until 1906, when it elected 30 members to Parliament, and it only secured major-party status after the First World War. This seeming anomaly is explained by analysts of British politics by the strength of *noblesse oblige* norms among the

aristocracy, who consciously served as a "protective stratum" for
workers by enacting factory reforms and welfare-state legislation,
activities that won the support of the workers (to be discussed in
more detail below).

In Latin countries such as France, Italy, and Spain, the strength
of revolutionary labor movements (anarchist, syndicalist, left socialist, and later communist) on the one hand, and ultra-reactionary
political tendencies among the middle and upper classes, on the
other, has been related to the failure of these societies to develop
a full-grown industrial system until after the Second World War.
The aristocracies in these countries had declined in power by the
late 19th century and did little to foster noblesse-oblige welfare
policies for the workers. At the same time, their business classes
in the late 19th and early 20th centuries were weakly developed
and resembled a semifeudal stratum whose position was tied to
family property. Not withstanding the Revolution of 1789, the
French social structure reflected, in Stanley Hoffman's words, a
"feudal hangover . . . traditional Catholic doctrines (notably concerning the evils of capitalist accumulation) left their mark . . . ;
the bourgeoisie in many ways imitated the aristocracy" (Hoffman
1963, p. 5). As Val Lorwin emphasizes, writing about the bourgeoisie
of France and Italy, "they flaunted inequalities by their style of
living. Their class consciousness helped shape the class consciousness of workers" (Lorwin 1958, pp. 342–43). This orientation, with
its emphasis on family and its concern for the maintenance of explicit status lines, was associated with a profound antagonism to
collective bargaining, labor legislation, and social security.

Strikingly, efforts to account for the moderate multiclass "people's party" orientations of the Belgian, Dutch, Swiss, and Danish
labor and socialist movements have pointed to the weakness of feudal elements in these societies. Carl Landauer notes that Belgium
had been much less of a *Staendestaat* than its neighbors.

> Belgium is a business country, with a weak feudal tradition—much
> weaker than in Germany, France, or Britain. . . . In Belgium, fewer
> upper-class people than elsewhere think that they owe it to their pride
> to resist the aspiration of the underprivileged. . . . [E]ven less than in
> Britain or France and certainly less than in Germany was exploitation
> motivated by the idea that the humble must be kept in their places
> (Landauer 1959, p. 479).

A similar thesis has been advanced by Hans Daalder for two
other small European countries, the Netherlands and Switzerland.
As he notes (1966b, p. 55), in both, "the position of the nobility
against that of burghers and independent peasants tended always
to be weak and to grow weaker as capitalism expanded." And writ-

ing of his native country, the Netherlands, Daalder points out that the historic "political, social, and economic prestige" of the Dutch bourgeoisie, which dates back to preindustrial times, fostered conditions which "dampened working class militancy, and eased the integration of the working class into the national political community" (Daalder 1966a, p. 197).

Preindustrial Switzerland "was one of small farms, with no considerable estates or landed aristocracy." Erich Gruner cites a comment by a Swiss writer in the late 1860s that "the poor man felt himself less oppressed, since he had the satisfaction of having his freedom in the community *(Gemeinde)* and province *(Landsgemeinde)* and the pride that, he, himself, counted for as much as the richest factory owner, which gave him self-respect and let him raise his head high" (Gruner 1968, p. 156). Factory and welfare legislation was enacted before 1900. Unlike the large German and Austrian Social Democratic parties, the small Swiss "Socialist movement . . . was on the extreme right wing of the Second International" before World War I (Cole 1956, p. 611).

The labor and socialist movements of Denmark have been the most moderate in Europe. One recent analyst of the Danish case notes that although the Social Democratic Party has been "the dominant force in Danish politics for the past half century," its pragmatic reformist orientation poses the same question as that raised for the United States, "why there is no socialism in Denmark," a question that can only be answered by reference to its past (Cornell, n.d.). While the explanation for Denmark, as for the United States, must be multivariate, part of it would appear to be, as Herbert Tingsten has noted, that feudalism and the nobility were much less important in Denmark than in Germany and Sweden. And in Britain, "moral responses to the miseries that existed . . . [were] sufficient to preclude any revolutionary movement" (Cornell, n.d., p. 19).

The clearest discrepancy in the relationship between status systems and working-class politics outlined here occurred in Norway. There is consensus among students of Scandinavian society that Norway was less affected by feudalism and aristocratic status norms than the other northern countries. Nevertheless, the major socialist movement in Norway decided in 1919 to join the Communist International and remained affiliated until 1923.

Analysts of Norwegian politics agree, however, that this development was an historic anomaly, an event response that was out of character with the behavior of Norwegian workers, as evidenced by the fact that the link with the Third International lasted only a few years. Norway appears to be "the exception that proves the rule." The Norwegian labor and socialist movements were weak and moderate until World War I. But the war, in conjunction with the development of cheap hydro-electric power, resulted in a period of sudden and very rapid industrialization and social dislocation, which created a large segment of workers without political traditions or loyalties who were prone to support of labor militancy and radicalism. The bulk of Norwegian workers were first organized at the time of the Russian Revolution and, as in many other countries, were swept up in the enthusiasm for the Revolution. But Norwegian socialism and trade unionism soon returned to the characteristic pattern of social democratic moderation. Thus, Norway fits the "pattern" up to 1914 and from the mid-twenties on. Even during the Great Depression of the 1930s, the Communists remained a weak party, securing less than 2 percent of the vote.

THE RIGHT TO PARTICIPATE

As emphasized at the outset, cross-national variations in working-class political activity were also affected by differences in the extent to which the proletariat was legally free to form class-based organizations and participate in the economic and political life of their societies. The greater the duration and intensity of state repression of working-class economic and political rights, the more likely workers were to respond favorably to revolutionary doctrines. As Max Weber concluded in his essay on the suffrage and democracy in Germany, "All the might of the masses is directed *against* a state in which they are only objects and not participants" (Weber 1958, p. 279).

The effect of participation may best be illustrated by examining the two principal paths by which the members of the working classes were accepted into the fabric of societies as political and economic citizens. The first involves their right to vote and to organize political parties that could play a constructive role in the polity; the second refers to the way working-class economic combinations, in the form of labor unions, were accepted as formally legitimate by the state and substantively legitimate by employers.

The absence of these rights throughout Europe for much of the 19th century emphasized the inferior status of the workers and peasants. The political organization of much of premodern Europe was based on functional representation by Estate or *Stand*. The lower classes, including the emerging proletariat, were not accepted as an Estate worthy of representation. And the parliaments of many European countries—Austria, Finland, Prussia, and Sweden, among others—were composed of members elected by the more privileged *Staende*. Some eventually created a new Estate for the outcaste groups. Thus their Constitutions legitimated the fixed hierarchical

status orders. The contradiction between such patterns of hierarchical representation and the universalistic norms of capitalism
and liberalism fostered efforts to secure plebiscitarian electoral systems, one man, one vote, as well as struggles for the right of free
association, particularly for trade unions. The fight for the vote
and the right to organize were perceived in terms of opposition to
hierarchical class role, as part of a broad struggle for equality.

The importance of the early granting of democratic rights for
political activity has been emphasized by social analysts and historians in numerous contexts. T. H. Marshall, for one, noted that extreme ideologies initially emerged among new strata, in particular
the bourgeoisie and working class, as they fought for the political
and social rights of citizenship. Along these lines, many writers
concerned with the question of "why no socialism in America?"
have pointed to the early enfranchisement of the white working
class as an important causal factor. Selig Perlman made this argument in *The Theory of the Labor Movement* when he suggested
that a major cause of the lack of class consciousness among American workers

> was the free gift of the ballot which came to labor at an early date as
> a by-product of the Jeffersonian democratic movement. In other coun-
> tries where the labor movement started while workingmen were still
> denied the franchise, there was in the last analysis no need for a theory
> of "surplus value" to convince them that they were a class apart and
> should therefore be "class conscious." There ran a line like a red thread
> between the laboring class and the other classes. Not so, where the
> line is only an economic one (Perlman 1928, p. 167).

This view was shared by Lenin, who maintained that the weakness of socialism in America and Britain before World War I
stemmed from "the absence of any at all big, nation-wide *democratic* tasks facing the proletariat" (Lenin, n.d., p. 51). Other countries, in which manhood suffrage and full democratic rights were secured in the 19th century, such as Australia, Canada, Denmark, and
Switzerland, were also resistant to efforts to create strong socialist parties.

Conversely, the denial of the suffrage proved to be a strong motive
for class political organization in many European nations. The first
major British labor movement, Chartism, was centered on the struggle for the vote. In some countries, general strikes were called by
workers to force through a change in the electoral laws (Austria,
1896 and 1905; Finland, 1905; Belgium, 1902 and 1913; and Sweden,
1902). The struggle for suffrage often had a quasi-religious fervor
and was viewed by its advocates as the key to a new and more
egalitarian society, since the poor outnumbered the rich and would

presumably secure a radical redistribution of income and opportunity if they had the necessary political rights. The existence of a
limited franchise based on property made it clear to workers that
political power and economic privilege were closely related. The
withholding of the franchise often became a symbol of the position
of workers as a deprived and pariah group. A restricted franchise
encouraged the ideologists of both unfranchised and privileged
groups to analyze politics in terms of class power.

The exclusion of workers from the fundamental political rights
of citizenship effectively fused the struggle for political and economic equality and cast that struggle in a radical mold. Thus, a
large number of European socialist movements grew strong and
adopted a radical Marxist ideology while the working class was
still unfranchised or was discriminated against by an electoral system that was explicitly class or property biased. Such was the history
of Austria, Germany, Finland, and Sweden, among others.

The variations in legal rights that influenced the character of
working-class politics also helped to determine the relationship of
trade unions to labor parties in different nations. Where both trade-
union rights and male suffrage existed at an early date, the unions
and the workers as a social force were able to press for political
objectives by working with one or more of the non-socialist parties.
And even when labor parties emerged, they did not adopt radical
objectives.

As Gary Marks has noted in his study of trade-union political
activity:

> Where trade unions were firmly established before party-political mobili-
> zation was underway, the resulting party had to adapt itself to an already
> "formed" working class with its cultural ties and institutional loyalties.
> Unlike the parties that were established before the rise of trade unions,
> these parties could not integrate the working classes into a singular,
> inclusive, and politically oriented sub-culture of radical or revolutionary
> resistance against capitalism. In this important respect, then, the Social
> Democratic Party, the early guardian and shaper of trade unionism
> in Germany, stands opposite the British Labour Party, which, in Ernest
> Bevin's telling phrase, "has grown out of the bowels of the T.U.C." (Marks
> 1982, p. 89; Sturmthal 1953, pp. 37–62; Derfler 1973, p. 73)

Labor unions in the English-speaking countries became legitimate pressure groups oriented to pragmatic and immediate economic goals. They were involved in many of the nonideologi-
cal issues of the day, such as protection versus free trade, and
immigration policies. Some of the more left or liberal nonsocialist bourgeois parties supported social legislation desired by labor
unions.

In those countries in which the trade union movement created a labor party, such as Australia and Britain, the original radical socialist promotion groups had comparatively little influence. The dominant working-class parties were controlled by trade unions and followed a pragmatic non-Marxian ideology. Socialists remained a comparatively small pressure group within these organizations or sought to build their own parties outside the labor parties.

In nations where the state repressed economic combination, unions were faced with a common and overriding task, that of changing the rules of the game. The more intensive and longer lasting the state repression, the more drastic the consequences. Where the right to combine in the labor market was severely restricted, as it was in Germany, Austria, Russia, France, Spain, and Italy, the decision to act in politics was forced on trade unions. Whether they liked it or not, unions became political institutions; they had first to change the distribution of political power within the state before they could effectively exert power in the market. At the same time, extreme state repression or employer opposition minimized the ability of privileged groups of skilled workers to improve their working conditions in a sectional fashion. In this important respect, then, repression fostered socialist or anarchist ideologies that emphasized the common interests of all workers.

Where fundamental economic rights were denied to workers, strong radical organizations were established before unions were well developed. This meant that the parties formulated their ideologies in the absence of pressures for pragmatic policies from trade unions.

Where the working class was deprived of both economic and political rights, those who favored social change were necessarily revolutionary. The identification of state repression with privileged and powerful groups reinforced political ideologies that conceived of politics in demonological terms. Perhaps the most important example of this pattern was Czarist Russia. There, every effort to form legal trade unions or establish a democratic parliamentary regime was forcibly suppressed. This situation provided the ground for revolutionary lower-class political movements under the leadership of intellectuals or others of middle- or upper-class origin.

Although the goals of party and union tend to differ when both are tolerated by the state, under repression there is much less space for diversity. Both share the task of changing the political status quo. As Lenin observed in the context of Czarist Russia:

> the yoke of the autocracy appears . . . to obliterate all distinctions between a Social-Democratic organization and trade unions, because *all* workers' associations and *all* circles are prohibited, and because the principal manifestation and weapon of the workers' economic struggle—

the strike—is regarded as a criminal (and sometimes even as a political) offense (Lenin 1973, p. 139).

The Leninist concept of the "combat party," with its reliance on secrecy and authoritarian discipline and its emphasis on the "conquest of power," developed as a reaction to the political situation of the time.

* * * * *

In Germany, to be discussed in more detail below, the continued domination of the Reichstag by traditional conservative forces, the absence of a democratic franchise in Prussia, and the strong repressive measures taken by Bismarck against the socialists in the 1870s and 1880s, bound the socialists and the trade unions formed by them into a distinct subculture having an explicitly revolutionary ideology. In practice, of course, as Robert Michels and many other contemporary observers argued, the bureaucracy of the party gradually became conservative and opposed any measures that threatened its organizational stability. Nevertheless, the position of the labor movement as a semi-legitimate opposition group helped to perpetuate its use of radical terminology.

In Austria, as in Germany, the intransigence of the upper class had a decisive influence on the character and ideology of the working-class movement. Anti-Socialist laws were in effect from 1866 to 1881, and a special law repressed the workers' party in many regions from 1881 to 1891. The party and the unions, which cooperated closely in the struggle for the suffrage, adhered to a radical class-conscious ideology. Manhood suffrage for parliamentary elections was only attained in 1907.

The achievement of this political goal, followed by a sharp increase in parliamentary representation, however, served to undermine the cohesion and radicalism of the workers' movement. As G. D. H. Cole notes, "the very success of the Austrians in winning the vote necessarily weakened their sense of the need for close unity. The main plank in their common programme having been withdrawn, it was none too easy to find another to take its place. Now that they had become an important parliamentary party the emphasis tended to shift to the struggle for social and economic reforms, especially for improved labour laws regulating conditions of employment and the development of social services on the German model. But these were poor substitutes because they tended to change the Socialist Party into a reformist party" (Cole 1956, p. 538).

The Socialist party and the trade unions continued to make significant progress after the defeat and breakup of the Hapsburg monarchy in World War I. Such a situation should have resulted in the development of working-class political and labor movements integrated into the body politic, and a further moderation of their ideology in the direction of the British and Scandinavian patterns. In fact, this did not occur. But the responsibility did not lie with the Austrian labor movement. Rather, the Austrian conservatives, whose support was based on the rural population and business elements, and who were tied closely to the Catholic church, aristocracy, and monarchism, refused to accept the rising status of labor. Faced with rebuffs from the conservatives, the church, and the business strata, the socialists responded by adhering to Marxian class-war principles. Within the Socialist International, the Austrian party was considered to be on the far left, before it was suppressed in 1934.

* * * * *

In analyzing the relationship between economic and political rights and working-class political behavior, I have thus far dealt primarily with formal rights, that is, whether adult suffrage existed, and whether trade unions could function without serious legal difficulties. In fact, however, legal rights were only partial indicators of the will and capacity of the upper and business classes to resist the emergence of the working class as a political force. The right to vote or organize unions did not necessarily mean that labor had acquired a legitimate place in society, or that the pressures toward radicalism flowing from the position of the worker as political outcast had disappeared.

It is possible to distinguish among three situations: total repression, legal existence but constant conflict (i.e., *de jure* but not *de facto* recognition), and *de jure* and *de facto* recognition. The existence of the first two conditions usually indicates that the business classes still desire to destroy the organized expression of the labor movement. Under such conditions, labor may be expected to react strongly against capitalism and, perhaps, the existing political system as well.

France before World War II, Spain before 1975, and pre-fascist Italy are examples of nations where unions were weak because the business and conservative classes refused to grant *de facto* recognition to them. The consequences of this for union strategy have been recognized by Fred Ridley:

> There is a close relationship between weak, unorganized labour movements and the outbreak of revolutionary or anarchist activity in Russia, Spain and Italy, as well as in France. The unions had little bargaining power when it came to across-the-table negotiations with employers; they had neither the membership nor the organization with which to

impress. Lack of funds, inability to pay strike benefits, meant that they could not hope to achieve their ends by ordinary peaceful strikes. They were thus forced to play for quick results: violence, intimidation and sabotage were the obvious weapons to choose (Ridley 1970, p. 18).

In much of Latin Europe, both the state and employers denied legitimacy to trade unions, i.e., their right to become the institutionalized representatives of workers, although in France manhood suffrage existed in the 1870s and in Spain from 1889. In France the Socialist party was able to gain electoral strength before unions were well developed. The party, however, had little success in fostering social legislation or trade-union organizations, given "the ferocity of bourgeois response to it" (Derfler 1973, p. 78; Sturmthal 1953, pp. 55–56). In countries where a wide franchise failed to provide "an effective lever in the hands of the masses, such 'democratic' reforms could paradoxically develop into a measure of plebiscitary control over them. This could result in an enduring alienation of sizable sections of the population rather than in their permanent integration in an effectively responsive political system" (Daalder 1966b, p. 54).

The French trade-union movement continued to face strong resistance from the state and the business class, both of which refused to grant unions a legitimate role as bargaining agents in the economy. The unions required a revolutionary ideology to motivate membership and leadership participation and thus sustain their organization. They found this ideology in syndicalism. As a number of historians have suggested, syndicalism, with its faith in violence and in worker spontaneity, was not merely an impractical flight of idealism, but a response to constraints that served to limit the alternatives facing unions. Ridley has noted:

> The law forced workers into opposition to the state; in a measure, indeed, it persuaded them to reject the state altogether. Its provisions, biased heavily in favour of the employer, excluded the worker from its benefits—left him to all interests an outcast—*hors du pays légal*. The syndicalist doctrine of autonomy, the insistence that the labour movement must develop outside the state, create its own institutions to reinforce it, can be understood in the light of its experience (Ridley 1970, p. 23; see also Stearns 1971, p. 13).

Distrust of parliamentary government and a strong emphasis on syndicalist and revolutionary class organization developed in Spain and Italy as well. As noted, Spain introduced universal male suffrage relatively early. But the government "continued to manage elections as it pleased, to the extent of deciding centrally who were to be elected, not only for its own party, but also to represent the recognized opposition groups." In the big cities, it counted the ballots; in small towns and rural areas, the "caciques," local bosses, controlled. In Italy, the Liberals, who dominated the government in the late 19th and early 20th centuries, rigged the election results among a more restricted electorate by a variety of corrupt practices, comparable to those used in Spain. "These practices . . . left a heritage of cynicism, highly politicized administrative machinery, corruption, and the absence of civic pride and of vital local government" (Barnes 1966, pp. 306–08). The expansion of the suffrage in 1912 was followed by an election in which the governing Liberals added to corrupt practices a heavy "dose of violence to ensure success" (Gaetano Salvemini, quoted in Barnes 1966, p. 308).

In both countries, trade union organizations were harassed by state institutions that claimed to represent the electorate democratically. Because unions were weak, the conditions for the emergence of a genuine working-class leadership were absent. Consequently, intellectuals or other upper-class radicals came to dominate the labor movement. The weakness and instability of trade unions also resulted in few achievements that could legitimate gradualist and pragmatic goals. As Juan Linz notes with respect to Spain:

> The bitterness of class conflict that ultimately led to semirevolutionary general strikes, local or regional insurrections . . . should not hide the fact that the labor movement was weak by comparison with other countries. Spanish labor lacked numbers, organizational and economic resources for strikes, success at the polls, and capacity for nationwide activities (Linz 1981, p. 368).

In Italy and Spain, as in France, the business classes continually resisted coming to terms with the trade union movement. Although unions had *de jure* recognition, the history of labor in these countries was characterized by constant warfare. Revolutionary syndicalism was strong in each country (Malefakis 1973, p. 5). In Italy, syndicalism gained strength as a reaction to the repeated suppression of local strikes and popular protest movements that often involved the use of violence. In Spain, anarchism grew in response to "alternate periods of legal toleration and savage repression." This pattern culminated in the triumph of authoritarianism in both Italy and Spain and the establishment of regimes that were primarily oriented toward maintaining the economic and class status quo. And as in France, the working class and its leaders responded by supporting extremist doctrines. Thus, in Spain, moderate socialism was relatively weak, whereas doctrines such as revolutionary socialism, anarchism, and even Trotskyism were strong. In Italy, anarchism and left socialism were influential before Mussolini, and moderate socialism, even today, remains relatively weak; the bulk of the working class supports the Communist party.

It is also worth noting that both Spain and Italy were industrially backward societies in the late 19th century when radical working-class movements emerged. Like fascism itself, anarchism has been viewed as an antimodern doctrine, a reaction against the strains of modernity. In this context, it should be noted that in France, too, syndicalism was strongest among craft workers in small-scale industries that were most threatened by industrialization and mass production.

The adoption of an anarchist or syndicalist political ideology had specific and identifiable consequences for trade-union movements. Syndicalism committed them to a loose, unstable, and relatively unbureaucratic organization. This structure, in turn, required the unions and their leaders to stress ideology at the expense of building loyalty on the basis of concrete gains achieved through collective bargaining. It also reduced those inhibitions on militant action that result from the need to protect an established structure.

In discussing the denial of legitimacy to socialists and trade unions, I have focused primarily on the influence this had on their activities and ideologies. But, obviously, the relationship is not a simple cause-and-effect one. The behavior of the left had its effect on the right. In particular, one should not ignore that France, Italy, Spain, and Austria are Catholic, which meant that the traditional struggle between the left and right was not solely, or even primarily, an economic class struggle but also was a confrontation between Catholicism and atheism or secularism. Many of the Catholic conservative leaders viewed the battle against Marxism and working-class institutions as part of the fight for their religion. To accept the legitimacy of a working-class movement that was Marxist and irreligious involved a much greater modification in their value systems than was necessary in situations where religious values were not involved, as in Britain and Australia.

In the Catholic societies of Western Europe, the church, in alliance with landed interests, attempted to establish trade unions and political organizations to counter the influence of socialism among the lower classes. The result was the "pillarization" of the working class into mutually antagonistic Catholic and socialist tendencies. In France, Italy, Spain, and Austria, socialist parties not only were rejected by the ruling powers, they were also opposed by a major segment of the working class. Both of these factors furthered the development of radical movements. Reformism tended to be more typical of working-class politics and unions in countries where labor was powerfully represented by unitary organizations that were accepted into the political and economic mainstream.[1]

EFFORTS AT INTEGRATION: BRITAIN AND GERMANY

The previous discussion indicates that radical ideologies were strongest where social and political groups attempted to reduce or destroy the influence of leftist or working-class movements by refusing them legitimacy and continually fighting them. In countries in which the working class was incorporated into the body politic at an early date, the chances that workers would come to support extremist or revolutionary doctrines were considerably reduced.

The American experience clearly illustrates the consequences for working-class movements of integration into society. There the absorption occurred as a result of social structures, values, and events that predated industrial society. The European experience offers insights into the effects of deliberate efforts to win the allegiance of the working class. An examination of Great Britain and Germany is particularly informative because in both countries, sections of the ruling strata consciously sought to reduce the class antagonism of the workers by accommodating their demands; yet the attempt succeeded in Britain and failed in Germany.

The conventional explanation of why Marxism is weak in Britain suggests that the landed aristocracy and their party, the Tories, who retained considerable power in 19th-century Britain, sought to stem the growing power and ideology of the rising industrial business class by winning the allegiance of the "lower orders." In their opposition to the new capitalist society and in a desire to preserve past institutions and values, Conservatives, led by Disraeli, often took the same position as the spokesmen of the working classes. As Hearnshaw points out:

> The "young England" Tories [which Disraeli joined] . . . with their curious affection for an idealized feudalism and chivalry, had much in common with the Chartists and other proletarian reformers of the early Victorian days. With them they deplored and resented the operation of the new poor law of 1834; they opposed the principles of laissez-faire; they hated the new machinery and the hideous mills in which it was

---

[1] It should also be noted that the involvement of workers in religious parties also helped move such groups to the left in social policies, once democratic institutions were stabilized. In the Low countries, in particular, the recognition of workers' rights by the religious groups helped to moderate the behavior of the socialists as well (Daalder 1981, pp. 207–08).

housed; they protested the repeal of the usury laws and the corn laws; they distrusted the new stock-jobbers and the joint-stock bankers . . . [their] principles flowed naturally from the mainstream of the conservative tradition (Hearnshaw 1933, pp. 219–20).

The Tories, however, maintained a traditional view of the relationship between rich and poor, one that was based on an idealization of class relations as they existed in pre-industrial society. They assumed that the lower classes should remain "dependent" on the upper class and that the latter, in turn, should be responsible for the welfare of the lower strata.

Some of the leaders of the aristocratic upper classes were able to perceive the extent to which the new industrial workers—despite occasional violent protest actions and increasing class consciousness—shared their view of "the good old days and the bad new days," and, more important, desired recognition and status within the existing order. Disraeli believed in the traditionalism of the lower classes. He was able to secure the passage of the Electoral Reform Act of 1867 as well as some social legislation. To this must be added the relative freedom that British trade unions attained in the last quarter of the 19th century, especially through the labor laws of 1875. The facts of political life, plus the steadily rising standard of living, demonstrated to workers and their leaders that it was possible to improve their position within British society. Both the Tories and Liberals formed workingmen's associations.

The reformist policies of British politicians in the late 19th and early 20th centuries helped to integrate workers into the national community, to reduce their hostility to existing political institutions (the state, the throne, and the major parties), and to adopt gradualist rather than revolutionary methods. Friedrich Engels noted that the absence of "a separate political working-class party" was to be expected "in a country where the ruling classes have set themselves the task of carrying out, parallel with other concessions, one point of the Chartists' programme, the People's Charter, after another" (Engels 1953, p. 466). Although a labor party gained strength in Britain in the early 1900s, following the Taff-Vale court decision that threatened the power of the trade unions, the leaders of the new movement did not view the other parties as class enemies who had to be eliminated. Rather, they conceived of a separate labor party as an electoral tactic, which would place labor in a better position to bargain with the older parties. The development of a stable, legitimate, labor movement created a stratum of working-class leaders who had secured position and power within the existing social system and consequently had close ties to it. The emergence of Fabianism as a political force in Britain is in large measure explicable by the fact that the Fabians, with their initial hope that the upper class could be converted to socialism, reflected the actual British historical experience of aristocratic intervention on behalf of the workers.

In Germany, a situation similar in certain important respects to that in Britain led to a comparable effort to integrate the lower classes into the society. The aristocracy, crown, and state bureaucracy sought to inhibit the influence of the rising liberal bourgeoisie. Bismarck, who was the chief exponent of this policy, established universal suffrage in the federal empire after 1867 so that he could use the votes of the rural lower classes, and to a certain extent of the workers themselves, against the urban middle classes, who, he realized, would dominate in a restricted property-based suffrage.

Unlike Disraeli and the British Tories, however, Bismarck had little confidence that the workers' organizations would become incorporated into the social order. This led him to outlaw the socialist movement in 1878 and to hope that by enacting social welfare measures advocated by the socialists he could win the loyalty of workers to the regime. The conservative *Sozialpolitik*, however, came too late. The workers had already begun to support the socialist movement; efforts to suppress it only served to undermine moderate representatives of the working class. This act of repression is generally recognized to be one of the chief sources of the difference in the political development of the German and British working classes.

Bismarck attempted to incorporate the proletariat by winning its loyalty to society without permitting workers to have their own organizations and leaders. By the time working-class political organization was legalized in 1890, the Social Democrats had acquired a revolutionary ideology that was difficult to discard even after the party had become a strong and stable movement, capable of antagonizing and frightening the middle and upper classes.

The Bismarckian policies deeply affected the outlook and strategy of German workers. First, and most important, they placed Social Democracy in a paradoxical position. On the one hand, the party was successful: it grew steadily from one election to the next, attracted hundreds of thousands of members and employed a large bureaucracy. It gradually adapted itself to the role of a parliamentary opposition, which anticipated coming to power through democratic means. On the other hand, however, the ideology developed during and immediately following the period of repression gave it the appearance of being devoted to purely revolutionary ends and legitimized the agitation of extreme leftists within its ranks. (The party rewrote its program in 1891, after 12 years of overt repression, to emphasize its intransigence.) Until World War I, the SPD refused to repudiate its formal belief in class warfare. In large part, the subsequent strength of left-wing socialists and Communists may be explained by the legitimacy the ideology of the Social Democratic party gave to such groups within the working class.

Second, Bismarck's policies, and the socialists' ideological reactions to them, prevented the SPD from becoming a legitimate national party in the eyes of other political movements. The socialist revolutionary rhetoric may have prevented many of the middle-class, white-collar strata from supporting the Party, while at the same time strengthening the potential for an alliance between the middle class and industrialists and large landowners.

Third, Bismarck's "social revolution from above" included a number of welfare programs that in other countries had been the responsibility of the unions themselves and had helped to stabilize conservative unions. August Bebel, the leader of the Social Democratic party, pointed this out in a speech in 1893:

> In Germany, the state system of workingmen's insurance took away from the trade unions that branch of activity, and has in effect cut a vital nerve, as it were. For benefit systems had meant enormously in the furthering of unionism in Britain and among the German printers. Labor legislation has likewise preempted many other lines of activity which properly belong to the trade unions (Bebel, quoted in Perlman 1928, pp. 77–78).

The fact that the state, rather than the unions, controlled welfare funds and dictated policies, which elsewhere were handled through collective bargaining, served to increase the awareness of workers and their leaders of the need to influence state policy. The potential for a syndicalist antistatist doctrine was reduced, since conservative state intervention stimulated the belief that workers should take over and use the state system. The trade unions, far from becoming antistatist, became more statist in their orientation. But at the same time, the elimination of various trade-union functions weakened the loyalty of workers to the labor movement and reduced the stability of the unions, which denied them the role in maintaining political stability that unions in various other countries, particularly Britain, assumed.

The effect of varying upper-class policies on the behavior of working-class movements can be illustrated within Germany as well as through international comparisons. As a number of political commentators have noted, the socialist movement in Prussia was quite different from that in southern Germany, especially Bavaria. In Prussia, which contained over half the population of the country, Bismarck pursued the same combination of repression and paternalism that he adopted for the federal empire. Prussia, a highly industrialized part of Germany, retained legal limits on the potential power of the workers even after the anti-Socialist laws were repealed. These restrictions were in the form of an electoral system based on three estates, which gave the middle classes and the landed nobility effective control over the Prussian legislature. The restrictions were, in large part, motivated by the fact that a purely democratic franchise would give a majority to the Socialists and the Catholic Zentrum, both antigovernment parties. And as Kautsky noted in 1911, the working-class movement in Prussia gave much more emphasis to class-struggle doctrines.

In the South, where governments were much less autocratic than in Prussia, in part because the old landed aristocracy was relatively unimportant and the rural and urban petty bourgeoisie proportionately stronger, the degree of political freedom was much greater. In Southern Germany, the Social Democrats cooperated with nonsocialist parties, in the process reducing their original emphasis on class struggle. The Revisionist doctrines of Eduard Bernstein were given their earliest and strongest support in the South. The Bavarian socialists, for example, broke with the tradition of the party and voted for the state budget.

Bismarck failed in his effort to destroy German socialism through force. His refusal to incorporate the socialist political movement in a democratic parliamentary system helped to perpetuate revolutionary rhetoric. But the fact remains that the Social Democrats eventually became a stable, moderate, opposition party. Its commitment to Marxism was largely aimed against the militarist imperial state.

The failure of Bismarckian policy is evident in the rise of large movements on the left of the Social Democrats after World War I. The momentum for such movements emerged from the prewar contradiction between Social Democratic party behavior and ideology. Although support for the Communists declined in the late 20s, they made considerable headway in the early 1930s. In Britain, on the other hand, communism and fascism were weak and found no social roots.

The identification of varying British and German policies with Disraeli and Bismarck is not intended to suggest that the sharply divergent histories of the two countries may be credited to the wisdom of one and the stupidity of the other. Rather, as Barrington Moore has emphasized, the structural histories of the British and German aristocracies differed greatly. A combination of factors led the British upper classes to collaborate economically with the rising bourgeoisie and to set their peasants free. The landed aristocracy developed "bourgeois economic habits" and accepted parts of liberal political doctrine. In Germany, on the other hand, the aristocracy continued to preside over a "labor-repressive agrarian system" and to work with the monarchy and the "royal bureaucracy" rather than the business classes. This relationship produced, or rather reinforced, an emphasis on obedience and control from the top. Thus, the divergent policies of British and German upper-class conservatives reflected basic variations in their nations' social structures (Moore 1967, pp. 413–50).

CONCLUSION

In this article I have analyzed some of the ways in which the character of working-class movements has been influenced by the varying status systems of different societies and by the degree to which workers and their organizations were able to participate legitimately in the economic and political decision-making processes. In the United States, and to a lesser extent in Canada, the absence of an aristocratic or feudal past, combined with a history of political democracy prior to industrialization, served to reduce the salience of class-conscious politics and proposals for major structural change. As Walter Dean Burnham has emphasized: "No feudalism, no socialism: with these four words one can summarize the basic sociocultural realities that underlie American electoral politics in the industrial era" (Burnham 1974, p. 718).

Conversely, in much of Europe, a "post-feudal" background was critical in shaping the political consciousness of the working class. As William Sewell, Jr. notes, "one of the most important roots of European class consciousness may have been the corporate cultural tradition of the pre-industrial European working class. This tradition made workingmen feel that their destiny was linked to that of their fellow workers, and predisposed them to collective, rather than individualistic, ideologies and modes of social and political action" (Sewell 1976, pp. 232–33).

The proletarian movements, born as *Staende,* adopted Marxism as their ideological cement and sought to achieve legitimation within the bourgeois order through constitutional reforms, the acquisition of citizenship. The emergence of radical politics originated as a consequence of the meshing of the hierarchical *Staende* with the inequalities of an emerging capitalist society differentiated into economic classes. Ironically, in trying to change the perception of the social hierarchy from *Stand* to class, radical working-class movements drew on and revitalized the sense of *Stand*-consciousness that they inherited. Many of the pre–World War I Social Democratic parties, as well as postwar Communist parties, also sustained corporative forms of group solidarity by creating a socially encapsulated working-class culture, in which their followers were involved in a plethora of party and union-related organizations.

Where the corporate tradition broke down or never existed, what developed were interest-group organizations and ideologies. As

Lenin and Perlman argued from contrary political perspectives, the orientation that stems from the class position of the proletariat is pure and simple trade unionism, or "economism," not revolutionary class consciousness. Against the background of Marxist theory, the outcome is paradoxical. For Marx and Engels maintained that the "logic of capitalism" would give rise to revolutionary movements, and that, to the degree that remnants of feudalism were removed and the victorious bourgeoisie established civic and political rights, class disparities would become the politically decisive facts engendering working-class consciousness and leading to proletarian revolution. The historical experience suggests that, with respect to the legacy of feudalism and political rights, the reasons for working-class radicalism were quite the opposite.

The impact of these variables is formalized in Table 1, which links the relationship between the social-class system and the rights to political and economic citizenship to the way in which workers responded in the decades before World War I. Table 1 illustrates both the weakness and strength of the type of comparative analysis undertaken here. The attempt to specify the kind of working-class movements that emerged under varying status systems and citizenship rights does not express the complexity of the phenomenon. Obviously, a static classification based on the dichotomization of three continuous variables cannot be expected to produce categories into which each national case fits through time. (For example, the United States and Denmark may both be classified as nonrigid status systems, although that of Denmark clearly has a greater continuity with a preindustrial corporate *Stand* tradition than the United States.)

The behavior of workers in western societies before and after

TABLE 1
Outcomes of Different Combinations of Social-Class Patterns and Citizenship Rights before World War I

Economic Citizenship	Political Citizenship	Nonrigid	Rigid
Early	Early	Low political consciousness, weak interest-group unions (U.S.)	Low political consciousness, strong reformist unions (Britain)
Early	Late	Strong reformist parties and unions (Low countries)	Radical parties, strong pragmatic unions (Germany)
Late	Early	Weak reformist parties radical unions (Switzerland)	Strong reformist parties, radical unions (France)
Late	Late		Revolutionary movements (Russia, Finland)

World War I was, of course, deeply affected by other variables, including the pace, extent, and shape of industrial development within their societies or how closely the objective social and economic situation "fit" the Marxist two-class model of an oppressive society. It is also important to recognize that these three factors are not independent of each other, although they may be distinguished analytically. Britain apart, the extension of postfeudal aristocratic power or values into the industrial era was associated with repressive political or economic patterns. And the British case may be explained by the fact that the aristocracy developed closer links to business than elsewhere. The emergence of democratic rights was in large measure tied to bourgeois hegemony. As Barrington Moore phrased it: "No bourgeois, no democracy" (Moore 1967, p. 418).

While the stress on the relationship between fundamental economic and political rights and the ideology of the labor movements is not meant to suggest that the character of contemporary movements is determined simply by their early history, the formative experiences did initiate certain trends or institutional patterns that took on a self-perpetuating character and hence affected ideology, structure, and political outcomes in later years. Most of the countries in which workers found it difficult to attain economic or political citizenship before World War I were the ones in which fascist and communist movements were strong in the interwar period: Austria, Finland, France, Germany, Italy, and Spain. Currently, commitment to democratic institutions appears strong in Austria and Germany, but, as Dahl notes, "it is untested by adversity" (Dahl 1966, p. 360). Although declining in electoral strength, communist movements are still very influential among workers in Finland, France, and Italy. Spain, democratic since 1975, remains problematic.

Although formative experiences continue to have an impact on the contemporary body politic, particularly in distinguishing the European from the overseas settler societies, it is obvious that many of the differences discussed here no longer hold for present-day Europe. Apart from Britain, postfeudal elements have declined greatly or have disappeared in the industrialized countries. The economic miracle of prosperity and growth that followed World War II changed occupational structures, status systems, levels of income, and the distribution of educational attainments in ways that reduced many of the social strains characteristic of prewar industrial societies. Logically, in terms of the analysis presented here, which derives from the approaches of Max Weber and Joseph Schumpeter, the amount of class-related political conflict should be reduced as the dynamics of an industrial society undermine the status mechanisms inherited from the feudal precapitalist order. The imposition on the stratification system of capitalism's or industrial society's stress on achievement and universalism should weaken rather than increase class-linked consciousness of kind. And significantly, the correlations between class and party voting have been declining steadily.

These changes, however, have given rise to new tensions reflective of an emerging postindustrial society. The new divisions can be understood as the most recent examples of the basic cleavages that structure comparative mass politics, systematically analyzed by Stein Rokkan (1970). I have discussed the character of these conflicts elsewhere and will not elaborate on them here (Lipset 1981, pp. 503–21). But it is important to note that the prominence of so-called postmaterialist issues, such as quality of life, ecology, sexual equality, international relations, and ethnic rights, have changed the divisions between the left and right and have affected their bases of support. These new issues are linked to an increase in middle-class political radicalism and working-class social conservatism.

The working classes in western society no longer have to undergo repression. They have acquired economic and political citizenship. It is still possible, however, to relate the forms of present-day politics, particularly party labels and formal ideologies, to the emergence of new social strata in the formative period of modern politics. Should the western world experience a major crisis, it is likely that national politics will vary along lines that stem from the past, much as they did during the 1930s. Political scientists of the future, who seek to explain events in the last quarter of this century, will undoubtedly find important explanatory variables in earlier variations in the behavior of the major political actors.

REFERENCES

Allardt, E., and Pesonen, P.   1967. Cleavages in Finnish politics. In *Party systems and voter alignments*. ed. S. M. Lipset and S. Rokkan, New York: The Free Press.

Aubert, V.   1974. Stratification. In *Norwegian society*. ed. N. R. Ramsoy, New York: Humanities Press.

Barnes, S. H.   1966. Italy: oppositions on left, right, and center. In *Political oppositions in western democracies*. ed. R. A. Dahl, New Haven: Yale University Press.

Bell, D.   1973. *The coming of post-industrial society*. New York: Basic Books.

Bendix, R.   1977. *Nation-building and citizenship*. Berkeley: University of California Press.

Brenan, G.   1950. *The Spanish labyrinth.* Cambridge: Cambridge University Press.

Buddenburger, T.   1922. Das Soziologische Problem der Sozialdemokratie. *Archiv fuer Sozialwissenschaft und Sozialpolitik* 49: 108–32.

Burnham, W. D.   1974. The United States: the politics of heterogeneity. In *Electoral behavior: a comparative handbook.* ed. R. Rose, New York: Free Press.

Carr, R.   1966. *Spain, 1808–1939.* New York: Oxford University Press.

Castles, F. G.   1978. *The social democratic image of society.* London: Routledge and Kegan Paul.

Cole, G. D. H.   1956. *A history of socialist thought,* Vol. III, *The second international, 1889–1914.* London: Macmillan.

Cornell, R.   (n.d.). Culture, values, and the development of socialism in Denmark. Unpublished paper, Department of Political Science, York University, Toronto, Canada.

Daalder, H.   1981. Consociationalism, center and periphery in the Netherlands. In *Mobilization, center-periphery structures and nation-building.* ed. Per Torsvik, Bergen: Universitetsforlaget.

_____. 1966a. The Netherlands: opposition in a segmented society. In *Political oppositions in western democracies.* ed. R. A. Dahl, New Haven: Yale University Press.

_____. 1966b. Parties, elites, and political developments in Western Europe. In *Political parties and political development.* ed. J. La Palombara and M. Weiner, Princeton, N.J.: Princeton University Press.

Dahl, R. A.   1966. Some explanations. In *Political oppositions in western democracies.* ed. R. A. Dahl, New Haven: Yale University Press.

Dahrendorf, R.   1967. *Society and democracy in Germany.* Garden City, N.Y.: Doubleday/Anchor.

de Man, H.   1928. *The psychology of socialism.* London: Allen and Unwin.

Derfler, L.   1973. *Socialism since Marx.* New York: St. Martin's Press.

Deutsch, K.   1953. *Nationalism and social communication.* New York: John Wiley.

Draper, T.   1960. *American communism and Soviet Russia.* New York: Viking.

Eckstein, H.   1966 *Division and cohesion in democracy. a study of Norway.* Princeton, N.J.: Princeton University Press.

Engels, F.   1936. Engels to Sorge, February 8, 1890 and December 31, 1982. In K. Marx and F. Engels, *Selected correspondence, 1846–1895.* New York: International Publishers.

_____. 1953. The English elections. In K. Marx and F. Engels, *On Britain.* Moscow: Foreign Languages Publishing House.

————. 1968a. Introduction to *Socialism: Utopian and Scientific*. In K. Marx and F. Engels, *Selected works*. New York: International Publishers.

————. 1968b. *The role of force in history*. London: Lawrence and Wishart.

Epstein, L. D. 1980. *Political parties in western democracies*. New Brunswick, N.J.: Transaction.

Friedberg, G. 1974. Comment. In *Failure of a dream?* ed. J. H. M. Laslett and S. M. Lipset, Garden City, N.Y.: Anchor Press/Doubleday.

Galenson, W. 1952. Scandinavia. In *Comparative labor movements*. ed. W. Galenson, New York: Prentice-Hall.

Gay, P. 1952. *The dilemma of democratic socialism*. New York: Columbia University Press.

Groh, D. 1973. *Negative Integration and revolutionaerer Attentismus*. Frankfurt/Main: Verlag Ullstein.

Gruner, E. 1968. *Die Arbeiter in der Schweiz im 19. Jahrhundert*. Bern: Francke Verlag.

Gulick, C. A. 1948. *Austria from Hapsburg to Hitler*, Vol. I, *Labor's workshop of democracy*. Berkeley: University of California Press.

Hartz, L. 1955. *The liberal tradition in America*. New York: Harcourt, Brace and World.

Hearnshaw, F. J. O. 1933. *Conservatism in England, an analytical, historical and political survey*. London: Macmillan.

Hoffman, S. 1963. Paradoxes of the French political community. In S. Hoffman et al., *In search of France*, Cambridge, Mass.: Harvard University Press.

Kautsky, K. 1910. *The class struggle (The Erfurt Program)*. Chicago: Charles H. Kerr.

Knoellinger, C. E. 1960. *Labor in Finland*. Cambridge, Mass.: Harvard University Press.

Laidler, H. 1927. *Socialism in thought and action*. New York: Macmillan.

Landauer, C. 1959. *European socialism*, Vol. I. Berkeley: University of California Press.

Landes, D. S. 1951. French business and the businessman: a social and cultural analysis. In *Modern France: problems of the third and fourth republics*. ed. E. M. Earle, Princeton, N.J.: Princeton University Press.

Lenin, V. I. (n.d.). Preface to the Russian translation of "Letters by J. Ph. Becker, J. Dietzgen, F. Engels, K. Marx and others to F. A. Sorge and others." In *On Britain*. ed. V. I. Lenin, Moscow: Foreign Languages Publishing House.

————. 1973. *What is to be done?* Peking: Foreign Languages Press.

Lidtke, V. L. 1966. *The outlawed party: social democracy in Germany 1878–1890*. Princeton, N.J.: Princeton University Press.

Lijphart, A. 1968. *The politics of accommodation: pluralism and democracy in the Netherlands.* Berkeley: University of California Press.

Linz, J. 1981. A century of politics and interests in Spain. In *Organizing interests in Western Europe.* ed. S. Berger, New York: Cambridge University Press.

Lipset, S.M. 1950. 1968. *Agrarian socialism: the cooperative commonwealth federation in Saskatchewan.* Berkeley: University of California Press (expanded edition, 1968).

————. 1977a. American "Exceptionalism" in North American perspective. In *The idea of America,* ed. E. M. Adams, Cambridge, Mass.: Ballinger.

————. 1977b. Why no socialism in the United States? In *Sources of contemporary radicalism,* ed. S. Bialer And S. Sluzar, Boulder, Colo.: Westview.

————. 1981. *Political man: the social bases of politics.* Baltimore: Johns Hopkins University Press (expanded edition of original, published in 1960).

Lipson, L. 1948. *The politics of equality. New Zealand's adventures in democracy.* Chicago: University of Chicago Press.

Lorwin, V. 1954. *The French labor movement.* Cambridge, Mass.: Harvard University Press.

————. 1958. Working-class politics and economic development: Western Europe. *The American Historical Review* 63:338–51.

Malefakis, E. 1973. A comparative analysis of worker movements in Spain and Italy. Paper prepared for delivery at the annual meeting of the American Historical Association, San Francisco.

Mannheim, K. 1936. *Ideology and utopia.* New York: Harcourt, Brace.

Marks, G. W. 1982. Trade unions in politics. Ph.D. dissertation, Department of Political Science, Stanford University.

Marshall, T. H. 1964. Class, citizenship and social development. Garden City: Doubleday.

Martin, W. C., and Hopkins, K. 1980. Cleavage crystallization and party linkages in Finland, 1900–1918. In *Political parties and linkages, a comparative perspective.* ed. K. Lawson, New Haven: Yale University Press.

Mayer, A. J. 1981. *The persistence of the old regime: Europe to the great war.* New York: Pantheon.

Meinecke, F. 1928. *Weltburgertum und Nationalstaat.* Munich: Oldenbourg.

Michels, R. 1906. "Die deutsche Sozialdemokratie. I. Parteimitgliedschaft und soziale Zusammensetzung. *Archiv fuer Sozialwissenschaft und Sozialpolitik* 26: 471–556.

Moore, B. Jr. 1967. *Social origins of dictatorship and democracy.* Boston: Beacon Press.

Murphy, D. J. 1975. Introduction. In *Labor in politics: the state labor parties in Australia.* ed. D. J. Murphy, St. Lucia, Queensland: University of Queensland Press.

Neumann, S. 1932. *Die deutschen Partein: Wesen und Wandel nach dem Kriege.* Berlin: Junker und Dumhaupt.

Parsons, T. 1969. *Politics and social structure.* New York: Free Press.

Payne, S. G. 1970. *The Spanish revolution.* New York: W. W. Norton.

Perlman, S. 1928. *A theory of the labor movement.* New York: Macmillan.

Pierson, S. 1979. *British socialists: the journey from fantasy to politics.* Cambridge, Mass.: Harvard University Press.

Pulzer, P. 1967. *Political representation and elections in Britain.* New York: Praeger.

Ridley, F. F. 1970. *Revolutionary syndicalism in France.* Cambridge: Cambridge University Press.

Rokkan, S. 1970. *Citizens, elections, parties.* New York: David McKay.

————. 1981. The growth and structuring of mass politics. In *Nordic democracy,* ed. E. Allardt et al. Copenhagen: Det Danske Selskab.

Rosecrance, R. N. 1960. The radical tradition in Australia: an interpretation. *The Review of Politics* 22:115–32.

Rosenberg, A. 1931. *The birth of the German republic 1871–1918.* Oxford: Oxford University Press.

Roth, G. 1955. *The social democrats in imperial Germany.* Totowa, N.J.: Bedminster.

Rustow, D. A. 1955. *The politics of compromise, a study of parties and cabinet government in Sweden.* Princeton, N.J.: Princeton University Press.

Sawyer, J. E. 1951. Strains in the social structure. In *Modern France: problems of the third and fourth republics.* ed. E. M. Earle, Princeton, N.J.: Princeton University Press.

Schultze, R. O. 1980. Funktion von Wahlen und Konstitutionsbedingungen von Wahlverhalten im deutschen Kaiserreich. In *Waehlerbewegung in der Europaeischen Geschichte.* ed. O. Buesch, Berlin: Colloquium Verlag.

Schumpeter, J. 1950. *Capitalism, socialism and democracy.* New York: Harper & Row.

Sewell, W. H., Jr. 1976. Social mobility in a nineteenth-century European city: some findings and implications. *Journal of Interdisciplinary History* 7:217–33.

Sharp, P. F. 1955. Three frontiers: some comparative studies of Canadian, American and Australian Settlement. *Pacific Historical Review* 24: 369–77.

Shell, K. L. 1962. *The transformation of Austrian socialism.* New York: University Publishers.

Siegfried, A. 1950. *Switzerland, a democratic way of life.* London: Jonathan Cape.

Sombart, W. 1976. *Why is there no socialism in the United States?* London: Macmillan. This book was first published in German in 1906.

Stearns, P. N. 1971. *Revolutionary syndicalism and French labor.* New Brunswick, N.J.: Rutgers University Press.

Sturmthal, A. 1953. *Unity and diversity in European labor.* Glencoe, Ill.: Free Press.

————. 1972. *Comparative labor movements.* Belmont, Calif.: Wadsworth.

Thompson, E. P. 1968. *The making of the English working class.* London: Penguin.

Tingsten, H. 1973. *The Swedish social democrats: their ideological development.* Totowa, N.J.: Bedminster Press.

Von Beyme, K. 1980. *Challenge to power, trade unions and industrial relations in capitalist countries.* Beverly Hills, Calif.: Sage.

Ward, R. 1959. *The Australian legend.* New York: Oxford University Press.

Waris, H. 1958. Finland. In *The institutions of advanced societies.* ed. A. Rose, Minneapolis: University of Minnesota Press.

Weber, M. 1946. *Essays in sociology.* ed. H. H. Gerth and C. Wright Mills. New York: Oxford University Press.

————. 1958. *Gesammelte Politische Schriften.* Tuebingen: J. C. B. Mohr.

Wells, H. G. 1906. *The future in America.* New York: Harper & Bros.

32

Revolution and Anomie

Bernard E. Brown

THE CRISES OF MODERNIZATION

One fruitful way of studying the complex process of modernization is to view it as a series of crises or challenges, to which a number of different responses are possible. A distinction can be made among the crises of legitimacy, participation, and tension-management (occurring roughly in that chronological order). As European societies went through the experience of modernization they necessarily had to cope with each of these crises. Feudal societies could not survive the Enlightenment, and the concept of divine right gave way to more rational theories of political legitimacy. With industrialization new groups emerged (an energetic entrepreneurial class, a managerial and clerical class, and a massive working class), and the existing political elites somehow had to deal with the demands of these new groups and integrate them into the political system. As the European economy became more complex each national society had to devise a system of controls, enabling it to coordinate the activities of increasingly specialized associations.

Nothing is fated to work out in favor of modernization in any of these crises. Revolt against the monarchy may be crushed; reactionary forces may overthrow a republic and reestablish monarchy; new or greatly expanded social groups, in particular the working class, may not be effectively integrated into the political system;

Source: Bernard E. Brown, *Protest in Paris: Anatomy of a Revolt* (Morristown, N.J.: General Learning Press, 1974), pp. 212–22. By permission.

and a society may be unable to cope with the problems of coordination. But punishment for failure is severe. A country that falls behind is likely to come under the influence or even the rule of those who have been more successful in meeting these challenges.

Each of the crises of modernization has posed serious problems for the French. Take, for example, the crisis of legitimacy. One of the basic assumptions of modernization theory is that as a society becomes more complex, the values serving to legitimize political authority become more rational. Or, rather than imply any causal relationship, rationalization of authority proceeds along with industrialization and increasing complexity of social structure. This assumption is borne out in a striking manner by the French experience, because of the great divide of the Revolution of 1789. The Tennis Court Oath, the August decrees abolishing feudalism, and the Declaration of the Rights of Man and Citizen marked an irrevocable break with absolutism and feudalism, and signaled the emergence of more rational principles of political legitimacy. Although France was converted almost overnight into a modern state as regards its official pattern of legitimacy, it did not thereby achieve a large popular consensus on its basic institutions. The revolution was repudiated by conservatives, and the revolutionaries were themselves divided. The result was a long period of constitutional instability. The transformation of French society continued. But the way in which the French tackled the successive crises of modernization was drastically affected by inability to agree on political structures. In the first great crisis of modernization in France, bursting forth in the Revolution of 1789 but continuing to this day, intransigeance rather than compromise became characteristic of the political process.

Dissensus carried over from one historical phase to another. When the French turned to the problem of integrating the working class into the political system a pattern of rejection, opposition, and violence had already taken hold and made it more difficult (though not impossible) to formulate policy. The French working and business classes, from the outset, have been reluctant to bargain with each other—although compelled to do so by circumstances. The heritage of class distrust and conflict continues to interfere with the smooth functioning of the political system. That 20 to 25 percent of the electorate votes fairly consistently for the Communist Party, and that the Communist-led CGT is the most powerful of the French trade unions, are indications of profound dissatisfaction within the French working class. In turn, exclusion of the Communist Party from governing coalitions drives the political balance to the right, placing the working class at a disadvantage in the political process and further intensifying feelings of class consciousness and alienation from the political system. Without having completely resolved the crises of legitimacy and participation, the French have plunged into the later phase of modernization, for the alternative is national decline. But the carryover of dissensus creates friction and grievances throughout the society. Much of the May Revolt—in particular the readiness of masses of students, workers, and even professionals to defect—can be explained by the relative failure of the French, compared with other industrial nations, to cope with the successive crises of modernization.

However, revolutionary dissent combined with an intensive destructive urge is a general trend among students and middle class intellectuals in all liberal-industrial societies today. The May Revolt never could have begun in a stagnant or traditional society. It came about in the first place only because, despite all the difficulties in their way, the French managed to create an advanced industrial nation by 1968. We are led to the paradoxical conclusion that not only the failures, but also the very *success* of a society in meeting the challenges of modernization may lead to its own downfall.

ANOMIE

Accompanying modernization in France, and everywhere else, is the phenomenon of *anomie*—a term popularized almost a century ago by Emile Durkheim. We have already encountered explanations of the May Revolt along the lines of Durkheim's theory, for example in Raymond Aron's *La révolution introuvable,* and the remarks of Georges Pompidou (before the National Assembly on May 14, 1968) and of General de Gaulle (during the television interview with Michel Droit on June 7, 1968). Durkheim asserted that the appetites and desires of men are infinite and that every society must impose a discipline or "regulator" in order to survive. In traditional society the family and religion constitute the regulator. Every person knows his role in family and religious activities; his desires are limited by his own perception of social status. But when a traditional society breaks up, the family structure and the church are brought into question. New values and new social structures arise (science, the republic, the corporation, the university, and so on); but frequently the individual in transition cannot accept them. Caught between the traditional and modern forms, his reactions may be those of resignation (ranging from apathy to suicide) or of rage against established authority. It is Durkheim's great insight that every modern society carries within itself the seeds of its own destruction. The more the individual is encouraged by society to realize his individuality, the greater is the risk that he will reject discipline and become perpetually discontent.[1]

The "anomic" reaction to social change in France has taken the form of violent opposition to the modern state and to urban industrial life. Hostility to industrial life has been especially vigorous in France among artists and writers, who have drawn a sharp contrast between bucolic nature and the polluted inhumanity of cities. As we have seen, under the influence of Proudhon and Bakunin, French anarchists have traditionally celebrated the glories of village and farm society. Such literary movements as Dada and surrealism have questioned science, rationality, and modern society, exulting instead in the gesture of the child, the unpredictable happening, and the immediate gratification of desires. The anarchist, dadaist, and surrealist traditions resurfaced in the May Revolt with astonishing force.

The anomic opposition to modernization is only one form of protest against poverty and exploitation. The dominant wing of the global revolutionary movement fully accepts modernization, though not through capitalism. The goal is to eliminate the capitalist, not science and technology—to base socialism on a modern, not a primitive economy. The question of whether to fight against exploitation by recapturing the spirit of traditional societies, or by transcending that spirit altogether has been a running controversy among revolutionaries ever since the Industrial Revolution started, and was especially pressing in May 1968.

Anomie is an unexpected consequence of the ability of modern societies to triumph over obstacles that seemed insurmountable a century ago. The development of science and technology has resulted in extraordinary increases in economic production and national wealth, in France and elsewhere; and though income differentials persist, it would require an excessive devotion to 19th-century Marxist texts to believe that workers in France, Britain, the United States, or any other industrial society have become increasingly miserable and impoverished in the past hundred years. There are always enough grave instances of social injustice, no matter how productive an economy, to inspire any number of protest movements—but this cannot account for the astonishing spurt of revolutionary activity in all modern societies today.

It is not only poverty that causes protest and revolt in a modern society, but also prosperity—a fatal defect in societies whose very

---

[1] For Durkheim's views on anomie: *De la division du travail social* (P.U.F., 1967, 8th ed.), pp. 343–65; and *Le suicide* (P.U.F., 1960), pp. 264–311. An excellent contemporary interpretation is in Robert M. MacIver, *The Ramparts We Guard* (New York: Macmillan, 1950).

rationale is to create more wealth. Poverty, however lamentable may be its consequences for individuals, is a school for discipline. A man fearful of losing his job because he will cease to eat is remarkably receptive to commands from his superiors. He may rebel from time to time but even in revolt he continues to carry out orders. In contrast, prosperity gives people the illusion that they are totally independent of others, that any obstacles can be overcome by an effort of individual will. When life is easy there is no reason to obey commands and no penalty for insubordination or indiscipline. When an individual successfully defies one authority he is tempted to defy another, and another, until finally the very notion of authority becomes unbearable. Prosperity unaccompanied by a strong sense of social responsibility undermines collective effort and may undo a society.[2]

The possibility of the dissolution of social discipline is especially great when wealth increases suddenly or when opportunities open up for a previously depressed class of people. It was precisely this kind of change in the condition of life that fascinated Durkheim from the time he first noticed that suicide rates increase sharply along with the progress of civilization. It is the dream of the poor that sudden wealth (winning first prize in the national lottery, an unexpected inheritance, a fabulous marriage) will open wide the gates of paradise—and in some cases it may. But the struggle to be successful may be more satisfying than success itself, in all walks of life. It is classic that the writer or artist who finally gains recognition after many years of effort goes through a crisis of confidence, fearing that he cannot repeat his success or, worse, so disappointed with the fruits of success that going on seems pointless. Similarly, the active businessman thrives on his work, telling himself that his goal is to retire young and enjoy life, only to discover later that he is incapable of savoring an existence without the challenge of work.

When the moorings of a society give way, everything goes—social discipline, political authority, the incentive to produce, and sometimes the incentive to live. As Durkheim perceptively remarked, "one cannot remain in contemplation before a vacuum without being progressively drawn into it."[3] He had in mind primarily suicide; lesser variations on the same theme are to "drop out" of normal society or to escape the real world through the use of drugs. This

---

[2] On the connection between poverty-wealth and discipline-anomie, see the suggestive comments of Durkheim in *Le suicide*, p. 282. Note also Raoul Vaneigem's call for a revolt against prosperity, in *Traité de savoir-vivre à l'usage des jeunes générations* (Gallimard, 1967), pp. 73, 88–91.

[3] E. Durkheim, *Le suicide*, p. 316.

form of anomic behavior is especially noticeable among the children of parents who themselves had to work hard to succeed. The corroding effect of prosperity is most evident at one remove.

Once in a condition of anomie, the individual may react in altogether unforeseeable ways. One tendency, we have noted, is toward renunciation, withdrawal, loss of zest for life, or suicide. But, as is stressed by Durkheim in a less well-known part of his analysis, anomie gives birth to a state of exasperation and irritated lassitude, "which can, depending upon circumstances, turn the individual against himself or against others."[4] He was referring not only to the extreme cases of suicide and homicide, but also to alternating political attitudes of apathy and violent attacks upon authority, the attempt either to escape from reality or to destroy it. Apathy and terrorism are related aspects of the same continuing reaction to modernization.

The May Revolt displayed many of the characteristics of the instability characterized by Durkheim as anomie. It took place in a society that had just experienced 20 years of unprecedented economic growth and was more prosperous than at any other time of its history. Poverty and injustice had hardly been eliminated, but the workers scraping along on the minimum wage, and other unfavored groups, took no initiatives and even throughout the general strike remained primarily concerned with improvement of material conditions rather than with revolution. Those who were in the forefront of the revolutionary movement were precisely those labeled by Durkheim as prime candidates for anomie—the children of the newly prosperous middle classes. It is significant that the most raucous and undisciplined campus in the entire French university system was Nanterre, whose students are drawn from the comfortable sections of the west of Paris. It was striking that students from modest backgrounds were more interested in their own social mobility than in abstract revolution in May.[5] Also noteworthy was the interaction and in many cases interchangeability between the two related anomic tendencies of apathy and rage. Once they had lost their ties to French society, many students and others glided back and forth between a diffuse counterculture of dropouts and

---

[4] Durkheim quote on the link between suicide and homicide, *Le suicide,* p. 322. See also, ibid., p. 408, and on the correspondence between suicide-homicide and apathy-terrorism, ibid., p. 424.

[5] That revolutionary students came in large proportion from "comfortable" situations is remarked by R. Boudon, "Quelques causes de la révolte estudiantine," *La Table Ronde* (Dec. 1968–Jan. 1969), p. 180. Also generously represented are Jews— corresponding to Durkheim's category of previously depressed groups suddenly enjoying new opportunities for advancement. Alain Krivine has publicly charged that the French police are now using Vichy records because so many Jews are in the New Left.

organized revolutionary groups. Extreme individualism blossomed into extreme collectivism only to disintegrate again upon meeting the slightest resistance. Those who wanted to escape all authority and those who wanted to impose iron discipline upon everyone else were the two marching wings of the revolutionary coalition; the ease with which many people switched from one to the other called attention to anomie as the common element of the diverse revolutionary groups.[6]

The May Revolt highlights in dramatic fashion the existence of a new dimension in the continuing crisis of participation or "entry into politics" of important social groups. Anomie was Durkheim's formulation of the problem of integrating the middle and working classes into political systems that had previously been dominated by a landed aristocracy. He saw that the working class was becoming increasingly isolated from the owning class. The life style of the capitalists was more and more remote from the reality of workday experience. A point is reached where it is beyond the capacity of workers and capitalists even to understand each other. He later broadened the meaning of anomie to include the lack of purpose in life under capitalism where individuals are engaged in the single-minded pursuit of wealth.[7]

In later stages of industrialization the social force undergoing the greatest rate of expansion is the intellectual class—the scientists, engineers, technicians, administrators, and so on—who receive their training in scientific institutes and universities. This newly massive intellectual class follows in the tradition of its predecessors

---

[6] We have previously commented on the way in which surrealists suddenly became Communists or Trotskyists, and just as suddenly returned to anarchism. Note the recent overnight conversion of a leading American activist to an Eastern religion. In a press conference reported by the *New York Times* (May 6, 1973) one of the "Chicago 7" defendants, Rennie Davis, relates that during a flight to Paris on his way to meet Vietcong negotiators in January 1973 he heard about a 15-year-old guru in India called Maharaj Ji. His immediate reaction was skepticism and even hostility. But he went to India and after eight days "received knowledge" from a disciple of the guru, whom he now calls "the one perfect master" on earth at this time. Although at first uncomfortable with the boy (who was about 10 years old at the time of the Chicago riots), Mr. Davis told the press conference that he now loved him. "I would cross the planet on my hands and knees," he said, "to touch his toe." The guru has been under investigation by the government of India on the charge of smuggling money, jewels and watches (all gifts from devoted followers) into the country.

[7] For general treatments of the "entry into politics" problem, see T. H. Marshall, *Citizenship and Social Class* (Cambridge: Cambridge University Press, 1950); S. M. Lipset, *Political Man* (Garden City, N.Y.: Doubleday Publishing, 1960); Reinhard Bendix, *Nation-Building and Citizenship* (New York: John Wiley & Sons, 1964); Barrington Moore, Jr., *Social Origins of Dictatorship and Democracy* (Boston: Beacon Press, 1967); and J. G. LaPalombara and M. Weiner, ed., *Political Parties and Political Development* (Princeton: Princeton University Press, 1966).

by making demands upon the political system. Just as hereditary monarchy was repudiated by the bourgeoisie, and parliamentary democracy questioned by the revolutionary wing of the working class, so many intellectuals find the dominant liberal synthesis inadequate. Liberalism seems to many to be a cover for the supremacy of money or numbers. Intellectuals are uncomfortable with political values that give an advantage to the wealthy and to demagogues. The life style of the intellectuals is also distinctive. In Durkheim's sense, many intellectuals are in a condition of anomie because they are increasingly isolated from the rest of society.

In addition, a certain amount of alienation is generated simply because there is a confrontation between an existing elite and a rising social group. At every stage of the modernizing process there is an anomic reaction due to the weakening of traditional values and the failure of the new values to replace them. The conflict between old and new norms must affect the intellectuals in the scientific civilization, as it affected workers in the industrial civilization. Just as the assembly line provoked irritation and revolt among workers, so the organization of social activity on the basis of scientific and rational criteria creates a feeling of "dehumanization" in many intellectuals. It is to be expected that a certain number of individuals will be left, at least during a transitional period, in a state of normlessness, or "deregulation." Those who repudiate the old and fear or disdain to accept the new display the symptoms of anomie.

That there should be an anomic reaction to modernization among intellectuals is not unusual; but the depth and intensity of this reaction—expressing itself in withdrawal and rage, political apathy and political terrorism—is startling. Why should the mass of anomie increase so sharply? At least three reasons may be suggested.

First, a large number of people break under the greater strain. In a scientific civilization there necessarily are rigorous standards of education and performance. There is no short cut to acquisition of scientific knowledge. Those who are not capable of acquiring this knowledge, or are not sufficiently motivated, fall by the wayside. Furthermore, the amount of knowledge to be mastered is increasing at an enormous rate, and with it the pressure on students. While examinations and student anxiety have always existed, in the past there have also been many ways of getting ahead on the basis of a modest education. When the major avenue to success is the university, those who cannot meet its demands are at a greater disadvantage than ever before.

Secondly, the productivity of the scientific civilization makes it possible to carry a marginal element within the society. Technically, it is feasible for any advanced industrial society to support a large class of dropouts and drones—provided that this class remains within manageable bounds and does not deprive the productive classes of their motivation to work. Many young people are able to enjoy—or endure—a life of anomie with the bemused support of their parents. Poverty is a highly effective social technique for imposing limits on anomie; prosperity, however, creates the conditions for the existence of a large alienated group.

Freedom itself may be a major cause of anomie in the intellectual class. Modernization makes possible a great expansion of individual freedom. As Durkheim points out, primitive man is merely an extension of the group, hemmed in by custom and taboo. He has no mind of his own. Modern man enjoys greater autonomy and is free to think as he pleases.[8] But the heavy responsibility of making a free choice can be utterly demoralizing, leading either to a desire to escape or to revolt. In authoritarian regimes the masses and the intellectuals can be conditioned, mobilized, and commanded. Problems may not actually be solved, but the over-pressured individual is relieved of the burden of choice. The disorder inherent in liberalism and the scientific civilization is eliminated. Anomic groups serve as pile drivers, splitting the foundations of the liberal state. Authoritarian elites pick up the pieces and impose the discipline that so many desperately crave.

In the scientific civilization what Durkheim called the "regulator" is more essential than ever. The intellectual must be imaginative, creative, and even enthusiastic if the collective scientific enterprise is to flourish. Doubts, hesitation, and withdrawal will block the system. The political integration of the intellectual class may well prove to be inherently more difficult than was the case for the capitalist and working classes. The landed aristocrats and capitalists were numerically weak in relation to the rest of the society and could be outmaneuvered in politics. But while the working class had the advantage of numbers, its function within the economy was to carry out orders rather than to give them, to obey rather than to innovate. As a class the workers were unable to direct themselves, let alone the rest of society. The intellectual class is not subject to the same handicaps. Unlike the old aristocrats or the capitalists, intellectuals are a large social force. Unlike the workers, they have ability, inculcated by their social function, to direct and command.

The question may be raised whether parliamentary democracies like France can cope with the entry of the intellectuals as a massive

---

[8] For Durkheim's views on freedom in primitive and modern societies, cf. *De la division du travail social*, pp. 35–102. See also Alvin Toffler, *Future Shock* (New York: Bantam Books, 1971), pp. 98, 319–22.

social force into the political system. Wherever freedom of criticism is permitted, opportunities for exploiting tensions are almost unlimited. In a climate of freedom the intellectuals are even more likely to rebel than the old working class, and more likely to withdraw their cooperation from the establishment. The parliamentary democracies that experienced great difficulty in securing the integration of the working class probably will continue to be unstable as they move into the scientific civilization and deal with the intellectual class. Even relatively consensual parliamentary democracies may have difficulty in adjusting to these new circumstances. It may well be that integration of the intellectuals into the political system can be accomplished only by an authoritarian elite (whether of the left or right) in order to eliminate that anarchy which is incompatible with the continued functioning and further development of a scientific civilization.

We are living through an era of reversal of values and of social relationships perhaps best comprehended through Hegel's parable of the master and the servant in which the servant, compelled to live by his work, becomes self-reliant, while the master comes to depend completely on the servant. Thus, capitalists may be overturned by proletarians, any dominant group may be subverted by any dominated group, the most contradictory and unforeseen developments may occur in the unfolding of history.

Most social scientists postulate that science is sweeping all before it, thrusting aside magic, superstition, and religion, bringing about the rationalization of social behavior, laying the basis for modern industry, unprecedented prosperity, and the full flowering of human freedom. In the model modern society it is assumed that the ideological conflict of early industrialization will be transcended and replaced by pragmatic negotiation among claimant groups for larger shares of ever increasing national revenues. The long-term trend would thus be toward stability, prosperity, and freedom. But, through an irony of history, mastery can be converted into dependence, political trends can be reversed. A complex economy can be paralyzed by the determined opposition of relatively few people in key positions. An abundance of material wealth can lead to dissipation of individual motivation and disintegration of social ties. The privilege of exercising a free choice can turn into an agony. From stability may come instability, from prosperity may come misery, and out of freedom may come a new and fearful discipline.

PART ONE. COMPARATIVE ANALYSIS: METHODS AND CONCEPTS

Almond, Gabriel A. and G. Bingham Powell. *Comparative Politics: System, Process, and Policy.* 2d ed. Boston: Little, Brown, 1978.

Apter, David E. and Charles F. Andrain, eds. *Contemporary Analytical Theory.* Englewood Cliffs, N.J.: Prentice-Hall, 1972.

Bill, James and Robert Hardgrave. *Comparative Politics: The Quest for Theory.* Columbus, Ohio: Merrill, 1973.

Blondel, Jean. *An Introduction to Comparative Government.* New York: Praeger Publishers, 1969.

Brown, Bernard E. *New Directions in Comparative Politics.* London: Asia Publishers, 1962.

Charlesworth, James C., ed. *Contemporary Political Analysis.* New York: Free Press, 1967.

Easton, David. *A Framework for Political Analysis.* Englewood Cliffs, N.J.: Prentice-Hall, 1965.

Eckstein, Harry and David E. Apter, eds. *Comparative Politics: A Reader.* New York: Free Press, 1963.

Finer, Samuel H. *Comparative Government.* New York: Penguin Books, 1974.

Friedrich, Carl J. *Man and His Government: An Empirical Theory of Politics.* New York: McGraw-Hill, 1963.

Greenstein, Fred I. and Nelson Polsby, eds. *Handbook of Political Science.* 9 vols. Reading, Mass.: Addison-Wesley Publishing, 1975.

Hempel, Carl G. *Aspects of Scientific Explanation.* New York: Free Press, 1965.

Holt, Robert T. and John E. Turner, eds. *The Methodology of Comparative Research.* New York: Free Press, 1970.

Kuhn, Thomas S. *The Structure of Scientific Revolutions.* 2d ed. Chicago: University of Chicago Press, 1970.

Landau, Martin. *Political Theory and Political Science.* Atlantic Highlands, N.J.: Humanities Press, 1972.

LaPalombara, Joseph. *Politics Within Nations.* Englewood Cliffs, N.J.: Prentice-Hall, 1974.

Levy, Marion J. *The Structure of Society.* Princeton: Princeton University Press, 1952.

Macridis, Roy C. *The Study of Comparative Government.* New York: Random House, 1955.

Mannheim, Karl. *Ideology and Utopia.* New York: Harcourt Brace Jovanovich, 1965.

Mayer, Lawrence. *Comparative Political Inquiry.* Homewood, Ill.: Dorsey Press, 1972.

Merkl, Peter H. *Modern Comparative Politics.* New York: Holt, Rinehart & Winston, 1970.

Merritt, Richard L. *Systematic Approaches to Comparative Politics.* Skokie, Ill.: Rand McNally, 1970.

Merritt, Richard L. and Stein Rokkan, eds. *Comparing Nations: The Use of Quantitative Data in Cross-National Research.* New Haven: Yale University Press, 1966.

Nagel, Ernest. *The Structure of Science.* New York: Harcourt Brace Jovanovich, 1961.

Parsons, Talcott. *The Social System.* New York: Free Press, 1951.

Popper, Karl R. *Conjectures and Refutations: The Growth of Scientific Knowledge.* New York: Harper & Row, 1968.

Przeworski, Adam and Henry Teune. *The Logic of Comparative Social Inquiry.* New York: John Wiley & Sons, 1970.

Scarrow, Howard A. *Comparative Political Analysis: An Introduction.* New York: Harper & Row, 1969.

Storing, Herbert J., ed. *Essays on the Scientific Study of Politics.* New York: Holt, Rinehart & Winston, 1962.

Weber, Max. "Politics as a Vocation" and "Science as a Vocation," in *From Max Weber,* ed. H. H. Gerth and C. W. Mills, New York: Oxford University Press, 1958, pp. 77–156.

PART TWO. CONTEMPORARY POLITICAL REGIMES

Democracies

Almond, Gabriel A. and Sidney Verba. *The Civic Culture.* Boston: Little, Brown, 1963.

_____eds. *The Civic Culture Revisited.* Boston: Little, Brown, 1980.

Aron, Raymond. *Democracy and Totalitarianism.* New York: Praeger Publishers, 1968.

Crozier, Michel; S. P. Huntington; and Joji Watanuki. *The Crisis of Democracy.* New York: New York University Press, 1975.

Dahl, Robert A. *Polyarchy: Participation and Opposition.* New Haven: Yale University Press, 1971.

————. *A Preface to Democratic Theory.* Chicago: University of Chicago Press, 1956.

————. *Who Governs?* New Haven: Yale University Press, 1961.

Eckstein, Harry. *Division and Cohesion in a Democracy: A Study of Norway.* Princeton: Princeton University Press, 1966.

Friedrich, Carl J. *Constitutional Government and Democracy.* 4th ed. Waltham, Mass.: Blaisdell, 1968.

Hamilton, Alexander; James Madison; and John Jay. *The Federalist.* New York: Mentor, 1961.

Linz, Juan and Alfred Stepan, eds. *The Breakdown of Democratic Regimes.* 2 vols. Baltimore: The Johns Hopkins Press, 1978.

Lowi, Theodore J. *The End of Liberalism.* 2d ed. New York: Norton, 1979.

Mayo, H. B. *An Introduction to Democratic Theory.* New York: Oxford University Press, 1960.

Moore, Barrington, Jr. *Social Origins of Dictatorship and Democracy: Lord and Peasant in the Making of the Modern World.* Boston: Beacon Press, 1966.

Nordlinger, Eric A. *On the Autonomy of the Democratic State.* Cambridge, Mass.: Harvard University Press, 1981.

Popper, Karl R. *The Open Society and Its Enemies.* 2 vols. 5th ed. London: Routledge & Kegan Paul, 1945.

Rawls, John. *A Theory of Justice.* Cambridge, Mass.: Harvard University Press, 1971.

Sartori, Giovanni. *Democratic Theory.* New York: Praeger Publishers, 1967.

Schumpeter, Joseph A. *Capitalism, Socialism, and Democracy.* 3d ed. New York: Harper & Row, 1950.

Authoritarianism: Old and New

Allen, William S. *The Nazi Seizure of Power: The Experience of a Single German Town, 1930–35.* 2d ed. New York: F. Watts, 1984.

Arendt, Hannah. *The Origins of Totalitarianism,* 2d ed. New York: Harcourt Brace Jovanovich, 1973.

Bracher, Karl D. *The German Dictatorship: The Origin, Structure and Effects of National Socialism.* New York: Praeger Publishers, 1970.

Bullock, Alan. *Hitler, A Study in Tyranny.* Rev. ed. New York: Harper & Row, 1964.

Collier, David, ed. *The New Authoritarianism in Latin America.* Princeton: Princeton University Press, 1979.

Friedrich, Carl J., and Zbigniew Brzezinski. *Totalitarian Dictatorship and Autocracy.* 2d ed. New York: Praeger Publishers, 1969.

Friedrich, Carl J.; Michael Curtis; and Benjamin R. Barber. *Totalitarianism in Perspective: Three Views*. New York: Praeger Publishers, 1969.

Gregor, James A. *Italian Fascism and Developmental Dictatorship*. Princeton: Princeton University Press, 1979.

Hamill, Hugh M., ed. *Dictatorship in Spanish America*. New York: Alfred A. Knopf, 1965.

Huntington, Samuel P. and Clement H. Moore. *Authoritarian Politics in Modern Society*. New York: Basic Books, 1970.

Jackson, Robert H. and Carl Rosberg. *Personal Rule in Black Africa: Prince, Autocrat, Prophet, Tyrant*. Berkeley: University of California Press, 1981.

Janowitz, Morris. *Military Institutions and Coercion in Developing Nations*. Chicago: University of Chicago Press, 1977.

Kirkpatrick, Jeane. *Dictatorship and Double Standards*. New York: Simon & Schuster, 1982.

Laqueur, Walter, ed. *Fascism: A Reader's Guide*. Berkeley: University of California Press, 1977

Neumann, Franz L. *Behemoth. Tn.. Structure and Practice of National Socialism*. New York: Octagon, 1963.

_____. *The Democratic and the Authoritarian State*. New York: Free Press, 1957.

Payne, Stanley G. *Falange: A History of Spanish Fascism*. Stanford: Stanford University Press, 1961.

Paxton, Robert O. *Vichy France: Old Guard and New Order*. New York: Alfred A. Knopf, 1972.

Perlmutter, Amos. *Modern Authoritarianism: A Comparative Institutional Analysis*. New Haven: Yale University Press, 1981.

Strauss, Leo. *On Tyranny*. Rev. ed. Ithaca: Cornell University Press, 1968.

Talman, Jacob L. *The Origins of Totalitarian Democracy*. New York: Norton, 1970.

Wiarda, Howard. *Dictatorship and Development: The Methods of Control in Trujillo's Dominican Republic*. Gainesville: University of Florida Press, 1968.

Communist Systems

Aspaturian, Vernon V. *Process and Power in Soviet Foreign Policy*. Boston: Little, Brown, 1971.

Bialer, Serwyn. *Stalin's Successors: Leadership, Stability and Change in the Soviet Union*. New York: Cambridge University Press, 1980.

Butterfield, Fox. *China: Alive in the Bitter Sea*. New York: Times Books, 1982.

Carrère d'Encausse, Helène. *Confiscated Power: How Soviet Russia Really Works.* New York: Harper & Row, 1982.

Conquest, Robert. *Power and Policy in the USSR.* New York: St. Martin's Press, 1961.

Dominguez, Jorge I. *Cuba: Order and Revolution.* Cambridge, Mass.: Harvard University Press, 1978.

Hazard, John. *The Soviet System of Government.* 5th ed. Chicago: University of Chicago Press, 1980.

Hough, Jerry and Merle Fainsod. *How the Soviet Union is Governed.* Cambridge, Mass.: Harvard University Press, 1979.

Meyer, Alfred G. *Leninism.* Cambridge, Mass.: Harvard University Press, 1957.

Pye, Lucian W. *The Dynamics of Chinese Politics.* Cambridge, Mass.: Oelgeschlager, Gunn & Hain, 1981.

Rubinstein, Alvin Z. *Soviet Foreign Policy Since World War II.* Cambridge: Winthrop, 1981.

Schapiro, Leonard. *The Communist Party of the Soviet Union.* Rev. ed. New York: Random House, 1971.

Skilling, H. Gordon and Franklyn Griffiths, eds. *Interest Groups in Soviet Politics.* Princeton: Princeton University Press, 1971.

Tucker, Robert C. *The Soviet Political Mind.* New York: Norton, 1972.

Ulam, Adam. *The Bolsheviks: The Intellectual and Political History of the Triumph of Communism in Russia.* New York: Macmillan, 1965.

_____. *Stalin: The Man and His Era.* New York: Viking Press, 1973.

Waller, Derek J. *The Government and Politics of the People's Republic of China.* 3d ed. New York: New York University Press, 1981.

White, Stephen. *Political Culture and Soviet Politics.* New York: Macmillan, 1979.

PART THREE. POLITICAL DYNAMICS AND PROCESSES

Political Authority

Bendix, Reinhard. *Nation-Building and Citizenship.* New York: John Wiley & Sons, 1964.

Berle, Adolf A. *Power.* New York: Harcourt Brace Jovanovich, 1969.

Buchanan, James M. and G. Tullock. *The Calculus of Consent: Logical Foundations of Constitutional Democracy.* Ann Arbor: University of Michigan Press, 1962.

Dahl, Robert A., ed. *Regimes and Oppositions.* New Haven: Yale University Press, 1973.

Denitch, Bogden D. *The Legitimation of a Revolution: The Yugoslav Case.* New Haven: Yale University Press, 1976.

Deutsch, Karl W. *The Nerves of Government.* New York: Free Press, 1963.

Inglehart, Ronald. *The Silent Revolution: Changing Values and Political Styles Among Western Publics.* Princeton: Princeton University Press, 1977.

Lasswell, Harold and Abraham Kaplan. *Power and Society: A Framework for Political Inquiry.* New Haven: Yale University Press, 1950.

Macridis, Roy C. *Contemporary Political Ideologies.* 2d ed. Boston: Little, Brown, 1982.

Mosca, Gaetano. *The Ruling Class.* New York: McGraw-Hill, 1939.

Pye, Lucian and Sidney Verba, eds. *Political Culture and Political Development.* Princeton: Princeton University Press, 1965.

Groups, Parties, and Elections

Berger, Suzanne, ed. *Organized Interests in Western Europe.* Cambridge: Cambridge University Press, 1983.

Brown, Bernard E., ed. *Eurocommunism and Eurosocialism: The Left Confronts Modernity.* New York: Irvington, 1978.

Butler, David et al. *Democracy at the Polls.* Washington, D.C.: American Enterprise Institute, 1981.

Duverger, Maurice. *Political Parties.* 3d ed. London: Methuen, 1969.

Ehrmann, Henry W., ed. *Interest Groups on Four Continents.* Pittsburgh: University of Pittsburgh Press, 1958.

Epstein, Leon. *Political Parties in Western Democracies.* New Brunswick, N.J.: Transaction, 1980.

Hirschman, Albert O. *Exit, Voice, and Loyalty.* Cambridge, Mass.: Harvard University Press, 1970.

LaPalombara, Joseph and Myron Weiner, eds. *Political Parties and Political Development.* Princeton: Princeton University Press, 1966.

Leiserson, Avery. *Parties and Politics: An Institutional and Behavioral Approach.* New York: Alfred A. Knopf, 1958.

Lipset, Seymour M. *Political Man: The Social Bases of Politics.* Rev. ed. Baltimore: The Johns Hopkins Press, 1981.

Lipset, Seymour M. and Stein Rokkan, eds. *Party Systems and Voter Alignments.* New York: Free Press, 1967.

Macridis, Roy C., ed. *Political Parties: Contemporary Trends and Ideas.* New York: Harper & Row, 1967.

Michels, Roberto. *Political Parties: A Sociological Study of the Oligarchic Tendencies of Modern Democracy.* New York: Free Press, 1958.

Neumann, Sigmund, ed. *Modern Political Parties.* Chicago: University of Chicago Press, 1954.

Ostrogorski, Moisei. *Democracy and the Organization of Political Parties.* 2 vols. Garden City, N.Y.: Doubleday Publishing, 1964.

Rae, Douglas W. *The Political Consequences of Electoral Laws.* New Haven: Yale University Press, 1967.

Rose, Richard. *Do Parties Make a Difference?* 2d ed. Chatham, N.J.: Chatham House, 1984.

Sartori, Giovanni. *Parties and Party Systems.* Cambridge: Cambridge University Press, 1976.

Truman, David. *The Governmental Process.* New York: Alfred A. Knopf, 1951.

Political Institutions and Performance

Aberbach, Joel D.; Robert D. Putnam; and Bert A. Rockman. *Bureaucrats and Politicians in Western Democracies.* Cambridge, Mass.: Harvard University Press, 1981.

Armstrong, John A. *The European Administrative Elite.* Princeton: Princeton University Press, 1973.

Barnard, Chester I. *The Functions of the Executive.* Cambridge, Mass.: Harvard University Press, 1968.

Blondel, Jean. *Comparative Legislatures.* Englewood Cliffs, N.J.: Prentice-Hall, 1973.

————. *The Organization of Government: A Comparative Study of Governmental Structures.* Beverly Hills, Calif.: Sage Publications, 1982.

Chapman, Brian. *The Profession of Government.* Winchester, Mass. Allen & Unwin, 1959.

Crozier, Michel. *The Bureaucratic Phenomenon.* Chicago: University of Chicago Press, 1964.

Dogan, Mattei, ed. *The Mandarins of Western Europe: The Political Role of Top Civil Servants.* New York: John Wiley & Sons, 1975.

Eckstein, Harry. *The Evaluation of Political Performance.* Beverly Hills, Calif.: Sage Publications, 1971.

Enloe, Cynthia. *The Politics of Pollution in a Comparative Perspective.* New York: David McKay, 1975.

Frank, Elke, ed. *Lawmakers in a Changing World.* Englewood Cliffs, N.J.: Prentice-Hall, 1966.

Groth, Alexander J. *Comparative Politics: A Distributive Approach.* New York: Macmillan, 1971.

Heidenheimer, Arnold J.; Hugh Heclo; and Carolyn Teich Adams. *Comparative Public Policy: The Politics of Social Choice in Europe and America.* 2d ed. New York: St. Martin's Press, 1983.

Hirsch, Herbert and M. Donald Hancock, eds. *Comparative Legislative Systems: A Reader in Theory and Research.* New York: Free Press, 1971.

Jackman, Robert W. *Politics and Social Equality: A Comparative Analysis.* New York: John Wiley & Sons, 1975.

Kornberg, Allan, ed. *Legislatures in Comparative Perspective.* New York: David McKay, 1973.

LaPalombara, Joseph, ed. *Bureaucracy and Political Development.* Princeton: Princeton University Press, 1963.

Loewenberg, Gerhard, ed. *Modern Parliaments: Change or Decline?* Chicago: University of Chicago Press, 1971.

Loewenberg, Gerhard and Samuel C. Patterson. *Comparing Legislatures.* Boston: Little, Brown, 1979.

Presthus, Robert V. *Elites in the Policy Process.* New York: Cambridge University Press, 1974.

Rose, Richard and Ezra Suleiman, eds. *Presidents and Prime Ministers.* Washington, D.C.: American Enterprise Institute, 1980.

Siegel, Richard L. and Leonard B. Weinberg. *Comparing Public Policies: United States, Soviet Union, and Europe.* Homewood, Ill.: Dorsey Press, 1977.

Siffin, William J., ed. *Towards the Comparative Study of Public Administration.* Bloomington: Indiana University Press, 1957.

Wheare, K. C. *Legislatures.* London: Oxford University Press, 1963.

Wilensky, Harold. *The Welfare State and Equality.* Berkeley: University of California Press, 1975.

PART FOUR. POLITICAL CHANGE

Modernization and Development

Almond, Gabriel A. and James S. Coleman, eds. *The Politics of the Developing Areas.* Princeton: Princeton University Press, 1960.

Apter, David E. *The Politics of Modernization.* Chicago: University of Chicago Press, 1965.

Bell, Daniel. *The Coming of Post-Industrial Society.* New York: Basic Books, 1973.

Binder, Leonard et al. *Crises and Sequences in Political Development.* Princeton: Princeton University Press, 1971.

Black, Cyril E. *The Dynamics of Modernization: A Study in Comparative History.* New York: Harper & Row, 1966.

————, ed. *Comparative Modernization: A Reader.* New York: Free Press, 1976.

Brzezinski, Zbigniew. *Between Two Ages: America's Role in the Technetronic Era.* New York: Viking Press, 1970.

Eisenstadt, Shmuel N. *Modernization: Protest and Change.* Englewood Cliffs, N.J.: Prentice-Hall, 1966.

————. *The Political Systems of Empires.* New York: Free Press, 1963.

Feit, Edward. *The Armed Bureaucrats: Military-Administrative Regimes and Political Development.* Boston: Houghton Mifflin, 1973.

Finkle, Jason L. and Richard W. Gable, eds. *Political Development and Social Change.* 2d ed. New York: John Wiley & Sons, 1971.

Horowitz, Irving L. *Three Worlds of Development.* 2d ed. New York: Oxford University Press, 1972.

Huntington, Samuel P. *Political Order in Changing Societies.* New Haven: Yale University Press, 1968.

Huntington, Samuel P. and Joan M. Nelson. *No Easy Choice: Political Participation in Developing Countries.* Cambridge: Harvard University Press, 1976.

Lipset, Seymour M. *The First New Nation: The United States in Historic. and Comparative Perspective.* New York: Basic Books, 1963.

Organski, A. F. K. *The Stages of Political Development.* New York A. Knopf, 1965.

Rustow, Dankwart A. *A World of Nations: Problems of Political Modernization.* Washington, D.C.: The Brookings Institution, 1967.

Dependency

Amin, Samir. *Accumulation on a World Scale.* New York: Monthly Review Press, 1974.

Cockcroft, James D., ed. *Dependence and Underdevelopment.* New York: Anchor Books, 1972.

Fanon, Frantz. *The Wretched of the Earth.* New York: Grove Press, 1966.

Frank, André Gundar. *Crisis in the Third World.* New York: Holmes & Meier, 1981.

————. *Dependent Accumulation and Underdevelopment.* New York: Monthly Review Press, 1979.

————. *Lumpenbourgeoisie, Lumpendevelopment: Dependence, Class, and Politics in Latin America.* New York: Monthly Review Press, 1972.

————. *Reflections on the World Economic Crisis.* New York: Monthly Review Press, 1981.

O'Donnell, Guillermo. *Modernization and Bureaucratic Authoritarianism: Studies in South American Politics.* Berkeley: University of California Press, 1973.

Wallerstein, Immanuel. *The Capitalist World-Economy.* Cambridge: Cambridge University Press, 1979.

————. *The Modern World-System.* 2 vols. New York: Academic Press, 1974 and 1980.

————. *The Politics of the World Economy.* Cambridge: Cambridge University Press, 1984.

Revolution

Arendt, Hannah. *On Revolution.* New York: Viking Press, 1963.

Brinton, Crane. *The Anatomy of Revolution.* Rev. ed. Englewood Cliffs, N.J.: Prentice-Hall, 1952.

Dunn, John. *Modern Revolutions.* Cambridge: Cambridge University Press, 1972.

Gurr, Ted Robert. *Why Men Rebel.* Princeton: Princeton University Press, 1970.

Johnson, Chalmers. *Revolutionary Change.* Boston: Little, Brown, 1966.

Rejai, Mostafa. *The Comparative Study of Revolutionary Strategy.* New York: David McKay, 1977.

Skocpol, Theda. *States and Social Revolution.* Cambridge: Cambridge University Press, 1979.

de Tocqueville, Alexis. *The Old Regime and the French Revolution.* Garden City, N.Y.: Anchor, 1955.

About the Editors

Roy C. Macridis is Wien Professor of International Cooperation in the Department of Politics at Brandeis University, and has taught previously at Harvard, Northwestern, Washington University, and the State University of New York at Buffalo. After receiving his B.A. from Athens College in Athens, Greece, he studied law in the University of Paris and received his M.A. and Ph.D. in Government at Harvard University (1947). Dr. Macridis has written or edited numerous publications. Among them are: *Modern Political Systems: Europe* (1986); *Contemporary Political Regimes: Institutions and Patterns* (1986); *Contemporary Political Ideologies* (1985); *The De Gaulle Republic: Quest for Unity* (with Bernard E. Brown, 1976); *French Politics in Transition: The Years after De Gaulle* (1976); and *The Study of Comparative Politics* (1956).

Bernard E. Brown is Professor of Political Science at the City University of New York (Graduate School and Lehman College), and has served as visiting professor at the universities of Paris, Saigon, Delhi, Dakar, and at McGill University (Montreal). He has received research awards from the Fulbright Commission, the Rockefeller Foundation, and the National Endowment for the Humanities. Among his many books are: *Socialism of a Different Kind: Reshaping the Left in France* (1982); *Intellectuals and Other Traitors* (1980); *Eurocommunism and Eurosocialism: The Left Confronts Modernity* (coauthor and editor, 1978); *The De Gaulle Republic: Quest for Unity* (with Roy C. Macridis, 1976); *Protest in Paris: Anatomy of a Revolt* (1974); *New Directions in Comparative Politics* (1963); and *American Conservatives* (1951).

A Note on the Type

The text of this book was set via computer-driven cathode-ray tube in 10/12 Century Schoolbook. Century Schoolbook is based on Century Expanded, a variation of the original face in the family Century Roman, which was drawn in 1894 by Lynn B. Benton and Theodore De Vinne for *The Century* magazine. Wider, with less variation between thicks and thins than Century Expanded, Century Schoolbook is classified a "Modern" typeface because of its symmetry, vertical stress, and sharply bracketed serifs. All these traits combine to make Century Schoolbook a bold, readable typeface.

Composed by Kingsport Press, Kingsport, Tennessee.

Printed and bound by R. R. Donnelley & Sons Company, Crawfordsville, Indiana.